SOCIOLOGY

Kenneth C. W. Kammeyer
The University of Maryland

George Ritzer
The University of Maryland

Norman R. Yetman
The University of Kansas

FOURTH EDITION

SOCIOLOGY

Experiencing Changing Societies

ALLYN AND BACON

Boston • London • Sydney • Toronto

A division of Simon & Schuster, Inc.
160 Gould Street
Needham Heights
Massachusetts 02194

Previous editions were published under the title *Sociology: Experiencing a Changing Society*, copyright 1987, 1982, 1979 by Allyn and Bacon.

Library of Congress Cataloging-in-Publication Data

Kammeyer, Kenneth C. W.
Sociology, experiencing changing societies / Kenneth C. W. Kammeyer, George Ritzer, Norman R. Yetman.—4th ed.
p. cm.
Ritzer's name appears first on the earlier edition.
Includes bibliographical references.
ISBN 0-205-12203-5
1. Sociology. 2. Social change. 3. United States—Social conditions. I. Ritzer, George. II. Yetman, Norman R. III. Title.
HM51.R46 1989
301—dc20 89-17547
CIP

Series Editor: Karen Hanson
Developmental Editor: Hannah Rubenstein
Production Administrator: Marjorie Payne
Cover Administrator: Linda Dickinson
Composition Buyer: Linda Cox
Manufacturing Buyer: Tamara McCracken
Photo Researcher: Laurel Anderson/Photosynthesis

Printed in the United States of America
10 9 8 7 6 5 4 3 2 1 94 93 92 91 90 89

Photo Credits

Chapter One Chapter Opener: Robert Harding Picture Library. p. 4: Mark Antman/The Image Works. p. 6: Acey Harper/Picture Group. p. 9: Gabe Palmer/The Stock Market. p. 11: Van Cleve/TSW. p. 13: Antro-Photo File. p. 16: R. Maiman/Sygma. p. 19L: Culver Pictures Inc. p. 19R: Bettmann Newsphotos. p. 20L&R: Culver Pictures Inc. p. 23: Mark Antman/The Image Works. p. 25: Willie Hill/The Image Works. p. 27: Jeffrey D. Smith/Woodfin Camp & Assoc.
Chapter Two Chapter Opener: John Curtis/Photosynthesis. p. 35: Tony O'Brian/Picture Group. p. 38: Ron Bell/Picture Group. p. 41: Rob Nelson/Picture Group. p. 44: Mark Reinstein/Click Chicago. p. 47: Leif Skoogfers. p. 48: Richard Steedman/The Stock Market. p. 50: Bob Daemmrich/The Image Works. p. 55: Larry D. Doell/The Stock Market. p. 56: Momatiuk/Eastcott/Woodfin Camp & Assoc. p. 58: Peter Turnley/Black Star.
(Photo Credits are continued on pages 743 and 744, which should be considered extensions of the copyright page.)

CONTENTS

CHAPTER 4 Forms of Social Life: Interaction, Groups, Organizations, and Societies 99

CHAPTER 5 Socialization 135

Cross-National and Cross-Cultural Perspectives

PREFACE

As we planned for this fourth edition, we asked ourselves what approach or emphasis would best reflect the nature of contemporary sociology. It was not difficult to find our new focus, since the authors, the editor, and the developmental editor all agreed that the time was ripe for an introductory sociology textbook with a distinctive emphasis on cross-national and cross-cultural studies. Sociologists (and most other observers) are increasingly recognizing that what happens in countries around the world can have an impact in every other country. And, increasingly, it is technically and politically possible to know *what* is happening in countries all over the world. For some years we have had the communications capabilities to see world events of the day on the evening news, and now there is a new political openness that allows us to know immediately of events in countries that were previously hidden from view. But it is not just news events that are known, for we are also getting more and more sociological information from nations in all parts of the world.

Since the countries of the contemporary world are mutually informed and interdependent, it is both interesting and important for sociologists to turn their attention to cross-national concerns. We must apply our sociological ideas and use sociological research to learn and understand as much as we can about other countries and societies.

Sociologists have always had an interest in comparative-societal studies and a fascination with the anthropological studies of nonliterate societies. Ever since the nineteenth century, sociologists have used the field studies of anthropologists. In this edition, we broaden our investigation of other societies and cultures to include contemporary sociological phenomena in nations worldwide. This is in line with the view of the American Sociological Association's former president, Melvin Kohn, who called for more cross-national research as "an analytic strategy for sociology." We have termed studies investigating sociological phenomena in one or more contemporary nations *cross-national* studies. Those studies that involve the more traditional, ethnographic investigations we have termed *cross-cultural* studies. Each chapter contains one such study, appropriately titled "Cross-National Perspectives" or "Cross-Cultural Perspectives."

Our cross-national and cross-cultural focus does not mean, however, that we neglect the society and culture of the United States. We continue to give major attention to the society that is most familiar, and probably of most concern, to the majority of our readers. We offer a more balanced consideration, however—one that takes American society as a primary focus, but also introduces data and analyses of other nations and societies, both contemporary and nonliterate.

Organization

The text is divided into four parts. Part One serves as an introduction to the fundamental ideas of sociology. In the first two chapters, we present key theories and research methods of sociology. The major sociological theories and classical theorists are introduced in

Chapter 1 and then referred to when appropriate throughout the text. The chapters that follow introduce the concepts of *culture, interaction, groups, organizations, society, socialization,* and *deviance*. Chapter 4, "Forms of Social Life: Interaction, Groups, Organizations, and Societies," covers small and large groups, organizations, and societies; it incorporates material from two chapters of the previous edition.

The final chapter of Part One—Chapter 7, "Sexual Behavior and Sexuality from a Sociological Perspective"—is a unique feature both to this book and to other introductory sociology texts. Here, we turn our attention to sexual behavior, a topic that is inherently interesting to most people. In this featured chapter we show how a sociological perspective can be usefully applied to this universal and fascinating human behavior. Our aim was to use the core sociological concepts presented in the first six chapters to illustrate to students how these basic sociological ideas can be applied to the study of sexual behavior and, by implication, to any other human behavior.

Part Two is concerned with the basic dimensions of inequality in societies. Again, whenever possible we introduce materials from other societies to supplement examples derived from the United States. Chapter 8 is concerned with socioeconomic stratification. Notable in this chapter is a discussion of the declining middle class, a relatively new social phenomenon not traditionally covered by introductory sociology texts. Chapter 9 explores race and ethnic stratification, and Chapter 10, gender and age stratification. In these chapters we discuss societal inequalities in Africa, Canada, China, India, and the Soviet Union, along with many other societies.

Part Three describes and analyzes in six chapters the basic institutions of societies—family, education, economy and work, health and medicine, religion, and politics. Once again the illustrative cases come from societies, both modern and preliterate, around the world. Part Four contains two chapters. One combines two societal features that have been especially important in the twentieth century: population growth and urbanization. This chapter presents succinctly an appropriate amount of introductory material on demography and urban sociology. The final chapter, Chapter 18, covers social change, social movements, and collective behavior.

"Connections"

The four "Connections" essays, which appear at the end of each part, are an integrative feature, one that illustrates key sociological concepts and theories within the context of real-world issues. In turn, they discuss the homeless, the fate of Mexicans who work along the United States-Mexico border, the phenomenon of working parents and "latchkey" children, and reproductive technologies such as surrogate parenthood and artificial insemination. After the social issue has been briefly described, the major theories (structural-functional, conflict, symbolic interaction, and social exchange) are applied to various aspects of the topic. How might structural functionalists view the issue of surrogate parenthood as compared to the way in which symbolic interactionists view the issue? What might social exchange theorists see as the key to understanding the relationship between the homeless and other members of society? How would conflict theorists describe the plight of the Mexican *maquila* workers in El Paso? Each "Connections" essay closes with a section entitled "Looking at the Research," in which we discuss what sociological research has told us about the issue, and, often, what additional research is needed. We believe this innovative and important feature will provide a useful and interesting break from the chapter-by-chapter pace that is so characteristic of introductory sociology classes.

"Critical Thinking"

At the end of each chapter, a set of approximately twelve Critical Thinking questions challenges one to probe more deeply for sociological understanding of the chapter. The questions can also serve as a springboard for classroom discussion.

Additional Pedagogical Aids

Each chapter has an introduction designed to draw the reader into the subject of the chapter. At the end of each chapter, a summary provides a convenient review of the chapter content. As a special convenience for the readers, each major sociological concept is printed in boldface, and a brief definition appears in the margin at the point of its first appearance. A complete glossary of terms appears at the end of the book, where fuller definitions and explanations are provided.

Study Guide. A Study Guide is also available for this book, which contains: Learning Objectives, chapter outline, key terms and definitions, key people, and self-tests (25 multiple choice, 20 true/false, 15 fill-in, 5 essay, glossary definitions, and answers to objective questions). Your bookstore can assist you, the student, in ordering this, if your instructor has not done so already. A computerized study guide is also available.

Instructor's Materials. Teaching aids for the instructor have also been prepared. These include: *Annotated Instructor's Edition,* Test Bank, Computerized Test Bank, Transparencies package, and video tapes from the Allyn and Bacon Video Library. Please contact Allyn and Bacon through your local sales representative, or write: Allyn and Bacon, Customer Service Department, 160 Gould Street, Needham, MA 02194.

Acknowledgments

Once again it is a pleasure to thank the many people who have helped us as we prepared the fourth edition of this book. Our first debt is to the hundreds of sociologists, and other scholars and writers, who carried out the basic research and did the writing that provided the material for this book. Sociology is an accumulated and still-growing body of knowledge and ideas that we have tried to bring together in a single text. We hope we have done justice to all of these many intellectual and scientific efforts.

We again wish to express our appreciation to the many sociologists and their students who have used the previous editions and have given us the benefit of their thoughtful critiques and suggestions. The most direct feedback came from the students in our classes at the University of Kansas and the University of Maryland.

In the course of preparing this edition we have called on many of our sociological colleagues to give us help, information, materials, and many other kinds of information. We especially wish to thank Barbara Altman, Bob Antonio, Bill Arnold, Jack Bremer, Ed Dager, Sue Dowden, Bill Falk, Sheryl Fyock, Jerry Hage, Lori Houk-Stephens, Pat Johnston, Tim Knapp, Joe Lengermann, Tim Miller, Jeremy Michaelson, Bob Minor, Alfredo Mirande, Alan Neustadtl, Stan Presser, John Robinson, Larry Sherman, Jay Teachman, Reeve Vanneman, and Sandi Zimdars-Schwartz. We especially wish to thank Pam Gindoff and Terri LeMoyne for their willingness to give us great amounts of their time and effort when they too were busy with their own work. We also want to thank our friends Mehrangiz Najafizadeh and Lewis Mennerick for the extraordinary contribution they made to the chapter on education. Among the staff members in the sociology department we have received continuing help from Dorothy Bowers, Cass O'Toole, Gerry Todd, Agnes Zane, Sue Harmon, Debbie Griffith, and many others.

We were encouraged to develop a fourth edition of this text by Karen Hanson, our editor. Her initial enthusiasm for the idea of an uncluttered, attractive, appealing book, with four-color photographs, gave us the impetus we needed to get the writing underway. Our developmental editor Hannah Rubenstein was, from the very beginning of her participation, deeply involved in every detail of the book. She gave her complete attention to every sociological concept and idea in the manuscript. Despite some formidable resistance from us on many occasions, she frequently made substantive contributions, and was often able to show us how our writing could be clarified, our ideas sharpened, and our book improved. This process of give and take between Hannah and her authors has often been intense, but it has surely led to a better book than it otherwise would have been. Marjorie Payne has been in charge of producing the book, a task that she has carried out with a gentle but firm hand. It isn't easy to get three different authors to complete tasks properly and on time, but Marjorie has worked toward this end with a balance of persistence and tolerance. She also made a number of substantive and clarifying contributions to the text during the production process. We want to express our thanks and appreciation to Karen, Hannah, and Marjorie for all they did to help us achieve our mutual goal of a fresh new introduction to sociology.

Our sincere thanks to Thomas and Sandra Dunn of Western Kentucky University for their excellent work in preparing the Annotated Instructor's Edition, Test Bank, and Study Guide that accompany this book.

We would like to give special acknowledgment to Dee Ann Spencer of Central Missouri State University for her work in conceptualizing, researching, and writing the initial drafts of the "Connections" essays. We would also like to thank Helen Fisk of the St. Paul Academy and Summit School for her work on the end-of-chapter "Critical Thinking" questions. It is our hope that this element of the book will help to stimulate the "sociological imagination."

Finally, we are very grateful to the following reviewers, whose comments and suggestions for improvement assisted us in the revision process:

Judy Aulette
University of North Carolina

Edward Duffy
Marshall University

Abe Levine
El Camino College

Susan Losch
Florida State University

Kathleen McKinney
Illinois State University

William McCoy
California State University—Dominques Hills

Lynn Mulkey
Hofstra University

Thomas Norton
Lafayette College

Raymond O'Connor
Holyoke Community College

Fred Pampel
University of Iowa

Ira Robinson
University of Georgia

Richard Senter
Central Michigan University

Dee Ann Spencer
Central Missouri State University

Jerry Shepperd
Austin Community College

J. Allen Williams
University of Nebraska

SOCIOLOGY

CHAPTER

1

A Brief Introduction to Sociology

A Definition of Sociology

What do sociologists study, analyze, and write about? To put the question somewhat differently, what is the subject matter of sociology? The answer can be found simply by looking at the front page of any newspaper (or, for that matter, at the comic strips or the sports pages). If you look at the front page of a newspaper the stories will be about what human beings are doing, sometimes as individuals, but often as groups, or organizations, or entire societies.

The headline of one day's newspaper reads, "Rifleman Slays Five At School," and sociologists ask, "What is it in the background of a person that would explain why he would do such a terrible and senseless thing?" Sociologists would try to make sense of this senseless act by looking into the social experiences of this man (perhaps his early family background, his military experience, his educational or marital history) to see what brought him to a point where he would kill innocent children in a schoolyard.

Another headline on the same day reads, "Miami Disturbances Continue Near Site of Police Shooting." This story is about black youths engaging in violent acts after an unarmed black resident was killed by an Hispanic police officer. Several sociological questions intersect in this story. What prompted the police officer to shoot an unarmed person? Is it significant that the police officer was Hispanic while the man killed was black? Are these events, the killing and the subsequent rioting, related to the social and economic conditions of blacks in the city of Miami? What is the relationship between blacks and Hispanics in this city?

But sociologists are interested in things other than violence and conflict. They are also interested in stories that appeared on the same day about the upcoming inauguration of a new President. One story, for example, describes how the major corporations of the country are paying most of the $30 million it will cost to celebrate the inauguration. Another story describes how primarily the rich, the powerful, and the famous will attend the inaugural events. But a human-interest story also appears about a homeless family that has been specially invited to the inaugural ball. These stories, too, will interest sociologists because they call attention to the differences between the rich and the poor of the society, and raise fundamental sociological questions about inequality, privilege, and power.

These few examples suggest that the subject matter of sociology is the ongoing human drama of social life, concerning itself with the actions of individuals and groups, at all social levels of the society, whether the actions are commonplace or unusual. Taking these examples as a starting point, we offer the following definition of sociology.

The subject matter of sociology is the drama of social life. The topics of concern to sociologists can be found on the front page of any newspaper.

Sociology is the systematic study of:

A. the social behavior of individuals;
B. the workings of social groups, organizations, cultures, and societies; and
C. the influence of social groups, organizations, cultures, and societies on individual and group behavior.

Although some people believe that sociology is concerned only with social groups and societal behavior, the definition above calls attention to the fact that sociologists are also interested in the social behavior of individuals. By using the word *social* to modify behavior, we are simply signalling that sociologists have a special interest in the behavior of individuals as it is influenced by social groupings. The definition shows also that sociologists are interested in the way various kinds of social groupings work, and especially how their workings influence human behavior.

Specialties of Sociology

Sociology is a wide-ranging way of studying human behavior. While sociologists generally accept the definition offered above, there are many different kinds of sociologists, and their approaches to the field are often very different. From the beginning it is important to understand this feature of sociology. *There is no one sociology; there are many sociologies.* It is therefore fruitless to look for the *real* sociology; it is more realistic to look for the ways in which sociologists and sociologies differ. To show this clearly we will identify in this section some of the most important differences among sociologists, beginning with their specialties and subfields.

Subfield Interests

A simple and direct way to learn how sociologists differ is to ask any sociologist, "What kind of sociologist are you?" (Your instructor will probably be your most convenient target, and you needn't be reluctant to ask, for no sociologist will consider the question odd. In any case, sociologists make a living by asking people questions, so they should be willing to answer some themselves.)

A sociologist who is asked this question will probably respond by listing his or her specialties, or subfield interests. Specialties or subfields are either some part of human behavior (deviant behavior) or some aspect of social life (political sociology), or ways of studying these things. At least 50 different specializations or subfields exist in sociology. Just to give you a flavor of the different kinds of sociological interests, consider the following list: sociology of the elderly and aging, sociology of art and literature, criminology, demography (the study of population), sociology of emotions (a relatively new specialty), medical sociology, military sociology, the sociology of race and ethnic relations, sociology of religion, social psychology, social stratification, and urban sociology. (Table 1–1 provides a more extensive list of sociological specialties.) Obviously, not every

Table 1–1. The Major Subfields and Specialties of Sociology

Aging, sociology of, or social gerontology	Mass communication and public opinion
Applied sociology and social policy	Medical sociology
Art and literature, sociology of	Mental health, sociology of
Collective behavior and social movements	Metatheory
Comparative or cross-national sociology	Methodology, qualitative approaches
Computers and sociology	Methodology, statistics, and mathematical sociology
Criminology and criminal justice	Military sociology and sociology of war
Cultural sociology	Occupations, work, and professions and industrial sociology
Demography or population studies	Political sociology
Development or modernization, the sociology of	Race and ethnicity, sociology of
Deviant behavior and social disorganization	Religion, sociology of
Economy and society	Rural sociology
Education, sociology of	Science, sociology of
Emotions, sociology of	Small groups, sociology of
Environmental sociology	Social change
Ethnomethodology/phenomenology	Social control
Family and marriage, sociology of	Social psychology
Gender, sociology of and women, sociology of	Socialization
History of social thought	Sociological theory
Human ecology	Sociology of knowledge
Language, sociology of, and social linguistics	Stratification, mobility and social class
Law and society	Urban sociology and community sociology
Leisure, sports and recreation, sociology of	World conflict and world systems, sociology of

There are many sociological specialties and subfields. The sociological study of the elderly and aging, called *social gerontology,* is just one of them.

subfield of sociology can be represented by a chapter in this book, although most will get some attention. But it will also be obvious that many chapters do represent major subfields of sociology, especially in parts 2, 3, and 4.

Most of these specialties can be further divided into subspecialties, which complicates the picture even more. All family sociologists, for example, study matters relating to marriage and the family, but any particular family sociologist will probably have special interests within this general area. Individual family sociologists can concentrate on the social history of marriage and the family, marriage and the family in different societies, the demography of marriage and the family, family problems (violence and divorce), sexual relations, childrearing, and so on.

Theoretical Preferences

It is possible that when you ask, "What kind of sociologist are you?" the answer will reflect the person's theoretical orientation. Later we will present four of the major theoretical approaches in sociology today. One is named symbolic interactionism, so some sociologists might answer by saying, "I'm a symbolic interactionist." You will learn some key features of this theory later, but for now it is enough to know that when a sociologist claims to be a symbolic interactionist it means that he or she attaches a special importance to the words and symbols that people use when they interact with each other. Many sociologists do not limit themselves to one theory. They can see the usefulness and validity of several theoretical approaches, depending on what issue or problem is being studied.

Research Preferences

Some sociologists have sociological identities that reflect their approaches to doing sociological research and scholarship. You have probably often read or heard about the results of surveys (e.g., surveys of how people feel about their work or about religion), so it would probably be fairly clear if a sociologist answered your question by saying, "I'm a survey researcher." It would mean that he or she does the research leading to survey results. In chapter 2 we will introduce major research methods used by sociologists, including a fuller description of what survey researchers do. We will also see that, in addition to surveys, sociologists use a variety of other research procedures to study human behavior.

With respect to research, sociologists can be classified according to whether they prefer quantitative research techniques or whether they favor a more qualitative approach. **Quantitative research** emphasizes numerical measurement and statistical analysis as a way of conducting sociological studies. **Qualitative research** relies more on verbal descriptions and analysis. Sociologists who prefer the quantitative approach often see the natural sciences as a model for sociology. Sociologists who prefer the qualitative approach emphasize that the subject matter of sociology cannot be easily reduced to mathematical formulae and statistical techniques. Although there are strong advocates of both the quantitative and qualitative approaches, many sociologists believe that both approaches are useful. Which approach is preferable at any given time is determined by the nature of the problem under study.

Quantitative research
Sociological studies that emphasize numerical and statistical analysis

Qualitative research
Sociological studies that emphasize verbal descriptions and analysis

Microscopic Sociology and Macroscopic Sociology

There is another major way that sociologists are differentiated, but usually this distinction is not so much a matter of personal identity. Sociologists can be classified according to the level of analysis that they use in their sociological work (Wiley, 1988). In the above definition of sociology we mentioned individuals, groups, organizations, cultures, and societies. These are all points along a continuum that extends from the smallest units of sociological analysis, individuals, to the largest units, societies. The smallest units are at the microscopic end of the social continuum; the largest are at the macroscopic end.

The terms *microscopic* and *macroscopic* are borrowed from the physical world, where microscopic objects are the smaller units of nature, e.g., molecules, viruses, and so on. Macroscopic objects of the physical world are the large units such as continents, planets, and galaxies. **Microscopic sociology** refers to the study of the smallest social units, namely, individuals and their thoughts and actions. **Macroscopic sociology** focuses on larger social units such as groups, organizations, cultures, and societies.[1]

Between microscopic social units and macroscopic units there are many different social phenomena, such as families, small groups (bowling teams), large groups (religious congregations), and organizations (the United States Navy). For convenience we can divide the range of social phenomena into the microscopic and macroscopic realms, but

Microscopic sociology
The study of the smallest social units—individuals, their thoughts, and actions

Macroscopic sociology
The sociological study of groups, organizations, cultures, and societies

[1] Sociologists often use the shortened terms, *micro* and *macro*, to refer to these different levels of sociological analyses.

we should recognize that many social phenomena fall in the middle of the continuum and are difficult to categorize as strictly microscopic or macroscopic.

To sum up the differences among sociologists: first, differences are based on their specialties or subfields, but differences may also exist in their preferred theories or in their ways of doing sociological research and scholarship. Differences are also noticeable in the social levels in which they work. While it is true that differences exist among sociologists, it is necessary at the same time to note that sociologists generally agree about many aspects of their field. We will focus on these fundamental ideas of sociology in the next section.

All of this diversity in sociology may seem a bit overwhelming, but it is important to recognize this diversity at the beginning. Although it may make sociology seem more complex, there is a bright side to the picture, too. Since there are many different parts of sociology (specialties, theories, methods, and levels), a number of things will be especially interesting to you. The truth is that all sociologists have personal preferences. As individual sociologists, we think some specialties are more interesting than others, some theoretical approaches are more significant than others, and some kinds of research and scholarship are more important than others. Some of us prefer to work at the micro level of social life, while others of us prefer the macro level. Throughout this book we invite you to sample the range and diversity of sociology and to discover some, perhaps many, features of sociology that will interest and engage you.

Some Fundamental Ideas of Sociology

Since we have called attention to the variety and diversity of sociological views, it is important to emphasize the points on which almost all sociologists agree. Most agree that the actions and behaviors of humans create social settings and social rules, but that these same settings and rules, in turn, influence the way humans act. This idea is both simple and complex, and it is certainly important enough to consider more fully.

Societies and Other Social Settings Are Humanly Created

The social settings in which people live, and the social rules by which they live, have all been humanly created. We know, for example, that the family system in our society today did not just spring up full grown one day. Yet it may be difficult to see how the family system and the rules that surround it were created by human actions. The difficulty we have in seeing how people's actions have created and changed the family system comes from our limited time perspective. We can see only what we have experienced, and changes do not often occur rapidly. A detailed example taken from some historical changes in the American family may help us see how, over time, social institutions can be changed by human actions.

During the first half of the nineteenth century in the United States, when a married couple with children divorced, the custody of the children was routinely given to the father. In the middle of the 1800s, significant changes began to occur. For example, if a child at the time of a divorce were still an infant, nursing at its mother's breast, the court might allow the child to remain with the mother. However, after being weaned, the child was often turned over to the father. As time went on, the courts started giving custody to mothers, even though the children were well beyond infancy. The courts, and the public at large, were more likely to think that any child at a "tender age" should be with its mother. Gradually the duration of the tender age increased and eventually included all minor children. By the 1920s, mothers were given child custody in almost every divorce case. By then virtually everyone had come to accept the idea that all minor children were better off in the care of their mothers.

In the last two decades, however, more and more people have questioned the assumption that mothers should always have sole custody. Many judges and courts are no longer presuming that mothers will have custody of all minor children. Today, in a small percentage of cases, custody is shared between the mothers and fathers, and in some instances fathers are getting sole custody (Ahrons and Rodgers, 1987; Luepnitz, 1982).

All these changes occurred because of human action. At first, actions were based on the belief that children were the property of their father's family (a belief that still prevails in many other societies). Then there was a gradual reversal as some people argued that small children were better off in the custody of their mothers. More recently, increasing numbers of people support the idea of joint custody between the mother and father. In a century and a half, the actions and beliefs about child custody have changed because some people in the society questioned the way things were done (Roman and Haddad, 1978).

The general sociological point is that every day people affirm or modify their social settings, and by doing so they maintain or change them. Whenever modifications and changes are made, resistance usually arises from those who prefer the existing social arrangements. Sociology is concerned with the way individuals—in the past and in the present—support or change their social settings.

Social Influences on Human Behavior

Now we turn to a second fundamental view of sociology: social settings influence and constrain human behavior. If we think of a newborn baby, for example, we have a human being that is apparently little more than a bundle of unrestrained reflexes. Over the years the baby's character is molded by agents of various social settings into an

Newborn babies may appear to be little more than bundles of unrestrained reflexes, but they soon reveal strong social tendencies as they interact with parents and others.

adult human being. In the early years of life, parents, as agents of the family and the society, teach the child some basic attitudes, values, and skills needed to survive in the social world (eat with utensils, talk, follow a variety of social customs). Later, teachers play an important part in teaching the child reading, writing, and arithmetic. More important, they teach a variety of standards for behavior and appropriate attitudes about many social objects. Throughout life, peers, friends, and colleagues shape the way a person behaves and thinks about all things, large and small.

Even as adults we are constantly being affected by social influences. Consider such everyday concerns as clothing and hair styles. At first a new style may not appeal to us. A new length of skirt or hair, or new clothing fashions, may seem odd and unattractive, and we vow not to change. But soon we see more and more people with the new styles and fashions, and perhaps someone comments that our own tastes are out of date. When this occurs, most of us change our preferences. Once we are wearing the shorter (or longer) skirt, longer (or shorter) hair, or new fashions, these styles come to feel natural and right because the social influences around us, from our closest friends to the mass media, have changed us.

Changes are not limited to the superficial level of styles and fashions. Our attitudes, beliefs, and behaviors about the most fundamental things of life—morality, politics, religion, work, entertainment—are also changed. Throughout our lives we are changed and modified as we enter different stages of life, different levels of education, new occupations, new communities, and new times.

Throughout this book we will see examples of how a wide range of social influences shapes people's lives. Yet even though we, as sociologists, are primarily concerned with the way human behavior is shaped by social influences, we should always remember, also, that individuals influence and modify the social groups, and even the cultures and societies in which they live.

The American People Finally Speak Up

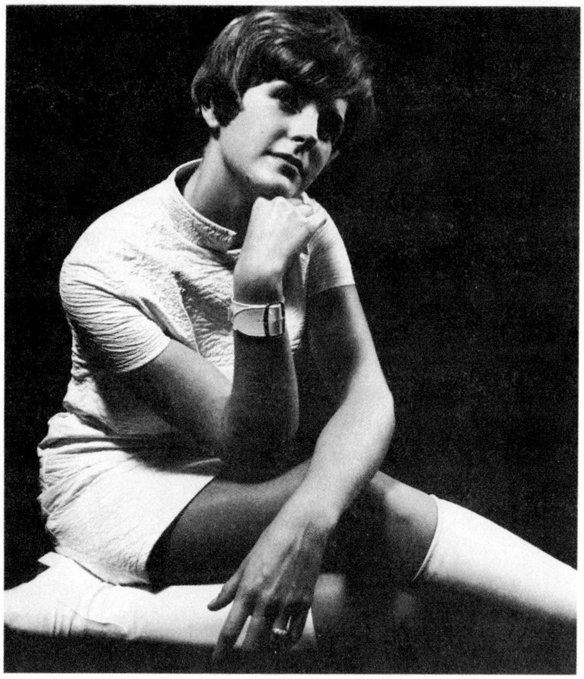

Social influences can be seen in everyday matters such as clothing and hair styles. The 1960s look affected by this young woman, who wears a miniskirt and white "go-go" boots, appears dated today.

How Can Sociology Be Useful to You?

Since you are just beginning your first course in sociology, we want to tell you about the benefits you may derive from your study of sociology, even if this introductory course is the only one you ever take. Other benefits, such as jobs and careers in sociology, can be attained only if you go on to take other work and perhaps even advanced degrees (a masters or doctorate) in sociology. But let us begin with what you may gain from this course alone.

Facts and Information

Most sociologists are fond of accumulating and relating facts and information about social behavior and the society in which we live (as well as other societies). They have a special preference for facts that are not widely known. Even better are facts that run contrary to popular beliefs. Therefore, both in this book and in your class, you will learn a few things about human behavior that you did not know before. Suppose you were presented with the following statements and asked whether you believed them to be true. What would you say?

- At the beginning of this century Americans married at an early age, often in their teens.
- The rate of suicide is higher among teenagers than any other age group in the society.
- Most elderly people in the United States are poor; most live below the poverty level.

What is your reaction to these statements? Are they true or false? Every one of those statements is *false*, though they are widely believed to be true. The facts are:

- At the beginning of the twentieth century, men were about 26 years old at the time of their first marriages; women were about 22 years old. Perhaps it is surprising that these ages are similar to the ages at which men and women marry today (Kammeyer, 1987).
- In the United States the rate of suicide among 15- to 19-year-olds is *lower* than the suicide rate for people in every older age group (U.S. Bureau of the Census, 1987). The suicide rate for people over 65 years is more than twice that for 15- to 19-year-olds.
- Most of the United States' elderly population (aged 65 and over) does *not* live in poverty. Among those people aged 65 and over, according to the current definitions of poverty, 12.2 percent are below the poverty level. This percentage is less than the national average, which is 13.5 percent. The percentage of children under six living in poverty is nearly twice as high at 22.8 percent (U.S. Bureau of the Census, 1988, p. 437).

The facts about marriage age, suicide, and poverty are statistical facts. Because they are fairly easy to document, the truth or falsity of such statements can be easily checked (although it is generally recognized that even statistical facts can be manipulated to prove a point). But you can learn many other kinds of facts in sociology. You can learn about the differences in marijuana use between black and white high school seniors, about the fastest growing occupations in the United States, about the nature of the social stratification system in the Soviet Union, or about the work load of Japanese college students. You may know something about these matters but, again, some of the facts may surprise you.[2]

Knowledge and Awareness of Other Societies

Sociologists have always had a great interest in societies other than their own. Early sociologists were especially intrigued by the work of anthropologists (and others) who described remote societies and their cultures—often small, non-Western societies with unusual and exotic customs. It was both fascinating and instructive to learn how differently societies could be organized, and how much the beliefs and values of people could differ from one society to another.

Sociologists today continue to be interested in the small non-literate societies, because there are still lessons to be learned and insights to be gained from such cases. The reports and descriptions of these and other distinct cultures have traditionally been called **cross-cultural studies,** and throughout this book we will be using them frequently to highlight or illustrate sociological points.

Cross-cultural studies Traditionally, studies that compare different, often small, non-literate societies

Today an even greater need exists for sociologists to understand other societies around the world. No longer are nations and societies on the other side of the earth

[2] On marijuana use, see chapter 2—Sociological Research; for the fastest growing U.S. occupations, see chapter 13—The Economy and Work; for a description of the Soviet stratification system, see chapter 8—Stratification: Living with Social Inequality; and for a description of the work done by Japanese college students see chapter 12—Education.

simply regarded as unusual and exotic places with no relevance for our personal lives. Travel and commerce among all nations of the earth are now commonplace. For sociologists, this means that we are now able to obtain information, both quantitative and qualitative, from nations previously closed to sociological scrutiny. We must know about other societies, not just because they are sociologically instructive but because we live in an interdependent global society. In sociology, **cross-national studies** examine sociological dimensions of two or more contemporary nations.

Cross-national studies Studies that examine sociological dimensions of two or more contemporary nations

Because an understanding of other societies is so critical today, we have purposely illustrated sociological issues with not only U.S. examples but examples from other nations around the world. Therefore, a primary theme is an emphasis on both cross-cultural and cross-national examples and data. You will find cross-cultural and cross-national illustrations and cases in every chapter. We believe these discussions will be both interesting and instructive.

What you learn about the many different societies presented in this text will be an important part of your introduction to sociology. Sometimes the information will be surprising and hard to believe; at other times it will be consistent with your expectations. Whatever the case, you will gain a substantial amount of new factual information from sociology, and, perhaps most important, new perspectives on the social world.

In sociology, cross-cultural studies have traditionally been anthropological studies of small non-Western societies, often with unusual or exotic customs.

Cross-National Perspectives

Sociology in China

As we will see later in this chapter, sociology had its beginnings in France in the nineteenth century. While sociology developed quickly in Europe and the United States, in the rest of the world it emerged later, and has often had an uneven history. The development of sociology in most of Asia has followed this pattern. China is an interesting example.

Sociology in China dates back to the beginning of the twentieth century, when Chinese scholars who had studied in Europe and the United States returned to their homeland with the ideas of this new field. Through the early decades of this century the Chinese scholars translated into Chinese a number of the classic American and European sociological studies, including Durkheim's *Division of Labor*. Through the first fifty years of the twentieth century, Chinese sociology grew steadily. Chinese sociologists were interested in both sociological theory and sociological research. The Chinese had a special interest in the study of social problems such as poverty, overpopulation, problems of rural life, and social welfare. In this respect, Chinese sociology had many of the same interests as American sociology.

However, things changed dramatically after the Communists came to power in 1949. Within a few years sociology departments in Chinese universities were being closed, and soon sociology had disappeared completely.

There were several reasons why the study of sociology was banned in China. First, in the early years of the revolution the Soviet Union was taken as a model by the Chinese. Since sociology was insignificant in the Soviet Union, the Chinese concluded that it was unimportant for them also. Second, the Chinese believed that Marxian theory could take the place of conventional Western sociology (as late as the 1950s Marxian theory was not strongly represented in American sociology). Third, the Chinese decided that their revolution would solve existing social problems, therefore, sociological studies were not needed. Fourth, sociology was thought to be a *pseudoscience* that opponents of Communism might use to attack the Communist party.

In 1957 a few Chinese sociologists tried to mount a defense of sociology, but they were severely criticized and seen as part of a right-wing conspiracy. The result was the complete disappearance of organized sociology in China. The only remnants of sociology during these years were the few sociologists who continued to work in academic settings, but as members of other academic departments such as history.

Chinese sociologists, like many other academics and intellectuals, suffered greatly during the Cultural Revolution of the 1960s. It was during this period that professors in many disciplines were forced out of universities and into the countryside where they were made to do manual labor on farms.

However, with the death of Mao Zedung and the defeat of his allies, the country moved in a more liberal direction. In 1979, a symposium was held in which the President of the Chinese Academy of Social Sciences announced that sociology had been "rehabilitated." The next day the Chinese Sociological Association was founded. However, those who sought to rebuild sociology faced a difficult task since almost all work in the field had been discontinued in 1952. Almost three decades of sociological development throughout the world was unknown in China. Most of the sociologists who practiced in 1952 were either dead or too old to begin learning all the new developments in the field. Young people who were gravitating toward sociology faced a shortage of well-trained faculty, facilities, and written materials.

Through most of the 1980s, Chinese sociology made dramatic strides. A number of foreign universities developed formal and informal arrangements with Chinese universities. Foreign sociologists were routinely brought to China to teach and do research. Many foreign works in sociology, both classic and contemporary, were translated into Chinese. Most important, many Chinese students began studying sociology abroad, especially in the United States, and this promised to create in China a whole new crop of professors who were knowledgeable about the latest developments throughout the world. Finally, native Chinese sociologists were creating their own distinctive brand of theory and sociological research.

However, the brutal crushing of the democratic movement in May, 1989, threatened to halt or even reverse these developments in sociology. At this point it is impossible to predict what will happen in the 1990s, however, the future of Chinese sociology does not look promising.

HANLIN, LI, FANG MING, WANG YING, SUN BINGYAO, and QI WANG. "Chinese Sociology, 1898–1986," *Social Forces* 65, 1987.

An Understanding of Human Behavior and Societal Life

As human beings we are always trying to understand ourselves, the people around us, and the events occurring in our society (or the world). The chances are good that you have wondered about some of the following: Why do children from the same family often have very different personalities? Why do some young people move into lives of crime, drug addiction, and alcoholism, while others from the same communities do not? Why do some married couples stay together for a lifetime, while others get divorced quickly? Why have there been so many scandals connected with religion in recent years? Why can't racial and ethnic groups get along more peacefully?

These kinds of questions are exactly the ones that many sociologists ask and try to answer. It would be foolish to promise answers to all these questions because no one has the complete answers to any of them. But we do believe that what you can learn from sociology will provide some insights into human behavior and societal life that will improve your understanding of these issues. Furthermore, these insights should be helpful to you far beyond the questions of today. You should be able to use them for problems and issues of the future, ones that we may not even be able to imagine now.

Throughout this book you will be introduced to many different sociological concepts (the technical terms of sociology). It is necessary in sociology, just as it is in economics or biology or physics, to learn the vocabulary of the field. We will alert you to the most important sociological concepts by providing a definition immediately after

Sociologists often try to answer the same questions that confront all of us in everyday life. For example, why have there been so many scandals connected with religion in recent years, such as the one involving evangelist Jimmy Swaggart?

Role conflict
Two or more people expecting one to do different and conflicting things

the concept is printed in boldface. These terms will also be defined briefly in the margins and fully at the end of the book. We believe that you will often find many of the terms and concepts applicable and useful, long after you have finished this course. For example, in chapter 13—The Economy and Work—you will learn about **role conflict.** One type of role conflict occurs when two or more people are expecting you to do different and conflicting things. Role conflict occurs mostly in the workplace, but it can occur in other areas of life as well (e.g., in your family life). This sociological concept and many others will prove to be useful throughout life.

In addition to concepts, we will also introduce you to a number of sociological theories. As we present and apply these theories we will show you how they can be useful tools for understanding current issues and problems. But equally important, these theories will provide the basis for understanding many issues and problems that will appear long after you have finished this college course in sociology. The usefulness of sociological theories is parallel to the way in which the theoretical principles of economics, biology, or physics can help you understand particular problems that you encounter in the economic, biological, or physical worlds. Thus, one of the important benefits of studying sociology is the general applicability of sociological theories to your personal and social worlds, in both the present and future.

Occupations and Careers That Use Sociology

You may be interested in the long-range occupational uses of a degree, or degrees, in sociology. With an undergraduate degree in sociology you can pursue a number of fields of advanced study. A bachelor's degree in sociology can be a basis for careers in social work, law, education, journalism, social policy, and other professional pursuits. The training that is part of a typical undergraduate degree program in sociology can also be useful for going directly into positions in government, research, marketing and sales, and human resources (personnel work). In addition, the skills learned in social research methods (see chapter 2) and statistical data analysis are skills often sought by businesses, research organizations, national and state associations and interest groups, and governmental agencies at all levels.

If you continue beyond the bachelor's degree and earn an advanced degree in sociology (master's or doctorate) the range of opportunities includes all those listed above as well as the role of professional sociologist. The most common career for professional sociologists is teaching, generally at the college level, from community and junior colleges to the largest and most prestigious universities. Some college teaching positions at the community and junior-college level may be held with a master's degree, but the Ph.D. degree is increasingly required for positions at any college beyond the two-year level.

More and more non-teaching jobs have become available for those with advanced degrees in sociology, especially for those with doctorates. Holders of these advanced degrees are often highly trained in research, data analysis, and in the analysis of organizational and governmental policies. Governmental agencies employ sociologists to carry out surveys and analyze data. Prominent federal agencies with sociologists on their staffs include the National Institutes of Health, the Census Bureau, the Civil Rights Commission, the National Science Foundation, and many others. Private organizations and businesses also hire sociologists who have been trained to design and carry out social research and policy analysis. Sociologists are employed by radio and television broadcasting companies, insurance companies, advertising agencies, and other businesses that must have valid information on public needs and interests.

Although only a few of you will go on to careers in sociology, every one of you should receive something of value from your introduction to the field. As we suggested earlier, one benefit will be an introduction to the major concepts and theories of the field. To begin, then, we will use the final section of this chapter to introduce you to the historical beginnings of sociology and to some of the major scholars who have shaped the field. We will close by presenting the major sociological theories that currently prevail.

The Beginnings of Sociology

No precise date can be given for the founding of sociology, but its beginnings date back to the early 1800s. General agreement prevails that the work of the French scholar Auguste Comte (1798–1857) gave sociology its name and an identity that eventually led to its status as a scholarly discipline. Of course, long before the term *sociology* was coined there were intellectuals, philosophers, and religious leaders who made observations about the nature of human behavior and human society. A brief look at the ideas of the nineteenth-century scholars who formed this distinctive new field of study will add to our understanding of sociology. We will begin with the founder of sociology, Auguste Comte.

Auguste Comte

Like many scholars of the nineteenth century Auguste Comte was influenced by the rapid changes occurring in European societies. During the years of Comte's young adulthood, French society had continued to experience repercussions from the French Revolution, which had started in 1789. The Revolution had brought about a considerable amount of chaos and disorder in France, and Comte viewed these developments negatively. Although Comte knew that a return to pre-Revolutionary conditions was impossible, he was looking for a way to bring greater order and tranquility to French society.

Comte thought that order could be restored if it were possible to understand more fully the way in which society worked. The fact that he lived in an age when the scientific approach had proved useful for understanding the physical world prompted Comte to put his faith in science. He rejected theological and philosophical approaches and concluded that the scientific approach was the way to achieve a better understanding of society. The appeal that the physical sciences had for Comte is revealed in the fact that he first called this new science of society *social physics*. Later, because that label had already been used by a Belgian scholar named Quetelet, Comte changed the name to sociology (Lazarsfeld, 1961).

Comte's work is important primarily because it advanced the idea that there could be (and should be) a science of society. He gave sociology a position among the other sciences of his time, and although it required the work of later scholars to solidify that position, Comte's pioneering effort deserves recognition. Also important in Comte's work is the idea that, as a science, sociology could solve social problems such as war, revolution, crime, and poverty. This idea continues to be a significant feature of sociology today.

As we move beyond the work of Comte and the beginnings of sociology, we encounter several major figures who either shaped the development of sociology as an academic discipline or had a major impact on the field since then. We will briefly examine their contributions to contemporary sociology, beginning with Emile Durkheim.

Emile Durkheim

After Comte, no sociologist worked more diligently to give sociology a place among the established scholarly disciplines than the French scholar Emile Durkheim (1858–1917). In the scholarly and intellectual communities of Europe in the late nineteenth and early twentieth centuries, sociology was by no means completely accepted. Durkheim made it a personal crusade to advance sociology and sociological explanations of human behavior.

Durkheim often wrote in an argumentative style in which he first rejected nonsocial explanations of human behavior, especially those based on biological or psychological reasoning. He used this approach in one of his major works, *Suicide* (Durkheim, 1897/1951), in which he sought to demonstrate the importance of social factors in explaining what seemed to be distinctively individual behavior. Even today our normal

(a) Auguste Comte (1798–1857)

(b) Emile Durkheim (1858–1917)

first reaction to a report of suicide is to try to understand and explain this event in individual, usually psychological, terms. Durkheim, however, demonstrated that the social contexts in which people live can explain variations in the frequency of suicide. For example, he collected and analyzed statistical data on suicide rates in various European countries, and found that suicide rates went up during periods of social upheaval and change. He reasoned that during times of revolution, war, or economic depression, the conventional rules of conduct would be in flux and, therefore, unclear. Durkheim called this societal condition *anomie*. **Anomie** literally means normlessness; it refers to situations in which individuals are uncertain about the norms of society. Suicide rates that go up during times of social upheaval (and thus presumed normlessness) illustrate what Durkheim called anomic suicide. Durkheim went on to identify other societal conditions that also led, in different ways, to variations in suicide rates.

Anomie
Normlessness; uncertainty about the norms of society

Durkheim's analysis of suicide is considered by many sociologists an excellent demonstration of the science of sociology. One reason that his work is considered exemplary is his use of suicide statistics that allowed him to do his analyses and report his findings in a quantitative form. The statistical analysis of social data has become a prominent feature of sociology. The second reason for holding up Durkheim's work on suicide as a sociological ideal is that he used social factors (in this case, societal conditions) to explain individual behavior. Durkheim demonstrated a basic sociological premise, which is that human behavior can be explained in social terms.

(c) Max Weber (1864–1920)

(d) Karl Marx (1818–1883)

Max Weber

Rationality
Goals and objectives set and achieved in the most efficient way possible

The German sociologist Max Weber[3] (1864–1920), like Durkheim, saw problems in the way European societies were changing. The key change, according to Weber, was the increase of rationality as the basis of human behavior. **Rationality** is a form of human action in which goals and objectives are set, and then achieved in the most efficient way possible. The choice of a behavior is based on how quickly and easily it will allow a person to reach a chosen goal or objective. Weber believed that, over the course of several centuries, the Western world had come to emphasize rationality so completely that it dominated every aspect of modern social life. Although rationality has obvious benefits, Weber also considered it a negative development in human societies. Furthermore, he believed that the trend toward an ever-greater emphasis on rationality would continue. For Weber, the problems of the modern world, with its emphasis on rationality, were like an "iron cage" from which there was no hope of escape (Mitzman, 1969).

We can illustrate Weber's concern with an example that will be familiar to anyone who has gone through the American educational system. Most large high schools and

[3] Sociologists use the German pronunciation for Weber, which is roughly *Vay-ber*.

many colleges and universities are based to some degree on the principles of rationality. That is, they are set up to process the largest number of students (to give them an "education") in the most efficient way possible. Often American college students receive their educations in large, mass-production-like classes. By assembling large numbers of students in a single lecture class, using multiple-choice or other objective examinations (often machine graded), only a relatively small amount of time will be required from one professor. Hundreds of students can earn credit for a course with a minimum of professorial effort. The emphasis on efficiency in systems of mass education is highlighted by comparing mass education with the undergraduate education in an elite British school where a student may spend hours in discussion with a professor and where a personal relationship often develops between teacher and student. A mass education system makes it almost impossible for college professors to know more than a few of their many students personally. And the students usually know their professors in only a most superficial and impersonal way.

The most visible symbol of rationality and efficiency to Weber (and to many Americans) was the bureaucracy. A large university, of the type just described, is one type of bureaucracy, but many other organizations are equally familiar examples. In a bureaucracy, the standards of rationality and efficiency reign supreme; work is carefully divided into simple precise steps and made routine. The emphasis is only on speed and efficiency, with little regard for whether the work is meaningful for individual workers. We will examine bureaucracies more in chapter 4, where we will note, as did Weber, that although it is easy to criticize the bureaucracy, many tasks can be accomplished with precision, speed, and continuity within a bureaucratic organization (Weber in Gerth and Mills, 1958, p. 214).

Karl Marx

The German-born social philosopher and social analyst Karl Marx (1818–1883) has a somewhat different place in sociology's history than has either Durkheim or Weber. Although he lived and did much of his writing before either of them, and therefore influenced the work of both, Marx was not a part of any effort to establish sociology as an academic or scholarly discipline. Marx was not a sociologist and did not consider himself to be one. He was an analyst and a critic of society, and as such, he and his ideas have had a profound effect on contemporary sociology.

Through his ideas, Marx has also had a significant impact on the events of world history—an influence that continues to the present. For Marx, as is well known, was not only an analyst of society; he was also a political activist. He believed that his ideas about society should play a part in solving the problems that he identified. It is important to recognize and keep in mind the distinction between Marx as the social theorist and Marx as the political activist. His social theories are the part of his work that make important contributions to current-day sociology.

When Marx examined the societies of his time, he was struck by the inequities that prevailed between the masses of people who were at the bottom of the society and those who were at the top. In societies that had a capitalist/industrial form of economic organization, the workers—the **proletariat**—sold their labor to the owners of the means of production. The owners of the means of production were the **capitalists,** the social class that owned the raw materials, the factories, the machines, and the equipment. Marx saw the relationship between the capitalists and the proletariat as one of struggle

Proletariat
The workers in a capitalist society who sell their labor to capitalists

Capitalists
The owners of the means of production in a capitalist economic system

and conflict. The capitalists had the advantage in this struggle because they controlled not only the means of production but also the ideas, the values, and information that prevailed in society.

While Marxian theory is highly complex, especially in the interpretations of contemporary Marxian scholars, Marx's view of society is still one that emphasizes the struggle between those who have power and those who do not. In particular, Marxian theory points out that power often resides primarily in the hands of those who have economic dominance in a society. Throughout this book, but especially in our consideration of social stratification systems (chapter 8), we will see the pervasive importance of this Marxian insight—how those who control economic resources have a special ability to influence, and be the beneficiaries of, educational systems, health care and medical systems, and many other advantages of the society. For this reason, any societal analysis that employs a Marxian perspective is likely to look first at the economic system, and especially at the class structure.

Conflict theory
A theory emphasizing that units of social groups or societies struggle for power

In the next section we will see that a general sociological theory, called **conflict theory,** is built on the principle that social groups and societies are composed of units that are often engaged in some kind of struggle for power. Thus, conflict theory can be identified as a direct descendant of Marxian theory.

To a lesser degree some of the other pioneers of sociology have a connection with contemporary sociological theories. Durkheim, with his emphasis on the importance of social factors and the structure of society, was a forerunner of structural-functional theory, which will also be discussed below. Weber, in much of his work, emphasized the importance of ideas in shaping the direction and nature of societies. This emphasis is closely connected with some of the fundamental features of symbolic interaction theory, which will be discussed next.

Sociological Theories

Theory
A set of ideas that provides explanations for phenomena

Sociological theories
Theories that explain human behavior and a variety of social and societal events

A **theory** is a set of ideas that provides explanations for a broad range of phenomena. By extension, **sociological theories** are those that explain a wide range of human behavior and a variety of social and societal events. A sociological theory designates those parts of the social world that are especially important, and offers ideas about how the social world works. Every sociological theory has special words or terms that are unique to that theory.

Certain sociological theories are related to the microscopic level of sociological analysis. These theories are not inevitably bound to the microscopic level, but sociologists concerned with the behavior, actions, and interactions of individuals tend to use them. Two of these theories are: symbolic interactionism and social exchange theory.

Symbolic interactionism
A theory that deals primarily with interaction between individuals at the symbolic level

Symbols
Words, gestures, and objects that communicate meaning when people agree on what they represent

Symbolic Interactionism

As the name implies, **symbolic interactionism** deals primarily with the interaction between individuals at the symbolic level. **Symbols** are the words, gestures, and objects that communicate meaning between people. In any given society, people share a common understanding of these symbols. Words are the most important symbols from a symbolic interactionist viewpoint. If someone were to walk into the room where you are reading

Interaction between people, including their words, gestures, and facial expressions, are of primary importance to symbolic interactionists.

and shout "Fire!" no further description or detail would be necessary. That single word would convey the message that something significant is burning, and is possibly dangerous to you. Of course, the expression on the person's face might also convey a message, and we have learned to read messages in the faces, hands, and bodies of other people. If a friend were to describe the actions of another person and simultaneously roll his or her eyes skyward, you would understand that the friend is saying something like, "Can you believe that?" That facial gesture might not be understood by people from another society, however, but it is a symbol that we have learned to interpret in a particular way.

Spoken and written words, as well as facial and bodily gestures, are important for symbolic interactionists. Human beings have an exceptional, and perhaps unique, ability to use words, and people make connections with other people through these words, or symbols. Infants and children acquire many of their early words from family members, especially parents. By the age of seven years, an average child has command of 8,000 words (Pfeiffer, 1985) but the first words they learn are the symbols for observable, concrete things, such as *mama, daddy, mouth, nose, cat,* and *ball.* Gradually, children learn more abstract symbols—symbols that indicate not just things but evaluations as well (e.g., naughty puppy, pretty kitty, dirty garbage). Obviously, most of the evaluations that children learn are those held by family members, especially parents. Parents and other family members are referred to as **significant others** because their views have such a great influence on young children. Later in life, friends, schoolmates, marriage partners, fellow workers, religious and political leaders, and others will also be significant others.

Significant Others
Persons whose views have great influence on an individual

In the process of learning language and symbols, children learn evaluations of themselves, just as they learn evaluations of other objects. In the same way that parents might convey the idea that "garbage is dirty," they might also convey the idea that "Doug is a good boy" when he plays nicely with his baby sister. It is through this process of learning symbols about themselves that children develop what symbolic interactionists call a **self concept,** that is, an individual's thoughts or feelings about himself/herself. (Rosenberg, 1979). Symbolic interactionism is, therefore, a theory that has something to say about how individuals think about themselves and, thus, how they act as individual human beings.

Self concept
An individual's thoughts or feelings about himself/herself

But symbolic interactionists also stress that the symbols people learn govern their responses to all other human beings and things. If someone were to show us a painting and say it was by Pablo Picasso, we would probably be in awe. We would probably respond as much to the name Picasso (a symbol) as to the painting itself. This example also illustrates how most members of any given society share a wide variety of symbols. The commonality of shared symbols at any given time gives symbolic interactionism a macroscopic dimension, as well as its predominant microscopic focus (Fine, 1990).

In summary, symbolic interactionists pay special attention to the symbols individuals use to interpret and define themselves, the actions of other people, and all other things and events. By understanding the meanings that people give to these things through the use of words and symbols, it is possible to understand much of human behavior.

Social Exchange Theory

A second important sociological theory is one favored by a substantial number of sociologists interested in individual behavior and especially in the interaction between individuals (or in some cases between groups). **Social exchange theory** (often simply called exchange theory) emphasizes that the motivations for human behavior are to be found in its costs and rewards. Every human action is seen as having some cost, and therefore, if carried out, it must have a reward. On the other hand, if an action is costly but unrewarded in some way, the individual will not likely repeat it (Blau, 1964; Cook et al., 1990; Ekeh, 1974; Homans, 1973).

Social exchange theory
A theory emphasizing that motivations for human behavior are found in its costs and rewards

As a simple example of the principles of social exchange theory, suppose you were to see an elderly man, with his arms full of packages, struggling to open a door. You might take the time to help him, even though you are in a hurry. The cost of your action, here, is your time and energy. Your reward might be the thanks of the man, or perhaps the smiles of other people who were passing by and saw how helpful you had been. According to exchange theory principles, you would more likely aid the next person who needs help because you received a reward for your actions. On the other hand, if the elderly man were to tell you to "Stop interfering and mind your own business!" you would probably have felt punished for your action, and you would not be as likely to repeat it in a similar circumstance.

Social exchange theory principles—that people are likely to behave in ways that have been rewarding in the past and not behave in ways that have been costly or painful—are thought by exchange theorists to explain most of human behavior and much interaction between people. Thus, for example, two young people dating will continue to see each other as long as each person is getting adequate rewards from the continuing interaction. It should be noted that the rewards can be anything that either of the two individuals finds of value, including gifts, opportunities for entertainment,

Social exchange theorists look at human interaction as an exchange between people. Every interaction involves giving and receiving.

the admiration of one's friends, an escape from boredom, the feeling that one is loved, sexual pleasure, and so on. When one person (or both) feels that there are more costs (e.g., time, effort, energy) than rewards coming from the relationship then, according to social exchange theory, the relationship will probably end.

A key concept of social exchange theory is reciprocity. **Reciprocity** is the socially accepted idea that if you give something to someone, that person must give something of equal or near equal value in return (Gouldner, 1960). If a fellow student asks you for your class notes or solutions to some problems the night before an exam, and you give them, you will normally expect that person to give you something in return. Once again, what you receive in return need not be the same thing. Your fellow student may give you some concert tickets, invite you to a party, or simply tell other people what a generous and smart person you are. If you do not feel you have received an adequate reward (reciprocity), you are likely to feel slighted, and you will probably not be as generous if you are asked again.

Reciprocity
Receiving something equal in value to what is given

The rules of reciprocity can be found at many levels of social life. We try to give people gifts that are similar in value to the ones they give to us; married couples try to entertain their friends in about the same way as they expect to be, or have been, entertained; friendly nations try to maintain a balance in their trading relations with imports roughly equal to exports. When there are violations of the principle of reciprocity, with one side returning less than it is receiving, relations between individuals, groups, or nations are apt to become strained. Too great a violation of reciprocity may result in anger and hostility and a breaking off of the relationship.

Although social exchange theory might have some applicability to the level of groups and societies, it is most often applied at the micro level of individuals. We will turn now to two theories that apply primarily to the macro level (groups, organizations, cultures, and societies): structural-functionalism and conflict theory.

Structural-Functional Theory

Structural-functional theory
Theory emphasizing that every societal pattern in some way contributes positively or negatively to society

Structural-functional theory, often called functional theory or functionalism, emphasizes that every pattern of activity (that is, every structure) in a society makes some positive or negative contribution to that society (Abrahamson, 1978; Turner and Maryanski, 1979; Alexander and Colomy, 1985; Ritzer, 1988). The two key words of structural-functional theory are *structure* and *function*. The term *structure* is used in this case as shorthand for social structure, which is a very basic sociological concept. A **social structure** is a regular pattern of social interaction or persistent social relationships. Examples of social structures include the socioeconomic status system of a society (the social class structure will be considered fully in chapter 8), the patterned social relationships between races and ethnic groups (chapter 9), or the patterns of family organization (chapter 11). These and other patterned social relationships are the structural features of a society.

Social structure
A regular pattern of social interaction or persistent social relationships

Structural-functionalists are interested in why certain structures exist in a society and especially what purpose, or function, they serve. A **function,** according to structural-functionalists, is a positive purpose or consequence—one necessary for the continued existence of a society (or some other social system). With regard to the family system in a society, the functions might include producing children, caring for them when they are young, and training them in the ways of the society. If a society does not have a fairly persistent structure for producing new members, caring for them, and socializing them, the society is not likely to survive.

Function
A positive purpose or consequence for the continued existence of a social system

Early structural-functional theorists believed that every structure of a society had a function—that is, made a positive contribution to the continuation of the society (Malinowski, 1925/1955). Modern-day functionalists still look for the positive contributions that various structures provide, but they also emphasize that some structures are detrimental to the survival of the society. When a social structure has a detrimental effect or consequence for the existence or well being of a society it is said to be **dysfunctional.**

Dysfunction
A detrimental effect or consequence for a society

To illustrate a possible dysfunction we consider again the example of marriage and family systems that produce children for the society. Throughout most of human history the death rates for infants and children were extremely high. In addition, many mothers died in pregnancy and childbirth. As a consequence, most societies developed marriage and family systems that encouraged people to have children, as many as they could. A marriage and family system that could produce many children under high-death-rate conditions was probably functional for most societies. However, in the twentieth century, the infant, childhood, and maternal death rates were greatly reduced in many countries. Nonetheless, the marriage and family structures continued to produce large numbers of children, who, consequently, had to be cared for and fed. The marriage and family system that had previously been functional was now viewed by many observers to be dysfunctional. The large numbers of children were seen as a threat to the survival of the society.

Manifest function
The intended and well-recognized purpose of some social structure

Latent function
A less obvious, unanticipated, or unexpected purpose of some social structure

Structural-functionalists are also inclined to compare the obvious functions of social structures with the less obvious functions. The **manifest function** is the intended and well-recognized purpose of some social structure. The less obvious, unanticipated, or unexpected purpose of a social structure is called a **latent function.** To illustrate, we may ask the question, "Why do we have organized crime in the United States?" At the level of manifest function, the purpose of organized crime is for criminals to make money from illicit activities. But what is the latent function, the function that is less obvious? To answer this question we must look for the less obvious, unanticipated, or unexpected consequences of organized crime.

Functional theorists would ask if organized crime serves a purpose for someone other than the criminals, or for the society as a whole? For starters, organized crime is allegedly involved in providing illegal drugs, prostitution, and gambling. The users of these "services" are generally involved in an illegal activity, but many think of themselves as "law-abiding." (Most people who bet illegally on sports events consider this activity a part of everyday life.) Organized crime is also said to distribute most of the pornography in the society—again, a "service" that many citizens are willing to pay for without asking too many questions. But what of those of us who have no need for drugs, or prostitutes, or pornography, or gambling? We, too, may benefit from the services of organized crime. Newspaper reports claim that organized criminal groups have systematically engaged in buying gasoline without paying high federal taxes. The gasoline is then sold to independent retailers who, in turn, may pass the savings on to us, the gasoline consumers. Other reports state that organized crime is engaged in the toxic-waste-disposal business. When legitimate companies want to dispose of their toxic wastes they may contract with organized criminals who will agree to do the job cheaply because they will dispose of the toxic wastes in any way possible—legal or illegal. Thus, they "provide a service"

The illegal dumping of toxic waste is just one of many "services" that organized crime provides for society. Structural-functional theory views organized crime as a structure that persists because it serves many functions for society.

by disposing of toxic wastes at a low cost. Of course, in the long run the effect of dumping toxic wastes in places where they will create health hazards will be dysfunctional to the society.

This functionalist analysis of organized crime helps to answer the otherwise perplexing question: "Why does organized crime persist in our society, even though most members of government, most law enforcement agencies and agents, as well as most citizens claim to want it stopped?" The answer is that organized crime, viewed as a structural feature of our society, provides a variety of services that are wanted and used by the rest of the society. It is in this sense that organized crime (as a structure) is functional.

The final major theory, conflict theory, also applies primarily to macroscopic analysis, that is, the analysis of larger social units such as social groups, social organizations, and societies.

Conflict Theory

In our discussion of Karl Marx we noted that his work sensitized sociologists to the fact that, in any kind of social group or system, from families to entire societies, inequities exist in the amount of power and resources held by the participants. Furthermore, these power and resource inequities are likely to persist over time. As we saw earlier, Marx believed that in a capitalist society the holders of the means of production are likely to have a persistent edge over the workers. Conflict theory is an extension of this idea, and thus as a general theory it emphasizes that in any social group, social organization, or society, certain positions (or statuses) are endowed with greater power than other positions or statuses. The incumbents of these positions, those with greater power and resources and those with less, are, according to conflict theory, engaged in a more or less continuous struggle. Those who have greater power and resources do not give them up voluntarily, and therefore those with less power and fewer resources try to wrest those resources from those who hold them (Coser, 1956; Dahrendorf, 1959; Ritzer, 1988).

As an example of how conflict theory can be applied, we turn again to the family. Even though we usually think of the family as a highly cooperative social unit, one where feelings of love and affection exist between the members, the principles of conflict theory are clearly applicable (Collins, 1971; Scanzoni, 1972). In our society (and in most others) two family statuses almost always have more power and control more resources: adults (compared to children and adolescents) and males (compared to females). The adult male in the family is therefore usually able to exercise power over other members of the family, which means that he can make other family members do (or not do) what he wants.

A simple, and probably familiar, example of the way the family members who are in the subordinate status struggle to get more power is found in the relations between adolescent children and their parents. Until adolescence the power of parents over their children is usually unquestioned by both parties. However, adolescence in our society is often a period of considerable conflict between parents and their children because the adolescents are striving to have a greater voice in deciding what they can and cannot do. A 16-year-old or 17-year-old is likely to want greater freedom and independence than parents are willing to give. Outright conflict sometimes results, but disobedience and subversion are more commonly the tactics of adolescents as they push for greater personal autonomy.

If there are conflicts and struggles for power in the family (and we have said nothing about husbands and wives), then clearly the same is apt to be true of other social groups, social organizations, and societies. Conflict theory can also be useful for the analysis of sororities and fraternities, schools, religious organizations, majority/minority relations, the politics of nations, and, of course, the relations between nations. In later chapters many examples will be provided of the inequities between those who have power and resources and those who do not, as well as descriptions of the conflict that ensues when the group with less power and fewer resources struggles for greater equity.

Summary

Sociology is the study of human behavior, in all its many forms. There is no single sociology, however; there are many sociologies. Sociological specialties or subfields focus on some part of human behavior and/or some aspect of social life. Sociologists have different theoretical preferences, research preferences, and levels of analysis (microscopic or macroscopic).

Although sociologists differ on a number of issues, they generally share some fundamental ideas and views. One is that societies and other social settings are humanly created. Every day, people affirm and modify their social settings, but these same social settings, in turn, influence and constrain human behavior.

Sociology can be useful in a number of ways. It provides a wide range of statistical and substantive facts about social conditions and trends. Sociology also provides an awareness and knowledge of cross-cultural and cross-national information. Through sociological concepts and theories, sociology can aid in understanding many issues and problems beyond the subject immediately under study.

Sociology offers training for a variety of occupations and professions. With a graduate degree in sociology, teaching at the college or university level is a professional option, but increasingly the research skills of trained sociologists are needed by governments, organizations, and businesses.

The beginnings of sociology can be dated to the early 1800s, when the work of Auguste Comte gave sociology its name and its place among other scholarly disciplines. Among the other pioneers of sociology, the most famous are Emile Durkheim and Max Weber. Karl Marx was an early analyst and critic of society whose ideas have had a profound effect on contemporary sociology.

There are four contemporary theories that dominate sociology. Symbolic interaction theory is oriented toward the interaction between individuals, especially at the symbolic level. The symbols that individuals learn through interaction govern their responses to other human beings, to things, and to themselves. Social exchange theory emphasizes the fact that the motivations for human behavior are found in the costs and rewards of human actions. Humans will continue actions and interactions that are rewarded, and will discontinue those that are not. Structural-functional theory focuses on macroscopic levels of analysis and emphasizes that every pattern of activity (structure) in a society makes some kind of positive or negative contribution to that society. Structural-functional theory also calls attention to less obvious functions of social structures; these are called latent functions. Conflict theory, which is an extension of some basic Marxian ideas, emphasizes that, in any social group, social organization, or society, positions of unequal power probably exist. The struggle for power is a source of conflict in these social groupings.

CRITICAL THINKING

1. What types of subjects might interest sociologists? List three to five topics that might be the subject of a sociological study.
2. Compare and contrast the advantages and disadvantages of qualitative and quantitative research.
3. Suppose a sociologist wanted to study education in the United States. What would be the focus of a microscopic study of education? What would be the subject of a macroscopic study?
4. Which groups in society have a vested interest in keeping the existing social arrangements in place? Which groups in society are likely to promote change?
5. Give examples from your own life that show how social settings have influenced or constrained your behavior.
6. In what ways is a knowledge of sociology useful to you in your personal or professional lives? Generate a list of issues or questions for which sociological research might prove useful.
7. Describe and compare the major contributions made to the field of sociology by Comte, Durkheim, Weber, and Marx.
8. Give examples of important symbols on your college campus.
9. Assume the beliefs of a social exchange theory sociologist. How would the idea of reciprocity apply to your relationship with your parents?
10. Give a brief explanation of how conflict theory might apply to union and management relations in the United States.

Social Psychology Quarterly
Journal of Marriage & the Family
American Sociological Review
Volume 54 • August 1989 • Number 4
DEMOGRAPHY
Sociological Forum
Volume 4, Number 2
June 1989
Official Journal of the Eastern Sociological Society
PLENUM PRESS • NEW YORK and LONDON
The British Journal of Sociology
AN INTERNATIONAL JOURNAL OF SOCIA
ASSOCIATED WITH THE SOUTHERN SOCIOLO
VOLUME 67, NUMBER 4 JUNE 198
Media Discourse and Public Opinion on Nuclear Power—Gamson and Modigliani
Structure after 50 Years—Camic
Fathers' Ages and the Social Stratification of Sons—Mare and Tzeng
Self-Perceptions of Black Americans—Hughes and Demo
Occupational Segregation by Sex—Jacobs
The University of Chicago Press
THE SOCIOLOGICAL QUARTERLY
Editor
GEORGE J. McCALL

CHAPTER

2

Sociological Research

Jennifer Hunt describes an incident that occurred when she was riding in a police cruiser in a large city:

> *One evening I was patrolling with a male officer when we observed people pouring out of a bar. A man then yelled, 'You better get in here quick. There's a helluva fight going on!' The officer ran out of the car while I grabbed the radio and requested a backup. . . . When I entered the door, I looked to my left and noticed a man sitting at the bar. He looked relatively harmless . . . most of the action was occurring at the far end of the room. People were yelling and crying. Three wounded suspects were all armed with knives. The police officer seemed to be pointing his gun in three different directions. When I approached the rookie officer, I grabbed an hysterical waitress reaching for a knife that she had apparently dropped on a stool. Meanwhile the rookie disarmed one man while the other voluntarily discarded his weapon* (Hunt, 1984, p. 290).

If Jennifer Hunt had been a regular police officer this incident would not have been extraordinary. But Jennifer was not, and is not, a police officer. She is a sociologist, and she was riding in the police cruiser to collect data for her doctoral dissertation. Her

Some sociologists have conducted research in dangerous settings, such as joining police on patrol. Like journalists covering a story, sociological observers can sometimes find themselves in violent or even life-threatening situations.

method of doing research is one that has a long history in sociology and it involves the researcher directly in the lives and activities of the people being studied. The researcher, then, is both a participant and an observer, and the research method is called participant observation. (For a full description of this method, see p. 46.)

Of course, very few sociologists are called upon to face dangerous citizens armed with knives when they do their research. In fact, many sociologists today carry out major sociological studies without coming into direct contact with people at all. There is some irony in such a situation because many people who become sociologists are initially attracted to the field through their interest in people and in human behavior. Yet it is only a slight exaggeration to say that significant sociological research is now possible without leaving the computer terminal. The information for such studies will have been obtained by others (often by skilled interviewers) and transferred to computer disks and tapes where it is stored until needed.

These two different sociological research methods show again the diversity of sociology. In this chapter we will explore the different ways of doing sociology by introducing and illustrating the most important research methods being used by sociologists today. But first we will consider some of the underlying ideas that guide most sociological research. We will begin with a brief look at what it means to use a scientific approach to study human behavior and social life.

A Scientific Approach to Knowledge

Most sociologists assume that human behavior can be studied by using a scientific approach. In today's world we are accustomed to having the results of scientific research for most major questions and issues we encounter. Certainly it is true of the physical world. We rely upon scientific studies to inform us about holes in the ozone layer that surrounds the earth and the dangers that such holes present. We look for scientific information about how the AIDS (Acquired Immune Deficiency Syndrome) virus is spread from one person to another because that information could help us make decisions about our own behavior. And, because most of us believe it is important to have scientific knowledge about the physical and biological worlds, we also expect to have scientific knowledge about our social and psychological worlds.

Although the scientific approach to understanding human behavior and the social world is widely accepted, studying humans is not quite the same as studying insects, the weather, or atomic particles. We therefore need to consider some of the basic elements of the scientific approach, but at the same time consider how the scientific approach must be modified to fit the subject matter of sociology.

Empirical Observation

Empiricism
The act of experiencing something with one's senses

One word that is critical for understanding the essence of a scientific approach is **empiricism,** which is the act of experiencing something with one's senses. Empiricism contrasts sharply with imagination and speculation, even though these two activities are also important parts of the scientific approach. We can imagine how some aspect of the social world will be, but we will not know what it is really like until we make some observations, or obtain information, either directly or indirectly. We can imagine what it is like to be a young rookie police officer, but our imaginings and speculations cannot substitute for the actual observations of researchers like Jennifer Hunt (1984, 1985).

Objectivity and Sociological Research

The central importance of empiricism in science leads directly to a consideration of a second feature of the scientific method—objectivity. **Objectivity** in science means, in general terms, that scientists conduct their research in such a way that their personal, subjective views do not influence the results of their research. This general statement may seem an easy rule to follow but, for sociologists, objectivity poses some special problems.

Objectivity
Conducting research in a way that personal, subjective views do not influence results

Objectivity has two dimensions. Objectivity is first an attitude of the scientist who must try to keep his or her personal views, beliefs, and values from influencing either the conduct or the conclusions of the research. The second dimension of objectivity is the use of research procedures described in sufficient detail so that other scientists may, if they choose, repeat (or replicate) a study. The attitudinal dimension of objectivity is much more difficult to achieve and maintain than is the procedural dimension, and we will deal with that first.

Objectivity as an Attitude. Scientists are expected to be objective about the subjects of their research. However, in everyday experience, scientists in all fields find it difficult to remain "value free." All scientists have personal views, attitudes, and values that could potentially affect the selection of particular problems for study, the conduct of the research, and the interpretation of the results.

In sociology, as well as in other social and behavioral sciences, special problems occur with this aspect of objectivity. Sociology often deals with issues, questions, and problems that are personally important in the lives of the sociologists conducting the research. Consider, for example, the issue of the death penalty for major crimes. One sociologist might be personally in favor of the death penalty, while another might be opposed. Will they likely ask the same research questions and carry out the same research? In an ideal world these two scientists with different views would not allow those views to influence the planning and execution of their research. However, in the real world these scientists might ask different research questions and reach different conclusions.

While some sociologists argue that all sociologists must be objective and value free at all times, others hold a more realistic view. This more realistic view acknowledges that sociologists have personal values, and, at least in some stages of their professional research, they may be allowed to use these values to influence their selection of issues and the types of questions they ask. For example, a sociologist might support the idea that women have a right to enter and succeed in occupations that have been previously male dominated. Such a sociologist could design a study to learn if women entering male-dominated occupations are treated and evaluated fairly. But, for validity, the study would have to be done fairly and the results repo.ted honestly.

Strong support for the death penalty is reflected in this demonstrator's call for the death of convicted serial killer Ted Bundy. Sociologists as citizens may also support or oppose the death penalty, but in the interests of scientific objectivity, their attitudes should not influence their research.

Attitudinal objectivity An attitude of fairness and honesty when planning and conducting research

Attitudinal objectivity requires scientists to maintain an attitude of fairness and honesty when planning and conducting their research. Researchers cannot intentionally design their studies in such a way that the results will be predetermined to support their views. They cannot design the questions or measures in such a way as to influence the outcome of the research. They certainly cannot interpret their results in a biased or dishonest manner in order to obtain the results they desire. An objective attitude must be rigorously maintained in the conduct of research, or one of the fundamental elements of science is sacrificed.

Procedural objectivity Performing and reporting research so that others will know how it was conducted

Objectivity as a Procedure. **Procedural objectivity** refers to the performing and reporting of all research tasks in such a way that any interested person will know exactly how the research was conducted. The research procedure cannot include any methods of observation that other qualified scientists are unable to repeat. For example, if an astronomer claimed to have heard a message from intelligent beings coming from outer space but then asserted: "The messages can only be heard on my recording instruments, and no one else may use my instruments," such a report, no matter how interesting, could not be accepted by other scientists or, for that matter, by the public. To be scientific, the methods of observation must be reported in such a way that other scientists will be able to use those same methods. Only then can other scientists verify or reject the results of the original research.

Although this standard is widely accepted by scientists and the public alike for the natural and biological sciences, a tendency exists to hold the social sciences to a less rigorous standard. But the standards of scientific inquiry should be uniformly applied. If, for example, a sociologist were to report that a "sample of 200 adults completed a questionnaire" and then reported the results of the research without providing any additional information about the sample, we should be skeptical about the report. As a minimum requirement, any interested person should be able to ask for information as to where and how the sample was selected.

Sociological researchers must also report, or be prepared to provide more details about, the specific questions asked in interviews or on questionnaires. If questions have been combined in certain ways so as to create general measures, these steps would also have to be described. Finally, any statistical procedures used to analyze the data must be reported.

Some sociological research methods do not involve samples, questionnaires, or statistical analyses but rather involve the observation of individuals or groups in natural social settings. With these methods the precise research procedures are often more difficult to document, but the researchers are nonetheless obligated to provide full reports of their methods if they are to measure up to the standards of procedural objectivity.

Ethical Issues of Social Research

When sociologists carry out research projects they may cause problems for, or even do harm to, the people they study. This possibility makes it necessary for sociologists to consider the ethical implications of their research. The basic question that any social researcher must ask is: If I carry out this research will it harm the participants or other people in some way? There are several types of potentially harmful or negative consequences that may come from social research.

Physical Harm

Although relatively rare, it is possible that a researcher's actions can cause physical harm to the people being studied. As an example, a social psychologist named Muzafer Sherif once conducted a field experiment with 12-year-old boys at a summer camp, and the final stages of the experiment had to be curtailed because the boys were in danger of being seriously hurt (Sherif, 1953). In this study the boys were divided into two groups, and then, through the manipulations of the researchers, the groups were brought into competition and conflict. For a number of days the conflict was limited to apple-throwing fights and to raids on each other's cabins, but in a final severe confrontation in the dining hall the two groups of boys faced off and the situation became dangerous. Some of the boys started to throw silverware and plates. The researchers quickly stepped in and stopped the hostilities (and that phase of the field experiment).

One of the objectives of Sherif's study was to observe how competition between groups could lead to conflict and then to learn about reducing conflict between those groups. Although that goal is surely desirable, it may have been outweighed in this case by the possible dangers to the subjects of the study.

Psychological Harm

The actions of a social researcher could possibly cause psychological harm as well, although anticipating when and how this might occur is often difficult. Researchers today frequently ask respondents about sensitive and personal issues, including questions about alcohol use, criminal acts, heterosexual or homosexual experiences, child or spouse abuse, deaths of relatives, mental illness, physical handicaps, and so on. For most people questions on these and similar subjects will not likely cause any psychological distress, but the possibility always exists that some respondents will suffer psychological harm. An example comes from a study of psychological depression in which interviewers asked subjects about an array of life's tragedies and about their symptoms of mental illness. The trained interviewers who conducted the pretest interviews reported that some of the interviewees were showing clear signs of depression after being questioned about these topics. The research directors became concerned that their interview was actually *causing depression*. Before the study could continue, the questions were broadened to include some more positive and "upbeat" topics (Converse and Presser, 1986).

Intrusions into Private Lives

Sometimes the intrusion into the private lives of individuals raises ethical questions for researchers. Especially problematic are the sociological studies in which people are observed without being informed that they are being studied, or being misinformed about the nature of the study. In a study that has become as well known for its ethical aspects as for its substantive findings, one sociologist secretly observed the homosexual behavior of men in public restrooms—called "tearooms" by those who frequent them (Humphreys, 1975). In order to study tearoom participants, Humphreys took the role of "watch-queen," a lookout who signals those engaged in homosexual acts that a stranger, or worse, a police officer, is approaching. Only a few of the men he studied knew that he was a sociological researcher. Although Humphreys took great care to disguise and protect the identity of the men he studied, a number of sociologists believed that, by deceiving the men under study, he was violating the ethical standards of social research. Humphreys subsequently reported that if he were to repeat the study he would spend more time "cultivating and expanding the [number] of willing respondents . . ." (Humphreys, 1975, pp. 229–231).

The Humphreys study is an extreme example of a concern that nearly every social researcher must have when collecting research data: How much must the researcher tell the respondents about the nature of a study in order to get their cooperation? Today most sociological research is conducted under rules of "informed consent," which means that, when people are asked to participate, they are told in a general way about the nature and purpose of the study and of any sensitive or dangerous aspects of the study. Of course, it must be clear that participation in the study is voluntary, and that the identities of participants will remain confidential. Most sociologists agree that, although it is sometimes inconvenient to go through the informed-consent procedures (and occasionally a study is changed or impeded because of them), it is better to err on the side of safety and to avoid problems of questionable ethics.

Steps in the Research Process

All research starts with a question, but the questions may come from very different sources. Sociologists commonly become interested in topics that have special importance in their personal lives or in topics that reflect current societal developments. For example, as women have entered the labor force in ever-increasing numbers, many sociologists (both men and women) have become interested in the occupational experiences of women. We now have a growing body of research-based knowledge about women in the labor force.

Reviewing the Literature

Even though a sociologist has selected a general area for research (e.g., women entering male-dominated occupations), he or she may not have decided on the exact question or questions for study. One often-used way of finding research questions is to turn to earlier studies on the same general subject, which is referred to as "reviewing the literature." For example, there have been a number of studies of women working in male-dominated occupations, including studies of women in corporate sales (Kanter, 1977), women in coal mining (Vaught and Smith, 1980), women in medicine (Lorber, 1984), and women in blue-collar occupations (Rosen, 1987).

There are many occupations that have been largely limited to males, such as piloting a helicopter in the military. But, as the options for women have opened, some women have managed to gain entry into what have been nearly exclusive male domains. As a result, women in these occupations are the subject of keen sociological interest.

Formulating Hypotheses

Hypothesis
A statement about how phenomena are expected to relate to each other

Reading the existing research literature will show what has been learned about a subject and what things remain unclear or uncertain. Previous research will also show which theoretical approaches have been used and have proved most useful for the study. Either the previous research literature or particular theoretical approaches may suggest specific hypotheses that need to be tested further. A **hypothesis** is a statement about how various phenomena are expected to be related to each other.

One of the ideals of scientific inquiry is for theories to provide hypotheses of relationships that can then be tested by research. A classic sociological example of a theory that provides hypotheses can be drawn from the work of social theorist Emile Durkheim, who was introduced in chapter 1. As you will recall, Durkheim studied the ways in which suicide is related to social conditions. (Anomie, or normlessness, was one such condition.) Durkheim also speculated (or theorized) that social integration would be related to suicide. He defined **social integration** as belonging to, or being a part of, social groups or the society. Using data from various nineteenth-century European countries, Durkheim found that the more socially integrated segments of populations had lower suicide rates. Married people, for example, were presumed to be more socially integrated because of marriage and family ties, and married people had lower rates of suicide (Durkheim, 1897/1951). Sociological researchers in the twentieth century continue to find support for Durkheim's idea that social integration, represented by marriage, reduces suicide (Breault, 1986; Gibbs and Martin, 1964; Gibbs, 1982). Two researchers have recently observed, however, that marriage today is less important as a deterrent to suicide than it was in earlier studies, especially for women. Occupational integration seems to be much more important today than marital integration (Stafford and Gibbs, 1985, 1988). These researchers conclude that both males and females today are more likely to get their sense of social belonging from their occupations rather than from marriage.

Social integration
Belonging to, or being part of, social groups or society

Durkheim's basic idea about the importance of social integration has provided hypotheses about other forms of behavior as well. For example, divorce rates in the United States have been found to be higher in areas where people are less socially integrated (Glenn and Supancic, 1984; Glenn and Shelton, 1985).

Since social integration has been found to be related to both suicide and divorce, sociological researchers might hypothesize that social integration is also related to other forms of behavior. A researcher might hypothesize that violence in the family (wife abuse, child abuse, elder abuse) would occur more often among families with low levels of social integration. The research literature on child abuse lends some support to this hypothesis because it has been found that when parents are more isolated (few friends, little contact with other relatives) they are more likely to abuse their children (Garbarino and Sherman, 1980).

Theoretical Concepts and Research Variables

Concept
A word or phrase that summarizes some meaningful part of the social world

A theoretical idea such as social integration is called a concept. The term used earlier, *male-dominated occupation,* is also a concept. A **concept** is a word or phrase that summarizes some meaningful part of the social world. An important part of social research consists of translating key concepts into observable phenomena. For example, to translate the concept of social integration into an observable phenomenon, Durkheim used the percentage of the population that was married. Of course, being married is not the only indication of social integration. One could also get an indication of the social integration level of individuals by asking how many friends they have or how much time they spend with family members. These observable phenomena are called **indicators**—in this case, indicators of the degree to which people are socially integrated.

Indicators
Observable phenomena that indicate the presence, absence, or level of a concept

When concepts are observed through the use of indicators, researchers often refer to the indicators as variables. **Variables** are defined as objects or phenomena that can change from one size, state, or degree to another. Levels of social integration are variable because some people, or some groups, are more socially integrated than others. Similarly, the degree to which occupations are male dominated is a variable because some occupations are almost entirely made up of males (engineers—94 percent male, police and detectives—89 percent male), while others are more evenly balanced between the sexes (real estate salespersons—49 percent male and 51 percent female). At the opposite extreme, some occupations are female dominated (bank tellers—91 percent female, kindergarten teachers—98 percent female) (U.S. Bureau of the Census, 1987).

Variables
Objects or phenomena that can change from one size, state, or degree to another

Independent and Dependent Variables

Social researchers divide variables into two basic classes: independent variables and dependent variables. **Independent variables** are those that are thought to produce a change in some other variable. Durkheim expected, on the basis of his theory, that the independent variable, social integration, would produce changes in suicide rates, the dependent variable. **Dependent variables** are those that are changed or influenced by independent variables. In everyday terms, independent variables are the presumed *causes* of changes; they produce *effects* on dependent variables. A researcher who wants to test the hypothesis that a low level of social integration will produce higher levels of child abuse would call social integration the independent variable and child abuse the dependent variable.

Independent variables
Variables that are thought to produce a change in some other variable

Dependent variables
Variables that are changed or influenced by independent variables

We have reviewed some of the basic elements of scientific research and turn now to the major research methods used in sociology. As we consider these research methods, further illustrations and elaborations will be given of the principles and processes already introduced.

Major Sociological Research Methods

Experiments

Experiments are typically set up in such a way that the independent variable is under the control of the researcher and its impact on a dependent variable can be observed directly. Such experiments are ideally suited for assessing causality. A hypothetical experiment will reveal some of the important elements of social experiments.

Experiments
Research method where the independent variable is under the control of the researcher

Sociologists are often interested in how education and instruction can change the attitudes of individuals. For example, let us suppose that a community wants to change the attitudes of high school students about drinking alcohol and driving. A film is made

A film showing alcohol-related automobile accidents might be the experimental variable in a field experiment designed to determine whether attitudes about drinking and driving can be changed.

showing how the use of alcohol contributes to automobile accidents and may cause serious injuries to young people. At the local high school, all seniors are given a questionnaire, called a pretest measurement, that will measure the students' attitudes toward drinking and driving. The **pretest measurement** is the measurement of the dependent variable (in this example, attitudes toward drinking and driving) before the introduction of the experimental variable (the film).

Pretest measurement
Measurement of the dependent variable before the introduction of the experimental variable

Shortly after the pretest measurement, the seniors are divided into two groups by some procedure that gives every student an equal chance of being selected for the experimental group (drawing names, for example, until half are selected and half remain). This technique, called random selection, is necessary to assure that all important characteristics of the students are distributed in the groups and that the two groups are as much alike as possible (Cook and Campbell, 1979).

Experimental group
Subjects in an experiment who are exposed to the experimental variable

Experimental treatment
Exposure to the independent variable in an experiment

Control group
Subjects not exposed to the experimental variable in an experiment

After the two groups have been randomly selected, one group, the experimental group, is shown the film on alcohol-related accidents and injuries. An **experimental group** is made up of the subjects who are exposed to the experimental variable, the film. (The film can also be thought of as the independent variable, since it may produce a change in the attitudes of the students.) In an experiment, exposure to the experimental variable is often called the **experimental treatment.** The other group of students, called the control group, will not be given the experimental treatment (will not be shown the film). A **control group** in an experiment is made up of subjects who are not exposed to the experimental variable. Shortly after the film has been shown to the experimental group, the attitudes of the students in both the experimental and control groups are measured again. This is called a **posttest measurement.** If the film has had an impact on the students' attitudes about drinking and driving, the students in the experimental group will have changed their attitudes, while the attitudes of the students in the control group will have remained relatively unchanged.

Posttest measurement Measurement of the dependent variable after the experimental treatment has been introduced

The experiment in this illustration—conducted in a normal school environment and involving the relatively normal activities of seeing a film and filling out questionnaires—is a field experiment. **Field experiments** are conducted in settings that are natural and involve activities that are relatively normal.

Field experiments Experiments conducted in natural settings involving normal activities

Sometimes sociologists conduct experiments under much more controlled conditions. These are called **laboratory experiments** since they are conducted in specially designed rooms that are equipped with one-way mirrors, audio systems, and video recording equipment. In a typical laboratory experiment, subjects are brought into a room or laboratory and asked to engage in some activity or task (solve a problem, judge or evaluate something). The experimenter will usually administer an experimental treatment to some of the subjects but not to others (who serve as the control group). The effects of the experimental treatment are then measured in some way.

Laboratory experiments Experiments conducted in rooms with special recording and observing systems

Laboratory experiments have the advantage of giving the researcher close control over experimental variables, but often the situation is artificial or unnatural. Therefore, the results of laboratory experiments, although effective for testing theoretical hypotheses, may be questioned for their applicability to real-life situations.

A distinction is often made between applied and basic research. **Applied research** is research designed and conducted to answer a specific practical question or to solve a particular social problem. **Basic research** tests hypotheses derived from theories, such as the test of Durkheim's social integration hypothesis discussed earlier. Applied research can be done with surveys and other research methods, but field experiments are often used to evaluate and assess the effectiveness of social programs or to test the desirability of proposed government policies that are designed to solve some social problem (Saxe and Fine, 1981).

Applied research Research to answer a specific practical question or solve a particular social problem

Basic research Research to test hypotheses derived from theories

Applied Research: A Field Experiment Example. Sherman and Berk (1984) used a field experiment to evaluate different police methods for dealing with domestic disturbances. Domestic disturbances are disputes and violence between family members that are sufficiently serious for the police to be called to the residence. When police arrive at scenes of domestic violence, they may take one of several courses of action. They may try negotiating or otherwise "talking out" the dispute, they may ask one of the parties to leave, or they may make an arrest.

In Minneapolis, a field experiment was conducted to see which of three different police responses was most effective in reducing the recurrence of violence committed by the same suspects. When called to a residence where domestic violence of a misdemeanor[1] nature had occurred, the police were to take one of the following actions: (1) arrest the alleged offender; (2) separate the offender from the person who was attacked or threatened by making the offender leave the residence; (3) give some form of advice, counseling, or mediation. The action to be taken by the police in any given

---

[1] A misdemeanor is a crime less serious than a felony; it is punishable by imprisonment for less than a year.

case was determined randomly through a color-coded pad of report forms. The color of the top sheet determined the officer's action. If, for example, the top sheet were blue, the officer would arrest the offender; if it were yellow, the officer would offer advice and counseling.

Conducting this field experiment required both the cooperation of the Minneapolis police department and careful supervision by the research team who took a number of precautions and made cross-checks to see that the police handled cases in the way called for by the experimental design. This experiment had no control group since the objective was to determine which of the three alternative police responses would be most effective in deterring future violence. Each response was an experimental treatment, and its effects could be compared to the effects of the other two treatments.

Two methods were used to establish which treatments were most effective: (1) monitoring police records for six months to see if a suspect's name appeared again in a case of domestic violence and (2) interviewing the original victims by telephone over a six-month period to find out if there had been a repeat incident with the same suspect.

The clearest finding of this experimental study was that suspects arrested in domestic violence cases were less likely to be involved in violence at a later date. Specifically, suspects who were arrested and temporarily incarcerated were less likely to appear on police records in the next six months. Also, when interviewed, victims of the original violence were less likely to report a recurrence of the violence (Sherman and Berk, 1984).

The findings of this field experiment have some obvious implications for the way police officers respond to incidents of domestic violence: if the police make arrests and incarcerate individuals who engage in domestic violence, there is less likelihood that the violent behavior will continue. In fact, the implications of this study have not been ignored by the nation's police departments. After these results were publicly announced and published in a sociological journal, many police forces changed their policies with regard to domestic violence. In 1984, only 10 percent of police departments in cities over 100,000 had a policy of arresting suspects in domestic violence cases. In 1986, 43 percent of these same departments had such a policy. Spokespersons acknowledged that the results of the Minneapolis experiment influenced them to change the way they dealt with incidents of domestic violence (Sherman and Cohn, 1989).

Participant Observation

Participant observation Research method in which a researcher interacts with and observes activities of people being studied

We noted at the beginning of this chapter that, when sociologist Jennifer Hunt collected data by riding in a police cruiser, she was engaged in a research method called participant observation. When sociologists do **participant observation** they make their observations by involving themselves directly in the lives and activities of the people whom they are studying. Participant observers observe what people say and do in the normal course of their regular activities; they talk to the subjects of their study about what they are doing and ask them what they are thinking. Participant observers may engage in informal interviewing by asking a number of subjects the same general questions. They also collect documents and other artifacts, and, most important, participant observers make extensive notes on what they see and hear (Simmons and McCall, 1985).

The gambling casino is a fascinating setting in which sociologists can observe human behavior. Sociologist Erving Goffman trained as a dealer so that he could work at Nevada's gaming tables and be a participant observer.

The degree to which participant observers become involved in the same activities as their subjects can vary greatly from one study to the next. For example, a sociological observer may actually be a member of some group of people (in an office or on an assembly line) and still observe what is happening from a sociological perspective. Sociological observers in these cases are called "insiders" (Burgess, 1984).[2]

One sociologist did participant observation where he was clearly an insider, by studying the hospital where he was confined with tuberculosis (Roth, 1963). Using his sociological training to observe the actions of doctors, staff, and other patients, he kept detailed field notes on conversations, routines, and activities. Even though he was like other patients, he was also acting in his role as a sociologist. After his recovery, he continued doing research by studying other hospitals, but as an "outsider" (Roth, 1963).

A second form of participant observation, more common than that involving true insiders, occurs when sociologists *act as if* they are bona fide members of the setting they are studying. A few people in the setting may be aware that sociological observations are being made, but most participants are not. When sociologist Erving Goffman (1967) undertook a study of gambling behavior, he trained so that he could work at the gaming tables of Nevada casinos. Although he did the same things as other casino employees,

[2] Some sociologists prefer to make the distinction between participant observation and non-participant observation. Non-participant observers are equivalent to what we are calling "outsiders."

throughout the experience he was a sociologist first and a casino employee second. Because most of the gamblers and staff did not know that their behavior was being observed, they probably behaved in normal, unself-conscious ways.

In the third (and by far the most common) form of participant observation, sociologists approach the people to be observed and openly declare their intentions of doing a sociological study. Using this approach, they are clearly recognized as outsiders and, because they are outsiders, the researchers must gain the confidence of those being observed. They do so by involving themselves in the activities of the group so that they will become both familiar and non-threatening to group members.

Sociologist Gary Fine (1987), who conducted participant observation research among Little League preadolescent boys, has reported how he first obtained permission from the league president to make his observational study. He described his research in general terms, explaining that he wanted to observe the behavior of preadolescent boys as they participated in Little League baseball and in their leisure time. When he was introduced to the coaches, and later to the boys, he made a similar statement. He informed the boys that he might eventually write a book, which gave him credibility and respect. In fact, the boys saw him as a kind of official chronicler and historian of the team, and occasionally asked him if some event were "going to be in the book."

Fine handled the issue of informed consent by telling the coaches that he would not study their teams unless they agreed. The boys were told that they did not have to answer his questions (including a questionnaire he handed out) or have anything to do with him if they did not want to. Each boy was given a letter to take to his parents

As a participant observer, Gary Fine studied the interaction among children on a Little League baseball team. Fine was forthright in identifying himself as a sociologist to the children and their parents.

that explained the central focus of the research; it invited the parents to ask questions, and informed them that if they had any objections he would respect their wishes. (Only two parents objected to the study.)

Sociological observers who are open about the aims and intentions of their research are often helped immeasurably by some members of the group who act as informants and interpreters (Trice, 1970; Wax, 1971). When Fine studied the boys on Little League baseball teams, he soon earned the trust of several boys who became his confidants. They interpreted events for him and alerted him when something special was occurring. On one occasion, a young boy sidled up to him and said, "Moons are shining tonight," which was a signal that several of the boys were at the edge of the baseball park, "mooning" the passing traffic. It was at this point that sociologist Fine knew that he had gained the confidence of the boys.

Studying Police Behavior through Participant Observation. Two recent studies of police behavior used participant observation as the primary research method (Hunt, 1984, 1985; Martin, 1982). Both studies were done by female sociologists, a fact of some importance since males and male values tend to predominate in the police world. Despite the obstacles this predominance created, the reported findings of these studies are interesting and sociologically important. A few highlights from the two studies will reveal some of the problems and issues of this research method.

Both Hunt and Martin became interested and involved in studying the police because women had recently been hired to work as patrol officers. Martin did her field work in the Washington, D.C., police department, and Hunt did hers in an unidentified large urban police department. (Hunt had previously spent a year studying New York City police officers.)

When Martin requested permission to do a study of women who had become patrol officers using police department data, the department refused her request. However, she had also applied to join the Police Reserve Corps and was accepted. This status allowed her to wear a uniform and join regular officers on patrol; it also gave her the access she needed to carry out her observations. During a nine-month period, Martin went out in patrol cars as often as three or four times a week. During the last three months of her study she also conducted interviews with more than 50 patrol officers (28 female and 27 male), and about a dozen higher ranking officers. She did her research without specifically informing the officials in her district that she was conducting a study, an action she later regretted both for ethical reasons and because it may have limited the scope of her research.

Several factors made it difficult for Martin to establish rapport with the officers with whom she went on patrol. First of all, she was not a regular police officer, only a reserve. The officers in her district soon learned that she was a college professor, and she did make it a point to tell the officers with whom she went on patrols that she was doing research. Martin believes that it was difficult to establish open relationships with some police officers because she was of a different social and educational background than they. The fact that she was a female in a department that was predominantly male was another problem and, finally, she feels that, because she was white, her relationships with black officers (both male and female) were inhibited (Martin, 1982, pp. 221–233).

Hunt used a more direct and dramatic approach as she set out to overcome the resistance of the police officers (especially the males) in the department where she did her study. She believes that a participant observer must change his/her perceived identity

Female police officers often find it difficult to be accepted by male officers. One strategy for gaining acceptance is for women officers to be aggressive and tough.

from being a person who is "untrustworthy" to one who is "trustworthy" in the eyes of those he/she is observing. Many police officers initially regard a researcher as a "spy" for the police department administration. To avoid that suspicion she deliberately displayed a defiant attitude and showed mild disrespect toward some senior police officers.

More important, Hunt behaved in a variety of ways that made the male officers either respect her or stand in awe of her. She displayed a "combat personality," occupying herself with guns, judo, and hand-to-hand combat. She repeatedly asked for patrols in high-crime areas of the city. She used profanity freely and, by her own description, "acted crazy." She behaved in unpredictable ways and deviated frequently from the behavior that male officers expected of a woman. In Hunt's words, ". . . my fieldwork involved the construction of a new category of female who combined elements of masculinity and femininity . . . . my new identity as 'street-woman-researcher' constituted a trustworthy category of person in the policemen's eyes" (Hunt, 1984, p. 293).

Martin's study of the Washington, D.C., police is particularly important for what it revealed about the problems that women encounter when they become police officers. She found that most male officers did not accept women as equals on the police force and that they considered women inherently unfit for police work. For women to overcome these barriers they had to adopt one of two responses. The first response put an emphasis on being a *police*woman. Women adopting this response were characterized by a strong need to succeed as police officers, to be accepted by male officers, and to differentiate themselves from women in general.

One woman who put the emphasis on being a *police*woman said:

> If you want to be treated like a Barbie doll you will be. If you demand to do the job and be treated with respect, they may test you and laugh at you but eventually you'll gain respect.
>
> I don't try to cut any slack. I don't primp or prance around. I'm fighting to get up front and see what's going on . . . (Martin, 1982, p. 188).

The second response put an emphasis on being a police*woman*. The women who adopted this response tended to accept the stereotypic female role. Thus, for example, one such police*woman* enjoyed it when the lieutenant called her "his little girl." Some women gained acceptance by being "mother confessors" to male officers, while others succeeded by being seductive and dating male officers. Despite such behaviors, or perhaps because of them, these women generally increased the perception that women were incapable of police work in the masculine tradition, and they tended to fail as police officers (Martin, 1982, pp. 194–198).

Social Surveys

The research method most strongly associated with sociology is the social survey. A **social survey** is a method of collecting information from a sample of people by means of questionnaires or interviews. **Questionnaires** are written sets of self-administered questions that are delivered to respondents by hand or through the mail. **Interviews** are questions asked by an interviewer or researcher, either in person or on the telephone.

Survey research has two basic objectives: description and explanation. **Descriptive surveys** are designed to obtain some basic information about a population, the simplest being public opinion polls and market surveys. Public opinion polls, now routinely conducted and reported, are familiar parts of contemporary American life. Although

Social survey
Collecting information from a sample of people through questionnaires or interviews

Questionnaire
Written set of self-administered questions delivered by hand or mail

Interview
Questions asked by an interviewer or researcher, in person or by telephone

Descriptive survey
Survey designed to obtain some basic information about a population

Drawing by M. Stevens; © 1989 The New Yorker Magazine, Inc.

"One final question: Do you now own or have you ever owned a fur coat?"

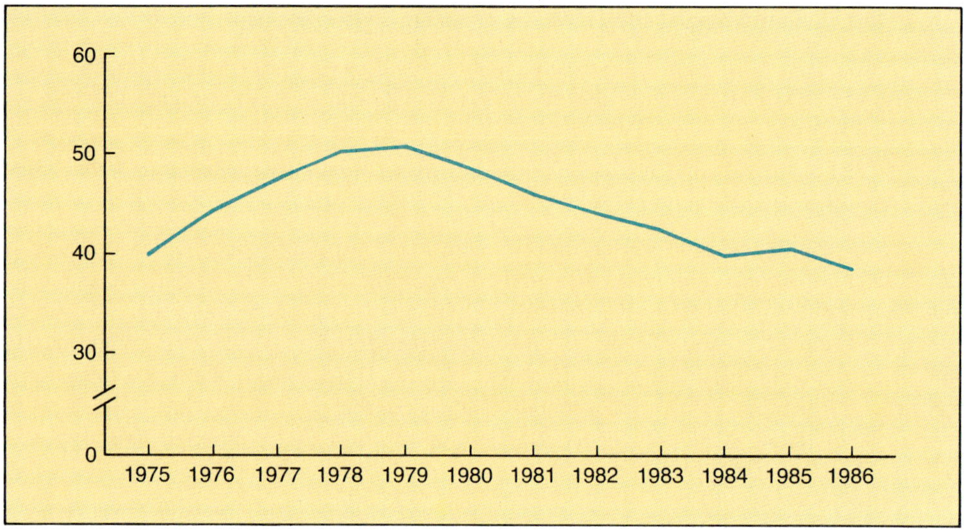

Figure 2–1. Marijuana Use among High School Seniors, 1975–1986. (*Source:* Backman et al., 1987)

such polls are sometimes conducted by sociologists and the results are of interest to sociologists, they are not a primary form of sociological research. The same holds true for marketing surveys, which are usually conducted by organizations specifically set up for the purpose of determining public tastes—for example, television viewing habits.

Sociologists conduct other types of descriptive surveys, often with the objective of identifying typical patterns of behavior or the distribution of attitudes in some population. For example, each year since 1975 the Institute for Social Research at the University of Michigan has conducted a survey among high school seniors in the United States. The reports of these surveys provide descriptive accounts of the life styles, values, and attitudes of young people in their last year of high school. Among other things, this survey has asked high school seniors since 1975 about their use of marijuana. (The survey is funded in part by the National Institute of Drug Abuse.) Figure 2–1 shows the percentage of high school seniors who reported marijuana use during the preceding year. These data make it clear that marijuana use among high school seniors reached a peak in 1979 (50.8 percent) and has declined since that time. In 1986, the percentage who had used marijuana in the preceding year decreased to 38.7 percent, which is lower than the 40.0 percent figure for 1975, the first year of the survey (Backman et al., 1987).

Often descriptive surveys raise questions about the reasons for certain patterns of behavior or about the sources of particular attitudes. We want explanations and answers to our questions. This, then, leads to explanatory surveys. **Explanatory surveys** attempt to find independent variables that will be related to, and possibly account for, differences in behaviors and attitudes (as dependent variables). In the case of marijuana use among high school students we might look for relationships with gender, race, and college plans. Table 2–1 shows these relationships.

Explanatory survey
Survey attempting to account for differences in behaviors or attitudes

Table 2–1 does not explain why some high school seniors use marijuana and others do not, but it does provide some clues that might be followed in more detailed

Table 2–1. The Percentage of High School Seniors Who Had Used Marijuana During the Preceding Year, by Gender, Race, and College Plans, 1986

		Percentage Using Marijuana
Males		40.5
Females		35.6
Whites		40.2
Blacks		25.3
Four-Year College Plans	Yes	36.1
	No	40.0

Source: Backman et al., 1987.

studies. The table shows that males are slightly more likely than females to be marijuana users. Marijuana use between college-bound students and those not planning to attend four-year colleges is also slightly different. The strongest relationship shown is between race and marijuana use. In this sample, black high school seniors were much less likely to use marijuana than were white seniors.

The relationship between race and marijuana could be analyzed further by bringing other variables into the analysis. For example, a researcher might ask, "Do black high school seniors use marijuana less because they are more religious?" In this survey we find that more than half of the black seniors (51.3 percent) say that religion is "very important" in their lives, compared to only 22.5 percent of the white seniors. As might be expected, the students who say that religion is very important in their lives are not as likely to use marijuana. Without actually doing the necessary analysis, one could speculate that the greater significance of religion in the lives of many black high school seniors might partially account for their lower use of marijuana. Of course, there may be many other explanations for the relationship between race and marijuana use, but this example illustrates how sociologists use survey data to search for explanations.

Samples for Social Surveys. The respondents questioned in social surveys are sometimes loosely referred to as the sample. However, a careful use of this term requires that the people who are questioned be drawn in some random way from a specified population (or universe of people). For example, to draw a **random sample** of the adult population of the United States, researchers would have to use a sampling procedure that would give each adult in the population an equal chance of being selected in the sample. Methods for drawing random samples have been well developed and are used regularly by major survey-research organizations, public-opinion polling organizations, and the federal government.

Random sample
A sampling procedure giving every person an equal chance of being selected

While random samples are highly desirable, many researchers in sociology use respondents who have not been randomly selected. The resulting sample is called a **convenience sample,** that is, research subjects who are conveniently available to com-

Convenience sample
Research subjects who are conveniently available to complete questionnaires or to be interviewed

plete questionnaires or respond to interviews. (College classes often serve as convenience samples.) Convenience samples are usually justified on the grounds that the research is exploratory.

Secondary Analysis

When individuals or organizations carry out the costly process of selecting a large sample of respondents, the interviews or questionnaires are usually long, many different types of questions are asked, and they produce more data than any single researcher can analyze. For this reason the data collected in surveys are made available to other investigators. (If federal government funds have been used in the collection of data, they must be made available to other researchers after a specified period of time and at a nominal cost.) For example, the surveys of high school seniors discussed above collected data on 1,300 different variables (Backman et al., 1987). These data are available in computer-readable form, which allows other researchers to have access to a large data archive at a minimal cost.

Secondary analysis
The reanalysis of data sets collected by other researchers

When new investigators analyze data sets from the surveys of other researchers it is called **secondary analysis.** These investigators often study issues that are very different from those studied by the original collectors of the data. Of course, in secondary analysis one is limited to the data originally collected so some compromises are usually required. The advantage of secondary analysis is that it is relatively inexpensive and is therefore an excellent way for beginning researchers to get involved in sociological research.

Government Archives for Secondary Analysis. The federal government of the United States conducts surveys and censuses of various types on a regular basis, and data from these are available to researchers. When the population of the United States is counted every ten years through a national census, the information obtained goes far beyond a simple count of men, women, and children. The census collects information on jobs, income, housing, marital status, childbearing, and many other aspects of American life. These data are available to the public and provide the raw material for many sociological studies.

The Census Bureau also conducts a monthly sample survey of the United States' population called the Current Population Survey. Its primary purpose is to provide an on-going evaluation of economic and social conditions in the United States' population. Again, many opportunities exist for researchers to use these data banks for sociological research. For example, the Current Population Survey data were used recently in a study of how having children influences the likelihood of parents' getting a divorce. It is fairly well established that when married couples have children their chances of marital disruption are lessened (Morgan and Rindfuss, 1985; Waite et al., 1985). Now, using data from the June, 1980, survey, researchers have found that whether a child is male or female also affects the likelihood of marital disruption. Specifically, the parents of a boy are less likely to divorce than are the parents of a girl. This fact is most clearly evidenced in the case of married couples with one child. If the child is a girl, the risk of marital disruption is 9 percent higher than if the child is a boy (Morgan et al., 1988). Researchers believe this difference indicates that fathers are more inclined to remain in the marriage when they have a son because they feel it is important to help with his training and upbringing.

The Historical-Comparative Method

Historical-comparative method
The examination of events and histories of societies or parts of societies

Sociological researchers who use the **historical-comparative method** examine the events and histories of whole societies, or the events and histories of major components of societies (e.g., religious systems, economic systems, governmental systems). The historical-comparative method is concerned with macroscopic types of social phenomena, to use the terminology introduced in chapter 1. This method also includes a comparative dimension, meaning, for example, that one society may be compared to itself at different historical periods or two or more societies may be compared to each other. Often the goal is to understand how historical events and conditions in different societies have led to different societal outcomes. Sometimes this method is used to explain why a society has changed in certain ways. To do this, researchers might study how conditions and events at one time in history led to different conditions at a later time. This study can be most effective when comparisons among two or more societies are made.

An example of historical-comparative research can be found in the work of Max Weber, one of the pioneering sociologists introduced in chapter 1. Weber, as we saw,

Max Weber's historical-comparative studies led him to compare the cultures of India, China, and European countries in an effort to learn why Western societies placed more emphasis on rationality and efficiency.

was interested in rationality, that is, human action based primarily on the criterion of efficiency. He was especially interested in why the Western world, primarily Europe and the United States, had come to place so much emphasis on rationality. Using a historical-comparative research strategy to study this question, Weber compared the cultures of India and China with those of European countries. He was looking for historical factors that might have led to an acceptance of rationality in the West and that might have inhibited its acceptance in non-Western societies. Weber concluded that the rise of Protestantism and the acceptance of its belief system in Europe was a key factor that led to an emphasis on rationality and efficiency and a striving for material success. When Weber examined the religious ideas of Eastern societies he found none that encouraged rationality in the same way that Protestantism had in Europe. Indeed, some Eastern religions inhibited rational approaches (Weber, 1904–1905/1958).

Because the historical-comparative method of social research requires an extensive knowledge of historical conditions in different societies, it is not widely used in contemporary sociology. A similar approach that puts less emphasis on historical processes and more emphasis on collecting quantitative data from different societies is called cross-national research (Kohn, 1987).

Cross-National Research

Cross-national research The collection of similar types of data in two or more countries

Cross-national research is the collecting of similar kinds of data in two or more nations for comparison. A major example of cross-national research is found in the work of Melvin Kohn and his research associates (Kohn, 1977; Kohn and Schooler, 1983).

Cross-national studies of childrearing, conducted in Poland and a number of other countries, have shown that the position of parents in the stratification system will influence their childrearing objectives.

Cross-National Perspectives

A Comparison of the Attitudes of Soviet and American Teenagers

Surveys of attitudes have become commonplace in the United States, but only in recent years has it been possible for American researchers to gain access to surveys of Soviet citizens. With the new Soviet policy of openness, called *Glasnost*, it is now possible for American researchers to ask and get answers to a wide array of interesting questions about Soviet citizens. Especially interesting are the questions that can be asked about the similarities and differences between Soviet and American youth. The young people of these two countries have grown up under very different political and social systems, and thus may have very different attitudes about the world, their countries, and their personal lives.

We may ask, for example, do Soviet or American teenagers have greater concerns about the possibility of nuclear war? How do Soviet and American young people compare in terms of worry about being victims of violent crime? About getting hooked on drugs? About the death of a parent? About not being liked? These and other questions were the subject of a cross-national survey conducted by five researchers and published in the *New England Journal of Medicine* in 1988 under the title, "American and Soviet Teenagers' Concerns about Nuclear War and the Future."

If you guessed that American teenagers were more worried about these social and personal issues, you would be wrong. The results of the survey indicate that Soviet teenagers express more concern about these issues than do American teenagers. Soviet teenagers worry more about virtually everything. This high level of anxiety is perplexing. While some of their concerns make sense, one is hard-pressed to understand how they could be more worried about being victims of violent crime or getting hooked on drugs since these problems are far less common in the Soviet Union than in the United States.

According to the survey results, American students tend to focus on personal problems (for instance, poor grades and their health), while Soviet students focus on global issues (nuclear war and world hunger). This seems to reflect the greater emphasis placed in the Soviet Union on doing good for society rather than for oneself.

In spite of their greater tendency to worry, however, Soviet students are much more optimistic about the future than are American students. Fewer than 10% of Soviet students thought a nuclear war probable in their lifetimes, compared with 40% of American students. The greater optimism of the Soviet students may be explained by such factors as the Soviet mass media, which depict Soviet leaders as working tirelessly for peace, and the fact that large numbers of Soviet students are likely to be actively involved in organized peace-related activities.

This cross-national survey of teenage attitudes points up both the value and the difficulties of such research. One difficulty is that, despite great effort, the researchers could not be sure that the wording of the questionnaire was interpreted in exactly the same way in the two countries. Another was the lack of familiarity on the part of Soviet students with such questionnaires since, unlike American students, they are rarely asked about their attitudes. Finally, the American students were probably far more likely to believe that the results would be confidential. It may be that the Soviet teenagers' responses are less than accurate reflections of their real attitudes toward these matters; they may not have believed that the questionnaires would be confidential and therefore gave answers that they thought officials would expect them to give. They also knew that their responses would be seen by an international audience and may have tried to give answers of which they thought such an audience would approve. Differences such as these could easily distort the results of this (and every) cross-national study. Thus, those who do this kind of research must be extraordinarily careful.

In spite of the greater methodological problems involved in cross-national surveys, however, they are well worth doing. In the case of the study discussed here, we certainly know more about the attitudes of Soviet teenagers (and how they compare to those of their American counterparts) than if some expert "Kremlinologist" had imagined or deduced what they think.

CHIVIAN, ERIC; ROBINSON, JOHN P.; TUDGE, JONATHAN R.H.; POPOV, NIKOLAI P.; ANDREYENKOV, VLADIMIR G. "American and Soviet Teenagers' Concerns About Nuclear War and the Future." *New England Journal of Medicine* 319, 1988.

Now that the Soviets have a new policy of openness called *Glasnost*, it is possible to conduct surveys of Russian high school students, whose attitudes can then be compared to the attitudes of American students.

Survey research studies of a similar nature were conducted over several years in the United States, Poland, Japan, Italy, and Taiwan. These studies showed that, in each country, the people who were higher in the social stratification system (more education, better jobs, higher incomes) were more likely to value self-direction. In raising their children, they tended to emphasize autonomy and to deemphasize simple obedience to rules. Since similar results were found in several different countries, these researchers concluded that a consistent relationship exists between social stratification and values that adults hold, especially with respect to rearing their children (Kohn, 1987). (This study will be discussed more fully in chapter 5.)

Statistics and Sociological Research

Statistics are techniques used to process the numbers produced by research and measurement. Statistics should always help us in some way: if they do not explain or clarify, they are of no use. Basically, statistics will do one of two things: (1) make the communication of information easier or simpler; (2) help us to make certain kinds of decisions. Statistics that help us communicate information about numerical data are called **descriptive statistics.** Statistics that help us to make decisions are called inferential statistics.

Statistics
Techniques used to process numbers produced by research and measurement

Descriptive statistics
Statistics used to communicate information about numerical data

Descriptive Statistics

Some of the most useful statistics are those that convey information about many numbers in a simple way—often with only a single number. When an instructor returns an examination to a class and says, "The average grade on the test was 92," he or she is using a single number to convey something about the scores of all the people who took the examination. The class is being told what the mean, the numerical average, is. The **mean** is calculated by adding all the scores together and dividing the sum by the number of people who took the examination. The mean is one type of statistic that is frequently used to say something about the central tendency of a group of numbers.

A second common measure of central tendency is the median. The **median** of the class's examination scores is the score in the center, or middle, of the distribution of scores. Roughly speaking, half of the students in the class would have scores that were higher than the median score, and half would have scores that were lower.

A third, less widely used, measure of central tendency is the mode. The **mode** on a set of examination scores would be the one single score received by the largest number of students.

Mean
A numerical average of a set of numbers

Median
The middle number of a distribution of numbers arranged from lowest to highest

Mode
The most frequently observed number in a set of numbers

Measures of Association and Correlation. Sociologists, as we have seen, are often interested in how different parts of the social world are related to each other. A number of statistical techniques show relationships between variables, and simple percentages are frequently used for this purpose. Let us suppose that, in a study of the relationship between level of education and divorce, we found that 21 percent of the women with less than a high school education had been divorced, but only 10 percent of women with college degrees had been divorced. This comparison of percentages would suggest that level of education is related to divorce.

Correlation
A measure of how much two variables are related or associated

Statisticians (some of whom are sociologists) have developed other statistics to summarize, often in a single number, whether and how much two variables are related. A widely used, but fairly complex, measure of relationships is called correlation. **Correlation** is a measure of how much two variables are co-related. When two different variables are measured numerically, they can be correlated. In the example of educational level and divorce, the former can be measured numerically by using the number of years of completed education. Divorce cannot technically be measured numerically because it is an "all or nothing" characteristic. (Sociologists will, however, sometimes use the correlation technique for analyzing this relationship by arbitrarily assigning numbers 0 and 1 to the divorced and nondivorced states, respectively.) Educational level could also be correlated with another measure, such as number of months engaged before marriage. A sample of married people could provide information on their educational level and the length of their engagement before marriage. Every person would then have two measures: number of years of education and number of months engaged.

We will not go into the complex statistical calculation for correlation here except to say that the product of the appropriate mathematical procedures is a single number. This number can range from −1.00 to +1.00. Usually it will be a two-digit decimal fraction preceded by a sign (e.g., −.43 or +.61). This number, called a correlation coefficient, will conveniently summarize the degree and the direction of the relationship for anyone who understands correlations, even minimally. For example, if the correlation between educational level and length of engagement is .00 (or near zero), one would probably conclude that no relationship or association exists between these two variables. On the other hand, if the correlation is +.53 or +.61, one would say that the two variables are positively correlated. An interpretation would be that those people with higher numbers on one of the variables would also generally have higher numbers on the other variable. Persons with long engagements are likely to have high levels of education. Notice that nothing is said about cause and effect. We might reasonably say that people with higher levels of education have longer engagements before marriage because they are more likely to wait until they finish college before marrying, but the correlation value alone does not provide conclusive proof of this assumption. The correlation technique tells us only whether two things are related (co-related) and the direction and degree of that relationship.

Inferential Statistics

Inferential statistics
Techniques that assist in making statements about a population from a sample

Inferential statistics are techniques that assist researchers in making decisions about whether, on the basis of a sample, statements can be made about the population from which the sample was drawn. For example, suppose we find a relationship between two variables in a sample of respondents in a social survey. Although the relationship holds for the sample, there is no certainty that it holds for the total population from which the sample was drawn. Even a randomly drawn sample may not *exactly* reflect the population. This is where statistical tests of inference become useful.

Some statistical tests will provide us with a probability statement that might, in a particular case, tell us something like the following: the chances are 99 out of 100 that the relationship found between two variables in our sample will also be found in the total population. If this probability is the result of the statistical test, we feel confident making an inference about the total population, even if we have studied only a sample from it. We could conclude that the relationship found in the sample is probably true of the total population, since the chances are only 1 in 100 that it would not be.

Summary

Although the research methods used by sociologists are varied and thus reveal the diversity of sociology, all are based on the idea that human behavior can be studied using a scientific approach. A key element in the scientific approach is empiricism, a reliance on experiencing something with one's senses. Objectivity, a second key element, is both an attitude of value neutrality and a clear description of the research procedures used.

When carrying out social research, sociologists must be concerned about the possible harm they may do to their subjects. In extreme cases they may do physical harm, but the more likely danger is psychological harm. Ethical considerations demand caution when intruding into the lives of research subjects.

The social research process begins with a question. Research questions may come from the personal interests of researchers, current societal developments, or sociological theories. Research hypotheses are derived from reports of previous research or from theories. Concepts are measured by indicators that can be empirically observed. When concepts have been converted into measures they are called variables. Independent variables are those that are thought to produce change in dependent variables.

Experiments are research techniques that are ideally suited for assessing causality. Sociological experiments are classified as field experiments or laboratory experiments. Field experiments are often used to test the effectiveness of social programs or the desirability of proposed government policies. Field experiments are more closely connected with the real world, but laboratory experiments are under the closer control of the researchers.

Participant observation is a research method in which researchers interact with and observe the behavior of those whom they are studying. Participant observers may be involved to varying degrees in the groups and social settings they are studying, sometimes as full-fledged participants, or insiders, but more commonly as outsiders.

Social surveys often involve random samples of populations. The people selected in samples are questioned, either with questionnaires or through interviews. The two basic forms of surveys are descriptive and explanatory.

Secondary analysis is the use of data collected by other researchers for new and often very different kinds of research questions. Data collected by the government (e.g., the census) are often used for secondary analysis.

Historical-comparative research examines the histories of societies and compares either different periods in the history of a single society or the histories of several societies. Cross-national research is the use of survey data collected from two or more nations so that the results can be compared. Cross-national research is more quantitative than classic historical-comparative studies.

Statistical methods used by sociologists are descriptive or inferential. Descriptive statistics convey information about the central tendencies of numerical data and associations or correlations between measures. Inferential statistics are tools that help researchers make decisions about their data when they have drawn samples from larger populations.

Appendix: Sociological Research

Interpreting Statistical Tables

Most people, in every society, marry at some time during their lives. In the United States, for example, approximately 90 percent of all people marry at least once, and a substantial number marry more than once. In many less economically developed and traditional societies such as India, the percentage marrying approaches 100 percent. However, even though most men and women marry, there is a much greater likelihood that, at the end of life, men will be married and women will not be. We will demonstrate this point with the accompanying table 2–2, which we present here as a way to illustrate the steps in reading and understanding a statistical table.

The first and most important rule for reading a table is to read the title carefully. Even experienced table readers can get confused if they fail to take the moment necessary to see what the title says. The title for table 2–2 is "The Percentages of Females and Males Who Are Married at Ages 35–39 and 65 and Over, for Selected Countries." Notice that the numbers in the body of the table are percentages. (In this table the percentage signs appear after each number; but in many tables they are omitted because the title or a heading makes them redundant.)

We will return to the percentages in the table shortly, but first there is more to be learned from the title. The title says that the table will be providing information on the marital statuses of both females and males, at two different age periods (35–39 and 65 and older), for a few selected countries.

The second rule for reading a table is to begin at the left side of the table and examine the headings. The first heading is "Country," which obviously refers to the

Table 2–2. The Percentages of Females and Males Who Are Married at Ages 35–39 and 65 and Over, for Selected Countries

Country	Age Category	Percentage Married	
		Females	Males
United States (1986)	35–39	76%	78%
	65+	40%	77%
Sweden (1981)	35–39	73%	66%
	65+	38%	67%
France (1980)	35–39	85%	84%
	65+	35%	73%
Japan (1980)	35–39	90%	89%
	65+	35%	81%
Indonesia (1980)	35–39	88%	96%
	65+	25%	81%

Sources: U.S. Bureau of the Census, *Statistical Abstract of the United States, 1988.* Washington, D.C., U.S. Government Printing Office, 1987. United Nations, *Demographic Yearbook, 1982.* New York: United Nations, 1984.

countries under consideration. The second heading is "Age Category," and it refers to age categories 35–39 and 65+. These age categories are shown for each country. It is customary to call the designations to the left of the data stubs.

The headings for the other columns of the table begin with an overall heading, "Percentage Married." Subheadings then divide the information according to gender: "Females" and "Males."

To see what kinds of information the body of the table provides we begin by inspecting the first percentage in the table—here the figure is 76 percent. This figure tells us that, in the United States among 35- to 39-year-old females, 76 percent are married. Moving along the same row to the next figure, we see that 78 percent of United States' males in the same age category are married.

If we now move down to the next row we can examine the percentages of United States' females and males who are married in the 65-and-over age category. We see that, while only 40 percent of the older females are married, 77 percent of the older males are married.

In a similar fashion we can examine the marital statuses of females and males in the other countries. We see the same pattern as that of the United States existing in all the other countries. In some cases it is even more extreme, as, for example, in Indonesia, where 81 percent of the males 65 and over are still married, while only 25 percent of the females in the older age group are married.

Table 2–2 shows that, in widely different countries, there is a consistent tendency for women in the later years of life to be unmarried. After age 65, only one-quarter to two-fifths of women are married, while two-thirds to four-fifths of older men are still married. The most obvious reason for this imbalance in marital status between males and females is the shorter life expectancy of males in many societies. However, an additional contributing factor is that, in many societies, males marry women who are younger than they, thus leaving many older women unmarried, even when there may be men of their age group still alive.

CRITICAL THINKING

1. What are the key features of a scientific approach? Why is it important in the study of sociology?
2. Sociologists must retain their objectivity about subjects that they study. If you were a sociologist, about which topics might you have difficulty maintaining a degree of objectivity?
3. Why should social sciences be held to the same rigorous standards of procedural objectivity as natural or biological sciences?
4. Discuss several ethical issues that need to be considered by sociologists when constructing research projects. Assume you are a sociologist interested in researching sexual behavior. Give examples of what you would consider to be ethical and unethical research practices for that topic.
5. Trace the basic steps in any sociological research project through an example.
6. Assume you wish to use twins to assess the degree to which heredity and environment influence our lives. What might be the dependent and independent variables in such a study?
7. Compare and contrast the advantages and disadvantages of the major research methods (i.e., participant observation, social survey, etc.) mentioned in this chapter.
8. Pretend you are a sociologist wishing to begin a research project on race relations in the United States. Develop several hypotheses that you might choose to test. What research methods would be most effective in testing these hypotheses?
9. Why must sociologists, and those who use sociological research, be wary of the statistics they use and see?
10. In what ways are statistics used in sociological research?

CHAPTER

3

Culture

Americans are learning more and more about the Japanese. The latest economic successes in Japan are now topics of routine conversation, as are the impressive educational accomplishments of Japanese school children. Japanese-manufactured products are often the standard by which we evaluate our own and other countries' products. Although we know what the Japanese can do, we are less sure of *how* they do it. This curiosity has led to a minor growth industry that analyzes the nature of the Japanese people. Indeed, the Japanese themselves are just as interested as the non-Japanese in analyzing their distinguishing qualities. Journalists, politicians, and scholars from the East and West are trying to identify and describe the key features of the Japanese people and their way of life (Kelly, 1988).

Included in most descriptions of the Japanese people are these qualities: a high regard for social obligations, a responsibility and loyalty to the group, and a respect for those in positions of authority. For example, Japanese workers are said to be intensely loyal to their companies or organizations. In turn, the companies are equally loyal to their workers, giving them lifetime security in their jobs. This emphasis on loyalty to the group may begin very early in the lives of the Japanese, even as part of their early childhood training.

The noted child psychologist Bruno Bettelheim (1985) has offered an illustration of the different childrearing methods of Japanese and American parents showing how the Japanese and American children might grow up with different views about the importance of responsibility to other people in the society. Bettelheim's example is the familiar situation of a young child (say, a boy) who does not want to eat his vegetables. An American parent might say, "You must eat your food, it is good for you, and it will make you grow." In contrast a Japanese mother might ask her son a question. "How do you think it makes the man who grew these vegetables feel? He grew them for you to eat and now you reject them." Or, "How do you think it makes these carrots feel? They grew so you could eat them, but now you will not" (paraphrase of Bettelheim, 1985, p. 58). The Japanese mother is making the child consider how his behavior will make others (even the carrots) feel.

Thus, the Japanese teach even their young children to be sensitive to the feelings of others. In contrast, the admonition of the American parent ("It will make you grow") emphasizes how the child himself will benefit from eating the vegetables. When the Japanese mother stresses how important it is for the child to be sensitive to the feelings of others, she is paralleling the notion of social responsibility and loyalty found between Japanese workers and their companies. Similarly, when the American parent stresses the well-being of the individual child she is reflecting an American concern with individual self-interest. These deeply embedded beliefs of desirable and proper behavior are examples of what sociologists call cultural values. Values are an important component of culture as we will see later, but for now, **cultural values** can be defined as standards of desirability, of rightness, and of importance in a society. For the Japanese, social

Cultural values
Standards of desirability, of rightness, and of importance in a society

A culture includes the ways that the people of a society have developed for meeting their needs, including food, clothing and shelter. Depicted here are a cheese seller in Bordeaux with a basket of French cheeses, a woman in traditional dress seen in a market in Cuzco, Peru, and houses in a village in Indonesia.

responsibility and loyalty reflect an important cultural value. For Americans, individualism is an important cultural value.

The Importance of Culture

The Meaning of Culture

Culture is the entire complex of ideas and material objects that the people of a society (or group) have created and adopted for carrying out the necessary tasks of collective life. As this definition suggests, cultures are human creations, but, of course, people inherit much of their culture from those who created it. In other words, every culture has a history. When children are born into a society they learn the elements of their culture, and they in turn pass them on, probably in some modified form, to those who follow them. Cultures, therefore, are also capable of change.

Culture
The entire complex of ideas and material objects for carrying out a society's collective life

One convenient way to think about culture is to recognize that the people of every society have an array of tasks to perform and problems to solve. All people must have ways of providing food, clothing and shelter, ways of producing and caring for children, and ways of solving disputes between members. Perhaps most important, all people must have a way of making life orderly and predictable.

In our daily lives it is important that we know that other people will behave with a certain amount of order and predictability. In the United States we expect all other drivers to keep to the right-hand side of the road and to respond to red, green, and yellow lights in a predictable way. The rules about driving are one example of cultural norms. **Norms** are rules for what should and should not be done in given situations. The norms with regard to driving are generally understood and followed by other drivers and by ourselves. Thus, cultural norms help us not only to predict what others will do but also help us to know what we should do.

Norms
Rules for what should and should not be done in given situations

A Cultural Explanation of Human Behavior

A cultural explanation of human behavior rests on the assumption that humans in any society will learn the basic cultural values and social norms of that society. To a considerable degree, the general behavior (and even individual behavior) of people in a society can be explained by that society's cultural values and norms. Sometimes a sociological analysis of culture operates in the opposite direction. By examining the individual behaviors of many people in a society, the cultural values of that society are deduced. Later in this chapter, we will consider some recent examples of this type of cultural analysis of American society.

Using culture to understand human behavior is not simply an abstract sociological exercise; it can frequently have practical applications as well. For instance, George Fields, an American advertising and marketing specialist, spent many years in Japan, where he worked at introducing American-manufactured products to the Japanese (Fields, 1983). Fields' parents were American, but he was born in Japan, and lived there during his youth. Fields' deep understanding of the Japanese people, their language, and their culture made him especially valuable when, as an adult, he worked for American businesses that wanted to market their products in Japan.

Although Fields was often successful in his efforts to introduce American products into the Japanese market, some of his failures revealed the significance of cultural factors even more clearly than his successes. One of Fields' more renowned marketing failures was his involvement in the attempt by General Mills to introduce cake mixes into the Japanese market in the 1960s. The problem was that, at that time, most Japanese kitchens did not have ovens. However, every kitchen had a rice cooker and, with some modifications in the mix, the cake could be baked in it. Fields helped introduce an intense advertising campaign; initially sales were good, but then they dropped off dramatically.

A group interview with Japanese housewives revealed that the reason for the decline was a concern about the vanilla and other flavorings in the mixes. One woman said, "I suppose you can wash it off, but . . . ." The Japanese women were worried about the possible contamination of their rice. Nearly every evening meal in Japan includes rice, which for the Japanese is not just a food, but a symbol of purity as well. The purity of the family's daily rice could not be jeopardized by baking a cake in the rice cooker.

When the Japanese women balanced the cultural significance of the purity of their rice against the attractiveness of serving cakes to their families, the purity of the rice was more important. The attempt to market cake mixes failed, and General Mills withdrew its product from the market. The power of a cultural symbol to influence human behavior was understood too late.

Culture is not the only way to explain human behavior. Two other frequently encountered explanations are "human nature" and a scientific theory called *sociobiology*. In considering these alternatives, we will show that cultural explanations are more useful and significant.

Human Nature versus Culture

Many people look for explanations of human behavior in what they call "human nature." The term *human nature* generally suggests that specific characteristics or traits that are found in all humans supposedly explain some particular behavior. Many times one hears people say, "It is just human nature to be selfish, . . . or jealous, . . . or friendly, . . . or aggressive." The speaker usually claims to explain some human or social behavior by invoking a particular characteristic.

On closer inspection, however, many aspects of human nature turn out to vary tremendously from one society to another. For instance, one society might value aggressiveness, while another might value nonviolence and peace. Quakers typically believe in and practice nonviolence. In contrast, some societies regard fighting as a pervasive way of life. The Yanomamo Indians, about 15,000 people who live in the Amazon rain forest, are constantly warring and fighting among themselves. According to data gathered over the last 23 years, 44 percent of the Yanomamo men over the age of 25 have killed someone (Chagnon, 1968; Rensberger, 1988).

When we compare the peaceful way of life of the Quakers and the violent way of life of the Yanomamo, we must question whether claims about a universally aggressive human nature have any validity or significance. A more satisfactory explanation of the difference between these two societies can be gained by examining the value that Quakers place on being peaceful and the value the Yanomamo place on violence and aggression.

The pervasive violence among the Yanomamo is evident in all parts of their lives, not just in their treatment of enemies. The males, for instance, are very violent with their own families. Yanomamo husbands often punish their wives brutally. As a minor punishment, husbands routinely jerk the small sticks that the women wear through pierced ear lobes. As a more severe punishment, they jab their wives with sticks or machetes, or burn them with glowing pieces of firewood. The Yanomamo women expect abuse by their husbands as a routine part of married life. An anthropologist who lived among the Yanomamo once heard two women talking about the scars their husbands had given them. One said that her husband must really care for her since he had beaten her on the head so many times (Harris, 1974).

As we would expect, the Yanomamo people rear their children in the tradition of violence. When small boys display aggressive behavior and engage in violence, they are encouraged and rewarded by their fathers. Understandably the Yanomamo have been called "The Fierce People" (Chagnon, 1968).

As the comparison between the Quakers and the Yanomamo shows, the human nature argument, which advocates the existence of universal, inborn, human characteristics, is extremely dubious. However, the idea that human behavior is shaped or determined by inborn, biologically based characteristics or traits continues to appeal to many people, and has formed the basis for a number of scholarly theories. For example, instinct theory, which dominated psychology during the early years of this century, attempted to explain any human behavior by attributing it to an instinct. Eventually it was recognized that positing an instinct for every human behavior was simply naming a behavior, not explaining it. (For example, having children might be attributed to a "parenting instinct.")

In recent years the most popular biologically based theory of human behavior has been sociobiology (Wilson, 1975). Because sociobiology has gained some prominence and popular acceptance in recent years, it is considered an alternative to the cultural explanation of human behavior.

Sociobiology

The fundamental idea of **sociobiology** is that human behavior reflects genetically inherited traits. Sociobiologists argue that humans are very much like other species of animals, that is, that human characteristics and behaviors are products of the Darwinian notions of natural selection and evolution. **Natural selection** is the idea that the fittest of any species will survive and spread its favored traits throughout the population (Gould, 1977).

Sociobiology
The fundamental idea that human behavior reflects genetically inherited traits

Natural selection
The fittest of any species will spread its traits throughout the population

According to this theory, we humans who are alive today have inherited the genetic characteristics that increased the chances of survival among our ancestors. The reasoning of sociobiology goes this way: if a specific trait appeared at some time in the genes of early humans, and that genetic trait made it more likely for the carrier and its offspring to survive, then that trait would more likely be passed on to the next generation. In the long run, through the process of natural selection, the traits that improved chances of survival would be found in the human population. Traits that detracted from survival, or were less advantageous for survival, would disappear or become rare. Sociobiologists conclude from this that any widely observed human behavior must have been beneficial for survival and, therefore, have been passed down genetically (Lumsden and Wilson, 1983).

As an example of the sociobiological approach, we have an attempt to explain the predisposition for human beings to feel love. The basic hypothesis was: "the great majority of women and men are born with a genetic capacity and need for forming durable attachments of an emotional character [love]" (Mellen, 1981, p. 139).

The sociobiological explanation for the human tendency to feel love is stated as follows: When early humans lived by hunting and gathering food, they had to cover a wide geographic area in pursuit of game and in search of other food. Hunting, especially, required speed and mobility. During the time when females were pregnant or were caring for their young, they were relatively immobile and needed assistance. The males, not similarly restricted, could range over large areas in search of food and game. If women—and, more important, their children—were to survive under these conditions, the males had to return with some food for them. Sociobiologists reason that males who were selfish might not return with the food, but if a male were born with a tendency to feel an attachment for the female who bore his child (a tendency to feel love), he would return to the female and child to share his food. If he did so, the child carrying his genes (perhaps including the gene that made him capable of feeling love) would be more likely to survive.

Or, consider the opposite scenario—a male who did not have the genetic tendency to feel love for a female. Because this male would probably not return as often to the female and her child, this child might die from lack of food, and the male's genes would not survive to the next generation. In this way, in the course of hundreds of thousands of years, the genes that produced a capacity for love would have survived in the human species (Mellen, 1981).

Many features of this sociobiological description are not proved facts; many may be unprovable. In fact, no one has actually isolated a gene that gives people the capacity to love. We also know very little about the lives of prehistoric humans, so that much of the scenario above is simply conjecture. Nevertheless, suppose it were all true. We are still left with the question, "Does it make any difference in our attempt to understand human behavior?" Perhaps all humans do have the capacity for love, but what difference does it make when love is viewed so differently in different cultures? Remember the Yanomamo wife who believed that her husband cared for her because he had beaten her on the head so much? A beating on the head is hardly considered an expression of love in American society.

Furthermore, although Americans believe in entering marriage on the basis of love, many societies consider love before marriage to be irrelevant. Often the bride and groom hardly know each other at the time of marriage, so they would not likely be in love. Why do the cultures of some societies emphasize love as a basis for marriage and other cultures deemphasize or ignore it? This interesting sociological question is one that the sociobiological point of view cannot address. Even if the sociobiological explanation were true (and that is by no means certain), sociobiology often misses interesting and important questions and issues such as why the people in different societies adopt such widely different behaviors (Bock, 1980).

Another way of seeing the power of culture is to observe how the people of every society tend to believe that their way of life is best. We will examine this view next, as we discuss ethnocentrism.

Ethnocentrism

When the ancient Greeks heard people speaking in other languages, the sounds they heard seemed meaningless. To the Greeks, such talking sounded like "bar, bar, bar, bar." Thus they called people with other languages *barbarians* (Ciardi, 1980, p. 18). The Greeks applied this word to all people who came from other societies whom they regarded as uncivilized.

People in all societies tend to think of themselves as the chosen people or, at the very least, as those at the center of humanity. From this view, it is understandable that people of any society would think their ways of doing things were the right ways, and the ways of other people were less right. This attitude is labeled *ethnocentrism*. **Ethnocentrism** is a view held by the people of a society that says that *they* are of central importance in the universe and therefore their way of doing things is the "right" way (Sumner, 1906).

Ethnocentrism
The view that one's own society's ways are the right ways

Obviously not every group of people can be right, since often the customs of one group are totally different from the customs of another. Also, if we had been born into another society, we obviously would have grown up thinking that the norms of that society were right and proper. It is the culture itself that makes things "right."

Cultural Relativism

The study of diverse cultural traditions often helps us to see how different customs can be equally acceptable. This view is the key to an important idea called *cultural relativism*. **Cultural relativism** is an approach that evaluates the behavior of the people of another society, not on the basis of the evaluator's culture but on that culture's own terms.

Cultural relativism
Evaluating the ways of other societies in terms of their own culture

In an extreme version of cultural relativism there are no rights and wrongs, only different cultural values and norms. A more moderate version emphasizes the fact that cultures vary, and other people's patterns of behavior are best judged in the context of their own culture. The following example illustrates the point.

Staphorst is a town of about 11,000 people in the Netherlands (Newton, 1978). If you were to drive into Staphorst you would find a picturesque community where the people still dress in traditional Dutch clothing, reminiscent more of the time of Rembrandt than of the twentieth century. You might be tempted to photograph these people but, if it were a Sunday, it would be better to refrain since the people of Staphorst are very religious and dislike having their photographs taken on their special day of worship. Indeed, the Staphorst people take Sunday so seriously that males and females do not spend time together on that day. They even separate their male and female farm animals on Sunday (Newton, 1978).

If you were to stay around Staphorst for a while you would learn that their Sunday behavior is only a minor reflection of their conservative religious views. The people of Staphorst are 95 percent Protestant (75 percent Calvinist and 20 percent Dutch Reformed). They follow a conservative religious tradition, and believe strongly in a literal heaven and hell. They are conservative in other ways, also, rejecting most of the ways of modern Dutch life. (Polio vaccine was resisted until 1971, when the town experienced an epidemic.)

If you were to delve into the courtship and marriage patterns of the people of Staphorst, however, you might be surprised at some of the customs (Gibney, 1948). When a young man of Staphorst becomes interested in a young woman, he gives her a signal by trying to snatch the rain cape she keeps tied to her waist. If the young woman is interested, she probably helps him succeed. The actual courtship begins when the young man starts coming to the young woman's house (which he will do on Monday, Wednesday, and Friday evenings) after she has retired to her bedroom. Even though the young woman's parents are in a nearby room and can obviously hear what is going on, the young man will crawl through her bedroom window. He will spend the night with her but leave before morning. Quite understandably, this practice often leads to the young woman's becoming pregnant. When this happens, it is time for the two young people to marry, which they do shortly thereafter.

To summarize the courtship system of Staphorst, young people *must* have premarital sex and the young woman *must* be pregnant before marriage is possible. In our society and in many others, premarital pregnancy is typically viewed as an unfortunate occurrence. Indeed, often people who are most religious are especially apt to be upset by a premarital pregnancy. Yet here we find the people of Staphorst, who are extremely religious, actually requiring pregnancy before marriage.

It would be difficult to argue that the acceptance of premarital sex and pregnancy by the people of Staphorst makes them "immoral." Judged by their standards, this practice is accepted as both moral and appropriate. Viewed from the perspective of cultural relativism, we as outsiders would accept the customs of the Staphorst people as part of their particular way of life.

The Staphorst example shows us that, if we take the time to look at the cultural traditions of other people, we can be more sensitive to the integrity of other cultures. In other words, we will be more inclined toward cultural relativity and less inclined toward ethnocentrism.

Cultural relativism, however, does not suggest that one must invariably accept the practices of other people regardless of what they might be. For example, when the Nazi government of Germany in the 1930s put into slavery or killed entire categories of people (Jews, gypsies, and the mentally retarded) one could not regard this phenomenon as just another example of cultural diversity. The idea of cultural relativity implies greater tolerance for cultural differences but not a blind acceptance of all forms of human behavior.

The Components of Culture

Earlier we defined culture as the entire complex of ideas and material objects shared by the people of a society. We are now ready to look more systematically at the major components of culture. We begin with a consideration of symbols.

Symbols
Words, gestures, and objects that communicate meaning when people agree on what they represent

People who live in the same culture generally understand each other, because they share the same symbols. **Symbols** are words, gestures, and objects that communicate meaning when people agree on and recognize what they represent. Every symbol has a social character because a group of people agree on the symbol's meaning (Charon, 1988; Meltzer, 1978). As we noted in our consideration of symbolic interaction theory in chapter 1, shared symbols are used by the people of any given society to communicate with each other and to create a certain order and predictability in daily life. Symbols can be divided into two types: nonverbal and verbal.

Nonverbal Symbols

In historical movies, when the Lord and Lady of the Manor ride through the village in their carriage, the tradesmen and shopkeepers often tip their caps and bow slightly. The symbolism of tipping one's hat to someone of high status is unmistakable: the lower-status person is showing respect for the high-status person. This act is an illustration of a **nonverbal symbol,** a physical display that has social meaning.

Nonverbal symbol
A physical display that has social meaning

In a time when men wore hats, they used to tip their hats when meeting women acquaintances on the street; this gesture was a nonverbal symbol of their respect. Tipping the hat as an act of respect is rarely seen today, but a vestige of this custom can still be seen in some instances. When the President of the United States steps out of his helicopter, he usually exchanges salutes with the military personnel in attendance. The military salute is an evolved version of tipping one's hat and is initiated by the lower-status person and returned by the higher-status person. It is a nonverbal symbolic act, a sign of respect for someone in a higher social position.

Another example of using nonverbal symbols to show respect for people of higher status can be seen among students in many military settings (e.g., West Point) who will come to attention when their instructors enter the room. They are seated only when told to do so. Coming to one's feet in the presence of someone of a higher status is a common display of respect found in many societies.

However, the meanings of nonverbal symbols are by no means the same from one society to another. Nonverbal symbols can sometimes have exactly opposite meanings in two different societies. In the United States, audiences and fans will often show their approval of performances by whistling. In Europe, however, audiences and fans whistle as a way of demonstrating disapproval and dissatisfaction.

The kiss, another nonverbal symbol, also varies widely in its meaning and use from one society to another. American male political leaders often have to brace themselves when they meet political leaders from the Middle East, some European countries, or the Soviet Union, because a common greeting among men in these countries is to exchange kisses on the cheeks. In American society, kisses on the cheek between men

The kiss varies widely in its meaning and use from one society to another. In many European societies, as well as others around the world, it is common for men to greet each other with a kiss.

and women are used as a way of greeting friends and acquaintances, but men do not usually exchange kisses unless they are close relatives—fathers and sons and brothers may kiss after having been separated for some time.

The kiss on the lips between lovers is not as natural as it may seem. The lip kiss was invented by the people of ancient India, although the earliest Indian records (about 2000 B.C.) indicate that their earliest custom was a nose or "sniff" kiss (Pike, 1976). By the time the famous Indian manual of sex and love, the *Kama Sutra,* was written in the fourth century, the lip kiss was well established. The practice of kissing with the lips spread westward to Persia, Syria, Greece, Italy, and eventually to the countries that make up Northern Europe. For Americans, who inherited their culture from these European countries, the lip kiss between romantic partners has always been an expression of love and affection. In many societies, however, lip kissing between lovers was unknown until it was introduced by explorers, traders, and missionaries from the West. According to reports from these observers, the people of most African societies did not kiss on the lips, nor did the New Zealand Maoris, the Australian aborigines, the Papuans, Tahitians, or other South Sea Islanders. It is said that the Chinese considered kissing vulgar because it reminded them of cannibalism. Among Eskimo tribes of the Arctic, the custom was for lovers to rub their noses together (Pike, 1976).

Cultural diffusion
The spread of a cultural trait from one society to another

Today the kiss on the lips between lovers is found in most societies around the world. This fact illustrates how a cultural trait can spread from one society to another as different peoples come into contact with one another. This process is called **cultural diffusion.** In the case of lip kissing, we may speculate that the worldwide distribution of American movies in the last 30 years greatly aided the process of diffusion. A few decades ago, American movies dealing with love had to be censored in Japan because the scenes showing men and women kissing were considered by the Japanese to be in very bad taste (Hughes, 1976).

Nonverbal symbols include many other things besides the physical acts performed by people. Many physical objects are also endowed with symbolic meaning. Flags, emblems, insignias, and coats-of-arms are some familiar examples of objects that have special meaning for people (Gusfield and Michalowicz, 1984). These objects are displayed on homes, automobiles, and clothing as a way of conveying messages to other people. In recent years the makers of clothing have adopted the practice of placing their names, logos and trademarks on the outside of clothing. The successes of clothing lines carrying these symbols suggest that aesthetics is not the only reason for a brand name to be written on the outside of one's shirt, blouse or pants. It takes only a little sociological imagination to see that recognizable names, logos, or trademarks send out a social message for the observers. Indeed, many different types of clothing convey messages to observers. Scientists, some of whom never go near a laboratory, nonetheless don their laboratory jackets as a symbol of their status as scientists (Joseph, 1986).

Verbal Symbols and Language

Verbal symbols
Verbal utterances that are part of the spoken or written language of a society

Although the nonverbal symbols of a culture are often interesting, it is the verbal symbols that have the most sociological significance. **Verbal symbols** are any verbal utterances that are part of the spoken or written language of a society. The language system shared by the people of a society serves as one of its most important social bonds. But more than that, language influences the way people of the same culture perceive reality.

The ability to learn and use verbal symbols is undoubtedly the most extraordinary ability that human beings possess, and using words and language is a critical element in people's social and cultural lives. At an early age, humans can learn hundreds—and then thousands—of different symbols, and can use them to communicate with other people. Not only do humans learn words but they also learn the rules of grammar and sentence structure that are characteristic of their particular language. English-speaking children, even as toddlers, learn to add an *s* to the end of a noun when they want to speak of more than one object. We find it humorous when small children say "mouses" instead of mice, but they are simply following a generalized rule that, in all likelihood, no one has explicitly taught them. Small children hear the plural form used for many nouns and then, quite reasonably, adopt the rule as a way of using the language properly.

The capacity to learn symbols, as well as the rules for using them, allows humans to store and transmit information, thoughts, and ideas with great ease. This ability gives language its particular importance as a carrier of culture. Through language we share not just the names for things but also the rules and values that shape and influence how we relate to these things. An example of this principle can be found in some recent controversies surrounding the rights and responsibilities of biological fathers.

In American society the term *biological father* is important; a biological father has certain rights and responsibilities with regard to any children he produces. However, in recent years new reproductive technologies have allowed women to conceive babies by being impregnated with the sperm of male donors. This practice has raised questions and created problems in some cases about the rights of the "biological father." In some cases the sperm donors have claimed their rights as biological fathers. For Americans this raises a perplexing question because sperm donors would not ordinarily have rights to a child, but a biological father (which the donor seems to be) does.

In some societies the notion of a biological father does not have the same meaning and significance as it does for Americans. For example, a few societies exist where two or more men are married to the same woman.[1] In such a case, there is often no way to determine which husband is the biological father. In one such society in the foothills of the Himalayas, the lack of concern about the biological father extends to cases where wives become pregnant while visiting their home villages. The pregnancy is accepted (even welcomed) by the woman's husbands, and the infant is considered theirs. Apparently the biological father is of no importance and has no rights to the child (Zorsa, 1982).

Americans might have a difficult time understanding how these Himalayan people could be unconcerned about the actual biological father and about his rights and responsibilities. But again, the reason is that Americans cannot easily ignore the social meanings attached to the term *biological father*. The words and symbols shared by the people of a society are important not simply because they convey information but also because they carry social rules and values.

The Sapir-Whorf Hypothesis. The words of any language seem to be symbols for elements that exist in the physical and social worlds. Clouds exist in the physical world, so a word has to be created so that we can refer to them. But another way to see the relationship between words and the physical and social worlds is to regard language as *shaping and influencing* what we see and perceive.

[1] This form of marriage is called polyandry. For a more complete description of this form of marriage see chapter 11.

Cross-Cultural Perspectives

Cross-Cultural Styles of Conversation and Interaction

Among the most interesting cross-national and cross-cultural comparisons to be found are how people converse and interact with one another in different societies. Conversing with another person may seem natural and obvious—in other words, a shared universal activity. In reality, there are dramatic differences in the conversational and interactional styles of people in different nations and cultures.

In the United States it is normal for people engaged in conversation to maintain a reasonable distance between themselves, although this distance may vary in relation to the topic at hand. For conversations about personal subjects, Americans prefer to be about two or three feet from one another and to confer in a soft voice and at low volume. If the conversation involves non-personal matters, the preferred distance is about five feet and full voice is used. Physical closeness (3 to 6 inches) is accepted only if the matter is top secret; the tone is then a soft whisper. This all seems natural from the point of view of most Americans, but the conversational habits of other societies are often very different.

In Latin America, the accepted distance between people involved in a conversation is much less than in the United States. For Americans of the United States, the degree of closeness preferred by Latin Americans evokes either feelings of hostility or stimulation. However, Latin Americans imply neither of these things with their physical proximity during a conversation. Thus, in conversing with Latin Americans, people of the United States are inclined to back up and move away. Latin Americans interpret such behavior in a negative way and they often see us as "distant or cold, withdrawn and unfriendly" (Hall, 1973). For our part, we often accuse Latin Americans "of breathing down our necks, crowding us, and spraying our faces" (Hall, 1973). Hall humorously describes the resulting relationships between Americans and Latin Americans:

> Americans who have spent some time in Latin America without learning these space considerations make other adaptations, like barricading themselves behind their desks, using chairs and typewriter tables to keep the Latin American at what is to us a comfortable distance. The result is that the Latin American may even climb over the obstacles until he has achieved a distance at which he can comfortably talk (Hall, 1973).

In Arab societies, much like Latin American societies, people are also much closer when they converse. Arabs prefer to breathe on the other person when they talk. Arabs find the smells of another person pleasing and consider the smells a way of deepening their personal involvement. They find the American pattern of not breathing in another person's face reveals a sense of shame, that Americans are ashamed of their breath. Thus, when American diplomats in Arab countries believe they are using their best manners by not breathing in their host's face, they may, in fact, be communicating to the Arab that they are ashamed of themselves and the way they smell.

The importance of the smell of people's breath is just part of the broader emphasis on odor in Arab society. Smell is a factor even in courtship and marriage.

When a marriage is arranged, the matchmaker will sometimes ask to smell the prospective bride, and the girl may be rejected if the matchmaker does not care for her smell. Consider an American suitor asking to smell his prospective bride and rejecting her because of her odor. For one thing, this would never be done. For another, it would not be effective because virtually everyone smells "nice" because their natural odors are concealed by deodorants, perfumes, colognes, and mouthwashes.

The emphasis on smell is not the only difference between Arabs and Americans in regard to the ways in which they interact and converse. For example, Arabs prefer not to have a conversation with another person while walking. They feel it is important that people look at one another when they are speaking with each other. Furthermore, interaction requires deep involvement and strong eye contact. Americans often feel uncomfortable interacting with Arabs because they find the amount and intensity of eye contact to be hostile or threatening, even though that is not intended by the Arabs.

HALL, EDWARD T. *The Hidden Dimension*. Garden City, New York: Doubleday and Co., Inc., 1966.
HALL, EDWARD T. *The Silent Language*. Garden City, New York: Doubleday and Co., Inc., 1973.

The idea that language shapes our perception of reality was developed by Edward Sapir and his student Benjamin Whorf in the 1930s; it is usually referred to as the **Sapir-Whorf hypothesis** (McCurdy and Spradley, 1979). This idea can be illustrated by observing how the people of some societies give to certain objects in their environment many different names with precise and detailed meanings. The Arabic language, for example, includes 6,000 terms that refer to specific types and variations of camels or that are derived from the basic word for camel. In Arabic, there are separate words for breeding camels, running camels, female camels, and camels in various stages of pregnancy (Gerth and Mills, 1953, p. 275).

Sapir-Whorf hypothesis The idea that perceptions of reality are shaped by language

Among the Eskimos the constant presence of snow and its importance in their lives is reflected in their language. The Kobuk Eskimos of northeastern Alaska have many different words for types and conditions of snow, including: *snow falling on the ground, falling snow, swirling or drifting snow,* and *snow that collects horizontally on trees* (Boas, 1911; Williams and Major, 1984).

When a language system has many different words to represent variable aspects of the same object, it enables people to have much more complicated perceptions of that part of reality. Most of us have only one word for snow, and thus we do not usually make distinctions among different types of snow. However, avid skiers do make distinctions between *powder* and *machine-made* snow, and they also have special words for various snow surfaces. These words make skiers more sensitive to variations in snow, supporting the hypothesis that language shapes our perception of reality.

The idea that perceptions of the world are shaped by language systems can be illustrated by an example from our everyday world. Americans are increasingly conscious of health foods, and natural ingredients have come to be associated with healthfulness. Health food stores, specializing in grains, fruits, nuts, and other vegetable products, and *organic* foods (another term loaded with symbolic meaning), flourish around the country. However, the food and advertising industries have quickly become sensitized to the

Because the camel is so widely used, the Arabic language has thousands of terms that refer to specific types and variations of camels.

important symbolic significance of the words *natural* and *natural ingredients,* with the result that these terms now appear on the boxes and packages of many commercially produced food products. We tend to perceive these as health foods—even when most of the "natural" ingredients are sugar, corn syrup, starches, salts, and vegetable oils. (Both ice cream and potato chips can, if the producer wishes, qualify as *all natural.*)

Knowledge and Beliefs

Knowledge and beliefs
A body of information created by the people of a society that influences behavior

Knowledge and beliefs taken together, constitutes a body of information created by the people of a society that influences behavior. Knowledge is presumed to be verifiable information, while beliefs are presumed to be difficult to verify. In practice, however, these forms of information are frequently interchangeable. Consider, for example, the following four statements about the sun:

- The sun is a god and should be worshipped.
- The sun is our primary source of heat and light.
- Sunbathing, which leads to a deep tan, is healthy for humans.
- Direct exposure to the sun over a period of time may produce skin cancer.

Which of these statements are knowledge and which are beliefs? Most of us would agree that the first statement is a belief, while the second is a factual statement and, therefore, knowledge. Statements three and four, however, are more troublesome. Some of us think that three is knowledge and four is only a belief, while others think the opposite is true. Furthermore, a true believer in a sun god would think it ridiculous to doubt the validity of the first statement. Knowledge and beliefs are not as easy to disentangle as one might suppose. An analysis of our reactions to this series of statements about the sun reveals the cultural nature of knowledge and beliefs. Those statements that we believe to be valid or true will influence how we behave. From a cultural viewpoint, knowledge and beliefs are accepted by substantial numbers of people in a society, and therefore shape general behavior. If we are to judge from the number of people who seek out beaches and swimming pools each summer, working assiduously at getting suntans, most Americans still seem to believe that a suntan is healthy.

However, knowledge and beliefs in every society undergo continuous change. As knowledge and beliefs change, behavior also changes. Even today, some people have modified their views about suntanning and have changed their suntanning practices. It is ironic that, if Americans begin to shield themselves from the sun at the beach or the swimming pool, their behavior will parallel the behavior of Americans a century ago. In that era, women in particular kept their faces, arms, and legs shielded from the sun, not because of a fear of skin cancer but because a tanned skin was associated with laborers and peasants whose work exposed them to the full day's sun.

We return now to what many regard as the key or primary component of culture: cultural values, or simply values. In comparison with knowledge and belief that focus on *what is,* values are related to what *should be.*

Values

We noted earlier that values are a society's standards of desirability, of rightness, and of importance. Values are expressions of what is good or bad, beautiful or ugly, pleasant or unpleasant, appropriate or inappropriate. Cultural values are shared by a substantial number of people in a society and therefore influence the behavior of most people. The social rules governing behavior (called norms) are generally consistent with, or reflections of, cultural values. We discussed earlier the importance that Japanese people place on social obligations and responsibility, loyalty to the group, and respect for those in superior positions. These could be called Japanese cultural values, and they influence how the Japanese act in a wide variety of circumstances.

Although it is possible to identify cultural values, not everyone in a society holds exactly the same values. Individual variation suggests the notion of personal values. **Personal values** are the values individuals use to make decisions about their personal lives and about the ways in which they respond to public issues. Personal values, like cultural values, deal, not with the trivia of life, but with fundamental and important aspects of our social lives. It is not a value to prefer The Grateful Dead or the movies of Eddie Murphy, although selecting any of them could perhaps reflect a more basic value. Personal values are likely to influence our occupational choices, our decisions about marriage mates (or about marriage itself), and our views about politics. Personal values influence our reactions to public issues: for example, our choice of a political party or our views on international relations, the environment, medical practices, and so on.

Personal values
The values individuals use to make decisions about their personal lives and public issues

Values are not neutral; they are positively or negatively charged. Cultural and personal values can also vary in degree from very strong to very weak. Some values are more important, more pervasive, and more influential than others. Later, in our discussion of American cultural values, we will look for our most important ones.

While youthfulness is highly valued in American society, in many societies of the world, older people are considered wise and valued advisors.

Values vary from society to society. What one group of people considers desirable may be viewed as undesirable by another group. For example, in our society a high value is placed on youth, beauty, and vigor. Many people make strenuous efforts to remain youthful in appearance. Health clubs, weight-loss spas, cosmetic surgery facilities, the clothing industry, and many related businesses thrive on the desire of Americans to stay young looking. In other societies, youth is not so highly valued. In many societies around the world, older people are considered wise and valued advisors.

Engaging in competition in order to win is another value not shared by the people of all societies. Americans generally believe that winning is much better than losing, and that it is inappropriate to play a game without trying to win. However, among the Tangu people of New Guinea, winning is not the object of their game, *Taketak*. *Taketak* involves spinning around dried fruit rinds ("tops") into masses of stakes that have been driven into the ground. Players from each of two teams take turns spinning the tops in the palms of their hands and throwing them into the masses of stakes, trying to hit as many stakes as possible. Stakes that have been touched are removed. The object of the game is not to have one team "win" by hitting all the stakes, but to have both teams hit exactly the same number of stakes, at which time the game ends. Ending in a tie expresses one of the primary values of the Tangu culture—the notion of moral equality among all persons (Burridge, 1957).

While we have already touched on some American cultural values, we now examine more systematically the dominant values in American society.

Dominant Values of American Society

Observers and social analysts have tried since the earliest days of American history to identify the dominant values of the people who settled on the land that is now the United States (de Tocqueville, 1961; de Crevecoeur, 1782/1981). The effort continues into the present, as contemporary sociologists try to isolate dominant values held by most people in the United States today (Bellah et al., 1985; Gans, 1988). It is interesting to note that some of the dominant American values observed in the earliest days of this society still prevail today. The most prominent among these is the way Americans value individualism.

Individualism. **Individualism** is the concept behind the special importance that Americans attach to the rights, freedoms and responsibilities of every person. Individual rights and freedoms and individual responsibility are key features of the American political philosophy that has its roots in the Judeo-Christian religious tradition. Americans believe that individuals have a fundamental responsibility for their own lives, and their successes or failures result from their own efforts and actions. This *belief* in individual responsibility leads directly to the *value* of individualism—the freedom of every person to do, think, say, and believe what he or she wants. Naturally, no individual has a right to harm other people or to infringe on their rights, but aside from those limitations, individuals have the freedom to lead their lives as they wish.

Individualism
The importance placed on the rights, freedoms, and responsibilities of every person

The value placed on individualism and personal freedom is especially strong in the art world. In this case, an artist has created his unique "work of art" from children's dolls.

The spirit of American individualism is expressed in the words of a California man, a top-level manager in a large corporation:

> I guess I feel like everybody on this planet is entitled to have a little bit of space . . . one of the things that makes California such a pleasant place to live, is people by and large aren't bothered by other people's value systems as long as they don't infringe upon your own. . . . if you've got the money, honey, you can do your thing as long as your thing doesn't destroy someone else's property, or interrupt their sleep, or bother their privacy, that's fine (Bellah, 1985, pp. 6–7).

Personal control
The idea that individuals cannot be made to do things that they do not want to do

Personal Control. Also a part of individualism, and closely related to personal freedom, is the notion of personal control. **Personal control** means that individuals cannot be made to do things they do not want to do by social, political or economic forces. In concrete terms, a person has

> . . . the right to be neighborly or to ignore the people next door. It is the ability to be distant from incompatible relatives and to be with compatible friends instead; to skip unwanted memberships in church or union; to vote for candidates not supported by parents or spouses or not to vote at all; and to reject unwelcome advice or demands for behavior change from spouses, employer, or anyone else (Gans, 1988, p. 3).

Americans value the right to be in control of their own lives.

Not only do Americans believe they have a right to control their lives, but they are confident that they can do so and are optimistic about meeting and overcoming every challenge (Spindler and Spindler, 1983). Again this idea is expressed in the words of the California corporation manager who said, "Given open communication and the ability to think problems out, most problems can be solved" (Bellah et al., 1985, p. 7).

Action. Americans also value being *active* over being passive when they face problems or encounter obstacles. This value is reflected in the way Americans respond to international problems, ranging from terrorism to the smuggling of drugs into the United States. Members of Congress have proposed using military aircraft to shoot down civilian planes suspected of smuggling drugs into the United States. The appeal of such a proposal is its direct and decisive action, although civilian pilots and passengers might be understandably apprehensive about this method of combatting drugs. In dealing with international problems, United States' presidents who have taken direct military action (air strikes, invasions, and so forth) usually receive strong public support as indicated by rising approval ratings in public opinion polls. Americans prefer to take action, even if it should fail; they do not like contemplation, hesitation, and waiting as ways of dealing with problems.

Hard Work, Success, and Personal Achievement. Americans also place a high value on work, personal achievement, and success. These values are certainly found in the occupational world, where most people (especially males in our society) act them out. The emphasis on work and success often becomes so important that people sometimes forget why they are working and striving to succeed. These three powerful values are pervasive in American life. Indeed, they extend into many areas of life beyond the work world. Some observers note that Americans work even when they are engaging in leisure-time activities (Kando, 1980; Gunter and Gunter, 1980). Sports are no longer

"That is incredible. Do you know that I, too, want as much as I can get as fast as I can get it?"

games but highly organized, serious competitions. Travel becomes a ceaseless driving marathon to see how many miles can be covered in a day, how many "points of interest" can be seen in a week. Childrearing is often measured more in terms of success and achievement than experienced as the joy of being with a child. Parents feel that they have "done a good job" when their children achieve good grades, win the most-popular-student award, make the football team or cheerleading squad, or graduate with honors.

Closely related to success is the value of materialism. **Materialism** is a preoccupation with acquiring more and more possessions and property. Sometimes the emphasis on acquiring cars, houses, video and sound systems, and recreational equipment is simply called greed. But material things are acquired for reasons other than the pleasure they give; possessions are also an indication of status. The term **conspicuous consumption** (Veblen, 1899), which is often used to describe this American tendency, means acquiring things simply to display them.

Materialism
A preoccupation with acquiring possessions and property

Conspicuous consumption
Acquiring things simply to display them

Many social critics claim that the late 1970s and 1980s have seen an upsurge in materialism, reflected in the "me generation" philosophy (Wolfe, 1976). A major news magazine referred to the late 1980s as a period of "mindless materialism" (*Time*, 1987). Although not denying that materialism is an important value of Americans, one sociologist has argued that Americans in the 1980s, who are employed in factories, service jobs, and as clerical workers, are not excessively materialistic; instead they buy largely for "comfort and convenience" (Gans, 1987, p. 105). That could be true, for as Gans says, these Americans have seen their real wages and salaries decreasing since the mid-1970s, and could hardly have engaged in rampant materialism. Nonetheless, it is hard to deny that when economic circumstances allow, Americans at all levels of the economic structure are inclined to acquire more and more material things.

Rationality. One important additional value of American society is rationality (Kalberg, 1980; Ritzer, 1983; Brubaker, 1984). *Rationality* as a value emphasizes the importance of setting goals and objectives and then achieving these goals in the most efficient way possible. Rationality reaches its peak when it is possible to calculate exactly which procedure will achieve an objective most quickly and with the least expenditure of effort.

Although the value of rationality has characterized much of the Western world in the last several centuries, it has a special prominence in the United States. Almost every part of life in the United States is in some way marked by an emphasis on efficiency and effectiveness. As a result, nearly everything is produced with an eye toward minimizing time and cost, and maximizing output and productivity.

A prime example of the application of the value of rationality can be found in the operation of the fast-food restaurant. Although there have been many imitators, the McDonald's restaurant chain led the way in rationalizing the fast-food industry. Efficiency and speed are dominant features of fast-food service. Because both the customers and the management value the speed with which food can be delivered and eaten, the restaurants offer a limited, simple menu with the food prepared and served in assembly-line fashion. While not noted by most customers, the speedy service offered is in the interests of the restaurant, not the customer. To ensure this efficiency, the seating is made intentionally hard so that customers will not linger after finishing their food (Luxenberg, 1985).

The emphasis on speed and efficiency, following the basic McDonald's model, is now found throughout the food service industry. But, these key features of rationality have now spread to many different aspects of economic and organizational life in the United States. Today, everything from lubricating one's car to getting one's teeth cleaned can be done in a system that follows the basic McDonald's model. One of the authors of this text has labeled this phenomenon the "McDonaldization of America" (Ritzer, 1983).

Norms

As we have previously noted in this chapter, norms are another major component of culture. While values are the general guidelines for evaluating behavior in society, norms deal with more specific situations and circumstances. We have defined norms as the rules for what one should or should not do in given situations (Williams, 1970, p. 442).

William Graham Sumner (1906) was one of the earliest sociologists to address the norms, or rules, of society. Sumner made the distinction between folkways and mores. **Folkways** are rules that generally govern everyday conduct. Violations of those rules usually bring no serious repercussions. The eating rules of a society often fall into the category of folkways. For example, eating an entire dinner with a spoon would be considered odd behavior for an adult, but it would not be a violation that calls for punishment.

Folkways
Rules that generally govern everyday conduct

Mores (pronounced *mor-ays*), by comparison, are rules relating to much more serious behaviors. Mores involve the moral standards of the society. Thus violations of the mores will result in severe punishments (often called **sanctions**) for violators. Stealing, robbing, killing, and espionage are considered to be immoral acts and are often punished severely.

Mores
Rules relating to serious behaviors and moral standards

Sanctions
Punishments for violating mores

The norms of a society define what one should or should not do in given situations. Many times the norms are simply understood by most people, but this sign declaring a "smoke-free environment" is explicit.

Frequently the rules that a society considers important are written into **laws** by the government. When norms are made into laws, the government takes on responsibilities for enforcing the rules. Many laws reflect the mores of the society.

Laws
The norms that are written and enforced by government

An illustration of the relationship between mores and laws can be found in the many towns and counties in the United States where business is prohibited on Sundays. These laws, called "blue laws," reflect a time when Sunday business was considered immoral. Today, some of these laws remain in effect, although most Americans do not consider shopping on Sunday immoral. This example shows that laws often reflect the norms of a society, but not invariably.

Variations in Following Norms. Although norms are the rules of behavior in a society, not everyone follows the norms at all times. One reason is simply a *lack of knowledge* about certain norms. Some people might not know what the rules are. Such is often the case with newcomers to a society, as illustrated by the immigrants in Israel who were unfamiliar with the norms that surround bus riding there. An Israeli bus driver described their plight:

> They don't know how to behave. They don't know what it means to stand in line; they haggle about the fare as if they were in the market; sometimes they even jump through the windows (Toren, 1973, p. 103).

Faced with such violations of the norms, the driver may take the role of teacher, educating the immigrants about the norms of bus riding:

> The driver may have to convince these passengers that it is not customary to cook and eat on the bus. Less dramatic is the need to explain the basic rules of the game—that fares are fixed and have to be paid, that buses run according to a time schedule, and that the driver has to comply with traffic regulations (Toren, 1973, p. 109).

Sometimes people are familiar with a norm, but they *do not accept it or choose not to follow it.* For example, although the norm of tipping for service in restaurants is generally understood in the United States, some people tip only when they consider the service to be of high quality. They do not accept the norm of routine tipping. (Some norms are easier to reject than others because penalties for rejection are not always severe.)

Often, societal norms are not followed because, although the norm still exists as an ideal, the behavior of substantial numbers of people has changed. In other words, many people may believe the norm is a good rule to follow, but in reality they deviate from it. A case in point is the norm prohibiting sex outside of, and especially before, marriage. In the United States, the prohibition against having sexual intercourse before marriage is a norm that most people are aware of and may even support, but evidence shows that more than 70 percent of American young people violate that norm (Hayes, 1987; Kahn et al., 1988; Zelnik and Kantner, 1980).

Ideal versus Real Culture

Ideal culture
Values and norms that most people are aware of and accept

Real culture
The everyday conduct of people that may differ from the ideal culture

The norm prohibiting sexual intercourse before marriage is one example of a distinction often made between the ideal and real cultures. The **ideal culture** reflects the values and norms that most people of a society are aware of and accept (premarital chastity). The **real culture** reflects what people actually do in the conduct of their everyday lives (premarital sex) even though it may differ from the ideal culture.

A second illustration of the distinction between the ideal and real cultures concerns a dominant American value discussed earlier: individualism. This value is undoubtedly supported by the vast majority of Americans, and it does influence behavior in the society. However, there are limits to how much individualism is allowed in the real world, even by those who accept the ideal of individual freedom. If homeowners in a suburban neighborhood decide to let their front yard become a "natural yard" by letting the grass, wild flowers, and weeds grow without mowing, it is very likely that the value of individual freedom would be severely tested in the neighborhood. This is one case among many that could be cited in which the ideal culture is overridden by the real culture.

Material Culture, Technology, and Cultural Lag

Material culture
The artifacts, objects, and tools used by the members of a society

The definition of culture presented earlier included both the "ideas and material objects that the people of a society have created. . . ." So far we have devoted most of our attention to cultural ideas, but now we will focus directly on the material objects of culture. **Material culture** includes all the artifacts, objects, and tools that are used in some way by the members of a particular society. In the United States, homes, cars, appliances, clothing, and works of art are all part of the material culture, as are the highways and roads, the machines that produce agricultural products and manufactured goods, television and radio networks and stations, and energy-producing facilities.

Technology
The interplay of machines, equipment, tools, skills, and procedures for carrying out tasks

The concept of technology is closely related to the material culture, but the two terms are not synonymous. Technology includes machines and production systems, which are, of course, material things, but there is more to technology than machines. **Technology** is the interplay of machines, equipment, tools, skills, and procedures for carrying out tasks. This broader view, especially with the inclusion of procedures, allows us to see that a technology exists for running churches, providing medical care, or conducting political campaigns. For example, today's political campaigns combine the technology of television with the technology of public relations. Political candidates are instructed by their staffs what to say, as well as how to say it and where and when to say it, in

The material culture of a society includes all the artifacts, objects and tools used by its members. Art objects, both those considered "fine" and "tasteless," are part of material culture.

order to maximize their coverage on the evening news (see chapter 16—Political Life). In this case the technology of media management is more important than the material aspects of television (cameras, videotape, transmission lines, etc.).

Technology in the contemporary world often changes very rapidly, usually much faster than social and cultural systems. Technological changes often make existing social practices or cultural forms obsolete, irrelevant, or even dangerous. Members of the society may not recognize the obsolescence of certain social or cultural practices and may continue to follow them. **Cultural lag** exists when social and cultural practices are no longer appropriate for prevailing technological conditions (Ogburn, 1922/1964).

Cultural lag
Social and cultural practices that are no longer appropriate under prevailing technological conditions

For example, cultural lag exists between the level of modern weaponry and the cultural view about war. Thermonuclear weapons have made warfare an irrational way of resolving international disputes. Yet political leaders around the world still talk as if the weapons available would only create a certain amount of damage to the enemy, not cause worldwide annihilation. The social invention called war has not been abandoned, even though the changed technology of war requires its abandonment.

Another contemporary cultural lag exists between the level of productivity possible with modern machines and automatic production systems, and the expectations that most people have about working. In a modern industrial society, fewer people are required to produce objects (cars, wheat, bricks, household appliances, and so on). Yet we cling to the ideas that everyone should work and that their work should produce "things" (although increasingly we consider services, such as tax consulting, public relations advising, or beauty counseling useful and productive). We also tend to think that everyone should work productively at least 40 hours a week. As machines take over even more tasks of production (and services), we will have to give people economic rewards for what we now consider "nonwork." Perhaps someday people will be routinely paid for creating artistic works, traveling, thinking, meditating, or having therapy. If this idea strikes us as strange or impossible, we might recognize our own reaction as an example of cultural lag.

Cultural Diversity

As we noted earlier, within any society some diversity exists in how the culture is understood and accepted. Not every American places the same importance on hard work and achievement or, for that matter, even uses the same language. In this section we will discuss ways in which cultural diversity exists, even within a single society.

Subcultural Groups

Subcultural groups (or Subcultures) A societal group that differs significantly from the dominant culture

For most societies we can identify a dominant culture. Our earlier description of American culture described the values, norms, and beliefs of the majority of Americans—the dominant culture. But often (and especially in the United States), identifiable groups of people have cultural characteristics that differ in some significant way from the dominant culture. These groups are called **subcultural groups,** or simply, **subcultures.** Some groups described as subcultures in the United States include Hispanic Americans, Native American Indians, Mormons, and residents of the "Old South" (Black and Reed, 1984; Mauss, 1984).

How does one identify a subculture? The illustrations above suggest that subcultures are identified by language, ethnicity, race, religion, region, or sometimes a combination of these factors. If one walks through certain parts of Miami, Florida, the prominence of Spanish, both in written and spoken form, signals that an Hispanic subculture (primarily Cuban) exists. Language obviously reflects an ethnic or national heritage, and therefore one would also find differences in foods, holidays, clothing, and other life-style characteristics. Although language and life-style differences are readily observable, the norms and values of a subculture are more subtle. They can, however, be identified by closer and more systematic observations, as we will see in our examination of Mormons and Hasidic Jews.

Because the people of any given subculture live in the context of a dominant culture, they often share the culture of the dominant society to some degree. Mormons, for example, have some identifiable norms and values that are distinctly Mormon, but they also hold many values and norms found in the dominant culture. Mormons of the nineteenth century had one norm that clearly set them apart from the dominant culture: the practice of polygyny (multiple wives). However, Mormons came to be influenced by the dominant culture, which vehemently opposed the practice of polygyny, and by about 1910 the practice had been officially dropped (Mauss, 1984). This example from the Mormon experience illustrates **cultural assimilation,** a process by which members of subcultures come to accept the values, beliefs, language, and behaviors of the dominant culture.

Cultural assimilation A process by which members of subcultures accept the ways of the dominant culture

A subcultural group must often take extraordinary measures to maintain its identity in the face of the dominant culture. In the Amish religious group of Pennsylvania, parents

The Cuban subculture of Miami, Florida, is clearly in evidence in many parts of the city.

remove their children from the public schools as soon as legally possible in order to minimize contact with the secular world (Kephart, 1976). The Hasidic Jews have made similar efforts to maintain their cultural identity, even though they are tightly surrounded by the dominant culture.

Hasidic Jews. Hasidic Jews had their beginnings in Poland in the early eighteenth century (Harris, 1986). Hasidism was innovative "in the way it redefined traditional Jewish values by placing prayer, mysticism, dancing, singing, storytelling, and the sanctification of daily life on an equal footing" with the study of traditional law (Harris, 1985a, p. 42). There are about 250,000 Hasidim in the world today (about one-fifth of the number that existed at the turn of the century); 200,000 live in the United States—half of them in Brooklyn. The Hasidim are divided into a number of groups, or "courts," the largest of which is the Lubavitchers (named after the city in Belorussia that was its original home). Despite many similarities among all Hasidim (e.g., all adult males are bearded), some differences exist (e.g., Lubavitcher men do not wear *peyes,* or long sidelocks of hair).

The Lubavitchers live in the Crown Heights section of Brooklyn. They live in a well-defined area characterized by synagogues, kosher butcher shops, and ritual bath houses. They follow a number of notable customs:

- Husbands and wives are forbidden to kiss or embrace each other in public.
- No physical contact between the sexes is permitted outside of the family.

- Few men attend college and work is not seen as an end itself, but rather as a means to earn a living so that they can follow a religious existence.
- After they marry, women cut off most of their hair and wear wigs.
- Most families do not own television sets or go to the movies.
- Women are not allowed to sing in the presence of men.
- Boys and girls go to separate schools and men and women are separated in synagogue.
- A woman may not have any physical contact with her husband during menstruation, or for a week afterwards. At the end of this period the woman is required to have a ritual bath at the *mikveh* before resuming sexual relations with her husband.

Since the Lubavitchers live in an enclave in Brooklyn completely surrounded by non-Hasidim, they frequently come into contact with people from the outside world. Even so they have been successful in maintaining their distinct cultural identity. Insofar as possible they treat outsiders as if they do not exist.

Countercultures

Counterculture
A societal group that is consciously in opposition to the dominant culture

Often in a society, groups emerge that are not just different in their ways, but are consciously in opposition to the widely accepted norms and values of the dominant culture. This type of group is known as a **counterculture** group (Yinger, 1960).

Generally, counterculture groups are not exceptionally large, and they often seem to appear and fade rather quickly. A listing of some of the most prominent counterculture groups of the United States over the past 30 years reveals how shortlived most of them are. In the 1950s the "beatniks" appeared, led by a relatively small number of literary and artistic people. Their key countercultural note was a rejection of conventional morality regarding sex, drugs, and work. The beatniks were superceded by the "hippies" of the 1960s and 1970s, who generally subscribed to the same philosophy. Much larger numbers of Americans became involved in the hippie movement, carrying forward the themes of individual freedom, antiwar, and antimaterialism. In more recent times "punkers" appeared as a prominent counterculture group. Their most distinguishing features were their devotion to certain types of music, and their adornment of bizarre clothing, jewelry, and hairstyles. All these life-style choices seem designed to demonstrate a dramatic rejection of conventional ways.

One group that has maintained a relatively long-term identity as a counterculture group is the Hell's Angels. This loosely knit, nationwide organization centers its activities around motorcycles and the heavy use of alcohol and drugs. Once again the life style manifested by this group seems designed to flaunt their rejection of conventional ways of life.

Counterculture groups are often highly critical of the established political systems, accusing them of being repressive, corrupt, or evil. These politically oriented groups often engage in illegal acts and terrorism. A recent example in the United States is a group calling itself "The New Aryan Nation." This organization models itself after the German Nazi party, is anti-black and anti-Jewish, and wants to return to a society in which whites are separate and in total control. Its members have engaged in killings and robberies in an effort to achieve their white supremacist objectives.

The "Skinheads" of the United States constitute a counterculture, holding explicitly racist and anti-semitic views, and having a tendency toward violence.

Also increasingly publicized are the activities of "Skinheads," a closely related counterculture group, easily identified by their shaved heads. They also hold explicitly racist and antisemitic views and have tendencies toward violence.

Summary

Culture is the entire complex of ideas and material objects that the people of a society (or group) have created and adopted for carrying out the necessary tasks of collective life. Cultural rules give the people of a society a guide for behavior and make their behavior relatively predictable.

As an explanation of human behavior, culture offers an alternative to a "human nature" explanation. The extensive differences in the behavior of people in different societies supports the importance of culture as an explanation.

Sociobiology offers another alternative explanation. It stresses that human behavior is influenced by genetically inherited tendencies. A major criticism of sociobiology is that it does not allow for cultural factors to override whatever genetically inherited tendencies humans might have.

Most people think of their own cultural practices as the best and right way—a perspective called ethnocentrism. The study of different cultures allows us to see that particular cultural practices are best judged in the context of the culture in which they occur—a view called cultural relativism.

The most important components of culture include the verbal and nonverbal symbols of a people. The verbal symbols, or language system, of a culture tend to shape people's perceptions of the real world (the Sapir-Whorf hypothesis). Knowledge and beliefs are also components of culture. Values, the standards of desirability within a culture, are centrally important for understanding culture. In the United States the most prominent value is individualism. Closely related is the importance placed on personal control of one's life. Other significant American values are hard work, personal success, personal achievement, materialism, and rationality.

Norms are the general guidelines for evaluating behavior in society. Folkways are norms that govern everyday conduct, while mores are norms that reflect the moral standards of the society. Norms are not observed uniformly by all people in a society.

An ideal culture does exist, which contrasts with the real culture—what people actually do in the conduct of their everyday lives.

Material culture and technology are also important elements. When the material culture and technology change, a cultural lag often results as other parts of the culture become obsolete, irrelevant, or, in some cases, dangerous.

Subcultural groups (or, simply, subcultures) are groups with identifiable cultural characteristics that set them apart from the dominant culture. Subcultures often get changed and influenced by the dominant culture through a process of cultural assimilation. To retain its distinctive ways, a subcultural group must make an effort to remain separate from the dominant culture. Groups with cultural characteristics that are consciously in opposition to the dominant culture are called countercultures.

CRITICAL THINKING

1. In what ways can a knowledge of the concept of culture be practical in business and travel?
2. Why (or why not) is a cultural explanation of human behavior more useful and significant than an explanation based on human biology or sociobiology?
3. Review the definition of ethnocentrism given in the chapter. Can you think of examples of American humor about peoples and cultures that are based on ethnocentrism?
4. The authors state that in order to be a cultural relativist one need not blindly accept all forms of human behavior. Give examples of human behavior (historical or other) that you feel are beyond the limits of tolerance. To what extent are your beliefs based on your culture's views of right and wrong?
5. Give examples of nonverbal symbols that you have used or seen in the past week.
6. Give an example of how new technology has shaped our verbal symbols and perceptions of reality.
7. Review the definition of cultural values presented in the chapter. List ten values you feel are dominant in American society. Then list ten values you personally feel are most important in your life. To what extent do your personal values match the societal ones you have mentioned? What might such a comparison indicate about your relationship to the dominant culture in America?
8. What norms govern your behavior as a college student? Would you classify these norms as folkways, mores, or laws?
9. Give three examples of discrepancies between our notion of the ideal culture and the real culture. How do you explain such discrepancies?
10. To what extent are technological changes responsible for cultural changes and cultural lag in the Third World today?
11. Make a fairly complete list of the subcultures and countercultures you believe exist in American society. Give an example of how each varies from the dominant culture. Is such diversity helpful or harmful for society?

CHAPTER 4

Forms of Social Life: Interaction, Groups, Organizations, and Societies

Human behavior is not random; it is patterned. Regularity and order can be found in the actions of all humans, whether they are Tibetans living in Katmandu, aborigines living in the Outback of Australia, or New Yorkers living on the Upper East Side of Manhattan. Average people living anywhere will know how to relate to the people with whom they come in contact in their daily lives. Imagine what would happen, however, if we were to take a person from any one of these places and put him or her in another society. The results would vividly reveal how the patterns of behavior in a society must be learned. We have only to recall two recent movies (*Moscow on the Hudson* with Robin Williams, and *Coming to America* with Eddie Murphy) to see the problems that emerge when a person encounters the social patterns of an unfamiliar society.

Because many of the social patterns of our own society are so familiar, we often give them little attention. In this chapter we will examine a wide range of different patterns of social relations. We will begin with a general concept that sociologists often use when describing a pattern of social relationships (social structure). Then, beginning at the microscopic level, we will see how interaction between individuals produces patterned behavior even in a two-person relationship. Next we will move to the level of groups and then to organizations. The chapter will conclude with a discussion of societies.

Social Structures

Social structures are regular patterns of social interaction and persistent social relationships. Social structures are constructed by the ongoing interaction of people, but at the same time, by observing these patterns of interaction, we can identify social structures. Social structures can be observed at any social level from the interaction between two people, through groups and organizations, to entire societies. To illustrate how a social structure is created through interaction, and, simultaneously, how social structures are observable in the regularities and patterns of everyday interaction, we will consider a familiar example.

Social structure
A regular pattern of social interaction and persistent social relationships

Imagine a number of college students who come together at the beginning of a school year to live on the same corridor of a dormitory. When they first move in they are probably strangers, or perhaps they know each other only casually. Over a period of time, however, through their interaction, they will start sorting themselves into sets of people who spend time together. These sets of people will talk, go to meals together, help each other with homework, and so on. Some of the emerging groups are apt to have special interests and activities—sports, dorm politics, partying, practical jokes, or studying. Using the words of the social structure definition, we can say that regular patterns of social interaction and persistent social relationships will occur among these students. For example, a resident of the corridor could easily predict which students would be doing what, and with whom, on any Friday night. In sociological terms, almost anyone living on this corridor will understand its social structure.

Social structures can also be sketched in a diagrammatic form. For example, in figures 4–1 and 4–2, the structures of the average American family and the leadership structure of a typical corporation are depicted diagrammatically. The structures of informal groups, organizations, governments, and societies can be similarly sketched.

Because social structures are created by people, they can change over time. But structures tend to have some persistence, and when sociologists speak of social structures they are talking about patterns of interaction and social relationships that persist over time. Included would be the major social structures found in societies, for they generally do not change rapidly. Examples in American society, to be examined later, are the socioeconomic-status system with its different social classes (chapter 8), and the major racial and ethnic groups (chapter 9). These stratification systems are, of course, social structures. The social class structure of the society is observable through the way people interact with each other, and these patterns of interaction do not change much over time. The same is true with respect to the relationships between racial and ethnic groups in the United States. Racial discrimination, for example, which places blacks and other racial minorities in disadvantaged positions, has existed for centuries and persists today.

Throughout this chapter we will be describing social structures at the various levels of social life. We will begin with the interaction between individuals, and then move

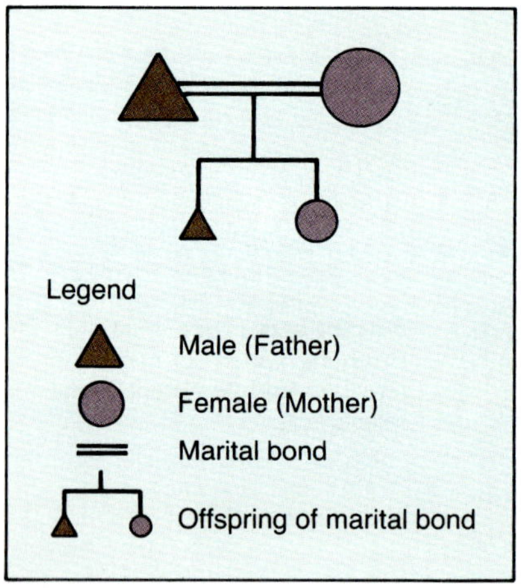

Figure 4–1. Diagrammatic Representation of the Structure of a Typical Family.

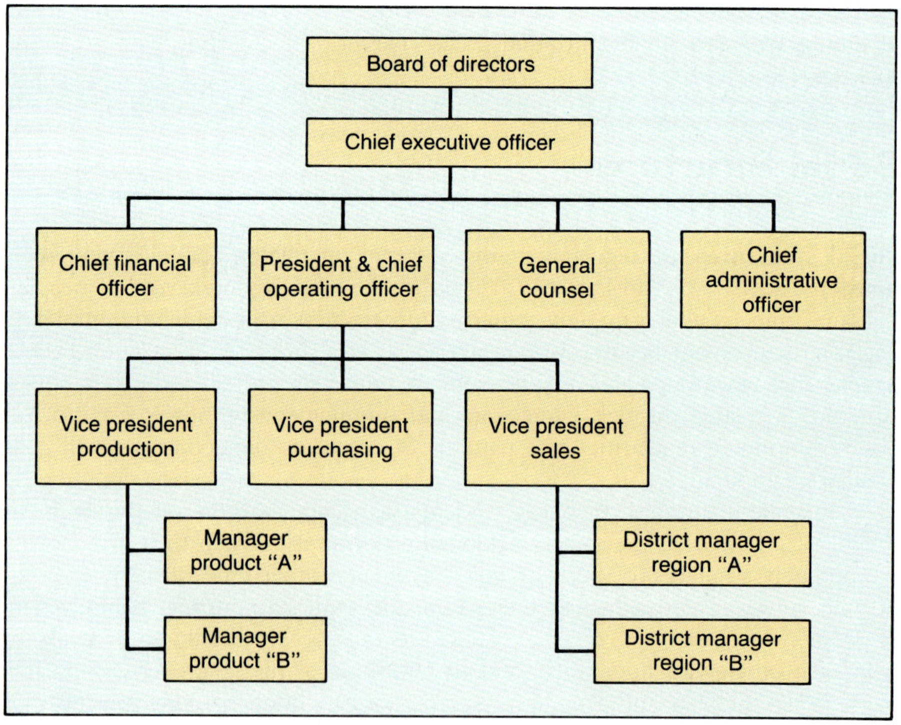

Figure 4–2. Diagrammatic Representation of a Formal Leadership Structure of a Corporation.

As people, in general, and students, in particular, interact with each other over time, they will form regular patterns of interaction that sociologists call *social structures*. Often these patterns of interaction, or structures, will center on special interests and activities.

on to groups and organizations. We will conclude, at the macroscopic end of the social continuum, with a consideration of societies.

Interaction

The ability of humans to meet and interact with other humans is a high-level skill, but most of the time we do it with ease. In an average day a person typically interacts with a wide variety of people, including friends, relatives, lovers, acquaintances, and strangers. As long as we share the same language with these people, we can negotiate almost any kind of situation, whether it is friendly or hostile, comfortable or awkward, casual or formal.

As we saw in our consideration of symbolic interaction theory in chapter 1, the human mind, with its ability to understand and use symbols (both verbal and nonverbal), makes interaction possible between people. People interact primarily through verbal symbols, or words, not only with others but with themselves. By using symbols to interact with themselves, people are able to evaluate other people and situations, and decide what actions to take. Again, this is an important principle of symbolic interaction theory.

"All right, now. I want you and Grandpa to run along and interact."

When interaction occurs between two people, two things happen, almost simultaneously. Each person in an interaction situation is *sending* words and cues and *receiving and processing* words and cues as they come in from the other person. The important feature of any interaction is the way people use their minds to interpret the words and cues of another person, deduce their meaning, and respond accordingly.

This abstract description of interaction makes it seem complex and unfamiliar, but if we take an everyday situation we can see how the process of interaction works. Consider a hypothetical yet commonplace situation in which a male and a female college student are getting acquainted. If they are in college and happen to sit next to each other in a class, over a period of time they may have a series of interactions that could ultimately result in their dating and becoming romantically involved. Their early interaction is important in this process. Two people seated side by side may rarely talk with each other at first. Gradually, however, they may start to interact. Of course, the very act of engaging in conversation when it is not necessary is in itself a symbolic act. When two people find themselves engaged in conversation they may recognize that their interaction could imply a mutual attraction. Even as they talk about something as mundane as the sociology professor or the next test, the young man might reflect to himself that he is attracted to the young woman and that she might be attracted to him.

As this interaction continues, different things might be happening at different levels simultaneously. Noncommittal ideas may first be exchanged, as the students talk about the professor or about studying for the next examination. The young woman may say she doesn't have anyone with whom to study, but if she makes this remark, the young man must interpret what it means. He has only a second or two to decide if she is saying that it might be pleasant for the two of them to get together outside of class, ostensibly to do some studying. At the same time, as he is assessing what her words really mean, he is formulating his response. If he responds to her objective statement inappropriately, he may look foolish. If he treats it as a suggestion that they get together outside of class and she did not mean it that way, he may be embarrassed. The young man must quickly select from his many possible choices: "I don't have anyone to study with either," or "I always find it helps to study with someone just before the test," or "Why don't we get together before the test?"

If the young man made the last of these statements, the young woman would have to decide exactly what his words meant. He could be asking for a date, or he could simply be suggesting that they study together. The woman must weigh all the evidence, again in just a second or two, and make some appropriate response. As a rule, a person in this situation will reply in such a way that the response will be appropriate regardless of the real intent of the statement. Or the young woman could simply say, "Are you asking me for a date or do you want to get together to study?" However, before doing so she will have to weigh the consequences of this response. Will the young man be shocked by her directness? Will her statement have the effect of acknowledging the previously unstated attraction between them?

The interaction just described goes on within the context of the cultural values and the social norms we discussed in the last chapter. In some societies, the norms of courtship would make it totally inappropriate for two young people to make a date of any kind. Often parents would have to be consulted and a chaperon obtained before two young people of the opposite sex could spend any time together. We can see from these normative constraints why human behavior is not random but is, as we said, patterned. The interaction between two people who are getting acquainted is partially open to their own creativity and inventiveness, but it is also patterned by the norms that prevail in a society.

But there is another important social constraint on the interaction between the young man and woman we have been describing. Both people have social statuses, or positions, and attached to these statuses are social roles. Status and role are important sociological concepts because they reveal why there is a great amount of regular and patterned social behavior.

Status and Role

The words and actions of the young man and woman described above will certainly be influenced and shaped, especially in the early interaction, by the fact of their genders. Many American young people still believe it more appropriate for males to initiate invitations for dates than for females to do so. This view is changing, but many young women still say, "I think it is fine for a woman to ask a guy for a date, *but I wouldn't do it.*" This statement tells us that although some young women do not see anything wrong with a woman initiating a date, many still feel that it might be inappropriate behavior. But why is it viewed as inappropriate? In order to understand why someone would feel this way and why this feeling is shared by many other people—young and old, female and male—we have to examine the importance of the sociological concepts of status and role.

A **status** is a socially recognized position in a social system. A **role** is the behavior generally expected of one who occupies a particular status. Again we can use gender as an example of status and role. In all societies, males and females have socially recognized positions, with certain expectations about what one will and will not do. However, males

Status
A socially recognized position in a social system

Role
Behavior generally expected of one who occupies a particular status

and females are not expected to act in the same way in every society. In chapter 10 we will examine some societies in which men and women are expected to act in ways that are very different from those traditionally expected of them in American society. But—and here is the important point—gender is always a status that carries with it some expected behaviors. Roles are always connected with gender.

Ascribed status
A status into which individuals move, or are placed, irrespective of efforts or capacities

Achieved status
A status that people acquire through their own efforts

Master status
A position so important that it dominates or overrides all other statuses

Statuses can be of two types: ascribed and achieved. An **ascribed status** is one into which individuals move or are placed, irrespective of their efforts or capacities. Examples of ascribed statuses include being male or female, young or old, black or white, son or daughter. We have little control over our ascribed statuses. (A few examples of efforts to control ascribed statuses are a black person "passing" as white, or a person of one gender undergoing a sex change.) In contrast, an **achieved status** is one that people acquire through their own efforts. Examples include becoming a college graduate, getting married, having children, becoming an astronaut, or even becoming a bank robber.

A related concept is that of master status. A **master status** refers to a position so important that it dominates and overrides all other statuses, both for the person and all other people. For example, being an AIDS victim may well be a master status for individuals because the disease might be so overwhelming that it shapes the person's self-image as well as other people's view of him or her. More commonly in our society, a master status is related to one's occupation. A person who is a Supreme Court Justice, a nun, a major league baseball player, or an opera singer is likely to be seen primarily in terms of his or her major occupational role—a master role.

Being manager of a major league baseball team (as Tommy LaSorda is) is an achieved status, and, because it dominates and overrides all other statuses, it is also a master status.

Another point about statuses and roles is that they have a reality of their own; they exist irrespective of the persons who fill them. Whoever occupies the status of the President of the United States, or is the center-fielder on a baseball team, or the anchorperson on a television news show must attend to certain expectations that accompany the status. In general, the people who fill a status understand the expectations and follow the behavior expected of them.

However, not everyone in a particular status behaves in exactly the same way. There are two reasons for this. First, the role expectations connected with a status are not fully detailed. Role expectations are not so precisely stated or understood that every detail of expected behavior is unambiguous. Second, individuals who hold statuses may have their own orientations toward the role. Let us deal with each of these issues separately.

Roles do not specify every exact behavior that a person in a given status must follow. In fact, roles often have only broad requirements within which a person must operate. Airline pilots, for example, are expected to be competent to fly planes in all kinds of conditions, and handle difficult and emergency situations in a calm and collected way. When pilots speak to the passengers they generally present themselves as steady, serious, and relaxed, even though they may not always feel that way. However, some pilots will occasionally inject humor, irritation (with delays, for example), or other emotions into their public presentations. When they are not within hearing or sight of the passengers, their behavior may be even more at odds with the general role expectations for airline pilots. Behind the scenes they are able to introduce their unique, personal characteristics and still fulfill the role expectations connected with a status. In other words, people do not simply conform to role expectations; they also actively modify their roles. This ability of individuals to modify (at least to some degree) their own roles has been called **role-making** (Hewitt, 1984, p. 81).

Role-making
The ability of individuals to modify their roles

Another way to see how individuals can vary their performance of a role is to note that the dominant view about what is expected of people in a given status need not be universal. Different orientations toward a role can exist. The college student role has broad outlines—enrolling, going to class, studying, taking exams—but different students might emphasize different features of the student role. These different emphases are called **role orientations.** Some students might emphasize the academic and intellectual aspect of the student role. With this orientation to the world of ideas and books, they take advantage of the opportunity they have to become involved in intellectual pursuits. Their role orientation toward their college-student status has been called the "academic-intellectual role orientation." In comparison, other college students are more oriented toward the vocational or professional training they receive in school. They see student life as an opportunity to learn a profession and gain entry into it. This orientation has been called the "vocational role orientation." Some students see their college experience as an opportunity to engage in an active social life or to learn social skills. For them, college is a learning ground for their future social lives. The fraternity/sorority scene may be a forerunner of the country club life that they expect to enter later. This role orientation of college students has been called the "social life role" (Bolton and Kammeyer, 1967).

Role orientation
An individual's emphasis on specific aspects of a role

As we have seen, the roles connected with statuses do not make individuals in the same status behave in the same way, but enough similarity is evident in role performance to produce some general patterns of behavior. These patterns, found among males and females, airline pilots, and students, and a vast array of other statuses, are sufficiently consistent to produce identifiable patterns in social life. However, statuses and roles can always be modified and changed over time, through the continuing actions and interactions of people.

Dyads and Triads

Dyad
Two people engaged in interaction

Triad
Three people engaged in interaction

When two people engage in interaction it is called a **dyad.** When a third person is introduced into the interaction it is called a **triad.** While both dyads and triads involve interaction, and both can be seen as groups, there are some interesting differences between two-person and three-person interaction. From a sociological and practical point of view, the triad is a much more complicated social arrangement (Simmel, 1950).

Triads are three-person groups in which it is often difficult to maintain a balance. Frequently in triads one of the three members becomes isolated from the other two.

A dyad has only one relationship, but a triad has three (A and B, A and C, B and C). That in itself makes the triad more complicated. Consider, for example, the common situation of a husband and wife dyad becoming parents of a new baby, thus becoming a triad. The relationship between the husband and wife becomes more complicated because each will now have a relationship with the baby. It is a fairly common occurrence for a new mother to devote so much attention to her relationship with the baby that her husband feels neglected. A substantial amount of research shows that satisfaction with marital relationships declines when married couples have children. Part of the reason can probably be attributed to the changes in interaction when a married-couple dyad becomes a triad.

Similar problems often emerge in three-person friendship groups. Although three-person groups can maintain a cohesive "three-musketeers" relationship, a balance is difficult to maintain. All pairs of relationships in a triad must be about equal in time spent together, displays of friendship, conversation, and so on. If this equality is not maintained, then one of the pairs will dominate, leaving the third person relatively isolated. Many people who have been in three-person friendship groups have had the experience of two members drawing closer together and shutting out the third.

Although dyads and triads are frequent forms of social interaction, the social group brings us to a more purely sociological level. We turn to this level next.

Social Groups

While the word *group* is used in various ways in everyday speech, and even in sociology, the technical sociological meaning focuses our attention on some important features of social life. A **group** may be defined as a relatively small number of people who interact with one another over time and thereby establish patterns of interaction, a group identity, and rules or norms governing behavior.

Group
A small number of people with patterned interaction, group identity, and norms

One of the key features defining a group is the interaction among all members. A larger entity such as a society (e.g., American society) differs from a group in that all the members of a society cannot possibly interact with each other because of their large number.

Although a large number of people cannot technically constitute a social group, a small number of people will not necessarily constitute a group either. Several people who meet briefly on an elevator are not a group, because they lack a group identity and because they do not interact on the basis of patterns they have established.

In-Groups and Out-Groups

According to our definition, a basic characteristic of a group is that the interacting individuals have a group identity. Therefore to qualify as a group, the people who compose it must define themselves as members and, conversely, those outside the group must be defined as outsiders. The emphasis on group identity leads to the distinction between *in-groups* and *out-groups* (Sumner, 1904). An **in-group** is one that members are involved in and with which they identify, while an **out-group** is one to which

In-group
A group that members are involved with and with which they identify

Out-group
A group to which outsiders belong

Urban gangs typically display a strong sense of group identity. They see their own group as the in-group and all others as out-groups.

outsiders belong. The importance of this distinction is the tendency for people to believe in the rightness and desirability of the in-group, and to reject the ways of the out-group. In contemporary Los Angeles (as well as other cities) groups of youths (typically labeled *gangs* by the public and the mass media) provide an extreme example of in-groups/out-groups.

Los Angeles has an estimated 600 gangs, and the rivalry between gangs is often intensely hostile. During 1987 in Los Angeles there were 205 gang-related killings, and during the first four months of 1988 there were 109 killings. Gang members are primarily black or Hispanic, but there are also Asian, Samoan, and white gangs (Reinhold, 1988). Typically gangs are identified with a particular neighborhood or, in the case of Hispanic gangs, a *barrio* (Mirande, 1987; Moore, 1985). The names of gangs often reflect where they live; for example, the Avenue Piru Bloods, Los Pocos Locos, or the Rock Mara, for the Maravilla area of East Los Angeles. The importance of gang names is revealed by the following example: because the Bloods and Crips are rival gangs, a Blood will not ask a friend for a cigarette (since it starts with the letter C), but will instead ask for a "bigarette" (Reinhold, 1988). Often gang members wear a near-uniform, clothing with distinctive colors and style. Gangs connected with the Crips wear blue, while the Bloods prefer red. The members of one Hispanic gang are identifiable by their khaki pants, camp or prison jackets, plain Pendleton shirts, and head bandannas or brim hats (Stumphauzer et al., quoted in Mirande, 1987, p. 80). In the areas of Los Angeles where gangs thrive, a gang member who strays into the neighborhood of a rival gang, or is found on the street wearing the wrong color clothing, might get beaten or killed. Life in these gangs represents an extreme example of in-group feeling, and hostility toward out-groups.

Primary and Secondary Groups

Sociologists also differentiate between primary groups and secondary groups. The concept of **primary groups** was developed by Cooley (1909) to describe groups "characterized by intimate face-to-face association and cooperation." Primary groups are typically small and close-knit. The relationships among the members are very personal. They strongly identify with each other as well as with the group as a whole. As a result of the closeness of the relationships, the primary group often has a profound effect on its members. As examples of primary groups Cooley cites the family, play groups of children, and neighborhood or community groups.

Primary groups Groups with intimate, face-to-face association and cooperation

Secondary groups, in contrast to primary groups, are typically large and impersonal. Members do not know each other as intimately or completely as do the members of a primary group. Members' ties to a secondary group are typically weaker than the ties to primary groups. Secondary groups have a less profound impact on members. They are usually formed for a specific purpose, and the members rarely interact with each other outside of the activities that are oriented toward the group goal. The members of a local Parent-Teacher's Association or a labor union are examples of secondary groups.

Secondary groups Groups that are typically large and impersonal

Reference Groups

Another sociological perspective on groups is revealed by thinking of how groups (both primary and secondary) serve as reference groups. **Reference groups** are any groups that a person takes into account when evaluating his or her actions or characteristics. As humans we are always trying to evaluate ourselves and our behavior. Am I attractive? Am I doing a good job? Should I wear these clothes tonight? One way we answer these

Reference groups Groups taken into account when one evaluates his or her actions or characteristics

It is often possible to deduce the reference groups of individuals by their clothing and behavior choices (note the can of dipping tobacco in the back pocket of the jeans).

questions for ourselves is to refer to the performance or the qualities of the members of some group. Although individuals often use groups of which they are members as reference groups, a person does not necessarily have to be a member of a group in order to use it as a reference group. Take, for example, a woman who is making reasonably good career progress and, after some years, becomes a manager in a major corporation. If this woman's reference group is made up primarily of the circle of friends with whom she went to high school, she will undoubtedly have positive feelings about her career progress. Many of her high school friends have probably not gone on to jobs in the corporate world; compared to them she is doing well. On the other hand, if this same woman manager takes as her reference group the fastest rising executives in her own corporation, she will evaluate her career success more negatively.

As this example shows, a reference group can be used to make comparative evaluations about oneself and one's performance. But reference groups can also provide a normative function by supplying an individual's norms and values. Thus, a young manager may not yet be a member of top management, but the latter can be his/her reference group, supplying the aspiring executive with the relevant standards of behavior. For example, if an aspiring young female manager notices that the successful female executives wear tailored suits and silk blouses, she too might stock her wardrobe with these items.

Religious group membership often provides an important reference group that has a profound influence on individual behavior. A study of American adults has shown that membership in different religious groups influences attitudes toward premarital sex, birth control, and abortion (Bock et al., 1983). Research evidence also reveals that religions as reference groups influence alcohol use (Cochran et al., 1988).

A person will likely have a number of reference groups, and those groups will probably change over time. Many college students have reference groups that include students who are socially popular figures, varsity athletes, and campus leaders. After graduation some of the characteristics and qualities of these types may seem superficial and irrelevant. Whatever one's reference groups are while in college, they are likely to change dramatically when one leaves the campus and enters the business or professional world.

Group Conformity—Three Classic Experiments

As the discussion of reference groups suggests, individual behavior is influenced by the groups to which one belongs and the groups to which one aspires. The tendency of individuals to respond to social groups and to allow them to influence behavior is one of the most intriguing aspects of human behavior. As we saw in the last chapter, Americans place great value on their individualism, and yet there is ample evidence that individuals have a tendency to *conform* to the behavior of other members of a group, even when no explicit demands are made to do so. That is, people seem to want to go along with the majority of group members even when those group members do not explicitly pressure them to conform.

The Sherif Experiment. An important study in this line of research is Muzafer Sherif's (1935) famous experiment, "A Study of Some Social Factors in Perception." Sherif was interested in studying what people would do when presented with an ambiguous phenomenon—one lacking in stable reference points. The phenomenon Sherif presented to his subjects was a single point of light in a completely dark room. Because no other objects in the room could be seen, there were no reference points, and the light appeared to move (even though it was not moving). This phenomenon is known as the autokinetic effect. In one part of this study individuals were first shown the light alone and then again in the presence of a group of people. When individuals alone were presented with the light, each one established a sense of the distance that the light had moved. When those individuals were then placed in the same situation with a group of people, each individual's judgment of the distance that the light moved tended to converge with the judgment of the group. It appears from this experiment that individuals prefer to be closer to the standards of the group; they preferred to be in conformity.

The Asch Experiment. In another classic experiment, Solomon Asch (1952) studied groups of seven to nine college students to examine the effect of group pressure on individuals. In each group, all but one of the members (the subject) were confederates of the researcher. The group was shown two sets of cards—the first card with a single vertical line and the second with three vertical lines. One of the lines on the second card was equal in length to the line of the first card. The other two lines were sufficiently different that, when asked to match lines on the two cards, the vast majority of people making decisions alone chose the correct line.

In the crucial experiment, Asch had his confederates choose an incorrect line on the second card. These choices were made out loud, within hearing of the subjects who were positioned toward the end of the group. Responding in turn, subjects showed that they were experiencing group pressure, even to the extent of making the same incorrect choice. In about one-third of the cases the subjects sided with the majority and made the incorrect choice. This tendency to conform to the majority opinion appeared even when the subjects apparently knew that they were making incorrect judgments. Although this experiment does demonstrate the pressure to conform to group opinions, it is important to remember that in about two-thirds of the cases the subjects resisted the majority and made the correct decision.

The Milgram Experiment. An experiment conducted by Stanley Milgram (1974) focused on a somewhat different aspect of conformity. He was able to demonstrate that many people will comply with the orders of someone who appears to be in a position of authority in an organization (the social form we will consider next). In the Milgram experiments subjects were asked to work with other individuals who, unknown to the subjects, were paid by Milgram to act out prearranged parts. The subjects always found themselves in the position of "teacher" in the study, while the confederates served as "learners." The learners were strapped into chairs and hooked up to electrodes. The teacher-subjects were placed in another room with a fake shock generator. Labels on the generator indicated the increasing intensity of its charge—from "Slight Shock" at the low end to "Danger: Severe Shock" and, finally, "XXX" at the other end. The shocks were not real, but the teacher-subjects did not know it. They were instructed to give the learner-confederates an electric shock for every wrong answer (intentional on the part of the confederate) and to increase the amount of shock each time. Learner-confederates reacted with screams, as if pained by the shocks. Almost two-thirds of the subject-teachers continued to administer shocks to the point marked "XXX"—a level they believed was potentially lethal. The researcher, dressed in white coat and projecting an aura of scientific respectability, was perceived by most subjects as an authoritative figure whose instructions were to be followed regardless of the resulting harm to other people.

Before the study, almost all of the subjects said they would never be able to bring themselves to inflict severe pain on someone in any foreseeable circumstances. The Milgram study indicates that, under certain conditions, many people, especially if they receive orders from authority figures, will violate their own moral norms and inflict pain, perhaps even at lethal levels, on other human beings.

These experimental studies reveal how people are influenced by the behavior of other members of groups and by authority figures in organizations. Furthermore, these reactions were produced in experimentally created groups and organizational settings. It is possible that the real groups and organizations to which individuals belong (families, friendship groups, schools, workplaces, and so on) may have even more influence on member behavior. Clearly groups and organizations can and do exert an influence on the behavior of individuals.

We are now ready to take a closer look at organizations and how they work. Of special importance is the bureaucratic form of organization that is so pervasive today.

Organizations and Bureaucracies

We live in a world that is increasingly characterized by large-scale organizations. Most of us were born in large hospitals or multipurpose medical centers; we have been educated in large school systems, have often worked for major corporations or businesses, and have dealt with complex governmental systems. Major portions of our lives are spent dealing with and working in large-scale organizations. We recognize increasingly that we cannot understand the society in which we live if we do not understand how organizations work and how the many different kinds of organizations—political, economic, and social—relate to each other (Clark, 1988).

To see just how enmeshed we are with large-scale organizations, we have only to open our wallets or purses. We carry social security cards, identification cards, registration cards, driver's licenses, medical insurance cards, draft registration cards (if we are male), credit cards, and a variety of other membership cards that verify that we belong to organizations. Not only do organizations surround us but they firmly implant themselves in our daily comings and goings. In other words, we live in an "organizational society" (Presthus, 1978).

Organization
A deliberately constituted collectivity with goals, statuses, roles, and rules

Sociologists use the term **organization** to describe a deliberately constructed collectivity aimed at achieving specified goals with clearly delineated statuses, roles, and rules. Thus, the U.S. Postal Service is an organization of managers, supervisors, postmasters/postmistresses, postal clerks, mail carriers, and many others whose task it is to deliver the mail. Mothers Against Drunk Drivers is a national organization with many community branches, established to draw attention to the harm caused by drinking drivers on the highways. Any neighborhood improvement association, with officers, members, and meetings, is an organization created to do something positive for a neighborhood.

These three examples show that many different types of organizations exist. Some are government agencies; some are private enterprises. Other organizations focus on causes or special interests and may be national or local in scope.

Another way to make distinctions among types of organizations is on the basis of how control is exerted over people who exist at or near the bottom of the organization—called the "lower participants." Three types of organizations have been identified on this basis (Etzioni, 1961).

Coercive Organizations. A **coercive organization** uses force to control those at the bottom of the structure. The major examples of coercive organizations are prisons and custodial mental hospitals. The lower participants in such organizations are prisoners and mental patients—people who have no personal commitment to these organizations. Because they are not deeply committed to the organization and, in fact, are probably highly alienated from it, coercion is needed to get them to do what the organization wants.

Coercive organization
Organization that uses force to control those at the bottom of the structure

A special name given to a certain extreme type of coercive organization is the total institution (Goffman, 1961). A **total institution** is an organization that is cut off from the rest of society, forming an all-encompassing social environment to meet all the needs of its members. Not all coercive organizations are total institutions; for example, some prisons and mental institutions allow inmates considerable flexibility (e.g., weekend leaves, conjugal visits, open doors). (See the accompanying Cross-National box on extremes in prisons.) On the other hand, some total institutions may not have the key characteristics of coercive organizations. For example, many large naval ships remain at sea for weeks and even months, providing the personnel on board everything they need for a full and complete life (food, personal and medical services, entertainment and recreation, religious services, and so on). Although these ships are total institutions, the people on board are not absolutely coerced into being there. We will have more to say about total institutions in chapter 5 on socialization.

Total institution
A closed organization that forms an all-encompassing social environment

Basic training in military organizations illustrates the characteristics of a total institution.

Cross-National Perspectives

National Extremes in Prisons

There are great variations in the way prisons are organized in different countries. Some prison systems are harsh, brutal, and repressive—consciously designed to break the spirit of inmates. Other prison systems give prisoners maximum freedom and show respect for individuality and privacy. Two examples will illustrate these extremes: the harsh and repressive political prisons of Uruguay in the 1970s and early 1980s, and the liberal system of the Netherlands' prison, *Schutterswei*.

Actually, repressiveness began for prisoners in Uruguay even before they entered prison. They were first detained for long periods in military units and tortured in various ways. Among the methods used were electrodes strategically applied to their bodies, suspending the prisoners by their arms, and immersing prisoners' heads under water for long periods. The torturers were quite expert and were able to punish their prisoners without leaving any physical traces. In fact, physicians were ordinarily present to be sure that the torture did not go too far. One of the shocking aspects of the Uruguayan system was the active involvement and cooperation of members of the medical profession.

Once the Uruguayan political prisoners entered prison the physical torture stopped, but it was replaced by psychological torture. In effect, the physicians were replaced by psychiatrists and psychologists. Said one of the psychiatrists involved in the system: "The war continued inside the prison. . . . Day after day, rule after rule—all was part of a grand design to make them suffer psychologically" (Weschler, 1989). In fact, the prisons were designed by psychologists to inflict the maximum amount of psychological damage. For one thing, life in the prisons was totally unpredictable. Orders were to be strictly followed, but the orders changed arbitrarily, dramatically, and without notice from one day to another. Inmates who wanted to obey, found it impossible to do so. And for those prisoners who found it impossible to obey, and that was everyone, there was always the possibility of long stays in *La Isla*, the much-hated group of isolation cells to which errant prisoners were sent for long periods.

In addition, the inmates were systematically dehumanized. They were allowed no names and were referred to by number. The guards were taught to be revulsed by the inmates, and they referred to them as "cockroach" or "diseased one." Whatever few possessions inmates were able to accumulate were arbitrarily confiscated at various times. They had no privacy and were constantly under surveillance through a system of peepholes and bugging devices. The nerves of the prisoners were randomly shaken with faked complete escapes with accompanying alarms, floodlights, and gun fire. After all this, and as a final humiliation, the prisoners or their families were expected to pay for the entire cost of imprisonment.

In contrast, the *Schutterswei* prison in the Netherlands is a model of a nonrepressive prison. One revealing feature of *Schutterswei* is that inmates have access to "sex cells," rooms with beds that prisoners can share with approved visitors. The only stipulation is that the visitor must be someone with whom the prisoner had a sincere relationship before coming to prison. The visitor may be a wife, a girlfriend, or a homosexual lover. The prison officials believe that such a system helps keep families together and personal relationships intact and keeps inmates from being broken mentally by incarceration.

The sex cells are not the only aspect of *Schutterswei* that stand in opposition to the more repressive types of total institutions. Prisoners are paid a wage of $27 a week that they can use as they wish, and many use it to furnish their brightly colored cells with television sets, stereo systems and coffeemakers. Some buy and keep pets (parakeets and fish being the most popular choices). Individuality is encouraged in the furnishing of cells and in the clothes inmates wear. There is a snack room where they can buy food and a kitchen where they can do their own cooking. Private telephone calls are permitted. In the final year of their sentences, prisoners may be allowed as many as six leaves of up to 60 hours each. Some conservatives in the Netherlands label these prisons "Hilton hotels."

Do such liberal prisons work? No one really knows, but it is true that the streets of Dutch cities are comparatively safe and the crime rate comparatively low. And the Dutch prison system is comparatively cheap despite its high staff-to-inmate ratio.

"Doing Time the Dutch Way." *World Press Review*. 35 May, 1988:53.
WESCHLER, LAWRENCE. "The Great Exception." *New Yorker*, April 3, 1989.

Utilitarian Organizations. A second type of organization is the **utilitarian organization** that uses money to control the people at the bottom. Industries and businesses are the most common types of utilitarian organizations. All employees and workers, but especially those at the bottom (clerks and those who do menial labor), are in the organization primarily for the wages they receive. Such workers are not likely to be highly committed to their organizations, although they tend to have a higher level of commitment than the "lower participants" in coercive organizations. They do what the organization expects of them because they are paid for it.

Utilitarian organization
An organization that uses money to control those at the bottom of the structure

Normative Organizations. Finally, in **normative** or **voluntary organizations** participants are controlled by the norms and values of the organization. Mothers Against Drunk Drivers, as well as many religious and political organizations, are major examples of voluntary organizations. Those at the bottom of such organizations may be believers, members, or volunteers. They tend to be highly committed to the organization's purposes or beliefs, and they do what the organization expects of them.

Normative or voluntary organization
An organization that controls participants by its norms and values

All of these types of organizations, especially as they grow in population size, tend to become bureaucracies. The bureaucracy has become the most common form of organization in contemporary life. Although the term is often used in a negative or derogatory way, it is necessary to take a more neutral and objective look at this form of organization.

What Is a Bureaucracy?

Bureaucracy
An organization with division of labor, hierarchical authority, rules, impersonality; selection and promotion is based on competence

A **bureaucracy** is an organization with a special set of characteristics:

1. A division of labor among the members, with everyone having specialized duties and functions;
2. A well-defined rank order of authority among members;
3. A system of rules covering the rights and duties of all members in all positions;
4. Rules and procedures for carrying out all tasks;
5. Impersonality in the relations among members;
6. Selection for membership, employment, and promotion based on competence and expertise.

Ideal type
A logical, exaggerated, and "pure" model of the phenomenon one is studying

These typical features of a bureaucracy are what sociologists call an ideal type. An ideal type is not, as it might seem, a best possible form of something. Rather, an **ideal type** is a logical, exaggerated, and "pure" model of some phenomenon that one wishes to study or analyze. It is a methodological tool developed by the German theorist Max Weber, whom we discussed in chapter 1 (Weber, 1903–1917/1949). Weber developed the ideal type as a tool for analyzing and studying real bureaucracies. By specifying the characteristics of the ideal-type bureaucracy, it is possible to see if, and to what degree, actual organizations are bureaucratic.

As an ideal type, a bureaucracy consists of a hierarchy of positions, with each position under the control and supervision of the one above it. Each position is assigned the task of performing a set of official functions, and procedures in each position are defined by a set of official rules. The individual in each position is granted the authority to carry out the functions of that position, but that authority does not extend beyond it.

In order for bureaucrats to apply the rules attached to their positions, they must receive specialized training. In general, only those who are formally qualified through specialized training are entitled to hold positions within a bureaucracy. Bureaucrats do not own the means of production—the offices, desks, and machines; the organization owns them and provides them to the bureaucrats as needed. Bureaucrats are not self-employed; they are employees. The written word is the hallmark of a bureaucracy because administrative acts, decisions, and rules are all put into writing.

Only the highest authority within a bureaucracy can obtain his or her position without going through bureaucratic selection procedures such as testing or presenting certain educational credentials. Often in the federal government the heads of departments or agencies are political appointees, perhaps chosen more for their special relationship with the President than for their specialized skills. Although such appointees may obtain their position through nonbureaucratic means, their authority, like that of those below them in the bureaucracy, is limited by the position they hold.

People become bureaucrats by their own choice, not because they have inherited a position in a bureaucracy. Bureaucrats are paid a salary, which is usually directly related to their positions in the bureaucratic hierarchy. The work associated with the official title is the sole, or at least the primary, occupation of the bureaucrat and is looked upon as a career. This opens up the possibility of moving to ever-higher positions within the organization. Upward mobility is based on merit and seniority. Promotion is determined by superiors within the organization.

Remember that this ideal-typical description may not pertain to any particular organization, but it should describe the characteristics that appear to some degree in any large organization (Blau and Meyer, 1987). One of these characteristics—the authority that is invested in the positions of a bureaucracy—requires some special attention.

Authority refers to "legitimate" power; it is the exercise of power accepted by those over whom it is exerted. It probably seemed quite natural when we stated above that people in the higher positions of an organization have authority over those in positions below them. But why is this true? How does a position in an organization give someone power over others in that organization? To understand the answer to this question we must examine how authority becomes legitimate (Weber, 1921/1968).

Authority
Legitimate power, accepted by those over whom it is exerted

Legitimation of Authority. In earlier times authority came primarily from the positions into which people were born. Kings and other royal family members in times past (and even in some places today) believed they were born with the *right* to exercise power over their subjects. But equally important is the fact that the people they ruled considered it their *duty* to obey the ruler's demands. This kind of authority is legitimized by **tradition**—the way things have been done for a long time in a society or social group. While traditional authority was more common in the past, tradition can also produce legitimacy for authority in modern organizations. In many businesses, leadership is passed directly from parent to child, and in some labor unions, parents have passed the presidency of the union to their children (Christie, 1956). Subordinates conform to the demands of such a ruler because it has been customary for them to do so. Therefore, one accepts the position of a traditional ruler because one has accepted it for a long period of time, or one's parents and grandparents accepted that rulership.

Tradition
The ways things have been done for a long time in a society or social group

A second way authority can be legitimized is by the charisma a leader claims—and is believed by followers to possess. **Charisma** is the extraordinary, sometimes supernatural, qualities of a person. Leaders of revolutionary social, political, and religious movements frequently derive their authority from their charismatic qualities. Examples of charismatic political leaders are Hitler, Mao Zedong, Castro, and Gandhi. Charismatic religious leaders include Jesus, Mohammed, Reverend Sun Myung Moon of the Unification Church, and Ayatollah Khomeini. Even some entertainment stars are sometimes believed by their fans to have charisma or a "larger-than-life" quality that gives them extraordinary power. The charismatic qualities of Elvis Presley would help to account for the continuing rumors that he has been seen alive some ten years after his death.

Charisma
The extraordinary (often believed to be supernatural) qualities of a person that serve as source of authority

Charisma is derived more from the beliefs of the followers than from the actual qualities of leaders. As long as a person believes he or she has special qualities, or it is believed by followers, authority will be derived from charisma.

Charisma is a very short-lived form of authority, generally limited to the life span of the charismatic leader and perhaps a short while thereafter. Attempts are frequently made to extend a leader's charisma beyond his or her own lifetime. This process, called the **routinization of charisma,** is accomplished when the qualities originally associated with a charismatic individual are passed on and incorporated into the characteristics of a group or organization. As an example, even after the death of Martin Luther King, the civil-rights movement in the United States was able to keep his charismatic qualities alive in order to advance the movement's objectives. Once charismatic leadership is translated into an organizational form, however, it eventually evolves into either a traditional or a rational-legal form of domination (Weber, 1921/1968).

Routinization of charisma
Qualities associated with a charismatic leader incorporated into a group or organization

National leaders Mikhail Gorbachev and Margaret Thatcher get their power primarily from the rules and regulations of the countries they head. Their authority is rational-legal authority.

Rational-legal authority Legitimization by the rule of law

In a system of **rational-legal authority,** leaders are legitimized by the rule of law. They derive their authority from the rules and regulations of the system rather than from their personal qualities or from tradition. For example, the office of President of the United States is legitimized by the Constitution, which defines the President's rights and responsibilities. The President's authority generally does not stem from his personal charismatic qualities or from tradition, although it may in some cases. His power is legitimized because people accept the rule of law and therefore accept the President's right to exercise the power of that office. When President Kennedy was assassinated, his Vice President, Lyndon Johnson, immediately assumed the powers of the Presidency. Whether the American people felt about Johnson the way they had felt about Kennedy was of no importance. The rule of law prevailed.

These ideas on the sources of authority relate closely to our concern with bureaucracy. Weber argued that each form of authority would manifest itself through some form of organizational structure. Rational-legal authority, with its emphasis on adherence to carefully defined rules and regulations, is conducive to the development of bureaucratic organization, while the other forms of authority spawned other types of organizational structures. Bureaucratization is the organizational form of rational-legal authority. Weber believed that as societies become increasingly rationalized, rational-legal authority would increasingly triumph over traditional and charismatic authority. In other words, the modern world would become increasingly bureaucratized.

In the early years of this century, before bureaucratic tendencies had reached anywhere near the proportions they have today, Max Weber predicted the triumph of bureaucracy in the modern world. His sociological prediction proved to be correct, but he was not happy about it. He deplored the tendency toward bureaucratization, saying that we were creating an "iron cage" from which there would be no escape (Mitzman, 1969). Weber thought that individuality and creativity would disappear in the face of the inexorable advance of bureaucratization. In Weber's view of the future: "Not summer's bloom lies ahead of us, but rather a polar night of icy darkness and hardness . . ." (in Gerth and Mills, 1958, p. 128).

The Realities of Bureaucracy

In the preceding section we have examined the ideal-typical features of bureaucracies: features that can be viewed as a rational system for accomplishing large numbers of tasks or great amounts of work. Indeed, bureaucracies do exactly that. Each year in the United States billions of pieces of mail are delivered, billions of checks are processed, and millions of student grade reports are placed on college transcripts. All of these tasks and many billions of others are accomplished by the people and computers of bureaucratic organizations. These monumental amounts of work are completed because the people and machines of bureaucracies apply precise rules and procedures in a uniform manner to every case processed. Also, because of the high degree of specialization, each person is doing a limited range of things in a highly repetitive manner. These features of the bureaucracy make it efficient in dealing with large numbers of tasks.

As everyone who has encountered a bureaucracy knows, however, bureaucracies are not very good at handling unusual or unique cases. The customer, or client, or student who has an out-of-the-ordinary situation or case nonetheless has the rigid rules of the bureaucracy applied, even though they are inappropriate or inapplicable. Under such circumstances many people become frustrated with bureaucracies and find them unfair as well as inefficient. But this reality of bureaucracies is just one of many that conflict with the organizational model of rationality and efficiency. We shall consider a few others next.

The Impersonal Treatment of Clients. The ideal bureaucrat is supposed to perform in a formal and impersonal manner. When bureaucrats come into contact with clients, however, the clients often perceive this behavior style as disinterest or even hostility. The impersonal treatment of clients has been called "service without a smile" (Hummel, 1987, p. 27). The client feels like a nonperson in the face of this impersonal bureaucratic treatment. Of course, now that much bureaucratic work is done by computers there is literally no live person with whom the client can interact.

Paperwork and Red Tape. As we noted earlier, the written word is the hallmark of bureaucracies. Not only is this true for the bureaucrats who must maintain written records of their actions, but it is also true for the clients of bureaucracies. Clients are frequently asked to complete various elaborate and detailed forms. Anyone who has ever

Drawing by Stevenson; © 1988 The New Yorker Magazine, Inc.

"Keep up the good work, whatever it is, whoever you are."

Bureaucracies maintain written records of almost every action and transaction: a record of written words that may threaten to inundate us all.

applied for admission to a college, applied for a credit card, or visited a doctor knows that the first step is to fill out an application. Bureaucracies ask for many different kinds of personal information, and through their computers they are easily able to retain files on massive numbers of people. Every adult in contemporary society has left a paper trail of his or her activities through encounters with bureaucracies.

Rules and Regulations. Bureaucracies have exact rules that are supposed to cover all situations and cases. The rules are to be followed precisely so that clients and cases will be uniformly treated. In this way the bureaucracy does not engage in favoritism and special treatment. However, sometimes the rules of the organization actually get in the way of what the organization is supposed to accomplish. The following account of an incident in a post office illustrates this point:

> I overheard a clerk telling a customer that he couldn't rent a post-office box unless he had a permanent address.
>
> "But the reason I need a box is because I don't have a permanent address," the man explained. "When you get a permanent address," the clerk politely explained, "you can get the box." "But, then I won't need it . . ." (Greenberg, 1979).

This example may be called a "Catch 22," a term first used as the title of a novel by Joseph Heller (1955). In this novel about military life during World War II, the protagonist, a bomber pilot named Yossarian, wanted to be excused from flying any more bombing missions by having the doctor declare him crazy. But the doctor explained that, even though there was a rule stating that a flier could be grounded if he were crazy, there was another rule—number 22—stating that anyone who wanted to get out of combat was not really crazy. Thus came about the origin of the phrase, "Catch 22."

The term **Catch 22** has become a part of the English language, and is used for a wide range of encounters with bureaucracies. Generally, the term is applied to situations in which the rules of an organization make it impossible to do what these same rules require.

Catch-22
Rules of a bureaucracy in conflict in such a way as to block action

The Bureaucratic Personality. Closely related to the issue of rules is the term **bureaucratic personality,** which is the tendency for bureaucrats to conform in a slavish manner to the rules of the organization. The person with a bureaucratic personality treats the rules as more important than the task or the objective of the organization. By adopting a bureaucratic personality, the bureaucrat can avoid guilt and personal conscience in dealing with clients (Hummel, 1987). The clerk who will not accept your check because the "company policy forbids accepting checks" can avoid personal blame or guilt for turning you down.

Bureaucratic personality
The tendency of bureaucrats to conform slavishly to organizational rules

The Informal System. According to the ideal-type characterization, bureaucratic organizations are built on the principle of impersonal relations among members. Members are supposed to be judged on the basis of objective measures of their performances, and relationships are based on rational principles. However, in reality, bureaucratic organizations always contain personal relationships and often close-knit social groups—primary groups of the type we discussed earlier. Some of the classic studies of sociology have shown how the informal groups in organizations, such as manufacturing plants, employment agencies, and the U.S. Army, influence behavior in ways that either subvert or override the objectives of the organization (Roethlisberger and Dickson, 1939/1964; Blau, 1963; Little, 1970).

The Tendency toward Oligarchy

Oligarchy
A small, powerful, controlling group at the top of an organization

Although positions in bureaucratic organizations, including leadership positions, are supposedly based on competence and expertise, such is not always the case. Apparently democratic organizations have an inevitable tendency to end up being undemocratic, or oligarchic. An **oligarchy** is characterized by a small group of people at the top of the organization having almost all the control and power. An early sociologist formulated the "iron law of oligarchy" to depict this tendency (Michels, 1915/1962).

To test out his thesis, Michels focused on the most unlikely places for oligarchies to arise—socialist political parties and labor unions. He felt that if he found oligarchical tendencies in such seemingly democratic organizations, he would find them anywhere and everywhere. In fact, Michels did find the existence of oligarchy in such organizations and concluded that the tendency toward oligarchy must be an "iron law" (Michels, 1915/1962, p. 50).

Michels attributed the oligarchic tendencies of organizations, in part, to the resources that came naturally to the people in positions of leadership. The leaders have higher quality information and more information than is held by the membership. Leaders also control the flow of information throughout the organization, through the organization's news media and by an agenda they choose to present to the organization's membership. Leaders are also likely to have and develop a higher level of political skill—making speeches, writing essays, and organizing group activities. Michels argued that leaders of organizations place their need to continue in a dominant position over the needs, interests, and values of the organization. In other words, power becomes more important to organizational leaders than does democracy. This means that the leaders of such organizations are perfectly willing to subvert the basic democratic principles of the organization in order to maintain their power.

Conflict in Organizations

The ideal-typical description of bureaucracy does not include conflict between individuals or groups within organizations. Yet conflict within organizations is pervasive. Of course, much conflict in organizations occurs between individuals, perhaps because they have incompatible personalities or because they are in competition for some scarce goal or resource. However, sociologists are often more interested in conflict that grows out of the characteristics of the organizations themselves (Clark, 1988; Perrow, 1986).

A major form of conflict within bureaucracies occurs when professionals such as physicians, lawyers, and scientists are employed in bureaucratic organizations. Professionals generally assume that their actions and performances should be judged and controlled only by other professionals. However, professionals employed in bureaucratic organizations are often subject to the supervision of nonprofessional superiors.

One study of Canadian doctors who were employed by companies found the doctors in conflict with managers over various medical and health issues. For example, pre-employment physical examinations were given to prospective employees, and the doctors were pressed by the company to disqualify any doubtful cases, even for minor medical reasons. The company wanted to minimize future risks, but this created conflicts with doctors who felt they were being pressured to violate their medical ethics. A number of other areas—plant safety, pressures for workers to return to work after injuries, and compensation for illnesses and injuries—revealed management interests that were in conflict with the medical autonomy of company doctors (Walters, 1982).

We have presented only one of many instances in which one group or sector of an organization has a nearly inevitable conflict with some other group or sector. For example, conflict almost always exists between sales and production people in industrial firms, between administrators and faculty in colleges, between doctors and nurses and administrators in hospitals, and between treatment and custodial staffs in prisons (Perrow, 1986).

Can Bureaucracy Be Eliminated?

While Max Weber was one of the first to fear and dislike the advance of bureaucracy, he was certainly not the last. Other scholars and intellectuals, as well as politicians and average citizens, have criticized the ever-larger bureaucracies and lamented the increasing number of bureaucrats (Blau and Meyer, 1987, pp. 194–195). Most contemporary observers, however, think that the clock cannot be turned back. "As much as we may wish otherwise, . . . large organizations operating on bureaucratic principles will remain part of the social landscape for some time to come" (Blau and Meyer, 1987, p. 195).

Another view of the future of bureaucratic organizations, however, sees profound changes occurring (Hage, 1988; Heydebrand, 1989). According to this view, the mindless rigidity of large bureaucracies is being replaced by smaller organizations characterized by informality and flexibility. Even though large organizations may continue to exist, their working subunits will be smaller, less formal, and more democratically organized. These working units will be mission, or task oriented. Two decades ago Alvin Toffler (1970) coined the word *ad-hocracies* to suggest the idea of temporary work groups composed of a wide variety of highly skilled workers brought together to solve specific, nonroutine problems.

An example of an ad-hocracy can be seen in the way a movie might be produced by a set of creative and highly skilled people. Few rigid rules would guide their behavior because most of the time they would be dealing spontaneously with emerging problems and questions. Some people believe that more and more circumstances will occur where these more informal and flexible work groups will emerge because they are best suited for the tasks at hand (Heydebrand, 1989; Toffler, 1970).

Although some social analysts foresee a future in which bureaucratic forms of organization will decline, the fact remains that the bureaucratization of life continues to expand. In the schools where we are educated, the organizations in which we work, and in virtually every other organization we encounter in our everyday lives, the form of organization is bureaucratic (Blau and Meyer, 1987; Meyer et al., 1985). On a worldwide basis the lives of more and more people are undoubtedly touched by governments and organizations that are increasingly bureaucratic. The bureaucratic form of organization may be modified, but it will not disappear in the foreseeable future.

Japanese workers are often required by their employing organizations to participate in formal exercise periods. This reveals the companies' interest in the well-being of the workers as well as their interest in rejuvenating their workforce.

The Contrast between Japanese and American Organizations

Because of the dramatic economic successes of the Japanese in recent years, much interest in Japanese organizations has arisen, especially in their business organizations (Ouchi, 1982). The following key features of Japanese organizations have been identified (with comparisons to American organizations):

1. Japanese managers have a long-run rather than a short-run perspective. In most major Japanese firms employees are guaranteed lifetime employment, which allows the managers to think in terms of the long-term success of the organization. *By comparison, American managers must produce positive results or they may be fired. With their jobs in jeopardy American managers are oriented to a short-run perspective.*

2. Japanese managers are rotated among a variety of specialties within the organization, which provides them with broad-range perspective. They can see the problems and needs of other parts of the organization. *American managers are often narrowly specialized, with a limited understanding of the problems and needs of other sectors of the organization.*

3. Japanese organizations have less of an adversary relationship between management and the workers. In fact a high level of mutual respect exists between workers and managers. *American workers and managers often see themselves as adversaries, or opponents.*

William Ouchi (1982) argues that American organizations could be more competitive in the international arena if some characteristics of the Japanese model were adopted. He does recognize, however, that this modification would have to take into consideration the realities of American society and culture. Among other recommendations he urges that American organizations place less emphasis on specialization, adopt more long-term employment guarantees, decrease efforts by management to control and routinize all work, place more emphasis on nonmonetary goals, and develop a stronger commitment to serving customers and contributing to the larger society. Although some of these changes could not be implemented immediately, they do represent some concrete management goals.

Changes and reforms of this type have already been implemented in some companies in the United States. These companies have been described as the "excellent" companies of the United States (Peters and Waterman, 1982). Among the best-known are Minnesota, Mining and Manufacturing (the 3-M Company, makers of Scotch tape), International Business Machines (IBM), Eastman Kodak (cameras), Johnson & Johnson (medical supplies), Procter and Gamble (household products) and Marriott (hotels and restaurants).

These companies show a willingness to experiment; they seek to foster, support, and protect the innovators in their organizations. They also show respect for the lower-status workers, and try to break down status distinctions between workers and management. Excellent companies are not simply motivated to maximize profits but have other values as well, among the most significant of which is remembering how important it is to meet the needs of the customers. These excellent companies, which place fewer people in central management, have very simple organizational structures. They are less bureaucratic (Peters and Waterman, 1982).

Organizations of the type we have been considering are parts of larger social units called institutions. Institutions will be introduced briefly at this point, and illustrated in part 3 of this book.

Institutions

An **institution** is a set of groups and organizations with norms and values that center around the most basic needs of a society. The major institutions are the family, education, the economy, health and medicine, and the polity. All of these institutions are found in one form or another in all societies because they carry out necessary societal tasks. As an example, societies must have some orderly way of ensuring that males and females produce enough offspring and care for them well enough so that a sufficient number will survive and the society can continue. The institution that accomplishes these tasks is, of course, the family. Following the definition offered above, the family as an institution has identifiable groups (families and kinship units); there are norms associated with the family (e.g., rules specifying how many spouses one can have); and there are values associated with the family (loyalty to family members).

Institutions
Groups and organizations, with norms and values, that attend to basic needs of society

Descriptions of the major institutions help to define the nature of a society. Indeed, all of the institutions, taken together, give a fairly clear view of a society. We are now ready to consider this major social unit, the society.

Society

Society
A population living in a given territory, with a social structure, and sharing a culture

Although sociologists sometimes focus on large portions of the world (Chirot, 1985) or on the relationships between parts of the world (Wallerstein, 1974, 1980) the largest social entity studied by sociologists is the society. A society typically is the most complete, the most all-encompassing unit of sociological analysis. A **society** is a population living in a given territory, with a social structure, and sharing a culture.

This definition covers a wide range of actual societies and therefore encompasses considerable diversity. For example, the population size of a society can vary greatly. With a 1990 population of approximately 250 million people, the United States is a society, but other societies in the world have only a few thousand people (the Yanomamo described in chapter 3), and some have only a few hundred. Even China, with its population of over a billion people (1.12 billion in 1990), is described as a society, although great cultural differences exist from one part of China to another.

Societies are most commonly described in terms of their economic systems. The long history of human existence has had only a few basic types of economic arrangements. We will summarize them briefly:

Hunting and Gathering Societies

Through hundreds of thousands of years of human existence, until about 7000 B.C., all humans lived by hunting and gathering their food. They hunted wild game or fished, and gathered wild fruits and plants. Hunting and gathering societies were not permanently fixed in one place because when the supply of food declined in a particular area it was necessary to move on to another. Only a few small hunting and gathering societies still survive in the world today. One, for example, is the !Kung[1] in the Kalahari Desert of Africa, a society that has been of great interest to anthropologists. The !Kung offer anthropologists an opportunity to study a hunting and gathering society and thereby gain insights into what the lives of prehistoric peoples might have been.

Horticultural Societies

Beginning about 9,000 years ago (7000 B.C.), some humans started growing part of their own food rather than gathering foods growing wild. In horticultural societies, food is typically grown in garden-like plots, which may be somewhat temporary in nature. When people started to grow their own food they also established more permanent communities and were not as likely to be nomadic.

Horticultural societies can still be found in the world today, as, for example, the Gahuku people of the New Guinea Highlands (Read, 1980). The Gahuku people have small personal garden plots that they cultivate with digging sticks. They raise mostly sweet potatoes, taro, and corn, though banana trees and other wild-growing fruits also provide food. These horticultural people also raise pigs, which provide food, especially for special ceremonial occasions.

---

[1] The exclamation mark before the name Kung reflects the fact that the !Kung have a clicking sound in their language that does not exist in English.

There are very few hunting and gathering societies left in the world today, but some exist in remote areas, such as that of these Tasmanian men.

Agrarian Societies

Agrarian societies appeared in about 3000 B.C. These societies differed from the horticultural societies by their larger scale of food production. Crops were regularly planted and harvested, often with the aid of plows pulled by draft animals. Generally the production of foods in agrarian societies was at a subsistence level, which means that the farm produce of one growing season was consumed during that year. As agricultural methods improved, however, some surpluses were produced, allowing some people in the society to engage in other kinds of productive activity. Since communities in agrarian societies could grow to larger sizes, the first cities emerged during this era.

The most prominent, early agrarian societies were in ancient Egypt, the Middle East, China, and later, in Medieval Europe. Agrarian societies exist today wherever most of the people rely on agriculture for their livelihood and subsistence.

Industrial Societies

Industrial societies are those in which the predominant economic activity is the production of manufactured goods. The Industrial Revolution, which opened the way for industrialization, is usually placed in the last half of the eighteenth century. England led the way by introducing a variety of machines, powered by steam, that produced manufactured goods in factories. Agricultural production must, of course, continue in industrial societies, but in the most highly industrialized societies only a small proportion of the population is engaged in agriculture. In the United States today, the figure is less than 5 percent.

Postindustrial Societies

Postindustrial society One primarily producing services and information, not manufactured goods

A recently introduced term for describing the economic base of a society is *postindustrial society* (Bell, 1973). The **postindustrial society** describes a society that was formerly industrial but is now primarily engaged in producing services and information rather than manufactured goods. In the United States today most people in the labor force are providing services of some kind instead of producing things. The postindustrial economy will be discussed more fully in chapter 13—The Economy and Work.

A Sociological Classification of Societies

While the economic systems of societies have been widely used as a basis for classification, the classic sociological way describes societies in terms of the social relationships that predominate. A question that can be asked about societies is, How do people generally relate to one another? Or, looked at historically, do people relate to each other differently in contemporary society (especially the large urban-industrial—or postindustrial—societies) than they did in societies of the past? A nineteenth century German sociologist named Ferdinand Toennies suggested that the relationships between people are different in modern societies than in societies of the past. He labeled historical societies *gemeinschaft* and modern societies *gesellschaft* (Toennies, 1887/1957).

Gemeinschaft societies feature very personal face-to-face relations in which the relationships are valued for their intrinsic qualities.

***Gemeinschaft* societies** are characterized by very personal face-to-face relationships such as those that exist in families, in rural villages, and perhaps in small towns. These highly personal relations between people are valued for their intrinsic qualities, not for the use they might be to us.

***Gemeinschaft* societies** Societies characterized by personal, face-to-face relationships

***Gesellschaft* societies** are characterized by relationships that are impersonal and distant. People interact with each other only in limited ways. The relationships are entered into only for what they might provide. Social relationships in a *gesellschaft* society are seen as means to ends.

***Gesellschaft* societies** Societies characterized by relationships that are impersonal and distant

Obviously any modern, industrial society today has both *gemeinschaft* and *gesellschaft* relationships. No society exists in which close personal relationships are totally absent. Similarly in historical, traditional societies, people did enter some relationships for self-interested reasons. The Toennies' distinction calls attention to the *prevailing* or *predominant* patterns of social relations in a society.

Summary

The way the people of any society relate to each other and organize their social lives is not random but patterned. Social structures are regular patterns of interaction and persistent social relationships. At a societal level, structures often reflect distributions of wealth, power, or authority, but structures can also be described along ethnic or racial lines.

Interaction between individuals is a complex process, but people do it with ease in their everyday lives. Although interaction has a creative and spontaneous dimension, it is patterned to some degree by cultural values and social norms.

Patterns of behavior are also produced by the statuses and roles that people occupy. Statuses are positions, and roles are the expected behaviors for a person occupying that position. However, people do not simply conform to a rigid set of role expectations, but may actively modify their roles.

Two people engaging in interaction is a dyad. When a third person is added, the dyad becomes a triad, making relationships much more complicated.

A key feature of social groups is that they are composed of a number of people who interact over time and thereby establish patterns of interaction, a group identity, and norms. Identifying with a group often produces in-group attitudes maintaining that the ways of one's own group are right, and those of out-groups are wrong. Primary groups are intimate, face-to-face groups, while secondary groups are larger and more impersonal. Reference groups are groups that people take into account in evaluating their behavior, even when they are not members of those groups. Experimental studies have shown that people tend to conform to the ways of groups they are in.

Organizations and bureaucracies are increasingly important in contemporary life. Organizations, divided according to how they control the members at the bottom, can be classified as coercive, utilitarian, normative/voluntary. Bureaucracies are organized along rational-legal lines, and in an ideal-typical sense are characterized by a division of labor, rank-ordered authority, a system of rules, impersonality, and membership based on competence or expertise.

The realities of bureaucracy include impersonal treatment of clients, paperwork and red tape, scrupulous observance of rules, a tendency toward oligarchy, and conflict. Although bureaucracies are often viewed negatively, they are not likely to disappear; however the future may see modifications and changes in bureaucratic organization. A number of distinct differences exist between Japanese and American organizations.

Institutions, such as the family, education, the economy, health and medicine, and the polity, are found in all societies. It is through the institutions that necessary societal tasks are accomplished.

Societies, the largest social entity typically studied by sociologists, are commonly distinguished by their economic systems: hunting and gathering, horticultural, agrarian, industrial, and postindustrial. Sociologically, societies can be described as *gemeinschaft* or *gesellschaft* types.

CRITICAL THINKING

1. Identify several social structures with which you might come in contact during an average week.
2. Give an example of a recent interaction that occurred in your life. How did your status affect your behavior in that interaction?
3. What statuses do you hold in life? Give an example of an expected behavior associated with each.
4. Are the following statuses achieved or ascribed: teacher, grandparent, female, judge, baby, nurse? How do you make the determination?
5. Give examples of groups that illustrate primary or secondary groups. Explain how the classification is made.
6. What reference groups are most important in your life? Explain how these groups may or may not influence your behavior.
7. Describe the Sherif, Asch, and Milgram experiments. What does each show us about human behavior in groups?
8. Use the first two pages of today's newspaper to identify two or three large organizations (using the term *organization* as sociologists would define it). Classify each organization as coercive, utilitarian, or normative.
9. The authors agree that the modern world is becoming increasingly bureaucratized. Give examples from this chapter and from your own life to support or refute this idea.
10. Give examples of both *gemeinschaft* and *gesellschaft* relationships in contemporary society.

CHAPTER

5

Socialization

In earlier chapters we have seen how the people of a society share a culture with many common values and norms. We have offered some clues as to how most people who happen to be born into a given society come to share the same values, norms, and ideas about roles. For example, we saw in chapter 3 how Japanese mothers are apt to use a different approach from American mothers in getting their children to eat their food and, in the process, teaching their children a lesson about social responsibility that will be remembered throughout life.

In the childrearing practices of the Japanese and American parents we had a glimpse of how children learn the cultural ways of their society. In this chapter we examine this learning process in detail, noting that children learn not only from their parents but also from siblings and playmates, from teachers and classmates, and from television and other mass media sources. Furthermore, socialization does not end with childhood. It continues throughout life as we go into jobs and professions, new organizations, and different stages of life.

The Nature of Socialization

Socialization is the process by which a person learns and generally accepts the established ways of a particular social group or society. The principal purpose of socialization is to make sure that the new members will do things in about the same way as they are currently being done. In other words, societies, groups, and organizations maintain a certain amount of continuity over time because of the socialization of new members. Generally, new members accept what is taught to them as the right and proper way of doing things.

Socialization
Process of learning and accepting the ways of a social group or society

In a similar way, from a cultural perspective, socialization passes on the values and norms to the new members, which allows them to persist from one generation to the next. Even when the new members of a society are not born into that society but come in as immigrants, various forms of socialization initiate these newcomers into the culture of the new society.

In addition to its significance at the level of the society and culture, socialization also contributes to the process of producing the characteristics and personality of the individual. The socialization that occurs early in life, in infancy and early childhood, is especially critical in this regard. Often called **primary socialization,** it is usually provided by the parents or other caregiver(s) and lays the foundation for personality development. In this process infants become social beings. The early stages of socialization nurture a tendency for the human infant to want and need interaction with other people—a tendency that generally endures for a lifetime.

Primary socialization
Socialization by parents (or caregivers) that lays the foundation for personality development

This Native American father is introducing his son to the ways of their society, both by what he says and by what he does. This is primary socialization, which provides cultural continuity and helps lay the foundation for the son's personality.

Socialization does not stop with the end of childhood. An older person returning to college will have experiences that provide socialization about many new subjects.

Socialization continues throughout the lifetime of every individual. As people move into new jobs, organizations, communities, and even new life stages they will learn the values, norms, and behaviors expected of them in these settings. Later in this chapter we will turn to the socialization that occurs during adolescence, adulthood, and old age, but first we will focus on the critically important socialization that occurs in infancy and early childhood.

The importance of socialization during infancy and early childhood can be understood by considering what human beings would be without contact with other humans. At this fundamental level we are not focusing on socialization per se although some socialization is occurring, but simply on the contact and interaction between infants and other human beings.

Acquiring a Human Nature

The human baby—born with biological needs and limited capacities—can make sounds—primarily crying—and has senses that allow him or her to experience comfort and discomfort. In the early days of life, babies cry when they are uncomfortable and stay relatively quiet when they are comfortable. Their usual discomforts are hunger, wetness, coldness, and pain. They cry reflexively when these discomforts occur. Because human infants are helpless, they must have some other human present to give them food and keep them warm, or they will not survive.

Although babies in these early days of life seem to be very limited and almost entirely biological in their nature, increasing evidence shows that they are already orienting toward the humans in their environment. Video camera observations have shown that infants, even in the first hours after birth, have a "quiet-alert stage" when they are attentive to their environment, especially to people. In the first few days or weeks of life infants will make eye contact with a parent, and will respond to a parent's facial expressions and voice sounds. This research on very young infants seems to show that the physical dependence infants have on other humans is augmented by an early tendency to be attracted to their primary caregivers.

Since the human infant begins responding to other humans at such an early stage of life, we might conclude that many other social and personal qualities normally found in humans are also inborn or inherent. But the evidence is to the contrary for, although human infants might have the tendency toward sociability, they must have sustained contact with other human beings or it will not develop. We can never know with complete certainty how an infant would develop if it were kept alive without contact with other humans, but a few documented cases of isolated children provide some insights. These substantiated cases of infants who have been raised in nearly complete isolation reveal all too clearly that, without human contact, the qualities we associate with humanness are almost completely lost.

Children Isolated from Human Contact

Mythological stories have been told of children who were reared by animals instead of human beings, and some cases of children who were allegedly found living in the wild with animals have been minimally documented. (They are called **feral**—meaning wild—**children.**) In one such case in India two children were found living with wolves. They were brought to an orphanage where they were cared for, observed, and photographed over a period of years. Long after they were found, these children continued to display

Feral children
Wild children—children allegedly reared in the wild by animals

There is increasing evidence that, at a very early age, babies are oriented toward the humans in their environment. They are especially responsive to their parents, who are the early caregivers.

animal-like behavior, such as walking on all fours, eating food with their mouths, and preferring to play with dogs (Singh and Zingg, 1942).

The reported cases of feral children are generally not as trustworthy as the cases of children who lived in human settings but were kept virtually isolated from human contact (Curtiss, 1977; Davis, 1940, 1947). In each case a family member placed the child in some isolated part of the home, providing only enough food and water to keep the child alive but offering no human contact. When found, the children did not talk, nor did they show the range of emotions that humans usually display (crying, smiling and laughing, responding to human gestures of friendship, and the like).

In one such case, a father locked his daughter in a room from age two until she was discovered at age 13 (Curtiss, 1977). The girl (called Genie) was placed by her father in a restraining harness, seated on a potty chair during the day, and placed in a straitjacket at night. The mother of this girl, terrorized by her brutal husband and further limited by blindness, had almost no contact with Genie after infancy. When Genie was finally found she was unable to speak because during her formative years her father had not allowed her to make any sounds. Even with intensive training after her discovery, Genie was unable to use language at more than a rudimentary level. Equally important, efforts to socialize her were only partially successful; long after she was found she persisted in behaviors that went beyond normal acceptability. One of Genie's teachers, who developed a close relationship with her, described how this 14-year-old girl "had many distasteful mannerisms and her behavior was often disconcerting and unpalatable" (Curtiss, 1977, p. 20). Genie would spit and blow her nose on everything and everyone around her. She also had a special fondness for plastic things and certain items of clothing or accessories:

> If anyone she encountered in the street or in a store or other public place had something she liked, she was uncontrollably drawn to him or her, and without obeying any rules of psychological distance or social mores, she would go right up to the person and put her hands on the desired item (Curtiss, 1977, p. 20).

Genie also masturbated whenever and however she could. Any object that she could use for masturbation attracted her. For more than four years after her discovery the professionals working with her were unable to limit this socially unacceptable form of behavior.

The information provided by Genie and the limited number of other cases of extreme isolation demonstrate that human beings do not become "human" if they do not have at least some human contact. Furthermore, there seems to be a critical formative period when infants and children need human contact and interaction or the effects upon their personalities are devastating and largely irreversible.

Early Socialization: "Getting Hooked on People"

How does a baby become human and develop personal traits? Most human infants eventually approximate the human qualities that are prominent in the particular group into which they happen to be born. To understand how this happens, we must go back to our earlier discussion of the human infant who cries when hungry and uncomfortable, and to the adult who attends to that crying by restoring comfort.

Because a baby absolutely needs adults for comfort and survival, adults control the situation. Although most parents first respond by freely gratifying their baby's every need, they do not do so for long. Eventually, adults start to assert their power. Parents continue to give what a child needs, but they start exacting a price. Mothers and fathers will feed and change the diapers of the baby, but eventually they want something in return, even if it is only a smile. If they get the smile, they may give something else—a hug, a cuddle, or a tickle. If the baby responds again, more comforting rewards are given.

This is the beginning of socialization for the norm of reciprocity (Gouldner, 1960). The **norm of reciprocity** calls for two interacting people to give one another things of equal or almost equal value. People want to continue to interact with one another if they are receiving something roughly equal in value to what they are giving.

Norm of reciprocity
A standard calling for two interacting people to exchange things of equal value

Reciprocity in interaction is probably the earliest social lesson. Campbell (1975) describes reciprocity from the point of view of what is happening to the infant:

> We have probably stumbled here upon a most important truth about socialization. . . . The human infant is both highly dependent and pleasure seeking. Put these two things together, and it follows clearly that he must have the help of others in securing his own gratification. This simple fact is the root-source of a process that we shall call, quite unscientifically, "getting hooked on people" (Campbell, 1975, p. 17).

By "getting hooked on people," Campbell means that after a while the baby needs more than the food and the dry diapers that the adult provides. The baby also needs the smiles, the attention, the hugs, and the comforting words of the adult who delivers the other necessities.

At first adults will give warmth and cuddling freely—but not forever. Adults soon start demanding more and more from their babies for what they provide. Thus babies must slowly give up their totally selfish ways. They have to start doing some things that they do not want to do and stop doing other things. Eating solid foods instead of warm milk, especially milk from the mother's warm body, comes just one step before sitting on the cold potty—and so the process of making a responsible member of society begins. Later, adults bestow smiles, praise, and affection for brushing teeth, keeping a room clean, sitting quietly during religious services, bringing home good grades on report cards, or writing thank-you letters promptly.

Parents and other adults also use negative sanctions, which they have at their disposal by virtue of their powerful position. They may augment their reward system by scolding, spanking, withholding desserts, or "grounding" to get the child or adolescent to do what is "right."

The use of reward and punishment to produce acceptable social behavior is not the only way to accomplish socialization; it is only a basic mechanism that is part of the larger process of socialization. Something else happens in this process that cannot be explained by the simple idea of rewarding good behavior and punishing bad behavior. Children do what their parents and others expect of them, even when their parents are not around to see what they are doing. Children will generally do the "right" things without constant reward or punishment. The following discussion explores how and why this happens.

Symbolic Interaction and the Social Self

In chapter 1 we introduced a theory called symbolic interactionism, and we noted that through symbols infants and children acquire an understanding of the world and themselves. Especially important is the way a child develops a sense of self through the

Significant others
People close to an individual who shape the self and define social objects

process of interaction with significant others. **Significant others** are those people in an individual's life who shape the individual's self and provide definitions for other social objects (Mead, 1934/1962). Usually parents are the most important significant others in the early stages of life. The recognition by symbolic interactionists that the self is essentially a social creation is probably the single most important insight of this perspective (Fine, 1990).

Looking-glass self
The self-image that reflects how others see a person

One of the early symbolic interactionists, Charles Horton Cooley, emphasized the social nature of the self with his concept of the **looking-glass self** (Cooley, 1902). This concept conveys vividly the notion that every child develops a self-image that reflects how others respond to her or him. Both as children and adults, we can see ourselves mostly through the responses and reactions of others. However, it should be noted that the actively creative human mind can also anticipate and imagine the responses and reactions of others. A boy who breaks a lamp while he is alone at home can probably anticipate or imagine his parents' response.

In a closely related sense, children and all humans can take an active, not simply a passive, part in the development of a social self. In taking some kind of successful action, a person does not necessarily need someone else to point out the success. A small child who bounces and catches a ball can evaluate that success independently. Humans have the capacity to assess the success of their own actions, and this ability contributes to their self-image (Gecas and Schwalbe, 1983).

Interacting with others gives people the ability to put themselves in the place of another person. As adults we do it almost constantly. If we are stopped by the police for a minor traffic violation, we try to decide quickly how to talk to the officer. Should we be flippant, penitent, aggressive, or humble? How will the officer respond to each of these approaches? Often we try to run through a scene as it might develop from these different approaches. We are not always successful in choosing the best strategy, but we try to anticipate how other persons will respond by putting ourselves in their places. The ability to respond to ourselves as objects, much as others respond to us, and the ability to anticipate how others will respond to our behavior or actions indicate a fairly high level of social being.

But one more step remains in the socialization process. We ultimately evaluate ourselves not only according to how specific individuals respond to us but also according to how others in general will respond. We consider what people will think if we do this or that. We want general social approval for what we do, not just approval from specific others.

Preparatory stage
First stage of a child's social development, largely imitation of others

Play stage
Second stage of social development, evaluating self from the view of significant others

Game stage
Final stage of social development, simultaneously assuming the roles of several others

Developmental Stages. George Herbert Mead, an originator of symbolic interaction theory, first described how children arrive at the point where they are concerned about how others *in general* will respond to their behavior. Mead postulated a three-stage developmental process during childhood. In the first stage, the **preparatory stage,** young children simply engage in meaningless imitation of those around them. They have little use for symbols at this stage. In the second stage, the **play stage,** children learn how to evaluate themselves and other social objects from the point of view of significant others. In this stage children learn to put themselves in another person's place. Last is the **game stage** during which children assume the roles of a number of other people simultaneously and respond to the expectations that these people have. During the game stage children acquire a sense of, and seek the approval of, what Mead called the generalized other.

The interaction between children and significant others gives children part of their self-image, but the child is not completely passive. The little girl at the keyboard is also evaluating her success in a positive way, and contributing to her own positive self-image.

Generalized other The internalization of the norms of the larger social group or society

The **generalized other** is the internalization of the norms of the larger social group or the society. As an example, most students will not cheat on an examination—even when there is no chance of being caught—because they have learned and internalized the idea that it is best to be honest. In a sense, they are rewarding themselves for living up to a standard they have learned and accepted. When people accept the ways of the society and generally behave in conformity to those ways, even when no specific punishment or reward will result from their conformity, then they are fully socialized.

To summarize, children learn to evaluate all objects (both abstract and concrete and including the self) largely from the people with whom they interact. Furthermore, their learning is not just superficial or calculated to get other people to bestow social rewards and approval. Nor is the learning of a society's ways done only to avoid punishment or penalty. The process starts there, but eventually humans internalize the ways of the society. They accept them as right for themselves and others, and they provide their own rewards when they conform to them.

This acceptance of societal ways does not mean that an effective social system will produce a society of conforming robots. People do cheat on tests; they also cheat in business deals and on marriage partners. Socialization to norms and values is never totally effective and certainly is not uniform throughout society. The rules and values of a society are themselves never universal or absolute. There is plenty of room for individual variation. Our description of early socialization explains why we have as much order and regularity in society as we do, and why it is possible to have a society at all. Although childhood socialization does not explain every individual's behavior, it does show how every individual is, to a great degree, a social product.

Agents of Socialization

Socialization is generally initiated by the people who are already members of a social system; they are called the agents of socialization, and they have the task of socializing new members. In the case of infants being born into families, the first socializing agents are the parents, but as children grow older, other agents of socialization also become important. Included among the other socializing agents are children's peers (often including siblings), teachers, and the mass media. We will begin with the most important early socializing agents, the parents.

Parents as Socializing Agents

Almost all parents recognize the responsibility of teaching their children the skills necessary to get along in life. From a sociological perspective, parents are responding to the social role of being a parent. Most adults learn the parental role through their own socialization.

Many parents also feel responsible for *shaping* the personalities of their children. Many contemporary parents have accepted the basic sociological and psychological view that personalities of children are shaped by environmental influences in general, and especially by parental influences on the child. However, parents cannot consciously set out to produce a certain kind of child and succeed in getting what they want.

Many young, modern, and well-educated parents seem to conceive of shaping the personalities of their children as a process of direct, straightforward teaching: "If I want my child to be independent, I will teach independence, and my child will be independent. If I want my child to be frugal or neat, I will teach those things." This naive view of the socialization process often causes parents to wonder "where they went wrong" when their children do not mature exactly according to their expectations.

Several factors explain why socialization is not a process of direct teaching. First, socialization is more complex than the direct-teaching idea suggests. To begin with, socialization usually involves two parents (or parent figures). Two socializing parents may send quite different messages to the child, and the result of mixed messages in the child's development cannot be anticipated. Even when parents are consistent, children often turn out differently from what their parents wish.

Second, the direct-teaching notion of socialization fails to take into account how pervasive and subtle socialization is. Socialization occurs as much by example as by direct verbal means. A father may tell his children to try to get along with other people and be friendly, but if he frequently engages in disputes with his neighbors and coworkers, the children get a different message. This father is socializing his children as much by his behaviors as by his words.

Furthermore, socializing agents other than family members influence a child. At a fairly early age children begin to be socialized by the communication media, especially television. Somewhat later, playmates and friends, the schools, and the print media (magazines, newspapers, and books) play a part in a child's socialization.

One final influence, biological inheritance, contributes an additional unpredictable factor. Although sociologists do not generally view personality characteristics as genetically inherited, the possibility does exist that certain natural endowments might moderate and interact with the socialization process (Rose, 1979).

Cross-Cultural Perspectives

Some Alternative Views of Children's Personalities

While Americans tend to believe that parents shape the personalities of their children, the people of certain other societies have distinctly different views. The Irish and the Hindus of India (to take examples from two very different cultures) place much more emphasis on the inherited characteristics of children. However, as we will see, there are other distinctive differences in the views of the Irish and the Hindus.

Irish parents do recognize that they play an important role in bringing up their children, and especially in teaching them right from wrong. They are likely to say, "Beware of the habit you give them" (Scheper-Hughes, 1979). But they also see a child's basic personality, talents, abilities, and nature as largely inherited. The Irish word that expresses this view is *dutcas*. *Dutcas* is translated as *blood, stock,* or *breeding,* but more specifically it refers to the personality characteristics one inherits from one's ancestors. Thus, when a mother throws up her hands in despair over her unruly sons, saying, "They're too full of their father's *dutcas*" (Scheper-Hughes, 1979), she is saying that the wildness of her sons is a trait they have inherited from their father.

An Irish child's *dutcas* does not have to come from an immediate parent, for the Irish believe that the characteristics of any ancestor can appear in the personality of a child. Thus, a daughter may be said to inherit her thriftiness from a particular grandmother, while a son may be seen as getting his laziness from a ne'er-do-well uncle.

A different view of inherited personality traits can be found among the Hindus of India (Kaker, 1979). Indian religious, medical, and folk beliefs hold that life begins at conception. It is here that the spirit from the body of someone who has lived previously is joined with the fertilized ovum. Thus, a major portion of the personality of a child comes not from immediate ancestors but from an already existing spirit that has lived in another body at a previous time. For the Hindu mother there is, however, an opportunity to modify the spirit while the fetus is still in the womb. The critical period for influencing the psychological development of the baby comes in the third month of pregnancy. According to Indian tradition, it is in that month that the feelings and wishes of the fetus, which come from its previous life, are transmitted to the mother. These are revealed to the mother in the form of cravings for particular foods. These cravings, which are really the wishes of the fetus, are not to be denied, for their fulfillment will ensure the proper psychological development of the child.

The personality of the Indian child is thought to be largely determined by the spirit from a previous life, though this might have been modified while in the womb. With this view in mind, it is not surprising that Indian parents are highly indulgent with their children. Mothers do not try to mold their children into a particular desired image. They are inclined to follow rather than lead the child in its development (Kaker, 1979).

These beliefs about the inherited personality traits of children, coming from the Irish and Hindu people, are not entirely unfamiliar to Americans. The personality traits of a child are sometimes seen as reflections of the personality of a particular family member—"She is just like her grandmother in her love of animals." There is also a long-standing folk belief in the United States that what a mother does during her pregnancy will affect the character of her baby. This parallels the Hindu belief described above. One American proponent of this view has collected cases that have led him to conclude that, from the sixth month of pregnancy, a fetus can begin to learn, and respond emotionally to its mother (Verny and Kelly, 1984). In one such case, a young musical conductor knew the entire score of a musical number, even though he had never seen it before. This is alleged to have occurred because his mother had played this piece of music while she was pregnant.

KAKER, SUDHIR. "Childhood in India: Traditional Ideals and Contemporary Reality." *International Social Science Journal* 31, 1979.
SCHEPER-HUGHES, NANCY. "Breeding Breaks Out in the Eye of the Cat: Sex Roles, Birth Order, and the Irish Double-Bind." *Journal of Comparative Family Studies* 10, 1979.
VERNY, THOMAS and KELLY, JOHN. *The Secret Life of the Unborn Child.* New York: Dell, 1984.

Because socialization is complex, pervasive, and subtle, and because outside socializing agents compete with familial ones, parents cannot expect to shape their children exactly as they desire. The scientific analysis of socialization and the experiences of many parents do not support the notion of socialization as a process of direct teaching.

Parental Differences in Socialization

The parents in any particular society will usually be in accord on a wide range of things they teach their children to do and not do. (Almost no parent, for instance, will consciously teach a child to lie, cheat, or use profanity.) But despite this general agreement, substantial differences exist in what the parents value in one part of the society, compared to the parents in another. Parents coming from different subcultural, ethnic, or religious groups, different social classes, and different critical historical periods will have differing notions of what they should teach their children (Peterson and Rollins, 1987).

The most extreme variations from mainstream socialization values typically occur in cases where parents are zealous about some cause or belief system. Recent newspaper accounts of certain fundamentalist Christians reveal how some parents will take extreme measures to socialize their children into the ways of their religious beliefs. Two fathers gave nearly identical accounts of how they terrorized their five-year-old children with a fear of going to hell so they could be assured that the children would be obedient and God-fearing.

In the words of one of these fathers:

> My daughter is 5 years old and—people say how inhumane—I let my daughter lay and cry herself to sleep for a week straight about the flames of hell. See my daughter personally lay at night and said, 'I don't want to go to hell, I don't want to go to hell,' and she'd be laying there crying.
>
> I could have ran right in there and gave her the Gospel and she could have made a profession of salvation, but I let it get deep into her memory. Know what I mean? That there is a Hell. And that will affect her whole life. That's why she is an obedient child (Naughton, 1988).

As a rule, parents try to teach their children lessons that they themselves have found to be useful or important in life. This rule has been most thoroughly documented with regard to the differences among socialization values of parents who are at different levels in the class structure (Kohn, 1977; Gecas, 1979, 1981).

Cross-National Findings. Studies conducted in the United States, Italy, Taiwan, Poland, and Japan have documented that parents at different levels of the class structure have different values that they communicate when they socialize their children (Kohn, 1983, Slomczynski et al., 1981, Naoi et al., 1985). The major findings of these studies can be briefly summarized: parents who are in the middle-class and upper-middle-class levels of the stratification structure (those with above average education and white-collar, managerial, or professional jobs) tend to value autonomy, creativity, and self-direction; by comparison, parents in the working class (especially those with blue-collar occupations) tend to value conformity to the rules and respect for external authority. In everyday terms, working-class parents are more likely to value obedience.

When parents engender in their children the value of autonomy and self-direction, they are portraying the world as a place that can be influenced by individuals who take initiatives. In contrast, parents who place a greater value on their children's obedience are reflecting their view of the world as a place of many rules and regulations, and where people in authority give orders. To make one's way in this world a person must learn obedience to the rules of those in authority.

When socializing their children, middle-class and upper-middle-class fathers wanted their children to be considerate of others, interested in how things happen, responsible, and self-controlled. These fathers were less likely to emphasize that their children should be well mannered, neat, clean, obedient, honest, and studious. These latter traits, however, were exactly the ones that the lower-class fathers strongly desired in their children.

Because of these different orientations, parents in the middle and lower social classes disciplined their children differently. Lower-class mothers punished their children directly or immediately after the child misbehaved, without asking questions. Middle-class mothers were more likely to punish or not punish their children according to how they interpreted the child's intention when committing the act. Middle-class parents judged the child's misbehavior by considering whether it seemed to violate the long-range goal that their child be able to demonstrate self-direction and individual responsibility. Working-class parents punished misbehavior if it violated some rule. They wanted obedience from their children—obedience to the rules that they had set down and obedience to the rules of the larger society.

In socializing their children, why do the middle classes value autonomy and the working classes value obedience to the rules? What is the relationship between position in the class structure and socialization values? According to the research of Kohn (1983) and his associates, the crucial factor is the occupational setting or work experience of the father. Middle-class fathers are typically employed in occupations that reward individual initiative and responsibility—autonomous behavior. The more they take initiatives, assume responsibility, and act independently, the more they are rewarded. In comparison, working-class fathers are typically employed in work settings where they must do exactly what they are told and where individual initiative is not especially valued or rewarded. People working on the assembly lines understand that they must do the work in the way they have been instructed if they want to keep their jobs.

When parents socialize their children they are often trying to impart the values they consider important for life. Obedience to rules is often valued more by working-class parents than middle-class parents.

Middle-class parents expect, at least implicitly, that their children will enter the occupational world at levels where they will be expected to show individual responsibility and self-direction. They socialize their children with this idea in mind, so that they will get along best and most successfully when they enter the white-collar, managerial, and professional occupations. Working-class parents have experienced a different kind of work world, one where they do what they are told, when they are told to do it. They assume that their children will enter the same kind of world, so they teach their children the importance of obedience in order that they will survive in that world. One might say that the arbitrary, absolute, and sometimes unfair demands for obedience that are often attributed to working-class fathers might be a way of forewarning their children about adult life. People in the lower strata of society are often treated arbitrarily by their superiors in the work world, as well as by other agents of authority (including police, the courts, and school personnel).

This line of research also shows how socialization is a contributor to the perpetuation of the existing class structure of a society. This socialization process may be *one* mechanism that pushes the children of working-class parents toward working-class occupations, whereas the children of middle-class parents move toward middle-class occupations. The different socializing influences that working-class and middle-class parents exert on their children actually help to keep the social class system more or less intact. As will be discussed in chapter 8, a relatively consistent and orderly continuation of the basic class structure persists from one generation to the next, perhaps due in part to class differences in parental socialization.

Increasing Emphasis on the Value of Autonomy

Social surveys taken between 1958 and 1983 provide additional information on the characteristics that American parents value in their children. While the social class differences discussed above persist, some overall shifts toward valuing autonomy are indicated (Alwin, 1984). For many years, sample surveys of parents in the Detroit metropolitan area have been taken, and since these surveys asked parents the same questions at different times, changes in their socialization values can be identified. The following question was asked in surveys taken in 1958, 1971, and 1983:

> If you had to choose, which thing on this list would you pick as the most important for a child to learn to prepare him [her] for life?
> a. To obey
> b. To be well-liked or popular
> c. To think for him [her] self
> d. To work hard
> e. To help others when they need help.
> Which comes next in importance? Which comes third? Which comes fourth?

In this question, the answer "To think for himself" is an indication of autonomy or self-direction. The answer "To obey" is clearly an indication of the value placed on obedience.

While parents in general have always ranked the "think-for-himself" value very highly, this value has been recently rising in favor, while the value placed on obedience has been declining. In all the surveys, including the one taken in 1983, the blue-collar parents are still likely to favor obedience more than white-collar parents do, but a clear shift has been seen in both classes toward autonomy and away from obedience. The only exception to this pattern is found among black parents in the Detroit sample, who, in the 1983 survey, had a slight tendency to prefer obedience more than they had in earlier surveys. Their preferences for autonomy, while high, have not appeared to change much over time (Alwin, 1984). The importance that many black parents continue to place on obedience may be a reflection of the fact that black Americans are often still in positions in which they must obey the rules, regulations, and orders of people in authority.

Reverse Socialization—Children Influencing Parents

Socialization is often viewed as a one-way process. In the case of parents and children the focus is primarily on the way the parents socialize their children. However, there is increasing recognition of the fact that children also influence their parents (Peterson and Rollins, 1987). Children's acting to change the behaviors, attitudes, or values of their parents is an example of reverse socialization. In general terms, **reverse socialization** occurs when people who are normally the ones being socialized are, instead, doing the socializing.

Reverse socialization
Those normally being socialized are, instead, doing the socializing

Reverse socialization in the family probably occurs most prominently after children have reached their teenage years. At this age the children are attuned to the mass media where they learn about recent changes and innovations. The children can then serve as sources of information in the areas where the parents are not as attentive (clothing styles, slang, music, movies, and so on). Reverse socialization from children to parents is apt to be found in societies that are changing rapidly (Mead, 1970).

Parents of teenage and young adult children are likely to acknowledge that they are influenced by their children (Peters, 1985). Sports, for example, is one area where parents reported the greatest increases in knowledge and participation because of their children. To a lesser degree, parents acknowledged the influence of their children in the areas of leisure, personal care, politics, and religion. Parents also agreed that their children had influenced their attitudes on social issues such as drug use, sexuality, the handicapped, minorities, and, most important, "perceptions of youth" (Peters, 1985, p. 929).

Peers as Socializing Agents

We noted earlier that the peers and siblings of young children also act as socializing agents. Older brothers and sisters, with their superior knowledge and verbal ability, have an obvious opportunity for introducing their younger siblings to many different aspects of life. Oldest and only children do not, of course, have older siblings to socialize them, which could account for some of the differences between children who are in different birth-order positions in the family (Polit and Falbo, 1987).

Although older siblings have the earliest opportunities for socializing young children, neighborhood and school friends are also soon acting as socializers. By the time children reach school age they have extensive daily contact with other children. In this context, away from parents and other adults, the interaction among children is probably influential in shaping attitudes and values.

An example of the intensity of peer-group socialization is found in a study of preadolescent boys participating in Little League baseball (Fine, 1987, ch. 4). The potential for socialization among these boys, aged 9 through 12, is very great because they feel free to discuss openly any topic that interests them, including topics that they would not discuss with adults. Furthermore, boys of this age take the comments and ideas of their peers very seriously (Fine, 1987, p. 79).

Preadolescent boys participating in Little League baseball establish and enforce appropriate behavior among their peers. While the adults who are coaching them are emphasizing teamwork, sportsmanship, winning and losing properly, and "hustle," the boys are more concerned about proper self-presentations. They are learning from their peers when to be tough and, if the situation calls for it, when to be fearful. They are learning to control their aggression, fears, and, most important, their tears. They are also learning that they must display a desire to win and a loyalty to team unity.

Boys on these teams are treated harshly when they forget that the team is more important than their individual concerns. For example, a boy who cries when his team has won (because he made a poor play earlier) is described by his fellows as "strange." Similarly, a boy must not display happiness when something negative has happened to the team, such as a player who smiled when he had just made an out. This boy, usually a poor player, hit a hard line drive that was caught by the third baseman. Even though he had made an out for the team, he returned to the dugout smiling. Some of the better players immediately let him know that his response was inappropriate. One snarled, "God, Jason, that's stupid, don't smile" (Fine, 1987, p. 82).

In a Little League setting young boys are often learning traditional male behavior from their peers. Through the reactions and words of their peers they learn how to control and channel their behavior in ways that are consistent with the male gender role. The sociologist who observed hundreds of preadolescent boys over three years says explicitly that, through socialization by peers, "Boys learn to act like men" (Fine, 1987, p. 86). The socialization is effective and may, in some cases, run counter to the child-rearing goals of the boys' parents.

The Mass Media as Socializing Agents

The media of mass communication, especially television, movies, and radio, but also magazines and newspapers, convey thousands of visual, aural, and verbal messages each day. These messages are embedded in dramas, comedies, news reports, music lyrics, comics, cartoons, news stories, and commercial advertising. In myriad ways these messages are defining social life for people of all ages. From childhood to old age, the media of communication are continuing the process of socialization.

While all the media of communication are important, television has undeniably overtaken all others in reaching and influencing people. In American households television sets are on more than seven hours each day (Liebert and Sprafkin, 1988).

Television as a Socializing Agent for Children

An average six-month-old infant in the United States will be in front of a television set one and one-half hours a day. By three years of age most children will be selecting their favorite television shows (Liebert and Sprafkin, 1988, p. 5). Television viewing continues to increase until it reaches a peak at about 11 years of age when an average child watches more than four hours a day.[1] Even among high-school seniors, however, television viewing is the recreational activity engaged in most often. (See figure 5–1.) "It has been estimated that by the age of 18 a child . . . will have spent more time watching television than in any single activity besides sleep" (Liebert and Sprafkin, 1988, p. ix). This massive exposure suggests that television is an important socializing agent for the children of contemporary society.

Over the last three decades many studies have been done on the influence of television on children. The two topics that have received the most attention are violence and male/female roles. With respect to violence the question has been, Does the portrayal of violence on television produce higher levels of violent and aggressive behavior in children? Regarding male/female roles, the primary question is, Do children learn stereotyped views of males and females from television?

Violence. Even a casual viewing of television reveals that violence is the mainstay of many programs: killing, hitting, fighting, verbal abuse, and threats are pervasive. These kinds of violence are found on Saturday morning cartoons and other children's programs, as well as in police and crime dramas, military and war stories, and space adventures. Even music videos have their share of stylized violence and aggression, as we will see below. According to a widely used index of violence on television programs, there are 9.7 acts of violence in every hour of television programming. In cartoons, there are 21.3 acts of violence per hour (Liebert and Sprafkin, 1988, p. 118).

[1] The reported *average* amount of television watching by children does obscure the fact that substantial differences exist among children with different backgrounds. Children in the lower social classes and from minority backgrounds watch much more than middle-class white children (Liebert and Sprafkin, 1988).

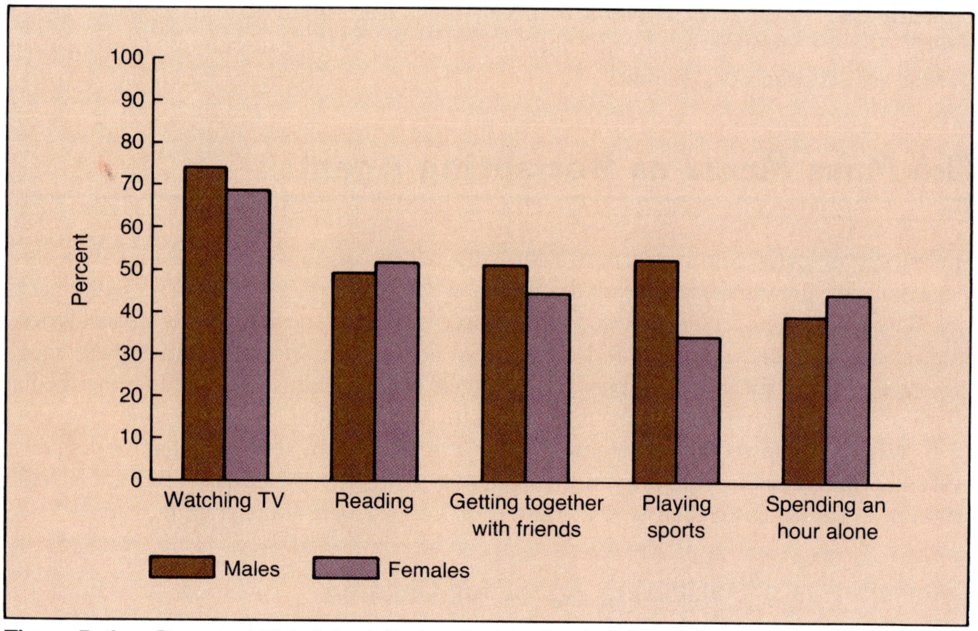

Figure 5–1. Percent of High School Seniors Participating in Selected Activities Each Day, by Sex: 1985. Of the activities listed, the most common daily activity for both male and female students in the class of 1985 was watching television. (*Sources:* U.S. House of Representatives, Select Committee on Children, Youth, and Families, *U.S. Children and Their Families: Current Conditions and Recent Trends, 1987. Original Source:* University of Michigan, Institute for Social Research, *Monitoring the Future,* various years.)

The hundreds of studies on the influence television violence has on children's behavior have produced an agreement that violence is learned from television (Liebert and Sprafkin, 1988). Aggressive behavior is found more often among the children who watch television most. A particularly interesting demonstration of the impact of television on the aggressive behavior of youngsters comes from a study conducted in Canada. This study focused on a Canadian community that did not have television reception until the mid-1970s because it was located in a geographic "blind spot" (Williams, 1986). The preschool and school-age children of this community—named "Notel" by the researchers—were studied both before and after television came to the community. Moreover, for purposes of comparison, the children in two other similar-sized communities were also studied. Both of these communities had received television broadcasts for many years, although one received only one channel (much like Notel was to receive). This natural field experiment provides important evidence on the impact of television on the aggressive and violent behavior of children.

The aggressive behavior of the children of Notel and the other two communities was measured before television came to Notel and again two years later. Aggressive behavior was measured by observations of children in their free-play time in school, and by teacher and peer ratings. Among the children of Notel, aggressive behaviors increased significantly after television was introduced into their community. During the same two-year period no similar increase was noted in the aggressive behaviors of the children in the two communities that had had television for many years. Further evidence was found when observations revealed that those children who watched the most television displayed the most aggressive behavior. Using several different measures and various kinds of analysis, this natural field experiment confirmed what other types of studies have also concluded: television viewing is related to more aggressive and violent behaviors among children (Joy et al., 1986).

Even though many studies have found television viewing to be related to violent and aggressive behaviors among children, the question still remains as to why a connection exists. Several types of answers have been offered (Joy et al., 1986; Liebert and Sprafkin, 1988):

1. *Observational Learning*—Children might, for example, see a "Kung Fu" kick on television and copy this method when fighting.
2. *Reduced Social Constraints*—Children who see violence used in many different situations might feel fewer social constraints against using violence.
3. *Arousal of Aggressive Tendencies*—Some children may have aggressive tendencies that may be aroused by seeing violence (or other exciting events) on television.

Male/Female Roles. A second major concern of many people is that television may contribute to stereotypes about males and females. The content of television has been analyzed many times, and the conclusions concerning the treatment of women are that women receive little recognition and respect. Women occupy only a quarter to a third of the roles on entertainment programs, and, when they are shown, they are usually in lower-status jobs or are unemployed. The personalities of women on television are generally passive, deferential, emotional, and weak. In comparison, men are usually active, dominant, rational, and powerful. Television commercials also show women less than men, and males are seen much more in dominant, forceful, and active roles (Kimball, 1986; Liebert and Sprafkin, 1988).

The study of the children of Notel uncovered further evidence that television does influence how children view males and females. Both before and after television came to the community the children were asked about "how suitable it was for boys (and girls)" of their age to: cry when hurt, do dishes, play rough sports, go out alone after dark, swear, learn to cook and bake, and so on. They were also asked about the suitability of various kinds of jobs for men and women (e.g., medical doctor, librarian, principal of a school, Prime Minister of Canada). These questions and others served as measures of how traditional the views of the children were about male and female roles (Kimball, 1986).

Before television arrived, the children of Notel had more egalitarian attitudes about males and females than the children in communities where television had existed for some time. This was especially the case for the boys of Notel. Two years after television was introduced, both the boys and the girls of Notel had much more traditional views of males and females. The results of this Canadian study are consistent with numerous other studies, documenting in a forceful way that television does act as a socializing agent regarding male and female roles. The persistent portrayal of males and females in traditional roles does influence children's ideas (Kimball, 1986).

Television as a Socializing Agent for Adolescents and Adults

Adolescents and adults are also socialized by television. If we take only one small segment of television programming—daytime and evening drama—we can see just how enormous the influence of the mass media can be. The average American adult sees 12 hours of television *drama* each week. If we think of this estimate in relation to the pretelevision era of history, it is equivalent to "*. . . five or six full-length stage plays a week!*" (Berger, 1987, p. 9).

Exactly how much these dramatic performances are influencing the attitudes and values of the American population is difficult to estimate, but we can be sure that the dialogue, actions, costumes, and settings of performances contain messages that help people define themselves and their behavior.

We should not overlook the fact that television dramas produced primarily for American television audiences are frequently sent to other countries around the world, where they also serve to socialize viewers. *Dallas*, *Dynasty*, and many other shows have enjoyed high levels of interest in Europe and elsewhere. One study has revealed that German viewers of *Dallas* see in this show a confirmation of their views of Americans. Although they know that the Ewing family is exceptionally rich, and therefore not like most Americans, they also believe that many Americans have a life that is made easier by money. Even though German viewers recognize the exaggerated character of life on *Dallas*—ruthlessness, dishonesty, greed—they nonetheless incorporate some of what they see in their attitudes about Americans (Massing, 1987). Very likely, the worldwide popularity of such television dramas as *Dallas* and *Dynasty* stem from their depiction of Americans as rich and aggressive.

Other television programs that have enormous potential for socializing adults and adolescents are the daytime talk shows—for instance, *Donahue*, *The Oprah Winfrey Show*, *Sally Jessy Raphael*, and *Geraldo Rivera*. These programs are immensely popular and are watched by millions of Americans each week. The standard format of these programs

Television programs have enormous potential for socializing viewers. Programs such as *The Oprah Winfrey Show* are very popular with adults and adolescents, and are probably important sources of views about social issues and problems of the times.

is to select a theme or issue for the day, invite special guests who have something to say on the topic, and then allow the studio and viewing audiences to ask questions or make comments. The topics under discussion purport to deal with important or interesting social issues or problems of the times. Viewers who perceive these programs as educational and informative, as well as entertaining, probably derive from them most of the information they possess on social issues. The opinions and attitudes of a great many Americans are very likely formed, and reinforced, by these television programs.

Although adolescents watch television dramas (including soap operas) and daytime talk shows, this age group, when compared to children and older adults, generally has the least interest in television (Williams and Boyes, 1986). One major exception is the great popularity of Music Television or MTV. This part of television programming appeals primarily to the age group between 12 and 25. Since both the song lyrics and accompanying dramatic presentations are conveying messages, the audience is being socialized about a wide range of highly important matters in their lives—romantic relationships, love, and sex, as well as hair, makeup, and clothing styles. A number of critics have spoken out against MTV for the way sexual material is presented. They charge that sexuality is often portrayed in a sadomasochistic way, mostly with women as the victims (Strouse and Fabes, 1985). If adolescents are influenced by television fare in the same ways as younger children, the socialization they receive from MTV may produce more aggression in male/female courtship relationships.

Adolescent and Adult Socialization

We have already seen how television is an important socializing agent for both adolescents and adults, so obviously people continue to be socialized after childhood. Indeed, socialization continues throughout life, as we will see in the remainder of this chapter. Some adult socialization occurs in connection with changes expected from one life stage to the next, changes that come largely from the process of aging, such as adolescence, for instance, and old age. Other life transitions come unexpectedly and often with suddenness, such as the loss of one's job, or getting divorced, or being widowed. Other adult socialization occurs in connection with entering occupations or professions, organizations, work settings, or institutions.

Adolescent Socialization

Adolescence in American society is generally thought of as a period of erratic and unpredictable behavior that begins with the onset of puberty and ends after high school. The biological changes that take place in the teenage years are often credited for causing adolescent behavior. The close connection with these biological changes obscures the fact that adolescence is a socially created stage in the life cycle. In American society and elsewhere, adolescent behavior is expected and prepared for, and therefore it does occur. Adolescence is an identifiable period in the life cycle of most people in our society—distinguished from childhood on the one hand and adulthood on the other.

In earlier times a distinctively adolescent period was not recognized, nor do some contemporary societies recognize it. Since adolescence is not universally found as a stage of the life cycle, it must be socially created in societies where it is found. In some societies (including our own), some useful purpose is probably served by having an

"While we're at supper, Billy, you'd make Daddy and Mommy very happy if you'd remove your hat, your sunglasses, and your earring."

identifiable period that comes after childhood and before adulthood. Young people do not have to marry and take jobs as soon as they reach their teens. Many young people also need to go through a formal educational system to acquire the skills necessary in a highly technological and bureaucratic economic system.

Anticipatory socialization
Learning what will be expected in a status before entering that status

People often learn what will be expected of them in a given status before they enter that status. Called **anticipatory socialization,** this process typically occurs in

Adolescence is a life stage that allows young people to lead a special life style before adult responsibilities. Adolescence is a social creation found most often in urban, industrial societies.

each stage of the life cycle. For example, young people learn, even before they reach the teenage years, that they will become adolescents. They learn that when they reach this stage their behavior and feelings will probably differ from the behavior and feelings of their childhood years. The words *adolescence* and *teenage years* become symbols with a self-fulfilling reality. In contemporary society, the economic system, augmented by mass advertising, sells the teenage years—a very lucrative market.

Teenagers are sensitized to the idea that they should like things that are clearly distinguished from childish and adult (or parental) things. Adolescents want to be clearly set apart from children and clearly set apart from parents and "old people." What adolescents define as their special domain is constantly being invaded by older and younger members of society. When preteen children start to idolize a music star first cultivated by teenagers, the teenagers quickly move on to someone else.

Adult Socialization

A number of important occasions arise in adult life when socialization occurs with special intensity. The term **adult socialization** refers to occasions in life when adults learn the new behaviors expected of them as they enter new occupations, professions, organizations, work settings, institutions, or life stages.

Adult socialization
Adults learning behaviors expected of them in new occupations, institutions, or life stages

Socialization in Occupations and Work Settings

There is more to be learned in a new job or organization than the specific tasks that one is assigned. One must also learn the norms and the expected role behaviors of the work setting or organization. Anyone who enters a large office, an academic department, a service agency, an industrial shop, or any other work group enters an ongoing social system. Every social system, in addition to norms and roles, will have—as we saw in the last chapter—a social structure (prevailing patterns of interaction). The social structure will include friendship patterns as well as patterns of privilege, deference, and respect among members. Newcomers must be sensitive to these features of the group they are joining.

Some occupations and professions feature intense training at the time of entry; often this training is a conscious effort at socializing new members. Military organizations are especially likely to begin this socialization as soon as new recruits arrive. A less well-known but striking example of early training/socialization is found in the way the airline industry trains flight attendants (Hochschild, 1983).

The training of flight attendants extends far beyond the technical aspects of their work. Equally important is the socialization that flight attendants receive on how to present themselves to the flying public. Above all, they must perform their duties in a way that makes them seem friendly, helpful, cheerful, and composed at all times. Flight attendants, especially the females, must smile easily and often. They are taught to display a friendly and cheerful presence, even when they are hurrying to complete their work, are being harassed by demanding and unruly passengers, or are facing a crisis.

The socialization of flight attendants begins even before they are hired. In an airline publication for prospective flight attendants, candidates are told how to conduct themselves at the hiring interview. This book tells candidates to be sincere, modest, and to display a friendly smile. Interviewees are also told to be enthusiastic, but with calmness and poise, to be "vivacious but not effervescent" (Hochschild, 1983, p. 96).

In any job or occupation the socialization of newcomers is provided by experienced workers. This socialization includes more than the work to be done, it also teaches the newcomer the norms and roles of the existing social system.

After flight attendants have been hired they are sent to an airlines' school where, in addition to learning the fundamental skills and tasks of the job, they are drilled intensively on proper behavior and demeanor. Airlines often have strict rules about what flight attendants may and may not do. In the Delta Air Lines school, flight attendants are told they may not drink alcohol while in uniform or for 24 hours before flight time. While on flights they may not knit, read, or sleep, and they are only allowed to smoke when seated (Hochschild, 1983, p. 99).

But the most important aspect of the socialization of flight attendants is that they must learn to control their real emotions and display the emotions that the airline demands. They must "manage" their feelings and emotions because they are being paid by the airlines to do so. Hochschild has called this behavior "emotion labor" (1983, p. 7). While we all learn to manage our emotions through the normal socialization processes, flight attendants are taught that managing theirs is part of their work. They are taught to deal with difficult passengers, and they are coached and drilled on how to control their anger.

Even though it is taboo to express anger toward passengers, flight attendants sometimes reach a breaking point. One flight attendant described an incident in which she finally did give vent to her anger toward a female passenger who had steadily complained about all the services, and then attacked one of the co-worker flight attendants with a racial slur. In the flight attendant's words:

> Then she began yelling at me and my co-worker who happened to be black. "You nigger bitch!" she said. Well that did it. I told my friend not to waste her pain. This lady asked for one more Bloody Mary. I fixed the drink, put it on a tray, and when I got to

her seat, my toe somehow found a piece of carpet and I tripped—and that Bloody Mary hit that white pants suit! (Hochschild, 1983, p. 114)

Of course, this kind of incident is an exception, and most successful airline flight attendants are able to control and manage their emotions, even under very adverse circumstances. Most are thoroughly and effectively socialized to provide the "emotional labor" that the airline requires of them.

Even though this type of formal socialization occurs in various occupations, equally important informal socialization occurs when new employees begin working. Older members of the group take on the task of training newcomers, which they accomplish both by example and direct instruction. Often the socialization message of veterans differs from that in the formal training process. Such was the case in the police department studied by sociologist Jennifer Hunt (1985), a study that was described in chapter 2.

When rookie police officers went on active duty they were quickly taught by veteran officers that it was permissible to use force, and even violence, when dealing with citizens. The veterans were quite aware that a discrepancy existed between police academy training about force and violence and the advice they were offering to rookies. Veterans often said, "It's not done on the street the way that it's taught at the academy."

Veteran street police quickly informed rookie officers that the weapons and nightsticks they had been issued were not adequate for the job on the street. Rookies quickly replaced their wooden batons with the more powerful plastic nightsticks. In the police academy recruits had been taught to avoid hitting people on the head or neck because blows there could cause serious injury or death. In contrast, on the street the standard was to hit wherever it would do the most damage in order to avoid danger to oneself.

The socialization of young police officers includes simulated experiences of when firearms should be used, or not used. What they learn at the police academy may differ from what veteran officers may teach them on the streets.

Veteran police officers carried out their socialization by showing their approval and support when rookie officers used force. One female officer was upset when she learned that she was the object of a brutality suit, and she was reluctant to face her male colleagues. When she did report for work, however, the men greeted her with a standing ovation. Their support also included a sexist compliment when they told this woman officer, "You can use our urinal now" (Hunt, 1985, p. 319). Thus, by praise and support as well as by example, rookie police officers learn that it is acceptable to use "normal" force on the street, even though the level of violence often exceeds what is legally permissible.

Both formal and informal socialization are likely to occur whenever one enters a new profession, organization, or work setting. Even when a person enters an organization or work setting in a position of authority, some socialization occurs. A new office manager or department head must usually take some time to learn the existing social system before making dramatic changes in working procedures (Gouldner, 1954).

When people enter prison there is an informal social system that new inmates must learn if they are to survive.

Resocialization in a Total Institution

Some instances of socialization in adulthood are so intense and pervasive that they can be called resocialization. **Resocialization** is the process of unlearning old norms, roles, and values, then learning new ones required by the new social environment. In the most extreme cases of resocialization the social self of the incoming person is stripped away or destroyed, so that the individual becomes dependent on the institution for a new self. This extreme often occurs when an adult enters a total institution such as a mental hospital or prison (Goffman, 1961).

Resocialization
The process of unlearning old norms, roles, and values, and learning new ones

As we saw in the last chapter, a total institution is usually cut off from the rest of society and forms an all-encompassing social environment that meets all the needs of the members. Prisons and mental institutions are prominent examples of total institutions. Total institutions are miniature societies, with all of the characteristics of societies: they have a cultural system with values and norms, as well as a social structure with statuses and roles. Another distinct feature of total institutions is the almost complete control they exert over the lives of people who exist within them. A total institution requires an extensive reorganization of the life of the entering individual. Because the old rules and roles of life can no longer apply completely in a prison or mental institution, resocialization must take place.

Jean Harris, a former headmistress of an elite girls' school who was convicted of murdering the best-selling diet-book author, Dr. Herman Tarnower, has vividly described her resocialization in a women's prison. One of the first things Harris learned is that prison discipline "has little to do with wrongdoing. It has a great deal to do with how people feel about you, or how fearful the staff is of the people who complain about you" (Harris, 1986, p. 201). In other words, discipline is often meted out arbitrarily. The same behavior by two different inmates will get different reactions from the guards. Harris describes how she received a misconduct charge for absent-mindedly leaving her government-issued coat in the exercise yard (the charge was "not taking care of government property"). In contrast, another inmate, sitting only seven feet from one of the guards, cut up her coat and made it into a vest. The guard said nothing.

Harris also describes the complex daily routine of obtaining an anti-depressant medication. If an inmate needs medication she must go to the dispensary for each administration. However, it is no simple task to get there because the round trip requires getting through eight locked doors. The guards stationed at each of these doors often keep the inmates waiting for considerable lengths of time before allowing them to pass through. Inmates requiring medication three times a day spend a considerable part of their day making these trips to the dispensary. In prison, even the simple task of taking a pill requires learning an intricate procedure and coping with a variety of complications and frustrations.

Resocialization for life in prison means that inmates must learn both a formal and an informal social system. The formal rules are made and enforced by the administrators and guards. The informal social system of a prison is controlled by the inmates. A sociological study of a women's prison, conducted by Heffernan (1972), shows how a new inmate must learn the informal system quickly or risk getting into trouble with the more powerful inmates. In the bathrooms certain sinks and showers are reserved for women with the highest status. When movies are shown in the recreation room the best seats are available only to these high-status women. In the words of the women inmates, "Some can, some can't." Should a new and unaware inmate accidentally select one of these preferred places, the result is a verbal or sometimes physical attack. New inmates in a total institution have few options; they must learn the rules of the new system (both formal and informal) and abide by them. The socialization is generally quick and effective.

Since total institutions are also places of work for many people, it is not surprising that there is also an informal social system that influences staff members as well. A young woman who had recently been a youth counselor at an institution for delinquent girls describes what she learned about making changes in the institution:

> When I first began to work here I was fresh out of college. You have all these ideas about all the changes you're going to make—to apply all the things you learned in college to rehabilitate. You try to express your views to the rest of the staff—that other ways of doing things might be more effective. But after you're here a while, you become institutionalized [socialized]. You find out that's not what's wanted. People who have been here a long time are the ones that make the decisions. They're the ones who call the shots. They really don't want change. . . . After a while you change. You do things just like they've always been done here (Giallombardo, 1974, p. 107).

The lesson is the same for the new inmate and the new staff member: the ongoing social system of rules and arrangements must be learned when one enters a total institution. What distinguishes total institutions from other groups and organizations is that total institutions influence all aspects of a person's life, and the influence is continuous. In other settings, one must adapt to the norms and rules of a new place of work, for example, but one can escape for many hours each day. In a prison, mental institution, nursing home, or monastery, or aboard a ship, such escape is not possible, and therefore the socialization is both more intense and more pervasive.

Socialization during Unexpected Life-Stage Transitions

As we have seen with adolescence, the expected changes from one life stage to another are often preceded by anticipatory socialization. However, some transitions in life are often unexpected or sudden. The death of a husband or wife, or the loss of a job can occur suddenly and unexpectedly. In these cases, socialization for the new status occurs when the unexpected event is in the process of occurring or has occurred.

Loss of Job. When people lose their jobs, especially if the loss means the termination of a long-time occupation or career, they are often ill-prepared to deal with their new status. One study of out-of-work scientists, engineers, and technical people reveals how unprepared many people are for being unemployed (Powell and Driscoll, 1979). Often, these professionals responded with relief when they were laid off because many had anticipated losing their jobs. After a period of relaxation, they made concerted efforts to locate new positions. When their best efforts failed they often started to experience serious self-doubt. Continued failure to find a job usually led to feelings of cynicism and discontent. Eventually these unemployed professionals ceased looking for work and had to adopt a new view of themselves and their occupational lives. Many admitted that they felt apathetic and listless about most aspects of their lives:

> I've lost all my drive and don't care.
>
> What's the use of looking? I'll just be turned down.
>
> I'm sick of being humiliated by people who act like they're doing you a favor just talking to you (Powell and Driscoll, 1979, p. 317).

A study of unemployed Canadian workers, covering a much broader occupational range, identified the most important adjustments that unemployed workers had to make (Burman, 1988). Because their incomes were curtailed, they had to learn how to economize and modify their spending habits. They also had to reconcile themselves to the fact that they were "losing ground" in the race for economic mobility. One of the most serious problems for the unemployed was learning how to use the many hours of the day when they had no job to occupy their time (Burman, 1988).

Widowhood. Losing a husband or wife through death is widely recognized as one of the most traumatic experiences of life. Learning to live without a spouse, especially after a marriage that has lasted a long time, requires a significant period of adjustment. Although the reactions of both males and females are likely to be similar, the chances are much greater for women to lose their husbands than for men to lose their wives. Women who have had traditional relationships with their husbands are often ill-prepared to take over many of the required tasks of contemporary life. The same is true of men if they have relied upon their wives for many of their daily needs. One woman, who lost her husband in middle age, describes the changes she had to make:

> It takes two years, say psychiatrists, before a widow absorbs what has happened and is capable of making decisions. Early [on] there is merciful numbness. . . . And the first thing you understand when your senses return is that although you are the same person, nobody else believes it. And after a while you see that they are right and you have to grow up in middle age (Mooney, 1981, p. D1).

"Growing up in middle age" describes vividly the socialization experience that accompanies the loss of a husband or wife.

Socialization for Retirement and Old Age

The life stages of retirement and old age are like the stages of adolescence and adulthood in the sense that they, too, are socially recognized and expected stages in life. Therefore a certain amount of anticipatory socialization is expected for these later life stages.

The transition to old age, however, is becoming increasingly complicated because of changes in the physical and economic characteristics of those in the elderly category. Retirement from the labor force is no longer as closely associated with old age as it was in the past. At the beginning of this century, the majority of men aged 65 were still active in the labor force. Today fewer than 20 percent of men over 65 are employed; an even smaller percentage of women over 65 are still employed—about 10 percent.

Retirement occurs at or before age 65 today because a greater proportion of the older population is economically able to retire. The payments of retirement plans and Social Security benefits, combined with personal savings, are allowing more and more people to retire at age 65 or earlier. Combined with the better economic conditions of the elderly is their better health. For most people over 50 in the United States today, retirement is no longer associated with idleness, illness, and poverty. These people approach their retirement years with expectations for many years of healthy and active life. (Chapter 10 discusses the elderly in greater detail.)

Of course, as the aging process continues, and especially as individuals reach age 75 and older, health conditions do lead to other changes in social status. As individuals are afflicted with more physical infirmities and often suffer from chronic ill health, they

Unemployed people, such as the thousands shown here waiting in line for thirty job openings, have to learn a new way of life after they lose their jobs.

become more and more dependent on the help of others. Frequently continuous care is required in this stage of life, many times in nursing homes and other institutions. In these settings they may be socialized to accept the inevitability of death.

Socialization for Dying. The ultimate and universal stage in the life cycle is death. Social systems, then, must have mechanisms for preparing people for death. Anticipatory socialization is an especially appropriate concept in this case, since preparation for death must occur before the actual event.

Funeral services, for example, are increasingly common occurrences as people grow older. For the elderly, the deaths of family members and friends become regular reminders of their own impending deaths. The rituals connected with death legitimize death; people learn to accept the deaths of others and also their own (Berger and Luckmann, 1967, p. 10).

A sociological study of a community of very elderly people (average age was 80) revealed that much of the social organization of the community centered around death (Marshall, 1980). Residents of the community were repeatedly made aware of the fact that death was more or less imminent both for themselves and others around them. The administration of the community repeatedly urged residents to plan the arrangements for their deaths—the disposition of their bodies, bequests, and other details. The residents did not treat death as a major philosophical issue but as a normal and expected occurrence (Marshall, 1980).

This example of socialization reveals again that social systems do not leave unattended the important passages from one life-cycle stage to another. Instead, the people in the system are prepared (socialized) to accept their movement into the next stage, even if that stage is death itself.

Summary

Socialization is the process by which a person learns and accepts the ways of a particular social group or society. Every social system makes sure that new members joining the system learn the accepted ways of doing things. Socialization is also important in producing the characteristics and personality of the individual.

The process of socialization begins in the very early stages of life, and through this process human qualities are acquired. Infants who are isolated from human contact during the early years of life do not show the characteristics we normally associate with human nature. Human infants develop reciprocal relationships with adults in which they learn to satisfy their basic needs by behaving in the way adults want them to. Through socialization, a child develops a social self, that is, the learned perception that a person has about his or her qualities and attributes. People learn to evaluate themselves through interaction with others, just as they learn to evaluate all other social objects. Social objects include the values, norms, and roles that prevail in the society.

Parents are important primary socialization agents, and many parents take very seriously the responsibility of shaping the personalities of their children. However, socialization is too complex and subtle for parents to achieve exactly what they desire in the socialization of their children.

Research on childhood socialization has shown that working-class families socialize their children differently from middle-class, white-collar families. Working-class families socialize their children to be obedient and to observe social rules. Middle-class parents socialize their children to take initiatives and to participate in decision making (autonomy). These two forms of behavior are related to the kinds of roles that children from different social classes are likely to play in the adult work world. Surveys have shown, however, that American parents are increasingly valuing autonomy over obedience. Reverse socialization occurs when children socialize their parents. Empirical evidence shows that children do teach their parents about some aspects of contemporary life.

Peers are important socializing agents for young children, and often the socialization of peers runs counter to that of parents. The mass media, especially television, are pervasive socializing forces in contemporary society. Children spend much of their time watching television, and evidence reveals that they are influenced by violence and by male and female characterizations seen there.

Adolescents and adults are also socialized by television, which is just one aspect of adult socialization. Adolescents receive anticipatory socialization for the adolescent stage of life. Adult socialization occurs when people enter new occupations, professions, organizations, work settings, institutions, or life stages. The total institution provides a particularly vivid example of adult socialization; this socialization is so extensive that it is referred to as resocialization.

Several life-stage transitions require learning new roles, but, for some of these there is little anticipatory socialization. Two examples are loss of job and a spouse's death. In contrast, a substantial amount of anticipatory socialization occurs for retirement and old age, and even death.

CRITICAL THINKING

1. Why is socialization important for the continuation of a culture? What would happen to a culture if all socialization ceased?
2. Explain how the socialization process in your culture taught you the following: how to say goodbye, proper table manners, and appropriate dress for religious occasions.
3. What evidence supports the claim that primary socialization is important to our "humanness"?
4. What is the norm of reciprocity? Give examples from your own life that illustrate this principle.
5. How do some of the values of middle-class and lower-class parents differ with regard to the socialization of their children? What accounts for this difference in values? How might this explain the perpetuation of the class structure in American society?
6. Explain how reverse socialization can take place between parents and children.
7. Evaluate some television shows in light of the information about violence and male/female roles presented in the chapter.
8. What evidence supports the notion that adolescence is a socially created stage in the life cycle rather than a biologically created one?
9. To what extent can anticipatory socialization help a person adjust to the socialization process?
10. What is adult socialization? What changes in a person's life might cause such socialization to occur?
11. Under what conditions is resocialization likely to occur?

CHAPTER

6

Deviance and Social Control

Ask a group of ordinary people to provide examples of deviance or deviant behavior, and you are apt to get an amazing array of responses. Indeed, when one sociologist asked people to do just that, he received 252 different descriptions. Among them, the following examples were offered:

> Movie stars, junior executives, perverts, perpetual bridge-players, psychiatrists, drug addicts, political extremists, conservatives, career women, prostitutes, liars, prudes, girls who wear make-up, priests, atheists, liberals, communists, alcoholics, the retired, criminals, divorcees, reckless drivers, and know-it-all professors (Simmons, 1965).

As we look at this list, we might wonder how the respondents could describe some of these examples as deviant. The fact that they did illustrates that deviant behavior is not as clearcut and obvious as we might suppose, nor is deviant behavior as fixed and unchanging as we sometimes think. To arrive at a sociological understanding of deviant behavior, we must first see that deviance is *socially defined,* and that social definitions of deviance differ from one society or social group to another.

The Social Nature of Deviance

To say that deviance is socially defined means that whenever most of the people of a given society, or social group, consider a behavior deviant, *it will be deviant.* As a result, a vast array of behaviors have been and are considered deviant in different societies. Even within the same society, significant changes often occur in what people consider deviant behavior. Cross-cultural and historical evidence provides many examples of the shifting nature of deviant behavior, showing clearly that it is socially defined.

We have seen indications of the variability of deviance in earlier chapters when we encountered behaviors in other societies that would be considered deviant in the United States. We saw in chapter 3 how the parents of Staphorst in the Netherlands expect their daughters to have sexual intercourse and become pregnant before marriage. These very religious people do not consider this behavior deviant since it follows their cultural norms. If, however, we were to hear of American parents who expected their teenage daughters to become pregnant before marriage, we would probably think of these parents as deviants.

Many other examples exist of different views about deviance from one society to another. Among the Plains Indians, young men were made to fast until they saw visions. A Plains Indian youth who could not see visions would probably have been considered deviant. Americans might consider a person who claims to see visions as a deviant. Among many Arabs the use of alcohol was prohibited, but smoking hashish was more likely to be accepted. An Arab who preferred alcohol to hashish would have been

This orange juice vendor is perceived as deviant only after we know that we are seeing a man dressed in feminine clothing and made up as a woman.

considered deviant by his own people, and yet most Americans would see the situation in exactly the opposite way (Simmons, 1965).

The Changing Nature of Deviance

The fact that deviance is socially defined becomes abundantly clear when we examine some recent changes in what Americans think of as deviant behavior. Some behaviors that, only a decade or so ago, were not considered deviant are now viewed as deviant. The reverse is also true.

Two centuries ago in the United States, for instance, being fat was considered good; it was certainly not considered deviant (Schwartz, 1986). But in contemporary American society many people consider obesity a form of deviance. To be fat today is to have a blemish on one's appearance and to be a social disgrace. Fatness is considered to be a morally reprehensible condition (Millman, 1980).

From Acceptability to Deviance. Smoking, especially in public places, is a behavior that has undergone a rapid transformation in the United States in a short span of years. By the end of World War II smoking had reached a peak of popularity in the United States. Cigarette smoking was viewed as glamorous and sophisticated behavior.

The tobacco industry even advertised that cigarette smoking was healthy ("as an aid to digestion," "to calm nerves," and "to control weight"). Smoking in public, even in closely confined places such as planes, cars, and restaurants, was perfectly acceptable behavior.

Personal attitudes about smoking began to change when the Surgeon General of the United States issued a report in 1963 showing that smoking was related to a number of illnesses, especially cancer and heart disease. Although many individuals decided to stop smoking, the social attitude toward public smoking did not change. Public smoking, even in confined spaces, continued to be acceptable behavior. Only gradually in the 1970s, and then rapidly in the 1980s, did the *social* definition of smoking in public change.

During the 1980s, more and more Americans openly contested the rights of smokers to smoke wherever they pleased. Today, the social definition of smoking is almost completely the opposite of what it was 25 years ago. Smokers who "light up" in the presence of nonsmokers will likely be told in very strong terms that their behavior is unacceptable. Smokers now often complain that their rights are being violated because they are made to feel like "criminals" when they smoke.

Although driving a vehicle while under the influence of alcohol has always been illegal, and thus a somewhat deviant act, recent changes in social definitions have clearly made drunk driving more deviant. In the past, most people hardly gave a second thought to driving after they had had a few drinks or more. Now, with growing concern about death and injury caused by drinking drivers, especially when innocent bystanders are killed or hurt, the social definitions are changing. Active campaigns against drunk driving by organizations such as Mothers Against Drunk Driving (MADD) and Students Against Drunk Driving (SADD) have heightened public awareness that driving after drinking is now apt to be considered a deviant act. In fact, the courts, too, are treating the offense of "driving under the influence" as a more serious crime, and jail sentences are not uncommon—especially for multiple offenders and in cases where innocent people are killed or injured. In 1982, 27 states passed new, stiffer laws against driving under the influence of alcohol (and drugs). Among other things, penalties were made more severe, and the certainty of punishment was increased (Kingsnorth and Jungsten, 1988).

From Deviance to Acceptability. Just as some behavior becomes more deviant over time, other behavior becomes less deviant, or more acceptable. Cohabitation before marriage is a case in point. In the 1950s and early 1960s some couples lived together without being married, but most people regarded their behavior as unacceptable. Such couples were commonly described as "living in sin." If an unmarried couple remained together long enough, and especially if they had children, the label "common-law marriage" was applied, always carrying a negative stigma, however. Couples involved in common-law marriages were looked down upon by most people in the community and were clearly regarded as deviants. Now, just a few decades later, many Americans accept cohabitation as a natural stage between dating and marriage. Even people who would not accept cohabitation for themselves do not attach much of a negative stigma to those who do.

The open discussion of sexual behavior is no longer taboo. Part of this change is borne of necessity, in response to the AIDS crisis. In large measure, however, candor in discussing sex reflects changing norms. For example, only a few years ago, condoms would never have been discussed openly, especially on television or in public settings. Since the spread of AIDS has become a national public concern, it has become acceptable, if not praiseworthy, to urge the use of condoms. Today, they are displayed, discussed, and demonstrated in a wide range of public forums. In the late 1980s the Surgeon General of the United States stood before a high school audience and demonstrated the proper use of a condom. Less than ten years ago that act would have been considered deviant.

Deviant Behavior as Defined by Specific Groups

Even within the same society, different social groups often define deviance differently. Groups of people who share the same norms and values will develop their own rules about what is and what is not deviant behavior. Their views may not be shared by members of the larger society, but the definitions of deviance will apply to group members. For example, the students in any high school will establish their own codes for dress, hairstyles, and behavior. Although not everyone has to have the same appearance, when an individual strays too far from the current fashion, that person is likely to be considered deviant.

The importance of group definitions of deviance among high school students can be illustrated by the case of gifted students who consider themselves deviant. One such student described all gifted students as "not really trying to get along with others, a little obnoxious about being smart" (Huryn, 1986, p. 178). Not only did gifted students consider themselves to be deviant but 77 percent of them felt that their peers at school regarded them as deviants. While the larger society, especially the adults, might view gifted students as the ideal for young people, the gifted students themselves may be considered deviant in their own social environments.

These illustrations indicate clearly that deviance is profoundly influenced by the society or social group in which the behavior or act occurs. Although deviance is often associated with individual behavior (individuals are considered bad, weak, corrupt, dishonest, or evil when they commit deviant acts), the sociological view emphasizes that deviance is a social phenomenon. We can only understand deviant behavior if we first recognize that societies and social groups define what is deviant, and what is not. Therefore, the sociological definition of **deviance** is any behavior that members of a society or social group consider a violation of group norms.

Deviance
Any behavior considered by a group to be a violation of its norms

The Social Functions of Deviance

As we saw in chapter 1, structural-functionalists look for the way societal structures (defined as regular patterns of interaction) may have some positive purpose for the ongoing functioning of the society. However, structural-functionalists also recognize that some social structures can have negative results (dysfunctions) for a society. At first glance, it would seem that most deviant behavior in a society (crime and other forms of unacceptable behavior) would be socially dysfunctional. However, since the work of Emile Durkheim (1895/1964), sociologists have recognized that deviant behavior can have positive functions for society. This paradoxical relationship can be explained by the fact that when a deviant behavior occurs, society's norms are reaffirmed. The deviant act serves to clarify the existing standards of social conduct. Without periodic violations of the standards of conduct, the standards would become less clear and thus less strongly held (Dentler and Erikson, 1959; Jensen, 1988).

Of course, we do not need cold-blooded murders to remind us that killing a person is a deviant act. Many areas of social life, however, lack clarity as to whether a behavior is deviant. These areas are ones in which the positive function of deviant acts is most clearly revealed. For example, during the Reagan administration, charges were brought against former White House officials (who had enjoyed close contact with the President and other staff members) for attempting to influence policy decisions in order to gain profitable contracts for their clients. Some charges resulted in convictions; in other cases, their actions were judged to be unethical.

These well-publicized activities—which highlighted what the media called "the sleaze factor"—have increased public sensitivity to the inappropriateness and illegality of "selling influence." When President Bush took office in 1989, one of his first acts was to appoint a commission that would prepare a code of ethics. He also spoke to all senior government officials, stressing the importance of avoiding even the "perception of unethical behavior." From a structural-functionalist perspective, this chain of events illustrates that deviant acts can have positive societal functions.

Sociological Theories of Deviance

Sociologists are concerned with why some people in a society engage in behaviors that violate, or run counter to, norms. Why do some people steal, rob, kill, and commit other illegal and anti-social acts? Theories of deviance attempt to answer these questions.

Strain Theory

Strain theory
The lack of congruence between institutional means and cultural goals

The **strain theory** of deviant behavior approaches deviance from the level of cultures and social structures (in other words, at the macroscopic level). According to strain theory, a discrepancy, or a lack of congruence, exists between cultural values and the means of achieving them. The strain can be thought of as a pressure that occurs when the culture values one thing, but the structure of the society is such that not everyone can realize the values in a socially accepted way. As we saw in chapter 3, the culture of the United States places a value on material or economic success. The structure of American society, however, does not give everyone the same chance for economic success. Many people in the lowest social classes have almost no chance to succeed economically. The result is that they may accept the cultural goal of "getting rich" but reject the socially accepted means of doing so. (Chapter 8—Social Stratification investigates the inequality inherent in the socioeconomic system.)

In the poor and minority areas of many American cities, many youngsters are pressured into deviant behavior because the conventional means for achieving economic success (education and careers) are both difficult and remote. For these youths, illegal activities represent other ways of achieving economic success, even extraordinary success. For example, selling drugs can be a means of making money. Many young men are willing to risk their lives selling "crack" and other drugs because in return they often make thousands of dollars a week.

As we will see later, however, deviance is also present in the upper levels of society. Wall Street traders and stock manipulators have made huge sums of money through a variety of illegal activities. In these cases, the cultural value of economic success has won out over prohibitions against breaking the law.

Merton's Typology. Strain theory does not excuse illegal behavior among the poor or the wealthy. Rather, it emphasizes that there are different ways of responding to cultural values (or goals), and some of the responses are deviant behaviors.

Sociologist Robert Merton (1938, 1957; Farnsworth and Leiber, 1989), who formulated strain theory, provides a typology of the different ways in which people respond to cultural values or goals. Merton labeled as **conformist** people who accept the cultural goals (achieving economic success) and who also accept the conventional or institutionalized means of achieving these goals (getting an education, working hard, and so on). In Merton's typology, conformists clearly are not deviants.

Conformists
Those who accept cultural goals and conventional means of achieving them

People who accept the cultural goals (economic success) but reject the conventional or institutional means of achieving them are called **innovators.** When large-scale cocaine dealers make great sums of money, they are innovators because they come up with new ways of achieving the cultural goal of economic success.

Innovators
Those who accept cultural goals but reject conventional means of achieving them

Those resigned to being unable to achieve cultural goals such as wealth and recognition, but who nonetheless slavishly adhere to conventional rules of conduct, are called **ritualists.** Ritualists continue to work at bureaucratic or dead-end jobs even though they have given up on any significant advancement in life. Because they have abandoned cultural goals, they, too, are in some degree deviant.

Ritualists
Those who cannot achieve cultural goals but continue to adhere strictly to conventional means of conduct

The **retreatist** rejects both the cultural goals *and* the conventional, institutionalized means. The retreatist response can be found among people who have given up on the system completely. They have no interest in economic success and thus have no reason to involve themselves in hard work or any other conventional, institutionalized means. Such people are almost always seen as deviant.

Retreatists
Those who reject both cultural goals and conventional means of conduct

A fifth type of response to cultural goals and institutional means is the rejection of both and the substitution of new cultural goals and means. These are the **rebels,** illustrated by revolutionaries who want to create a new type of society. The new society might have entirely new cultural goals (harmony and cooperation rather than individual economic success) and new institutional means (meditation, communing with the spirit world, etc.).

Rebels
Those who reject both cultural goals and means and substitute new ones

The different responses to cultural goals and institutional means are summarized in table 6–1.

Strain theory is most effective in showing how deviant behavior can be a product of the relationship between cultural goals and the structural characteristics of a society. As a theory of deviance, it is most closely associated with structural-functional theory (see chapter 1). Strain theory shows how some structural features of society (social classes, the impoverished, racial minorities) can be dysfunctional by keeping many people from realizing important cultural goals. Deviant behavior is often the result.

Strain theory is less effective as an explanation for deviance among those who are members of advantaged groups. As we noted earlier, when deviant behavior occurs among Wall Street brokers, it cannot be attributed to their position in the social structure. Their position in the social structure has not blocked their paths to success. Thus, the explanation for their choosing deviant behavior lies elsewhere (Akers and Cochran, 1985).

Table 6–1. A Typology of Modes of Conformity and Deviance

	Culture Goals (getting rich, etc.)	Institutionalized Means (working hard, etc.)	
I. Conformity	Acceptance	Acceptance	Non-deviance
II. Innovation	Acceptance	Rejection	Types of deviance
III. Ritualism	Rejection	Acceptance	Types of deviance
IV. Retreatism	Rejection	Rejection	Types of deviance
V. Rebellion	Rejection and substitution	Rejection and substitution	Types of deviance

Source: Adapted from Robert K. Merton, *Social Theory and Social Structure*, rev. ed., p. 140. Copyright 1957 by The Free Press.

Deviance as Learned Behavior

As we saw in chapter 5, people learn both norms and values through socialization. We also saw that the norms and values that people learn vary greatly. Values and norms depend upon the society in which one lives and the social groups of which one is a member. Two theories of deviance are built on the idea that some people learn values and norms that lead to deviant behavior.

Differential Association Theory. Edwin Sutherland (1947), who originated this theory, saw deviant behavior as the result of socialization. **Differential association theory** emphasizes that individuals may be socialized by a group of people who engage in and accept deviant behavior. The name of the theory reflects the idea that what people do is influenced by the differences in the people with whom they associate. This argument is akin to a folk belief about the dangers of "keeping bad company." People learn to be drug addicts, alcoholics, or car thieves by keeping company with others who engage in or admire such behavior.

Differential association theory
People learn deviant behaviors by being socialized by a deviant group

In a classic sociological study, Howard S. Becker (1963) pointed out the importance of friendship groups in the process of learning to smoke marijuana. When people start using marijuana, they usually rely on their friends to supply the drug until they are relatively experienced users. Furthermore, people *learn* how to enjoy the effects of marijuana from their friends.

It is widely held in the drug culture that people who say they cannot get high on marijuana have been improperly instructed in how to smoke it, and that people who say they do not enjoy being high did not smoke with people they like or trust. Research has confirmed the importance of social support for marijuana use (Akers and Cochran, 1985; Goode, 1969).

Subcultural Theory. These studies are consistent with a second, and closely related, theory of deviant behavior, which is also based on learning deviant behavior from a social group. This second theory is called the subcultural theory of deviance (Cohen, 1955; Cloward and Ohlin, 1960). **Subcultural theory** puts the emphasis on the carrier of deviant ideas, and identifies subcultures that have norms and values quite different from those of the larger society. Therefore, deviant behavior is really conformity to a

Subcultural theory
Deviant behavior involves conformity to the norms/values of a deviant group

set of norms and values accepted and taught by a particular social group. But when these norms and values are not held by the majority of people, the resulting behavior will be frowned on and labeled deviant by the dominant groups in society.

One of the pioneering studies using this approach was Albert Cohen's (1955) analysis of a gang of delinquent boys. Considering this group as a deviant subculture, Cohen found that the group held values that constituted a sort of "anti-culture" or negative reflection of the "straight" middle-class world. The boys in the gang held other people's property in contempt and expressed their feelings by acts of wanton destruction and vandalism. They also seemed to derive malicious satisfaction out of making "straight" people feel uncomfortable. They were "negativistic" in that they often turned middle-class values upside down. Thus Cohen sought to establish that the deviant group he studied was a particular kind of anti-establishment subculture. He also generalized the idea that most deviant groups are simply negative reflections of the majority culture.

Deviant subcultures are very similar to the countercultures described in chapter 3. We noted there that in the United States many groups have held values and subscribed to norms that were in opposition to the most widely held values and norms. Various kinds of bohemian groups from beatniks to hippies to punks have been considered deviant because they held values and accepted norms that were at odds with the majority. Examples of deviant subcultures can be found in every large society.

The Violent Subculture of British Soccer Fans. In England today there are groups of fans, generally teenage and young adult males, who clearly reveal the way deviant behavior can be learned from a subcultural group (Dunning et al., 1986). These football hooligans (as they are called) generally come from the lowest rungs of the British working class. They consider drinking, fighting, and other aggressive behaviors a natural and normal part of being a fan at a soccer match.

Football hooligans identify passionately with their hometown teams, and when they go to matches they consider it part of the fun to attack and fight with the fans of other football clubs. These attacks include throwing objects (often dangerous items such as darts, metal discs, broken seats, bricks, slabs of concrete, and fireworks) at opposing-team fans. A common practice is for the fans of one team to "invade" the fans of an opposing team, either in the stadium or at the railway or bus stations as the visiting-team fans depart after the game. These invasions lead to fist fights, kicking, and other forms of violence. The most notorious of these invasions occurred at the European Cup matches in 1985 when a violent clash between British and Italian fans led to the deaths of 38 people. Many Britons consider it too dangerous to go to stadiums for the soccer matches because the threat of being accidentally harmed is too great. Most citizens clearly identify the football hooligans as deviants.

Various attempts have been made to explain the routine and nearly ritualized violence of British football fans. One explanation focuses on the norms and values learned by a segment of British youths, and thus it is consistent with both subcultural and differential association theories. Most of the violent youths come from working-class neighborhoods and housing projects where the norms and values are supportive of violence. In many of these neighborhoods it is a mark of prestige for a young man to prove his ability to fight and be aggressive. Indeed, many of these young men learn to enjoy fighting. A man 26 years of age describes the great satisfaction he gets from fighting:

> I go to a match for one reason only: the "aggro" [aggression and fighting]. It's an obsession, I can't give it up. I get so much pleasure . . . that I nearly wet my pants. I go all over the country looking for it. . . . every night during the week we go around looking for trouble (Dunning et al., 1986, p. 222).

In the neighborhoods and housing developments where these young English males grow up, they do not learn to value educational and occupational success. Instead, they learn to value "physical intimidation, fighting, heavy drinking, and exploitative sexual relations" (Dunning et al., 1986, p. 234). The deviant behavior of the football hooligans of England is easily identified as the product of the values and norms these young men have learned on the streets of their neighborhoods.

U.S. Outlaw Motorcycle Gangs. In the United States there are subcultural groups who share norms and values that are very similar to the football hooligans of England. The most widely known are motorcycle gangs, such as the Hell's Angels, who also value fighting and getting into trouble. A related characteristic of male motorcycle-gang members is that they, too, are exploitative of their female companions. The female bikers are expected to engage in prostitution in order to earn money for the dominant males. But this is only part of the broader subordination of females to male bikers. Beyond prostitution, a biker's regular girl friend (his "Ol' lady") can be bought and sold (for anywhere between 50¢ and $500), and the sexual favors of other females (those who do not have regular boyfriends) are freely shared by group members. Beyond sexual abuse, female gang members are generally treated quite brutally by the male members.

In the United States, motorcycle gang members often value fighting and getting into trouble. Their female companions are often the objects of sexual exploitation.

Obviously, these and other forms of behavior are greatly at odds with the norms of the larger society (Quinn, 1987; Watson, 1980).

Puerto Rican Women Gang Members. Deviant female groups have also been the subject of sociological study. Young female members of several Puerto Rican gangs in New York City were studied and found to have a consistent set of values and beliefs (Campbell, 1987). The young women make a clear distinction between the recreational use of drugs and drug addiction. Gang members both use and sell marijuana, and at parties they occasionally use both amphetamines and LSD. However, they strongly condemn the use of heroin, and are very negative about "skin popping" (injecting drugs) because it is regarded as a sign of drug dependence.

In the subculture of these Puerto Rican women, many crimes are not considered criminal. Although they condemn people they do consider "criminals," they do not include as criminals those involved in ". . . drug selling, inter-gang warfare, organized crime, prostitution, domestic violence, stripping abandoned buildings and automobiles, shoplifting, and burglary of businesses" (Campbell, 1987).

Theories of deviant behavior that rely upon learning or socialization do not, of course, explain why different norms and values arise in the first place. When a general societal norm exists that is negative about criminal activity, why do some social groups (subcultures) place a positive value on criminal behavior? These theories also do not explain why some individuals do, and others do not, choose to associate with groups that hold different norms and values. Individuals do make choices; their behavior is not totally determined by their social environments. Examples abound of people who break away from the subcultural environments in which they find themselves.

Despite these criticisms, the importance of socialization as an explanation for deviant behavior cannot be denied. The evidence in support of socialization is found in virtually every form of deviance, from drug use and juvenile delinquency to adult and organized crime (Hazani, 1986; Orcutt, 1987).

Conflict Theory of Deviance

In chapter 1 we saw that conflict theory rests on the premise that, in any society, inequalities in resources and power will exist. When focusing on deviant behavior, conflict theorists emphasize the ways in which a society is organized to serve the interests of the rich and powerful members, often at the expense of other members of the society. To many conflict theorists, the ultimate source of deviance in American society is the capitalist economic system (Gordon, 1981). This view is well summed up by the title of a book, *The Rich Get Richer and the Poor Get Prison* (Reiman, 1979). Since inequality is built into the very basis of the system, many conflict theorists hold that the only real solution lies in the system's total overhaul—a replacement by a much more equitable system in which the gap between the "haves" and the "have-nots" will be minimized.

Although deviance is found at every level of society, the nature, rate, and punishment of deviance are frequently related to the social-class position of the deviant individual (Berk, Lenihan, and Rossi, 1980; Braithwaite, 1981). Generally those from the upper strata of society—the wealthy, the powerful, the influential—play a major role in defining what is, or is not, deviant. These individuals are able to influence the moral and legal definition of deviance in numerous legal ways, including lobbying, making financial contributions to political campaigns, selecting candidates for office, and participating in various policy-making bodies. The result is that a society's moral and legal system reflects the interests of the powerful. The behavior of those whose interests are not represented is therefore much more likely to be defined as deviant. For instance, upper-class people are seldom, if ever, likely to be caught for, and charged with, vagrancy—an illegal behavior for which lower-class persons are frequently caught, charged, and convicted. As Anatole France (1922) once sarcastically commented, "The law, in all its majestic equality, forbids the rich as well as the poor to sleep under bridges on rainy nights, to beg on the streets, and to steal bread."

Elite Deviance. Although deviance is usually equated with acts such as vagrancy, burglary, robbery, kidnapping, and assault—for which members of the lower classes are more likely to be convicted—as we have seen, society's elites also break laws and deviate from the accepted morality. Conflict theorists have a special interest in **elite deviance,** or the deviant and criminal acts committed by the wealthy and powerful. Cases of elite deviance are often much more costly in economic terms than other types of crime, yet punishment is more lenient.

Elite deviance
Deviant or criminal acts committed by the wealthy and powerful

Elite deviance can take many different forms and may range from unethical or immoral acts to criminal acts punishable by fines and imprisonment. Stock manipulation and embezzlement of company funds, for example, are clearly illegal, although a public official who lies to his constituency or gives special favors to friends may be called immoral or unethical yet may be immune from prosecution. Some elite deviant acts result in personal economic gains (such as a senator's accepting a bribe). Other acts result in economic gain for a business or corporation (as in the case of price fixing or kickbacks or bribes to secure business contracts). While elite deviance is generally less visible, dramatic, and overtly violent than other forms of deviance, it may still be injurious to the public's health, safety, or financial well-being. For example, in 1967 the President's Crime Commission estimated that the nation's annual loss to white-collar crime was 27 to 42 times as great as the loss through traditional property crime (robbery, burglary, larceny, and forgery) (Thio, 1978, p. 355).

Even when criminal convictions are obtained, the penalties for elite deviance are often relatively light. When the E.F. Hutton company, a major financial institution, was caught in a fraudulent check "kiting" scheme, a crime for which ordinary citizens would generally be penalized, no company officials were criminally indicted. Even though the company officials were systematically writing checks when they had insufficient funds in bank accounts, and were therefore fraudulently taking the bank's money, the U.S. Justice Department did not choose to prosecute.

In the 1980s a scandal occurred on Wall Street involving the illegal buying and selling of stocks on the basis of "inside" or advance information about stocks that were going to rise in value. This is called "insider trading," and it is illegal. The insider trading case that rocked Wall Street in 1986 centered around Ivan Boesky (nicknamed "Ivan the Terrible," or "Piggy" because he was so greedy). Boesky was a multimillionaire stock market speculator who ultimately admitted that his unbelievable economic successes (for which he was greatly admired) were the result of advance information he had acquired about corporate takeover deals. With this information Boesky was able to buy into the companies before their stock prices rose, and he could therefore make great profits. By the time these illegal dealings came to light, Boesky had amassed a huge fortune.

When his crimes were uncovered, Boesky agreed to help the government find others involved in insider trading. He eventually agreed to pay $100 million in penalties and was banished for life from professional stock trading. In exchange, the government allowed Boesky to sell $440 million in stock he controlled *before* the announcement of his penalties was made. In other words, Boesky was allowed to sell his stock before the price was to plummet *because* of the announcement of his penalties. Boesky was clearly treated quite gently by the authorities and emerged from the scandal with a significant portion of his fortune intact.

Boesky was also sentenced to a three-year prison term (he could be paroled after a year of his imprisonment) at the prison of his choice; he chose the minimum security facility in Lompoc, California. The California climate is gentle, and the prison is set on 44,000 acres of rolling hills and manicured lawns. It offers the inmates a gym, tennis courts, a weight-lifting room, and an outdoor track. It is hard to imagine a burglar or robber who has stolen hundreds of millions of dollars being given such preferential treatment and such a light sentence in a "country-club" prison.

Conflict theorists argue, as we have noted, that elite deviants commit much larger crimes and receive lighter punishments than average citizens. This viewpoint can be illustrated by comparing the Boesky case (or the E.F. Hutton case) with that of William J. Rummel. Rummel was convicted of three offenses by the courts of Texas. His crimes were the following:

1. forging a check for $28.36;
2. obtaining $80 by fraudulent use of a credit card;
3. taking a check for $120.75 in return for a false promise to repair an air conditioner.

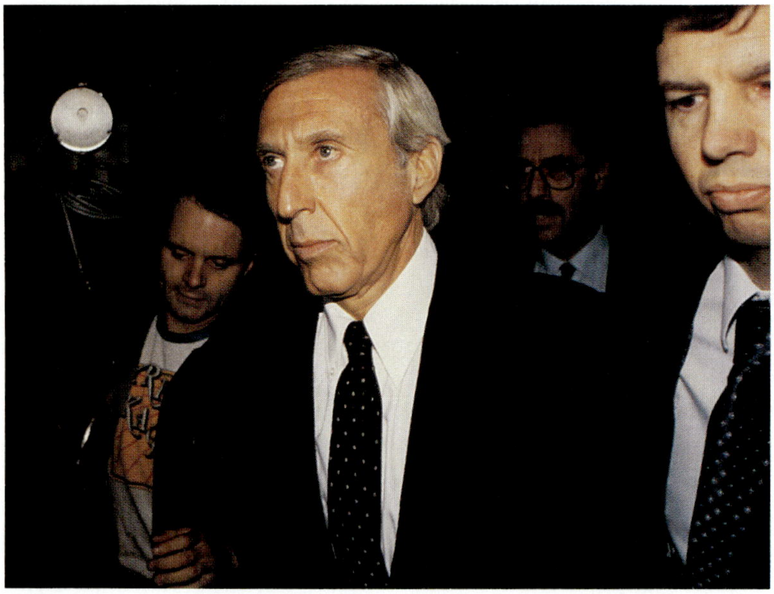

Elite deviance is illustrated by the insider trading crimes of Ivan Boesky. Even though he was convicted, he retained some of the hundreds of millions of dollars acquired through his illegal activities.

"I'm quite content. This was my prison of choice."

Although none of these crimes involved physical injuries to the offended parties, these convictions all happen to be felonies, and under Texas law conviction for a third felony carries a mandatory sentence of life imprisonment. The constitutionality of the law was sustained by the Supreme Court (*New York Times*, 1980a, p. A24). Thus, for crimes involving a total of $229.11, William Rummel faces a life behind bars.

Conflict theory emphasizes the inequalities of power and money in societies. Many conflict theorists, following Marxian theory, see the inequalities as growing out of a capitalist economic system. However, other conflict theorists have noted that inequalities in power and authority also exist in countries with socialist or communist economies (Dahrendorf, 1959).

We will turn next to a theory of deviance that shares with conflict theory the view that inequalities between groups of people in a society can influence who is and who is not considered deviant. Called labeling theory, it is associated with symbolic interaction theory (chapter 1) because it places great emphasis on the symbolic labeling of people as deviants.

Labeling Theory

Labeling theory focuses on the social nature of the process by which some individuals in the society are able to label other individuals as deviant. Also of interest is how the labeled person accepts or adopts the deviant label for himself or herself (Dotter and Roebuck, 1988; Gove, 1980).

Labeling theory
Focuses on the process by which some people are labeled deviant by others

Labeling theory is concerned with which people will be labeled "criminals," "alcoholics," "drug addicts," or "mentally ill." When such labels are applied, the labeling process begins. It involves a person or group doing the labeling (the labeler) and a person or group to whom the label is applied (the labelee). Those who do the labeling are social control agents. Often these agents, such as the police or psychiatrists, label as part of their official functions. Labeling also occurs in very informal contexts, such as when a family member or friend labels someone a drunk, a nymphomaniac, or a liar. Those who are labeled in this process are the deviants. Thus, from a labeling perspective, a deviant is someone to whom a deviant label has been successfully applied (Becker, 1963, p. 9).

The process of becoming deviant usually begins when people perform acts that are disapproved of by certain members of society. Some people rape, steal, or become mentally ill. These forms of deviance may be due to personality problems, a particular kind of home life, community conditions, peer-group influence, or other factors. Although some sociologists focus on the causes of deviance that lie within individuals or their environments, many have come to focus on the official and unofficial social control agents and the labels they create and apply. If no deviant labels were created by social control agents, then there would be no deviance. According to labeling theorists, in order for behavior to be considered deviant, it must be labeled as such:

> . . . social groups create deviance by making the rules whose infraction constitutes deviance and by applying these rules to particular people and labeling them as outsiders. From this point of view, deviance is not a consequence of the act the person commits, but rather a consequence of the application by others of rules and sanctions to an "offender" (Becker, 1963, p. 9).

In other words, no specific behavior is inherently deviant; behavior becomes deviant only when others define it as such.

As we have shown, the deviant label is not applied uniformly. The poor, minority groups, and the disadvantaged are more likely to be labeled deviant for a given act than are more advantaged individuals who behave in the same way. In cases of extreme offenses, such as murder, the community's selectivity in labeling people as deviant is not as clear, but it is quite clear in less extreme forms of deviance: "Some men who drink too much are called alcoholics and others are not; some men who act oddly are committed to hospitals and others are not; some men who have no visible means of support are hauled into court and others are not" (Erikson, 1964, pp. 11–12). These realities have led observers to argue that people are more likely to be labeled mentally ill when they are poor, work in low-status occupations, or are in similarly devalued circumstances (Goffman, 1959a). A person in a more advantageous social situation often escapes being labeled deviant, despite manifestations of the same forms of behavior.

Labeling theory has also been used to help us to understand deviance from the perspective of the victim of deviant acts. In cases where husbands have abused their wives, it is frequently the woman, the *victim,* who is labeled as the deviant (Carlson, 1987). The abusing husband will often successfully label his wife as deviant, charging her with being inadequate, perhaps not living up to the expectations of some ideal female role. Many abused wives report that their husbands convinced them, often for years, that *their* inadequacies were the cause of the beatings. Second, if an abused wife tries to do something about the violence, she is likely to be labeled as deviant by the larger society for revealing that her home and marriage are "defective." Thus, labeling contributes to violence against wives and to their reluctance to do anything about it. The abusive husband may ultimately be labeled as a deviant, but before that occurs, the female victim is likely to have acquired that label.

Primary versus Secondary Deviance. When deviance is viewed from a labeling perspective, the focal concern is not individual, isolated acts of deviance. Labeling theorists are not concerned with explaining why previously "straight" people steal their first orange from a fruit stand, embezzle their first dollar from their employer, or assault their first victim. Such early, nonpatterned acts of deviance are called **primary deviance.**

Primary deviance
Non-patterned acts of deviance

Virtually everyone commits some acts of primary deviance. In a study of 1,689 adults in New York City, Wallerstein and Wyles (1947) found that 91 percent of the respondents in the study admitted that they had broken a law after their sixteenth birthday. Sixty-four percent of the men and 29 percent of the women could have been convicted of a felony. Between 80 percent and 90 percent of all the men and women studied had stolen something. One-fourth of the men admitted to having stolen an automobile, and one out of ten had committed a robbery. Thus, isolated acts that would be labeled deviant by social control agents are widespread.

Labeling theorists, however, are chiefly concerned with **secondary deviance,** which refers to forms of deviance that persist in individuals and that cause them to organize their lives and personal identities around their deviant status. Labeling theorists focus on the process whereby individuals become labeled as criminals, and the label comes to override all other definitions of self.

Secondary deviance
Persistent forms of deviance around which people organize their lives

Although the labeling approach focuses on the degree to which others label an individual, it is also possible for individuals to label themselves (Thoits, 1985). For example, persons who are sick label themselves as ill in the hope that others will recognize this label and respond appropriately—by expressing sympathy, curing the illness, or excusing the sick person from normal activities and responsibilities. Deviants, then, sometimes label themselves before anyone else does and proceed to act in accordance with that label (Lorber, 1967).

Although a number of criticisms have been leveled against labeling theory, it persists as a powerful sociological perspective on deviance (Bazemore, 1985; Klein, 1986; Sommer et al., 1988). Much of the following discussion, in fact, is a reflection of the insights of labeling theory.

The Process of Social Control

Having defined deviance (and various theories of deviance), we now come to the problem of analyzing the reciprocal process of social control, which is an important part of labeling deviants. **Social control** refers to the process whereby a group or society enforces conformity to its demands and expectations. Social control involves those with power who seek (often successfully) to label as deviant those who do not conform. Those who develop labels and engage in the labeling process are the social control agents. Those successfully labeled are the deviants. From the perspective of labeling theory, deviants and social control agents cannot exist without each other. We also can differentiate between two broad types of social control agents: rule enforcers and rule creators (Becker, 1963).

Social control
Process by which a group/society enforces conformity to its demands and expectations

Acting as Rule Enforcers

When we think of rule enforcers, we generally think of the formal agents involved in the social control process—the police, the courts, prisons, even parents (Birenbaum and Sagarin, 1976). Arrest by police, conviction and imprisonment by the courts, and punishment by parents are all examples of the exercise of social control through rule

Rule enforcers
Those attempting to maintain social control through the use of undesirable labels

enforcement. Each of these social control agents is clearly implicated in the labeling process. Arrest and incarceration serve to label an individual as a murderer, thief, or rapist. Even parental admonishments can label a child lazy, dumb, or mean. **Rule enforcers** attempt to maintain social control and order through the threat or actual application of undesirable social labels.

Although most of us think of formal agencies when we think of rule enforcement, we are somewhat less likely to think of ourselves as rule enforcers. All of us, however, act as rule enforcers on a fairly regular basis in our day-to-day activities. If people around us violate a social norm, we act in a variety of ways to indicate that they have done so, in an effort to bring them back into line. We are likely to act as rule enforcers when we observe someone spitting on the floor, cutting in at the head of a line, or hassling an innocent passerby. Even a raised eyebrow, a grimace, or a frown can serve the function of social control. We can also engage in more extreme forms of rule enforcement such as a raised voice, a clenched fist, or even a blow to the head. Such interpersonal social control devices, both subtle and blatant, are far more widespread than the formal means employed by the police, the courts, and other social control agencies.

Rule Creators and Social Change

Rule creators
Those who create the rules, norms, and laws

The **rule creator** devises the rules, norms, or laws. Without rule creators, we would have no deviance, since we would have nothing from which to deviate. This is what we mean when we say that deviance is created by social control agents who establish a society's normative system. While some laypersons may believe that norms, rules, and laws represent eternal and incontrovertible truths, sociologists see these rules as generally produced to protect the vested interests of the rule creators and those they represent.

A number of studies have shown that social rules are the product of the vested interests of social control agents. One illustration is found in Chambliss's analysis (1964) of the history of vagrancy laws—laws that came into being when feudalism was breaking up. Medieval landowners needed a large pool of cheap labor when they could no longer depend upon serfs to carry out their work. Vagrancy laws provided this cheap labor by forcing people to work in order to avoid being arrested for vagrancy. With the final breakdown of feudalism, the need for vagrancy laws disappeared. For a long time the laws lay dormant, little changed and rarely applied. However, as commerce and trade developed in Europe, the vagrancy laws were renewed and applied to different people. They were directed at the rogues and vagabonds who threatened to disturb the orderly flow of commerce by robbing and stealing. In short, vagrancy laws, first created to aid landowners, fell into disuse, only to be revived later and redefined to suit the new, powerful, commercial class. Vagrancy laws exemplify the fact that rules are the result of the vested interests of agents of social control.

Computer abuse
Unauthorized altering, stealing, or sabotaging someone else's computer data

Computer Abuse and Rule Creators.

A contemporary example of rule creation is found in the criminalization of computer abuse. **Computer abuse** is the unauthorized entry into someone else's computer data for the purpose of altering, stealing, or sabotaging it (Hollinger and Lanza-Kaduce, 1988). These acts are unusual types of deviance in that they can be committed without the use of force or even without the perpetrator's being physically present. The first law against such computer crime was passed in Florida in 1978. The interesting sociological question is why such laws came into existence.

Drawing by S. Gross; © 1987 The New Yorker Magazine, Inc.

The mass media played a key role in the development of computer crime laws. The fact is that few people would be aware of computer crime without the mass media's doing stories on them. The number of newspaper articles on computer crime, describing the threat it poses, has increased dramatically, as has public perception of computer crime as a serious problem. Unlike the case of vagrancy laws, no specific interest group played a central role in the passage of computer crime laws. (The news media have an interest in publishing stories on computer crime in order to help sell newspapers, but they have no vested interest in the passage of legislation against it.) A key role was played by state and federal legislators who were attracted to the issue by media attention and found in it a cause that would give them wide media exposure without alienating any powerful interest group. Thus, rules and laws may come into existence because of the action of groups with vested interests, but other forces (like the mass media) may also play a key role. Furthermore, laws may be created by interest groups, but they may also come into existence because social conditions (e.g., the rise of the computer, the increasing awareness of computer abuse) change and require new legislation (Hollinger and Lanza-Kaduce, 1988).

The Personal Experience of Deviance

Becoming Deviant

Although some people come to be labeled deviant without having committed a deviant act, we begin our discussion with the assumption that some act has been committed that some rule-enforcement agents consider deviant. Some people who commit a deviant act once or twice may never commit another; others will proceed only partway through the process of becoming deviant; still others move from primary deviance to secondary deviance (Lemert, 1967).

If an act of primary deviance is observed, the person committing it may be punished by rule-enforcement agents. Despite punishment, some people commit additional acts of primary deviance. Assuming that these acts are observed by social-control agents, further and probably more severe punishments will occur. Although punishment may deter some people, others will engage in still further acts of deviance and possibly develop hostility and resentment toward those who punish them. This leads to a crisis level in the community's ability to tolerate more deviance. The most likely result is some formal action by social-control agents that labels the individual. For some, this strengthens their deviant identity and increases their deviant conduct. Ultimately, the individual who moves through the entire process comes to accept deviant social status and attempts to adapt to it. The end product is secondary deviance, or a person whose life and identity are organized around a deviant label.

Although some people consciously enter into a deviant career, most seem to simply respond to circumstances and situations in which they find themselves (Lemert, 1972, p. 80).

Coping with Deviance—Goffman's Theory of Stigma

More than anyone else, Erving Goffman has contributed to our understanding of how people, having been labeled deviant, cope with their own deviance. Goffman's work was done primarily in the tradition of symbolic interaction theory. He was especially interested in the way people interacted with each other, and in the messages they were sending by their words and gestures. In one of his most influential books, he studied people with certain characteristics that others would find unusual, unpleasant, or deviant (Goffman, 1963). Goffman called these characteristics *stigmas,* and he was particularly concerned with how people who have stigmas, cope with them.

Goffman's analysis begins with physically stigmatized people and gradually introduces a wide array of other stigmas. In the end, readers realize that they have not been reading about a remote person who has a physical deformity, but about themselves. As Goffman (1963, p. 127) says: "The most fortunate of normals is likely to have his half-hidden failing, and for every little failing there is a social occasion when it will loom large, creating a shameful gap."

Discredited stigma A stigma that is known about and visible

Discreditable stigma A stigma that is unknown and not immediately visible

Goffman deals with two basic types of stigmatized individuals. The first type, the individual with a **discredited stigma,** "assumes his differentness is known about already or is evident on the spot." The second type, the individual with a **discreditable stigma,** assumes that his stigma "is neither known about by those present nor immediately perceivable by them" (Goffman, 1963, p. 4). Discredited or discreditable stigmas can take the form of physical deformities, as when a person has lost a limb; character blemishes, as when a person has a prison record or a history of mental illness; or membership in an ethnic or racial group that is often viewed negatively by others (gypsies, for example).

In Goffman's view, people with discredited stigmas (readily visible) face different problems from those with discreditable stigmas (not immediately obvious). With a discredited stigma, the person can be prepared for some expected (often hostile) responses in social interaction with other people. On the other hand, persons with discreditable stigmas often try to manage interaction so that others will not learn of their characteristic. Concealment often becomes cumbersome. For example, there is the case of Mrs. G. whose husband was in a mental hospital. In order to keep the neighbors from discovering

Tony Melendez, playing a guitar with his toes, is coping with what Goffman called *a discredited stigma*. Since his differentness is readily visible, he can anticipate, and be prepared for, the negative reactions of some of those who see him.

what she believed to be a stigma, she told them that he was in the hospital because of a suspected cancer. Every day she would rush to get the mail before her neighbors picked it up for her as they used to do. She abandoned second breakfasts at the drug store with the women in the neighboring apartments to avoid their questions. Before inviting her neighbors in, she hid any material that identified the hospital, and so on (Yarrow, Clausen, and Robbins, 1955, cited in Goffman, 1963, p. 89).

AIDS and Stigma. A major example of stigma in the United States today is AIDS. There is great fear of the disease and at least in some segments of American society, substantial hostility toward those with AIDS. In the early stages of the disease, AIDS patients have a discreditable stigma, since there are usually not any overt signs of the disease. Victims will then often attempt to manage information so that others do not learn that they have AIDS. However, as the disease progresses, concealment of the stigmatized characteristics becomes increasingly difficult. AIDS victims are likely to lose substantial amounts of weight, look unwell, require frequent hospitalization, and perhaps develop the visible skin lesions of Kaposi's sarcoma. In Goffman's terms, AIDS victims in the later stages of the disease have discredited stigma; their disease is very visible. Rather than concealing information, AIDS victims come to focus on managing the tension produced by people who know that they have the dreaded disease. They may be shunned by friends, may lose their jobs, and may be badly treated by health personnel. The social aspects of having AIDS are easily understood as a contemporary example of Goffman's insightful analysis of stigma.

Those who have AIDS often feel that they are shunned by the public because they have been stigmatized. Friends of AIDS victims often make special efforts to show their acceptance and support.

Leaving the Deviant Role

Once imposed, the deviant label is difficult and sometimes impossible to remove. However, many deviants do manage to shed the label and leave the deviant role. Our concern in this section is not with those who can escape the deviant label relatively easily (such as someone defined as slightly overweight, who can go on a diet), but rather with those whose label is difficult to remove. Although we will focus on alcoholics, the same points apply to many other deviant roles.

Delabeling
A deviant label is shed and replaced by an acceptable label

The problems of leaving a deviant role are illustrated by sociological studies of Alcoholics Anonymous (AA) (Trice and Roman, 1970; Denzin, 1986, 1987). In AA, one finds examples of successful **delabeling,** that is, cases in which alcoholics were able to shed their deviant label and replace it with a socially acceptable one, "recovering alcoholic."

Delabeling can occur in three basic ways:

1. Deviants can organize to change the rules, norms, or laws of society to make an offending behavior acceptable, as the gay liberation movement has done to delabel homosexuals.

2. Professionals, who frequently are the ones who initially apply a deviant label, also can establish delabeling ceremonies in which they publicly announce that an offending behavior has ceased to be deviant and an individual is eligible to return to the broader community. An event along these lines occurred when the American Psychiatric Association removed homosexuality from its list of mental illnesses (Spector, 1977).

3. Mutual-aid organizations can encourage the deviant individual to return to conformity to social norms. These organizations can also help create a socially acceptable stereotype about the reformed deviant. Alcoholics Anonymous is a mutual-aid organization that "provides opportunities for alcoholics to join together in an effort to cease disruptive and deviant drinking behavior in order to set the stage for the resumption of normal, occupational, marital, and community roles" (Trice and Roman, 1970, p. 539).

Alcoholics Anonymous uses various methods to help alcoholics shed their deviant label. AA believes that alcoholics have a biological predisposition to become alcoholics. This interpretation of the causes of alcoholism counters the alternate belief that alcoholics are responsible for their actions or that alcoholism is a form of mental illness. To help further in the delabeling process, AA argues that since alcoholics' deviance stems from their drinking, once they stop drinking, their deviant status ends. AA also has constructed a rather unusual repentant role. By admitting that they are alcoholics, alcoholics will supposedly embark on the road to delabeling and acquiring the new "more respectable role" of ex-alcoholic. AA also stresses the degradation of drinking. By showing how far down some alcoholics have descended, they set the stage for stories of glorious comebacks.

Although AA is more successful than most organizations in helping people leave a deviant role, few hard data are available on its success ratio. AA has been a middle-class organization with little attraction for individuals from the lower classes. And, it could be argued that voluntary membership makes AA successful because those who decide to join AA are the ones most motivated to solve their drinking problem. AA, however, does help some people modify or change their deviant label.

Crime: A Major Form of Deviance

In this final section we turn our attention to a significant aspect of deviant behavior: crime. **Crime** is deviant behavior that violates the law and is subject to formally sanctioned punishment by the larger society (U.S. Bureau of Justice, 1983, p. 2). The study of crime, criminal behavior, and the treatment of criminals is a subfield of sociology called criminology.

Crime
Deviance that violates the law and is punishable by the larger society

Types of Crime

One way of differentiating crimes is to distinguish between crimes against people and crimes against property. **Crimes against people** (or **violent crimes**) involve the threat of injury, or threat (or use) of force, against victims. Violent crimes include four major types:

Crimes against people (violent crime)
Threat or use of injury and force against victims

1. Murder and non-negligent homicide (all willful homicides as distinguished from deaths caused by negligence);
2. Forcible rape (including assault to rape, threat of force, and attempted rape);
3. Robbery (stealing or taking anything of value by force or threat of force);
4. Aggravated assault (assault with intent to kill or to do great bodily harm) (U.S. Department of Justice, 1988a).

Property crime
Crime aimed at gaining or destroying property unlawfully

Property crimes do *not* involve the threat of injury, or the threat (or use) of force, against victims; the objective is to gain or destroy property unlawfully. The following are the major types of property crime:

1. Burglary (breaking or unlawful entry into a structure with the intent to commit a felony or theft—includes attempts);
2. Larceny-theft (unlawful taking of another's property without force, violence, or fraud—excludes embezzlement and forgery);
3. Motor vehicle theft (theft or attempted theft of a motor vehicle);
4. Arson (willful and malicious burning of, or attempt to burn, houses, buildings, vehicles, personal property, and the like, of another person).

Index offenses (street crimes)
All crimes against people and property crimes

Felonies
More serious crimes punishable by a year or more in prison

Misdemeanors
Minor crimes punishable by less than a year in prison

White-collar crime
Crime committed by upper-status people in the course of their occupations

Political crime
Crime committed within or against a political system

Organized crime
Structured associations obtaining profits through illegal means

Victimless crime
Crime in which participants choose to be involved

Juvenile delinquency
Illegal or antisocial behavior on the part of a minor

The FBI calls all eight of these violent crimes and property crimes **index offenses.** They are also often called **street crimes**—a term used frequently in the mass media.

Another important way to differentiate crimes reflects the ways they are handled by the criminal justice system. **Felonies,** more serious crimes (e.g., homicide, rape, and robbery), are punishable by a year or more in prison. **Misdemeanors,** minor offenses (e.g., drunkenness, shoplifting, and disturbing the peace), are punishable by imprisonment for less than a year.

Although this section focuses on street crimes, at least five other major types of crime can be identified. A major social problem is **white-collar crime** (Braithwaite, 1985), or crime usually committed by upper-status people in the course of their occupations (e.g., computer data theft, embezzlement, consumer fraud, and bribery). Elite deviance, which we discussed earlier, is part of white-collar crime. Another type is **political crime,** which is misconduct and crime committed within or against a political system. As a result of government scandals such as Watergate, the Iran-Contra affair, and other questionable behavior of a variety of government officials (e.g., illegal campaign contributions and "influence peddling"), political crime is an issue of growing importance. Another facet of political crime is terrorism, which is an act carried out to influence or change existing governments. **Organized crime** refers to "those self-perpetuating, structured, and disciplined associations of individuals, or groups, combined together for the purpose of obtaining monetary or commercial gains or profits, wholly or in part by illegal means, while protecting their activities through a pattern of graft and corruption" (U.S. Bureau of Justice Statistics, 1983, p. 3). We usually think of the Mafia when we think of organized crime. In **victimless crime** (Schur, 1965) it is difficult to identify a victim: the participants choose to be involved in the activities (e.g., selling and buying pornography, prostitution). Finally, **juvenile delinquency** refers to illegal or antisocial behavior on the part of a minor.

Official Crime Statistics

The best-known crime statistics in the United States are gathered from official law enforcement agencies and collated and published by the FBI as the *Uniform Crime Reports* (U.S. Department of Justice, 1988a). Local police agencies send the FBI monthly and annual summary reports on crimes in their jurisdictions, which provide the basis for the *Uniform Crime Reports* statistics. These reports include data on the number of offenses discovered by, or reported to, these law enforcement agencies.

For 1987, according to the FBI, 13.5 million criminal offenses were reported to the police in the United States. Of these, about 12 million (about 89 percent) were *property* crimes—burglary, larceny, motor vehicle theft, and arson. The 1.5 million *crimes against people* (violent crimes) included approximately 20,000 homicides, 91,000 forcible rapes, 518,000 robberies, and 855,000 aggravated assaults. The vast majority of crimes in the United States are crimes against property and *not* crimes against people (U.S. Bureau of Justice Statistics, 1988a).

The great volume of crime in the United States is revealed by the frequency of various crimes. On the basis of the crimes reported in the *Uniform Crime Reports,* the FBI has prepared a Crime Clock, which is shown in figure 6–1. Among other facts, this clock shows that in the United States one violent crime is committed every 21 seconds, and one crime against property, every 3 seconds.

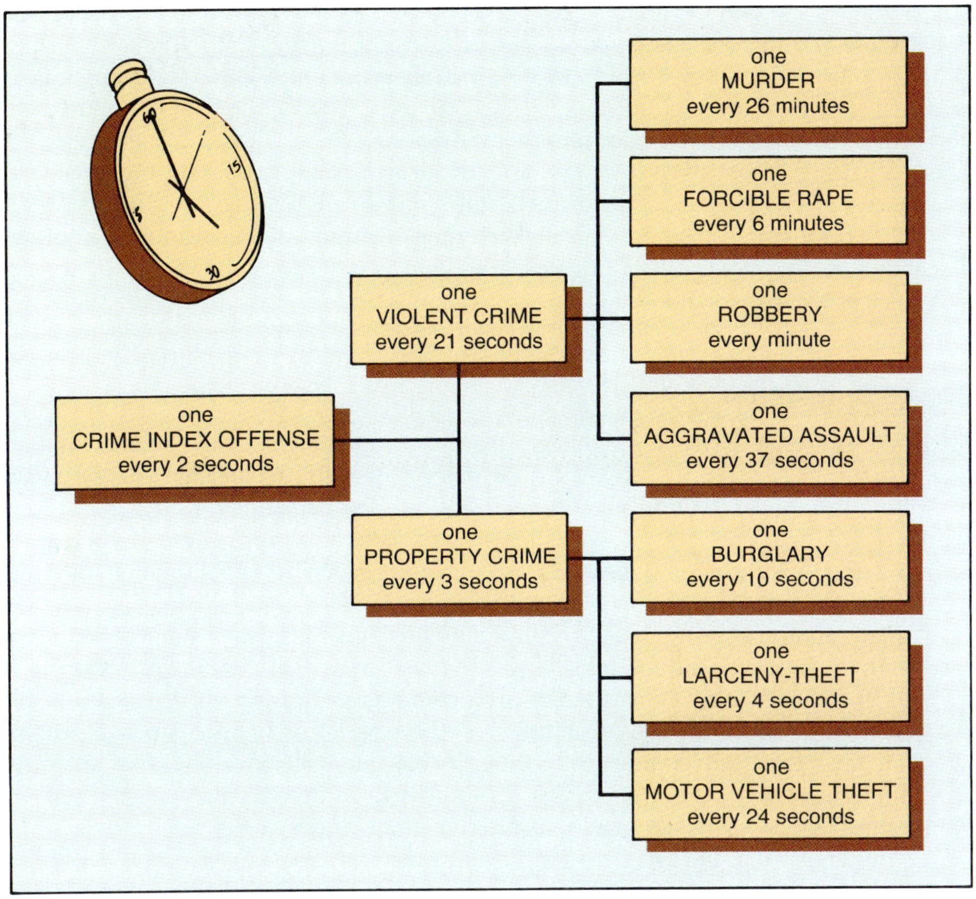

Figure 6–1. Crime Clock, 1987. The crime clock should be viewed with care. Being the most aggregate representation of Uniform Crime Report data, it is designed to convey the annual reported crime experience by showing the relative frequency of occurrence of the Index Offenses. This mode of display should not be taken to imply a regularity in the commission of these offenses; rather, it represents the annual ratio of crime to fixed time intervals.

Murder in the United States. The Crime Clock reveals that in the United States a murder is committed every 26 minutes. Compared to other countries, the United States has an exceptionally high homicide rate. For example, in 1980 23,000 murders were committed in the United States. This number of murders was committed by a U.S. population of 227 million people. As a comparison, the combined populations of Denmark, the Federal Republic of Germany, Greece, Japan, and Poland had populations totalling 230 million. Yet these countries had only slightly more than 2,300 murders (U.S. Bureau of the Census, 1984, p. 181). The United States has a murder rate that is ten times higher than these widely dispersed countries of the world.

Crime in Urban and Rural Areas

In 1987 the metropolitan areas of the United States (called MSAs, or Metropolitan Statistical Areas[1]) had a violent-offense rate of 720.0 per 100,000 (that is, there were 720.0 known violent offenses for every 100,000 people living in MSAs), whereas the comparable rate in rural areas was 177.7 per 100,000. In the same year, cities had a property-offense rate of 5,575 per 100,000, whereas the comparable rate in rural areas was 1,723 per 100,000 (U.S. Bureau of Justice Statistics, 1988a). These figures underscore the extent to which crime is disproportionately an urban problem. Violent crimes are about four times more likely to occur in cities than in rural areas, and the likelihood of property crimes in cities is about three times that in rural areas.

One probable reason for the higher crime rates in urban areas is the greater likelihood of drug use in cities. An increasing body of evidence shows that drug sales and use are related to crime rates.

Drugs and Crime

Drug abusers, especially heroin addicts, frequently commit crimes in order to support their habits. In New York City, almost 80 percent of men arrested for serious crimes tested positive for the recent use of illegal drugs. It is estimated that 40 percent of New York's 1,672 murders in 1987 were drug-related (Hamill, 1988). Furthermore, most people believe that official statistics greatly underestimate the actual amount of crime committed by drug addicts.

Many addicts become skilled criminal entrepreneurs in order to support their drug needs. Heroin addicts tend to specialize in a particular type of crime, which they refer to as their "main hustle." For males the most common main hustle is drug sales, while for females it is shoplifting and prostitution. As they specialize, they become increasingly adept at their particular crimes with the result that they will probably avoid arrest for committing the crime. This gives us one reason why the crime statistics on drug addicts, while still high, are probably greatly underestimated (Faupel, 1986).

The drug-crime linkage is rocking many American cities; in fact, it is disrupting many of the world's cities. Several Latin American countries are increasingly under the

---

[1] A Metropolitan Statistical Area "includes a central city of at least 50,000 population or an urbanized area of at least 50,000. The county containing the central city and contiguous counties having strong economic and social relationships to the central city and county are also included" (U.S. Department of Justice, 1988a, p. 317).

In the major cities of the United States, the sale and purchase of drugs has become so widespread that business is conducted openly. Drugs account for the majority of crimes in urban places today.

control of drug dealers. (See the box on Colombian drug traffickers: "Drugs and Political Power: The Case of Colombia.") Although the United States as a whole is not in the grip of drug gangs, certain areas of a number of our major cities are controlled by heavily armed drug gangs (with the Uzi machine gun as the weapon of choice) who deal viciously with those who seek to cut in on their territories. In Washington, D.C., during 1988, 372 people were killed, and approximately 80 percent of the deaths were described by the police as "drug related."

In order to deal with the increasing problems produced by drugs, a number of law enforcement and political leaders such as Kurt Schmoke, the Mayor of Baltimore, have urged decriminalization of drugs. Decriminalization means that using drugs would not be a crime, and some agency of the government would dispense drugs to those who wanted them (perhaps even free of charge). Those who support decriminalization do not usually support the *legalization* of drugs, which would allow private business to sell drugs that are now illegal (e.g., cigarette companies could sell marijuana cigarettes).

The interest in decriminalizing drugs stems from a belief that little can be done at the moment about the seemingly insatiable demand for drugs in the United States. Slogans such as "Just say no" are not likely to have much of an impact on hardcore drug abusers. Furthermore, it is impossible to completely seal off the borders of the United States in order to cut off the supply of drugs. Therefore with little to be done about demand or supply, decriminalization might be tried.

Decriminalization would squeeze the criminal element out of the business because, if the government dispensed drugs at no cost, or at a nominal cost, the profits would be taken from the illegal drug business. The presumption is that illegal drug dealers would lose interest in supplying drugs to addicts if they could not make enormous profits.

Cross-National Perspectives

Drugs and Political Power: The Case of Colombia

One of the most ominous developments in the arena of drugs is the degree to which Latin American countries are coming to be controlled by the drug kings. Government officials who stand up to, and attempt to arrest and prosecute, the drug lords often find themselves in grave danger, and many have been killed for their efforts. In Colombia alone, between 1985 and 1988, the drug cartels have killed an attorney general, a minister of justice, more than fifty judges, and more than a dozen journalists. In their efforts to control drug sellers, more than 400 police and military personnel have been killed. Any Colombian official who speaks out against the drug traffickers is likely to receive death threats. Many end up on a death list (Isikoff and Robinson, 1989). The result is that fewer and fewer government officials are willing to oppose the drug kings.

Not only are the governments less willing to oppose the drug kings, but the drug kings are *becoming* the government. The most notorious example is the leader of Panama, General Manuel Noriega. Beginning in 1988 the United States launched a campaign to oust Noriega, who was reputed to be a leading figure in the international drug trade. Among other acts, the United States imposed a variety of economic sanctions against Panama, including a refusal to pay Panama Canal tolls. Despite years of trying to topple Noriega, however, he has remained in political power in Panama.

Colombia supplies about 80% of the cocaine smuggled into the United States and earns between $2.5 and $3.0 billion from the business. In fact, the drug business is now larger than Colombia's other famous product—coffee. A leader of one Colombian drug cartel is Rodriguez Gacha. Gacha lives in a small town with his private military-style defense force of 110 gunmen. In addition, he controls the city government, which has responsibility for the transfer and promotion of police officers. Recently, Gacha's cartel participated in local elections and gained control over five more towns in the northern part of the country. This area could easily be turned into a "drug state" within the nation of Colombia. Beyond control over local governments, drug traffickers control one-twelfth of the productive farmland, one of Bogota's four main television stations, a nationwide chain of radio stations, car dealerships, office buildings, discount drug stores, and at least six of the nation's professional soccer teams. Said an executive of one of the country's largest newspapers: "These people are more powerful than the state" (Isikoff and Robinson, 1989).

Further buttressing the power of the drug lords is the fact that they employ many people who owe their livelihoods to them. In addition, the drug cartels have engaged in "narco-philanthropy," that is, giving money to the poorest members of society who, in turn, feel deeply indebted to and are ardent supporters of the drug traffickers. Another Colombian drug lord, Pablo Escobar, built 450 homes with running water, electricity, and telephone service—all rarities for the poor in Latin America. No one in the *barrio* has ever paid any rent. As a result, one of the people who lives in this *barrio* said: "We love Don Pablo [Escobar]. . . . He is a man of great tenderness" (*Washington Post*, 1989). A nine-year-old boy said: "He is the father of us all" (*Washington Post*, 1989). Not only is Escobar loved, but he is a member of the Colombian Congress and *Forbes* magazine rates him the fourteenth wealthiest person in the world.

While we may think of these problems occurring in distant lands, there are growing signs that American drug dealers, too, are growing more powerful. There are mounting concerns that the police in the United States are outgunned by the drug gangs. Does what has happened in Latin America represent the future of the United States? Not likely, but it seems clear that drug traffickers who grow more powerful will seek greater legitimacy.

It is possible to interpret what has taken place in Latin America, and what could happen in the United States, from the point of view of Marxian theory. That is, one basic Marxian view is that those people in society who control the means of economic production are likely to control the government and the minds of the people. Marx, of course, focused on legitimate capitalists, but the drug lords can be seen as illegitimate capitalists who own the means (that is, the drug factories) of drug production. Given this power base, they are able to exercise control over the government and over the minds of the people through television and radio stations and newspapers they own.

ISIKOFF, MICHAEL and EUGENE ROBINSON. "Colombia's Drug Kings Becoming Entrenched." *Washington Post*, January 8, 1989.
"Drug Lord's Largesse Wins Friends." *Washington Post*, January 8, 1989.

Decriminalizing Drugs: The Dutch Experience. Those who advocate decriminalization cannot take much heart from the experience of the Netherlands. The Dutch have had a very liberal attitude toward drugs. Designated shops dispense marijuana. Amsterdam has a city-owned houseboat where cocaine and heroin are openly used. Specially designed buses travel around the city and dispense methadone at regular locations. In spite of this liberalness, or perhaps because of it, crime in Amsterdam has risen dramatically, with hard drug users blamed for the vast majority of the crimes. Drug abusers from many nations have gravitated toward Amsterdam because of its liberal policies. Some businesses have been hurt, and the city's image as a tourist attraction has been tarnished.

The American Justice and Penal Systems

Americans today expect that people who have been convicted of crimes will spend time in jail or prison; however, it has not always been that way. During the colonial period most convicted criminals were fined, whipped, or confined in stocks. If their crimes were serious enough, they were hanged. The colonists did not conceive of imprisoning criminals for a specified period of time (Rothman, 1971). Only after colonial times did the idea of imprisoning criminals become an accepted practice.

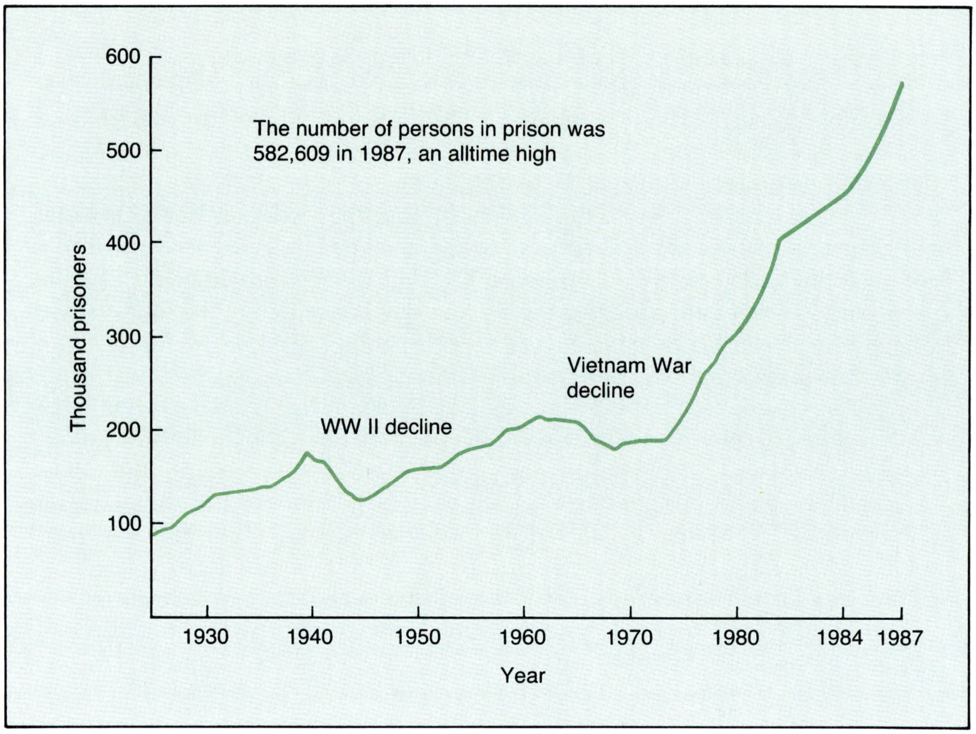

Figure 6–2. Number of Persons in Prison: 1925–1987. (*Sources:* U.S. Bureau of Justice Statistics, *Report to the Nation on Crime and Justice* (Washington, D.C.: U.S. Department of Justice, 1983); U.S. Bureau of Justice Statistics, *Prisoners in 1987* (Washington, D.C.: U.S. Department of Justice, 1988c).)

In the United States today the overcrowding of prisons has become a serious problem. The population of state and federal prisons in 1987 was 582,609 (U.S. Bureau of Justice Statistics, 1988). In the 1980s the number of people in prison grew by more than a quarter of a million, an increase of 76 percent. (See figure 6–2 for the growth of prison inmates since the 1920s.) One striking change is the increase in the number of female prisoners, which has grown faster than male inmates in every year since 1981.

The High Cost of Imprisonment. Unfortunately, the mere custody of prisoners (let alone treatment) is very expensive. In 1983 (the last date for which data are available), municipal, county, state, and federal governments spent approximately $10.4 billion for corrections (U.S. Department of Justice, 1988b). This is more than a quadrupling of the $2.3 billion spent on such facilities a decade earlier, in 1973 (*Sourcebook of Criminal Justice Statistics—1983*, 1984, pp. 2–3). Beyond correctional costs, the costs of police, courts, prosecutors, and public defenders swelled the total cost of the U.S. justice system in 1983 to almost $40 billion.

Specific deterrence Specific punishment supposed to deter a person from committing future crimes

Arrest and Imprisonment as Deterrents to Crime. The threat of imprisonment is supposed to serve as a deterrent to crime. We can differentiate between two types of deterrence. In **specific deterrence** the actual punishment of an individual is supposed to deter him/her from committing other crimes in the future. **General deterrence** involves the threat of punishment and the idea that people will not commit crimes because they fear they will be caught and sent to prison (Miranne and Gray, 1987).

General deterrence
The threat and fear of punishment that is supposed to prevent crime

The question posed by specific deterrence is whether an offender will be more or less likely to commit another crime after arrest or punishment. A recent study shows that arrested offenders will be less likely to commit a future crime than offenders who are released by the police. This was true for novice (first-time) offenders, but it was especially true of experienced offenders (Smith and Gartin, 1989). Persons who are arrested for criminal acts are less likely to commit a crime at a later date than those persons who are released by the police. This conclusion is nearly the same as the field experiment described in chapter 2, in which men arrested for domestic violence offenses are less likely to repeat their offenses than men who are not arrested (Sherman and Berk, 1984).

Although arrests seem to deter people from future criminal acts, the same is not true for imprisonment. One study has shown that the severity of punishment (imprisonment) does not reduce the likelihood of a return to crime; being imprisoned actually *increases* the likelihood of another criminal offense (Shannon, 1980). Other studies have shown that about one-third of the people who serve time in prison, and are released, return to prison at a later date. This is called **recidivism** (Waldo and Griswold, 1979). If one-third of the people who spend time in prison are not deterred from further crime, it suggests that something about the prison experience may lead to further crime for some people. Moreover, even though it might be supposed that prison would be a special deterrent for white-collar crime, a recent study has suggested that even white-collar criminals are not deterred from future crime by prison sentences (Moore, 1987).

Recidivism
Reimprisonment for crimes committed after having been previously released

Summary

Deviance is socially defined, which means that whenever most of the people in a given society, or social group, consider a behavior deviant, it will be deviant. It can be shown that many behaviors that were at some time acceptable are now deviant; similarly, many behaviors that were deviant at an earlier time are now acceptable. Deviant behavior can often serve to define for the society what is and is not acceptable behavior.

A number of theories of deviance exist: strain theory, deviance as learned behavior (differential association and subcultural), conflict theory, and labeling theory. Each one has a different perspective on deviant behavior.

From a social control perspective, there are attempts to keep most people in conformity with the prevailing norms of the society. Although the most powerful people in the society are most likely to define acceptable and deviant behavior, everyone at some time or another acts as rule enforcers and rule creators.

Three different stages of a career of deviance can be defined. The first stage is becoming deviant, the second is coping with deviance, and the third is leaving the deviant role. Important social aspects are involved in all three of these stages.

Crime is the most attention-getting aspect of deviant behavior. Several distinct types of crime can be defined, including crimes against people (violent crimes), property crime, white-collar crime, political crime, organized crime, victimless crime, and juvenile delinquency. Most crime in the United States is crime against property, but this country also has a high murder rate, especially compared to other nations. Crime is higher in urban areas than in rural areas, and this is probably attributable in part to the extensive use of drugs in today's society. Drug use has become such a serious problem in the United States that some law enforcement officials and political leaders have suggested decriminalizing drugs.

Persons convicted of crimes in the United States are expected to spend time in jail or prison. As a result, the American prison system has been charged with controlling ever-larger numbers of inmates. Serious questions have been raised about whether arrest and punishment will deter individuals from further crime. Recent studies have shown that arrest is a deterrent, but the severity of punishment is not.

CRITICAL THINKING

1. Use examples from the chapter to illustrate that deviant behaviors are socially defined behaviors that may vary from group to group.
2. What determines the nature of deviant behavior in a society or social group?
3. According to the structural-functionalists, how might deviant behavior have a positive societal function?
4. Depending on your cultural group, how might certain behaviors represent both conformity and deviance?
5. How can sociology be used to explain the extreme behavior of certain British soccer fans?
6. Use examples from the chapter to explain how conflict theorists explain deviant behavior. From the perspective of conflict theory, how does social class influence society's response to deviance?
7. How would a labeling theorist respond to a mother's statement that "her young son was just naturally naughty?" Would the sociologist consider her son's behavior an example of primary or secondary deviance?
8. In what ways have you acted as a rule enforcer in your day-to-day activities?
9. Give examples of rules that are produced to protect the vested interests of the rule creators in the following social organizations: United States Congress, high schools, prisons.
10. Use a daily newspaper to identify examples of the following types of crimes: property crimes, misdemeanors, white-collar crime, political crime, and organized crime. Compare society's punishments for each of these types of offenses.

CHAPTER

7

Sexual Behavior from a Sociological Perspective

A NOTE FROM THE AUTHORS: *This chapter on sexual behavior has a special purpose at this point in the book. The first six chapters have introduced you to some fundamental concepts and ideas of sociology. Throughout the rest of the book, many of the concepts you have learned, such as values, norms, roles, reference groups, and so on, will help you to analyze and understand various aspects of social life. Similarly, the sociological ideas introduced in the preceding chapters will continue to provide insights about human social behavior in the remaining chapters. As an example, a fundamental sociological idea is that human behavior is influenced by cultural values, by social norms, by membership in groups and organizations, and by the verbal and nonverbal symbols that we share with other people. This chapter on sexual behavior will present applications of many of the basic concepts and fundamental ideas of sociology.*

Sexual behavior is a strategic area to choose for applying sociological concepts because it is explained so frequently by biological characteristics or psychological mechanisms. Although both biology and psychology are important in understanding sexual behavior, we will show that sociological concepts and ideas are also significant. With this approach we hope to strengthen your understanding of these concepts and ideas and, most important, give you the experience of seeing how helpful and relevant a sociological perspective can be.

- Sexuality is a basic human characteristic.
- Sexual behavior is universal, found in every society.
- Sexual behavior at its most fundamental level is a physical and biological act.

These facts are nearly indisputable, and as such they seem to suggest that a sociological perspective might have little relevance to sexuality and sexual behavior. Yet in chapter 3 we considered the people of Staphorst who insisted that their children have premarital sex before marriage; this case reveals how important cultural customs can be in determining sexual behavior. To demonstrate more fully the importance of cultural norms and values, we begin this chapter with a brief examination of how much sexual behavior, and even sexuality, varies from one society to another. These cultural variations will make it clear that we learn much of our sexual behavior from the cultures of the societies in which we live (Reiss, 1986).

Cultural Differences in Sexual Behavior

The culture of every society defines, limits, and controls sexual behavior. Even the boundaries of what is, and what is not, sexual are defined by the culture. Some societies exist in which a brother and sister eating at the same table is considered a mildly sexual type of act and is therefore prohibited (Davenport, 1977). In the United States, of course, nothing is sexual about a brother and sister eating a meal together, even if they are alone.

In contrast, other societies have patterns of sexual behavior that we would consider unusual or unthinkable—though we would agree that the behaviors are sexual. It is well known that in the classical period of Greek history (500 to 300 B.C.) many Greek men had sexual relations with young boys. Often these men were teachers or military men, and the boys were their students or apprentices. Many of the men had wives and had fathered children, obviously having had heterosexual relations, but that fact did not preclude sexual relationships with boys as well.

Although the practice of having sexual relations with young boys was widespread in classical Greece, it was not accepted universally. Aristotle, for example, one of the great philosophers of that era, thought that men who engaged in such relationships were depraved.

A similar cultural pattern has been observed among the Azande people of the Southern Sudan in Africa, where the men also routinely had sexual relations with young boys. Among the Azande the unmarried warriors had young boys who lived with them as personal aides. A boy would take care of the daily needs of his "husband," which included the soldier's sexual needs (Evans-Prichard, 1970).

Another cultural variation in sexual behavior is found in the way husbands and wives relate to each other during sexual intercourse. In chapter 3 we saw that among the Yanomamo people of the Amazon Valley, violence is common between husbands and wives, and this violence extends into their sexual relations. Similarly, the Gusii of southwestern Kenya define sexuality as a hostile and antagonistic relationship between men and women. Both sexes regard intercourse as a situation in which the man overcomes the natural resistance of the woman. Women are expected to frustrate men with sexual taunts and insults. Gusii men are said to experience greater sexual gratification when women protest and cry during intercourse (Davenport, 1977).

The Gusii view of sexuality is taught to the children when they are young and is especially emphasized at the time of puberty rituals. If girls display any signs of sexuality when they are young, they are punished; signs of sexuality among young boys, however, are both encouraged *and* punished. When these youngsters of the Gusii reach adolescence, they are taught sexual antagonism through the puberty rituals. The adolescent boys are circumcised at a secret initiation ceremony, after which the adolescent girls are brought to where the boys are. The girls are naked and perform erotic dances, while making negative remarks about the boys' mutilated genitals. The girls' dances are supposed to arouse the boys sexually, giving them erections, which will cause them pain since they have just been circumcised (Davenport, 1977). It is little wonder, then, after these childhood and adolescent experiences, that the Gusii think of sexual relations in the context of antagonism and hostility.

In contemporary Islamic societies, sexual relations between husbands and wives are greatly influenced by interpretations of female sexuality based on the *Koran*. Women's sexual needs are seen as very strong, and husbands must meet these needs if their wives are to remain virtuous. Female sexuality is often viewed as dangerous because women, if not under strict control, can be "fatal attractions" for men. A married man can too easily be distracted from his social and religious obligations by a woman other than his wife. Therefore, all women must be kept secluded in their homes, and when they enter public places their faces should be veiled and their bodies completely covered with clothing (Mernissi, 1987).

In Islamic societies, women's sexual needs are seen as very strong; therefore, women must remain in their homes or keep their bodies and faces covered when in public. This will help to protect them from the advances of men.

Cultural Definitions of What Is Sexual

Not only does sexual behavior vary from one culture to another but definitions of what is considered "sexy" differ as well. For example, in American society, popular magazines often publish articles that claim to reveal which parts of the male and female anatomy are most sexy. Females are often said to favor the buttocks as the sexiest part of a male. Males are similarly attracted to the *derriere* as one of the sexiest parts of a woman, but breasts and legs also evoke some favor. Apparently, almost no American males select the armpits as one feature of a woman that arouses them sexually. Fewer still choose the neck as sexually exciting. Yet there are males in different parts of the world who would select these as the sexiest parts of a woman's body. Indeed, they would think it strange that men in other societies would not consider them sexy. For instance, among the Abkhasians, a group of people living in the southern part of the Soviet Union, the female's armpit is especially exciting sexually (Benet, 1974). It would be unthinkable among the Abkhasians for a woman to allow a man other than her husband to see her armpits. Japanese males, on the other hand, consider a woman's neck as a particularly sexual part of her body. They are especially attracted to a long, swanlike neck. For a number of years the Hollywood film actress Audrey Hepburn was very popular among Japanese men, precisely because one of her most striking features was a long, slim neck. Although this feature might have appealed to some American males, it is doubtful that very many would have seen it as sexually arousing.

Women's breasts are considered objects of sexual attraction and erotic stimulation in almost every society, even those where the breasts are normally uncovered. However,

The beach wear of American women at the turn of the century reveals the different standards of attractiveness in earlier times.

among the Mangaia of Polynesia, women's breasts have no sexual significance. Because the males of this society do not find them erotic, women's breasts have no place in heterosexual foreplay or in sexual communication (Davenport, 1977).

History provides other examples of diversity regarding what was considered sexual. In Hawaii, before the influence of Western cultural ideals, extremely obese women were viewed as highly erotic, especially among the aristocrats and members of royalty (Davenport, 1977). In the United States, as recently as the beginning of this century, if one were to judge from the photographs of women who were considered sexually appealing, the ideal woman's body was much heavier and well rounded than the ideal body of today. The beginning of the twentieth century was also a time when American women wore floor-length dresses, which made the sight of a woman's ankle or calf sexually arousing to males.

Although the sexual attractions of females are most often noted by contemporary Western people, sometimes the males of a society are the objects of sexual attention. Among the Wodaabe, a nomadic tribe in Central Africa, young males are the center of attraction, especially during ceremonies held several times a year. Dances are performed by the young males, who compete with each other to be chosen the most beautiful and charming (Beckwith, 1983). Their costuming and makeup, along with the parading and performing before tribe members, are comparable to a Miss America contest in the United States. The most handsome young men of the tribe stand in a kind of chorus line where their attractiveness is judged largely on the basis of their exaggerated facial expressions. An observer describes the scene as follows: "Eyes roll; teeth flash; lips purse, part and tremble; cheeks, inflated like toy balloons, collapse in short puffs of breath" (Beckwith, 1983, p. 508).

These facial features, especially the large rolling eyes, are particularly alluring to the women of the tribe, who may cry out in ecstasy when a man performs well. The charm and magnetism of these facial gestures may bring multiple wives to the most handsome young men of the tribe. American women would probably not find these facial gyrations sexually attractive, but the Wodaabe women clearly do.

These examples of cultural variations in sexual practices illustrate some of the many ways in which sexual behavior is culturally defined. Variations in definitions can also be seen in the context of a single society *over time,* when there are changing definitions of sexuality. As an example, definitions of sexuality and norms governing sexual behavior have changed dramatically in the United States throughout its history, as a brief review will reveal.

Historical Views of Sexuality in the United States

The historical evidence we have about the sexual lives of nineteenth century married couples in the United States comes from diaries, journals, reports of doctors and midwives, folk songs, sayings, stories, and poems. As we will see later in this chapter, social research on sexual behavior, especially the systematic use of interviews and questionnaires (social surveys), were not undertaken until well into the twentieth century. Although the qualitative historical evidence we have must therefore be accepted cautiously, it does give us some insight into the views of many men and women of that time.

Social historians believe that marital sex was very different in the United States a century or two ago. In the nineteenth century the authority and supremacy of the husbands and fathers in many families (called **patriarchy**) dominated most of family life. In regard to sex, patriarchy meant that many husbands simply dictated when they would have sexual intercourse with their wives. In this powerful position, men often showed little regard for either the feelings of their wives or the physical repercussions of their actions (Shorter, 1982).

Patriarchy
Authority and supremacy of husbands and fathers giving them dominance over family life

In the patriarchal family the husband and father dominated family life, including the sexual life of the married couple.

This example of the attitudes prevailing in the nineteenth century about marital sex shows one way in which sociological theories can be important in understanding sexual behavior. Conflict theory, which was introduced in chapter 1, emphasizes the importance of power and conflict in any social group, including the family. Power differences between husbands and wives, which were especially pronounced in this patriarchal era, made marital sexual relations an area of conflict within the family.

The indifference that many nineteenth century husbands displayed to the physical and emotional well-being of their wives is shown in the words of one social historian who said: ". . . intercourse in the traditional family was brief and brutal, and there is little evidence that women derived much pleasure from it" (Shorter, 1982, p. 9). Evidence reveals that many husbands did not abstain from having sex with their wives either during pregnancy or immediately after the birth of a child. Despite warnings of doctors and midwives that the health of women would be endangered during these periods, especially by infections, many wives reported with embarrassment that their husbands paid "no heed" (Shorter, 1982).

Of course, not every pre-twentieth century man behaved in this brutish and insensitive way. Certainly there were loving and considerate husbands who were sensitive to the emotional and physical feelings of their wives. We are describing only a general condition that prevailed in many marriages of that era.

And how did pre-twentieth century women regard sex? Many probably viewed it with fear because sexual intercourse often meant another pregnancy. Most women of the nineteenth century, especially those living in rural areas, had no knowledge of contraception or even of a safe period during their menstrual cycles. For women of a childbearing age, the only preventions against pregnancy were being pregnant already and—maybe—breastfeeding. An average married woman in the nineteenth century typically had seven or eight pregnancies, and perhaps as many as six live births. In addition to the difficulties of pregnancy itself, the very real danger of death during childbirth always existed. In the light of all these dangers, added to the insensitivity of many husbands, it is understandable that many married women would view sexual intercourse with apprehension and probably dread.

Another indication of the way definitions of sexuality have changed over time comes from the marriage manuals of the nineteenth and early twentieth centuries. One main theme found in marriage manuals of the 1800s was the belief that women have very little sexual desire. Women had sex with their husbands primarily because it was their wifely duty. An 1869 marriage manual asserted the following:

> As a general rule, a modest woman seldom desires any sexual gratification for herself. She submits to her husband, but only to please him and but by the desire of maternity . . . (Hayes, 1869, quoted in Gordon and Shankweiler, 1971, p. 460).

A second theme of nineteenth century marriage manuals is also reflected in the statement above—the claim that women are interested in sex only because of a desire for maternity. This is often called the **procreative view of sex**—sex for reproduction only.

Procreative view of sex
Sex viewed as for the purpose of reproduction only

Writers of this period, including many who were doctors, also tended to see sex as a "draining," "exhausting," and "debilitating" activity. Men, especially, were thought to have a "loss of vital body fluids" when they had sexual intercourse, leading to negative effects on health and vitality. The view that men lose strength and vital fluids from having sex is a widely held notion in other cultures around the world. Many Hindus in contemporary India believe that men are born with a fixed amount of semen, which must be conserved if a man is to live to an old age (Harris, 1981).

Not until the twentieth century did marriage manuals start to acknowledge that women as well as men could have sexual desires, and that they, too, could enjoy the physical pleasure of sex. In the nineteenth century, this idea was only grudgingly admitted, and women who revealed their sexual desires too openly were often labeled mentally ill or deviant. Deviant behavior, as we saw in the last chapter, depends on what people, at a particular time, consider deviant. Thus, although a woman of the nineteenth century who was actively interested in sex was considered deviant, in contemporary American society a woman who claimed to have *no* sexual desire would probably be the one considered deviant (Barker-Benfield, 1976).

As we consider these changing historical definitions of sexuality and different norms for appropriate sexual behavior, we should note that views about sexuality and sexual behavior are in some way a reflection of the general characteristics of the society in which they are found. The place of women in nineteenth century America was subordinate to that of the patriarchal male, so it is not surprising that sexual life would reflect this societal feature. But other general characteristics of society may also influence the nature of sexual behavior. We will consider this possibility next.

A Societal Perspective on Sexual Behavior

A basic sociological premise holds that the general nature of a society will shape and influence all types of behavior, including sexual behavior (Schur, 1988). In the case of the United States, it can be argued that sexual relations, as a reflection of the characteristics of the society generally, have become *depersonalized, commercialized,* and increasingly *coercive* and *aggressive*.

Depersonalization of Sex

Many social analysts have observed that social relations in modern society have become more and more impersonal. In chapter 4 we saw how the early sociologist Toennies used the term *gesellschaft* as a label for a type of contemporary society in which personal relations tend to be impersonal and based primarily on individual self-interest. A parallel feature of contemporary society is that many people are given much more personal freedom than are people who live in more close-knit traditional societies (Simmel, in Wolff, 1950). If these characteristics (impersonality, self-interest, and personal freedom) describe life in contemporary American society, and there is considerable evidence that they do, we might expect that they would also be found in sexual relations. Thus, the **depersonalization of sex** is defined as sexual interaction that is impersonal and self-interested.

Depersonalization of sex Sexual interaction that is impersonal and self-interested

There is little disputing the fact that, since the late 1960s in the United States, personal freedom with regard to sex has greatly increased (Reiss and Lee, 1988; Talese, 1980). The most obvious example has been the acceptance of sex as a recreational activity. Many Americans, especially in the 1970s, came to see sex as an activity they could engage in simply for the pleasure it gave them. Sex was viewed as just one more pleasurable form of recreation, with little or no meaning beyond the immediate expe-

The smug look combined with the message on the shirt indicate that this man thinks depersonalized sex is the ideal.

rience.[1] However, if sexual partners are seen only in terms of the pleasure they can provide, the relationship between the two people is very likely to be of no particular importance. Treating sexual acts and sexual partners as unimportant is the essence of depersonalized sex (Schur, 1988).

Commercialization of Sex

Commercialization of sex
Sex bought and sold as any other commodity of the marketplace

Commercialization prevails when everything can be bought and sold, when everything has a monetary value and can be purchased if one has the money to pay. The **commercialization of sex** refers to the fact that sex is bought and sold just like any other commodity in the marketplace. Americans are accustomed to purchasing their recreation, and since sex is seen by many as a form of recreation, it follows that sex is something to be purchased. Some obvious ways in which sex is purchased are prostitution, soft and hardcore pornography, erotic telephone services, R-rated and X-rated movies and videos, and subscriptions to sexually oriented television networks. Also included is a substantial market in sexually oriented clothing and other sexual paraphernalia that are widely advertised and displayed. Almost all of these sex-related products and services can be legally purchased (with the only exceptions being some extreme forms of pornography and prostitution).[2] It is estimated that the legal "sex industry" adds up to $5 billion yearly (Schur, 1988).

Another dimension to the commercialization of sex goes beyond the obvious commercial transactions for sex or sexually related materials. A widely held view exists

---

[1] Although many Americans came to view sex as recreational, that should not obscure the fact that most sexual behavior, in the context of a relationship, has some significance to the participants.

[2] Even prostitution is legal in a few Nevada counties.

The commercialization of sex has become a commonplace item on theater marquees, but now an even more blatant form of commercialization can be found on the television screen.

that says that women are often "purchased" and displayed as the sexual property of men. Sociologist Randall Collins has said that, "With male dominance, the principal form of sexual property is the male ownership of females" (Collins, 1971, pp. 7–8). Even in dating situations, when males pay for meals and entertainment, there is often the implicit assumption that the females owe something in return. That something may be sex.

Cross-Cultural Perspectives

Societal Reactions to Erotica and Pornography

The people of prehistoric times produced artifacts, drawings, and paintings showing their keen interest in the sexual features and sexual acts of males and females. Most of the major historical cultures of the world—Greece, Rome, India, China, Japan, Africa—have produced art or writing that depict sexual behavior and sexuality. In the contemporary world there is a continuing outpouring of paintings, sculptures, photographs, films, and writing about sexuality and sexual behavior. Despite the universality of interest in sexuality and sexual behavior, the societal responses to sexual representations and descriptions are extremely varied, and often the source of great controversy.

The very words used to describe visual representations and written descriptions of the human body and sexual acts indicate how differently people react to sexual subjects. It is common to hear people speak of *dirty pictures* and *dirty books,* words that often reflect the speaker's negative feelings. The word *pornography* also carries a negative connotation about sexually explicit materials. On the other hand, the word *erotica* is apt to indicate a neutral, or even positive, reaction to sexual images, objects, or writing.

Sociologist Ira Reiss (1986) defines *erotica* as any material designed predominantly for sexual arousal. *Pornography* is the term applied to erotic material that is distasteful or obscene to the person who uses the label. From this perspective erotica is a more general, neutral, or less judgmental term, while pornography indicates that certain material is considered beyond a societal or personal standard of acceptability.

The differences and changes in the social acceptability of erotica is a sociologically interesting issue, because the standards and the justifications for acceptability are so varied. When Michelangelo, the Italian Renaissance artist, was asked by Pope Clement VII to paint a biblical scene on the wall behind the altar of the Sistine Chapel (twenty-five years after he had completed the ceiling paintings) he painted all the figures, including Christ and the Virgin Mary in the nude. The Pope, however, considered these paintings objectionable, and, although he first wanted the paintings destroyed, he later agreed to have another painter (nicknamed by the Italians, the *breeches-maker*) add clothing to the figures (Bullough, 1976; Lewinsohn, 1958). Indeed, over the next two hundred years other painters continued to add clothing to the figures in Michelangelo's painting.

Late in his life Michelangelo painted *Leda and the Swan* for an Italian duke. This painting also depicted a nude woman, and if it had survived it would be invaluable today. It was ultimately burned, however, because the authorities of the time considered it objectionable (Bullough, 1976; Lewinsohn, 1958).

In India, many of the ancient temples of the Hindu religion are adorned with sculptures of a sexual nature. These sculptures do not simply show nude human figures, but depict males and females engaging in sexual intercourse. In fact, these Indian temple sculptures are noted for the variety of sexual positions of the participants.

In contemporary times, in many societies, sculptures and paintings of male and female bodies and people engaged in sexual acts continue to be produced and displayed. Especially important today are the erotic materials produced by photographers and the motion picture industry. Often, this form of erotic material makes no claim to being art, but is openly aimed at sexual stimulation. Reiss (1986) has called this form of sexual material *commercial erotica*. In the late 1960s Denmark and Sweden were among the first countries to change their laws about erotic materials, making them easily available to their citizens. In these countries it has been possible for many years to purchase virtually any kind of visual or literary erotic material.

Many countries of the world, including the United States, have followed the lead of the Scandinavian countries and have made commercial erotica available to the public. The major exceptions are the Islamic and Communist countries (Russia, China, and Cuba, for example) where erotic materials are severely restricted.

In the United States the widespread availability of erotic materials is opposed and decried by several groups who consider such material pornographic. Among the most vocal opponents are religious leaders and political conservatives whose objections are on religious and moral grounds. But feminists, also, have raised an important challenge to pornographic materials, claiming that they perpetuate the subjugation, objectification, and debasement of women (Reiss, 1986).

BULLOUGH, VERN L. *Sexual Variance in Society and History*. New York: John Wiley & Sons, 1976.
LEWINSON, RICHARD. *A History of Sexual Customs: From Earliest Times to the Present*. New York: Harper & Row, 1958.
REISS, IRA L. *Journey into Sexuality: An Explanatory Voyage*. Englewood Cliffs, N.J.: Prentice Hall, 1986.

Our understanding of the commercialization of sex in the United States can be enhanced if we apply the insights of structural-functional theory. As we have just seen, the commercialization of sex is a structural feature of the society that maintains and perpetuates the exploitation of women. In functional theory terms, this commercialization is functional for males who often control more economic resources, but it is dysfunctional for females because it continues their exploitation.[3]

Functional theory also stresses how societies tend toward a consistency and integration among different structures. In the present case the general commercialization of many aspects of social life, but especially entertainment, is consistent with the commercialization of sex. The commercialization of sex "fits" with the commercialization of many other aspects of contemporary American society—a point Schur also makes.

Sexual Coercion

The third aspect of sexual behavior in American society is **sexual coercion,** which is forced sex, or rape. Rape is alarmingly widespread. Official statistics on rape reflect only reported cases, and the record shows 90,000 attempted or actual rape cases in the United

Sexual coercion
Sex through force, or rape

[3] The usefulness of structural-functional analysis is not pointed out by Schur, but the argument presented here reflects his presentation (Schur, 1988, p. 13).

States in 1986 (U.S. Bureau of the Census, 1987). Some people maintain that a level of "sexual terrorism" exists in contemporary American society that allows males to frighten, and therefore dominate, females. Sexual terrorism makes it necessary for women to ask themselves ". . . whether to go to the movies alone, where to walk or jog, whether to answer the door or telephone" (Sheffield, 1987, p. 171).

Official statistics on rape undoubtedly understate the case, however, since many instances of rape are not reported to authorities. Many women are forced to have sex against their will by men they know, such as acquaintances, friends, former boyfriends and former husbands, as well as current dates and romantic partners (Brownmiller, 1975). The prevalence of date-rape or acquaintance-rape is literally uncounted, but surveys have shown that one-fourth to one-half of all women will experience rape or attempted rape in their lifetimes (Schur, 1988, p. 140). Rapes committed or attempted by acquaintances and dates are obviously related to the view that women are often regarded as sexual property.

An extreme view of coercive sex is expressed by feminist Andrea Dworkin, who argues that almost all acts of sexual intercourse are a demonstration of male domination (Dworkin, 1987). Dworkin's view is a minority position, but it does point to the potential for domination and coercion in sexual behavior.

According to Schur's societal analysis of sex in American society, both the society at large and sexual behavior in particular are characterized by depersonalization, commercialization, and coercion/aggression. The fundamental assumption of this view is that the characteristics of a society will be reflected in the sexual realm. Although the resulting depiction of sex in American society may not be accepted by everyone (it is controversial), it does shed some light on contemporary American sexual patterns.

The Sexual Norms of Societies

All societies have rules and norms about sexual behavior. These norms sometimes require people to act in certain ways (have sexual intercourse if they marry, for instance); but more often, norms relating to sex prohibit certain behaviors. One prohibitory norm that has special sociological significance is the rule that prohibits sexual intercourse between closely related individuals—or the **incest taboo.**

Incest taboo
Prohibitions of sexual intercourse between closely related individuals

Every known *contemporary* society has a norm (almost always supported by laws) that prohibits sexual relations (and, of course, marriage) between close kin members. In every case the norm prohibits sex between parents and children and between siblings. With regard to other relatives, the rules are much less consistent. In many societies first cousins are prohibited from marrying and thus from having sexual relations. However, even in the United States, some states permit first cousins to marry; and in many of the societies studied by anthropologists, marriage between cousins is actually preferred.

The prohibition of sex between close relatives has been nearly universal, but in a number of historical circumstances it has been allowed (Hopkins, 1980; Middleton, 1962). Generally, such exceptions to the rule permitted members of royal families to marry each other in order to retain royal power. In the Egyptian, Incan, and Hawaiian royal families, marriages between immediate family members kept the royal bloodline "pure," and retained privilege and power in the family. In one documented historical period, however, marriage between brothers and sisters, as well as fathers and daughters,

Among the royal families of Egypt it was common for brothers and sisters to marry each other, and when the Romans ruled Egypt the same was true for commoners.

occurred frequently among commoners. When the Romans ruled Egypt during the first to the third centuries A.D., such marriages were widely recorded. By allowing marriage between family members, Egyptians prevented family wealth and property from being confiscated by the Roman authorities through inheritance laws (Hopkins, 1980).

Although the norms prohibiting incest are nearly universal and applicable to both genders, a pervasive complex of norms is applied differently to males and females. This complex of norms, called the **double standard,** gives males much more sexual freedom than females, especially when it is applied to young unmarried men and women. The following are the most familiar specifics of the *traditional* double standard:

Double standard
Sexual norms that give males more sexual freedom than females

- Young men may have sexual intercourse before marriage; young women should not.
- Young men may have sexual intercourse with women even when there is no emotional feeling or commitment; young women may have sexual intercourse when they are in love, or when there is a mutual commitment.
- Young men may have multiple sexual partners; young women should not have multiple partners.

- Young men may have sexual intercourse with women who are much lower in social status, or are "immoral" women; if a young woman were to have sexual intercourse with a man of lower status, it would be viewed even more negatively than with a man of her own status.
- Young men may have sexual intercourse for recreation or to gain sexual experience and expertise; young women are not allowed to have these motives or objectives.

Because of the undeniable liberalization of sexual norms in the United States during the 1970s, the rigidity of the double standard of sexual behavior has been somewhat relaxed. Perhaps among some individuals, and in certain groups in the society, the double standard is not as strongly enforced as it once was, but evidence shows that it still influences people's reactions to women who violate the norms. In the words of two researchers who have looked carefully at American sexual behaviors and norms, the double standard "remains very much alive" (Blumstein and Schwartz, 1983). They point out that some women have claimed for themselves the same sexual freedoms as men enjoy, and they may have been successful in freeing themselves from guilt and self-recrimination for their liberated sexual behavior. However, ". . . when they act on their beliefs, they are treated differently from men by the people around them" (Blumstein and Schwartz, 1983).

The liberalization of sexual norms has modified some of the more rigid aspects of the double standard, but women are often still more constrained than men.

In an experimental study conducted among college students, researchers asked the subjects to evaluate a specific person on the basis of his or her sexual behavior. (The person was fictitious, but the subjects were led to think it was a real person.) As one aspect of the experiment, subjects were asked to evaluate either a male or a female who had a first sexual intercourse experience in a casual relationship at age 16. Both male and female subjects gave more negative evaluations to a female than to a male who had done so. The researchers concluded that some aspects of the double standard still exist (Sprecher et al., 1987).

Another kind of evidence that suggests the persistence of the double standard is found in the terminology that teenage boys and young men still often use to distinguish between "girls they would go out with for fun" and girls they would be serious about. Also, the array of slang names applied to males and females who are sexually active indicate many more negative labels for the females than the males. Even the preadolescent Little League boys studied by Gary Fine (1987) frequently referred to girls as "sluts" and "prosties" [apparently a reference to prostitutes]. After listening to and observing these preadolescent boys, Fine concludes: ". . . boys generally wish to be seen as sexually potent, whereas girls lose status by having the same reputation—the double standard is very much in existence in preadolescence" (Fine, 1987, p. 107).

The verbal symbols used by preadolescent boys demonstrate, once again, the importance of symbolic interaction theory. The symbols the boys used to refer to girls ("sluts" and "prosties") carry important meanings, and they obviously influence the boys' behavior. In contrast, some of these boys who were successful with girls were called "ladies' men" or "Casanovas," which were generally positive labels. In specific cases, boys were greatly influenced by negative labels that their friends applied to girls. If one boy referred to another boy's girlfriend as a "dog," for example, the boy might hide the relationship or stop seeing the girl completely (Fine, 1987, pp. 105–114).

The behavior of these preadolescent boys also shows, as we would expect from our discussion of peer socialization in chapter 5, that attitudes about sex (in this case, about the double standard) are learned from social sources. Of course, socialization by peers is just one of the socialization sources through which young people learn about sexual norms and sexuality. In the next section we will examine how sexual socialization occurs and how it shapes the sexual attitudes and behaviors of young people.

Socialization for Sex

Most Americans say that children should learn about sex from their parents. The general assumption is that if parents take responsibility for the socialization of their children regarding sex, the values of the children will be healthier and their behavior will be more responsible. The alternatives to parental socialization about sex are formal sex education programs in the schools, learning about sex from peers, and learning about sex (either directly or indirectly) from the mass media—especially movies, magazines, music, and television.

Although most people believe that children *should* learn about sex from their parents, the fact is that parents do a very poor job of teaching their children about sex (Fox, 1980; Fox and Inazu, 1980; Roberts et al., 1978). To the extent that the sexual socialization of young people does occur in American families, it is largely left to mothers,

The ideal of most Americans is to have young people learn about sex from their parents. In general, parents do a very poor job of teaching their children about sex, but the most common circumstance is for mothers to talk with their teenage daughters.

and the greatest amount of communication about sex is between mothers and daughters. Mothers are as likely as fathers (and some studies have shown them to be more likely) to discuss sex with their sons (Aldous, 1983; Fox and Inazu, 1980).

The minimal amount of sexual socialization received by sons, from either parent, is especially noteworthy. In one study of over 1,400 parents in Cleveland, Ohio, less than 2 percent of the fathers and only 9 percent of the mothers had discussed premarital sex with their adolescent sons (Roberts et al., 1978). Furthermore, the sex education programs in schools have a tendency to focus on premarital pregnancy and thus give more attention to adolescent girls than they do to adolescent boys. This reflects the double standard of sexual conduct that assumes that boys can take care of themselves in sexual matters. The result is that adolescent males are short-changed in their sex education (Shapiro, 1980).

Since mothers and daughters are the most likely combination of parents and children to discuss sex, their communication has been studied most extensively. The topics mothers and daughters talk about most frequently are menstruation and dating/boyfriends. Over 90 percent of both mothers and daughters in one study said they had discussed these topics. The least likely topics are sexual intercourse and birth control, with about 70 percent of the daughters saying that they had discussed these matters with their mothers (Fox and Inazu, 1980). Since these percentages are higher than are reported in most other studies, they probably represent the best of circumstances.

On the basis of an observational study of parents and their ninth-grade-level children (both boys and girls), one sociological researcher concluded that *both* parents and children generally try to avoid talking about sex-related topics (Aldous, 1983). In this observational study the parents and their teenage child could choose to discuss or not discuss any of a series of topics presented to them. One of these topics was "The ABC's of Birth Control." While most parent-child groups did not avoid the discussion completely, they used a number of techniques to either keep the subject impersonal or otherwise limit the discussion. One method was the "cut-off," in which one member of the family would say something that effectively ended the discussion. When the parents of one boy started talking about birth control, the son cut off the discussion quickly by saying, "Um hum." Then, pushing on to the next topic, he said, "Next?" (Aldous, 1983, p. 33).

In another family, the father cut off the discussion of birth control by first saying to his son, "What do you think of that, Dale?" But then the father immediately blocked the reply by saying, "Of course, you're not thinking of anything like this yet, huh?" (Aldous, 1983, p. 33).

Even when parents did try to engage their children in a discussion of birth control, the children were very reluctant and noncommittal on the topic. The following one-sided conversation shows that the daughter, Debbie, wanted nothing to do with the topic:

MOTHER: What do you think, Debbie?
DAUGHTER: Nothin'.
MOTHER: How would you plan your family?
DAUGHTER: I don't know.
MOTHER: Well, say you were 18 and married. Would you want a family right away?
DAUGHTER: No.
MOTHER: Well, how would you prevent it?
DAUGHTER: I don't know. (Aldous, 1983, p. 35)

If, as it seems from this study, both parents and children prefer to avoid personal discussions about sexual topics, what is the explanation? One possible explanation grows out of the tendency of both parents and their children to act as if the other generation does not have a sexual life (Aldous, 1983; Jones and Placek, 1981). Thus, any conversation that moves into this area is likely to lead to embarrassing revelations. Children may not want to reveal how much they know or what their sexual experiences have been. Parents, for their part, may not *want* to know how experienced and knowledgeable their children are about sex, because to learn these things would require that they acknowledge the sexual nature of their children (Aldous, 1983).

Adolescents may not be eager to discuss sexual matters with their parents, but the topic is a very popular one when they talk with their peers. Among the 11-year-old and 12-year-old Little League boys observed by sociologist Gary Fine (1987), sexual topics ranked with aggression as the two major themes of their discussions. Boys of this age have relatively little sexual experience—apparently kissing and limited petting are the major activities of the most active boys—but their interest level is high. When they talk about it, they are trying to show that they are interested and knowledgeable about heterosexual relations. Through the talk, banter, joking, and teasing about sexual matters, the "boys learn what is expected of them by their peers" (Fine, 1987, p. 110).

While these preadolescent boys talk a great deal about heterosexual relations, they also make frequent references to homosexual topics. This often takes the form of derogatory expressions such as "God, he's gay," "He's the biggest fag in the world," and "What a queer." Although these phrases are not generally used to refer to actual homosexual behavior, and are often used among friends in a good-natured way, the rhetoric of homosexuality is a flexible and abusive part of the preadolescent's language (Fine,

1987, p. 115). Probably this negative use of homosexual terminology is a way in which many boys are trying to define their own sexual identity.

Socialization by the Mass Media

In the early 1960s the word *pregnant* was not allowed on television, and movies and television did not show married couples in the same bed (twin beds were the standard). However, in recent years the amount of sexual content in the mass media—especially television, movies, and magazines—has increased dramatically. Today television and movies are important sources of information and values about sexual matters for many children and adolescents. In 1977 a religiously oriented group that was concerned about the amount of sexuality on television monitored the networks and found 2.81 references to sex per hour of prime-time viewing. Their calculation was that over the course of a year television "viewers would be exposed to 9,230 scenes of suggested sexual intercourse or sexually suggestive comments" (quoted in Liebert and Sprafkin, 1988, p. 199). Although much of the sexuality on television in the 1970s was verbal, it is now much more likely that actual sexual behavior will also be shown (Liebert and Sprafkin, 1988). Perhaps most important, couples shown on television having sex are not usually married. Unmarried sexual intercourse "occurs five times as often as married intercourse on the prime-time series adolescents watch most often" (Liebert and Sprafkin, 1988, p. 201).

There is little doubt that television programs and movies are providing children and adolescents with information and normative standards about sexual behavior. Studies have shown that even young adolescents can understand the sexual talk and innuendos on prime-time television. When public opinion pollster Louis Harris asked youngsters themselves about the relative importance of prime-time television as a source of information about sex, they ranked friends, parents, and courses in school as more important; but, of course, the messages of television sex may be more subtle and indirect than adolescent viewers recognize.

Premarital Sexual Behavior

We have seen that sexuality and sexual behavior in general are defined in very different ways from one society to another, and from one time to another. The varying views about sex can be further illustrated by the way in which people view sex before marriage. We will begin by looking at premarital sex in two societies—Iceland and Ireland—where views about adolescent sex are almost diametrically opposed.

Premarital Sex in Two Contrasting Societies: Ireland and Iceland

Iceland and Ireland are both small island societies in the North Atlantic, but it would be hard to imagine two societies in which views and behaviors with regard to premarital sex could be more different. In the case of Iceland, for example, young people report that they generally start having sexual intercourse at about 15 or 16 years of age. When asked about their reasons, the Icelandic youngsters say that they are apt to have sex out of "curiosity" or for a "sense of adventure" (Tomasson, 1980, p. 98). The Icelandic young people speak openly about their sexual relations; they show little evidence of associating sex with guilt, shame, or secretiveness.

Since Icelandic adolescents engage in "recreational" sex, it is not surprising that as they grow older, cohabitation becomes common. Even pregnancy is not a reason for immediate marriage. An estimated three-fourths of all first births occur to women before they are married. It is a popular custom for Icelandic couples to combine their marriage ceremony with the baptism of their first child (Tomasson, 1980).

The case of Ireland is very different. Less than 5 percent of all reported births are illegitimate, and approximately this same percentage has persisted for nearly a hundred years (Kennedy, 1973, p. 174). Of course, the Irish may also have some premarital pregnancies that lead to hurried marriages, but even these are likely to be minimal because many marriages in the rural areas are arranged, and there is almost no courtship period. Furthermore, the Irish are very moralistic about sex, and rigidly control the contact and interaction between young men and women.

An example of the rigid and puritanical sexual morality of Ireland has been carefully documented in studies by Messenger (1969, 1971). Messenger and his wife, both professional anthropologists, lived on the Island of Inis Beag (a fictitious name) off the Irish coast where they studied and observed the lives of the people. These especially isolated Irish peasants probably represent an extreme in Irish traditionalism, but their behavior is at least approximated in many other parts of Ireland.

As a beginning point, sex among the Irish people of Inis Beag is rarely spoken of *by anyone*. The result is an exceptional lack of knowledge and much misinformation about sexual matters. Young people, especially girls, are told almost nothing about sex. The boys usually hear something about sex from their peers. If young women are told anything, it is about menstruation. What little information they receive is often flawed or inadequate because their mothers have many misunderstandings and prejudices about the subject. Since most young women get no information at all, their first menstrual period is usually a very traumatic experience. In general, all things connected with sex are viewed as shameful and are mentioned as little as possible, especially by women.

Sexual intercourse is viewed as a "duty" for women, something that, as wives, they are obligated to "endure." Evidence indicates that many of these people do not know that females can have orgasms. If they have heard of the idea, they consider it deviant behavior. Men are recognized as needing and wanting sex more than their wives, but even men believe that sexual intercourse and ejaculation can weaken them.

Boys and girls are separated in most activities at an early age, a pattern that continues through life. During adolescence, the two sexes are kept apart almost completely. Courtship and dating are not part of the lives of young people. The people of Inis Beag and the anthropological observers are in agreement that on the island of Inis Beag, premarital sexual intercourse does not occur. Some young men did boast that they had engaged in petting with women tourists and also a few local girls. The extent of this sexual activity was limited to kissing and some fondling outside the young women's clothing. The young men believe that the few girls who do participate in this sexual activity get no pleasure from it.

In summary, sex and sexual intercourse among the Irish of Inis Beag are limited, secretive, and guilt-ridden. Sexual intercourse is something that comes after marriage where its only legitimate purpose is procreation. Women are not expected to feel pleasure from sex, and even for men it is viewed as primarily a physiological need that is periodically satisfied.

Premarital Sex in the United States: Different Sexual Scripts

Sexual scripts
Definitions of when and with whom sex is appropriate and what it means

In a society as large and heterogeneous as the United States, not everyone views premarital sex in the same way. Young people have different social influences and experiences, through which they develop different attitudes toward premarital sex. The term *sexual script* is widely used to describe the different attitudes about sexual behavior (Gagnon and Simon, 1973; Gagnon, 1977). Sexual script gets its meaning from the word *script,* taken from the language of the theater where it refers to the instructions and words that actors are given so they will know how to act. In a similar but less specific way, **sexual scripts** are social definitions about when sex is appropriate, with whom it is appropriate, and what it means to have sex.[4] For example, one kind of sexual script is that sex is recreational: it is primarily a physical act that one engages in for physical pleasure. Another alternative sexual script is that sex is relational, emphasizing that sex is an integral part of a relationship and has the purpose of strengthening emotional or psychological intimacy (DeLamater, 1987).

We can further illustrate sexual scripts by describing the most prominent premarital scripts found today in American society.

Sexual Scripts among American Dating Couples

A study of dating couples coming primarily from four colleges in the Boston area (Rubin et al., 1981) provided some interesting information on sexual activities (Peplau et al., 1977). These couples, when they entered the study, thought of themselves as "going with" each other. We can assume, therefore, that they had some type of emotional involvement and at least a partial commitment to each other. Since these couples were college sophomores and juniors, it is perhaps not surprising that 82 percent of the couples had had sexual intercourse in their current relationship. Further, 74 percent of the men and 62 percent of the women had had sexual intercourse with one or more *other* partners. Even though these figures suggest a generally liberal attitude toward sex, not all of the couples in the sample had the same sexual scripts. Three different orientations toward sex (sexual scripts) emerged.

Sexually Traditional Couples. One set of 42 couples (18 percent of the total) had not had sexual relations in the current relationship. In some cases the males in these couples might have had some previous sexual experience, but the women were almost always virgins. Such couples were likely to reflect the double standard in their sexual attitudes, since much greater significance was placed on the virginity of the woman than the man.

Although these traditional couples often expressed love for each other, this love did not justify having sex. Indeed their love was partially responsible for keeping them from having sex. These couples often indicated that abstaining was a way of showing their respect and love for each other. It also showed that their feelings for each other were not simply based on physical attraction. For these couples with a traditional sexual

[4] Our use of the term *sexual script* is now sometimes called *sexual scenario*, but the meaning is virtually the same. See DeLamater (1987).

script, sex would have to wait until marriage. As the following example shows, however, they might engage in petting that stopped just short of coitus.

> **Paul and Peggy.** . . . Peggy is firmly opposed to premarital sex for herself. Raised a devout Catholic, Peggy believes that intercourse before marriage is wrong. She explained that she "can't imagine anything that would cause me to change my mind. Even if I were engaged, I wouldn't feel right about having sex." Many of Peggy's girlfriends are having sexual affairs, which Peggy accepts "for them." It's not right for Peggy, however, and she believes that Paul respects her views. For his part, Paul indicated that he would like to have intercourse with Peggy. They have engaged in extensive petting, and sometimes enjoy lying together nude. Paul commented that he sometimes finds these sexual activities more frustrating than satisfying, but added that intercourse "just isn't all that important for me." He says of Peggy, "She's more conservative than I am. I'm trying to gradually win her over to my way of thinking" (Peplau et al., 1977, p. 97).

Love Justifies Sex. The most prominent sexual script in this sample of dating couples was one that viewed sexual intercourse as permissible if the two people loved each other. This script is the equivalent of what Reiss (1967) has labeled *permissiveness with affection*. This script does not necessarily require that the dating couple have a long-term commitment to each other. They might be engaged or planning marriage (perhaps vaguely), or they might not be. The key elements of this sexual script are that mutual love is the prerequisite for sex and that sex is an appropriate expression of the emotions and feelings of love.

For couples who held the love-justifies-sex script, sex usually came through a gradual increase in sexual intimacy. These couples did not accept "instant sex" because it did not fit with their romantic view of sex as an expression of love and caring. The following case illustrates this sexual script:

> **Tom and Sandy.** . . . Before they met, Sandy was a virgin, while Tom had had coitus with three different women. Three weeks after their first date, Tom told Sandy that he loved her. She was in love, too, and their relationship grew quickly. In a few months they were spending weekends together at one of their dorms. They slept in the same

Sexual relationships between adolescents are frequently based on the sexual script which holds that *love justifies sex*.

bed, but did not have intercourse. Although Tom was very attracted to Sandy, he was slow to initiate intercourse. "I didn't want to push it on her," he said. "I felt that we shouldn't have sex until our relationship reached a certain point. Sex is something I just can't imagine on a first date." Just before becoming engaged, Tom and Sandy first had intercourse with each other. For Tom, "Sex added another dimension to our relationship; it's a landmark of sorts" (Peplau et al., 1977, p. 98).

Sex as Pleasure (or Sex for Intimacy). Some of the dating couples[5] held a liberal view of sexual behavior, that sex did not have to be tied directly to love or commitment. Having love was a desirable condition, but it was not a precondition for sex. Reiss (1967) labeled this sexual standard *permissiveness without affection*. Others have called it *casual sex* or *recreational sex*. Individuals or couples with this sexual script are likely to view sexual intercourse as a pleasurable activity, one that is both expected and desired in any significant dating relationship. From this point of view, sex stands on its own merits and need not be justified by either love or commitment. The following couple exemplifies this sexual script:

Diane and Alan. . . . Before they met, both Diane and Alan had had intercourse with several partners. About two weeks after they started dating, Alan asked if Diane would like to make love. She declined, saying she wasn't ready yet, but implying that she would be soon. Since they were alone in Alan's apartment, she jokingly suggested that he go "exhibit himself" across the room so she could get used to his body. They spent the weekend together, and by Sunday Diane felt ready for coitus. Diane told us that she and Alan were not in love when they first had intercourse. Nonetheless, she enjoyed the sex and felt it was "part of our getting to know each other. It led to an obvious closeness." Diane and Alan view sex as fun, and the events surrounding first intercourse suggest this playful orientation. For them, sex served as a way of developing a closer relationship. Within several months, both were in love, and their relationship continued for several years (Peplau et al., 1977, pp. 98–99).

These three sexual scripts do catch what seems to be the essence of much contemporary thinking. The love-justifies-sex script is predominant in this particular sample of dating couples, and it is highly likely that it prevails as the sexual script for most unmarried couples today.

A Note on Sex Research in the United States

Before we consider the data on premarital sex behavior of young people in the United States today, we should take a brief look at the source of our information, which is predominantly produced by social research, especially survey research.

Several earlier discussions have been based on the research results of sociologists and other scholars. For example, participant observation methods were used to study the Irish of Inis Baeg, as well as the preadolescent Little League baseball players. The cultural customs of the Azandi, the Gusaii, and the Mangaia of Polynesia were based on the ethnographic field work of anthropologists. The historical studies cited earlier have generally relied on documents and other written records of the past. So far we

[5] Peplau et al. (1977) do not indicate how many couples fall into this category. It is probably a small proportion of the total number.

have said little about survey research on sexual behavior. Today, much of the information we have about contemporary sexual behavior comes from social surveys where, through questionnaires and interviews, respondents have been asked about their sexual lives. It is now an accepted practice to ask people about their sexual attitudes and behaviors, but it has not always been so. Except for a few isolated studies of college students, it was nearly unthinkable 50 years ago for a social researcher to ask people questions about their sex lives. But a pioneering study of sexual behavior by Alfred Kinsey changed that, and for this reason alone it deserves some special attention.

The Kinsey Studies

The name of Dr. Alfred C. Kinsey continues to be associated with the study of sexual behavior, even though his early recognition and reputation came from work as an entomologist studying an insect called the gall wasp. In the late 1930s, however, in connection with a university course on marriage, Kinsey began collecting sexual histories through personal interviews. Over the next decade Kinsey and his associates collected over 11,000 sexual histories (5,300 males and nearly 6,000 females). In 1948 Kinsey and his associates published *Sexual Behavior in the Human Male*, and in 1953, *Sexual Behavior in the Human Female*. These two books were probably the most widely discussed (as well as criticized and joked about) books of their time (Pomeroy, 1972).

Kinsey's studies still provide baseline information on the sexual behavior of American men and women. Because he asked his subjects to recall their lifetime sexual histories, some sexual data go back into the nineteenth century. As an example of the kind of information Kinsey collected, he found that women who were born before 1900 reported having sexual intercourse with their husbands more often than women who were born after 1900. One interpretation of this difference can be found in our earlier discussion of the nature of marital sexual intercourse in the nineteenth century. As we noted above, women a century ago were likely to view sexual intercourse with their husbands as a wifely duty, and husbands were apt to believe that it was their prerogative to demand sex whenever they wanted it. Under these conditions, sex may have been more frequent, simply because husbands demanded their sexual rights and disregarded the wishes of their wives.

Although the sexual information found in the Kinsey studies continues to be useful and informative, the research methods he used have not escaped criticism. Despite the thousands of males and females interviewed, the samples were not drawn randomly from the total population (in other words, all adults did not have an equal chance of being drawn into the sample). Kinsey's method of obtaining case histories was to interview anyone who would agree to his request, and he asked virtually everyone he met. He often spoke before organizations and groups, and then asked for permission to interview all the members (Pomeroy, 1972). As a result of his procedures, Kinsey's samples were strongly biased toward people who had higher levels of education (20 percent of the women in his sample had some graduate education—far higher than the average for that era).

Although Kinsey's sampling methods can be criticized, he made a tremendous contribution to the scientific study of sexual behavior. His own status as a natural scientist lent credibility to his inquiry. Despite the uproar of opposition that came from people who were outraged by his studies, Kinsey established that sexual behavior is a legitimate topic for social research (Madge, 1962).

Today, interview and questionnaire surveys that ask detailed questions about sexual behavior and attitudes are conducted on a nearly routine basis. Many of them are either sponsored or conducted by the federal government, with samples covering adolescents as well as adults in the population (Hayes, 1987; Zelnik and Kantner, 1980; Zelnik and Shah, 1983; Kahn et al., 1988). From these studies we now have extensive and reliable information about the sexual behavior of American adolescents and adults.

Sexual Behavior among American Adolescents

The facts of sexual behavior among American adolescents are well documented by repeated sample surveys conducted over the last three decades (Hofferth et al., 1987; Kahn et al., 1988). From one of the most recent surveys we have extensive information on the sexual activity of unmarried American young people aged 14 to 19 (Mott and Haurin, 1988). Some of the key findings of this study are shown in table 7–1.

Table 7–1 shows that by the age of nineteen, 78.2 percent of American males and 67.6 percent of females have had sexual intercourse. Even by age 17 about half of the males (48.4 percent) and one-third of the females (33.2 percent) have experienced sex. Among black adolescents the percentages are higher, with 93.5 percent of the males and 79.1 percent of the females having had sexual intercourse by age 19. Hispanic males fall between white males and black males, but Hispanic women have the lowest percentage (58.4 percent) of all adolescents who have had sexual intercourse by age 19.

A number of factors are associated with adolescents having had sexual intercourse. For example, the sexual behavior of this national sample was related to adolescents' use of alcohol and drugs. Among younger adolescents (those under 16 years of age) the majority had not used alcohol or drugs and had not had sexual intercourse (about one-half of the males and two-thirds of the females had not done any of these three things). On the other hand, by age 19, about half of the males and nearly one-third of the females had used both alcohol and marijuana, and had had sexual intercourse (they had done all three). However, among the females, only two years earlier, at age 17, only about 8 percent had used both alcohol and drugs, and had had sexual intercourse. For all three activities males started at earlier ages than females. Although this study found some evidence that the start of one of these activities increases the likelihood of starting one or both of the others, no certain causal connection can be proved. For example, young men and women who start using marijuana or alcohol under age 16 are more likely to remain virgins in the following year than they are to have sexual intercourse (Mott and Haurin, 1988).

In a different study of adolescents the researchers asked whether the sexual activities of one's friends influenced one's own sexual activity (Billy and Udry, 1985). The assumption was that adolescents who had not had sex would be more likely to begin having sex if their friends were sexually active. Over a two-year time period for both black and white adolescents, only white females were more likely to start having sex if their friends were sexually active. These research findings do not mean that in general friends are without influence in sexual matters; other studies have shown repeatedly that adolescents themselves rate their peers as a most important source of information about sex (Strouse and Fabes, 1985).

Table 7–1. Percentages of Adolescents Who Have Experienced Sexual Intercourse Prior to Given Ages, by Gender and Race/Ethnicity

Race/ethnicity and Age	Percent Who Have Experienced Sexual Intercourse	
	Males	Females
Total		
14	10.2	3.3
15	17.2	8.4
16	29.1	17.6
17	48.4	33.2
18	64.8	50.9
19	78.2	67.6
N	5,396	5,450
White		
14	6.8	3.2
15	12.5	7.9
16	23.5	16.6
17	43.3	31.3
18	60.8	49.2
19	75.5	66.2
N	3,219	3,230
Black		
14	30.4	4.9
15	44.3	12.5
16	61.4	24.2
17	78.6	45.7
18	87.3	64.2
19	93.5	79.1
N	1,362	1,365
Hispanic		
14	9.9	2.0
15	18.3	6.1
16	31.8	15.2
17	49.9	28.5
18	68.0	42.3
19	80.3	58.4
N	815	855

Source: Mott and Haurin, 1988.

Some Consequences of Premarital Adolescent Sex

One obvious consequence of premarital sex is premarital pregnancy and childbearing. The increase in sexual activity among unmarried teenagers has contributed to increases in births to unmarried women in the United States. About one in every five births today is to an unmarried woman, but, of course, not all of these mothers are teenagers; only about one-third of unmarried mothers are 19 or younger. However, the number of unmarried teenage mothers would be much greater except for the fact that about 60 percent of unmarried teenagers who become pregnant have abortions (U.S. Bureau of the Census, 1987).

Teenage women who bear children before marriage tend to have disrupted educations, low-paying jobs, and to be dependent upon public welfare (Hayes, 1987). When women who bear children before marriage do marry they have higher separation and divorce rates (Teachman, 1983). Perhaps the most important consequence of premarital childbearing for adolescent women is that, compared to their classmates who do not become mothers, they "consistently experience greater difficulty in realizing life plans" (Furstenberg, 1981).

Being sexually active does not necessarily lead to premarital pregnancy, since contraception is available and tends to be used more frequently than it was two decades ago. A survey of American teenagers in 1970 found that only about 12 percent of those who were sexually active were using contraception (Zelnik and Kantner, 1980). A 1982 survey found that nearly 70 percent (68.6) of sexually active teenagers were using some form of contraception (Hofferth and Hayes, 1987). These survey results probably do not reflect the effects, if any, of recent educational campaigns that have urged all sexually active people to use condoms as a protection against AIDS (see the discussion of AIDS and sexual behavior below).

Since a high percentage of American teenagers are sexually active, considerable interest has arisen in other, more social, consequences of having premarital sex. The study of Boston area couples discussed above asked whether having sex had any consequences for a couple's interpersonal relationship. The researchers found that having sex, or not having sex, did not seem to affect either the quality or the length of a relationship. When couples were interviewed two years after their first interview, it made no difference when the couple had started having sex, or if they never had sex at all. About the same percentage had broken up in the two-year interval (Peplau et al., 1977).

Another study of premarital sex sought to determine if having sex before marriage had an influence on self-concept (MacCorquodale and DeLamater, 1979). In our previous discussions of symbolic interaction theory, especially in chapter 5, we saw the importance of the thoughts and feelings people have about themselves (called the self-concept). One dimension of the self-concept, the degree to which people think well of themselves or have positive views of themselves, is called **self-esteem.** In this study of college students and noncollege young people of the same age, there was a tendency for those who had the most sexual experience to have the highest levels of self-esteem. In particular, the sexually active males were more likely to feel that they were socially desirable and to feel more positive about their bodies and faces. Among the females, less of a relationship existed between being sexually active and having positive self-esteem, although females with the greatest variety of sexual experience were more likely to think of themselves as socially desirable and attractive.

Self-esteem
Positive views of one's self; a dimension of the self concept

One intriguing question cannot be answered from this research because it is based on correlations: Do the positive self-images come before or after the premarital sexual experiences? Young people who are, in fact, more socially desirable and attractive (thus their self-image may be partially based on fact) might move into heterosexual relationships more easily and at a younger age. This would lead them toward a longer history of sexual intimacy by the time they reach college age. There is ample evidence that the earlier one begins, the sooner one will have more "advanced" sexual experiences (DeLamater and MacCorquodale, 1979). In concrete terms, kissing comes before French kissing, while breast and genital fondling comes before sexual intercourse, which, in turn, comes before oral-genital contact. The process is sequential, and the earlier a person begins the process, the more extensive that person's experiences will be at any given age. This fact could account for the correlations between positive self-images and sexual experiences. Those young people with positive self-images may have had more opportunity to start the process earlier and to arrive at sexual intercourse sooner (as well as to experience more sex and more varieties of sex).

The other possible reason for the relationship between sexual experience and positive self-image is that self-image may develop positively from the sexual experience. For males especially, since for them sex may be viewed as an accomplishment, having success in the area of sex could enhance their self-images. For females the same reasoning may not hold, but the greater satisfaction with attractiveness by the sexually active women might reflect the positive evaluations they have received from their male partners.

While the causal direction of the relationship between self-image and sexual experience cannot be conclusively determined by this research, there is one statement that can be made with assurance: for this sample of students and nonstudents there is no evidence to support the notion that premarital sex produces a decline of self-image or self-esteem. Apparently, among most young people today there is not a strong feeling that they are being deviant or breaking an important societal norm when they engage in sexual relations before marriage. At least if such feelings do exist, they are not strong enough to produce a negative self-concept or lowered self-esteem.

Marital Sex

A married couple that remains married for 25 or 30 years will probably have sexual intercourse more than 3,000 times. This average is based on the responses that married persons give to questionnaire and interview questions about the number of times they have sexual intercourse weekly. Since the responses come from couples in all stages of marriage it is possible to construct a composite picture of the total amount of sex in a long marriage. Based on the findings of a number of different studies of marital sex, there is some indication that the frequency of marital sex increased after 1970 (Kinsey, 1948; Tavris and Sadd, 1977; Westoff, 1974; Blumstein and Schwartz, 1983). The 1970 date corresponds roughly with what has been called a "sexual revolution" in the United States when there was a general liberalization of sexual behavior throughout the society.

The so-called **sexual revolution** of the 1970s, or the "new sexual ethic," is generally related to nonmarital sex—premarital sex, cohabitation, and extramarital sex. However, the increase in sexual intercourse among married couples after 1970 is an indication that the sexual revolution carried over into marriages as well. Indeed, studies of working-class married couples have found that the general liberalization of sex during this period created problems for many wives. Many said they felt caught between the old definitions of sex, learned when they were young, and the new sexual ethic (Rubin, 1976).

Sexual revolution
1970s liberalization of sexual norms, especially about premarital sex, cohabitation, extramarital sex

Often the husbands of these working-class couples became aware of the new, liberalized views of sex before their wives, and they found it relatively easy to adopt the new ideas. For example, the husbands (perhaps being socialized by magazines like *Playboy* and *Penthouse*) learned about the greater expression of sexuality among women. These working-class husbands were no longer the stereotypical insensitive men who thought only of their own satisfaction. They wanted their wives to enjoy sex and be interested in sexual experimentation. But the wives often found their husbands' new attitudes a mixed blessing. Most wives grew up having learned a very narrow definition of what is sexually appropriate, especially for women. Indeed, for many of these women sexuality was something they had learned to control and repress. When it came to sex, the guiding principle had always been, "Men *use* bad girls, but *marry* good girls" (Rubin, 1976, p. 136). Again, the double standard is reflected here, which the women in this social class had been thoroughly socialized to accept. Now, after some years of marriage, many of these women were being asked by their husbands to learn a new definition of sexual behavior.

AIDS and Sexual Behavior

Acquired Immune Deficiency Syndrome, commonly called AIDS, is the most deadly sexually transmitted disease in history. While the long-term effects of syphilis and gonorrhea can also kill, medical treatments now exist that usually lead to recovery. AIDS has no cure, and the possibility of a vaccine apparently lies some distance into the future. Therefore, the only protection against AIDS is to avoid contracting the disease.

AIDS is contracted when the blood or semen from an infected person enters the bloodstream. Sexual intercourse, therefore, is a central means of passing the disease from one person to another. Of course, AIDS can also be contracted by using an infected hypodermic needle (a problem for intravenous drug users), by transfusions of infected blood, and by the direct transmission of an infected woman's blood to a fetus in her uterus.

Table 7–2 summarizes the adults' and adolescents' AIDS cases known to the Centers for Disease Control of the United States Public Health Service through March 1989. The known cases are divided into two time periods: the cumulative total number from 1981 to 1988 (April) and the cases that have been identified in the most recent twelve-month period (April 1988 through March 1989). This breakdown makes it possible to see how AIDS is being transmitted through the population and which types of exposure are related to the transmission of currently known cases.

The AIDS cases of the most recent twelve-month period reveal that, while homosexual and bisexual males still make up the majority of all new cases (57 percent), their percentage of the total is dropping. By contrast, heterosexual intravenous drug users are increasing their percentage of the total, from an earlier 18 percent to 23 percent.

The *number* of new AIDS cases coming from heterosexual contact increased greatly in the last year, compared to earlier years, but the percentage of the total rose only 1 percent (from 4 percent to 5 percent). The majority of these heterosexually contracted cases (55 percent) were the result of having sex with an intravenous drug user (not shown in the table).

There are now also nearly 1500 cases of AIDS among children under thirteen. More than one-third of these cases appeared in the last year. The vast majority of these (79 percent) are infants who contracted the disease from their mothers, half of whom were IV-drug users.

Sexual transmission of the AIDS virus is most probable when lesions or cuts are present through which infected semen or blood can enter the bloodstream directly. Thus,

Table 7–2. AIDS Cases among Adults and Adolescents (13 and over) by Exposure Category, Cumulative Number of Cases from 1981 to April, 1988, and New Cases from April, 1988, through March, 1989

	Cumulative Cases 1981 to April, 1988		New Cases between April, 1988–March, 1989	
	Number	Percent	Number	Percent
Male homosexual/bisexual contact	36,658	(64)	18,347	(57)
Intravenous (IV) drug use (heterosexuals)	10,398	(18)	7,601	(23)
Male homosexual/bisexual contact and IV drug use	4,337	(8)	2,070	(6)
Hemophilia	549	(1)	316	(1)
Heterosexual contact	2,333	(4)	1,629	(5)
Blood transfusion	1,414	(2)	822	(3)
Other/undetermined	1,452	(3)	1,575	(5)

Source: Centers for Disease Control. *HIV/AIDS Surveillance Report,* APRIL, 1989, pp. 1–16.

for example, a woman who has active herpes may be in greater danger of contracting AIDS from an infected partner, since the herpes lesions will admit the infected semen. Similarly, anal intercourse, which has a higher likelihood of tearing rectal tissue, may also produce higher rates of transmission. Public health authorities and the medical professionals have repeatedly urged the American public to change their sexual behavior as a way of reducing the chances of contracting AIDS through sexual activity.

Two major modifications in sexual behavior have been urged: (1) males are urged to wear condoms when engaging in sexual intercourse, as a protection against giving

Drawing by P. Steiner; © 1987 The New Yorker Magazine, Inc.

SAFE SEX

Since the outbreak of the AIDS epidemic there have been massive communication efforts to get Americans to change their sexual behavior. This Los Angeles billboard is urging gay males to "Play Safely."

the AIDS virus to their partners; (2) all persons are urged to know their sexual partners. The ideal is the knowledge, based on medical testing, that one's sexual partner does not have the AIDS virus. Because this level of knowledge is usually not available, sexually active people are urged to know as much as possible about the sexual histories (and drug-use histories) of their partners. One clear implication of the latter recommendation is that one should not engage in promiscuous or casual sex.

Over the decade of the 1980s the campaign to slow the spread of AIDS in the population has become more intense and widespread. Few people in the United States can be unaware of AIDS, and most should have heard what actions to take to avoid this disease. However, this raises the obvious question: Have Americans changed their sexual behavior (and attitudes) since the beginning of the AIDS outbreak?

No doubt the concern about AIDS has opened up communication about sex and contraception. Public discussions are now held about different sexual practices, both heterosexual and homosexual, and about the use of condoms. Many sexual topics that could not have been mentioned in public a few years ago, such as anal intercourse, are now discussed explicitly. The Office of the Surgeon General of the United States mailed an informational brochure on AIDS to every postal address in the United States, in which many previously taboo sexual subjects were discussed. Schools throughout the United States have initiated AIDS educational programs, often beginning at the elementary school level.

New evidence shows that gay men, especially in the major urban centers where the earliest concentration of AIDS cases occurred (San Francisco and New York), have modified their sexual behavior considerably. After initial resistance, the gay community in San Francisco, for example, recognized that social and behavioral changes had to be made. The gay baths there, where promiscuous and impersonal sex was the standard, were closed, and it was done with the support of the gay community (Fineberg, 1988).[6]

The majority of the population has not shown any substantial evidence yet that their sexual behavior has changed very much, even though they are aware of the AIDS danger and the protective actions required. In a national survey 90 percent knew how AIDS could be contracted, but 90 percent also said they viewed their risk as low or nonexistent. In surveys conducted in New York City, 80 percent of the respondents agreed that sexually active people should carry condoms and that women should tell their sexual partners to use them. However, more than 60 percent of those interviewed said they had not used condoms more than some of the time (Fineberg, 1988, p. 130). Furthermore, the numbers and frequency of sexual contacts among these respondents had not changed in the preceding month. According to an NBC/*Wall Street Journal* poll, concern about AIDS has had no effect on the way in which 92 percent of the people in the population lead their lives (Carroll, 1988).

A study of college students found that they are concerned about AIDS, which, over half of the sexually active students said, had affected their behavior. However, although these students often claim to have become more selective in their sexual partners, most of them have not entered into exclusive dating relationships (Carroll, 1988). This study does show awareness and concern among college students, as well as some early indications that they see the need for making changes in their sexual behavior.

The evidence about changed sexual behavior, except among homosexual males, is still limited, but it must be remembered that AIDS was unknown to the population in the early 1980s. The longer-term influences of this disease are yet to be seen and probably depend on how the AIDS virus moves into the heterosexual, nondrug-using population of the United States.

Deviant Sexual Behavior

In our consideration of deviant behavior in chapter 6 we saw that almost every behavior has been defined as deviant by the people of some society at some time. We also saw that virtually every kind of behavior has been socially acceptable at one time or another. Thus, when we ask, "What is deviant sexual behavior?" we should be prepared to find that it depends upon who is defining the behavior and when.

In this chapter we have already seen that in Egyptian society for a period of more than 200 years (longer than the United States has been a country) many marriages occurred between brothers and sisters. Obviously sexual relations between brothers and sisters were not considered deviant by the Egyptians in that time. Yet, as we have also noted, societies existed in which a brother and sister were not allowed to eat a meal together because to do so had sexual connotations.

In light of these facts we can only approach sexual deviance from the social perspective of the people of one society during a particular time. We can try, for example, to assess what sexual deviance is in the United States during the last decade of the present century. But the task will not be easy because we have already seen with respect

[6] However, the other high-incidence group, intravenous drug users, have not yet shown signs of modifying behavior and, as a result, is the fastest growing category of AIDS victims.

to premarital sex that segments of the population hold very different views. Several ways have been suggested for evaluating whether a sexual behavior is deviant (Bryant, 1982).

One measure of deviance is whether a particular sexual act is against the legal statutes of a nation or state. Acts that are illegal are presumably deviant to some degree. The problem with using the law as a measure of deviance is that laws often remain on the books for many years, even when they are no longer enforced. For example, many states have laws against fornication, prohibiting sexual intercourse between people who are not married. A law against fornication would make almost every cohabitating couple lawbreakers. In the state of Virginia a cohabiting couple attempted to get the state's law against cohabitation declared unconstitutional, but Virginia's court of appeals rejected their lawsuit. From the legal perspective, the most important consideration is whether violations of a law are prosecuted. In the case of cohabitation, in Virginia as well as other states, it is unlikely that the laws prohibiting sexual intercourse between unmarried individuals will be enforced against cohabiting couples.

A second indication of sexual deviance is the statistical frequency of some act. If a particular sexual act is widespread, involving large numbers of people, it is not likely to be considered deviant. Again, the case of cohabitation is instructive, since the number of cohabiting-couple households in the United States now exceeds more than two million. A second example is adultery, which is contrary to existing social norms as well as against the law in most places. However, estimates show that at least 60 percent of all married men and 50 percent of all married women have adulterous sex before they reach age 40. Among high income men—those earning $60,000 or more a year—an estimated 70 percent have extramarital affairs. Many of the women who are the mistresses of such men do not consider themselves deviant; they accept these affairs as a normal part of their lives (Richardson, 1985).

A third standard that can be used to evaluate the deviance of a sexual act is the degree to which one person is a victim. Being a victim indicates that one person in a sexual act is coerced or forced to do something against his or her will. Homosexual behavior, for example, almost always occurs between consenting adults, which leads some people to conclude that no deviance is involved. Similarly, prostitution is a sexual act that involves two people who agree, through a commercial transaction, to engage in sex. However, since many female prostitutes are addicted to drugs, have no other means of making a living, or are under the control of a male pimp, some question does arise about whether they are free in making their decisions.

Several sexual acts clearly involve victims. One obvious case is rape, in which one person, through force or threat, makes another person perform a sexual act. Closely related are all cases when children are sexually abused. The sexual abuse of children can occur either in the family or outside it. Inside the family, the most common circumstance is for a young girl to be sexually abused by either a father, brother, or other male relative living in the home. It is also possible for young boys to be sexually molested in similar circumstances, but the incidence is considerably lower. Even if the sexual abuse occurs outside the family, the aggressor is typically either a relative or friend of the family, or someone who has been charged with responsibility for the child. The results of a study conducted among college students at the University of New Hampshire showed that 19.2 percent of female students and 8.2 percent of male students had been "sexually victimized" sometime during childhood (Finkelhor, 1979).

A fourth measure of deviant sexual behavior is the degree to which a given act is viewed as socially reprehensible. One aspect of the sexual abuse of children is the

The sexual abuse of children is considered one of the most reprehensible forms of sexual deviance.

revulsion that most people feel when they learn that a small child has been sexually violated or molested. The deviant nature of incest and rape is also reflected in the negative reaction that people have to the aggressors. Even some less deviant sexual acts such as voyeurism and exhibitionism are primarily deviant because the actors are considered socially reprehensible. The voyeur, or Peeping Tom, if unobserved, does no actual harm to his victim, but people abhor the way he invades another person's privacy.

Many kinds of sexual deviance, including some of those discussed above, depend to some degree on the situation or context in which they occur. For example, exhibitionism is the act of showing one's body in a public place, and yet people who go to nudist camps or nude beaches often emphasize that their action is neither sexual nor deviant (Bryant, 1982).

This sociological analysis of sexual deviance leads us back to where we started. Sexual behavior, both that which is acceptable and that which is deviant, is determined to a considerable degree by the norms, values, and roles of the particular society in which people live.

Summary

Sexuality is a basic human characteristic, sexual behavior is universal, and sex is a biological act; but many societal and cultural differences exist in sexual behavior and sexuality. All of these variations and differences, including historical changes from one period to another, indicate that sexual behavior is influenced as much by social factors as it is by biological factors.

A number of societal characteristics of the contemporary United States are reflected in the sexual behavior of Americans. These characteristics include the depersonalization of sex, the commercialization of sex, and coercive and aggressive sex.

Sexuality is normatively controlled in every society. The most nearly universal norm is the prohibition of sex between closely related individuals—the norm prohibiting incest. However, the norms vary from one society to another, and there are historical exceptions to even the most widely held prohibitions—parent-child and sibling sexual relations.

The double standard is a complex of norms that gives males greater freedom in their sexual behavior than females. Although the rigidity of the double standard of sexual behavior might have lessened, it is still very much alive in American society today.

Children learn about sex through the socialization process. Although there is widespread agreement that children should learn about sex from their parents, evidence reveals that most parents communicate to their children very little information about sex. Children and adolescents learn about sex from their peers and the mass media, especially television and movies.

Premarital sexual behavior varies greatly from one society to another. Ireland and Iceland, for example, are very different in the amount of premarital sex that is allowed for their young people. The United States has different premarital sexual scripts for young people. Three prominent scripts are "traditional," "love justifies sex," and "sex as pleasure."

Sex research in the United States has a relatively short history, with the Kinsey studies being the most important early landmark. Since Kinsey, many surveys have obtained information on the sexual behavior of both teenagers and adults.

Surveys of teenagers show a rapid increase in premarital sexual behavior in the 1970s. The consequences of premarital sex include premarital pregnancy and childbearing. For teenage women, premarital childbearing leads to a number of negative outcomes, including greater difficulties in realizing life plans. However, premarital sex has no influence on the continuation of couple relationships. Premarital sex does not decrease self-esteem, and, in fact, may enhance it for some adolescents.

Marital sex increased somewhat during the period of the "sexual revolution." Among working-class couples the sexual revolution may have put new and unwanted demands upon the wives.

AIDS has introduced a new factor into the sexual behavior of Americans. More open discussions are held now about sexual matters, and awareness of sexual issues has increased. The chances of contracting AIDS can be reduced by certain modifications of sexual behavior, which most Americans understand, but there is little evidence of change except in the gay male community.

Sexual deviance, like all other forms of deviance, is socially defined. Sexual deviance can be defined by the laws of a society, but the laws may fall into disuse. The frequency of a sexual behavior also indicates whether it is deviant; previously deviant acts often become more commonplace and thus less deviant. Deviance is also indicated by the degree to which a sexual behavior victimizes another person. Rape is one such deviant act. Sexual deviance is also indicated by the degree to which an act is viewed with revulsion. The sexual abuse of children is an act of sexual deviance that is considered especially reprehensible.

CRITICAL THINKING

1. Why is sexual behavior a good subject to demonstrate how fundamental human behavior is influenced by culture?
2. How do our beliefs about sexuality reflect the general characteristics of our society? Give contemporary and historical examples to support your answer.
3. Do the ideas of sexual coercion, commercialization, and depersonalization find support in any recent movies you have seen? Give examples.
4. In your view, are there still norms about sexual behavior that support a double standard for males and females? How do you explain the existence of such a standard?
5. What differences exist between the ideal roles and real roles of parents in socializing their children about sex? What other sources of socialization influence a person's sexual behavior and beliefs?
6. Contrast premarital views and behavior in Iceland and Ireland. Are these differences accounted for by psychology, sociology, or biology? Explain.
7. Which sexual script described in this chapter best describes the dominant pattern you see on your college campus?
8. How do changes in the ability of sociologists and other researchers to gather data about sexual behavior reflect changing views about sex in society at large?
9. Two major modifications in sexual behavior have been suggested as a result of the AIDS epidemic. To your knowledge, to what extent has behavior changed to comply with these suggestions? What societal conditions might promote rapid compliance?
10. What standards might be employed in determining whether a particular sexual behavior is deviant?

CONNECTIONS

The Homeless

Introduction

The conditions under which people are made homeless have existed throughout the history of the United States. However, homelessness became especially acute during the economic depression of the 1930s. When unemployment rates soared, some people were forced to "take to the road" in search of employment. Some became "hobos," unemployed wanderers who illegally used the railroads as their means of transportation. The struggles, sorrows, and desperation of these people were shared by folksong writer and singer Woody Guthrie (1912–1967), who traveled with the homeless and recorded their lives in such songs as "The Hobo's Lullaby."

> Go to sleep you weary hobo
> Let the towns drift slowly by
> Can't you hear the steel rails hummin'
> That's a hobo's lullaby
>
> Do not think about tomorrow
> Let tomorrow come and go
> Tonight you're in a nice warm box car
> Safe from all the wind and snow
>
> I know the police cause you trouble
> They cause trouble everywhere
> But when you die and go to heaven
> You won't find no policemen there
>
> I know your clothes are torn and ragged
> And your hair is turning grey
> Lift your head and smile at trouble
> You'll find happiness someday
>
> Go to sleep you weary hobo
> Let the towns drift slowly by
> Don't you feel the steel rails comin'
> That's a hobo's lullaby

The lyrics of "Hobo's Lullaby" take on particular relevance in the 1990s because of significant increases in homelessness. The homeless today, however, are different from those in Guthrie's time because then homelessness was likely to be either a chosen lifestyle or a temporary condition based on extreme economic situations. Today, homelessness is a more serious problem because few people freely choose such a life and it is likely to be a far more permanent condition. Furthermore, the homeless are seen by most Americans as outcasts, deviants, and burdens to our society (Kornblum and Julian, 1989). Many wonder how it is possible that the United States, with its great wealth, can have up to 3 million people living on its streets without even the most basic human needs of food, clothing, and shelter.

Who are the homeless and where do they come from? Fischer and Breakey (1986) have identified four categories of the homeless: (1) the chronically mentally ill who have been deinstitutionalized from hospitals or other mental health facilities, and who are more likely to exhibit the aberrant behaviors that people often associate with the homeless; (2) street people, such as "bag ladies" and "grate men," who live isolated lives, shun other people, and exist on what resources they can scavenge from the streets; (3) chronic or skid-row alcoholics whose lives revolve around ways to gain and drink alcohol; and (4) the situationally distressed who are unemployed, have been evicted from their homes, or are in transience seeking work. The last category includes families as well as single people.

The alarming rise in the homeless is among families. Bassuk and associates (1986) estimated that families comprised over 20 percent of the homeless population in 1985 and projected that their numbers would double in 1986. In New York City alone there are 4,000 homeless families, totaling 14,530 individuals, of which 9,590 are children. The typical homeless family in Boston was headed by a single black woman under 30 years old, who had not completed high school, and who had 2.4 children (Bassuk, 1986). These women had experienced trauma in their childhoods, had personality disorders, had inconsistent or nonexistent work histories, had extreme difficulty parenting, and sometimes physically abused their children. Not surprisingly, their children also had serious medical and emotional problems. The population composition of the homeless cross-cuts categories of gender, race, age, education, and occupation. The homeless are much younger than in the past, and are more likely to have a psychiatric disability, to be drug abusers, to have extensive medical problems, and to be women (Garrett and Schutt, 1986).

From these descriptions of the homeless it is apparent that as a category the homeless are people who are often seen as deviating from the majority of the population on two counts. The very fact that they have no home makes them different from most people. But, in addition to being homeless, they may also have a mental illness, or be alcoholic, or be drug addicts, or be unemployed, or be in extreme poverty. The homeless often carry the burden of a double-deviant label.

For a fuller examination of the homeless, we will consider their conditions and problems from the perspective of the four major sociological theoretical perspectives.

Structural-Functional Theory

Structural-functionalists, as we saw in chapter 1, are primarily interested in the functions of different social structures. Functionalists look at the structures of a society and consider what purposes or functions they serve. For example, some functionalists see inequality in society as having a purpose or a function. Inequality is seen as the natural outcome of a system in which rewards are given to those who perform tasks that require special skills, or talents. Some people live in affluence because they have these skills and talents, and use them to perform important societal tasks, while others live in poverty because they lack the skills and talents. According to this perspective, economic inequalities are functional because the important tasks of the society get accomplished. Inequality is also functional because the poor are motivated to work harder in order to rise above their deprived economic position.

The social position of the homeless can be seen as similarly functional in various ways. For example, the homeless are, as we have noted, deviant—often doubly so—but their deviance can be functional for the majority of the society. The aberrant behaviors of the homeless serve to reaffirm the values and norms of the rest of the society and thus strengthen their social unity. Further functions of the homeless can be found in their absence

from the work force, for that opens up jobs for others. Also, the needs of the homeless lead to the expansion of various occupations such as social service workers, which can provide work for many members of the middle class.

Functionalists, however, are concerned not only with functions but also dysfunctions. Dysfunctions are the negative or detrimental outcomes of social structures. The homeless are dysfunctional to society by the strains they place on the economic and political systems. For example, when the homeless become ill, the costs of health care are borne by the public. The homeless certainly represent a severe drain on the time and resources of the police. Furthermore, many people feel that the presence of so many homeless people represents a threat to the quality of life within our cities.

Conflict Theory

For conflict theorists, the homeless provide an example of the inequality inherent in American society. The homeless often wander past, or set up "homes" on the grates near, the homes and office buildings of the most affluent members of our society. The inequality in our society is rarely clearer than when the affluent members of our society are forced to walk by, or step over, homeless people. There is clearly much mutual disdain and hostility between them.

Conflict theorists would also point to the powerlessness of the homeless, their lack of resources, and their resulting inability to change their situation. That our society largely ignores the homeless and the conditions under which they live on our city's streets, provides conflict theorists with evidence of the extent of the powerlessness of this underclass.

The lack of power among the homeless is illustrated in their inability to gain affordable housing. In many cities housing once occupied by the poor has been either destroyed or purchased by corporations and renovated for rental or sale to the wealthy. Gentrification of inner city housing shoves the poor into smaller, more expensive living spaces, sometimes shared with many relatives. Continued increases in rents squeeze some people from these cramped spaces and into the streets.

In the past, the government has sought to satisfy the basic needs of the poor by building public housing. However, Kozol (1989) points out that the government is no longer building public housing, and "the waiting time to get to the top of the 200,000-family-long list is 18 years" (1989, p. 3G). The lack of affordable housing has led to an increase in public shelters that serve as temporary housing for the homeless. Bassuk (1986) has referred to shelters as "a stop-gap, band-aid response to a festering problem." Kozol describes these shelters as a "rational and antiseptic way to isolate and containerize the poor" (1989, p. 3G). Conflict theorists might view the growth of shelters as a way of placating the homeless and, more generally, the poor. Kozol contends that by the year 2000 the United States "may well be operating the most nicely decorated poorhouse in the world" (1989, p. 3G). To the conflict theorists, a poorhouse, no matter how nicely decorated, is a clear indication of profound inequality in society.

Symbolic Interactionism

Symbolic interactionists would be interested in how homelessness is experienced by people, how they make sense of their situation, and how they form relationships in the impersonal world of city streets. Instead of discussing homelessness in the abstract manner of the functionalists (e.g., the functions and dysfunctions of homelessness), symbolic interactionsts are likely to observe it personally and to discuss it in far more individual terms. Those who have observed and talked to the homeless describe them in such a stark way that we may be shocked at the lifestyle of this segment of our population. For example, Jon D. Hull (1987) lived among the homeless on the streets of Philadelphia and described his interaction with a homeless man.

> Though he is now dying on the streets, Gary used to be a respectable citizen. His full name is Gary Shaw, 48, and he is a life-long resident of Philadelphia and a father of three. He once worked as a precision machinist, making metal dies for casting tools. "I could work with my eyes closed," he says, "I was the best there was." But he lost his job and wife to alcohol. Now his home is an old red couch with the springs exposed in a garbage-strewn clearing amid abandoned tenements. Nearby, wood pulled from a building burns in a 55-gallon metal drum while the Thunderbird [a cheap wine] is passed around. When evening falls, Gary has trouble standing, and he believes his liver and kidneys are on the verge of failing. His thighs carry deep burn marks from sleeping on grates, and a severe beating the previous night has left bruises on his lower back and a long scab across his nose. The pain is apparent in his eyes, still brilliant blue, and the handsome features of his face are hidden beneath a layer of grime (1987, pp. 94–95).

Symbolic interaction, as the name suggests, reflects a concern with symbols. From this point of view, it is interesting to reflect on "bag ladies" (Shulman, 1981). The "bag" is often a shopping bag. In our society a shopping bag is a symbol of success. Carrying a shopping bag out of a supermarket is a sign that the person is at least able to support her(him)self and perhaps a family. Carrying a shopping bag with a department store label is a symbol of an even higher level of success. Furthermore, there is even a symbolic hierarchy based on the prestige of the department store whose name is on the shopping bag. Thus, a bag from Nieman-Marcus is of higher status than one from Macy's which, in turn, is of higher status than a bag from K-Mart.

The shopping bag has symbolic importance for bag ladies. It allows them to demonstrate that they are not very much different from most other women in society. As Shulman puts it, the shopping bag is a "universal female sign in our culture, [which] commonly adorns the arms of even comfortable women." In spite of this symbolic unity, there are clearly important differences between middle- and upper-class women and bag ladies. As Shulman says, "While most of us have drawers, closets, some even attics and cellars in which to store our possessions, the homeless . . . have only their shopping bags. Compare their contents with your dresser and kitchen drawers and the mystery of the bags disappears." Thus, in this case symbolic unity cannot conceal substantial material differences.

Social Exchange Theory

We can use exchange theory to look at one aspect of the lives of many homeless people—panhandling and begging. Homeless people do more than simply wander the streets, sleep in parks, sit on curbs, or scavenge garbage dumps for food. Some "earn" money by panhandling or begging. Some may simply sit with their hands out hoping for passersby to toss them coins, others are more aggressive and block the way of pedestrians, others are boys who jump on the hoods of cars to wash windshields, and still others are mothers with children who stand in busy intersections to solicit money from drivers. They may have signs that tell people such things as "Please help, have family, need job, money for rent, food, thanks!" or "God bless the happy giver" (Gibbs, 1988, p. 70).

Exchange theorists might look at panhandling as an example of reciprocity among drastically different economic segments of our population. When panhandlers are successful, they gain at least a meager subsistence. For their part, those who give panhandlers money relieve their guilt about the conditions under which panhandlers live in comparison to their own domestic comforts. For this reason, particularly successful beggars are the handicapped and women with small children since most people feel especially guilty when passing them. Another gain for those who give to panhandlers is relief from fear. Many panhandlers create this sense of fear by yelling at people, acting menacingly, and approaching people in isolated and dangerous places, such as in subways. Thus, there is a kind of reciprocity in the relationship between panhandlers and those who give them money. The panhandler gains money to survive, while those who give reduce guilt feelings and feel less fearful.

People are ambivalent in their attitudes toward giving to panhandlers. Some feel that helping beggars simply encourages them to continue living on the streets, ripping off the hard-earned money of working people. For example, billboards of unknown sponsorship appeared in 1988 in El Paso, Texas, which said, "Please don't give to beggars, they cause traffic problems" (Gibbs, 1988). Others have a more charitable attitude and give to beggars because they feel they are victims of our society and should be cared for.

Looking at the Research

Research on the homeless is difficult for many reasons. For one thing, they are plagued with problems (e.g., drugs, alcohol, mental illness) that may make it difficult to get accurate information from them. For another, they may well resent talking to social scientists who are apt to come from the far more successful sectors of society. Furthermore, the homeless may be difficult to study and re-study because they are such a rapidly growing and changing population. No one really knows exactly how many homeless there are, exactly what their demographic and social characteristics are, how they survive on the streets, or why and under what conditions they leave the streets. All these factors vary because homelessness is not necessarily a permanent condition, that is, many are only temporarily homeless. For example, they may have been evicted from their homes but after a few months move in with relatives. We do know, as seen in the research reported by Bassuk (1986), that the increase among homeless families is dramatic. Because these families are often headed by women, there has been a "feminization of homelessness" that is a reflection of the "feminization of poverty" in our country.

In general, the public is fearful of the homeless. Although they may toss the homeless some loose change, the public does not want to spend time with them and get to know them. As a result, misconceptions and myths about the homeless persist. For example, a widespread assumption is that most of the homeless suffer from some form of mental illness. However, one sociological study might cause us to reevaluate this conception. David Snow and his associates (1986) studied the issue of whether the homeless were mostly mentally ill people. Their 20-month study in Austin, Texas, of homeless men and women revealed that only about 16 percent of this group had ever been labeled as having a mental health problem, and only 10 percent had ever been institutionalized. These findings help dispel the myth of the ubiquity of mental illness among the homeless. Instead of being mentally ill, they are mostly unskilled workers who have gone in and out of the job market in dead-end, low-paying jobs that do not enable them to get off the streets. These people, like most of the homeless, are trapped in poor economic conditions that lead to further poverty and despair.

Although sociological theories and research help us to better understand the homeless, this work in and of itself does not help society to deal with the problem any better. Until there is a widespread consensus to do something about homelessness, and to use the work of sociologists and others in a constructive way, the future of the homeless, and their place in our society, is bleak.

References

BASSUK, ELLEN L. "Homeless Families: Single Mothers and Their Children in Boston Shelters." In Ellen L. Bassuk (ed.), *The Mental Health Needs of Homeless Persons*. San Francisco: Jossey-Bass, 1986.

BASSUK, ELLEN; RUBIN, LENORE; and LAURIAT, ALISON S. "Characteristics of Sheltered Homeless Families." *American Journal of Public Health* 76, 1986.

FISCHER, PAMELA J., and BREAKEY, WILLIAM R. "Homelessness and Mental Health: An Overview." *International Journal of Mental Health*. 14, 1986.

GARRETT, GERALD, and SCHUTT, RUSSELL K. "Homeless in the 1980s: Social Services for a Changing Population." Paper presented at the Eastern Sociological Society, New York City, 1986.

GIBBS, NANCY R. "Begging: To Give or Not to Give." *Time*, September 5, 1988.

HULL, JON D. "Slow Descent Into Hell." *Time*, February 2, 1987.

KORNBLUM, WILLIAM, and JULIAN, JOSEPH. *Social Problems*, 6th ed. Englewood Cliffs, N.J.: Prentice Hall, 1989.

KOZOL, JONATHAN. "A Nicely Decorated Poorhouse." *The Kansas City Star*, April 9, 1989.

SHULMAN, ALIX KATES. "Bag Ladies." *New York Times*, September 29, 1981.

SNOW, DAVID A.; BAKER, SUSAN G., and ANDERSON, LEON. "The Myth of Pervasive Mental Illness Among the Homeless." *Social Problems* 33, 1986.

CHAPTER

8

Stratification: Living with Social Inequality

All societies face the basic problem of how to distribute scarce and desirable resources and social rewards—money, power, influence, and respect—among their members. Seldom, if ever, are they distributed equally; differences in social rank appear in virtually all human societies, even those that claim to be egalitarian. Throughout human history, some people have possessed greater wealth, prestige, and power than others, regardless of the society in which they lived, and this phenomenon shows no sign of disappearing. **Social stratification** refers to the structure of social inequality in each society—the manner in which scarce resources and social rewards are distributed among different social categories.

Social stratification
The structure of social inequality in a society

An individual's position in a system of stratification affects **life chances,** a term referring to the likelihood of realizing a certain standard of living or quality of life. For example, in American society the life chances of the poor for education, nutrition, life expectancy, quality of housing, and treatment by the criminal justice system differ dramatically from those of the rich. This chapter will be concerned with the nature and consequences of social inequality and social ranking: wealth and poverty, power and powerlessness, dominance and subordination, prestige and degradation, and the ways in which advantages and disadvantages are passed from one generation to another.

Life chances
The likelihood of realizing a certain quality of life

Although social stratification is virtually universal, societies differ in the ways in which they allocate scarce resources. Therefore forms of stratification systems vary widely. Even though most societies have been stratified in some way, however, this does not necessarily mean that a society must be stratified. "A system of ranks does not form part of some natural and invariable order of things, but is a human contrivance or product, and is subject to historical changes" (Bottomore, 1966b, p. 10). In other words, social stratification is not "natural" or inevitable. A classless society is a possibility, if not a probability.

Social stratification is a *social* phenomenon. A system of stratification in any group or society is *not* determined by the biological characteristics of individuals or by supernatural laws. It results from human actions in both the present and the past. Earlier generations create a system of stratification that influences each succeeding generation. Throughout their lives people learn the structure of, and their places in, their society's stratification system.

Dimensions of Stratification

In a complex society such as exists in the United States, determining one's position in its stratification system is frequently difficult because several criteria may be used—wealth, prominence, prestige, influence, and ancestry. Although wealth is obviously an important determinant of one's place in the American stratification system, it is not the only one. People are evaluated differently depending on how their wealth is attained. For example, members of the U.S. House of Representatives have annual salaries of $89,000. However, they have a different location in the stratification system from a professional baseball player, a cocaine dealer, a plumber, a lottery winner, a small-town business owner, or a playboy whose annual incomes are the same or much higher. Each of these different sources of income carries differences in prestige and power which, in addition to wealth, must be considered in evaluating how people are distributed in a system of stratification.

Class
Social ranking on the basis of economic factors

Status
Social ranking on the basis of prestige

Power
The ability to impose one's will upon others even if they resist

Because social stratification in modern societies is influenced by different factors, Max Weber distinguished among three basic dimensions: class, status, and power. **Class** is a social ranking made on the basis of economic factors. **Status** in the context of stratification refers to a social ranking on the basis of *prestige,* that is, the esteem, honor, and social approval accorded an individual or group. **Power** is a social ranking based on the ability to make others do what you want them to do.

Class

Although Weber recognized wealth as an important dimension of stratification, it was Karl Marx who especially emphasized the role of economic factors in determining social ranking. He identified two basic social classes that are distinguished by their relationship to property. The dominant class—composed of landowners, slaveowners, and factory and business owners—owns and controls the means of production (such as land, machines, and tools). The subordinate class includes industrial laborers, peasants, serfs, and slaves who work for the dominant class.

Proletariat
The subordinate class that sells its labor to the owners of the means of production

Capitalists
The owners of the means of production in a capitalist economy

In a capitalist society, industrial laborers (the **proletariat**) are forced to sell their labor to those who own the means of production (the **capitalists**). To achieve profits, capitalists exploit workers by paying wages that are less than the value of the goods the workers produce. As capitalists compete with each other and seek to achieve ever-greater profits, they try to cut costs by reducing wages paid to the workers. Marx described different ways—among them, employing children and lengthening the work days—in which capitalists in the nineteenth century sought to increase their profits.

Contemporary industrial capitalism differs greatly from capitalism in Marx's day, and critics have argued that his analysis no longer applies. Dahrendorf (1959), for example, contends that Marx focused too narrowly on the idea of ownership of property. The distinctive feature of capitalism today is the corporation, which is owned by hundreds of thousands of shareholders, not by one or even a handful. Such corporations, however, are controlled and run by a small number of people—corporate managers and executives. Therefore, *control,* not *ownership,* of the means of production is the factor that distinguishes classes in modern capitalist societies.

New Class
The powerful stratum of managers, executives, and intellectuals in bureaucratically dominated societies

In analyzing changes in the economic structures of modern societies, several writers have suggested the emergence of an important new social stratum—a "**New Class,**" consisting of intellectuals, bureaucrats, managers, executives, scientists, and other professionals who wield power. This New Class appears not only in capitalist countries of the West but in the USSR, in its Eastern European satellite states, and in the Third World of developing nations as well. According to this analysis, economic changes have produced a changing occupational structure that creates new positions of power and authority in the economic, political, social, and cultural spheres.

Status

Although Max Weber did not ignore the special significance that Marx attributed to property and economic factors, he believed that stratification was based on prestige and power as well as on economic factors. Whereas one's class position is determined by wealth and income, Weber argued, one's status is based on the prestige that attaches to the positions that people occupy in society. Usually one's status position is intimately related to one's class position, but it is possible for individuals to be ranked differently on these two dimensions. Status, therefore, according to Weber, refers to groups of people who share similar life chances resulting from social estimation of honor or prestige.

For example, despite a popular egalitarian ideology, one source of status in American society is lineage or family background. Considerable prestige is connected with membership in such hereditary societies as the Daughters of the American Revolution, the Society of Mayflower Descendants, and the National Society of Colonial Dames. Although many such organizations tend to draw their membership primarily from those with considerable wealth, the primary criterion is ancestry. Similarly, inclusion in the *Social Register*, a published listing of about 65,000 families and single adults that has been used by sociologists as an index of upper class America, is based on social standing, not on wealth alone.

Power

Weber argued that a third dimension of stratification exists—power—that is different from class and status. Power refers to the ability to get others to do what you want, even against their own will. The nature and distribution of power and the struggle among groups vying for power have been among the central concerns of sociologists. Although class, status, and power are closely related, Weber felt that they were theoretically separate—that is, there are situations in which those wielding the greatest power in a society do not necessarily possess great economic resources or prestige. Thus power is a crucial part of any system of social inequality. The President of the United States, for example, has extraordinary power, both in this country and throughout the world, but he is not necessarily wealthy. We would not argue that basketball star Michael Jordan, pop star Michael Jackson, or even one of the wealthiest Americans—billionaire Sam Moore Walton (the founder and owner of Wal-Mart)—are as powerful or are accorded prestige equal to that of the President of the United States. We will examine the nature and distribution of power more fully in chapter 16, Political Life.

How Are Stratification Systems Justified?

Stratification systems are systems of inequality, and it is important that the majority of people accept that inequality. The people in privileged positions generally can accept the inequality easily, but even they can feel more comfortable if something justifies their position. People lower in the system must have some basis for accepting the inequalities they experience. For these reasons stratification systems usually have an ideology. An **ideology** is a set of ideas that explains reality, provides directives for behavior, and expresses the interests of particular groups. An ideology is used to legitimize and justify the existing social order and to maintain the inequalities in wealth, power, and prestige.

Ideology
Set of ideas that explains reality, directs behavior, and expresses group interest

The ideology, which contains a set of rules that explain how and why the society's resources are distributed as they are, frequently becomes accepted by those in subordinate as well as dominant positions. Different stratification systems have developed different kinds of ideologies, which may include religious, political, economic, or "scientific" elements.

Religion has frequently provided an ideology to support social inequalities. American slaveholders, for example, maintained that the Bible supported slavery—that blacks were condemned to eternal servitude by the curse of Ham. Similarly, the Indian caste system, characterized by a system of rigidly defined social ranks and an extremely high degree of social inequality that has endured for thousands of years, is justified by the Hindu religion. Hindu belief emphasizes the importance of reincarnation—the process whereby one's soul is reborn in another person after one's death. However, whether one's soul is reincarnated in a person higher or lower in the caste system depends on how faithfully one has accepted and observed one's duties in the previous life. Failure to observe the rules of the caste system could condemn someone to be reincarnated as an "outcaste," the lowest and most despised position in the system.

Science has also been widely used to justify social ranking. In American society for more than a century, so-called scientific findings have shaped views on race. In the nineteenth century scientists conducted numerous studies to prove the existence of a racial hierarchy in brain size, and therefore intelligence, with northern Europeans highest on the scale and blacks lowest. Today intelligence testing has replaced such anatomical studies as a way of "scientifically" validating the superiority of socially dominant groups. Differences in test scores between whites and blacks—affected by social class, cultural backgrounds, and the settings in which the tests are given—are frequently used to reinforce the system of racial inequality in the United States.

Meritocracy
An ideology that justifies social inequality by emphasizing equality of opportunity

Finally, inequality in American society today is widely justified by **meritocracy** as an ideology. The basic belief in this ideology is equality of opportunity—all Americans have equal chances to achieve success, and inequalities in the distribution of wealth, power, and influence reflect the qualifications or merit of individuals in each stratum. Affluence is perceived to be a result of the personal qualities of intelligence, industriousness, motivation, and ambition, whereas poverty is perceived to exist because the poor lack those attributes. Thus Americans generally accept the idea that those at the top of the economic pyramid deserve to be there, and they attribute the responsibility for poverty to the qualities of the poor themselves (Huber and Form, 1973). Ryan (1971) labels this explanation of poverty "blaming the victim." He contends that this view fails to recognize the ways affluence and poverty are a result of the structure of opportunities available to people in different socioeconomic statuses.

Structural-Functional and Conflict Theories of Social Stratification

Sociologists have developed two broad theories to account for social stratification—structural-functional theory and conflict theory. These competing conceptions of social inequality have generated considerable controversy.

Structural-functionalists are inclined to see social stratification as an expression of common values in society. Therefore, since American society values economic success, it accords those with more money higher status in the stratification system. Since the stratification system supports basic American values, it contributes to societal integration and stability. In contrast, conflict theorists view stratification as an expression of conflicting group interests. The various strata are seen as emerging from the conflict over scarce, valued resources.

The **functional theory of stratification** views the stratification system as equitable because people get what society seems to say they deserve (Jeffries and Ransford, 1980). Those at the top are seen as deserving greater power, prestige, and life chances than those at the bottom, who deserve much less of each. Functionalists see inequality in the distribution of rewards as beneficial to both individuals and society because society's tasks are accomplished by the best-qualified people. Conflict theorists, on the other hand, view the existing distribution of rewards as unjust and detrimental to most people as well as to society as a whole.

Functional theory of stratification
Social inequality is necessary to motivate the most able people to fill society's most important tasks

To structural-functionalists, power and coercion do not play a central part in maintaining a system of rewards and privileges. In their view, the system is maintained because most of a society's members believe in and accept common values. Once again, conflict theorists disagree. They do not believe that most Americans accept the fact that some have a right to greater rewards. We accept it, they say, because those in power have forced us to, perhaps by propagandizing us into believing in their greater rights.

Structural-functionalists contend that the major function of stratification is to motivate the relatively few capable people to occupy higher-level, more prestigious positions in society. To encourage people to want to occupy these more "important" positions, Davis and Moore (1945) argue, they must be offered greater rewards, in the forms of more money, power, and prestige. Therefore, a society must not only be stratified, but it must be stratified in such a way that the higher a person rises in the system, the greater are the rewards attached to a position. So, the argument goes, if we want the most talented people to become physicians, politicians, or business managers, we must offer them greater rewards. If we do not, the structural-functionalist says, then not enough of the most talented people will enter these positions.

Conflict theorists ridicule this idea. They argue that these positions will prove intrinsically attractive to many people, with no need to offer greater rewards. Conflict theorists argue that since members of the upper classes occupy these positions in large numbers, they have a vested interest in attaching great rewards to them. They contend that the functional theory of stratification simply perpetuates the privileged position of people who already have power, prestige, and money. The functional theory also can be criticized for assuming that simply because a social structure has existed in the past, it must continue to exist in the future. Possibly future societies can be organized in other, nonstratified ways.

Critics of functionalism also challenge the idea that positions vary in their importance to society. Are garbage collectors really less important to the survival of society than advertising executives? Despite the lower pay and prestige of the garbage collectors, they may actually be more important for the survival of the society.

Even in cases where one position obviously serves a more important function for society, greater rewards do not necessarily accrue to that position. The registered nurse may be more important to society than the movie actor, but the registered nurse has far less power, prestige, and income than the actor.

Other critics question whether there really is a scarcity of people capable of filling high-level positions. In fact, evidence suggests that many people who may possess ability are prevented from obtaining the training needed to achieve prestigious positions. Moreover, formal educational credentials may themselves be unrelated to job performance and, therefore, serve to exclude capable people from jobs that they could effectively perform (Persell, 1977, pp. 158–163). In general, many able people may never get a chance to show that they can handle high-ranking positions.

Finally, functionalists see the American stratification system as open, with the ability to rise in it generally dependent on personal talent and motivation. This expresses the American belief that those with ability and ambition can make it to the top. Conflict theorists reject this notion as well. They argue that ability and motivation are insignificant; what really matters is being born into the upper strata where people have greater access to educational facilities, the best universities, and the "right" contacts. Conflict theorists hold that status in the American stratification system is often ascribed, rather than achieved. That is, more people remain in the position into which they are born than achieve higher positions through personal effort.

Social Inequalities in American Life

Having identified the various dimensions of social stratification and competing explanations for its existence, we now turn to an examination of social inequalities in American life.

Inequalities of Class

Wealth
Accumulated economic resources that people have acquired over time

Income
The money that people obtain during a specified period of time—usually a year

What is the nature of economic inequality in American society? How equally is the economic "pie" divided? How concentrated are economic resources in the United States? In examining economic inequalities, we must first distinguish between wealth and income. **Wealth** refers to the total economic resources that people *have,* while **income** refers to how much money people obtain during a specified period of time, usually a year. Although there is frequently a close relationship between the two, an individual could possibly have substantial wealth and little income or vice versa. Therefore wealthy landowners might be "land poor"—that is, they may own considerable amounts of real estate but derive little income from it. On the other hand, some people might have a very high income but spend or lose most of it and thus have accumulated little wealth. In the discussion below we shall examine data on trends in the distribution of wealth and income in the United States.

Income. Income is specifically the wages, salaries, dividends, interest, and rents received each year by individuals or family units. Median family income in the United States in 1987 was $30,850 (U.S. Bureau of the Census, 1988a). This means that half the families earned more than that amount and half earned less. However, this figure is somewhat misleading because it tells nothing about the range of incomes above $30,850. Much more room exists at the top for high incomes than at the bottom for low incomes, as the annual earnings of many corporate executives, professional athletes, and entertainers demonstrate. In other words, the incomes of the bottom half of Americans range from $0 to $30,850 annually, but the incomes of the upper half range from $30,850 to over $1 billion. However, the earnings of most American families are far closer to the figure of $30,850 than the huge sums earned by the super rich.

Only 1 percent of American families earn more than $150,000 a year, and although all of them could be called rich, marked differences exist between the rich and the very

Children of the wealthy have expensive toys that mimic those of their parents. Children of the poor often live in poor and dilapidated housing, with few resources and little hope.

The working environments of people in high-status occupations are dramatically different from those in lower-status jobs.

Drawing by Joe Mirachi; © 1988 The New Yorker Magazine, Inc.

"The poor are getting poorer, but with the rich getting richer it all averages out in the long run."

rich. Physicians and other health professionals, lawyers, and accountants are most highly represented in the $100,000–$150,000 range. Avery and Elliehausen (1986) found that the occupations producing the highest incomes (the top one-half of 1 percent—those with incomes of $280,000 or more) were commercial and investment banking, insurance, and real estate.

The data in table 8–1 show that little overall change has occurred since World War II in the distribution of income to various strata. Since the late 1960s, however, the poor have grown poorer and the rich richer. In 1967 the bottom 40 percent of American families received 17.9 percent of income, and the top 40 percent received 64.3 percent. By 1987 the bottom category had declined to 15.4 percent, and the top category had increased to 67.7 percent. Moreover, in 1987 the share of the poorest fifth of the American population (4.6 percent) fell to the lowest it has been since 1954, while the share of the richest fifth (43.7 percent) rose to an all-time high.

Table 8–1. The Distribution of Before-Tax Family Income among American Families

	Percentage of Total					
American Families	Lowest fifth	Second fifth	Third fifth	Fourth fifth	Highest fifth	Index of concentration
1947	5.0	11.9	17.0	23.1	43.0	.376
1957	5.1	12.7	18.1	23.8	40.4	.351
1967	5.5	12.4	17.9	23.9	40.4	.348
1977	5.2	11.6	17.5	24.2	41.5	.364
1987	4.6	10.8	16.8	24.0	43.7	.392

Source: U.S. Bureau of the Census, *Current Population Reports*, Series P-60, no. 159, 1988.

However, focusing on the top 40 percent or even the top one-fifth of the population obscures the increasing concentration of income at the very top. In 1987 the top 5 percent included families with incomes above $86,300. The top 5 percent received 16.9 percent of all income, which is more than the total income for the entire lowest 40 percent of the population. These recent increases in income inequality are measured by an index of income concentration (technically called the Gini index). As income is distributed more equally, the index declines; as overall income inequality increases, so does the index. Although the index of income concentration is characterized by periodic fluctuations, it declined between 1947 and 1967 and since then has risen steadily, reaching in 1987 its highest level (.392) in the post-World War II period. By 1987 the income gap between rich and poor families had reached its greatest level in 40 years.

The income inequalities in the United States shown in table 8–1 are especially striking when compared to other Western industrialized countries. As the data in figure 8–1 indicate, only in France and Austria do people at the lower end of the economic

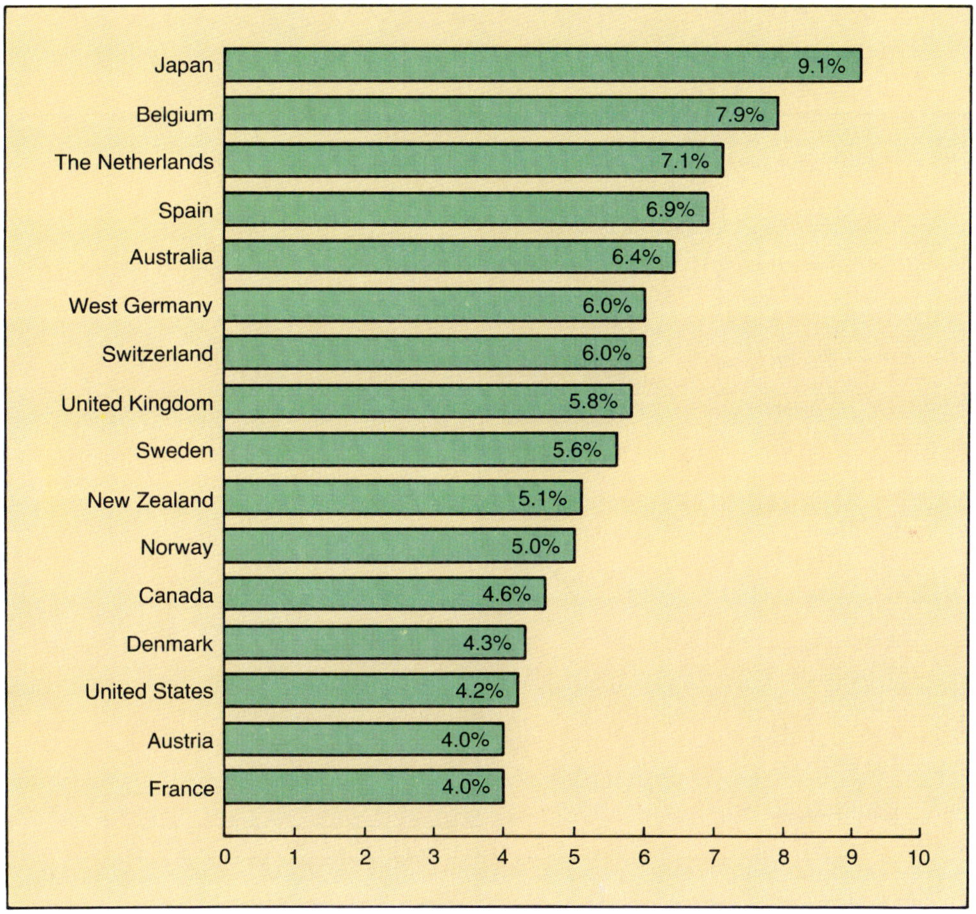

Figure 8–1. The Percent of a Country's Total Income Going to the Poorest 20 Percent of the Population, for Selected Countries. The poorest 20 percent receive the greatest proportion in Japan and the least in Austria and France. (*Source:* United Nations Department of International Economic and Social Affairs, "National Account Statistics: Compendium of Income Distribution Statistics," *Statistical Papers*, Series M, No. 79. (New York, United Nations, 1985.))

scale receive so small a share as in the United States. For example, the bottom fifth of the population receives more than twice as much income in Japan as in the United States (United Nations Department of International Economic and Social Affairs, 1985, pp. 6–9).

The Declining Middle Class. During the first two decades after World War II, Americans experienced unprecedented prosperity and increases in family income. Between 1947 and 1967 average weekly earnings rose by 50 percent, and real median family income nearly doubled—increasing from $15,423 in 1947 to $27,004 in 1967 (in 1987 dollars) (U.S. Bureau of the Census, 1988a, p. 35). Moreover, as we have seen in table 8–1, between 1947 and 1967 a trend toward more equitable income distribution appeared. Widespread prosperity and more equitable distribution of income contributed to the image of the United States as a "middle-class society" and reinforced the widespread belief among Americans that the quality of their lives would always improve over that of their parents and that the quality of their children's lives would exceed theirs.

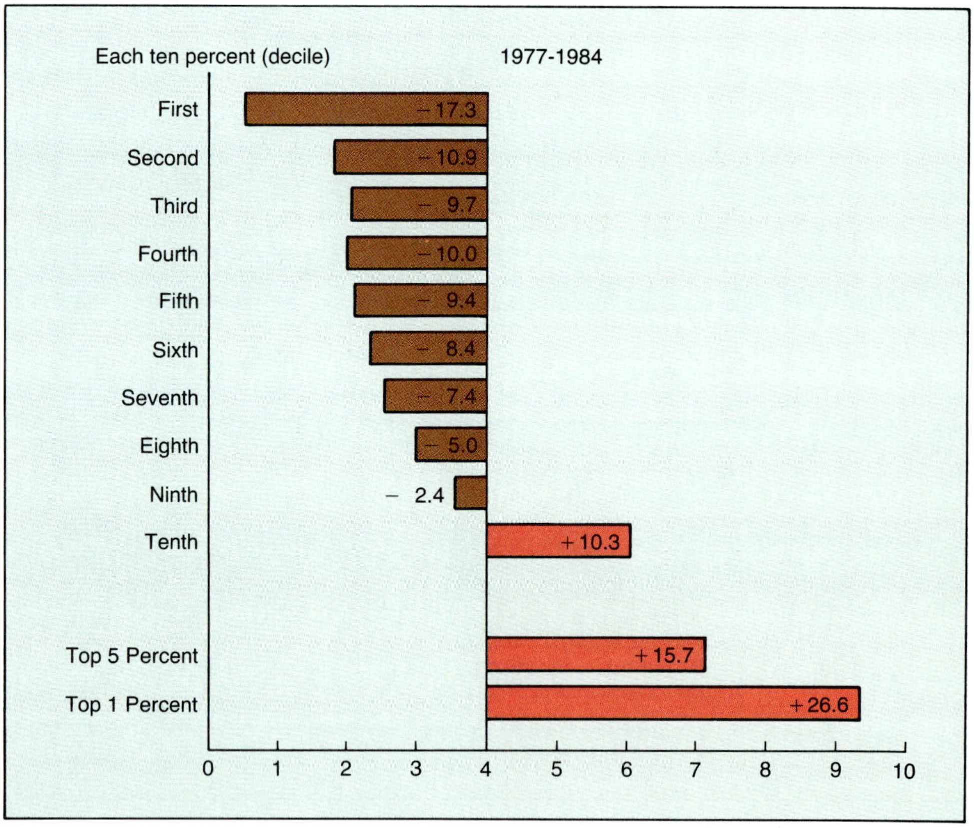

Figure 8–2. Percentage Changes in Average Family Income for Each Ten Percent of the Population, 1977–1984. (*Source:* Adapted from Congressional Budget Office, *The Changing Distribution of Federal Taxes: 1975–1990* (Washington, D.C., October 1987).)

However, since the late 1960s and early 1970s the economic position of the American middle class has stagnated. Real median family income, which achieved an all-time high of $30,820 (in 1987 dollars) in 1973, failed until 1987 to reach that level again. Real median family income for 1987 ($30,850) was virtually the same as in 1973; not once during the intervening 14 years did it reach the 1973 level. The period of rapidly rising American prosperity had ended.

Moreover, as shown above, since the late 1960s a steady trend has been seen toward increasing income inequality, with the more affluent sectors of the population receiving a greater percentage of the nation's income. The Congressional Budget Office study cited above examined changes in income distribution between 1977 and 1984 and projected changes through 1988. Data from that study, shown in figure 8–2, showed that *all except the highest 10 percent of American families experienced a decline in income between 1977 and 1984*. The only increases were to the highest income category, and these increases were greatest among the richest 1 percent. The study further projected that by the end of 1988, the lowest 80 percent of families would experience an income decline. However, the richest 10 percent would see their incomes rise by 16.5 percent; the richest 5 percent, by 23.4 percent; and the richest 1 percent, by 59.2 percent.

The ability to own one's home has been a prominent component of the American dream and for many Americans it represents participation in the broad middle class. Therefore, another index of the declining middle class and the growing gap in living standards between the rich and the poor is in housing costs. Increasingly, the United States is becoming a nation of housing haves and have-nots. In 1987 the median price of a first home was nearly $67,000, four times the 1975 price ($16,530) and almost double the 1975 price of $34,800 (in 1986 constant dollars). In some regions of the country (especially the Northeast and the West), increases in housing prices have been even more dramatic. These rising costs have made it increasingly difficult for low-income and moderate-income—especially young—households to purchase a home. As table 8–2 indicates, between 1974 and 1987 the rate of homeownership declined for households with annual incomes under $35,000, and this decline was especially pronounced for households with incomes under $5,000 (Apgar and Brown, 1988).

Table 8–2. Household Income and Homeownership

Thousands (1986 Dollars)	Number of Households (in thousands)		Percent Homeowners	
	1974	1987	1974	1987
Under 5	4,705	7,204	42.8	36.7
5 to 10	8,755	10,984	48.7	45.9
10 to 17.5	11,436	15,326	53.8	51.9
17.5 to 25	11,152	13,063	58.7	60.0
25 to 35	13,277	14,636	69.3	68.3
35 to 50	11,638	14,177	78.6	79.3
50+	9,891	14,089	86.2	89.1
Total	70,854	89,478	64.7	64.0

Source: Apgar, William C., Jr. and Brown, H. James. *The State of the Nation's Housing.* Cambridge, Mass.: Joint Center for Housing Studies of Harvard University, 1988, p. 7.

The New York Stock Exchange and other major financial institutions provide the stocks, bonds, and trust holdings that are especially concentrated among the very wealthy families of the United States.

Wealth. Measures of income inequality alone do not adequately measure a society's stratification system. To gain an accurate picture of the distribution of a society's economic resources we must also examine wealth—which includes savings, investments, homes, and property. Wealth represents accumulated or "stored-up" purchasing power.

Historical trends in the distribution of wealth show that the Colonial and immediate post-Revolutionary periods were the most egalitarian in American history (Smith, 1984; Williamson, 1980). In other words, wealth was more equally distributed during this period than at any other time. Between the early nineteenth century and the beginning of the Great Depression in 1929, economic inequalities increased. During the Great Depression and World War II the distribution of wealth became significantly more equal. From the end of World War II to 1963 an overall increase occurred in the concentration of wealth, but then it declined, so that by 1976, for the first time in the twentieth century, the wealthiest 1 percent of Americans owned less than 20 percent of the nation's total assets. However, the most recent data available indicate that that trend has reversed; wealth is again more heavily concentrated among the very rich. By 1983 the richest 1 percent of the population owned nearly one-third (32.9 percent) of the nation's wealth (Wolff, 1987; Joint Economic Committee, 1986). Today the distribution of wealth is much more highly concentrated in the upper extremes than income is.

Since the 1983 data probably do not reflect the impact of changes in national tax policies in the 1980s—changes that disproportionately benefitted the very rich—they may actually underestimate the current concentration of wealth. A Congressional Budget Office study found that federal tax changes enacted between 1978 and 1986 had their most dramatic effects at the extremes of income distribution. Between 1977 and 1988 the tax burden of the poorest 10 percent of taxpayers increased by 20 percent, while the tax burden of families in the highest 10 percent of income declined 6.4 percent (Congressional Budget Office, 1987, pp. 43–48).

The concentration of wealth in American society is even more apparent if one distinguishes between net worth and net financial assets. Most studies of the distribution of wealth have relied on measures of **net worth,** which refers to the difference between a household's assets and liabilities. For example, in 1984 the Census Bureau conducted the most comprehensive survey yet undertaken of the net worth (which includes assets such as homes, bank accounts, stocks and bonds, and liabilities such as mortgages and loans) of American households. The study found that nearly one-fifth of American families had zero or negative net worth—that is, their financial liabilities exceeded their assets. It also found that the net worth of a typical white household was 12 times that of a black household and eight times that of an Hispanic household. The median net worth for white households was $39,135; for black households, $3,397; and for Hispanic households, $4,913 (U.S. Bureau of the Census, 1986, p. 19).

Net worth
Household wealth based on the difference between assets and liabilities

However, the net worth of many Americans who have accumulated some wealth is held almost exclusively in the equity that they have in their homes and automobiles. Oliver and Shapiro (1989) have therefore argued that the most accurate measures of the concentration of wealth in the United States should exclude equity in homes and vehicles since these can seldom be converted to other purposes (such as financing a college education, establishing or expanding a business, or paying for emergency medical expenses). The term **net financial assets (NFA)** refers to household wealth after the equity in homes and vehicles has been deducted. If this measure of wealth (rather than

Net financial assets
Household wealth after equity in homes and vehicles has been deducted

The greatest portion of the wealth of most Americans is their homes and cars, and in many cases this wealth is quite modest.

net worth) is used, figures on the overall wealth of American households and inequalities in the distribution of wealth in American society change dramatically. Although the overall household median net worth is $32,609, household median net financial assets are $2,599. Moreover, "whereas the top 20 percent of American households earn over 43 percent of all income [see table 8–1], the same 20 percent holds 67 percent of net worth and nearly 90 percent of NFA" (Oliver and Shapiro, 1988). Stocks, bonds, and trust holdings are especially concentrated among very wealthy families. The richest one-half of 1 percent of American families own 40 percent of the nation's corporate stock. As these recent trends indicate, then, the United States is a society in which both income and wealth are unequally distributed, and these inequalities appear to be increasing.

Poverty. For most of human history the vast majority of people have been poor. Because poverty was so widespread, it did not appear to be a significant problem. It was simply taken for granted and perceived to be inevitable, a perception that the Bible reinforced: "For ye have the poor always with you" (Matthew 26:11) and "The poor shall never cease out of the land" (Deuteronomy 15:11). In modern American society, however, the most affluent in human history, the existence of poverty appears as a glaring contradiction, one that has been the subject of considerable debate (Murray, 1984; Harrington, 1984).

Obviously, poverty is a relative concept. The lives of poor families in rural Mississippi are considerably better than those of impoverished families in Calcutta, India, who are forced to live, eat, sleep, and die on the streets. Similarly, poor Mississippi families today live better lives than most families did in preindustrial times.

However, we do not live hundreds of years ago, or in Calcutta today. Americans live in a society that takes for granted many gains in the quality and security of life. We find it intolerable that people should live on the streets or die at an early age of minor ailments (as they did in preindustrial times). Nevertheless, even in the United States today, the poor suffer from hunger, inadequate shelter, and premature death.

Income sufficiency
Amount of money needed to purchase basic necessities of life

The most widely used definition of poverty in America is based on the idea of **income sufficiency**—the amount of money needed to purchase the basic necessities of life. Although several standards might be used to determine what level of income is sufficient, the measure used by the Social Security Administration has become the official government index of poverty.

Poverty index
Annual income necessary to meet minimal yearly living costs in the U.S.

The **poverty index** utilizes U.S. Department of Agriculture estimates of the costs of a minimal food budget, adjusted to the size of the family. The per person daily food budget is multiplied by three to determine the approximate level of funds needed for all other living costs—housing, clothes, medical care, heat, light, and other necessities. Therefore, in 1987 the index classified as poor all families of four with an income of less than $11,611 (U.S. Bureau of the Census, 1988c, p. 1). By this measure 32.5 million Americans, 13.5 percent of the population, lived below the poverty line in 1987.

Working poor
Working people whose incomes fall below the poverty line

Who are America's poor? Many Americans think of them as the "dregs" of society, its most disreputable members. The poor are often visualized as skid row winos, "bag ladies," able-bodied adults who prefer welfare to working, and so on. However, the reality is that the poor do not fit our stereotypes so clearly. For one thing, there are large numbers of **working poor**—people who earn so little from their work that their income is below the federal poverty line. In 1985 the working poor totalled 2.1 million.

Moreover, another 5.4 million people wanted full-time jobs but had to settle for part-time work (Pear, 1986, p. 18).

Some recent data (U.S. Bureau of the Census, 1988b; Duncan, 1984; O'Hare, 1985, 1987) indicate the following characteristics of the poor:

- Black poverty is more than three times as common as white poverty, and the poverty rate for Hispanics is nearly three times that for whites. However, two-thirds (66 percent) of the poor are white.
- Most poor adults aged 22–64 are working or looking for work.
- Many poor people live in two-parent families. However, one of the striking trends in the United States has been the "feminization of poverty"—the increasing percentage of impoverished families who are headed by women. In 1986 more than half (51 percent) of families in poverty were headed by women.
- Of the 32.5 million poor Americans in 1986, 40 percent (12.9 million) were children under 18 years of age.
- About 11 percent of the poor (3.5 million) were aged 65 and older.
- Forty percent of the population below the poverty level do not receive welfare.

This profile of poverty in America shows that the stereotypical portrait of the poor is overly simplistic. First, many of those living in poverty are doing so because of economic conditions beyond their control. For example, thousands of blue-collar workers in "smokestack" industries have lost their jobs as manufacturing plants have shut down or moved; thousands of family farmers, caught between rising production costs and falling prices for their products, have been forced into bankruptcy. Second, many of those living in poverty are working or seeking more stable work. Third, many of those included in the categories discussed above—children under 18, some people over 65, the handicapped or disabled—are unable to work. Finally, the poverty category contains a disproportionate number of single mothers. Therefore, whereas some people are poor because employment is not available or because their employment does not pay a living wage, a great many poor people are unemployable under existing conditions rather than unemployed. The vast majority of the poor did not create their condition of poverty and are virtually powerless to change it on their own.

During the past quarter-century changes have occurred in the extent of poverty in the United States. In 1959, the first year for which comparable data were collected, 39.5 million people, or 22.4 percent of the population, were below the poverty line. Those figures declined steadily throughout the 1960s until by 1973 they reached low points of 23.0 million people, or 11.1 percent of the population. The major decline occurred during the middle 1960s when poverty programs initiated by the Kennedy and Johnson Administrations were in full-scale operation. The **poverty rate** (the percentage of the population below the poverty line) remained fairly stable through the 1970s until the recession late in that decade, when it began to rise (see figure 8–3). This increase was further spurred by substantial cuts by the Reagan Administration in social welfare assistance programs. The number of people in poverty continued to climb until 1984, when the poverty rate fell to 14.4, its first decline since 1978. By 1987 the poverty rate had fallen to 13.5, about the same level as it had been in 1981.

Poverty rate
Percentage of the population below the poverty line

The poverty rate provides us with an annual "snapshot" of the percentage of people experiencing poverty at one point in time—for example, in 1987 about one-seventh (13.5 percent) of the American population lived below the poverty level. Such figures convey the impression of a permanent and well-defined group of "poor people." However, these figures obscure the turnover among the low-income population. An intensive study of American families between 1968 and 1978 revealed that one-quarter of all Americans lived below the poverty level for at least one year during that period, but only slightly more than half of those living in poverty in one year were still poor the next year (Duncan, 1984).

When Americans lose their jobs and their means of making a living, they can fall into poverty very quickly. That has happened to many industrial workers and farmers in recent years.

While there are many children in the United States who live in poverty, they may still be relatively advantaged when compared with children in many other parts of the world. These boys in the Philippines must live on, and get their livelihood from, this mountainous garbage dump.

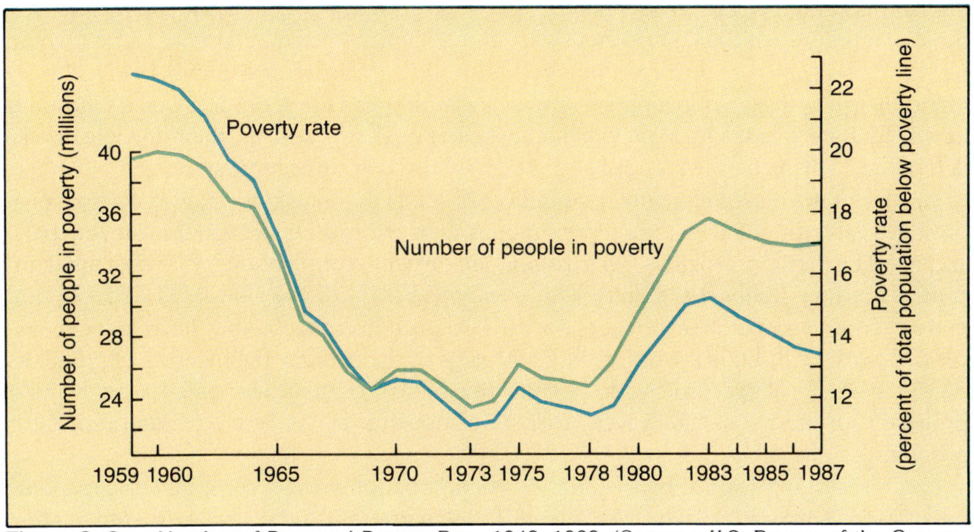

Figure 8–3. Number of Poor and Poverty Rate: 1948–1988. (*Sources:* U.S. Bureau of the Census, "Money Income and Poverty Status in the United States: 1987." *Current Population Reports*. Series P-60, No. 161, 1988c. U.S. Bureau of the Census. "Poverty in the United States: 1986." *Current Population Reports*. Series P-60, No. 160, 1988e.)

Underclass
Most impoverished segment of American society for whom poverty is relatively permanent

A Permanent Underclass? Although a substantial minority of the American population lives in poverty at some point in life, for most of the poor this condition is not permanent. However, several scholars have recently begun to study the lives of the most impoverished segment of American society—those people in persistent poverty. They contend that this social category at the very bottom of American society, referred to as the **underclass,** represents a steadily increasing form of poverty in the United States. Found primarily in the nation's inner cities, the underclass is characterized by high rates of unemployment, out-of-wedlock births, female-headed families, welfare dependence, homelessness, and serious crime. Although the underclass is disproportionately black and Hispanic, it also includes a substantial portion of whites.

William J. Wilson (1987, 1989) has argued that the growth of the urban underclass—the "truly disadvantaged"—results from major economic changes in American society that have caused extremely high levels of inner city unemployment. Earlier in the twentieth century, relatively uneducated and unskilled native and immigrant workers were able to find stable employment and income in the area of manufacturing. Today, however, manufacturing jobs have moved from inner cities to the suburbs, the Sun Belt, or overseas; and the jobs created in the cities demand credentials for which most inner city residents are unqualified. Thus inner city residents find themselves without prospects for work. Moreover, as many stable working-class and middle-class residents with job qualifications have moved from the inner cities into better residential neighborhoods, the stability of neighborhood social institutions (e.g., churches, schools, and recreational facilities) has been undermined, and the social fabric of community life has deteriorated. The underclass has become increasingly isolated, socially and economically.

Inequalities of Status

The importance of status as a key dimension of stratification in American society was demonstrated in one of the classic studies in American sociology. Analyzing a New England community he called "Yankee City," W. Lloyd Warner began his research on the community's stratification system with the assumption that economic factors would be the most important in determining stratification (Warner and Lunt, 1941). But he found that the prestige of people's social backgrounds and life styles (e.g., neighborhoods in which they lived, clubs to which they belonged), as well as their income levels, determined where they were ranked by others in the stratification system.

One of the most frequently used indices of status in modern societies is occupational prestige. Table 8–3 shows the prestige ratings given to various occupations in American society. The most prestigious occupations are usually compensated by substantial incomes, but they frequently require highly technical skills or are associated with political power. Thus, occupational categories with low prestige can possibly have incomes exceeding those with higher prestige. In many areas of the country the incomes of plumbers exceed that of college professors, despite the higher prestige associated with being a professor. In most cases, however, a close relationship exists between class and status positions.

One striking feature of the studies on occupational prestige is that occupational rankings in American society have shown little change since the first such studies were conducted in 1947. Moreover, considerable research has demonstrated that strong similarities exist in the occupational prestige rankings in most industrial countries and

Table 8–3. Occupational Prestige Rankings

Occupation	Score	Occupation	Score
Physician	82	Real estate agent	44
College professor	78	Firefighter	44
Judge	76	Postal clerk	43
Lawyer	76	Advertising agent	42
Physicist	74	Mail carrier	42
Dentist	74	Railroad conductor	41
Banker	72	Typist	41
Aeronautical engineer	71	Photographer	41
Architect	71	Plumber	41
Psychologist	71	Farmer	41
Airplane pilot	70	Telephone operator	40
Chemist	69	Carpenter	40
Minister	69	Welder	40
Civil engineer	68	Dancer	38
Biologist	68	Barber	38
Geologist	67	Automobile mechanic	37
Sociologist	66	Jeweler	37
Political scientist	66	Watchmaker	37
Urban planner	66	Blacksmith	36
Mathematician	65	Bricklayer	36
Secondary school teacher	63	Airline stewardess	36
Registered nurse	62	Meter reader	36
Pharmacist	61	Mechanic	35
Veterinarian	60	Baker	34
Elementary school teacher	60	Shoe repairman	33
Accountant	57	Bulldozer operator	33
Economist	57	Bus driver	32
Artist	56	Truck driver	32
Actor	55	Cashier	31
Librarian	55	Sales clerk	29
Statistician	55	Butcher	28
Social worker	52	Housekeeper	25
Funeral director	52	Child care worker	25
Computer specialist	51	Longshoreman	24
Stock broker	51	Gas station attendant	22
Reporter	51	Taxi cab driver	22
Office manager	50	Elevator operator	21
Bank teller	50	Bartender	20
Electrician	49	Waiter/Waitress	20
Machinist	48	Farm laborer	18
Police officer	48	Peddler	18
Insurance agent	47	Maid/servant	18
Musician	46	Garbage collector	17
Secretary	46	Janitor	17
Computer operator	45	Bootblack	9

Source: Davis, James A. and Smith, Tom W. *National Data Program for the Social Sciences: General Social Survey Cumulative Codebook, 1972–1982.* Chicago: National Opinion Research Center, 1986, Appendix F.

industrializing societies, such as China, as well (Inkeles and Rossi, 1956; Treiman, 1977; Lin and Xie, 1988).

As Warner suggested, however, status is not determined solely by occupation. Ancestry, religious affiliation, place of residence, lifestyle, amount of education, and many other factors have all been associated with an individual's status. There may be contradictions among these different factors: for example, sex and race might affect the prestige attached to occupants of a particular occupation. Acker (1980) found that predominantly female ("pink-collar") jobs have a lower average prestige than traditionally male occupations. This finding was reinforced by Bose and Rossi (1983), who found a substantial overall difference in the prestige ratings of traditionally women's jobs (e.g., housekeeper, dental assistant, private secretary, registered nurse) and predominantly men's jobs (e.g., garbage collector, electrical engineer, building construction contractor, plumber).

Some Consequences of the American Stratification System

In this section we focus on the effects or consequences of one's place in the system of stratification. We will concentrate on the differences in lifestyle and life chances for people in various strata, especially the poor. We have already mentioned that life chances—the likelihood of realizing a certain standard of living or quality of life—are influenced by position in the social hierarchy. Numerous factors, including life expectancy, cause of death, and mental and physical health, are all related to the people's positions in the stratification system. Conversely, people's places in the system affect their lifestyles—tastes, fashions, preferences, and other ways in which they lead their lives. Lifestyles may include such items as one's type of home, vacation, leisure-time activities, reading habits, and sexual behaviors.

Health

As we will see more fully in chapter 15 on Health and Medicine, economic inequalities in American life are significantly related to physical and mental health. In the United States and most other societies, people in the lower classes are more likely to suffer from poor physical and mental health than those in the higher socioeconomic groups (Syme and Berkman, 1981; Rainwater, 1968; Hollingshead and Redlich, 1958; Cockerham, 1986). For example, a disproportionate number of poor people suffer the disabling effects of chronic illnesses. In fact, the rates of disability among the poor for the major chronic illnesses—heart disease, arthritis and rheumatism, back and spine ailments, impairments of the legs or hips, and hypertension—are nearly double those of the nonpoor (Newacheck et al., 1980). Similarly, the relationship between health care and economic circumstances is reflected in a 1984 study of trends in infant mortality prepared by the National Center for Health Statistics. This study noted that in 1984 the infant mortality rate stopped going down partly because of cutbacks in federal medical funding for the poor (*Kansas City Star*, October 18, 1984, p. 7A).

On the basis of their systematic review of the relationship between income and illness, Newacheck and colleagues conclude that there is "a substantial health gap between 'poor' and 'nonpoor' families in the United States" (Newacheck et al., 1980, p. 143).

Summarizing a considerable body of research dealing with the impact of social class factors on health, Cockerham (1986) comes to a similar conclusion: "On nearly every measure, membership in the lower classes carries health penalties. . . . To be poor is by definition to have less of the things (including health care) produced by society" (Cockerham, 1986, p. 49).

Life Expectancy

Life expectancy refers to the average number of years that people in a particular demographic or social category will live. The effect of social class on life expectancy is dramatically illustrated by the fate of passengers on the luxury liner Titanic, which sank in 1912. Of the 143 first-class female passengers on board, only four perished, and of those four, three chose to remain with the ship. Of the 93 second-class female passengers, 15 perished. However, 81 of the 179 third-class female passengers died as the ship went down (Lord, 1955). On the Titanic, as in society in general, life expectancy is related to one's position in the social hierarchy.

Life expectancy
Average number of years that people in a demographic or social category are expected to live

In a survey of a number of studies on the relationship between social rank and life expectancy, Antonovsky (1967) found that socioeconomic position has a significant effect upon life expectancy. In societies in which overall death rates are either very low or very high, only small differences exist between classes. Low death rates reflect great achievements in the battle against death, while high death rates reflect people's helplessness. In these extreme cases, position in the stratification system makes little difference. However, in societies where moderate progress has been made in reducing the death rate, differences are likely to be great because relatively scarce resources (such as new drugs and new medical techniques) are more available to members of the upper strata.

Studies conducted in American society for more than 50 years have persistently supported the conclusions of Antonovsky's research (Kammeyer and Ginn, 1986). Two national studies, one conducted in the 1960s and the other in the 1970s, found that when educational level is used as a measure of social class position, those with higher educational attainment have much lower mortality rates than those with lower educational attainment (Kitagawa and Hauser, 1968; Rosen and Taubman, 1979). Rosen and Taubman's study, which was limited to the white population, found that the least-educated people had death rates that ranged from 40 to 60 percent higher than the most educated people (Rosen and Taubman, 1979). A pronounced difference was also noted when family income was used as a measure of social class. The death rate for the lowest income groups was 2.75 times higher than for the highest income groups. A study of the causes of the deaths of over 48,000 white Oregon residents between 1976 and 1984 found that residents of the poorest census tracts had the highest mortality rates for all causes of death; the wealthiest had the lowest. The greatest difference between the poorest and wealthiest groups was found in deaths attributed to alcoholism, in which the lowest income group's index of potential life lost was 11.7 times higher than the index for the most wealthy group (United States Centers for Disease Control, 1988).

The higher death rates of people in lower social classes may be the result of a variety of factors. Since the economic resources of the middle and upper classes are greater, they may put their resources toward better environmental conditions or more extensive health care. The lower classes may have little money left for medical care after they provide for the necessities of food, clothing, and shelter (Rosen and Taubman, 1979).

People are also becoming increasingly aware that the occupations of members of the lower social strata are directly related to their higher mortality rates. One reason for the lower prestige of certain occupations is that they are more dangerous to health and life. Occupations such as underground mining, lumbering, oil drilling, and construction all have a greater chance of leading to accidental deaths. But although accidents may cause some deaths, evidence has also shown that conditions of the workplace may have delayed effects on health, thus reducing the length of life. Coal miners and cotton mill workers are known to have a high incidence of respiratory diseases (black and brown lung diseases) that lead to higher mortality rates. The long-term effects of working with asbestos materials, lead, and various petrochemicals are almost certainly injurious to health, and probably produce higher death rates (Fox and Adelstein, 1978).

Criminal Justice

The impact of social class on life chances is strikingly apparent in the area of criminal justice. The sociological literature on the relationship between social class and criminal behavior, however, has produced contradictory findings. On the basis of an extensive review of studies examining this relationship, Tittle, Villemez, and Smith conclude that "class and criminality are not now, and probably never were related, at least not in the recent past" (Tittle, Villemez, and Smith, 1978, p. 652). However, Braithwaite (1981), who conducted a review of studies of social class and juvenile crime, concluded that there is an inverse relationship between social class and crime; lower-class people commit more crimes against people—which are more likely to come to the attention of the police—than middle-class people do. Finally, depending on how social status is defined, Thornberry and Farnsworth (1982) found that social class background is not related to criminal behavior by juveniles. Among adults, however, an individual's educational attainment and job stability are both inversely related to criminal behavior; those with low educational attainment and unstable jobs have higher rates of criminal behavior.

However, most studies analyzing the relationship of social class and criminal behavior have not dealt with white-collar crime (including embezzlement, fraud, and bribery), which is almost exclusively an upper-class and upper-middle-class phenomenon. It is also more lucrative than other forms of crime. For example, the U.S. Chamber of Commerce estimates that white-collar crime costs over $40 billion annually, over 250 times the amount of all bank robberies, and more than ten times the annual amount in thefts (Reiman, 1979, p. 106). Yet the rates of arrests and convictions and lengths of sentences for white-collar crime are nowhere near as severe as those for index offenses, or street crimes.

The poor are disadvantaged in their relationship to the criminal justice system in several ways. First, they are much more likely to be victims of violent crimes. Moreover, they are more likely to be suspected of crimes by the police, and as a result, they are more likely to be arrested and charged with crimes. Higher-class individuals arrested for the same offenses are more apt to be released without being charged (Reiman, 1979). Once arrested, the poor are less able to afford bail. Often they must stay in jail until they are tried, which limits their ability to gather information for their defense. Because they probably cannot afford a private lawyer, they are forced to use overworked public defenders who often lack the resources of private lawyers. In court they are likely to appear guilty because their dress, manner, and speech differ from that of judges and jury members, who are usually members of the middle or upper classes. If they are convicted, the poor cannot often afford to appeal their cases. When they do get out of jail, their poverty and their jail records prevent them from getting good jobs or perhaps any jobs at all. This situation, of course, leads some people into a vicious cycle of crime and incarceration that lasts a lifetime.

Education

In our society education is a crucial factor in determining one's chances of success in virtually every realm of life. College, postgraduate, and professional degrees are essential to occupational and economic success in our credential-oriented society, and socioeconomic factors have a strong influence on the level and quality of education that an individual is able to attain. Several studies have demonstrated that students with the same academic records but varying social-class backgrounds have different probabilities of obtaining education past high school. For example, Sewell (1971) found an extremely strong relationship between parents' socioeconomic status (SES) and college attendance: "the lower the SES group, the more limited the opportunities at each level" (Sewell, 1971, p. 795). He found that a student from a high SES background has almost 2.5 times as much chance as a low SES student *with the same academic ability* to attend some kind of post-high school educational institution. The advantage was 4 to 1 for access to college, 6 to 1 for graduation from college, and 9 to 1 for attaining a graduate or professional education. Similarly, Bowles and Gintis (1976) found that children from the lowest tenth in socioeconomic status are only one-twelfth as likely to complete college as those in the highest 10 percent.

A variety of factors prevent the poor from obtaining the amount and kind of education needed for vocational success. The quality of public elementary and high school education available to the poor is generally inferior to that available to the middle and upper classes. Also, many lower-class children either cannot afford to start college or are forced to drop out before they finish because they must go to work to support themselves and their families. Even when those from lower- and working-class backgrounds do attend college, they are much more likely to attend two-year community colleges or four-year colleges of lesser quality and prestige (Cohen and Brawer, 1982).

Open and Closed Systems of Stratification

Societies differ in the extent to which they permit and encourage **social mobility**—the movement of persons from one social class to another. An **open class system** of stratification is one in which few obstacles exist for people who are changing their social positions; success is unaffected both by the constraints of disadvantaged social origins or by the privileges of advantaged social class backgrounds. All people, regardless of birth (sex, race, religion, ethnicity, social background), have genuinely equal opportunity to change positions and move up or down in the stratification system. The greater the degree of social mobility, the more open the class system is. In an open class system emphasis is placed on achievement.

Social mobility
Movement of persons from one social class to another

Open class system
Stratification with few obstacles to social mobility

By contrast, a completely closed stratification system allows virtually no social mobility. A **closed class system** is one in which children inherit their parents' social position. In a closed class system people's places in a social hierarchy are fixed or ascribed (that is, based on qualities such as race, ethnicity, social background, or sex, over which they have no control). In a closed class system little possibility exists for social mobility.

Closed class system
Stratification in which social mobility is almost impossible

People are born into a position and cannot, under normal circumstances, move out of it.

Caste system
The most rigid and closed of stratification systems

The most rigid and closed of all stratification systems is a **caste system.** A caste system is endogamous, which means that people must marry within their own caste. A person who does not marry within his or her caste will probably be punished severely. Intimate contact, such as eating with someone of a different caste, is prohibited. Typically elaborate systems of rituals and customs are developed to limit interaction between caste members. As an example of a completely closed system, we will consider the traditional caste system of India.

The traditional Indian caste system, the basis for organizing Indian society since the fifth century B.C., is the classic example of caste. The system can be divided into five broad strata, each of which contains thousands of internal distinctions based primarily on occupation. At the top of the hierarchy stand the Brahmans, the priests, scholars, and teachers of basic religious principles, who provide religious support for the social order (Mayer and Buckley, 1970). Occupying the lowest and most despised position are the *Harijans,* a term meaning "people of God," which was popularized by Gandhi. These people are the outcastes, whom Indians believe fall outside the caste system. They are frequently called "untouchables" because the outcastes are not permitted to touch members of the upper castes. Indians believe that they can be contaminated even if an outcaste's shadow touches their clothing, food, or person. Outcastes are so despised that in rural areas they are frequently barred from the villages during the early or late part of the day when they cast long shadows and are therefore more likely to contaminate other villagers.

Since 1949 discrimination on the basis of caste has been outlawed, and the coming of modernity to India has undermined and disrupted the traditional caste system, especially in large metropolitan areas. In the modern Indian world of bureaucracies, factories, and schools, contact among castes has increased. Despite these changes, however, the Indian caste system persists, especially in the rural areas, where 75 percent of

India has vast numbers of impoverished people, many of whom are in the lowest castes of the society, and thus have little chance of escaping their poverty.

Cross-National Perspectives

Japan's Outcastes: The *Burakumin*

The term *caste* refers to an extreme case of a closed system of stratification that is characterized by a hierarchy of social statuses into which people are born and must remain throughout their lives. The case of the Japanese *Burakumin*—Japan's "invisible race"—reflects the continuing impact of a caste system in one of the world's most modern, rational, and technologically advanced nations. Physically indistinguishable from other Japanese, the *Burakumin* are acknowledged to be completely Japanese, but of such lowly social origins that they are constantly subjected to prejudice and discrimination (DeVos and Wagatsuma, 1966).

The contemporary Burakumin are descendants of the untouchable *eta* caste. The degree to which the *eta* were despised by the rest of Japanese society is revealed in the name itself: *eta* means "filth abundant." Under the feudal system of Tokugawa, Japan, from the seventeenth to the nineteenth centuries, the *eta* occupied an outcaste status below the four superior castes (the ruling caste of warriors and administrators, the peasants, artisans, and merchants) that constituted Japanese society. The *eta* were discriminated against in every aspect of their lives, and a number of laws were enacted to reinforce their inferior status. For example, as outcastes they were restricted to the dirtiest, most defiling, and least desirable occupations (e.g., as butchers, leatherworkers, grave tenders, and executioners). They were legally segregated from the rest of the Japanese people and forced to live in isolated ghettos. Moreover, they were required to walk barefoot and to wear special clothing that identified them as *eta*. Because they were considered innately inferior and "impure," their marriages were restricted to other *eta;* intermarriages with non-*eta* were virtually nonexistent.

The *eta* were legally "emancipated" during the mid-nineteenth century, and the laws that had formerly restricted their lives and discriminated against them were formally abolished. Although emancipation provided legal freedom, discrimination against the outcastes (subsequently known as *Burakumin,* or "village people") persisted. Among the popular prejudices about the *Burakumin* that persisted well into the twentieth century were the following:

> One rib is lacking; they have a dog's bone in them; they have distorted sexual organs; they have defective excretory systems; if they walk in the moonlight their necks will not cast shadows, and, they being animals, dirt does not stick to their feet when they walk barefoot (quoted in Neary, 1986, p. 558).

Today there are an estimated one to three million *Burakumin* living in Japan, a nation of 123 million. During the twentieth century the *Burakumin* have organized social movements to protest the discrimination they continue to encounter in employment, education, and housing. Although the Japanese government has enacted legislation designed to end the cycle of poverty and discrimination and to improve their living conditions, *Burakumin* continue to be found in overcrowded slum-like ghettos and their lives are characterized by low incomes, high unemployment, and high dependence on welfare. They are often the "last hired and first fired." The *Burakumin* continue to be viewed by most Japanese as "mentally inferior, incapable of high moral behavior, aggressive, impulsive, and lacking any notion of sanitation or manners" (Wagatsuma, 1976, p. 245). The power of these stereotypes and the fear they elicit are reflected in the importance attached to family registration records, which certify "proper" social backgrounds. Such records are frequently required in connection with applications for jobs, loans, and admission to schools. Above all, it is not unusual for families to undertake exhaustive investigations of the lineages of their children's prospective spouses to ensure that their families will not be "contaminated" by *eta* origins.

DEVOS, GEORGE and HIROSHI WAGATSUMA. *Japan's Invisible Race: Caste in Culture and Personality*. Berkeley: University of California Press, 1966.
NEARY, IAN J. "Socialist and Communist Party Attitudes toward Discrimination Against Japan's *Burakumin*." *Political Studies* 34, 1986.
WAGATSUMA, HIROSHI. "Political Problems of a Minority Group in Japan: Recent Conflicts in Buraku Liberation Movements." In Willem A. Veenhoven and Winifred Crum Ewing (eds.), *Case Studies on Human Rights and Fundamental Freedoms*. Vol. III. The Hague: Martinus Nijhoff, 1976.

the Indian population lives. In rural villages people still find it unthinkable to marry someone from another caste and would face the threat of ostracism from their group if they did (Weisman, 1988).

A caste system is not unique to India. For example, in Japan members of a caste called *Burakumin* are economically and socially discriminated against and are considered mentally inferior by the rest of Japanese society; marriages between the *Burakumin* and the upper caste are considered a tragedy (by upper caste members) and are strongly discouraged. (For a further discussion of the *Burakumin,* see "Japan's Outcastes: The Burakumin" in the Cross-National box.) As we will discuss more fully in chapter 9, the structure of relations between blacks and whites in the United States historically has resembled a caste system. Hereditary factors (skin color, hair texture, lip form) were used as the criteria for determining opportunities for full participation in society. Blacks were relegated to an inferior status, and their access to politics, education, jobs, and housing were restricted. Moreover, throughout the South, interpersonal relations between black and white were governed by what was known as the "etiquette of race relations," which required patterns of deference by blacks to whites. Although the legal basis for the caste system has been eliminated by judicial rulings and by federal legislation, the issue still remains controversial as to how closely black/white relations today resemble a caste system.

In the same way that a genuinely classless society probably has never existed, pure caste and class systems probably do not exist either. No stratification system is totally closed or totally open. Virtually all societies display ascription and achievement in some form, and thus fall somewhere between the two extremes.

A Sociological Analysis of Mobility

Lee Iacocca is one of the most prominent and celebrated businessmen in contemporary society. Born of parents who had immigrated to America from Italy, he experienced the hard times of the Great Depression as he grew up in Allentown, Pennsylvania. He worked his way through college, and, through the classic virtues of hard work, ingenuity, and industriousness, became president of two of the nation's largest corporations—the Ford Motor Company and, later, the Chrysler Corporation (which he rescued from near bankruptcy and transformed into a once-again prosperous company). His name has been prominently mentioned as a possible presidential candidate.

In 1984 Iacocca published his autobiography, *Iacocca*. Although books describing how to achieve success appear frequently on the best-seller list, *Iacocca* remained on the list for more than two years, a phenomenal feat for any book. One reason for the book's sensational success is that Iacocca's life story epitomizes the American dream. His is the classic success story—humble origins, an unquenchable desire to gain an education, a commitment to hard work, and a meteoric rise to the top of America's corporate world. Well-publicized success stories such as Iacocca's reinforce the widespread belief among Americans that their society provides great opportunities for social mobility (Huber and Form, 1973).

Two types of social mobility can be described. One is **horizontal mobility,** which refers to movement from one social position to another of equal rank. Iacocca's shift from the presidency of the Ford Motor Company to the same position at Chrysler exemplifies this type.

Horizontal mobility
Movement from one social position to another of equal rank

However, popular interest in, and sociological research on, social mobility has centered on **vertical mobility,** which refers to movement upward or downward in the stratification system. Iacocca's rise to fame, fortune, and power is an example of upward vertical mobility; an example of downward vertical mobility would be if the son of a lawyer were to spend his career as a carpenter.

Vertical mobility
Movement upward or downward in the stratification system

In analyzing the nature of social mobility, sociologists have focused on two main types: intragenerational mobility and intergenerational mobility. **Intragenerational or career mobility** refers to the movement of individuals in the stratification system during their lifetimes. Studies of this type of mobility focus on the life span of individuals, examining where people begin their careers and where they finish them. Someone who starts as a laborer and ends as a lawyer has clearly experienced upward mobility. On the other hand, someone who ends up on skid row after beginning as a physician has experienced downward mobility.

Intragenerational or career mobility
Movement in the class structure by individuals during their lifetimes

Intergenerational mobility refers to differences between the social-class position of children and the social-class position of their parents. Studies of this type of mobility compare the social class of parents with those of their children, most often with that of a son. If the children have more money, have more education, or occupy a higher-status occupation, they have experienced upward mobility. If they are lower than their parents on any of these dimensions, they have experienced downward intergenerational mobility.

Intergenerational mobility
Movement in class position comparing parents and children

Any assessment of the extent of social mobility in American society must consider the effects of **structural mobility**—mobility occurring as a result of changes in a society's occupational structure. Structural mobility is caused by large-scale structural changes in the society as a whole. Among the structural changes that have had a profound effect on the class structure of many countries, including the United States, are technological innovations, wars, economic fluctuations (e.g., depressions or recessions), and urbanization. If the nature of the economy and the occupational structure change over time—for example, if the number of white-collar workers increases over blue-collar workers—then the possibility of upward social mobility from blue-collar to white-collar occupations will be increased because more higher-status jobs will be available. On the

Structural mobility
Mobility resulting from changes in a society's occupational structure

other hand, if an increasing percentage of the population has earned college degrees, the proportion of their children who can achieve mobility through college graduation will decrease. Thus Hout found that opportunities for changes between social origins and current occupations have recently diminished for both men and women. "[The] origins and destinations of workers in the early 1980s are more similar than were the origins and destinations of workers in the early 1970s" (Hout, 1988, p. 1382). This observation is especially true in high-status salaried professional and management occupations where workers in the 1980s are more likely to have fathers with those occupations than was the case in the 1970s.

Patterns of Social Mobility in the United States

Some general conclusions can be drawn from the large body of recent sociological research on social mobility. First, most social mobility is modest; it occurs in steps between adjacent strata, that is, by moves from the lower-middle class to the middle class, or from a parent's occupation as a small-town merchant to the offspring's occupation as a lawyer or doctor. Large jumps from the lower class to the upper class (the classic rags-to-riches story) are rare; for example, Lee Iacocca's rise from humble origins to corporate success is the exception, not the rule.

Moreover, occupational inheritance is greatest at the top and at the bottom of the occupational structure. Men from upper-middle-class and unskilled blue-collar backgrounds are most likely to have occupations similar to their fathers, and children whose fathers had occupations between these two extremes are most likely to experience mobility. Studies of the highest levels of American society indicate that recruitment for the most powerful corporate positions is largely restricted to individuals from upper-class and upper-middle-class origins. A recent study of the social origins of the chief executive officers of 243 major corporations in 1986 showed that nearly two-thirds had been raised in upper-middle-class or upper-class families (Boone, Kurtz, and Fleenor, 1988; see also, Kerbo, 1983; Tumin, 1985).

Second, patterns of social mobility in the United States have not changed substantially over time. Although most historical studies of social mobility are limited to cities and do not represent the nation as a whole, such studies tend to show that patterns of social mobility at the turn of the twentieth century and at mid-century were about the same. Furthermore, historical studies of business elites show patterns of recruitment from the upper class similar to the contemporary elite (Kerbo, 1983, pp. 346–348). However, Hout's recent analysis supports the notion of "expanding universalism." This phrase means that, increasingly, occupational status in the United States cannot be inherited but must be attained by actual achievement. Although high-status origins remain an advantage, advantaged offspring are less likely today than in the past to occupy high-status positions without competing with individuals from other social origins (Hout, 1988, p. 1381).

Finally, the overall rates of social mobility in the United States do not differ substantially from those in other Western industrialized countries. Although differences do exist in the historical experiences and occupational structures of the 16 countries they studied, Grusky and Hauser concluded that "industrialized societies share a common pattern of mobility" (Grusky and Hauser, 1984, p. 35). Similarly, Kerckhoff, Campbell, and Winfield-Laird (1985) found substantial similarities in the amount of intergenerational occupational movement of men in Great Britain and the United States. Consistent

When young adults live amidst wealth and have a luxurious lifestyle it is often because they were born into positions of affluence.

with the findings cited earlier, both studies found the greatest degree of inheritance of occupational position among the highest-status and lowest-status occupations, with the greatest mobility occurring among those in between. "The picture that emerges is one of severe immobility at the two extremes of the occupational hierarchy and considerable fluidity in the middle" (Grusky and Hauser, 1984, p. 35). Such studies contradict the notion that the United States is more open in terms of social mobility than other nations.

Social Stratification in the Soviet Union

Until this point our discussion of social stratification has focused primarily on patterns of social inequality and social mobility in the United States. The distinctive features of structured social inequality become even more apparent by a comparison with the Soviet Union—a modern, highly industrialized society whose social system is legitimated by an egalitarian ideology. The Soviet Union is today the world's most powerful communist society, yet its system of social ranking and the distribution of scarce resources among those ranks differ considerably from the classless society anticipated by Marx.

Stratification in the USSR, as in the United States, has been shaped by economic and technological forces. Increasing division of labor and occupational specialization have produced an economic system in which technical expertise is highly valued, and the educational system has become a major factor in determining how people are distributed in the work force. As the number of skilled manual and nonmanual occupations has expanded, so also have opportunities for upward occupational mobility.

However, the occupational structures of the two countries differ substantially. The Soviet Union has continued to have a greater proportion of industrial workers than the United States because its economy has concentrated more on heavy industry and less on services, consumer goods, and marketing. The USSR also continues to have a higher proportion of farmers in its labor force than the United States does.

Despite differences in occupational structures, Inkeles (1968) found a remarkable agreement on the relative prestige of occupations among the United States, the Soviet Union, Japan, England, New Zealand, and Germany. Moreover, Soviet sociologists have identified a prestige hierarchy of occupations that is broadly similar to that found in the United States. Thus professional occupations, such as engineering and scientific jobs, are highly ranked, while agricultural, sales, and service occupations have low prestige (Dobson, 1977, p. 301).

Yet in the Soviet Union the working-class or skilled manual labor categories are consistently ranked above many low-level nonmanual or white-collar occupations. This fact may be explained by Soviet ideology that extols the virtues of the worker and by the higher relative incomes obtained by the working class.

Because of the role that the Soviet state has in organizing and regulating economic forces, power and privilege are more likely to flow from political position than from occupation. The most highly ranked figures in Soviet society are the political elites, who gain their privilege because of their position within the structure of the Communist Party, whose members consist of less than 10 percent of the adult population.

The other path to elite status is to achieve celebrity status as a musician, writer, artist, dancer, actor, or athlete whose prominence has been perceived as a contribution to the power and prestige of the Soviet system. Although celebrities have considerable personal prestige, they have little power in the Soviet Union (Smith, 1976, p. 29).

Data on wage and salary distribution indicate that the Soviet Union is far from an egalitarian society. It has a wage ratio of 50 to 1, which means that the top salaries are 50 times greater than the minimum wage. In the United States, the ratio has been calculated at 300 to 1, or six times greater than the range in the Soviet Union (Lenski, 1978, p. 370). If one considers total income, including wages, stock dividends, and interest, the 50 to 1 ratio for the Soviet Union would hardly be affected, but the 300 to 1 ratio for the United States would be dramatically increased. In other words, income is far more equally distributed in the USSR than in the United States.

In contrast to the official ideology, in Soviet society some people are "more equal than others." Soviet elites—the "privileged" class—have access to goods, services, and luxuries, and enjoy a life style unavailable to ordinary Russian citizens. The elites have access to special stores that insulate them from chronic shortages and provide them with scarce consumer items (Smith, 1976). Prominent Communist Party officials enjoy the most conspicuous symbol of rank and privilege—chauffeur-driven limousines; they also have access to private cars, often expensive foreign models, which are limited in number and extremely expensive. In a society with severe housing shortages, the elites receive the most desirable housing—fashionably equipped urban apartments and lavishly furnished country estates. Moreover, admission to exclusive medical clinics, restaurants, and clubs are all allocated according to rank. Overall, the Soviet elites are "far better clothed, fed, housed, and medically cared for than the rest of the population" (Smith,

1976, p. 43). In addition, they are among the few individuals who are permitted to travel to other countries, to vacation in expensive resorts, and to have access to Western movies, books, and magazines that are banned for ordinary Russians. Finally, in a society in which educational attainment is a critical determinant of upward mobility, elites are able to ensure that their children attend the most prestigious universities (Smith, 1976; Dobson, 1977; Matthews, 1978).

Until recently, Soviet authorities maintained that poverty was a social ill found only in capitalist societies, and they officially banned public discussion of the existence of poverty in the USSR. However, the policies of *glasnost* (openness) under Soviet leader Mikhail Gorbachev have enabled economists and sociologists to examine poverty in Soviet society much more critically and publicly. Soviet sociologists estimate that at least 20 percent of the Soviet population—compared with 13.5 percent in the United States—now live in poverty. However, Matthews contends that this figure is much too low, and that nearly 40 percent of the nonpeasant labor force earns less than the minimum subsistence level necessary to sustain an urban family. The existence of a substantial stratum of people living in poverty is therefore one of the primary social problems confronting Gorbachev in his program of *perestroika* (restructuring or reformation) (Fein, 1989, p. 1; Matthews, 1986, p. 176).

Despite considerable social inequality and the existence of a substantial poverty class in the USSR, social mobility from the lower classes into the political elite appears to be greater in the USSR than in the United States. A majority of the highest Party and administrative positions in the political bureaucracy are filled by males from peasant and working-class origins. Therefore political participation has been a very important channel of upward mobility for the children of peasants and workers in the Soviet Union. However, the upper-middle stratum just below the elite—the intellectuals, scientists, and scholars—is likely to be drawn from upper-middle-class backgrounds. Studies of trends in social mobility in the Soviet Union suggest that, especially among the urban intelligentsia, occupational continuity is increasing across generations; that is, their children do not experience mobility but tend to have occupations similar to those of their parents (Dobson, 1977). Matthews (1978) suggests that fewer and fewer people in the lower social classes are experiencing social mobility because those selected for upward mobility are hand-picked by the current elite for their talent as well as their support of elite policies. Nevertheless, Matthews (1978, p. 163) contends that the Soviet elite is more open in terms of class origins than other modern societies, including the United States. However, Dobson argues that the relatively high rates of intergenerational mobility found by Soviet sociologists result primarily from changes in the economic structure of the Soviet Union—the expansion of bureaucratic and technical positions—rather than from "conscious socialist policies designed to promote mobility" (Dobson, 1979).

In addition to some income inequality between classes, the Soviet Union also has inequalities based on gender. (See chapter 10 for a discussion of gender inequality in the United States.) About 90 percent of Soviet women aged 30 to 49 work outside the home, which is roughly twice the percentage in the United States. About 68 percent of Soviet physicians are women, along with 75 percent of the teachers and 33 percent of the engineers. Yet most of the female labor force is found in unskilled manual positions or low white-collar jobs. Even those women in higher occupational positions usually have less authority than men (Swafford, 1978, p. 670; Browning, 1987).

The political power of Soviet women (or lack thereof) is similar to that of their American counterparts. Only one-quarter of the members of the Communist Party are women, and women hold no real positions of power in the *Politburo,* the powerful elite body that makes national policy. So striking is the absence of women from positions of power that it was a major news story in 1986 when Soviet leader Mikhail Gorbachev appointed the first woman in 25 years to the Secretariat, the 11-member body that carries out policies and supervises the nation's affairs (*New York Times*, March 7, 1986, p. 3).

Summary

Social stratification, or structured social inequality, is a universal feature of human societies. Social inequalities and social ranking are usually justified by reference to an ideology, a set of ideas used to explain and justify the inequalities. The inequalities in American life are justified by a meritocratic ideology that emphasizes an ideal of equality of opportunity.

Sociologists have distinguished three basic dimensions of social stratification: class, status, and power. Class is an economic variable strongly emphasized by Marx as the determinant of social stratification. However, Weber argued that status, or prestige, and power were also important dimensions in a system of social stratification. An examination of the American stratification system reveals that, despite an egalitarian ideology, considerable inequality exists in contemporary American society. Inequalities in the concentration of wealth and income in the United States are pronounced and have persisted over long periods of time. Inequality is also manifested in differences among the social classes in both life chances and life styles.

Stratification systems differ in the extent to which they are open or closed. An open class system is one in which there are few obstacles to social mobility, which is the movement between positions in a system of stratification. In a closed class system little possibility exists for mobility; people's positions in a social hierarchy are determined almost completely by birth. The most closed of all stratification systems is a caste system, which is exemplified by traditional Indian society.

There are different types of social mobility. Vertical mobility can be either upward or downward. Horizontal mobility involves the movement between comparable positions in the social structure. Sociologists have examined both intragenerational, or career, mobility and intergenerational mobility, in which parents' occupational positions are compared with those of their offspring. In general, studies of social mobility suggest that, despite a widespread belief that American society has provided unique opportunities for social mobility, upward social mobility is no greater in the United States than in other Western industrialized nations.

Despite an egalitarian ideology, patterns of social inequality and limitations on social mobility in the Soviet Union are clear. Elite status is drawn primarily from positions within the Communist Party and is reflected in unequal access by Party officials to scarce resources. Although the existence of poverty in the USSR was, until recently, officially denied, new studies indicate a substantial class whose incomes fall below official minimum subsistence levels. Social mobility from the lower classes is most pronounced in the political arena but is more limited among nonpolitical occupations.

CRITICAL THINKING

1. The authors state that a "classless society is a possibility, if not a probability." What conditions need to exist in order for such a society to be possible? Which existing society comes closest to this ideal?
2. Review the definitions of class, status, and power presented in the text. To what extent does each affect the following occupations in American society: judge, nurse, firefighter, mechanic, janitor?
3. Meritocracy has been a predominant ideology in American society. What are the basic tenets of this ideology? Review the data presented in the chapter to determine the validity of this ideology. Does it justify the existing social order? How did you learn about this ideology as you grew up? Give examples.
4. Explain the key differences between the structural-functional and the conflict interpretations of social inequality. What evidence presented in the chapter supports each theory?
5. How do the income data in the chapter support the contention that dominant and subordinate classes exist in American society?
6. America has been stereotyped as a "middle-class society" in which each generation is more successful than the previous one. Does the evidence in the chapter support this idea? How has the distribution of income been affected by America's move to a post-industrial society?
7. How can you explain the existence of an underclass in American society?
8. How are our lives (health, education, life expectancy, etc.) affected by social stratification?
9. What characteristics does a closed-class system have? To what extent is American society closed?
10. Examine the experience of a grandparent, parent, and yourself to assess the intragenerational and intergenerational mobility in your family. In addition, assess each individual's horizontal and vertical mobility. Does your family's experience tend to prove or disprove the authors' main conclusions?
11. Compare and contrast social stratification in the United States and the Soviet Union. Be sure to include a comparison of ideology, occupational structure, power, and standard of living.

CHAPTER

9

Racial and Ethnic Inequality

MINORITY-GROUP RESPONSES TO DOMINANT GROUP PRESSURES

Acceptance

Resistance

Avoidance

SUMMARY

CRITICAL THINKING

As we have seen in chapter 8, human societies are almost universally stratified or differentiated into categories of superiority and inferiority, dominance and subordination. Throughout history, racial and ethnic factors have frequently been used as criteria for ranking a society's members into categories of unequal wealth, power, and prestige.

Prejudice, discrimination, and conflict based on racial and ethnic distinctions are widely found throughout the world today—between black, white, colored, and Indian in South Africa; English-speaking and French-speaking in Canada; Tutsi and Hutu in Burundi; East Indians and Blacks in Guyana; Armenians and Azerbajanis in the Soviet Union; Kurds and Iraqis in Iraq; Tamils and Sinhalese in Sri Lanka; Serbs, Croatians, Montenegrins, and Albanians in Yugoslavia. Indeed, in the last few decades more people have died in ethnic conflicts around the world than in the Korean or Vietnam wars

The Azerbaijani are one of many ethnic and minority groups in the Soviet Union who are demanding greater recognition. Sometimes, as in other ethnic conflicts around the world, there has been violence and death as Soviet ethnic groups clash.

combined. In this chapter we consider the dynamics of racial and ethnic relations. We will focus especially on how different patterns of racial and ethnic relations are achieved and maintained.

Ethnic and Racial Groups

Ethnic group
A group socially defined on the basis of its cultural characteristics

Ethnicity
The sense of belonging to and identifying with a particular ethnic group

Race
A group socially defined on the basis of physical characteristics

The word *ethnic* is derived from the Greek word *ethnos,* meaning "people." **Ethnic group** refers to a group that is socially defined on the basis of its cultural characteristics. **Ethnicity**—the sense of belonging to a particular ethnic group—thus implies the existence of a distinct culture or subculture in which group members feel themselves bound together by a common history, values, attitudes, and behaviors. Other members of the society also regard them as distinctive. Ethnic groups may differ in cultural characteristics as diverse as food habits, family patterns, sexual behavior, modes of dress, standards of beauty, political orientations, economic activities, and recreational patterns. In its broadest sense, the term *ethnic* implies a sense of common peoplehood. In American society, Chicanos, Italians, Jews, Poles, Filipinos, and white Anglo-Saxon Protestants all can be considered ethnic groups.

The terms *race* and *ethnicity* are often used interchangeably, but they should be distinguished. An ethnic group is socially defined on the basis of its *cultural* characteristics; the term **race** refers to groups that are socially defined on the basis of *physical* characteristics. A group is defined as a race when certain physical characteristics of the group are selected for special emphasis by members of a society.

The term *race* is meaningless in a biological sense since there are no "pure" races. The crucial aspect of any definition of a group as ethnic or racial is that the characteristics that distinguish it are *socially defined.* Thus the criteria selected to make racial distinctions in one society may be overlooked or considered insignificant or irrelevant by another society. In much of Latin America, skin color and the shape of the lips—important differentiating criteria in the United States—are much less important than hair texture, eye color, and stature. A person defined as black in Georgia or Michigan might be considered white in Peru. Among the Tutsi (where men average a height of over six feet) and the Hutu (who stand slightly over four feet) peoples of central Africa, the physical characteristic of height is the basis for group distinctions. Therefore, the recent conflict between these two peoples, which resulted in the murders of thousands of the minority Hutus, is racial.

The principle that racial differences are socially defined is vividly shown by laws in the United States that prohibited interracial marriages. Until recently, many states stipulated that any person with one-fourth or more black* ancestry (that is, with one black grandparent) was legally defined as "black" and therefore prohibited from marrying someone "white." However, some states enacted more restrictive definitions of race. A

* Over the last two-hundred years, a variety of terms—*Colored, Negro, Afro-American, Black*—have been used to refer to Americans of African descent. Recently, many black leaders have urged the adoption of the term *African-American.* However, when this book was written, no consensus on terminology had emerged. Therefore, we will use both *African-American* and *black American* in this chapter, and the more customary *black American* in the remainder of the book.

recent example of this enactment occurred in Louisiana, when Susie Guillory Phipps, a light-skinned woman with Caucasian features and straight black hair, found that her birth certificate classified her as "colored." Mrs. Phipps, who contended that she had been "brought up white and married white twice," challenged a 1970 Louisiana law declaring that anyone with at least one-thirty-second "Negro blood" was legally classified as black. Under this law an individual who had *one* great-great-great grandparent who was black (and thus had only one-thirty-second "black" and thirty-one thirty-seconds "white" ancestry) was legally defined as black. Although the state's lawyer conceded that Mrs. Phipps "looks like a white person," the state strenuously maintained that her racial classification was appropriate (Trillin, 1986).

That racial classifications are social, not biological, categories is today nowhere more apparent than in South Africa, where all people are required to be classified in one of four legally defined racial groupings—white, black, colored, and Indian. The lives of all South Africans, including the jobs they may hold, the schools they may attend, where they may live, and whom they may marry, are dramatically determined by the category in which they are placed. The arbitrary nature of such categories is revealed in circumstances in which an individual's legal classification—and thus the entire range of opportunities that flows from it—is changed. A South African newspaper recently reported:

> Nearly 800 South Africans became officially members of a different race group last year. . . . They included 518 coloreds who were officially reclassified as white, 14 whites who became colored, 7 Chinese [who are classified as "honorary whites"] who became white, 2 whites who became Chinese, 3 Malays [who are classified as colored] who became white, 1 white who became an Indian, 50 Indians who became colored, 54 coloreds who became Indian, 17 Indians who became Malay, 4 coloreds who became Chinese, 1 Malay who became Chinese, 89 blacks who became colored, 5 coloreds who became black (Uys, 1988, p. 27).

What Is a Minority Group?

Sociologists usually use the terms *majority* and *minority* to refer to social relations in which racial and ethnic criteria are employed in the society's system of stratification. The distinctive feature of a **minority group**, or **subordinate group,** is that it occupies a *subordinate* or inferior position of prestige, wealth, and power in a society. A minority group is typically excluded from full participation in a society and is the object of discrimination by the majority group.

Minority, or subordinate, group
A group that occupies an inferior position of prestige, wealth, and power

The term *minority* does not refer to the numerical size of a group. For example, under the system of apartheid in South Africa today, blacks are a numerical majority (69 percent) of the total population, yet they are systematically excluded from full social, economic, and political participation. Numerical superiority, therefore, does not necessarily ensure that a group will be dominant.

The crucial variable in majority/minority relations is **power**—the ability of one group to realize its goals and interests, even in the face of resistance. Power may be based on the superior population size, weaponry, technology, property, education, or economic resources of the dominant group. Superior power is crucial to the establishment

Power
The ability of a person or group to realize its goals and interests, even in the face of resistance

Majority, or dominant, group
A group that occupies a position of superior power and privilege

of a system of ethnic or racial stratification. Moreover, having achieved power, a **dominant group,** or **majority group,** is reluctant to give it up voluntarily, but instead usually strives to maintain and perpetuate its privileged position.

Race and Ethnicity in the American Experience

The United States, which has been called a "nation of nations," is one of the most racially and ethnically diverse societies in the world. Despite an ideology formally committed to human equality, racial and ethnic criteria have frequently determined social status in American society. Figure 9–1 presents data on the distribution of major racial and ethnic groups in the United States. Presently members of the largest racial and ethnic minorities (African-Americans, Hispanics, Asians, and Native Americans) comprise nearly one-quarter (23 percent) of the population.

One of the most prominent features of the American experience is the competition among numerous racial and ethnic groups for economic, social, and political dominance. Moreover, in the future the impact of racial and ethnic factors will probably be even more pronounced. By the year 2000 one-third of all school-age children will be either Hispanic, African-American, Asian, or Native American (American Council on Education, 1988). Furthermore, in some states (e.g., California) the *majority* of working-age adults in 2000 will be members of these minorities (California Assembly Office of Research, 1986). Thus minority peoples will affect the nation's prosperity more substantially than

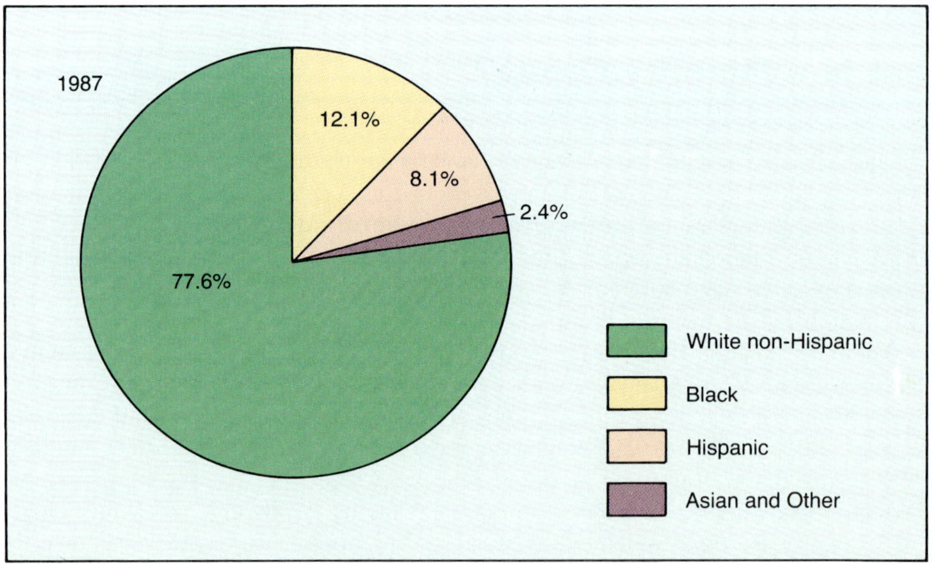

Figure 9–1. Racial and Hispanic Population of the United States, 1987. (*Sources:* Population Reference Bureau, *Charting the Change.* (Washington, D.C.) 1988; U.S. Bureau of the Census, "The Hispanic Population of the United States," Series P-20, No. 418, September 1988i.)

ever before in American history. In this section we sketch some key features of ethnic and racial relations in the American experience, beginning with the earliest inhabitants—Native Americans—and concluding with a discussion of some characteristics of contemporary immigration to the United States.

Native Americans

The first Americans migrated from Asia 20,000 to 40,000 years ago, slowly dispersing throughout North, Central, and South America. Native American peoples developed a great diversity of cultures with widely different levels of technology, cultural complexity, and languages. Great differences can be found among Native American tribes to the present day, despite the popular perception of North American Indians as a single distinct ethnic group.

The arrival of Europeans significantly affected Indian cultures. From the 1600s onward, as Europeans began to migrate in increasing numbers, their demand for land on which to settle became the primary source of conflict with Native Americans. The process of European expansion westward involved the expulsion of Indians from their tribal lands. Although Indians resolutely resisted domination, the advance of white settlement eventually overwhelmed Indian resistance. Armed with superior military technology and bolstered by increasing numbers, whites moved inexorably westward. Indian tribes were forced to retreat as the control of lands they had formerly occupied was passed to whites. Their land base, which initially had been over 2 billion acres, dwindled to 155 million acres in 1871 and 90 million acres in 1980 (Dorris, 1981). Diseases such as smallpox, scarlet fever, measles, and cholera were fatal to large numbers of Indian peoples, who for centuries had been physically isolated from the Old World and had developed little or no resistance to these diseases. Moreover, substantial numbers of American Indians died as a result both of warfare with Europeans and of the deliberate extermination of Indians by European invaders. The Native American population, which had numbered between 5 and 6 million when Columbus arrived in the New World, dwindled to 237,000 by 1900 (Thornton, 1987, p. 32). Traditional Indian cultures and patterns of authority were undermined as their economic resources were eroded and as Indian affairs became controlled by whites.

By the turn of the twentieth century, whites believed that Indians were a vanishing race, and that the few remaining Indians should be forced to assimilate—to give up their cultural heritages and to adopt the white values of rugged individualism, competition, and private enterprise. To ethnocentric whites, these values represented more "civilized" forms of behavior.

However, a striking feature of Indian life in the twentieth century has been an ability to endure. Despite strong pressures to assimilate into the mainstream of American society, they have clung tenaciously to their cultures. Today Native Americans are one of the most rapidly growing ethnic categories in the United States.

A substantial portion of Indian lands were ceded to colonists and early settlers by treaties, first between Indians and colonial British governments and later with the United States government. These treaties form the basis of the unique legal and political status of Native Americans today. In contrast to other American racial and ethnic minorities, American Indian tribes "are due certain privileges, protections, and benefits of yielding some of their sovereignty to the United States" (Dorris, 1981, p. 54). Among these rights

Despite strong pressure to conform to the norms, values, and traditions of the dominant group, Native Americans have maintained their distinct ethnic identities.

are the obligations of the federal government to protect their lands and to provide Indians with social, medical, and educational services.

During the nineteenth century, American Indians were removed to isolated areas not then coveted by whites. Solemn treaties signed with the United States government guaranteed that Indians would retain sovereignty over these lands in perpetuity—"as long as the grass shall grow and the rivers shall run." Although the lands held by Indians today represent only a small portion of those guaranteed in those treaties, they hold vast and extremely valuable agricultural, water, timber, fishing, and energy resources. However, these resources are being developed and exploited primarily for economic interests that are national and multinational, not Indian.

As a consequence, Indians are increasingly challenging their political and economic domination by outsiders, and are seeking to exert Indian control over reservation resources. Indian activists have mounted legal challenges to ensure that the federal government honors the terms of the treaties it has made with Indian tribes. Indian activism has also been reflected in their efforts to develop organizations to advance Indian economic interests by resisting external exploitation of their resource base. One of the most prominent of these has been the Council of Energy Resource Tribes (CERT), which was formed to promote Indian economic interests in the substantial coal, gas, oil, and uranium reserves that are found on Indian lands (Snipp, 1986). As the powerful economic and political pressures intensify over increasingly scarce and valuable Indian resources, it seems inevitable that conflicts will only increase in the future (Erdrich and Dorris, 1988).

European Ethnic Groups

The first European immigrants to settle permanently in what is now the United States were almost exclusively English. The economic, legal, and political traditions that English settlers brought established the English character of American institutions, language, and culture. Ethnic groups who migrated later were forced to adapt to the cultural and social systems that the English had created.

Although the English composed the greatest proportion of the early colonial population, the middle colonies (New York, New Jersey, Pennsylvania, and Delaware) were settled by substantial numbers of Germans, Dutch, Scotch-Irish, Scots, Swedes, and French Huguenots. Here the idea of America as a "melting pot," in which diverse cultures come together to form a new people, was first formulated. In 1782, a Frenchman, Hector St. John de Crevecoeur, wrote,

> What then is the American, this new man? . . . Here [in America] individuals of all nations are melted into a new race of man, whose labors and posterity will one day cause great changes in the world (de Crevecoeur, 1782/1981, p. 39).

However, relations between different ethnic groups sometimes fell short of this ideal. Because German settlers in Pennsylvania insisted on maintaining their own language, churches, and culture, their presence generated some of the earliest recorded conflict among European ethnic groups in America, which was openly expressed by Benjamin Franklin:

> Why should the *Palatine Boors* [Germans] be suffered to swarm into our Settlements, and by herding together, establish their Language and Manners, to the Exclusion of ours? Why should *Pennsylvania,* founded by the English, become a Colony of *Aliens,* who will shortly be so numerous as to Germanize us instead of our Anglifying them . . . ? (cited in Dinnerstein and Reimers, 1987, p. 6).

Immigration to the United States was greatest in the century between 1820 and 1920, when more than 30 million immigrants entered the country. Between 1820 and 1895 immigrants were drawn principally from countries of northern and western Europe—from Germany, Ireland, Great Britain (England, Scotland, and Wales), and Scandinavia (Norway, Sweden, and Denmark). With the exception of the Catholic Irish, the "**old**" **immigration** (as the immigration from these countries became known) was heavily Protestant.

"Old" immigration
People from northern and western Europe who immigrated to the U.S. primarily between 1820 and 1895

"New" immigration
People from southern and eastern Europe who immigrated to the U.S. primarily between 1890 and 1920

Immigration to the United States reached its peak between 1890 and the outbreak of World War I in 1914, and those who entered were drawn from countries different than those of the old immigrants. The "**new**" **immigration**—including Greeks, Croatians, Italians, Russians (primarily Jewish), Poles, Hungarians, Czechs, and Lithuanians—hailed from southern and eastern Europe. Unlike the old immigration, which was heavily Protestant and followed agricultural pursuits in the United States, new immigrants were overwhelmingly Catholic or Jewish and were attracted primarily to the economic opportunities in the nation's rapidly expanding cities.

Native-born whites held deep-seated prejudices against the new immigrants, believing that they were innately inferior to previous immigrants. The U.S. Commissioner of Immigration described the new immigrants as "beaten men from beaten races; representing the worst failures in the struggle for existence. They have none of the ideas and aptitudes which fit men to take up readily and easily the problem of self-care and self-government" (quoted in Saveth, 1948, p. 40).

Table 9–1. White Ethnic Backgrounds, 1980*

Ancestry Group	Number
English	49,598,000
German	49,224,000
Irish	40,166,000
French	12,892,000
Italian	12,184,000
Scottish	10,049,000
Polish	8,228,000
Dutch	6,304,000
Swedish	4,345,000
Norwegian	3,454,000
Russian	2,781,000
Czech	1,892,000
Hungarian	1,777,000
Welsh	1,665,000
Danish	1,518,000
Portuguese	1,024,000

Source: U.S. Bureau of the Census, "Ancestry of the Population by State: 1980," *Census of Population, Supplementary Reports*, Washington, D.C.: U.S. Government Printing Office, 1983, p. 2.
* Restricted to ancestry groups with 1 million or more.

Such beliefs in the racial and cultural inferiority of new immigrants provided the foundation for American immigration policy from 1917 to 1965, which was designed precisely to discriminate against new immigrants by restricting their numbers while still permitting substantial numbers of old immigrants to enter.

White ethnics
Contemporary descendants of the "new" immigrants

Despite fears that they were undesirable and unassimilable and that they represented a threat to American society, the descendants of the new immigrants, today referred to as "**white ethnics,**" have achieved considerable socioeconomic success. Greeley (1976) has characterized their socioeconomic achievements as the "ethnic miracle." By the 1970s, Jews had attained the highest income levels of all European ethnic groups in American society, and they were followed by Irish, German, Italian, and Polish Catholics, not by white Anglo-Saxon Protestants. Moreover, when parental educational levels are held constant, Catholic ethnics show higher educational achievement than any other European group except Jews. Yet, despite their economic and educational achievements, white ethnics still retain a sense of cultural identity with their ethnic and national roots. Table 9–1 presents data on the national backgrounds of Americans of European descent.

African-Americans

From the earliest settlement to the present, the principal racial division in American society has been between white and black; no other minority group has experienced discrimination so intense, pervasive, and enduring as African-Americans. Numbering more than 29 million—more than 12 percent of the total population—African-Americans are today the largest racial minority in American society. Their numbers total more than

Many ethnic and nationality groups were treated harshly when they first arrived in this country, but today many of their descendants proudly celebrate their ethnic heritage.

the entire population of Canada or of the Scandinavian countries of Sweden, Denmark, Norway, Finland, and Iceland combined. Only Nigeria, Ethiopia, and Zaire have larger black populations than the United States.

Slavery and Caste. During the first 200 years of their existence in American society, the lives of African-American people were defined primarily by their role as slaves, a status in which individuals are involuntarily placed in perpetual servitude, are defined as property, and are denied rights generally given to other members of society.

Equally important in understanding the dynamics of race relations in the United States is that even those African-Americans who were free during the slavery era (more than one-tenth of the black population) did not have the same rights and privileges as whites and were not accepted into society on an equal basis. In contrast to slaves in many other societies, slaves in the United States were subject to *racial* discrimination as well as legal servitude. Therefore, the most distinctive and enduring feature of black/white relations in the United States has been that African-Americans—slave or free—have occupied a lower caste status, both during the more than 200 years of slavery and long after it was legally abolished in 1865.

The Aftermath of Slavery. Patterns of black/white relations formed under slavery were not automatically changed by emancipation; freed blacks were formally given freedom but not the means (that is, economic, political, and educational equality) to realize it. African-Americans remained largely unskilled and illiterate, most of them living in enforced dependence upon the dominant whites. The result was a black peasantry dominated by an agricultural system that ensured dependence upon the land and isolation from the main currents of the society. Intimidation and violence in the form of lynching and terrorism were used to maintain the subordinate status of blacks long after slavery had been legally abolished.

To ensure that white dominance would be perpetuated, the "Jim Crow" system of racial segregation was created. During the late nineteenth century, Southern legislatures passed a variety of statutes requiring racial separation. In 1896, in the famous *Plessy v. Ferguson* decision, the U.S. Supreme Court provided legal support for the doctrine of "separate but equal." Thereafter virtually every aspect of contact between whites and blacks was legally regulated.

From Plantation to Ghetto. In response to these oppressive conditions, African-Americans began to leave the South during the early twentieth century. They migrated primarily to Northern urban areas, where their settlement was both legally and informally restricted to areas in which other blacks lived. This migration out of the rural South has been one of the most significant aspects of the African-American experience and one of the most important demographic changes in American history. In 1900, almost 90 percent of the black population lived in the South; by 1980 the percentage was only slightly more than one-half (52 percent). In 1900 African-Americans were primarily rural residents, with only 22.7 percent living in urban areas. By 1980, more than four-fifths (81.3 percent) of the African-American population lived in urban areas, indicating that blacks have become a more urbanized population than whites. Although a substantial portion of this increase in urban blacks occurred in the North, many Southern blacks also moved into cities. Table 9–2 shows the percentage of the African-American population residing in major American cities for the years 1920, 1950, 1970, and 1980.

The massive migration of African-Americans out of the South was one of the most important factors underlying the protest movement that swept the nation during the 1950s and 1960s. Although discrimination against African-Americans in education, employment, housing, and the administration of justice also prevailed in the North, greater opportunities were available for them in Northern urban areas than in the South. Especially after World War II, an educated and articulate black middle class played an important part in legal challenges to the Southern Jim Crow system. These actions culminated in the Supreme Court's 1954 *Brown v. Board of Education* decision that segregated schools were unconstitutional. The *Brown* decision, which overturned the Court's 1896 "separate but equal" doctrine, symbolized the beginning of an era in which the legal basis for the caste system would crumble.

The Changing Status of African-Americans. During the late 1950s and early 1960s African-Americans employed numerous forms of direct protest—such as nonviolent sit-ins, boycotts, and voter-registration drives—to effect changes in the existing

Table 9–2. African-American Population as Percent of the Total Population of the 12 Largest U.S. Cities,* 1920, 1950, 1970, and 1980

	1920†	1950†	1970	1980
New York	2.7	9.8	21.1	25.2
Los Angeles	2.7	10.7	17.9	17.0
Chicago	4.1	14.1	32.7	39.8
Philadelphia	7.4	18.3	33.6	37.8
Houston	24.6	21.1	25.7	27.6
Detroit	4.1	16.4	43.7	63.1
Dallas	15.1	13.2	24.9	29.4
San Diego	1.2	4.5	7.6	8.9
Phoenix	3.7	6.0	4.8	4.8
Baltimore	14.8	23.8	46.4	54.8
San Antonio	8.9	6.7	7.6	7.3
Indianapolis	11.0	15.0	18.0	21.8

Sources: U.S. Census of 1920; U.S. Census of 1950; U.S. Bureau of the Census, *Negroes in the United States, 1920–1932*, Washington, D.C.: U.S. Government Printing Office, 1935; "Characteristics of the Population," *Statistical Abstract of the United States, 1972*, pp. 21–23; *Statistical Abstract of the United States, 1984*, pp. 28–30.

* These were the 12 largest cities in the United States in 1980.

† Figures pertain to "nonwhite" population, of which over 90 percent was black.

system of race relations. During the 1960s federal, state, and local governments and private organizations made efforts to eliminate black inequality. The Civil Rights Act of 1964 substantially reduced public discrimination in restaurants, hotels, and business establishments. It also provided the impetus for substantial integration of public school systems in the South and for "affirmative action" efforts to ensure nondiscriminatory job hiring. The Voting Rights Act of 1965 enabled African-Americans throughout the South to exercise their right to vote. Finally, the Civil Rights Act of 1968 banned discrimination in the sale or rental of housing.

The effects of these and other changes were most marked in politics and education. Between 1964 and 1989 the number of African-Americans elected to public office increased from 103 to more than 7,200 (still, however, less than 2 percent of all elected public officials). Moreover, the number of African-American mayors increased from *none* in 1964 to more than 299 in 1989. Many major American cities have now had black mayors, including Los Angeles, Chicago, Detroit, Philadelphia, Atlanta, and Washington, D.C. The increasing significance of African-American political power was apparent in 1984 and 1988, when Jesse Jackson's presidential candidacy not only electrified the African-American community (and was instrumental in registering thousands of new black voters) but gained the support of a substantial number of white voters as well.

Since the Civil Rights Movement of the 1950s and 1960s, African-Americans have also achieved substantial gains in education. In 1957 the proportion of whites aged 25–29 who had completed high school (63.3 percent) was almost double the proportion of blacks (31.6 percent). By 1987 the proportions of each racial group who were high school graduates were nearly equal—86.3 percent for whites and 83.3 percent for blacks. Moreover, between 1957 and 1987 the ratio of white to black college graduates declined.

When Jesse Jackson campaigned for the presidency in 1988, he received the support of many white Americans as well as the overwhelming majority of votes of African-Americans.

In 1957 11 percent of whites but only 4 percent of blacks age 25–29 had completed four or more years of college; but by 1987 comparable figures were 23 percent for whites and 11.4 percent for blacks (U.S. Bureau of the Census, 1988a, pp. 75–76). In the early 1970s a steadily increasing percentage of blacks began attending college, so that by 1977 the percentage enrolled was nearly proportional to the black population as a whole, a striking increase over the college attendance rates of blacks in the mid-1960s (Jones, 1981). These gains of the 1960s and early 1970s have recently eroded, however, threatening to reverse the movement toward educational equality. Since 1975 black college attendance and completion rates have declined, as has the proportion of black students enrolled at four-year colleges and in graduate and professional schools (American Council on Education, 1988, p. 8).

Moreover, the overall economic status of African-Americans has shown little improvement since the mid-1960s. Although many blacks have experienced socioeconomic mobility during the past decade, African-Americans remain underrepresented in high-status professional, technical, and managerial positions, and overrepresented in service occupations, traditionally recognized as low-status jobs in American society (Farley and Allen, 1987). Furthermore, an enormous gap still separates black and white family incomes. As figure 9–2 shows, since 1950 income levels for both African-American and white families have risen substantially. White median family income nearly doubled, increasing from $16,264 (in 1987 dollars) in 1950 to $32,274 in 1987. The median family income for blacks increased more than 125 percent, reaching $18,098 by 1987. Although the gap between black and white incomes tended to narrow slightly during

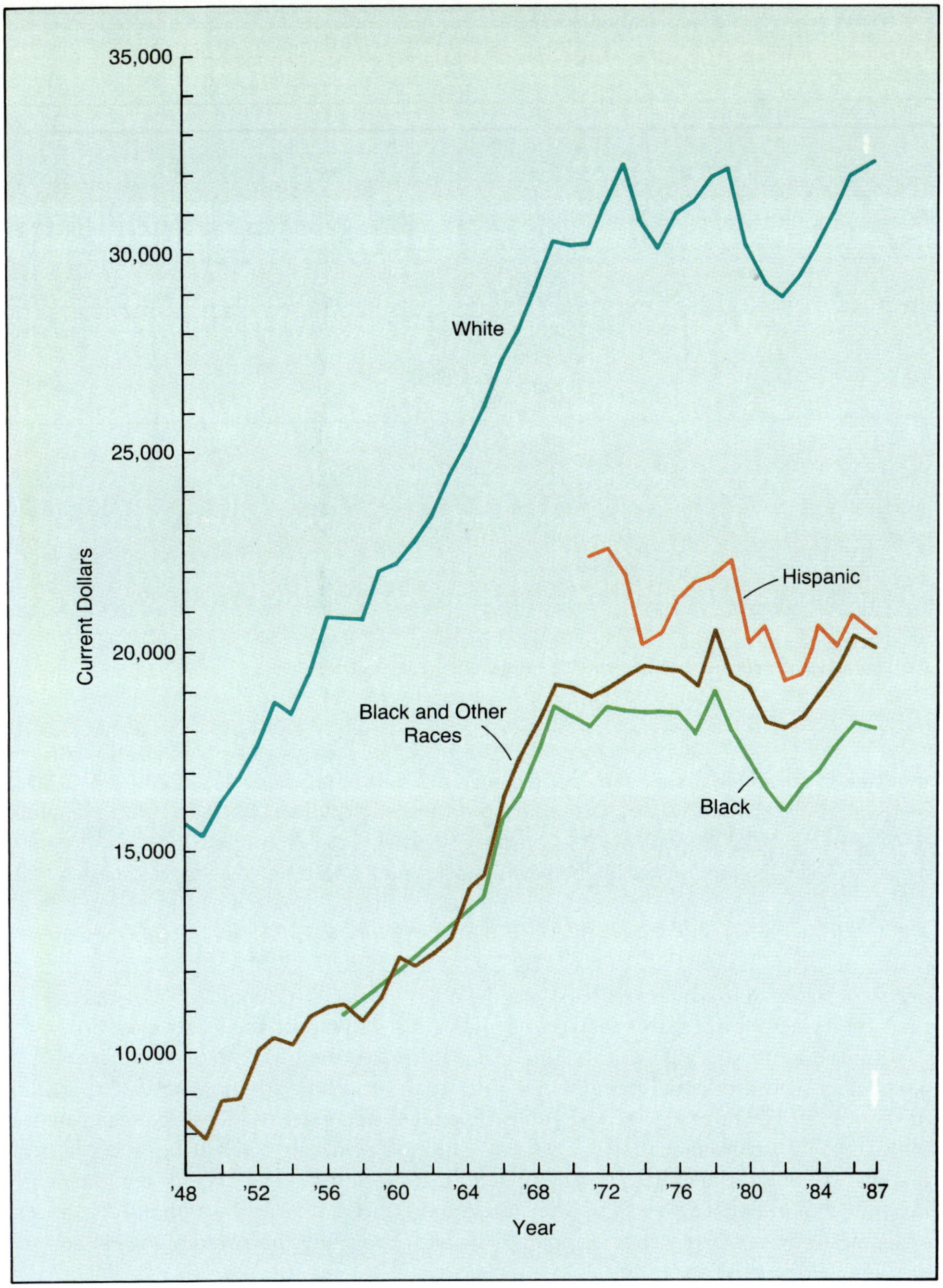

Figure 9–2. Median Income of Black, White, and Hispanic Families, 1948–1987 (in current U.S. dollars). (*Source:* U.S. Bureau of the Census, *Current Population Reports*, Series P-60, 1948–1988d.)

While some black Americans have been able to move into the middle class, the overall economic status of black Americans has shown little improvement since the 1960s.

the 1960s, since 1970 this gap has recently increased (see figure 9–2). In 1970 black median family income was 61 percent of white family income. By 1987 it had declined to 56 percent (U.S. Bureau of the Census, 1988d).

An even greater disparity between blacks and whites has been revealed by the Census Bureau survey of net worth of American households discussed in chapter 8. (In 1984, white households had a median net worth of $39,135, while the median net worth of black households was $3,397.) As a result of all the economic inequities between blacks and whites, both past and present, white households average nearly 12 times more net worth than black households (U.S. Bureau of the Census, 1986).

The gap separating African-Americans from the mainstream of American life is also reflected in residential patterns. Despite federal legislation outlawing discrimination in the sale of housing, blacks and whites remained nearly as residentially segregated in 1980 as they had been in 1970. This segregation is primarily a result of racial discrimination, not class differences; even affluent blacks continue to live in predominantly black neighborhoods. Other American racial and ethnic minorities—notably Asians and Hispanics—do not experience comparable levels of housing discrimination (Massey and Denton, 1987, 1988).

The patterns of discrimination responsible for black residential segregation include efforts by some people in the housing industry who discourage blacks from buying homes in white neighborhoods and organized neighborhood resistance to proposals for low-income and moderate-income housing. Another crucial source of housing discrimination involves home loans. A study that analyzed over 10 million applications for home loans from every savings and loan association in the country between 1983 and

1988 showed that black applications were rejected more than twice as often as the applications by whites. Moreover, the applications of high-income blacks were rejected more often than those of low-income whites (Dedman, 1989). Thus the substantial differences separating black and white Americans economically, educationally, and residentially have not been eliminated, and in some respects they have widened in the past decade.

Hispanic-Americans

Hispanic-Americans constitute one of the largest and most rapidly growing ethnic categories in the United States today. During the 1980s the Hispanic population grew nearly five times faster than the rest of the population, reaching a total of 19 million, or 8 percent of the total population, in 1987. Although Hispanics are more likely than the rest of the population to be Spanish-speaking, Catholic, and poor, they do not constitute a single ethnic category; there are widely diverse cultural, historical, and geographic backgrounds among them. They also differ in their socioeconomic status and in their regional distribution. Although there are more than 3 million "Other Hispanics" (which include Salvadorans, Guatemalans, Nicaraguans, Dominicans,, Colombians, and Ecuadorans), we focus here on the three largest Hispanic ethnic groups: Mexicans, Puerto Ricans, and Cubans.

Mexican-Americans (or Chicanos) are the largest Hispanic group and (after blacks) the second largest minority group in American society. More than 12 million Chicanos

Mexican citizens in search of a way to make a living continually attempt to enter the United States. Often, the U.S. Border Patrol apprehends them and returns them to Mexico.

live in the United States, about 90 percent of them in the southwestern states of Texas, New Mexico, Arizona, Colorado, and California. The earliest Mexican-Americans became a minority through the annexation of Mexican lands by the United States in the nineteenth century. However, most Mexican-Americans are descended from immigrants who came to the United States in the twentieth century. Mexican immigration is still a major factor in American society; today Mexicans are the largest national category of both legal and illegal immigrants to the United States.

Several indicators reveal that Mexican-Americans lag considerably behind the mainstream of American society in socioeconomic status. Despite some evidence of improvement among younger generations, Mexican-Americans lag behind both whites and African-Americans in educational attainment. Long stereotyped as primarily rural farm workers, today Mexican-Americans are overwhelmingly urban residents. However, they tend to be found primarily in low-paying blue-collar and semi-skilled occupations (although some evidence reveals that during the 1970s the proportion of Mexican-Americans in skilled, higher-paying occupations increased). As table 9–3 indicates, median family income for Mexican-Americans is only 63 percent of median family income for whites (Davis, Haub, and Willette, 1985; U.S. Bureau of the Census, 1988d).

Other Spanish-speaking peoples have immigrated primarily to urban areas on the East Coast, particularly since the end of World War II. Although the number of immigrants from countries throughout the Caribbean and Central and South America has increased markedly during this period, Puerto Rico and Cuba have been the two primary sources.

Puerto Ricans, who, unlike other immigrants, are American citizens, began migrating to the mainland primarily after World War II. Today nearly two-thirds of the more than 2 million mainland Puerto Ricans live in New York City, which has been the principal magnet for Puerto Rican immigrants. This migration to the mainland has been prompted primarily by economic pressures among the impoverished lower strata of Puerto Rican society. Consequently, Puerto Rican immigrants have been concentrated in blue-collar, semi-skilled, and unskilled occupations, and their income level (47 percent of white median family income) is the lowest among all American ethnic groups.

Table 9–3. Median Family Income, 1986

	Income	% of White Income
All races	$29,458	
White	30,809	
Black	17,604	57
Hispanic	19,995	65
Mexican	19,326	63
Puerto Rican	14,584	47
Cuban	26,770	87
Other Hispanic	24,240	79

Sources: U.S. Bureau of the Census, "Money Income of Households, Families, and Persons in the United States: 1986," *Current Population Reports,* Series P-60, No. 159, 1988d; "The Hispanic Population of the United States," *Current Population Reports,* Series P-20, No. 418, 1988i.

Cuban immigrants and their families are heavily represented in many neighborhoods in Miami, from the most affluent to the poorest parts of the city.

Cuban immigrants have been primarily political refugees. Approximately 750,000 Cubans have entered the United States since Castro's rise to power in 1959, and today they number about 1 million. In contrast to most previous immigrations to the United States, early Cuban immigrants tended to be drawn mainly from the upper social and economic strata of Cuban society. With these backgrounds, they brought skills (educational, occupational, business, and managerial), entrepreneurial values, and substantial amounts of capital that enabled them to achieve rapid socioeconomic success. In less than 25 years since their initial migration, Cubans have become the most affluent of all Hispanics and are an integral part of the economies of a number of American cities, especially Miami, Florida, which they have transformed into a major commercial center with ties throughout Latin America.

Asian-Americans

Asians are an extremely diverse category that includes Chinese, Japanese, Filipinos, Koreans, Asian Indians, Vietnamese, and many other national or ethnic groups. Compared to the millions of Europeans who have immigrated to the United States, Asian immigration has been slight. By 1987 Asians represented 2.2 percent of the American people. Today, as a result of changes in American immigration laws, which before 1965 had virtually excluded them, Asians are proportionately the nation's fastest growing minority. During the 1970s the Asian population increased by 141 percent, Hispanics by 39 percent, and African-Americans by 17 percent. Between 1980 and 1984 Asians constituted nearly half (48 percent) of all legal immigrants (Gardner, Robey, and Smith, 1985).

During World War II, suspicion of the Japanese in the United States was so great that those who lived on the Pacific coast were interned in concentration camps. Only recently have the federal courts ruled that damages should be paid to the Japanese who lost their homes and businesses during their period of internment.

Historically the Chinese, Japanese, and, later, Filipinos have been the most prominent Asian groups; Asian Indians, Koreans, and Vietnamese are more recent arrivals. The initial migration of Chinese, who were the first Asians to immigrate to the United States, reached its peak from 1873 to 1882. Initially welcomed as a source of labor, the Chinese soon became perceived as an economic threat to native labor, and they were subjected to various forms of discriminatory legislation. In 1882 Congress passed the Chinese Exclusion Act, the first law to restrict a specific nationality from immigrating to the United States.

Anti-Asian sentiment was revived when many Japanese immigrated to the United States in the early twentieth century. Although the Japanese represented an extremely small proportion of the total population, their presence generated intense hostility. Like the Chinese before them, the Japanese were the object of legislation to harass them and diplomatic efforts to prevent their further immigration. In 1924 all Asian immigration to the United States was restricted, and it remained limited until 1968, when a new immigration law went into effect.

Despite early anti-Asian prejudice and discrimination, in particular toward the Japanese during World War II (which resulted in their evacuation from the West Coast and their internment in concentration camps), Asians have recently made significant socioeconomic gains, especially in education. By 1980 more than half of 20–21-year-old Asian-Americans were enrolled in school compared with a third of whites of the same age (Hirschman and Wong, 1986, p. 1). So extraordinary have Asian educational attainments been that charges have been raised that many of the nation's most prestigious universities have placed limitations on the percentage of Asian students they would admit (Mathews, 1987).

Similarly, reflecting a dramatic decline in labor market discrimination against them, by the 1980s the income levels of American-born and immigrant Asians were not significantly different from whites who had comparable skills. However, there were differences in income levels among Asian groups: Japanese, Chinese, and Koreans earned more than whites; Filipinos, Asian Indians, and Vietnamese earned less. Moreover, poverty rates for native-born Chinese, Japanese, and Korean families were lower than for whites (U.S. Commission on Civil Rights, 1988).

Contemporary Immigration

Since 1968 the traditional patterns of immigration into the United States have been radically transformed. This recent wave of immigration promises to produce the most dramatic and far-reaching changes in the ethnic composition of the United States since the massive waves of new immigrants in the late nineteenth and early twentieth centuries. Since the early 1970s, the number of permanent immigrants to the United States has increased substantially. By 1986 more than 600,000 legal immigrants were admitted, a number greater than immigrants to all other nations of the world combined. Moreover, experts estimate that, in addition to 450,000 new residents who are added to the population of the United States each year as a result of net legal immigration, there is a net annual increase of 100,000 to 200,000 illegal immigrants (Bouvier and Gardner, 1986). (Net legal immigration is calculated by subtracting the number of people leaving the country from the number entering the country.)

The changes in the national origins of contemporary immigrants are as dramatic as their increasing numbers. Until 1968, immigration to the United States was overwhelmingly European, ranging from a high of 96 percent of all immigrants for the decade 1891–1900 to 53 percent between 1950 and 1960. Today, as a result of changes in American immigration laws, only a small percentage (10 percent in 1986) of immigrants come from Europe. The predominant sources of immigration are Third World nations in Central and South America, the Caribbean, and Asia. In 1986 *none* of the leading countries from which the United States received immigrants—Mexico, the Philippines, Korea, Cuba, Vietnam, India, the Dominican Republic, and the People's Republic of China—was a traditional European source (U.S. Bureau of the Census, 1988h). Given the declining birth rate of the American population, some demographers estimate that, if current trends in birth rates and immigration rates continue, a century from now 40 percent of the American population will be made up of post-1980 immigrants and their descendants—at least 80 percent of whom will be Hispanic, Caribbean, or Asian (Bouvier, 1981).

The settlement patterns of today's immigrants differ from previous flows into the United States. Whereas previous immigrants settled primarily in the industrial states of the Northeast and Midwest (New York, Illinois, New Jersey, Pennsylvania), immigrants today are much more dispersed geographically. States with the largest foreign-born populations in 1980 were California, New York, Florida, Illinois, and Texas (U.S. Bureau of the Census, 1982, pp. 14–19).

When Americans think of immigrants to the United States, they often have an image of "huddled masses" who are poor, unskilled, and uneducated. That perception of immigrants may have been valid at one time, but today it is seriously out of date. The changes in America's immigration laws have affected the occupational composition of the present immigrant population. Today the range of immigrants' occupations much more closely resembles that of the native population than immigrant populations have in the past. Whereas immigrants during the first two decades of the twentieth century were overwhelmingly unskilled, blue-collar workers, preferences today for those with skills needed by the United States has meant that immigrants entering now are much more highly educated than in the past. Physicians, nurses, scientists, architects, artists, entertainers, engineers, and others with highly technical skills have contributed to a "brain drain," first from Europe and later from Third World nations that can least afford to lose such skills.

Today the overall educational level of immigrants to the United States is not especially low when compared to the United States' population as a whole. For example, 16.2 percent of American adults aged 25 and over have completed college, while 15.8 percent of immigrants have done so. Immigrants from Asia and Africa are especially well educated; almost half of African (46 percent) and Asian (44 percent) immigrants in 1980 had completed college (Bouvier, 1986, p. 24). About half of all Asian immigrants between 1966 and 1975 were professionals; for Asian Indians the figure was 90 percent (U.S. Commission on Civil Rights, 1988, p. 5). The preference for immigrants with skills has meant that, unlike the situation between 1840 and 1920, it has become almost impossible for unskilled laborers to enter the United States unless they can claim a close family relationship or refugee status.

The emphasis on occupational skills has also meant that, increasingly, the less skilled have resorted to illegal means of entering the country. Today the largest category of immigrants consists of those who enter the country illegally (although, as we noted earlier, the estimated annual net increase from illegal immigrants is lower than from legal immigrants). By 1986 1.8 million illegal immigrants from 93 countries were apprehended, with the vast majority from Latin America (Bouvier, 1986, pp. 36–38). Estimates of the total number of "undocumented aliens" living in the United States range from 3 million to 6 million (Kammeyer and Ginn, 1986).

As was the case in the early part of the twentieth century, concern over the impact of immigrants on American society has created a growing sense of alarm among many Americans. One debate about immigration that has a long history deals with questions regarding the impact that immigrants have on jobs, wages, and the domestic economy in general. No doubt many immigrants have in the past taken, and continue today to take, jobs and occupations that other American citizens do not want. The newest immigrants, especially those with low levels of education, often take the menial and service jobs that are the least desirable and lowest paid. Even immigrants with professional skills, such as medical doctors, often practice in less desirable settings and institutions.

One study of the impact that immigrants have on employment and wages in southern California during the early 1980s concluded that Mexican workers did not increase unemployment among non-Hispanic California residents. Furthermore, the immigrants generally took the lower-status jobs, while the longer-term residents moved up the occupational ladder (Muller and Espenshade, 1985). This study is not conclusive evidence about the impact of immigrants on jobs, wages, and the economy, but it does counter the fears that many people have about the negative impact of immigration. Therefore, no matter how the issue of contemporary immigration is resolved politically, it seems inevitable that, given the prominence of America throughout the world, the United States will continue to attract immigrants, legal and illegal—thus reinforcing and recreating the ethnic diversity that, almost from its founding, has characterized American society.

Majority/Minority Relations

The diversity of racial and ethnic groups in American society provides an opportunity to examine several of the different ways in which racial and ethnic groups interact and to explore the conditions under which different kinds of intergroup relations occur. We examine first how members of the dominant group define the role of minorities and, next, the experiences of minorities in responding to the policies of majority groups.

Prejudice and Discrimination

Prejudice and discrimination are important elements in all majority/minority relations. The term *prejudice* (derived from two Latin words, *prae* [before] and *judicum* [a judgment]) denotes a judgment before all the facts are known. **Prejudice** refers to a set of rigidly held negative attitudes, beliefs, and feelings toward members of another group. **Discrimination,** on the other hand, involves unfavorable treatment of individuals because of their group membership. Unlike prejudice, which is an attitude and an internal state, discrimination involves overt action or behavior.

Prejudice
Rigidly held negative attitudes, beliefs, and feelings toward members of another group

Discrimination
Unfavorable treatment of people because of their group membership

Clearly, however, a close relationship frequently exists between prejudice and discrimination. Because they are related, an extensive amount of research has been carried out concerning the nature and causes of prejudice. Attitude surveys conducted since the 1940s have shown a significant decline in anti-black prejudice; increasingly, white Americans have come to support broad principles of racial integration and equal treatment in public accommodations, employment, public transportation, schools, and housing. For example, in 1942, 32 percent agreed that whites and blacks should attend the same schools; by 1982 this figure was 90 percent. In 1944, 45 percent thought that blacks should have as good a chance as whites to get any kind of job, and by 1972, 97 percent agreed. The percentage approving integration in public transportation rose from 46 percent in 1942 to 88 percent in 1970. Moreover, whites have indicated increasing willingness to participate personally in desegregated settings (Schuman, Steeh, and Bobo, 1985). These changes are a result of two factors. First, they reflect attitude changes among individuals over their lifetimes. Second, younger people generally exhibit less racial prejudice than their elders, and as younger, more tolerant, cohorts have replaced older, more prejudiced ones, overall racial prejudice has declined (Firebaugh and Davis, 1988).

However, the same striking agreement does not appear among Americans on how to combat discrimination or segregation. Although today white Americans endorse broad principles of nondiscrimination and desegregation in important areas of American life, they are much less likely to support policies for translating these principles into practice. For example, despite their strong support of the principle of integrated education, the percentage of white Americans who felt that the federal government should ensure that black and white children attend the same schools declined between the 1960s and the 1980s. Moreover, widespread white opposition was raised to busing as a means of desegregating schools (Schuman, Steeh, and Bobo, 1985).

The substantial gap between people's support for broad principles of equality and their support for specific programs to implement these principles indicates the complexity of racial attitudes. The relationship between prejudicial attitudes and discriminatory behavior is equally complex. Prejudice does not always produce discrimination, although it has frequently been treated as the cause of discrimination. An individual, however, may be prejudiced without *acting* in a discriminatory manner. In recent years it has become less fashionable to express racial prejudice publicly. Overt forms of discrimination such as exclusion from public accommodations, jobs, and colleges and universities—which in the past were tolerated by most whites—are now often prohibited by the law and condemned by public opinion. Therefore, whether prejudice is translated into discrimination depends on the social context within which the prejudice occurs.

Because sociologists are primarily concerned with understanding human behavior, the primary focus in our analysis of racial and ethnic relations is on discrimination, which may range from mild slights (Polish jokes, for instance) to systematic oppression (slavery) to violence (lynching, pogroms, and massacres). Discrimination is a means of preserving the unequal status of the minority group and the disproportionate power of the majority. We can distinguish two different types of discrimination: attitudinal and institutional. They are interrelated and serve to reinforce each other.

Attitudinal Discrimination

Attitudinal discrimination
Discrimination that stems from prejudicial attitudes

Attitudinal discrimination refers to discriminatory practices that stem from prejudicial attitudes. The discriminator either is prejudiced or acts in response to the prejudices of others. Attitudinal discrimination is usually direct, overt, visible, and dramatic. Despite increasing white acceptance of principles of nondiscrimination and racial desegregation, African-Americans especially have been confronted with attitudinal discrimination in virtually every aspect of their lives. For example, in 1985 and 1986 alone, 45 cases were documented of arson and cross-burnings after minority families moved into predominantly white neighborhoods. Although such "move-in" violence was found throughout the country, the majority of cases occurred in the North and Midwest. The U.S. Justice Department reported 276 violent attacks by whites against blacks in 1986 alone. Moreover, during the 1980s hundreds of incidents of intimidation, harassment, and vandalism occurred against racial minorities, including many on college campuses (Southern Poverty Law Center, 1987; *Time*, 1987).

In Philadelphia a black couple were forced to move from their new home after they were threatened by a crowd of 400 whites, who jeered at them with taunts of "Beat it" and "We want them out" (*U.S. News and World Report*, 1985, p. 12). In Kansas City, a white man used gunfire and explosives in an effort to drive a black man from the neighborhood in which he lived (Dauner, 1987, p. B1). In Cleveland, a 66-year-old African-American woman was killed in her home when it was firebombed. In Chicago,

The white citizens of Forsyth County, Georgia, demonstrate in opposition to any kind of racial integration in their county. This is a vivid example of attitudinal discrimination.

a neighbor of black victims of arson justified such violence to a reporter: "I don't think [arson] is right. But it's also not right for them to come into a neighborhood when it's all white" (Southern Poverty Law Center, 1987, p. 7).

Attitudinal discrimination does not always occur in so virulent or so direct a manner. It can be manifested less dramatically merely by the adherence of members of the dominant group to social definitions of traditional subordinate group roles. Malcolm X, the charismatic black protest leader who was assassinated in 1965, recalled how his well-meaning white high school English teacher, Mr. Ostrowski, was bound by cultural norms concerning the "proper" caste roles for blacks.

> I know that he probably meant well in what he happened to advise me that day. I doubt that he meant any harm. . . . I was one of his top students, one of the school's top students—but all he could see for me was the kind of future "in your place" that almost all white people see for black people. . . . He told me, "Malcolm, you ought to be thinking about a career. Have you been giving it thought?" . . . The truth is, I hadn't. I never have figured out why I told him, "Well, yes, sir, I've been thinking I'd like to be a lawyer." Lansing certainly had no Negro lawyers—or doctors either—in those days, to hold up an image I might have aspired to. All I really knew for certain was that a lawyer didn't wash dishes, as I was doing.
>
> Mr. Ostrowski looked surprised, I remember, and leaned back in his chair and clasped his hands behind his head. He kind of half-smiled and said, "Malcolm, one of life's first needs is for us to be realistic. Don't misunderstand me, now. We all here like you, you know that. But you've got to be realistic about being a nigger. A lawyer—that's no realistic goal for a nigger. You need to think about something you can be. You're good with

your hands—making things. Everybody admires your carpentry shop work. Why don't you plan on carpentry? People like you as a person—you'd get all kinds of work" (Malcolm X, 1966, p. 36).

Institutional Discrimination

Institutional discrimination Organizational practices and societal trends that exclude minorities from economic opportunity, power, and prestige

The concept of **institutional discrimination** reflects organizational practices and societal trends that exclude minorities from economic opportunities and from positions of power and prestige. Institutional discrimination is central to one of the most controversial interpretations of recent American race relations. In *The Declining Significance of Race* (1978) and *The Truly Disadvantaged* (1987), William J. Wilson argued that in the past, attitudinal discrimination was the major factor responsible for the unequal economic, political, and social status of African-Americans. He acknowledges that in many areas of American life, such as housing, education, and municipal politics, attitudinal discrimination is still pervasive and serves as a barrier to black participation in the mainstream of American society today.

However, Wilson contends that the overall economic position of urban blacks has recently deteriorated not only because of instances of attitudinal discrimination such as those cited above; it has also occurred because of impersonal economic changes that have little to do with race. These include "the shift from goods-producing to service-producing industries, the increasing polarization of the labor market into low-wage and high-wage sectors, technological innovations, and the relocation of manufacturing industries out of the central cities" (Wilson, 1987, p. 39). Relatively unskilled blacks concentrated in the nation's central cities are especially vulnerable to the relocation of manufacturing jobs that in the past provided economic opportunities for several generations of relatively unskilled workers—native and foreign, black and white. The economic opportunities of the African-American underclass, who lack the educational and occupational skills necessary for the highly technological jobs being created in the cities today, are therefore rapidly diminishing.

Although the African-American underclass's lack of educational and occupational skills reflect a legacy of historic attitudinal discrimination, institutional factors—the broad structural changes in the economy mentioned above—play a crucial role in sustaining black economic inequality. Even if all racial prejudice were eliminated, the African-American underclass would still lack the necessary qualifications to participate in the mainstream of the economy and would continue to be found primarily in the unskilled sector where unemployment is extremely high and wages very low. In other words, in the economic sphere institutional discrimination has become an important source of continuing African-American inequalities.

Institutional discrimination is thus more subtle, more complex, and less visible than attitudinal discrimination Because it does not result from the motivations or intentions of specific individuals, it is more impersonal than attitudinal discrimination. Nevertheless, it has the same discriminatory consequences for minority group members. In examining institutional discrimination, therefore, we must consider the *effect* of a particular policy or practice upon a minority group rather than the motivations of the majority group.

Patterns of Racial and Ethnic Relations

The efforts of dominant groups to create and maintain their positions of power have been expressed in many different patterns of racial and ethnic relations, ranging from violent conflict to peaceful coexistence. The following discussion reviews the range of patterns of racial and ethnic relations. The patterns are not mutually exclusive; a majority group may adopt more than one of these policies at the same time or at different times. For example, as our discussion of Indian-white relations indicated, Native Americans at different times have been subjected to policies ranging from extermination to expulsion to forced assimilation.

Extermination

The most repressive and destructive dominant-group pattern of majority/minority relations is **extermination,** or **genocide,** which denies the subordinate group's very right to live. According to William O'Brien, genocide refers to actions intended "to destroy, in whole or in part, a national, ethnic, racial, or religious group." His definition includes:

Extermination, or genocide
Practices that seek to reduce or destroy a minority population

> (a) killing members of the group; (b) causing serious bodily or mental harm to members of the group; (c) deliberately inflicting on the group conditions of life calculated to bring about its physical destruction . . . ; (d) imposing measures intended to prevent births within the group; (e) forcibly transferring children of the group to another group (cited in O'Brien, 1968, p. 516).

Although examples of genocide are not confined to the twentieth century, some of the most notorious examples have occurred relatively recently in human history. In 1915 1.5 million Armenians were massacred by the Turks. Between 1935 and 1945 the Nazis exterminated more than 6 million Jews and other "non-Aryan" groups (such as Gypsies). In the small African country of Burundi more than 100,000 minority Hutu (about 3.5 percent of the population) were murdered by the dominant Tutsi people in 1972, and in 1988 another 5,000 to 20,000 were killed. (Refer to the Cross-National box: "Ethnic Conflict in Africa" for further discussion of this topic.)

Since genocide violates the sanctity of human life, an ideology of racism is often developed to justify genocidal actions. **Racism** involves a belief in the inherent superiority of one racial group and the inherent inferiority of others. Its primary function is to provide a set of ideas and beliefs that can be used to explain, rationalize, and justify a system of racial domination. By denying that a racial minority has human qualities or by depicting it as subhuman or destructive of human values and life, the minority's extermination is made morally justifiable and acceptable. For example, in 1876 an Australian writer defended efforts to annihilate the native people of New Zealand (Maoris), Australia, and Tasmania: "When exterminating the inferior Australian and Maori races . . . the world is better for it. . . . [By] protecting the propogation of the imprudent, the diseased, the defective, the criminal . . . we tend to destroy the human race" (quoted in Hartwig, 1972, p. 16).

Racism
Belief in the inherent superiority of one racial group and the inherent inferiority of others

Cross-National Perspectives

Ethnic Conflict in Africa

Ethnic conflict and violence are not restricted to Western countries. During the past quarter century there have been several violent intertribal conflicts in Africa. In the process, thousands have died and many thousands more have been forced to flee their homes, creating in Africa one of the world's largest refugee populations. In Nigeria, conflict among Yoruba, Ibo, and Hausa tribes resulted in a bloody civil war that, between 1968 and 1970, cost a million lives. In Uganda dictator Idi Amin slaughtered more than 100,000 Ugandans, mostly members of the Baganda, Langi, and Acholi tribes. Today ethnic divisions still create conflicts in many African countries, including Ethiopia, the Sudan, Benin, Ivory Coast, and Angola. While many Westerners have been aware of these conflicts, most know nothing about the severe violence and killing in the tiny east African country of Burundi, which in the past twenty years has experienced one of the largest massacres since the atrocities of Nazi Germany (Lemarchand, 1975).

Burundi is a landlocked country of central Africa, situated between the republics of Zaire and Tanzania. During its colonial period, which ended in 1962, Burundi was controlled by the Belgians. As in several other African countries, independence from European colonialism brought deep-rooted and long-repressed tribal rivalries to the surface. In 1972 a wave of violence swept the country. An estimated 100,000 people were killed, or 3.5 percent of the total population. A comparable annihilation of the American population would have resulted in the deaths of about 8 million people.

The violence in Burundi reflects the rivalry of the country's two major ethnic groups: the Tutsi and the Hutu. The Tutsi, a tall and slender people, make up only about 15 percent of Burundi's population. For centuries before the arrival of European colonial powers, the Tutsi had held the Hutu, a people of smaller stature, in a form of serfdom. During the colonial period the Belgians supported the social divisions of a Tutsi aristocracy and a Hutu servant class. When independence was achieved in 1962, many Hutu were hopeful that, since they represented 85 percent of the population, the promise of majority rule would bring an end to Tutsi domination. However, Hutu frustration grew in the years following independence as the more politically astute Tutsi effectively blocked Hutu efforts to change the status quo.

In 1972 small bands of Hutu revolted against Tutsi rule. They killed and mutilated any Tutsi they could find, including women and children, as well as any Hutu who refused to join them. The Tutsi-dominated government of Burundi responded with a wave of counterviolence. In many villages all Hutu of any wealth, community influence, or educational level above grade school were systematically shot or beaten to death. The killing was selective, aimed at all influential Hutu. The objective of the annihilation of the Hutu elites was to crush any Hutu threat to Tutsi power. The Tutsi sought to eliminate "not only the rebellion but Hutu society as well, and in the process lay the foundation of an entirely new social order" (Lemarchand, 1975).

This wave of genocide ensured Tutsi political and economic power in Burundi and led to the systematic exclusion of Hutu from the army, civil service, the university, and high schools. In 1988 the long-simmering tension between these two groups flared once again into violent conflict. At least 5,000 more people were killed in another Hutu uprising and the Tutsi reprisal that followed, and more than 50,000 Hutu fled to the neighboring country of Rwanda, where Hutu are the tribal majority (Brooke, 1988; Perlez, 1988). The conflict between Tutsi and Hutu is but one example of how ethnic and racial hatreds continue to produce bloodshed and violence throughout the modern world.

BROOKE, JAMES. "In Africa, Tribal Hatreds Defy the Borders of State." *New York Times*, August 28, 1988.
LEMARCHAND, RENE. "Ethnic Genocide." *Society* 12, 1975.
PERLEZ, JANE. "Burundi's Army May Have Inflamed a Deadly Tribal Revenge Born in Fear." *New York Times*, August 29, 1988.

Expulsion and Exclusion

The objective of extermination is to reduce or eliminate contact between majority and minority, and to create an ethnically (or racially) homogeneous society. A similar rationale underlies the process of **expulsion,** that is, the ejection of a minority group from areas controlled by the dominant group. Expulsion can be of two types: direct and indirect (Simpson and Yinger, 1985, pp. 19–20). **Direct expulsion** occurs when minorities are forcibly ejected by the dominant majority, often through military or other governmental force. The policy of direct expulsion was at no time more pronounced in American history than during the nineteenth century, when thousands of American Indians were removed from the East to areas beyond the Mississippi River.

Expulsion
Practices that seek to expel minorities from areas controlled by the dominant group

Direct expulsion
The forcible ejection of a minority group by a dominant group, often by military force

Numerous examples of direct expulsion can be found in recent history. Nazi Germany sought to achieve a pure "Aryan" people not only by extermination but also by expelling numerous minorities from its borders. In contemporary Israel, Meir Kahane, an American-born rabbi, has gained increasing political support for his proposal to resolve the problem of Arab-Jewish tensions in that country by removing all Arabs from Israel and its occupied territories and making Israel into an exclusively Jewish state (Friedman, 1985, p. 1).

Indirect expulsion occurs when harassment, discrimination, and persecution of a minority becomes so intense that members "voluntarily" choose to emigrate. Harassment and persecution of minorities, particularly religious minorities, led many groups to seek refuge in the United States. Persecuted Protestant sects were among the earliest European immigrants to the American colonies, and the tradition of America as an asylum for the oppressed has continued into the present. Since the early Christian era, Jews periodically have been forced—either directly or indirectly—to leave the lands in which they have settled. The most dramatic emigration in modern Jewish history occurred in the late nineteenth and early twentieth century when millions (more than one-third of all Eastern European Jews) fled czarist Russia.

Indirect expulsion
Use of harassment, discrimination, and persecution to expel minorities

Achieving or retaining ethnic homogeneity is also attained when a host society refuses to permit another group entrance because that group is perceived as a threat to

Exclusion
Policies that refuse to admit culturally different groups into a country

the society's basic social institutions. When countries have policies that refuse to admit culturally different groups it is called **exclusion.** As we noted earlier, between 1917 and 1965 American immigration policy was based on the assumption that immigration from southern and eastern Europe and Asia should be substantially or completely restricted. This assumption was embodied in the 1924 immigration legislation, which established numerical quotas for each nation. More than four-fifths of the quotas were assigned to those nations of northern and western Europe whose ethnic characteristics most closely coincided with those of the "original" settlers of the country. Although Great Britain had an admissions quota exceeding 65,000, Italy was allocated less than 6,000, and Hungary, less than 1,000. Asians were almost completely excluded. This policy remained virtually intact until its repeal in 1965.

Oppression

Oppression
Policy that exploits a minority group by excluding it from equal participation in society

Oppression involves the exploitation of a minority group by excluding it from equal participation in a society (Turner, Singleton, and Musick, 1984, pp. 1–2). Oppression "depends on exclusiveness rather than exclusion" (Bonacich, 1972, p. 555). Unlike extermination, expulsion, or exclusion, a system of oppression accepts the existence of minorities but subjugates them and confines them to inferior social positions. The majority group uses its power to maintain its access to scarce and valued resources in a system of social inequality.

Slavery, in which the slave's labor was a valuable resource exploited by the slave owner, was an example of oppression in American society. Even after slavery was legally abolished, the Jim Crow system of racial segregation that ensued was organized to exploit blacks for the benefit of the dominant whites. After taking a tour of the South at the turn of the century, a journalist remarked upon the exploitative nature of black/white relations:

> One of the things I saw in the South—and I saw it everywhere—was the way in which the people were torn between their feelings of race prejudice and their downright economic needs. Hating and fearing the Negro as a race (though often loving individual Negroes), they yet want him to work for them; they can't get along without him. In one impulse a community will rise to mob Negroes or to drive them out of the country because of Negro crime or Negro vagrancy, or because the Negro is becoming educated, acquiring property and "getting out of his place;" and in the next impulse laws are passed or other remarkable measures taken to keep him at work—because the South can't get along without him (Baker, 1964, p. 81).

Apartheid
The South African legal system of "separate development" that perpetuates white power and privilege

A classic contemporary example of oppression is the South African system of **apartheid,** or "separate development," which functions to maintain the privileged position of whites, who enjoy one of the highest standards of living in the world but who represent only 15 percent of the country's population. On the other hand, South African blacks, who comprise more than two-thirds (69 percent) of the population, are excluded from genuine participation in the nation's political system and are legally confined to rural reserves, or "homelands," that represent only 13 percent of the land. However, black labor provides a cheap labor supply for South African mines, farms, manufacturing, and domestic help that is essential to the South African economy and the system of white privilege. Therefore, the entire system of state controls restricting black political

The South African system of apartheid, which segregates the races in almost all areas of life, is often maintained by repressive police power.

power, residence, and education is designed to perpetuate the system of white privilege (Cohen, 1986).

Assimilation

In general, the majority group's response to ethnic minorities in America has been to seek their assimilation. **Assimilation** involves efforts to integrate or incorporate a group into the mainstream of a society. As with other majority group policies previously discussed, the objective of assimilation is a homogeneous society. In American society two distinct conceptions of assimilation have existed: Anglo-conformity and the melting pot.

Assimilation
The integration or incorporation of a minority into the mainstream of a society

Anglo-Conformity. The principal assimilationist model in the American experience has emphasized conformity by minority groups to dominant-group standards. In the United States this has been termed *Anglo-conformity*. **Anglo-conformity** assumes that ethnic minorities should give up their distinctive characteristics and adopt those of the dominant group (Cole and Cole, 1954). It can be expressed by the formula $A + B + C = A$, in which A is the dominant group and B and C represent ethnic minority groups that must conform to the values and life styles of the dominant group if they want to achieve positions of importance and prestige in the society (Newman, 1973, p. 53).

Anglo-conformity
American concept of assimilation that assumes that minorities should adopt traits of the dominant group

A policy of Anglo-conformity not only seeks a homogeneous society organized around the idealized cultural standards, institutions, and language of the dominant group; it also assumes the inferiority of the cultures of other ethnic groups. Many Americans retain vivid and painful recollections of the ridicule of their cultural ways and the pressures for them to become "Americanized." Many tried to rid themselves of their traditional beliefs and practices. A daughter of Slovenian immigrant parents recalls her childhood:

> In the 9th grade, a boy said to me, "You talk funny." I wondered what he meant. I listened to my friends, and I did not think they "talked funny." Then, that great American experiment, the public high school, opened my ears. I heard the English language spoken as I had never heard it spoken. . . . I began to hear that I did indeed pronounce my words differently, and so did my friends. I practiced [English] in secret, in the bathroom, of course, until I could pronounce properly the difficult "th" sound, which seemed the most distinctive and, therefore, the most necessary to conquer. How superior I felt when I had mastered this sound . . . ! Alas, however, I refused to speak Slovenian (Prosen, 1976, pp. 2–3).

Melting pot
Concept of assimilation that ethnic groups contribute to the creation of a new and different society and culture

The Melting Pot.

Like Anglo-conformity, the ultimate objective of a melting pot policy is a society without ethnic differences. More tolerant than a policy of Anglo-conformity, the **melting pot** sees ethnic differences as being lost in the creation of a new society and a new people—a synthesis unique and distinct from any of the different groups that formed it. Unlike Anglo-conformity, none of the contributing groups is considered to be superior; each is considered to have contributed the best of its cultural heritage to the creation of something new. The melting pot ideal can be expressed by the formula A + B + C = D, in which A, B, and C represent the different contributing groups and D is the product of their synthesis (Newman, 1973, p. 63). As Ralph Waldo Emerson expressed it in the mid-nineteenth century:

> . . . in this continent—asylum of all nations—the energy of Irish, Germans, Swedes, Poles, and Cossacks, and all the European tribes—of the Africans, and of the Polynesians—will construct a new race, a new religion, a new state, a new literature . . . (quoted in Gordon, 1964, p. 11).

Cultural Assimilation and Structural Assimilation.

To what extent has ethnic assimilation actually occurred in American society? Milton Gordon (1964) pointed out that assimilation is not a single phenomenon but involves several processes. The two most important of these are cultural assimilation and structural assimilation. Most of the previous discussion has concerned cultural assimilation, or **acculturation**—that is, the acquisition of the *cultural* characteristics of the dominant group, including its values, beliefs, language, and behaviors. But many ethnic groups have become fully acculturated to the dominant American culture and still have not been able to achieve full *social* participation in the society. Sharing the same language, norms, and culture does not ensure access to informal social organizations, clubs, cliques, and friendship groups.

Acculturation (cultural assimilation)
The acquisition by minorities of the cultural characteristics of the dominant group

Structural assimilation
The integration of minorities into primary and secondary social relations with the dominant group

Structural assimilation occurs when there is social interaction among individuals of different ethnic backgrounds. Two types can be distinguished: secondary and primary. Secondary structural assimilation refers to the ethnic integration of social situations characterized by impersonal secondary relationships: jobs, schools, political organizations, neighborhoods, and public recreation. However, even sharing membership in such secondary groups does not necessarily involve primary-group associations—informal social organizations, friendships, and, ultimately, intermarriage. Primary structural assimilation is achieved when these kinds of interethnic associations occur.

Considerable research has recently focused on measuring rates of assimilation among different American racial and ethnic groups who have been compared in terms of educational attainment, income levels, occupational characteristics, residential distribution, and intermarriage (Hirschman and Wong, 1981). These data show that, overall, European ethnic groups and Asians have experienced considerable socioeconomic, educational, residential, and marital assimilation in American society. However, these patterns of assimilation are not duplicated among Hispanics, American Indians, and African-Americans (Yetman, 1985).

Pluralism

Pluralism refers to a system in which different cultures can coexist and be preserved. In modern times such a system has seldom been the policy of a majority group. In American society, the primary advocates of pluralism have been minority spokespersons. According to this notion, the strength and vitality of American society is derived from its ethnic diversity. Belonging to a "nation of nations," each group should be permitted to retain its unique qualities while affirming its allegiance to American society. This ideal can be expressed by the equation A + B + C = A + B + C, in which A, B, and C are each ethnic groups that maintain their distinctiveness over time (Newman, 1973, p. 67).

Pluralism
Ethnic or racial groups coexisting equally while preserving their identities

Pluralism is the most tolerant of the several policies we have considered, for it implies recognition of cultural equality among ethnic groups, not the superiority of one. It accepts cultural heterogeneity and may even include some form of geographic or social separation. The basic difference between a policy of *pluralism* and one of *exclusion* is that under pluralism the minority is relatively autonomous and may voluntarily choose to place itself apart, whereas under a policy of exclusion the separation is dictated by the majority group. Under a policy of pluralism the majority does not require separation of ethnic and racial groups; it simply allows their existence. The few examples of pluralism in American history typically involve religious groups, such as Hasidic Jews, the Amish, and the Hutterites, who are culturally distinct and who have maintained their distinctiveness with a minimum of external interference from the larger society.

Minority-Group Responses to Dominant Group Pressures

How do minorities experience and respond to demands of the dominant group? The previous discussion has emphasized the role of the dominant group in setting the limits within which minority groups may function. Minorities, however, are not simply passive recipients of dominant-group policies; they actively respond in a variety of ways to majority pressures for subordination.

Sociologists have distinguished three general categories of minority-group responses: acceptance, resistance, and avoidance. Acceptance involves the minority's moving toward the majority. Avoidance and resistance involve a rejection of, or moving away from, the majority. At different times, individual or group responses may change from one of these responses to another.

Acceptance

A minority may accept the dominant group's definition of its subordinate status. Given the majority's superior power, acquiescence may be necessary for survival. The Southern caste system was for many years relatively stable because most blacks, at least on the surface, accepted the elaborate system of racial etiquette and segregation. The most severe violence against blacks—lynchings and terrorism—was committed when blacks made, or whites perceived them to have made, an effort to reject the traditional subordinate roles ascribed to them. Alvin Poussaint, a prominent African-American psychiatrist, graphically recounted how he was forced to accept the traditional role of black submissiveness:

> Once last year [1967] as I was leaving my office in Jackson, Miss. with my Negro secretary, a white policeman yelled, "Hey, boy! Come here!" Somewhat bothered, I retorted: "I'm no boy!" He then rushed at me, inflamed, and stood towering over me, snorting, "What d'ja say, boy?" Quickly he frisked me and demanded, "What's your name, boy?" Frightened, I replied, "Dr. Poussaint. I'm a physician." He angrily chuckled and hissed, "What's your first name, boy?" When I hesitated he assumed a threatening stance and clenched his fists. As my heart palpitated, I muttered in profound humiliation, "Alvin."
>
> He continued his psychological brutality, bellowing, "Alvin, the next time I call you, you come right away, you hear? You hear?" I hesitated. "You hear me, boy?" My voice trembling with helplessness, but following my instincts of self-preservation, I murmured, "Yes, sir." Now fully satisfied that I had performed and acquiesced to my "boy status," he dismissed me with, "Now, boy, go on and get out of here or next time we'll take you for a little ride down to the station house!" (Poussaint, 1971, p. 349).

The Southern caste system placed African-Americans in a position of permanent subservience. Most European ethnic groups, however, were not so rigidly proscribed from seeking equal status with "native" whites. Nevertheless, the pressures of Anglo-conformity frequently led ethnic minorities to accept dominant-group standards. These standards included degrading perceptions of their own cultures, which caused them to feel ambivalent about their background and sometimes to reject it. The son of Italian immigrant parents describes his childhood in the following way:

> I enter the parochial school with an awful fear that I will be called Wop. . . . I begin to loathe my heritage. . . .
>
> I am nervous when I bring friends to my house; the place looks so Italian. Here hangs a picture of Victor Emmanuel and over there is one of the cathedrals of Milan, and next to it, one of St. Peter's, and on the buffet stands a wine-pitcher of medieval design; it's forever brimming, forever red and brilliant with wine. These things are heirlooms belonging to my father, and no matter who may come to our house, he likes to stand under them and brag.
>
> So I begin to shout at him. I tell him to cut out being a Wop and be an American once in a while. Immediately he gets his razor-strap and whales hell out of me, clouting me

> from room to room and finally out the back door. I go into the woodshed and pull down my pants and stretch my neck to examine the blue slices across my rump. A Wop! That's what my father is. Nowhere is there an American father who beats his son this way (Fante, 1966, pp. 391–394).

Some minority-group members have shown a willingness to lose their ethnic identity and adopt the characteristics of the majority group. The eagerness and intensity with which assimilation was sought are exemplified in Abraham Cahan's classic novel of immigrant adjustment, *The Rise of David Levinsky*. To enhance his ability to function in American society, Levinsky, a Russian Jewish immigrant, enrolls in an evening English class, where his teacher becomes one of his first American role models.

> At first I did not like him. Yet I would hang on his lips, striving to memorize every English word I could catch and watching intently, not only his enunciation, but also his gestures, manners, and mannerisms, and accepting it all as part and parcel of the American way of speaking. . . . If I heard a bit of business rhetoric that I thought effective I would jot it down and commit it to memory. In like manner I would write down every new piece of slang, the use of the latest popular phrase being, as I thought, helpful in making oneself popular with Americans . . . (Cahan, 1917/1966, pp. 129, 292–293).

Resistance

Some minority-group members respond to majority-group pressures by refusing to accept majority-group definitions of their status. Resistance may include boycotts, strikes, legal action, political activity, nonviolent mass protest, and violence. Each of these techniques has been used by American minority groups to achieve greater equality in American life.

Despite murder, lynching, terrorism, and harassment—the tactics whites have used to enforce black subordination—black Americans have an enduring tradition of resistance to the caste system. This spirit of resistance is typified by the following account by Fred Shuttlesworth, an African-American minister and leader of efforts to end racial segregation in Birmingham, Alabama, during the late 1950s and the 1960s. Shuttlesworth barely escaped death when his house was demolished by more than a dozen sticks of dynamite. Shuttlesworth recalls the experience:

> That house was about fifty years old, all that black dust and stuff, dynamite smoke and stuff, and I came out. On the way from around the back of the house, this Klans—this policeman who was a Klansman—said to me, . . . I think it shook him, he said, "I know some people. I know some people in the Klan. They're really after you." He said, "If I was you I'd get outa town as quick as I could."
>
> I said, "Well, you tell them that I'm not going out of town." I said, "You see all this I've come through?" I said, "If God could save me through this, then I'm gon' stay here and clear up this." I said, "I wasn't saved to run . . ." (quoted in Raines, 1978, p. 166).

Throughout the twentieth century the black protest movement has used the legal process to resist a minority status. Most noteworthy among these was the historic 1954 Supreme Court decision of *Brown v. Board of Education,* which declared segregated schools unconstitutional. Bolstered by the knowledge that segregation was unconstitutional, during the Civil Rights Movement of the 1950s and 1960s African-Americans used a variety of tactics—public confrontations, boycotts, picketing, and civil disobedience—to bring about social change. However, these tactics were supplanted in the 1970s by more traditional political activity (Sitkoff, 1981, p. 229).

The black protest movement has been instrumental in generating resistance among other racial and ethnic minorities. Although American Indians have for generations resisted pressures for assimilation, they have recently shown a willingness to use many of the tactics of direct protest (such as sit-ins) employed by African-Americans. Indians also are appealing to the courts to challenge present and past treaty violations. Resistance among Chicanos has increased as well. One of the most dramatic manifestations of increased Chicano militancy was the armed confrontation of the charismatic Reies Tijerina, who advanced claims for millions of acres of Mexican land guaranteed to Mexican residents under the 1848 Treaty of Gaudalupe Hidalgo. On another front, Cesar Chavez has led agricultural workers, primarily Mexican-Americans, in a struggle to improve their status. Chavez's efforts have contributed substantially to a heightened sense of identity among the more than 12 million Americans of Mexican descent. Recently the political impact of Hispanics in general and Mexican-Americans in particular has become apparent. Given their rapidly increasing numbers in American society, they have become an important political factor, particularly because of their concentration in such key electoral states as California, New York, Texas, and Florida (Wicker, 1988).

Avoidance

Another response to minority status is avoidance, in which the minority neither accepts nor resists the dominance of the majority. Rather, they seek to set themselves apart from the majority and to keep contact minimal. Such a stance shields minority group members from prejudice and discrimination by the majority group and enables them to preserve their own culture and social institutions with minimal outside interference.

Throughout the American experience many ethnic groups have tried to avoid the pressures for complete assimilation with the dominant society by embracing a form of ethnic pluralism as the most appropriate means of adjusting to American society. The adjustment of the immigrant Irish typifies a pluralist response that is characteristic of many other ethnic groups. Although the objects of discrimination by Protestant Americans, the Irish avoided much of the hostility directed toward them by creating a society within a society, a separate institutional system centered around the Roman Catholic Church. The institutional system that developed around the church—its schools, hospitals, orphanages, asylums, homes for the aged, charitable and athletic organizations, and informal groups—integrated the Irish community and served to maintain Irish-American solidarity and identity.

Separatism
Minorities' choosing to be isolated from the majority group

The most extreme form of avoidance is **separatism,** in which little, if any, interaction occurs with the majority. The impulse for separatism frequently has been created by considerable conflict with the majority group and a desire to avoid a recurrence of the discrimination or subjugation that a group has encountered. For example, this impulse was an important factor contributing to the creation of the state of Israel. The goal of a separate nation was also the objective of the pre-Civil War colonization movement that aimed to return American slaves to Africa and of the Back-to-Africa campaign of Marcus Garvey during the 1920s.

The idea of separate ethnic areas or states has been advocated by spokespersons of a number of different ethnic groups in America—by African-Americans, Indians, and Germans, among others. Religious groups that seek to protect their unique identity from the influences of the larger society have been among the foremost advocates of separatism. Having endured great persecution for their beliefs during the mid-nineteenth century, the Mormons sought to isolate themselves from the corrupting influences of the larger society by establishing, in the words of a Mormon hymn,

> . . . a place which God for us prepared
> Far away in the West
> Where none shall come to hurt or make afraid
> There the Saints will be blessed.

Summary

Societies are frequently stratified by ethnic or racial categories. The term majority or dominant refers to a group's relative power—its ability to realize its own objectives and interests. A minority group, in contrast, is subordinate to the majority group and is relatively powerless. An ethnic group is identified on the basis of its cultural characteristics. A racial group, on the other hand, is distinguished by its physical characteristics. Both racial and ethnic phenomena are socially defined—that is, the same racial or ethnic group may be perceived and responded to differently in different societies.

The ethnic diversity of the American people was created by the migration of European, African, Asian, and Latin American peoples during the past three and one-half centuries. The greatest period of immigration to America occurred between 1820 and 1920. The old immigration, composed of peoples from northern and western Europe, occurred primarily prior to 1895. Immigrants from southern and eastern Europe—the new immigrants—came mainly between 1890 and 1920. Asian immigration, initially from China and Japan and more recently from Korea and Southeast Asia, occurred during the late nineteenth and twentieth centuries. During the second decade of this century, Spanish-speaking peoples began to enter the country in increasing numbers. The largest number of these were Mexican-Americans, who entered in substantial numbers prior to the Great Depression of the 1930s and since World War II. Puerto Rican and Cuban migrations are essentially post-World War II phenomena.

African-Americans are the largest racial minority in contemporary American society. Both attitudinal discrimination and institutional discrimination have contributed to black inequality. Despite considerable changes brought about by federal, state, and local laws barring discrimination, African-Americans still remain considerably outside the mainstream of American society.

The adaptation of ethnic groups is influenced by both the policies of the majority groups and the characteristics of the minority group. Among the range of majority-group policies toward racial and ethnic minorities, extermination, or genocide, is the most repressive. Expulsion and exclusion also aim for an ethnically homogeneous society but do not resort to genocide to achieve their goal. A system of oppression accepts the existence of ethnic differences but excludes minorities from full and equal participation in the society. Assimilation involves the integration or incorporation of a minority into the mainstream of a society. In the United States this assimilation took either the form of Anglo-conformity, in which there was an insistence upon conformity to the majority's cultural standards, or the form of the melting pot, in which diverse peoples each contributed to the creation of a new culture and society. Finally, pluralism involves a system in which different ethnic groups coexist equally and preserve their own cultural characteristics.

Minorities also respond actively and differently to majority policies, and their responses influence their adaptation. Acceptance involves acquiescence to the dominant group's definition of their status. Resistance may involve direct protest and action. Avoidance involves neither acceptance nor resistance; instead, minority people seek to separate themselves from contact with the majority. Its most extreme form is separatism.

CRITICAL THINKING

1. What is the difference between an ethnic and a racial group? Give examples to show that the characteristics of each of these types of groups are socially defined.

2. Give examples of majority and minority groups in American society. Does a majority group need to be numerically superior in order to be dominant? Give at least one example to support your ideas.

3. Why is the migration of African-Americans from the rural South to the urban North an important demographic trend in American society?

4. Explain how legal decisions have changed the status of African-Americans. Have laws produced true equality for African-Americans in society? What would?

5. Compare and contrast the experience of Hispanic-Americans and Asian-Americans with that of African-Americans. How do you explain the similarities and differences that you see?

6. Speculate about the impact of the population growth of minority groups on American society. Does an increase in numbers necessarily mean an increase in power? Explain.

7. Give examples of at least three ethnic groups in American society. How do the cultural characteristics of these groups differ? Which ethnic group do you feel is dominant in American society? Why?

8. In what ways are majority and minority groups in our society stereotyped? How do these stereotypes help perpetuate the existing social order?

9. Compare and contrast the power basis of the majority groups in the United States and South Africa.

10. How do dominant groups maintain control of subordinate groups? List the policies explained in this chapter and give an example of each.

11. How do minorities respond and adapt to majority policies?

CHAPTER 10

Gender and Age: Stratification and Inequality

We are born either male or female, and, except for a tiny number of people who take the dramatic step of changing their sex, there is little we can do about it. The sex of a person is determined by certain physical characteristics, including the reproduction organs by which the sexes are biologically identified. Age is also a biological characteristic, but unlike sex, which is relatively stable, the process of aging goes on continuously. These two biological characteristics—sex and age—are part of our makeup at all times. What makes sex and age sociologically important is that every social group attaches significance to them.

The term commonly used to indicate that being male or female is socially significant is *gender*. **Gender** can be defined as the social distinctions made between males and females that are used to organize social arrangements and influence social behavior. Gender distinctions are made despite the many similarities between males and females, and the wide variations that can easily be observed within either gender category (Hess and Ferree, 1987).

Gender
Social distinctions between males and females in social arrangements and for social behavior

Age is also used as a basis for organizing social activities and behaviors. Societies are strongly organized on the basis of arbitrary age categories despite the similarities of people in different ages, and the wide variations among people of the same chronological age (Riley et al., 1988).

The organization of societies around gender and age distinctions are of considerable importance because, as the title of this chapter suggests, the result is often one of inequities, or systems of inequality. We have already seen in chapter 8 on social stratification and chapter 9 on race and ethnic groups how inequalities exist in wealth, power, and access to many of society's opportunities. In this chapter we examine how being male or female, or being young or old, leads to different social arrangements and social behaviors. Although these differences do not inevitably lead to negative results, we will see that gender and age distinctions often produce inequalities.

We will begin by considering the positions of males and females, both in American society and in societies around the world. Later in the chapter we will focus on age groups, especially the elderly.

Gender in Different Societies

Three key social dimensions describe the relationship between males and females, and define the position of each gender in a society. These dimensions are power, division of labor, and gender roles. Power is the ability to impose one's will upon others, even if they resist. Power can only exist when there is a relationship between individuals, between groups, or between classes of people. In this chapter we are interested in the power relationship between sexes—males and females.

Gender is a strong determinant of appearance and behavior as seen in this Tuareg woman from West Africa. From a sociological view, gender will be related to power, division of labor, and role.

Division of labor
The specialization of occupations in a society

Division of labor by gender
The society-wide assignment of different work tasks to males and females

Gender roles
Activities and behaviors expected of males and females

Division of labor is also a general sociological term, commonly used to describe how the occupations of a society are specialized so that any individual has only one major occupation or task. When we use the term *division of labor* in connection with *gender,* we refer to the society-wide assignment of different work tasks to males and females. We will refer to this as **division of labor by gender.**

Gender roles are the expectations that prevail in a society about the activities and behaviors that may and may not be engaged in by males and females. These expectations are widely understood and produce social pressures such that people feel the need to comply with them. These role expectations are socially learned through the process of socialization.

These three concepts—power, division of labor, and gender roles—are closely related to each other. They also reflect inequalities between different groups of people. With regard to power, obviously if one set of people has power over another, inequality results. With regard to division of labor and gender roles, the inequality is not as immediately obvious, but a closer examination will show how each concept leads to inequality between males and females. We will begin by looking at differences in male and female power in different societies.

Power and Gender

In most societies around the world, males have greater power than females, both in the personal and public spheres. For example, males have generally been the political leaders, historically (e.g., classical Greece, Imperial China, and the Roman Empire) and in contemporary modern societies. Notable contemporary exceptions to the overall pattern include Great Britain's Prime Minister Margaret Thatcher, the recently elected Benazir Bhutto of Pakistan, the late Golda Meier of Israel, and Indira Gandhi of India. The male dominance of political leadership is also the standard among the vast majority of nonliterate societies on which we have ethnographic information.

At the private level the picture is almost identical. In the family, for example, males almost always have greater power than females. Much of the power of males within the family comes directly from a patriarchal tradition. Patriarchy means that a husband or father has unquestioned authority or dominance over other family members. Also, an organization—or, indeed, an entire society—may be based on the principle of patriarchy. In the case of Western societies, including the United States, support for patriarchy can be found prominently in the sacred writings of the Judaic and Christian religious traditions. Although these sources of male power might have diminished somewhat in recent years, their influence has certainly not disappeared. As an example, a contemporary spokesperson for the patriarchal view is Phyllis Schlafly, who draws on religious doctrine to conclude: "If marriage is to be a successful institution, it must . . . have an ultimate decision maker, and that is the husband" (Schlafly, 1977, p. 50).

In non-Western cultures the basis for male power in the family is also found in religious and ideological systems (Bernard, 1987; Giele, 1988, 1977). In the Islamic world males are given ultimate authority, both within their families and in the larger society where they predominate (Mernissi, 1987). Hinduism also gives primary power to males, again both inside the home and in the public world.

Before we examine some explanations as to why males in so many societies have been given more power than females, we should first note that considerable differences

Women generally have less power than men, especially in the political world, but there have been some notable exceptions in recent decades. Benazir Bhutto was elected President of Pakistan, despite the fact that women in the Moslem world are often subordinated to men.

In most societies of the world, men have more power than women to make decisions for their groups. Often this power is based on the principle of patriarchy—the unquestioned cultural assumption that men should be in control.

exist in the relative power of males from one society to another and in different historical periods. A careful examination of the anthropological record shows that in some societies, under certain economic and cultural conditions, women have power that is at least equal to, and sometimes greater than, that of men (Sanday, 1981; Tanner, 1974; Okonjo, 1976). Furthermore, in some societies where males have formal authority and dominance, females may have informal power. Among the Mundurucu, who live in the tropical rain forests of South America, men monopolize the formal positions of authority, but the Mundurucu women do not think of themselves as inferior to men. In fact, the Mundurucu men do not think of the women as subordinate to themselves (Sanday, 1981).

In the societies where women have had power that is equal to, or greater than, men, one of two conditions has had to prevail: (1) the economic or historical circumstances make men dependent upon the activities of women; and (2) a long-standing magical or religious association exists between the fertility of women and the general well-being of the social group (Sanday, 1981).

When women in a particular society carry out an activity critically important for the physical survival of the group, they often increase their power. For example, among the African tribe called the !Kung, who live in the Kalahari Desert, food supplies depend upon hunting animals and gathering vegetation from the "bush." The !Kung women do the gathering, which requires that they go far out in the bush. From this activity alone they provide between 60 percent and 80 percent of the tribe's food. But the women do more than gather food; while out in the bush, they watch for signs of animals. Although the women do not hunt the animals themselves, they report their findings to the men who do the actual hunting. The contribution of the !Kung women is obviously great, and their power in tribal decision-making is equally great. The !Kung society is essentially egalitarian, as are other societies where the economic contribution of women is significant compared to that of men (Draper, 1975; Sanday, 1981).

A recent cross-national study of 111 contemporary societies confirms anthropological studies showing the importance of women's economic contributions (South, 1988). This study shows that the more that women participate in the labor force, the less males are able to exercise power over them. Specifically, men are less able to restrict women to traditional roles (early marriage, high fertility, and illiteracy) if women participate in the labor force (South, 1988).

Similar conclusions about the importance of women's economic contributions have been reached by studying families in the United States. For example, if we take husbands' helping with the housework as an indication of greater female power, some studies show that higher income from the wives is related to greater contributions by the husbands. A sample of couples in which the wives were college and university administrators showed that the higher the wives' incomes, the more likely it was that their husbands would share in family tasks (Bird et al., 1984). Two major studies using national random samples of adults have supported the same conclusion. As a woman's income increases relative to her husband's income, his share of the household work increases (Huber, 1986; Ross et al., 1983).

In the *public* sphere, however, there are only limited indications that women gain very much public or political power in societies where they make greater economic contributions. American women, for example, are contributing greatly in the economic realm, but, as we will see later in this chapter, their positions of power in the political or economic realms are still very limited.

In addition to the power that women may gain from their economic contributions, a second suggested basis of power for women is connected with religions or magic systems. Cross-cultural studies have shown that when religions or magic systems give prominence to women as the producers of life, they are also likely to have greater power. In many such societies the childbearing ability of women is closely associated with the fertility of the soil (Sanday, 1981). In West Africa, where such a view of women prevails, the women say, "Whether the male chief is big or small . . . what matters is that he was given birth by a woman" (Sanday, 1981, p. 115). The women may also express this power by action:

> Such women protest a chief's action by treating him like a child. They either rely on shame or ridicule to get their way or, if pushed to an extreme, will march scantily clad with bared breasts while men stand by in a state of embarrassed silence and passivity, as if they had been overcome by a superior military force (Sanday, 1981, p. 115).

A male in this case holds the political position of chief, but, despite this formal position of power, women exercise influence over him and other men. According to anthropologists, this occurs in a number of societies where women are portrayed positively in the magical or religious systems (Sanday, 1981).

The Iroquois tribe in North America provides an historical illustration of this point. The Iroquois believed the earth belonged to women, and they highly valued the fertility of the soil, for which the women were responsible (Sanday, 1981). As a result, the Iroquois women had considerable power in village and tribal decision-making (Wallace, 1969).

Despite the existence of societies in which women exercise power at least equal to that of men, in the overwhelming majority of societies males have had dominance over females.

Therefore, the question that needs to be addressed is, Why do males so often have greater power than females?

One of the oldest and most frequently used explanations for the greater power and prestige of males is biological. Contemporary sociobiologists argue that males evolved as the hunters and food providers, while females evolved as specialists in having and caring for babies and in taking care of the home (Tiger, 1969; Goldberg, 1973). The related assumption is that the male activities are more important, and thus they receive greater power and prestige. One major flaw in this argument is that it is not supported by the facts we have about food sources in hunting and gathering societies. In the hundreds of thousands of years before the development of agriculture, humans had to get their food by hunting animals and gathering edible vegetation. We know from contemporary hunting and gathering societies that women typically get most of the food (just as we saw in the case of the !Kung above). If pre-agricultural hunting and gathering societies were at all similar, it is hard to see how females could have been genetically programmed to leave the "breadwinning" activities exclusively to males (Collins, 1988).

One of the early economic theories of male domination goes back to the work of Friedrich Engels (1884/1972). The key to most economic explanations of male dominance lies not in who does the work, but in who controls the means of production (e.g., land, tools, machines). Contemporary scholars who advance the economic hypothesis point out that the power of women has usually been less in agrarian societies where women have not typically been the owners of the land (Blumberg, 1984). Women's power is especially low in societies where the inheritance system passes land from fathers to sons and where, at marriage, a woman must leave her home and live in her husband's family residence.

Division of Labor by Gender

In societies around the world, men and women are usually assigned different work tasks, which is another way of saying that labor is typically divided by gender. Exactly why a division of labor is so commonplace is a matter of considerable discussion. Some argue that certain tasks are assigned to men because of their greater physical strength. Whatever the validity of this explanation, it cannot account for all differences in gender-related work. An analysis of 50 types of work in 186 societies identified two tasks invariably assigned to men: (1) the hunting and butchering of large animals, and (2) the processing of hard and tough materials, such as mining and quarrying rocks and minerals, smelting metal ores, and doing metalwork (Murdock and Provost, 1973). Women, on the other hand, were most likely to be responsible for grinding grain, carrying water, and cooking. At first glance, it would appear that this division of labor is based purely on physical strength, but carrying water—a woman's task—requires considerable physical strength. Furthermore, women in many societies carry heavy loads including—in addition to water—firewood, food, and various other products. According to reports, African women, who often carry heavy loads by balancing them on their heads, can carry as much as 70 percent of their body weight. This means that a woman weighing 140 pounds could carry nearly 100 pounds on her head (Rensberger, 1986).

Women in many societies perform work that demands great physical strength. Thus, the division of labor between the genders cannot be explained solely by body size and muscularity.

In addition, there are more societies in which women are responsible for erecting and dismantling shelters than there are societies in which men have this responsibility. Women are responsible just as often as men for preparing the soil and planting seed, as well as for tending and harvesting crops (Murdock, 1937).

Evelyn Reed (1971) has argued that when agriculture was done primarily with a digging stick, this task was left most often to women. With the taming of animals and the development of the plow, agriculture was taken over by men. But farming done with a digging stick must have been just as backbreaking as farming done with draft animals and the plow. Physical strength alone, therefore, does not account for variations in the division of labor by gender.

Some scholars have suggested that differences in male and female work may reflect a desire, especially by men, to establish a clear male identity. Many people define themselves as male or female on the basis of what they do. For females, childbearing (and nursing) is unarguably their exclusive responsibility: "Perhaps because women have ways of signaling their womanhood, men must have ways to display their manhood"

(Sanday, 1981, p. 78). From this point of view, men in all societies must have a way of demonstrating maleness in an activity prohibited to females. One activity frequently reserved for males is fighting battles and waging wars (Collins, 1988). There is a symmetry in this idea: women are responsible for producing life, while men are responsible for taking life (Sanday, 1981). Even in contemporary American society where women are widely used in the military, they are prohibited by law from serving in combat.

Gender Roles in Three New Guinea Societies

The well-known studies by anthropologist Margaret Mead (1935) provide vivid support for the argument that the gender-role differences familiar to us are not universal. Mead studied three separate tribes in New Guinea that happened to have dramatic differences in their gender roles. She lived first with the Arapesh, a society in which both the males and the females generally had characteristics and behaviors that we would associate with the feminine role. Both sexes among the Arapesh were passive, gentle, unaggressive, and emotionally responsive to the needs of others. In contrast, Mead found that in another New Guinea group, the Mundugumor, both the males and the females were characteristically aggressive, suspicious, and, from a Westerner's view, excessively heartless and cruel, especially toward children. The striking feature of these two cultures is that males and females were expected to be very alike, and they were.

Mead then studied a third New Guinea tribe, the Tchambuli. In this group, the gender roles of the males and females were almost exactly reversed from the roles traditionally assigned to males and females in Western society. Mead reported in her autobiography that "among the Tchambuli the expected relations between men and women reversed those that are characteristic of our own culture. For it was Tchambuli women who were brisk and hearty, who managed the business affairs of life, and worked comfortably in large cooperative groups" (Mead, 1972, p. 214). The children also exhibited these characteristics. Girls were the brightest and most competent, and displayed "the most curiosity and the freest expression of intelligence." The Tchambuli boys "were already caught up in the rivalrous, catty and individually competitive life of the men" (Mead, 1972, p. 214). Mead reported also that while the women managed the affairs of the family, the men were engaged differently: "Down by the lake shore in ceremonial houses the men carved and painted, gossiped and had temper tantrums, and played out their rivalries" (Mead, 1972, p. 215).

This cross-cultural examination of gender roles shows vividly how the behavior and the seemingly "natural" personal attributes of the sexes can vary greatly. Most of what we think of as normal, typically male or typically female behavior is the outcome of the social life in which we are immersed and in which we become what is generally expected of us.

Traditional Gender Roles

We have now seen important variations in power, division of labor, and gender roles in different societies. These differences clearly imply that gender roles and associated behaviors are learned in the society where one is socialized. We now take a closer look at the nature of traditional male and female roles as they have prevailed in Western societies in general and the United States in particular. We begin by distinguishing two key dimensions associated with traditional views of males and females: personality traits and expected behaviors (Kammeyer, 1964).

Stereotyped Personality Traits of Males and Females

Many people believe that certain personality traits are inherently related to being either male or female, that males and females are born with distinguishing drives and characteristics. This way of thinking creates stereotypes. A **stereotype** is a belief that a certain category of people has a particular set of personal characteristics. Stereotypes exist for racial groups, religious groups, ethnic groups, and, in the case at hand, males and females.

Stereotype
Belief that a category of people has some particular set of characteristics

For example, females are often stereotyped as emotional, whereas males are supposed to be unemotional. Males are believed to be less affected by things that would deeply touch females. Males are thought to be more aggressive, and women are seen as more passive. Many people believe that these and other personality traits come with the biological makeup of males and females. Refutations of these stereotypes are all around us, but the beliefs persist. Consider the following poignant statement by a young man describing an event with his girlfriend.

> There was an occasion when I went to Susan's one night, a happy man, and left feeling like a disheartened boy. She wanted to know why I didn't make a move on her and why I wasn't aggressive. . . . I know I'm not as aggressive as other men are or as I "should be" but I told her that it shouldn't matter. . . . I took her in my arms and asked her if she knew I loved her and she said she didn't know. I know she said it in disgust but it really hurt me. I began to cry. Man, I just about ran out of the door because I didn't want her to see me cry. I was not a man: I wasn't aggressive and I didn't hide my emotions and I really felt bad (Forisha, 1978, p. 160).

It is clear from this young man's reactions to his own behavior how deeply embedded the stereotyped views are of male personality traits. He shows shame and even disgust at his own characteristics and behavior. He failed by not being as aggressive as men are supposed to be, and he compounded the sin by displaying his emotions in front of his girlfriend.

Women, of course, are often equally trapped by the stereotypes about female personality traits. When they sometimes want to express aggressiveness, they may have to restrain themselves because it would be viewed as unfeminine.

A number of other personality traits are associated with being either male or female. Women are thought to be followers rather than leaders. Women are thought to be more sympathetic, sensitive, compassionate, and concerned about others. They are portrayed as more inclined toward artistic and aesthetic activities. They are assumed to be less inclined toward mathematics, science, and even intellectuality. Women are often thought to be more moral, more religious, or, in some cultures, "purer" than men.

Men are thought to be better leaders, more objective, aggressive, independent, active, dominant, competitive, logical, scientific, calculating, tough, strong, and unsentimental.

Believing in the stereotyped personality traits of males and females serves as a support or justification for many kinds of gender inequality. If males are believed to be better leaders and decision-makers, it would, of course, follow that men should be given positions of leadership. If women, on the other hand, are thought to be more sensitive, compassionate, and concerned for others, then they would "naturally" fit better into the tasks and jobs that call for these skills (caring for children, the ill, or the elderly, for example). But the occupations so often reserved for women have much less prestige than the leadership jobs allocated to men.

In general, a belief in stereotyped male and female personality traits is found among people who prefer a traditional allocation of tasks between the sexes. Most important, men are more likely to believe in stereotyped personality traits than women are. Studies have found also that age is related to beliefs about stereotyped personality traits, which means that older people believe in the stereotypes more than younger people do. Also, better educated people are less likely to believe in stereotyped personality traits, while the religious people are more likely to do so (Mirowsky and Ross, 1987).

Although men are more apt to believe in the stereotyped personality traits of the sexes, a recent study has shown that husbands and wives are likely to influence each other's views. Interestingly, neither husbands nor wives seem to dominate in this process of mutual influence between spouses. Wives who do not accept the stereotyped view of the sexes pull their husbands closer to their views, but, on the other hand, husbands who do believe in the stereotype pull wives in their direction. Furthermore, husbands and wives who are in agreement, either for or against the stereotyped view, tend to reinforce each other's views and become more extreme (Mirowsky and Ross, 1987).

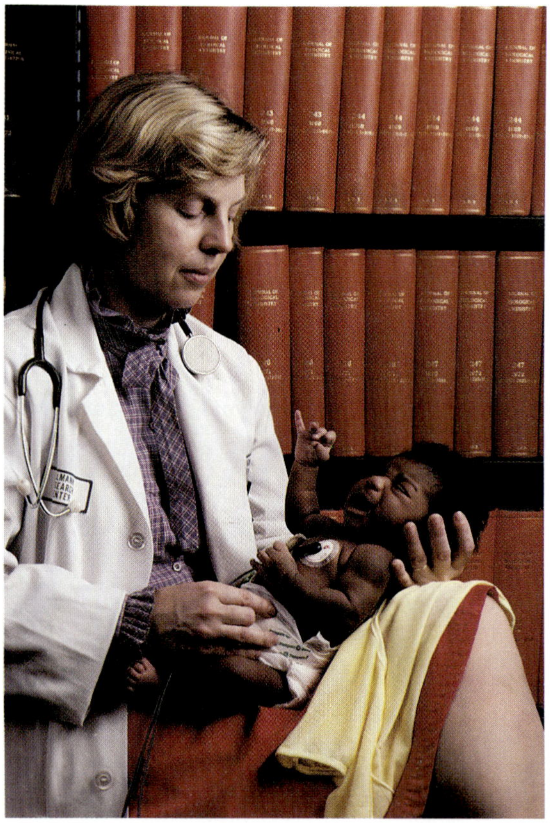

In spite of their increasing entry into the medical profession, many women are found more often in specialties like pediatrics that are consistent with traditional gender roles.

Expected Behaviors of Males and Females

The prescriptions for male and female behavior, according to the traditional gender roles, fit the stereotyped personality traits like a glove fits a hand. As we previously noted, whenever people hold stereotyped views of male and female personality characteristics, they are likely to hold traditional expectations about male and female behavior.

Although traditional gender-role expectations are found in almost every sphere of life, they are revealed most clearly in the family. According to the traditional feminine role, women are expected to perform supportive tasks within the family, and in general are expected to be subordinate to men. Women have the primary responsibility of taking care of home and children. The traditional expectation for men is that they will provide for and, if necessary, defend their families. Although these traditional female and male role expectations may seem exaggerated and even out of date, they still exist for substantial numbers of people in contemporary society. For example, in a modern-day family (with or without young children) it would still be acceptable for a wife to remain in the home while her husband was the sole wage earner. However, it would be considered very unusual if a husband stayed at home while his wife was the sole breadwinner.

Current Attitudes about Gender Roles

Traditional views about the feminine and masculine roles have been undergoing significant changes since the feminist movement began in the 1960s. The reduced support for the traditional gender roles that occurred during the late 1960s and early 1970s have been described as a "revolution in attitudes" (Mason and Lu, 1988, p. 39). However, some researchers have suggested that during the 1980s this change in attitudes slowed down, as a possible "backlash" against feminism. Yet in 1985, a national sample of American adults expressed more profeminist views than a similar sample had in 1977. Both men and women, in every age group from 18 to over 65, showed less acceptance of the traditional feminine role in 1985 than they had less than a decade earlier (Mason and Lu, 1988).

Despite the declines in public expressions of support for the traditional female role, substantial numbers of adults still hold traditional views. For example, in the 1985 survey, 50 percent of the men and more than 45 percent of the women agreed with the statement: "It is much better for everyone if the man is the achiever and the woman takes care of the home and family" (Mason and Lu, 1988).

Surveys of adolescents show that many of them also accept traditional views about the feminine gender role. When a national sample of high school seniors was asked how they felt about the statement above, one-third agreed that it is better if the "woman takes care of the home and family." However, high school males agreed with the statement more than females (46 percent of the males, compared to only 21 percent of the females) (Backman et al., 1987).

These survey results indicate that attitudes are changing about some of the strongest expressions of traditional gender roles, especially among women. Substantial evidence still exists, however, that many Americans consider it best if men are employed and women are taking care of home and children. For example, when high school seniors were asked about the most desirable arrangement for a married couple with preschool

Surveys have shown that traditional attitudes about gender roles are changing. Like this mother, parents may make a conscious effort to teach their boys to do household work that is traditionally relegated to females.

children, their first preference was for the husband to work full time and the wife not to be employed at all (Backman et al., 1987). These results among today's young people show the widespread acceptance of traditional gender roles in American society. To see how traditional gender-role expectations are learned, along with stereotyped views about male and female personality traits, we will examine the process of gender-role socialization.

Socialization for Gender Roles

To document the ways in which girls are socialized to exhibit female personality traits, and boys, male personality traits, is much like trying to document the ways in which people learn how to talk or use proper sentence structure. This socialization is such a continuous and ever-present experience that examples are both obvious and subtle.

Gender roles can be learned in a variety of ways, including direct training. Direct training occurs when significant others, especially parents, in the child's environment reward the child for behaviors that are consistent with traditional gender roles. If a three-year-old boy falls and skins his knee, his parent might say, "Oh, you are such a brave little man, you won't cry. Will you? If you don't cry we will let the puppy in the house."

If significant others respond one way to boys and another way to girls, and if their responses reinforce the expected gender-role behaviors, then male and female behavior will likely be shaped and modified accordingly.

While everyday observations lead us to believe that such gender-role reinforcement does go on, it has not been easy to document this reinforcement in scientifically controlled observational studies (Losh-Hesselbart, 1987; Maccoby and Jacklin, 1974). What is demonstrable is that parents and others often provide toys and clothes that are consistent with their expectations and beliefs about how children of each sex should behave. This type of reinforcement is found somewhat more often for boys than girls, which indicates that adults are somewhat more tolerant of "tomboy" behavior in girls than feminine behavior in boys. Some observers have reasoned that this is true because "male-type" behavior is more highly valued in our society. Perhaps this is why it seems more tolerable when a girl behaves like a boy than when a boy behaves like a girl. At least, the reasoning goes, the tomboy female is aspiring to a "higher-status" position, while the boy who is more "feminine" is actually "lowering" himself. Perhaps this is why young girls can more successfully deviate from the traditional gender role. They cannot safely do so, however, much beyond the age of 10 or 11.

Modeling is a second way in which traditional gender roles may be learned. **Modeling** occurs when children observe significant others of the same sex (again, often parents) engage in a behavior and then imitate that behavior. For example, girls see their mothers (and other females) applying makeup and may imitate that behavior in play. Of course, modeling is based on the assumption that children can determine which sex they belong to and thus which behavior to model. This process may be aided by parents and significant others who will make it clear which sex is the appropriate or inappropriate model. If a boy begins to apply lipstick in imitation of his mother, he may be told that "little boys do not wear lipstick."

Modeling
Children learning gender roles by observing significant others of the same sex

The mass media, and especially television, may also serve as important gender-role models for children. Evidence shows that children respond to television portrayals

"Gosh, Grandma, what a big office you have!"

of the sexes, in that children who watch the most television are more likely to hold gender stereotypes (Losh-Hesselbart, 1987).

A Theory of Gender-Role Learning

In addition to acquiring appropriate gender-role behavior through social rewards, children also acquire gender roles as a result of the organization of the ideas and experiences they have encountered in early life (Kohlberg, 1966). The mental organization of ideas and experiences is a fundamental learning process and is actually an extension of the idea of the self concept discussed in chapter 5. Children develop a sense of self from interacting with other persons. They learn that they are *boys* or *girls* because they are so identified by parents and significant others. Kohlberg describes this extension of the self for a boy:

> The . . . basic sexual self-concept (his categorization as a boy . . .) becomes the major organizer and determinant of many of his activities, values, and attitudes. The boy in effect says, "I am a boy, therefore I want to do boy things," therefore the opportunity to do boy things (and to gain approval for doing them) is rewarding (Kohlberg, 1966, p. 89).

Kohlberg's view of gender-role development starts with the idea that children organize their worlds as simply and efficiently as possible. Gender is already a part of most children's understanding by the age of three and is firmly fixed by the age of five or six. Once children have an idea of their gender, they tend to build their values and attitudes around this basic dimension. Parents start this process of gender-role differentiation, and normal developmental processes characteristic of all children then complete the process of acquiring a gender identity. **Gender identity** is a recognition of one's gender and an acceptance of characteristics typically associated with that gender.

Gender identity
Recognition of one's gender and acceptance of characteristics associated with that gender

Learning gender identity depends on symbolic communication with others, especially with significant others. At first children simply learn labels for themselves, much as they learn any other label for any other object. More than half of two-and-a-half-year-old children do not give the correct answer when they are asked their gender. By the time they are three years old, however, from two-thirds to three-fourths of children will answer the question correctly.

Although young children may recognize that *boy* or *girl* applies to them, they do not necessarily recognize that these words apply to entire categories of people. A young girl named Susan may know that she is both Susan and a girl, but she may not recognize that *girl* is a word that can be applied to a whole set of young females. At the age of two or three, children usually focus on superficial social characteristics, such as clothing styles and hairstyles, not on genital or other gender-related physical differences. This focus is reflected in the anecdote about the three-year-old who came home and announced to her mother that she had seen a new baby at her friend's house. When asked if the baby was a boy or a girl, she said she didn't know because "it wasn't wearing any clothes."

Kohlberg argues that the structuring of a child's world goes on at the same time as gender-role stereotypes are being learned. The male child recognizes not only that he is a boy but also that *boy* is a general category of people of which he is a part. Furthermore, he learns that boys are part of the general category called males and men.

Girls learn the same kinds of things. When boys and girls begin to identify with their respective categories, they begin to value characteristics that are associated with their category.

Children tend to value things that are the same as, or similar to, things they already know and like. A boy, for example, learns to value certain games, toys, and active and sometimes aggressive behaviors because they are consistent with being a boy. Thereafter the boy will look for, and be interested in, activities that are associated with his already accepted male-like behavior. The same process occurs for girls.

There is a steady interweaving of the mental development of the child and the social learning that occurs with socialization. Through this process, males and females learn, and generally accept as appropriate, the major dimensions of the gender roles of their society. Through the remainder of this chapter we examine the ways gender roles continue to influence the behavior of males and females.

The Impact of Traditional Gender Roles

A few general statements describe the overall effects of traditional gender roles found in American society.

1. Gender roles, as traditionally defined, place women in subordinate and less-valued positions than men.
2. The traditional feminine gender role calls for women to make more sacrifices than men.
3. Traditional gender roles work to the disadvantage of women in most spheres of life, but especially in what is called the "public world" beyond the family.

Before examining evidence supporting these conclusions, we should note another point of view. Some argue that the traditional masculine role has significant disadvantages for men, just as the traditional feminine role has disadvantages for women (Lewis, 1981; Pleck and Sawyer, 1974).

An empirical study of college men uncovered many who experienced strains in their intellectual, sexual, and emotional relationships with women (Komarovsky, 1976). The source of these strains came, at least partially, from trying to live up to the standards of the traditional masculine role. For example, about one-third of these men—seniors in an Ivy League school—acknowledged that intellectual rivalries with women were troubling to them. One young man commented:

> I enjoy talking to more intelligent girls, but I have no desire for a deep relationship with them. I guess I still believe that the man should be more intelligent (Komarovsky, 1976, p. 49).

Another young man admitted that he had broken off a relationship with a young woman because "she bested me in arguments too often for comfort" (Komarovsky, 1976, p. 49). Although the majority of college men in this study did not display such attitudes and behaviors, those who did were disturbed when they could not live up to the masculine role ideal of being intellectually superior to women.

The catalogue of problems that men are said to experience because of the demands and limitations of the traditional masculine role include the following:

1. Males are not allowed to show their emotions because that would be seen as unmanly (recall the young man who cried in front of his girlfriend).
2. Males are expected to be brave and "macho" in the face of danger and threats.
3. Males are expected to perform sexually and, indeed, to be eager for sex at all times.
4. Males are expected to have jobs (unemployment is often very distressing for men) and to be competitive and successful in their work.
5. Males are often precluded from extensive contacts with their own children, often because of their intense work schedules and almost invariably in the case of divorce.

Many scholars hold that such expectations and restrictions cause male stress and anxiety (Lewis, 1981). From this point of view, the traditional masculine role may explain why males exceed females in stroke and heart attack deaths, suicide, death as the victims of homicide and accidents, alcoholism, and mental illness (Lewis, 1981).

Although the pressures and constraints of the traditional masculine role may cause certain hardships and difficulties for males, moderating factors do exist. The first and most obvious point is that in many ways the traditional gender roles give males the dominant position in social relations. Furthermore, despite the importance assigned to the traditional masculine role, men may have much more latitude, or a wider range of options, than we sometimes assume. Sociologist William Goode has asked: "If socialization and social pressures are so all powerful, where are all the John Wayne types in our society?" (Goode, 1982, p. 135).

Goode observes that relatively few men live up to the most frequently discussed prescriptions for traditional masculine behavior (tough, aggressive, striving, unsentimental). He notes further:

> The *macho* boy is admired, but so is the one who edits the school newspaper, who draws cartoons, or who is simply a warm friend. There are at least a handful of ways of being an admired professor. Indeed a common complaint against the present system is that women are much more narrowly confined in the ways they are permitted to be professors, or members of any occupation (Goode, 1982, p. 135).

This observation about the relatively greater range of options for males, compared to those for females, illustrates a special case of the general sociological observation that "oppressed groups are *typically* given narrow ranges of social roles, while dominant groups afford their members a far wider set of behavior patterns" (Goode, 1982, p. 135).

We thus return to our original position: women are especially disadvantaged by traditional gender roles. We do not deny some negative impacts of the traditional masculine role, but women are adversely affected in more pervasive and critical ways.

We begin consideration of the impact of traditional roles by looking at several everyday behaviors. Gender roles, as we will see, are associated with the way people touch each other, how they sit and stand, and how they speak to each other. Although these behaviors may seem relatively unimportant and even trivial, their implications are often greater than we might first suppose.

Gender Roles and Male/Female Interaction

The pervasive influence of traditional gender roles can be found in many aspects of everyday life. For example, in daily behaviors, such as touching, standing, or sitting, males and females differ, and the differences are associated with traditional gender roles.

Touching, Sitting, and Standing. Observational studies of everyday interaction have shown that there is a general pattern of more powerful people touching less powerful people. Bosses, for example, are much more likely to touch workers than workers are to touch their bosses. With regard to male/female interaction, studies have shown that men are much more likely to touch women than women are to touch men. When males touch females, it may often be in a playful or friendly spirit, but it is also a way of demonstrating that the male has some control over the female.

Sitting and standing are both forms of body language. Again, observational studies of males and females indicate differences between the sexes. Males take up more physical space by the way they place their legs and arms. These differences in the way males and females sit and stand indicate that males are in a position of greater freedom and have greater control over space (Henley, 1977).

Speaking and Language. Studies have shown that when males and females engage in conversation, males are much more likely to interrupt females than vice versa. In one study, undergraduate male and female students who did not know each other were brought into a social laboratory for an experiment. They were introduced and told to get to know each other before the "actual" experiment. Their conversations during that get-acquainted period were recorded, and 54 deep interruptions were observed. Seventy-four percent of these interruptions were by males interrupting females, while only 26 percent were initiated by females. In same-sex couples the interruptions were nearly equal between the two conversers. In another study, where the same researchers observed conversations in "natural" settings—drug stores, coffee shops, libraries—males in cross-sex conversations made 96 percent of the interruptions (West, 1978).

When males interrupt females they are probably reflecting the greater power and authority that reside in the male gender role. Females have been shown in other studies to be more tentative in their speech, often qualifying their statements with remarks such as "I think," "I suppose," "I guess," and "I believe." Women also tend to speak more softly and use "softer" words. As one writer noted, there is a great difference between "Oh, my, what a lovely idea," and "Damn, yes, that's a tremendous idea" (Richmond-Abbott, 1983).

Some research shows that females are treated differently even by parents, who are more likely to interrupt their daughters than their sons (Weitzman, 1979). Other research has found that teachers in elementary and junior high schools also treat males and females differently in the classroom (Sadker and Sadker, 1985). Even though teachers claim that boys and girls are treated the same, observational studies of classroom behavior have shown that boys dominate communication in the schools. Even in language arts and English classes, where girls traditionally outperform boys, the boys still command more of the teacher's attention when they speak. In part, this male dominance in communication comes from boys' being more assertive, but, in addition, teachers respond differently to boys than they do to girls (Sadker and Sadker, 1985).

According to Kohlberg's theory of gender-role learning, children will adopt behaviors, speech and language, and modes of dress that they associate with their gender.

When boys call out answers without raising their hands, teachers are likely to accept their responses. However, when girls call out their answers, teachers have a greater tendency to reprimand them for not raising their hands. Teachers also give more attention to boys and praise them more often when they answer questions. The following dialogue illustrates a typical pattern in the classroom:

TEACHER:	What's the capital of Maryland? Joel?
JOEL:	Baltimore.
TEACHER:	What's the largest city in Maryland, Joel?
JOEL:	Baltimore.
TEACHER:	That's good. But Baltimore isn't the capital. The capital is also the location of the U.S. Naval Academy. Joel, do you want to try again?
JOEL:	Annapolis.
TEACHER:	Excellent. Anne, what's the capital of Maine?
ANNE:	Portland.
TEACHER:	Judy, do you want to try?
JUDY:	Augusta.
TEACHER:	OK (Sadker and Sadker, 1985, p. 56).

This classroom interchange illustrates how males often receive support, which helps them move toward the right answers, and they receive praise when they answer correctly. Girls, on the other hand, are given less information about the quality of their answers and less praise (Sadker and Sadker, 1985).

The communications patterns in the family, in male/female conversations, and in the schools all reinforce the same general pattern. Female contributions are less highly valued than those of the male. If we think of how these patterns can make important differences in college, in organizations, in political groups, and in the work-world, we will realize that they are not trivial or inconsequential. When what men say is considered more important than what women say (perhaps by both men and women in many instances), then men will have an advantage in obtaining job positions, being promoted, and receiving career rewards. In the political world men will be more successful in running for office and getting elected. We turn now to the public world to see how women have fared in the worlds of politics, occupations, and careers.

Men and Women in the Public World

It is not difficult to document the dominance of men in all realms of public life. The political and occupational worlds are major areas in which males are greatly overrepresented in leadership positions. Using income as a measure of the positions people hold, or as a reward for their work, men have consistently had the advantage. The world of politics provides an excellent example of the underrepresentation of women in leadership positions of the American system of government.

The Political Arena

When the Constitution and the Declaration of Independence were being written and were adopted, substantial debate centered on the inalienable rights of "men." When the founders of the new country used the word *men,* they may or may not have been using it to refer to *all* people, both men and women. Perhaps they were, but in fact they set up a form of government in which women (as well as slaves and Native Americans) were denied the right to vote. Not until the ratification of the Nineteenth Amendment to the Constitution in 1920—a century and a half later—did women finally receive the vote.

Although the United States was not the first nation in the world to grant women the vote, it was certainly not the last. On a worldwide basis, New Zealand was the first country to grant women suffrage, in 1893. Other countries that preceded the United States in giving women the vote include Australia (1902), Denmark (1915), the Soviet Union (1917), England (1918), and (in 1919) Luxembourg, the Netherlands, and Austria (Giele, 1988). Some European countries did not allow women the vote until after World War II (France, 1944; Hungary, 1945; Yugoslavia, 1946; Italy, 1947; Belgium, 1948; and Switzerland, 1971). Japan did not allow women to vote until 1945. A number of countries, especially in the Islamic Third World, still have not given women the vote (Giele, 1988).

Since women in the United States were not allowed to vote until well into the twentieth century, it is not surprising that women are poorly represented in the political realm today. Among the 100 members of the United States Senate in 1989, only two were women. In the House of Representatives in the same year, 26 of the 435 members were women. Among these national lawmakers, about 7 percent are women, although over 50 percent of the population is female.

Cross-National Perspectives

Global Feminism

Feminism in the last half of the twentieth century has been called the "second feminist revolution," to distinguish it from the suffragette movement of the earlier part of the century. In the United States this second feminist revolution is usually thought to have started in the early 1960s. But from an international point of view, the new feminist movement may not have originated in the United States at all, and, as it has unfolded in the last 25 years, it has certainly not been limited to the United States.

As early as 1949 the French intellectual and social critic Simone de Beauvoir wrote a book called *The Second Sex*, in which she identified some of the social and economic causes of the subordination of women, and outlined some of the ways the status of women could be changed. It was fully a decade later before the feminist movement started to take shape in the United States.

Since that time feminism has spread around the world, and there is hardly a country where some efforts are not being made to improve the status of women. The global feminist movement has not, however, been homogeneous, and attempts at communication and organization at the international level have not always been smooth. The fundamental problem for feminists from different countries and regions is that there are great differences in the societal and economic conditions of women around the world. The objectives of feminism in different nations and continents become intertwined with very different economic and political events and objectives. This diversity, and related controversies, of the feminist movement has been revealed most clearly at a series of international conferences for women.

The first major International Women's Conference was held in Mexico City in 1975. The objectives as outlined at that conference included "eradication of underdevelopment, the quest for peace, and the pursuit of equality for women" (Cagatay et al., 1986). Five years later in Copenhagen, Denmark, a second meeting was held to assess progress toward these goals. This meeting was not harmonious, largely because of disputes between First-World and Third-World women. The women from the most developed nations wanted to focus only on issues that were common to all women, while women from the Third World argued that the oppression of women could not be separated from the oppression of racial groups (*apartheid* in South Africa), national groups (Palestinians in the Middle East), and social classes in many countries.

More recently, in 1985, there was a third international conference of women in Nairobi, Kenya. At this meeting there were 13,500 attendees, and for the first time they were more representative of all the women of the world. There were more delegates from the Third World and more diversity by social class and economic background. The Nairobi meeting proved to be more harmonious and therefore productive.

The Nairobi conference achieved a widespread consensus that women's issues were closely connected with the political and economic issues of individual countries, as well as with issues of the international economy. When there is political oppression or economic distress in a country, or in a region of the world (Africa, for example), it is usually women who are the most oppressed and who must bear the greatest burden. Perhaps because this third women's conference was held in Africa, and many more delegates were African, the women from all countries were sensitized to the plight of poorer women and women of color. Because of a heightened sensitivity to the problems of women in the Third World, the Nairobi conference was marked by less divisiveness and more constructive dialogue.

The Nairobi conference dealt with a list of wide-ranging issues important to women, including world peace, ecology, child care, battered women, lesbian women, female employment, development planning, women's studies, and many others. Many of the delegates to the Nairobi conference came away with a new optimism about the possibilities of an international feminist movement. When the meetings finally ended the feelings of achievement, camaraderie, and satisfaction were spontaneous. By one account, "It was like the end of summer camp, women embracing and crying, exchanging addresses and bits of jewelry, exhausted and aware that something momentous was coming to an end" (Bernard, 1987).

DE BEAUVOIR, SIMONE. *The Second Sex*. New York: Alfred A. Knopf, 1953 (originally published in 1949).
BERNARD, JESSIE. *The Female World from a Global Perspective*. Bloomington, Ind.: Indiana University Press, 1987.
CAGATAY, NILUFER; GROWN, CAREN; and SANTIAGO, AIDA. "The Nairobi Women's Conference: Toward Global Feminism?" *Feminist Studies* 12, 1986.

Women in the United States won the right to vote in the twentieth century, primarily because of the efforts of the Suffragettes of the "first" feminist movement. The second feminist movement, the "second wave" had its beginnings in the 1960s, and, like its predecessor, it uses both demonstrations and political action to advance women's causes.

The World of Work

Men and women hold very different positions in the world of work. Many occupations exist in which either men or women predominate. Figure 10–1 shows the gender distributions of some selected occupations in which there is a strong imbalance between males and females. As part of "Managers and Professionals," nurses, elementary school teachers, and librarians are overwhelmingly female. The professions at the opposite

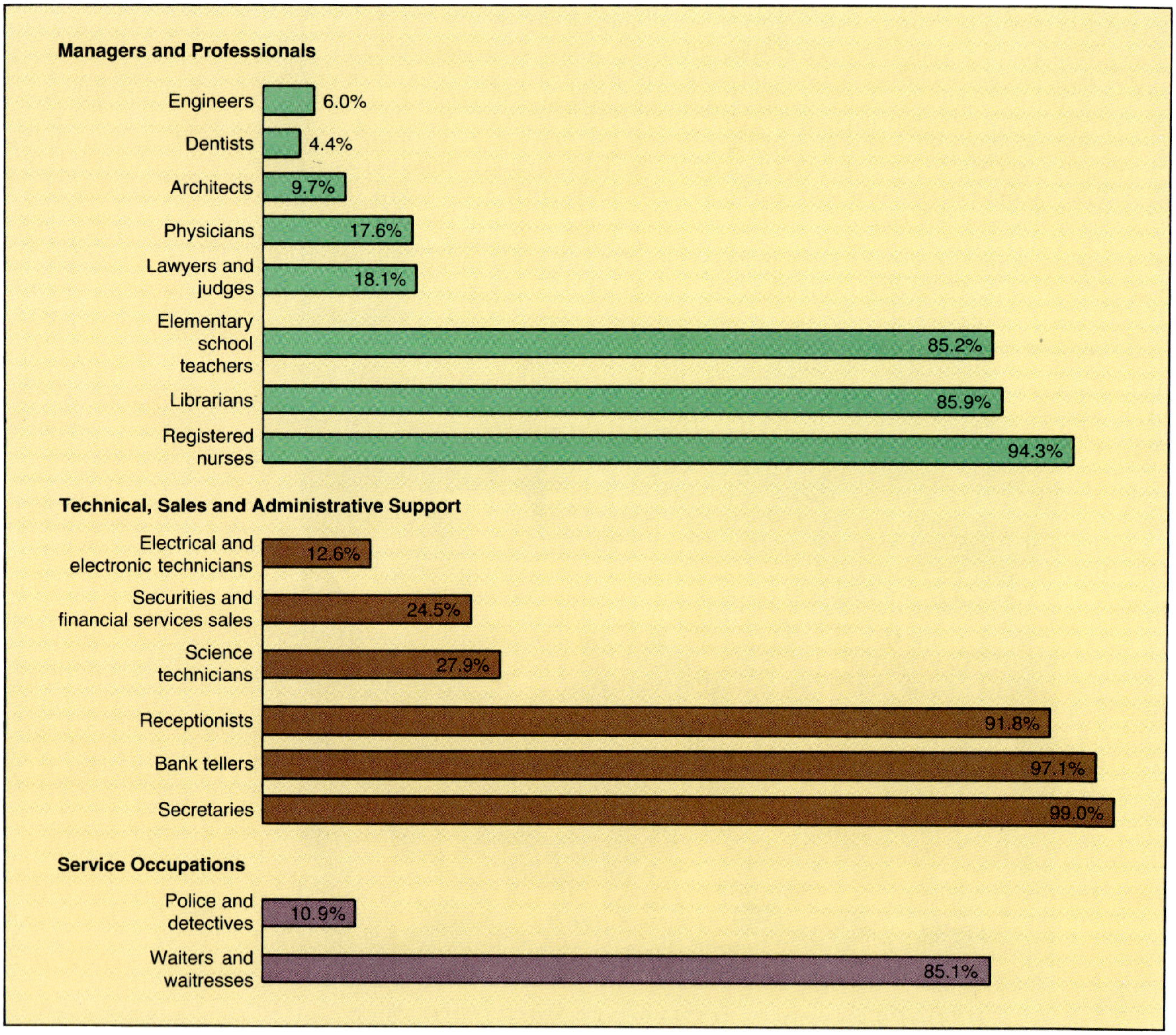

Figure 10–1. Females in Selected Occupations, as a Percent of the Total, 1986. (*Source:* U.S. Bureau of the Census, *Statistical Abstract of the United States, 1988* (Washington, D.C.: U.S. Government Printing Office, 1987), Table 627, pp. 376–377.)

extreme, all having at least 80 percent male membership, are engineers, dentists, architects, physicians, and lawyers/judges. Not only are these male-dominated professions more highly paid but they also enjoy greater prestige than the female-dominated professions. The male-dominated fields are closely associated with traditional male roles (such as engineering), while the most female-dominated fields relate closely to traditional female roles (such as nursing and elementary school teaching).

However, finding men and women in different occupations, with different levels of compensation and prestige, is not entirely explained by the different gender-role orientations of the sexes. Factors contribute to the places of men and women in the occupational world that go far beyond gender-role socialization. One is sex segregation.

Sex Segregation in Occupations

Sex segregation in occupations means that certain occupations and jobs are filled primarily by women, while others are reserved for men. Sex segregation in the workplace is a product of both restriction and choice, but a study conducted for the National Academy of Sciences has concluded that restrictions, especially on women, have been more influential than choice (Baron and Bielby, 1985; Bielby and Baron, 1986; Reskin and Hartmann, 1986).

Sex segregation
Filling certain occupations and jobs with women and reserving others for men

Recent studies of the occupational careers of women who work in organizations and bureaucracies have shown that sex segregation begins at the time women (and men) are hired. One influential study of over 400 work organizations in California, ranging in size from two to almost 8,000 employees, determined that sex segregation existed in the majority of organizations. Approximately 60 percent of the organizations studied were completely segregated by sex—"that is, workers of one sex were either excluded entirely or were concentrated in job titles filled exclusively by the same sex" (Baron and Bielby, 1985, p. 236). Even in the 40 percent of work organizations that were not completely segregated, less than 10 percent of the employees were in jobs that included both sexes. This overwhelming pattern of sex segregation in jobs makes it clear that the segregating was done by employers. It is highly unlikely that males and females, if they had been given free choices, would have been so consistent and thorough in selecting different jobs.

The widespread segregation of jobs by sex has significant influences on career mobility. It is not uncommon for men and women to have different entry-level jobs in an organization, even though the tasks are nearly identical. For example, in a California ordnance plant, the entry-level job for women was "assembler," while the entry-level job for men was "production worker." The tasks carried out were nearly the same, but the career opportunities for the male production workers were much greater, with a higher percentage of men being promoted to the next job level in the organization (Baron and Bielby, 1985).

A similar pattern was found in a study of federal government employees. This study is especially important because federal law makes it illegal to discriminate by sex, and one might suppose that the law would be more faithfully followed in the federal work force. However, that proved not to be the case since female federal employees were generally hired at lower levels than male. Newly hired women were concentrated in female-dominated jobs in the lower tier of the job ladder, precisely the ones that offered the least opportunity for advancement. Even more important, women in the middle grades of federal workers were promoted at lower rates than men. This study also found that the most difficult kind of promotion for women was from the middle-level ranks to supervisory and managerial jobs (DiPrete and Soule, 1988).

Some alternative explanations have been offered for the widespread existence of sex segregation in occupations (England et al., 1988). One alternative has been offered by economists, who argue that women intentionally select occupations that are easy to get into and out of, while still providing moderately good incomes. An extension of this economic argument is that women also select occupations that allow them to take time out when they want to have children and remain at home. Obviously, this economic explanation is in line with the view that women *choose* to be in sex-segregated occupations. Although this economic theory sounds plausible, a national sample of male and female workers did not find support for its major assertions (England et al., 1988).

The results of this study and many others suggest a more sociological explanation for sex segregation of occupations and the accompanying lower wages for women. This explanation first emphasizes the mutual or two-way influence between gender-role socialization and discrimination by employers. Traditional gender-role socialization leads many women to the view that certain jobs are more appropriate and available for them. Employers conclude from this that women do not want certain male-dominated jobs. This may feed their already existing belief that women are "by nature" not suited to certain jobs. The general view that one sex is inherently superior to the other sex is called **sexism.** Sexism often serves as the basis for overt discrimination against women in the occupational world, keeping occupations sex segregated and, as we will see, women's pay less than men's pay.

Sexism
The view that one sex is inherently superior to the other

Even in the absence of overt discrimination by employers, structural or institutional factors act to keep women in sex-segregated (and often lower-paying, lower-status) jobs. These structural or institutional impediments to promotion and higher pay have been called institutional sexism. **Institutional sexism** is defined as the day-to-day operations, rules, and policies of organizations and institutions that result in the discriminatory treatment of women. An important aspect of institutional sexism is that it can operate without individuals being prejudiced against women or intentionally discriminatory. However, when organizations and institutions have rules or policies that directly or indirectly impede or limit women, the effect can be just as important as when prejudice is blatant and discrimination, intentional.

Institutional sexism
Day-to-day operations, rules, and policies of organizations and institutions that discriminate against women

An example of institutional sexism may be found in the practice of having female jobs in organizations that lead only to other female jobs—jobs that have relatively low pay and status. Other such institutional practices that work to the disadvantage of women include giving preferences to military veterans (which favor many more men than women), limiting public advertising for jobs (which might give the male friends of already employed men a better chance of being hired), and designing machines and tools for the average height and strength of men rather than women (England et al., 1988). As an example of the latter, some female police candidates in training programs are unable to use large caliber firearms effectively and are therefore unable to meet the training requirements. In actual police work, however, smaller caliber weapons are often used by officers.

Another example of institutional sexism stems from employee policies about child care, which may have a significant effect on female employees. Few American employers provide child-care services in the work setting. (Employers in societies like Sweden are far more likely to provide adequate child-care facilities.) Since the traditional feminine role expectation is that women will care for children, women with children are apt to face more problems and strains than men working for the same employer. The employer cannot be blamed personally for creating the problems of their female employees with children, and the employer certainly cannot be charged with prejudice. The point remains that a company policy that does not provide adequate child-care services does affect some women adversely.

Then there are organizations and institutions that specifically limit the activities of women—particularly activities that are important for moving up in the organizational structure. For example, in the United States military women cannot serve on combat ships at sea or in other combat zones. For the officer corps these are very important assignments during a career, since they are often considered prerequisites for gaining the highest military ranks. Obviously, if the rules of the military preclude women serving in these positions, then women are severely disadvantaged when they try to compete for the highest military ranks.

A number of religious organizations have created similar institutional impediments for women. Barred from serving as ministers, priests, rabbis, or elders, women are automatically excluded from the higher offices and positions of authority within the religion. In most major religions today, males have retained the positions of leadership for themselves simply by blocking the first steps in the hierarchy. Opposition groups have occasionally emerged, however; an unofficial group of Roman Catholic priests has issued a "Pastoral Letter on Equality in the Church," which calls for ending the "sin" of gender discrimination (Hyer, 1985). This is a recognition of, and an effort to combat, the institutional sexism that exists in religion.

The Economic Impact of Sex Segregation on Women

Sex segregation of occupations, which is the combined product of gender role choices, discrimination in hiring and promotion, and institutional sexism, has some obvious impacts on the relative earnings of women compared to men. In the late 1980s the relative earnings of women in the labor force had reached about 70 percent of male earnings. Nearly 20 years earlier, in 1967, women in the labor force earned 62 percent of what men earned, revealing that, during these two decades, employed women made only small economic gains relative to men. Male and female incomes in the major occupational categories are compared in figure 10–2.

A recent study completed for the National Academy of Sciences estimates that 35 percent to 40 percent of the disparity in male and female income is accounted for by sex segregation (Perl, 1985). Although some reduction did occur in the amount of sex segregation during the 1970s, progress toward integrating workplaces slowed during the 1980s. The National Academy of Sciences report concluded with the following warning:

> Decreases in federal enforcement that have occurred since 1981 and recent changes in the philosophy of enforcement, including reversals of federal civil rights policy in some areas, are likely to negatively affect women's future employment opportunities (Perl, 1985, p. A15).

The future of women in the labor force is difficult to predict, although it appears from the above study that constant surveillance will be necessary if equality is to be achieved. Both overt discrimination and institutional sexism are still found throughout American society. On the other hand, increasing numbers of women are moving into a wide range of occupations and professions, and as they do some of the barriers created

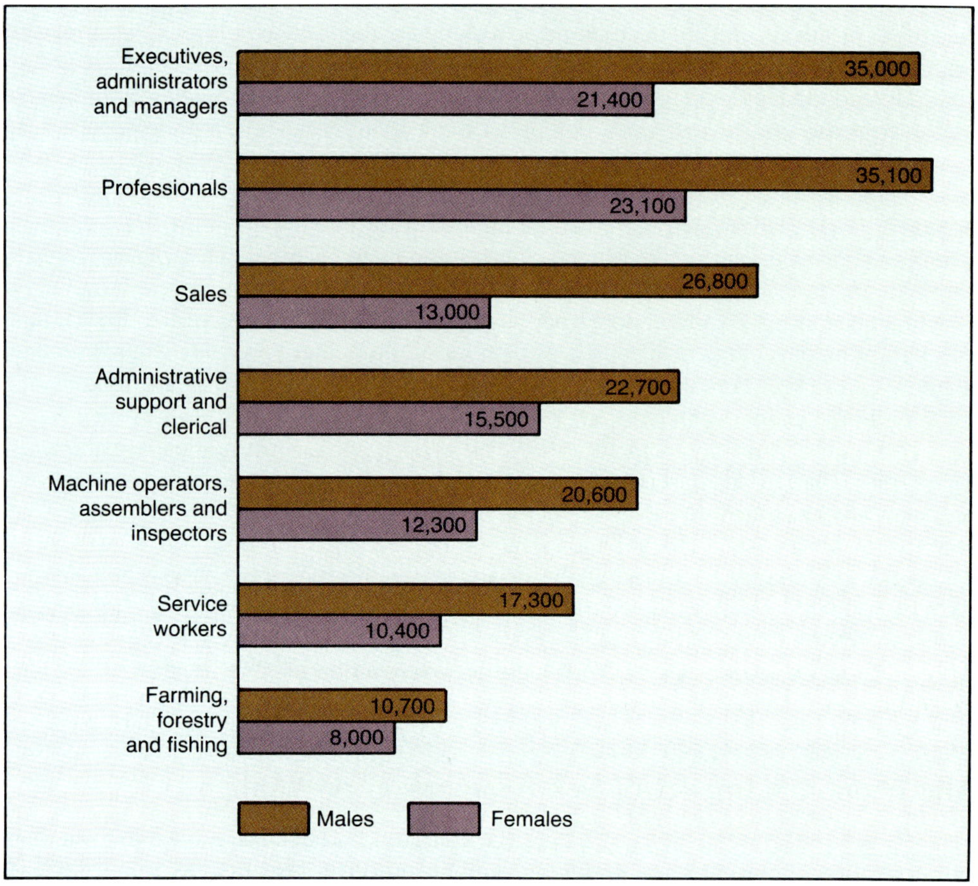

Figure 10–2. Median Incomes of Males and Females in Selected Occupational Categories. (*Source:* U.S. Bureau of the Census, *Statistical Abstract of the United States, 1988* (Washington, D.C.: U.S. Government Printing Office, 1987), Table 653, p. 395.)

by sexist attitudes and institutional barriers are likely to be reduced and broken down. While gender equality in the workplace might be achieved in some future time, that time has not yet arrived (England and McCreary, 1987; Ferree, 1987).

Age Stratification and Inequality

A society may be stratified by age, just as it is stratified by economics, power, race, ethnicity, or gender. Age may be used to divide a population into significant categories that are treated in special ways. Different age groups in a society will be given different rights, opportunities, rules, and limitations. Often the old or the young age groups, since they tend to be dependent on the rest of the adult population, are at a disadvantage and therefore receive unequal treatment in the society. Although every society makes some distinctions on the basis of age, the nature of age stratification systems differs from one society to another and has changed from one historical period to another (Riley et al., 1988).

Children and Society

Since childhood appears to be a normal and natural stage of life, it is interesting to find that for much of Western history, childhood was not thought of as a distinct life stage. This, at least, is the view of social historian Philippe Ariés (1962), who assembled evidence to support the thesis that in the Middle Ages a child went from infancy directly into a kind of adulthood. The most common image of the medieval child, as Ariés found in the paintings of that period, was that of a kind of miniature adult. Obviously, if parents did not recognize a stage of life that we recognize as childhood, they were likely to treat their children differently than they are treated today.

Children at a very early age were expected to participate in productive work. Because of their size they could not do all things that adults could do, but they were not allowed to spend their time in frivolous play. In the nineteenth century in the United States, children of poor and working classes were expected to contribute to the family income and production by working. Even in the twentieth century, children of farm families often left elementary school to help with farm tasks.

Today, the situation is quite different, with children rarely entering the work force until at least high school age. Again the exceptions are likely to be on family farms, or other farm labor, and family businesses. Usually children are not expected to work, but they are also denied a wide range of rights and privileges. Children and adolescents in contemporary families are usually rather closely controlled and limited by parents. The assumption is that their immaturity makes it imprudent to give them too much freedom. Although some agitation has occurred for greater children's rights, no significant social movement has emerged (Farson, 1974).

Some rights that were earlier granted to adolescents and young adults have been withdrawn in recent years. Many high schools adopted liberalized policies of dress and behavior in the 1970s, which have been withdrawn or retracted in the 1980s. Smoking, for example, was often allowed in specified areas of high schools, but in recent years many schools have discontinued this privilege. In a similar way, many states and localities in the 1970s lowered the age for drinking alcoholic beverages to 18. In the 1980s the laws were changed, raising the legal drinking age in most places to 21.

Again, these changes illustrate how the social definitions of age groups can change from one time to another, even in the same society. When age categories are socially defined, certain rights and limitations will be attached to the people in that category. This system is referred to as **age stratification.**

Age stratification
A system of socially defined rights and limitations based on age categories

The attitude that limitations and restrictions can be based on age is called **ageism.** Although the term *ageism* is applied primarily to the treatment of the elderly, it can generally refer to any instance when an individual's age is the primary basis for evaluating and dealing with that person. An example of ageism would be a 63-year-old worker's being released from a job, while younger workers who are no more productive are retained. But ageism could also be illustrated by a brilliant teenager who has been denied entry into college simply because of age.

Ageism
Attitude that limitations and restrictions can be based on age

In the next section we will turn our attention to the elderly, a growing and increasingly important part of the population. Much of our discussion will reflect the work being done in a field of study called *social gerontology*. **Social gerontology** is the study of the impact of social and cultural conditions on the process of aging, and also the social consequences of age changes in the population of a society (Hooyman and Kiyak, 1988).

Social gerontology
Study of social and cultural influences on aging and societal consequences of age changes

The Elderly Population

Old age cannot be precisely defined in terms of years of life because just as the meaning of childhood has changed, so also has the meaning of old age. In the United States it is both the legal and social custom to use the 65th birthday as the beginning of old age. When the Social Security Act was passed in 1935, age 65 was set as the age when retirement benefits could be received. Thus, in the public mind, 65 became linked with old age. However, the laws have changed periodically, and for several decades Americans have had the option of receiving partial Social Security benefits at age 62. In the 1980s Congress passed legislation providing that, in the year 2000, full Social Security benefits cannot be received until age 67. Furthermore, as a way of combatting age discrimination in the occupational world, Congress also passed legislation that allows most classes of workers to work until age 70, if they wish.

Even though this legislation gives older people the right to remain in the labor force until they are well past 65, the actual trend in retirement has been in the opposite direction. For the last 100 years American workers have been retiring at younger and younger ages. In 1890, 70 percent of males over the age of 65 were still in the labor force. Today, less than 15 percent of Americans over 65 are employed (in 1986, 16 percent of males and 7 percent of females). By ages 62 to 64 less than half of all males (45.4 percent) are still in the labor force (Soldo and Agree, 1988). The percentage of women still working at that age is even lower, but the retirement trend for women is different than that for men. Among women aged 55 to 64 the percentage in the labor force has been edging upward since 1950, from 30 percent to over 40 percent. This increase among women, however, is probably just a reflection of the generally larger numbers of women in the labor force. The fact remains that between the ages of 55 and 65, less than half of American men and women are still employed. Although some of these people may be unemployed or may have given up looking for work, the majority have probably retired voluntarily.

Who Are the Elderly Today?

The legal and social trends just discussed are indications of who the elderly are in our society, but some of these indicators are providing different pictures. If time of retirement means old age, then old age is coming earlier than ever before; and yet the laws governing Social Security benefits, and prohibiting mandatory retirement, suggest that old age is coming later. Obviously, any definition of old age is very arbitrary, depending on the way in which age is socially defined. In the contemporary United States, many people still view age 65 as the beginning of old age, but new definitions are emerging, particularly from the older people themselves. Often people at age 65 and even older do not think of themselves as old because they have a level of health and a style of life that they do not associate with old age.

Third quarter of life
From age 50 to age 75

To reflect the changing conditions of older people, it has been suggested that we think in terms of the *third quarter of life*. The **third quarter of life** is defined as beginning at about age 50 and continuing until about 75 (Pifer and Bronte, 1986). Clearly, this concept minimizes the significance of reaching age 65 and emphasizes the fact that most people today continue to live active lives until age 75. The age of 50 is chosen in part because many people make important changes in their lives at that point—usually their children have established independent lives, their occupations and careers (and incomes) have often reached about the highest level that will be attained, and retirement emerges as a serious consideration. Age 75 is suggested as an upper limit for the third quarter of life because many people begin then to experience significant declines in physical and mental abilities (Pifer and Bronte, 1986).

Obviously a third quarter of life would have to be followed by a **fourth quarter of life,** the years between 75 and 100 years of age. The idea that an average person could live to 100 is not as extraordinary as it may sound. The life span (the maximum length of human life) has long been over 100 years, although only a few people in most populations reach this maximum. However, some responsible biologists and demographers are suggesting that by the middle of the next century (2050)—well within the lifetimes of many readers—life expectancy may be near or at 100 years (Siegel and Taeuber, 1986).

Fourth quarter of life
From age 75 to 100

Another refinement on the definition of the elderly is found in the already widely accepted terms *young-old* and *old-old*. The **young-old** are people aged 65 through 74, while the **old-old** are aged 75 and older. Again, the young-old category is a recognition of the fact that many people over 65 are still vigorous, healthy, and active; the old-old category of 75 and older marks the beginning of, in many cases, physical and mental decline, although some people are still independent and active well beyond that age.

Young-old
Ages 65 through 74 when most people are vigorous, healthy, and active

Old-old
After age 75, when many people experience some physical and mental decline

Today, many people aged 65 and over are still vigorous, healthy, and active. The stereotyped image of the elderly as sick, frail, and sitting in a rocking chair is no longer appropriate for many of today's older people.

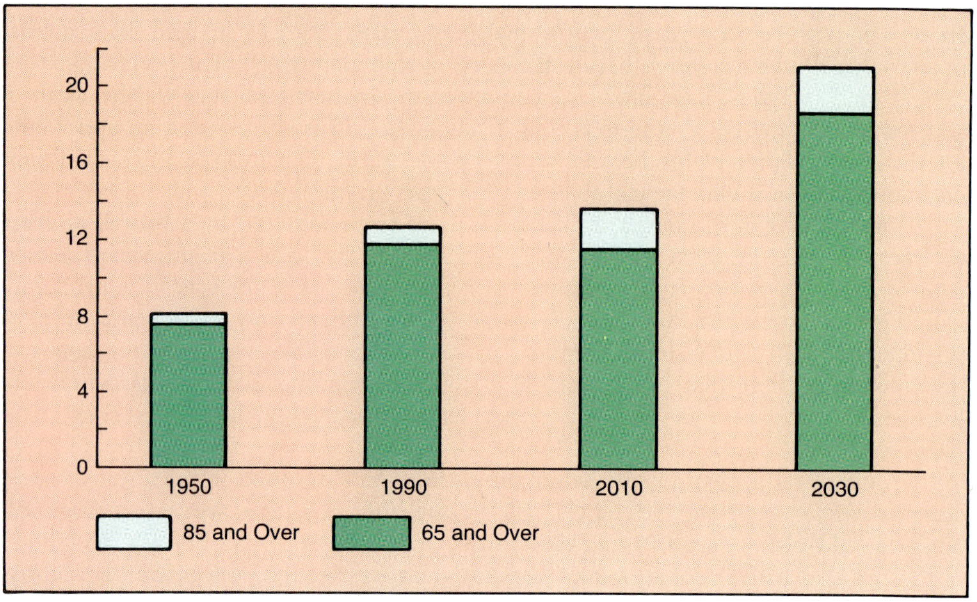

Figure 10–3. Older Population as Percent of Total U.S. Population: 1950–2030. (*Source:* Population Reference Bureau, Soldo and Agree, 1988.)

The Size of the Older Population in the United States

Regardless of how the older population is defined, it is certain that in the next half century both the *number* of elderly people and their *proportion* of the total population will increase.[1] In fact, the older population has been growing rapidly for the last 50 years. In 1990 over 31 million Americans will be aged 65 and older, while in 1940 there were only 9 million in that category. In a half-century from now, in 2040, there will be an estimated 67 million people aged 65 and over. If we look at the elderly as a percentage of the total population, we can see in figure 10–3 that people 65 and older have increased from about 8 percent of the total in 1950 to nearly 13 percent in 1990. However, the greatest increase in the percentage of older people in the population will come in the next century, when by 2030 the 65-and-over population will have grown to 21 percent.

Since about 1970 the increasing numbers of elderly in the population have been produced primarily by decreases in deaths due to chronic diseases (as opposed to infectious diseases). The major chronic diseases are heart disease, cancer, and stroke. Except for cancer, the death rates from these causes have declined since 1968. Furthermore, these three causes of death, which account for three-fourths of the deaths among the elderly, are all occurring at later ages than they did 20 years ago (Manton and Meyers, 1987).

---

[1] Throughout the remainder of this chapter, unless we specify otherwise, the terms *elderly* and *old* will refer to the conventional age group of 65 and older. This designation is still necessary because most available data use age 65 as the beginning of old age.

The Economic Condition of the Elderly

Just as the physical lives of many older people have been improving, so have their economic lives. There is definitely a bright side to the economic condition of the elderly population today, but there is also a dark side. We will deal with the bright side first because it probably reflects the majority of the elderly. We have already seen an indication of the improved economic conditions of the elderly in the historical trends in retirement. We saw that in 1890, 70 percent of all males 65 and over were still employed, while in 1986 that figure was 16 percent and going down. The high percentages of early retirement among men today simply reflects the fact that they are economically able to retire. Although the incomes of retired persons are lower than when they were working, they are not generally living in poverty. Nor are they wealthy, since the primary source of income for those 65 and over comes from Social Security benefits. In 1988 Social Security payments averaged about $500 per month for a retired worker. Of course, some retired workers receive additional pensions from previous private and public employment (Soldo and Agree, 1988).

Annual income is not the only economic resource of the older population, however. The majority of older people have some economic resources in real estate, savings, and investments. Over three-fourths of elderly householders own their own homes, which, in most cases, are mortgage free. Among elderly *couples,* 88 percent own their own homes, but only 65 percent of elderly females *living alone* own their own homes. Although the health care costs for the elderly are greater than for other age groups, Medicare now covers the major portion of their medical costs. In many cases taxes (both personal income and state and local property taxes) are reduced for people over 65. With these economic resources, many of today's elderly are able to live relatively comfortably, but certainly not in affluence (Soldo and Agree, 1988).

But now we turn to that part of the elderly population where the economic picture is much darker. Some people have reached old age who are perhaps in poor health and with physical disabilities, who do not own homes, and who have no savings or other assets. Often, their monthly rent takes a substantial part of their only money income—Social Security benefits. These elderly people live in very precarious economic conditions, often in poor, dilapidated housing. They are truly the impoverished elderly.

In 1986, according to the federal government's poverty standard, more than 12 percent of the elderly were living in poverty—with the old-old having a higher percentage in poverty than the young-old. However, the most serious poverty exists among elderly women and elderly minorities. Elderly women have a significantly higher level of poverty (15 percent) than elderly men (8 percent). Elderly blacks have a much higher poverty level than elderly whites (31 percent compared to 11 percent), while elderly Hispanics are at an intermediate level (22.5 percent). The most seriously impoverished are elderly black women who live alone; a full 60 percent of these women are below the poverty level. These official poverty levels may actually be missing some of the poorest people in the society, for some elderly may be so poor that they live with relatives and thereby may reside in households that are not below the poverty level (Soldo and Agree, 1988).

Economic Comparisons between the Elderly and Children

Although many elderly in the United States are poor, even more poverty exists among the children of the society. In 1986, 21 percent of all children under 16 years old were living in households where incomes were below the poverty level. Among black children

In the United States today, one child of every five lives in poverty. Children who live with single mothers are especially likely to be in poverty.

the percentage was 43.8 percent; among Hispanic children it was 38.4 percent. Since we have already seen that only about 12 percent of the elderly have incomes below the poverty level, clearly these children as a group are more disadvantaged than old people, especially because children (and their parents) are not likely to have the economic assets of many older people (homes, savings, investments). Furthermore, over the last 25 years the poverty rate among children has increased at the same time that the poverty rate among the elderly has decreased (Preston, 1984).

If one looks at expenditures by the federal government as a measure of the relative concern about the elderly and the children of the society, the balance is overwhelmingly in favor of the elderly. In 1984, federal expenditures per child for education, the Aid to Dependent Children program, food stamps, Head Start, nutrition, and health programs added up to only 9 percent of the per person expenditures for the elderly (Preston, 1984). If one considers government expenditures at all levels (federal, state, and local), and thus includes the educational system, expenditures are still estimated to be three times greater for the elderly than for children (Soldo and Agree, 1988).

Why are Americans choosing to devote more of their government expenditures to the dependent elderly than to dependent children? One explanation can be found in the competing voter interest groups, which have different levels of political power. In a democratic society the decisions that allocate different levels of resources to the dependent parts of the population are made by voters. Which groups of voters are more likely to support expenditures for the elderly? The elderly themselves would be justified in looking out for their own economic interests. As a group, the population over age 65 votes more than any other age category (U.S. Bureau of the Census, 1989). The elderly are now a significant voting block in the United States, and through organized interest groups, such as the American Association of Retired Persons, they are becoming stronger. But the middle-aged voting population is also likely to support expenditures for the elderly, for two self-interested reasons. The first is that, if the government does not support their elderly parents, it will fall to them to do so. The second is that the adults in the population, especially those who are middle-aged, may be looking ahead to when they reach old age, and they prefer to have governmental programs in place for their own support.

In contrast, none of these adult voting groups, except the parents of children, have a direct interest in supporting children. The matter has been put succinctly in the following statement:

> Children don't vote; and adults don't vote on behalf of their own children, which is water over the dam. I daresay that if we passed through life backwards, adults would insist that conditions in childhood be made far more appealing (Preston, 1984, p. 385).

A Cross-National View of the Elderly

Just as the older population is growing in the United States, it is also growing in much of the Western world. (See figure 10–4.) Most of the countries of northwestern Europe have a higher proportion of elderly in their populations than the United States does (12.0 percent in 1985). Among them the highest percentages in 1985 were Sweden (16.9 percent), Norway (15.5 percent), the United Kingdom (15.1 percent), and Denmark (14.9 percent). As figure 10–4 shows, the developing countries all have lower proportions of elderly because health and living conditions cause earlier deaths, and high birth rates add larger numbers of children to the population each year. The countries with the smallest proportions of elderly in their populations are found in Africa and the Arab Middle East (Soldo and Agree, 1988).

All of the countries of western Europe spend higher percentages of their gross national product (GNP) on their elderly than does the United States (7.4 percent). Austria has the highest expenditure on social programs for the elderly (21 percent of its GNP). In Scandinavian countries and Great Britain, when old people are taken care of by their relatives, the government provides some compensation for the services they render. Other European countries provide tax deductions and early retirement pensions for people who assist in the care of their older relatives (Soldo and Agree, 1988).

China, because of the sheer size of its total population, has a larger number of elderly people than any other nation on earth. In 1985 China had more than 50 million people aged 65 and over. In the culture of traditional China, elderly people were highly honored and respected. However, in the last 40 years, since its communist revolution, China has broken down many of the traditional cultural customs and values, and has at the same time engaged in an intense effort to modernize its economy. This raises the question of how the elderly of China are being treated today (Olsen, 1988).

Evidence shows that China continues to give special attention to the elderly in its population through programs that have been created, especially since 1978. The most important of these programs are pensions and medical care for the retired elderly, homes for the aged, and special efforts to give the elderly Chinese satisfying activities after retirement. For economic and political reasons the Chinese are encouraging their elderly to retire at a relatively early age (60 for men and 55 for women). Early retirement allows the Chinese to bring younger and better trained workers into the urban labor force. The

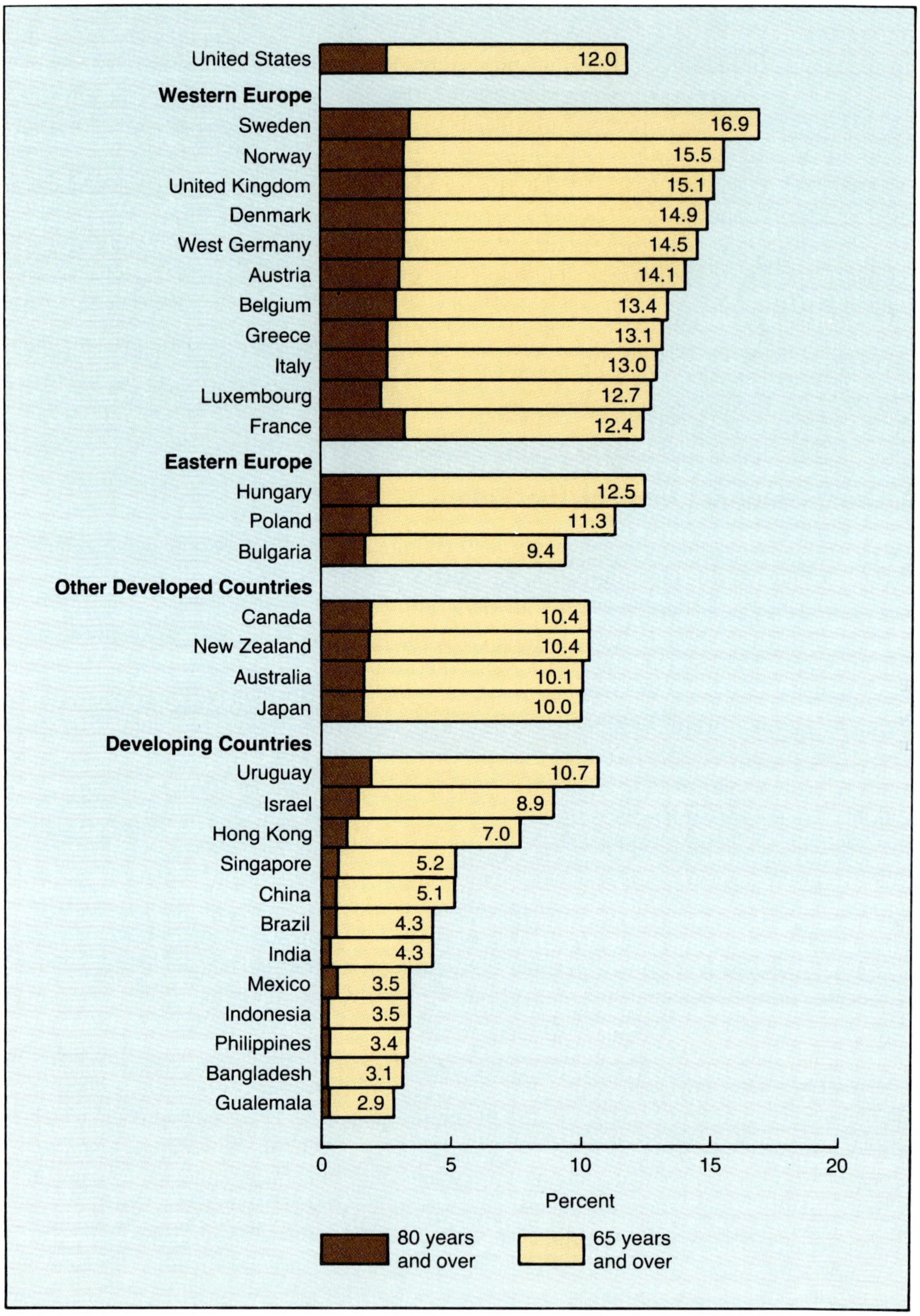

Figure 10–4. Percent of Elderly Population in Selected Countries, 1985. (*Source:* Population Reference Bureau, Soldo and Agree, 1988.)

Chinese leaders are particularly concerned about the discontent among the retired elderly when they no longer have the meaningful activities of work. A prominent slogan of the Chinese today is: "The old are entitled to continue doing, to study, to be cared for, to enjoy themselves, and to receive medical care" (Olsen, 1988, p. 255). It appears that the elderly do receive respect and consideration in contemporary China, but the reasons may have just as much to do with the political and economic aims of the government as with China's cultural tradition of venerating the elderly.

Summary

Every society is organized to some degree on the basis of gender and age categories, and often the results are inequities or systems of inequality. The inequalities between males and females can be analyzed in terms of three separate but closely related concepts: power, division of labor by gender, and gender roles.

In most societies males tend to have greater power and more privileges than females, but some exceptions are notable. Women have greater power in societies where they carry out activities on which men are dependent and where there are long-standing magical and religious associations between the fertility of women and the general well-being of the social group. In societies around the world, men and women are typically assigned to different work. The division of labor by gender often finds men doing heavy and dangerous work, but there are many instances when females, too, are assigned heavy and arduous tasks.

Cross-cultural evidence shows that the gender role differences familiar in American society are not universal and therefore are not inborn characteristics of the sexes. Anthropological studies give evidence that gender roles are learned through the socialization process.

The stereotyped personality traits associated with males and females attribute certain traits (emphasizing achievement and action) to males and other traits (emphasizing emotional support and comfort) to females. Therefore, traditional feminine and masculine roles in American society emphasize that females should participate in activities that are supportive and expressive, while males should participate in ones that are active and instrumental.

Attitude studies among Americans show that traditional gender-role attitudes have been reduced; but many Americans, both young and adult, still accept some traditional expectations, especially for women.

The socialization for gender roles occurs through social rewards provided by significant others and by models provided by males and females in the child's environment. Also, children themselves develop a gender identity and actively adopt the behaviors and attitudes associated with the different genders.

In general, the gender roles in American society (and many other societies) place women in subordinate and less-valued positions than men. However, the argument can be made that traditional gender roles also impose significant disadvantages on men. The traditional masculine role places expectations on men that may be stressful and perhaps places restrictions on their behavior. However, on balance, women are still more disadvantaged than men by traditional gender roles.

The impact of traditional gender roles can be seen in everyday behaviors, such as how males and females touch each other, how they sit and stand, and how they speak. In the schools the responses of boys and girls are treated differently by teachers.

In the public world, especially in political and economic life, women are underrepresented in the more prestigious positions. Sex segregation in occupations, produced in large part by sexism and institutional sexism, continues to leave women less rewarded in the work world.

In the stratification of society by age, the elderly and children are the most disadvantaged. Children and young adults are defined by the rest of the society as being less than mature, and thus limitations are placed on their rights.

The definition of old age is changing in the United States because of the improving health and economic positions of many people over age 65. The elderly population is growing rapidly, and will continue to increase in numbers and as a proportion of the population. Many elderly people today are reaching old age with considerably greater economic resources than in the past. However, elderly women who live alone, especially if they are members of minority groups, have much higher than average levels of poverty than other categories of the elderly.

When the poverty levels of the elderly and children are compared, higher rates of poverty are found among children.

Cross-national studies of the elderly find their numbers growing in most developed countries. All western European countries spend higher proportions of their economic resources on the elderly than the United States does. China, with the highest numbers of elderly in the world, has instituted special programs to care for this population.

CRITICAL THINKING

1. What relationship exists between economic contributions, power, and gender in our society?
2. How do Margaret Mead's studies of gender roles in New Guinea societies show that such roles are the result of society rather than biology?
3. List some common gender-related stereotypes. How are these stereotypes reinforced in the mass media?
4. Give examples of gender role expectations in your family.
5. Give examples from your own childhood of how you learned the gender roles expected of you in society.
6. In what ways are gender roles in evidence in everyday behaviors such as touching, standing, sitting, speaking, etc.? Can you think of examples of these differences from your own experiences?
7. Is sexism and gender stereotyping likely to decrease in the future? Explain, using information from the chapter as well as your own ideas.
8. Compare and contrast the rights and restrictions associated with old age and childhood.
9. Give examples of inequalities in our society related to gender and/or age.

CONNECTIONS

The United States-Mexico Border

Introduction

It is a warm spring Sunday as I drive into El Paso, Texas. The sun is shining, as it always does in this desert-mountainous region; my car windows are down to enjoy the warm rush of air, and a lively *conjunto* band is playing on a Mexican radio station. The Border Highway is aptly named as it follows the course of the Rio Grande River, which serves as the borderline between the United States and Mexico. On my left, on the Mexican side, families are picnicking on its banks and splashing and swimming in the shallow river, crossing the invisible borderline at times. Above the banks are the *colonias,* or poorest housing districts, in the huge city of Juarez, where adobe houses line dirt streets. Most homes don't have running water so residents must wait for the water truck to come with their weekly supply. When it doesn't come there is no water, and some of their babies die of dehydration caused by dysentery from the polluted, contaminated waters in which they are now swimming. Farther down the river people walk through a large hole in the fence ("Tortilla Curtain") intended to restrict Mexicans from illegally entering the United States, to spend the day in El Paso. The green vans of *La Migra,* or Border Patrol, watch them but decide instead to chase another group and return them to the border. Since it is Sunday, not a work day, the daily cat-and-mouse chase game is played in a more relaxed way.

To my right, on the U.S. side of the highway, I also see *colonias* similar to those across the border; in them diseases that have disappeared in other parts of the United States are rampant. I wonder at these Third-World conditions as I drive farther north into El Paso, past sprawling homes with manicured yards, some with swimming pools, and others with maids' quarters that house the women who come from Mexico for low wages to take care of these homes and children.

On Monday morning a different picture emerges on the Border Highway. Traffic is congested on the bridges connecting the two cities; exhaust from cars sends pollution into the air to join with that from industrial smokestacks. Workers in Juarez take buses to the many *maquiladoras,* assembly plants built in Mexico by American corporations. There, American-made parts are assembled into consumer goods (e.g., televisions, refrigerators, clothing, toys) by Mexican workers and then returned, virtually duty free, to the United States for sale. Plant managers cross the bridge from the United States to join these workers, then cross back to their homes in El Paso, hoping to avoid the tangle of traffic compounded by trucks that carry goods from the factories.

Some people from Mexico come to work in the United States, both legally and illegally, for daily wages that far surpass the $3.00 minimum *daily* wage they find in Mexico. Most do manual labor, including the many women who work as maids. To avoid *La Migra* some cross on "mules"—a name for men who wade across the river with people on their backs so they will not get wet.

El Paso and Cuidad Juarez together comprise the second largest metropolitan area along the U.S.-Mexican border. The intersection of these two border cities reveals the economic, social, and cultural contrasts of the United States—an affluent, advanced industrial society—and Mexico, a less industrialized Third World country. In this discussion we will look at the complex set of social relations that characterizes the U.S.-Mexico border from the viewpoint of four theoretical perspectives, focusing especially on some of the consequences of the growth of *maquiladoras,* or American assembly plants, in Mexican border cities.

Structural-Functional Theory

In chapter 8 we saw that functionalists view stratification as a normal arrangement in societies, perpetuated by people's values and beliefs in a system that allocates jobs and wealth to people according to their training and expertise. This system is seen as functional because it assures that all jobs in society get done and that people get what they deserve in terms of money, power, and prestige.

If we look at the development of American corporations in Mexico from a functionalist perspective we would focus on how *maquiladoras* have been beneficial to both countries. Major corporations, such as General Motors, Zenith, Ford, and RCA, have built over 1,000 assembly plants in Mexico over the past few years to take advantage of cheap labor, low shipping costs, and tariff duties payment charged only on the value added in Mexican plants. A manifest function for corporations, then, is the greater profit earned on products made in Mexico than if the products had been manufactured in Asia, the Caribbean, or, especially, the United States. Functionalists would contend that *maquiladoras* have been beneficial to the Mexican economy and to Mexican workers because they have brought thousands of people into the workforce who were previously unemployed or were working at even lower wages than the *maquila* workers.

Functionalists might also point to a latent function of *maquilas* in reducing the number of Mexicans coming into the United States illegally to seek work. This helps to provide a stability to the socioeconomic structures of both countries, as well as providing special benefits to the United States because Mexican workers spend approximately one-half of their paychecks there (Tiano, 1987).

Conflict Theory

Conflict theorists would disagree with the functionalists' view of the growth of American factories in Mexico. They point out that *maquiladoras* represent an excellent example of a "runaway shop" or "off-shore assembly plant" that has contributed to the process of deindustrialization in the United States. As we noted in chapters 8 and 9, manufacturing employment in many American cities has declined as employers have sought cheaper sources of labor, and one result has been the social problems associated with a permanent underclass.

Conflict theorists would also focus on the ways in which American corporate interests have exploited *maquila* workers in order to gain the greatest possible profits. Workers in Mexico, for example, are paid a minimum wage of $3.00 a day, and in *maquilas,* $.80 to $1.20 an hour. For years Mexican *maquila* workers received wages that ranged from one-fifth to one-seventh of those paid to American industrial workers, and recent devaluations of the Mexican peso have reduced these figures to as little as one-fifteenth of their American counterparts (Cockcroft, 1986, p. 110).

Conflict theorists would also point to inequities in the division of labor by looking at age and gender stratification in *maquilas.* As many as 85 to 90 percent of *maquila* workers are women in the 16- to 25-year-old range; many of them become the economic mainstays of their families while still in their teens. María Patricia Fernández-Kelly, who has conducted extensive field research among women factory workers, summarized a typical reason given by plant managers for hiring females.

> We hire mostly women because they are more reliable than men; they have finer fingers, smaller muscles, and unsurpassed manual dexterity. Also, women don't get tired of repeating the same operations nine hundred times a day (Fernández-Kelly, 1983a, p. 181).

Fernández-Kelly challenges this assumption and says that *maquila* work has become a sex-segregated occupation as justification for subordinating women in the workplace, and has resulted in a patriarchal power structure since most managers are men. Because there is an abundance of unemployed workers and these young, unskilled women are easily replaceable, they are relatively powerless to influence the conditions of their work. High turnover rates in *maquilas* further limit possibilities for career mobility among women, as does their lack of skills, which also keeps them in the lowest paying positions. Finally, many women are made ill by the unhealthy working conditions and by age thirty are unable to continue working in the *maquilas*.

Symbolic Interactionism

As we have seen, symbolic interactionism is less interested in broad macroscopic issues, such as cross-cultural economic development, than on microscopic issues, such as the ways in which people communicate and interpret the meanings that situations have for them. People make plans and choose courses of action based on their interpretations of the meanings of situations. At times, there is a discrepancy between the expectations people have for situations and what they actually experience when in that situation. Again, let us look at *maquila* workers in Mexico to illustrate this idea.

Not all *maquila* workers are young, female, unskilled, and uneducated. Some are highly trained, educated females and males who have left the teaching profession. Why would *maquila* work appeal to teachers? In Mexico there is a discrepancy between the perception of teaching as respected work and the reality of teachers' lives. For example, although teachers are among the most highly educated in the country, the average teacher earns only slightly over $150 per month; most do not own a house or car; they pay 75 percent of their salaries for rent in the poorest areas of cities; and most teach in two schools, with few teaching materials for their large classes (Campa, 1989). This situation has led to widespread dissatisfaction among teachers and a strike of 100,000 teachers in Mexico City in 1989 (*K.C. Times*, 1989). For Mexican teachers, symbolic representations, in the form of extrinsic rewards such as good pay and good working conditions are lacking, as expressed in one man's comments: "What else can we lose, we've already lost our purchasing power and if maids earn more than teachers with 15 years of formal education?" (Campa, 1989, p. 9).

Symbolic interactionists might focus on the loss of self-esteem and role conflict that stems from the discrepancy between teachers' expectations for their work and the low rewards given to them. Zurcher (1983) says that this type of situation requires that some kind of action take place to reduce discomfort or strain. He says there are a number of kinds of action teachers might take, such as leave the role, stay in the role and "grin and bear it," "distance" themselves in such a way as to let others know they no longer care about the strain, or make a new role within the situation. From the symbolic interactionist perspective, we would assume that being a *maquila* worker would magnify role conflict between teachers' perceptions of the value of their education and training, and the semi-skilled work they must take to support their families.

Social Exchange Theory

Exchange theorists, like symbolic interactionists, are more interested in individuals' behaviors but in a different way. Whether people continue in situations or leave them is related to the rewards or costs they experience. If relationships are reciprocal, people will maintain them. As an example of this exchange relationship we will leave *maquilas* and look at another border situation: the relationship between Mexican domestic workers (maids) and their employers. Most Mexican domestics cross the border illegally because the benefits of domestic work far outweigh the work and wages available to them in Mexico—such as those in *maquilas*. The Border Patrol is not interested in stopping them because they perform jobs that Americans do not want (Ruiz, 1987). Although on the border they earn less (about $15 to $20 a day) than domestics in other parts of the country, their wages far exceed those in Mexico ($3 a day). To support their own families, women domestics care for the homes and children of Americans while leaving their own children in the care of relatives. According to the rules of reciprocity, this arrangement is beneficial not only to domestics but also to their employers who are relieved of housework and child care at a very low cost. Furthermore, for employers, the benefits are greater because they typically do not pay social security taxes on the salaries of domestic workers (Ruiz, 1987).

Reciprocity is sometime strained, however, and violated to the point of termination of employee-employer relationships. As Ruiz (1987) has found, both Anglo and Mexican-American employers are unappreciative of their maids, and in fact some Hispanics treat them worse than Anglos do. Ruiz also found evidence of discrimination in newspaper ads for domestics through such statements as "must be clean" or, more blatantly, a refusal to accept Mexican domestics. Ruiz concludes that Mexican domestics experience a "quadruple whammy"—discrimination based on their low social class, their gender, their ethnicity, and their Mexican citizenship. In this example, the exchange relationship would not be equal, or reciprocal. Some women restore the balance by resigning, others by regarding other benefits as worth the costs they experience.

Looking at the Research

A growing body of research—called border studies—examines issues arising from the dynamic interaction along the 2,000-mile U.S.-Mexico border. This research reflects some of the different perspectives discussed above. For example, sociologist and border scholar Ellwyn Stoddard (1987), who has conducted extensive research on the growth of *maquiladoras,* has found that most Mexicans who work in *maquilas* have no desire to move to the United States. *Maquila* workers receive

higher wages and greater benefits, such as transportation to work, bonuses for good attendance, and cafeteria privileges, than do workers in Mexican-owned factories. He contends that the presence of *maquilas* has curbed unrest and actually prevented people from moving to the United States. Stoddard also reports that *maquila* workers are satisfied with their jobs and have little interest in union activities. Therefore, *maquila* growth has been beneficial to both countries—to Mexico by providing jobs, training, and capital, and to the United States by enabling corporations to produce goods at lower costs than would be possible in other parts of the world. Finally, he points out that *maquila* workers spend about one-half of their paychecks in the United States, thus stimulating American businesses and the expansion of jobs.

However, critics of the *maquiladoras* point out that, no matter how contented workers may be in their *maquila* jobs, these factories serve as a magnet encouraging migration to the Mexican border cities for a population much larger than they can absorb (Bustamante, 1983;

Fernández-Kelly, 1983b). By 1974 one-third of the people on the Mexican side of the border were migrants, but only 3 percent were employed in *maquiladoras* (Cockcroft, 1986, p. 109). Therefore, as the population of Mexican border cities increased after the introduction of the *maquiladoras,* so also did the unemployment and underemployment rates. One of the consequences of the extremely high proportion of women *maquila* workers is that employment opportunities for men in border cities, such as Juarez, are far less plentiful. Mexican men in these cities, therefore, seek work in the United States, while female members of their households work in the *maquilas* (Fernández-Kelly, 1983a, 1983b). Thus, critics contend that, rather than reducing the flow of illegal immigrants, the presence of *maquiladoras* has actually increased their numbers.

Finally, the *maquiladoras* are unstable; if threatened with labor unrest in the form of demands for higher wages or for improved working conditions, they will simply move elsewhere in Mexico or to other countries where wages are lower and workers more compliant, leaving behind a mass of unemployed workers (Bustamante, 1983; Cockcroft, 1986). Critics also point out that, although American corporations profit from the reduced labor costs of Mexican workers, American workers who lose their jobs when American plants are closed and moved to Mexico are the losers.

The *maquiladoras* are therefore influenced by a wide variety of social, cultural, economic, and political forces, and their presence in Mexican border cities such as Juarez has contributed to the unique quality of life on the U.S.-Mexico border. So closely intertwined are cities such as Juarez and El Paso that some have described the border region as a third country in which food, language, and music, as well as social, economic, and political structures, are shared. As described by Miller, border cities such as Juarez and El Paso "couple like reluctant lovers in the night, embracing for fear that letting go could only be worse" (Miller, 1985, p. xii).

References

BUSTAMANTE, JORGE A. "Maquiladoras: A New Face of International Capitalism on Mexico's Northern Frontier." In June Nash and María Patricia Fernández-Kelly (eds.), *Women, Men, and the International Division of Labor*. Albany: State University of New York Press, 1983.

CAMPA, HOMERO. "Siete Veces Ha Cerrado La Puerta Bartlett A Los Lideres de la Disidencia Magisterial." *Proceso*, No. 643, February 27, 1989, pp. 6–9.

CROCKCROFT, JAMES D. *Outlaws in the Promised Land: Mexican Immigrant Workers and America's Future*. New York: Grove Press, 1986.

FERNÁNDEZ-KELLY, MARÍA PATRICIA. *For We Are Sold, I and My People: Women and Industry in Mexico's Frontier*. Albany: State University of New York Press, 1983a.

FERNÁNDEZ-KELLY, MARÍA PATRICIA. "Mexican Border Industrialization, Female Labor Force Participation and Migration." In June Nash and María Patricia Fernández-Kelly (eds.), *Women, Men, and the International Division of Labor*. Albany: State University of New York Press, 1983b.

Kansas City Times. "100,000 Striking Teachers in Mexico Demand Raises," April 25, 1989.

MILLER, TOM. *On the Border: Portraits of America's Southwestern Frontier*. Tucson, Ariz.: The University of Arizona Press, 1985.

RUIZ, VICKI L. "By the Day or the Week: Mexicana Domestic Workers in El Paso." In Vicki L. Ruiz and Susan Tiano (eds.), *Women on the U.S.-Mexico Border: Responses to Change*. Boston: Allen & Unwin, 1987, pp. 61–76.

STODDARD, ELLWYN R. *Maquila: Assembly Plants in Northern Mexico*. El Paso, Tex.: Texas Western Press, 1987.

TIANO, SUSAN. "Women's Work and Unemployment in Northern Mexico." In Vicki L. Ruiz and Susan Tiano (eds.), *Women on the U.S.-Mexico Border: Responses to Change*. Boston: Allen & Unwin, 1987, pp. 17–39.

ZURCHER, LOUIS A. *Social Roles: Conformity, Conflict, and Creativity*. Beverly Hills: Sage, 1983.

CHAPTER

11

The Family

Because the family is a familiar social form, we can all describe what a family is and how it works. Our description would probably begin by stating that the family consists of a number of people with different statuses, such as wives and husbands, mothers and fathers, and children. But at this point we would have to pause because we may already have a problem. For example, there is a society in southern India called the Nayar who, according to the anthropological record, had a family system without husbands and fathers. In the eighteenth and early nineteenth centuries the men of the Nayar had no continuing relationships with their wives or children, nor did they assume responsibility for them. Thus, in the Nayar family system, the men did not occupy the status that we generally think is important for the family.

While the Nayar still live in southern India, their family system is no longer organized as it was in the eighteenth century, primarily because, when the British colonized India, they forced the Nayar to change. However, before the British arrived, young Nayar girls between the ages of seven and 12 were married at a group ceremony. Each girl was given a specific boy as a husband, and for four days she would cohabit with him. At the end of that time, the boy would return to the home of his mother, and the girl would return to her mother's. Throughout her life this male would be her formal husband, even though she might never see him again.

The girl would reach maturity in the home of her mother, where she would receive overnight visits from her lovers. When she became pregnant, one of her lovers would be designated as the father of the unborn child. This nominal father would give a few symbolic gifts and pay the costs of the child's birth, but thereafter he would have no rights to, or responsibilities for, the child. The child would be reared in the home of its mother and grandmother.

The Nayar household was headed by the grandmother, who was the matriarch of the family. The sons of the matriarch also lived in the household, but only part of the time because the Nayar men were warriors. (In India's caste system the caste of the Nayar was responsible for military tasks and warfare.) These sons would help with economic support of the household, and when they were present they would also help with the childrearing (especially of the boys), but the Nayar household was primarily centered around the females (Gough, 1960).

It is easy to see why the Nayar might have developed a family system that de-emphasized the importance and prominence of males. If the men of the caste were frequently gone on military expeditions or were taking part in military training, they could not be counted on to carry out key family tasks. Furthermore, since the men were engaged in fighting, they might be killed and thus lost to the family at any time. This example shows how family systems have a tendency to adapt to external conditions and why the family has been called an *adaptive institution*. This characteristic of the family will be discussed below.

Although the Nayar family system is unusual—nothing quite like their system has been observed in any other society—it does allow us to see some important sociological points. First, family systems can be organized in very different ways. In more sociological terms, the family structure and the statuses and roles of different family members can vary greatly from one society to another.

A second point to be made about the Nayar example is that, in describing the family, we may find it best to begin with what the family does instead of what its organization or structure is. What activities, purposes, or tasks does the family perform? These functions of the family, as they are often called, are sometimes described as tasks necessary for a society's survival. Many efforts have been made to identify the *essential* or *universal* functions performed by the family, but these efforts usually reveal alternative (nonfamily) ways of accomplishing the same task (Reiss and Lee, 1988).

A better way to look at the functions of the family is to see them as variable from one society to another and from one historical time to another. This view still allows us to see that some important societal tasks, or functions, are nearly always carried out by the family. In the next section we will examine some major functions of the family, beginning with those that are found most widely, and moving toward those that are found less often or are of diminishing importance.

The Functions of the Family

An analysis of family functions has an obvious connection with structural-functional theory described in chapter 1. Structural-functionalism focuses attention on the positive and negative contributions of a structure (in this case, the family) to a society. In chapter 1 we noted that the family contributes to society by producing children, caring for them when they are young, and training them in the ways of the society. Since these tasks are performed in some manner by the family in nearly every society, they are the near-universal functions of the society. There are, however, societies in which these functions are either not performed by the family, or they take such a different form that they deserve special attention.

Reproduction. For a society to continue, replacements must be provided for the members who die, a task accomplished primarily through childbearing. (Sometimes the reproduction function is called *replacement*.) In almost every society, men and women who are married are the preferred producers of children. The Nayar family system, of course, is an exception since the father is not part of the family unit. Also, societies exist in which children are produced by couples who are not formally married, but they may have **de facto unions** because they have cohabited for extensive periods of time. In addition, children are born to unmarried women, and in these cases, even with the fathers absent, mothers and their children are usually accepted as family units.

de facto unions
Couples who are not formally married who produce children

Care and Nurturance of Children. As we have previously noted, the human infant is incapable of caring for itself. It must be given physical care or it will not survive. We also recognize more and more that the human infant must have emotional support and nurturance. Family sociologist Ira Reiss, who has searched for the universal family functions, has concluded that every family system, regardless of form, provides emotional support and nurturance for its children (Reiss and Lee, 1988).

The care and nurturing of children is one of the nearly universal functions of the family. It is especially important that children be provided with emotional support during their early years.

Socialization. If some degree of order and continuity is to exist in a society from one generation to the next, infants must also be taught the society's cultural and social ways. In chapter 5 we discussed the importance of parents' socializing their children, but we also noted that in many societies the mass media and schools are also significant socializers.

Meeting Economic Needs. The family is a societal unit in which members cooperate to satisfy their common economic needs. Sometimes people live in other larger social units in which there is economic cooperation (e.g., communes, *kibbutzim*). Also, many individuals in the United States today live alone; nearly one-fourth of all households (23.9 percent in 1986) had only one person. Obviously, for many people in contemporary American society, having family members in the same household is not a necessity for meeting economic needs. In many societies, however, the family has been, and continues to be, both an economic-producing unit and a consuming unit. Production within the family, through farming, a family business, or family handicrafts, has been most common through history. However, in contemporary, economically developed societies, the family is primarily integrated through its consumption, not its production. Nonetheless, the family continues to provide for the economic needs of its members, especially those who are dependent, such as children.

Intergenerational and Kin Support. Long after childhood, support—physical, economic, and emotional—continues between generations within families. Parents continue to help and support their adult children in a variety of ways, and adult children reciprocate by giving help, respect, and attention to their parents. In many societies,

Even though the United States is a society in which the nuclear family predominates, family members of different generations—the extended family—continue to give each other physical, economic, and emotional support throughout life.

and among ethnic or nationality groups in the United States, more distant family members also give each other support and help. The nature and amount of family and extended kin support varies considerably, but the family continues to perform the support function in many societies.

Regulation of Sexual Behavior. Marriage is often a way of controlling sexual behavior. Many societies have norms prohibiting sex before marriage, as well as having strong prohibitions against extramarital sex. In restricting sex to marriage, these norms regulate sexual behavior. However, in such societies the restrictions are often imposed on women more often than on men—again, an example of the double standard of sexual behavior. Furthermore, in chapter 7 we saw that, in the United States and many other societies, the norms prohibiting premarital sex, and even extramarital sex, are not very effective. Although marriage systems can be, and often are, strong regulators of sexual behavior, many exceptions also exist.

Social Placement. In many societies, the family is a mechanism for placing new members into the existing structure of the society. In rigidly stratified societies, the family into which one is born will determine for life one's place in the society's structure. Obviously, in more open societies, this social placement function of families is much

The nuclear family is defined as being made up of husband, wife, and children. However, many families do not conform to this ideal-type definition.

less determinant, but even when upward (or downward) mobility is possible, one still starts from the level of one's family of birth.

Reproduction, care and nurturance of children, provision of economic necessities, kin support, regulation of sexual behavior, and social placement, then, are the major functions of family systems; and although other functions have been identified, such as education, religious training, and recreation, they are much less widespread and significant. The family system of every society will carry out at least some of these tasks, and in many societies the family performs most of them.

Even though the same functions are performed by the family systems of many different societies, the actual family structure may vary greatly from one society to another. We will consider next some of the major differences in family types.

Two Basic Family Types

The simplest distinction of forms of the family differentiates between nuclear families and extended families.

Nuclear Family. When a family unit is made up of a husband, wife, and children living in the same house, it is called a **nuclear family.** The primary bond of loyalty in the nuclear family is between the husband and wife.[1]

Nuclear family
A family unit made up of a husband, wife, and children

[1] This description, and other family structures and norms, are *ideal types*. In chapter 4 an ideal type was described as a logical, exaggerated, and "pure" model of some phenomenon that one wishes to study or analyze. A nuclear family could still exist if a husband and father were living in another place (e.g., on military active duty).

Family of orientation The family into which a person is born that gives orientation (socialization)

Family of procreation The nuclear family that one creates by marrying and having children

Extended family A family of three or more generations living in the same household

Most people are members of two different nuclear families during their lifetimes. The nuclear family into which one is born is one's **family of orientation.** (This is the family that gives a person his or her orientation, or socialization.) The nuclear family that one creates by marrying and having children is one's **family of procreation.**

Extended Family. When a family unit is made up of three or more generations living in the same household or very close together, it is an **extended family.** An extended family thus includes first generation parents, their married sons or daughters, their spouses, and their children. Extended family units have a high degree of economic cooperation across all generations, and primary loyalty is usually given to the oldest generation.

Table 11–1 provides the names and descriptions for other major variations in family norms and structures.

The Family and Social Change

The preceding section and table 11–1 have shown that family systems can take many different forms, the norms that govern family relations can vary greatly, and the functions of the family differ from society to society, from one time to another. All of these facts indicate that the family is not a fixed and unchanging social arrangement, but that it can and does change. This statement raises the question about how and why the family changes from one time to another.

Because the family is widely accepted as a basic social institution of the society, it is often thought that the family shapes or influences the rest of the society. Although that can be true in some instances, it is usually the case that the alternative is true—the family as an institution is often shaped and changed by the rest of the institutions of the society. For this reason the family is appropriately called an *adaptive institution.* The family typically adapts, or makes adaptive changes, when some other part of the society changes.

The most familiar case of the family as an adaptive institution is found in the way the family adapts to changing economic conditions. History provides many examples: when economic times are bad—times of depression, for instance—families typically cut back on the number of children they have. In the United States, during the depression of the 1930s, Americans cut back on their childbearing, and this was before the time when contraception was easily and widely available. The birth rate was lower during that period, in part because Americans postponed marriage (an adaptation in itself), and if they were married, they had fewer children.

Ireland experienced a devastating famine in the middle of the nineteenth century (which killed more than a million of their 8 million people), and the people of Ireland thereafter completely reorganized their family system. Instead of allowing their children to marry early, as they had done before the famine, the Irish started using a system of inheritance and dowries that kept their children from marrying until they were quite

Table 11–1. Family Types

	Rules of Descent	
Matrilineal	**Patrilineal**	**Bilineal**
Descent comes from mother and her kin Inherits property from, and owes primary allegiance to, that family	Descent comes from father and his kin Inherits property from, and owes primary allegiance to, that family	Descent comes equally from mother's and father's family Allegiance is shared.
	Rules of Residence	
Matrilocal	**Patrilocal**	**Neolocal**
Newly married couples live with wife's family.	Newly married couples live with husband's family.	Newly married couples establish new, separate household.
	Authority	
Matriarchy	**Patriarchy**	**Egalitarian**
Authority held by oldest female, usually mother	Authority held by oldest male, usually father	Husbands and wives share authority equally
	Number of Marriage Mates	
Monogamy	**Polygamy**	
One partner at a time	Two or more partners (either husbands or wives) at a time	
	Polygyny	**Polyandry**
	A husband having more than one wife	A wife having more than one husband

old (men were often in their thirties or older). This new system also kept as many as a quarter of the Irish from marrying at all (Kammeyer, 1976).

These are but two examples of the way family systems adapt to changing external conditions. But the family also adapts to many political actions as well. Family systems are changed by immigration laws, tax laws, abortion laws, military conscription, social security systems, housing regulations, and many other government actions and policies. Overall, the family is an institution that is more apt to adapt to changes in other parts of society than it is to produce basic social changes.

Cross-Cultural Perspectives

Polyandry: A Rare Marriage Type

Polygyny and polyandry are forms of marriage that involve more than one mate. Polygyny—the practice of having more than one wife or female mate at one time—is very common in societies around the world. About 75 percent of all the societies that have been studied by anthropologists and sociologists allow polygyny. By contrast, polyandry—the practice of having more than one husband or male mate at one time—is very rare. Only about 1 percent of the world's societies have practiced polyandry.

The most fully documented polyandrous societies are the Toda (a non-Hindu tribe of India), the Marquesan Islanders in the South Pacific, and various groups in Tibet and the Himalayan region generally. The Nayar, whom we have already described, are also usually classified as polyandrous, because Nayar women typically had several lovers. These lovers, however, did not live in the woman's household, and this sets the Nayar apart from other polyandrous societies. These few examples of polyandry provide the bulk of the information we have about this unusual marriage form.

Often the polyandrous men who share wives are brothers. This was true of the Toda, where women understood that when they married a man they were also marrying his brothers. Even a brother who might be born after the marriage would be considered a woman's husband. Tibetan polyandry, also, is typically a case of two or more brothers married to the same woman. The Marquesan Islanders are an exception, however, since the co-husbands were apparently not brothers.

The ethnographic reports of polyandrous males insist that there is very little jealousy among husbands. Anthropologists were generally told that jealousy is a ridiculous idea, and that displays of jealousy would be socially disapproved. Of course, if a wife with two or more husbands became pregnant there would be no way of knowing who the biological father was. The people of polyandrous groups consider this a special advantage since every baby will have several fathers to give it special care and attention.

Often in areas where polyandry occurs, resources and land are limited. Polyandry may emerge in these places as a way of eking out a living from an inhospitable environment that requires the energies of several men to provide for one family unit. For example, in mountainous villages it can be advantageous if one husband cultivates the land, while another herds the sheep in a distant pasture. A third brother can gather wood, or cut grass for cattle food. Also, a wife in these places may be safer if at least one of her husbands is at home while others are away (Zorsa, 1982).

One other economic advantage of polyandry is that the small parcels of land owned by a family do not have to be divided up among their sons. When two or more sons marry one wife and live in the same household, the land can remain intact from one generation to the next.

In societies where polyandry exists, some families move toward group marriage (multiple husbands *and* wives). If, for example, the family's resources allow, the husbands of a woman may take a second wife. Since sexual relations may occur between any pair of wives and husbands, the result is group marriage.

The dark side of polyandry is that it is frequently associated with female infanticide. Since the ratio of males to females is normally equal, or nearly so, there will be too many females for a polyandrous marriage system to work. In order to create an imbalanced ratio that has two or three times more males than females, polyandrous societies are apt to let some female children die in infancy.

The best theoretical perspective on polyandry is provided by structural-functional theory. Polyandrous marriage patterns can be functional in an environment with limited land and scarce resources. Polyandry allows all men to have sexual access to a woman and to experience parenthood. At the same time, this practice keeps the society's birth rate in balance with its resources, the family's land remains intact, and cooperating husbands have an easier time of providing for the needs of a family. The females who reach adulthood are likely to have an easier life with multiple husbands; in one polyandrous village the people said they pitied any woman who had only one husband (Zorsa, 1982).

GOLDSTEIN, MELVYN. "Pahari and Tibetan Polyandry Revisited." *Ethnology* 17, 1978.
STEPHENS, WILLIAM N. *The Family in Cross-Cultural Perspective*. New York: Holt, Rinehart and Winston, 1963.
ZORZA, VICTOR. "When Brothers Share Wives, Age Counts." *The Washington Post*, May 2, 1982.

The Processes of Marriage and Family Life

To examine the marriage and family systems we can consider some typical processes that people experience as they enter marriage, have children, and, in many cases, divorce and remarry. We know that all people do not follow the same steps in the same order—some people have children before marriage, some married couples do not have children, spouses sometimes die at an early age, and not every married couple divorces. Nonetheless, a review of some of the typical processes, from courtship through remarriage, can reveal much about current-day marriage and family life.

Choosing Marriage Mates

In many countries of the world today, young people have almost complete responsibility for finding and selecting a mate for marriage. The United States is among the most prominent of these countries, and it has been so since the earliest days of the American experience. Even in colonial times Americans gave their children considerable freedom and autonomy in the selection of their marriage mates. Young people were allowed to spend time together in recreational settings where they could enjoy each other's company. Many European visitors in the eighteenth and nineteenth centuries believed that Americans, especially young women, were given far too much freedom.

Mate selection in the United States is based on romantic love, and it has been since colonial times. However, in most societies of the world, it is considered unwise to base the selection of a marriage mate on emotion.

The mate selection system in the United States has almost always been based on the idea of romantic love, or mutual attraction. The people of every society recognize that two people can develop an intense emotional attachment, but they often do not consider this emotion a sound basis for choosing a marriage mate. In fact, many societies regard it as foolish to select a mate on the basis of this heightened emotional state. Marriage is too important and serious an institution to be based on an emotion that will almost certainly diminish (Goode, 1959).

Nevertheless, the idea that romantic love should be a precondition of marriage did take root and thrive in the United States (Goode, 1959). It can be said that choosing one's marriage mate on the basis of attraction and love is consistent with the emphasis that early Americans placed on personal freedom and individual rights. The Declaration of Independence gave every individual the right to life, liberty, and the pursuit of happiness, a concept that was certainly consistent with choosing one's own marriage partner. Emphasizing romantic love as a basis for marriage gave participants great control over the selection of marriage mates in the past, just as it does today.

Arranged marriage
Parents select marriage partners for their children

In contrast, most societies have had, and many continue to have, arranged marriages. In **arranged marriages** the parents select marriage partners for their children. Often the young people scarcely know each other, and it is not assumed that they will love each other at the time of marriage. In arranged marriage systems it is hoped that a couple will develop an affectionate and warm relationship after they are married, and that they will continue to have pleasant companionship for life.

Many Islamic societies use systems of arranged marriages. In Iran, for example, the parents of a young man will interview the families of some potentially marriageable young women. They will inquire about the general characteristics of the family (their standing in the community, economic resources, educational attainments, occupational levels, etc.), and they will ask about the qualities of the marriageable daughter. The parents of the young man will then make a recommendation to their son, and in most cases he will follow their advice. In societies where arranged marriage is the custom, the young people often consider it a very difficult and imposing task to select a marriage partner. Young people in these societies will often say that they are too inexperienced to make this decision, and they would prefer to have their parents do so because they are wiser and more knowledgeable.

The Japanese have had a history of arranged marriages, but that history has also included marriages based on mutual attraction, or "love matches." Indeed, in preindustrial Japan (before 1870) the Japanese lived primarily in small rural villages where youth groups were formed that allowed teenaged boys and girls to spend time together. The youngsters would often spend nights together in the youth lodge, which produced many marriages based on mutual attraction and free choice. However, even though these were love matches, parents had to give final approval for the marriage (Hendry, 1985).

In some places in preindustrial Japan a form of premarital sex was also allowed. A young man would visit the home of a young woman at night. If the parents approved of him as a possible marriage partner, they would allow their daughter to sleep near the door so that she could receive his night visits. If the parents disapproved, or the daughter was not interested, the parents would hide her in an interior room of the house (Hendry, 1985).

Near the end of the nineteenth century the Japanese developed a strong negative reaction to love matches because they associated them with unwanted Western influences. They believed that love matches ignored the sacred responsibility that young people had to their families and their family homes. Love matches were associated with personal weakness and animal lust. During this period, the first half of the twentieth century, Japanese marriages were primarily arranged. After World War II love marriages re-emerged, and today many young Japanese enter marriages based on mutual attraction. However, that does not mean that arranged marriages have disappeared. Parents still arrange meetings for their children, but the first meeting is now often followed by a series of "dates," and if the match is not suitable, either party can terminate the relationship (Hendry, 1985).

"Joyce, I'm so madly in love with you I can't eat, I can't sleep, I can't live without you. But that's not why I called."

Social Influences on the Selection of Marriage Mates

Homogamy
Marriage between people with similar characteristics—religion, race, ethnicity, nationality, social class

Marriages in any society are likely to occur between two people with similar social characteristics. This pattern is called **homogamy**—marriage between people with similar characteristics—such as religion, race, ethnicity, nationality, and social class.

Marriages are apt to be homogamous, even in a society like the United States, where the selection of a mate is based on love and personal choice. Homogamous marriages are the result of many social influences on the selection of marriage partners. Parents today may not choose marriage mates for their children, but they do influence their children's choices—sometimes directly, sometimes subtly. Parents make inquiries about the dating partners and the opposite-sex friends of their children. They ask about the families they come from, and in particular they ask about religion, socioeconomic status, and perhaps about nationality and race. Through such questions parents find out if their children are likely to be interested in someone coming from different social, cultural, racial, or economic origins. If these possible marriage mates are viewed as too different, and thus unacceptable, parents will often discourage the continuation of the relationship.

When children are still living at home, parents often try to influence the selection of mates by placing their children in social settings where they are less likely to meet members of the opposite sex who are "different." By selecting homes in neighborhoods with certain preferred characteristics, parents can reduce the chances of their children meeting and ultimately wanting to marry someone of a different race, religion, ethnic group, or social class. Similarly, sending children to school, especially to college, may

One custom of the traditional Jewish wedding calls for the bride to walk around the groom several times. Religious traditions, along with many other factors, encourage *homogamy*, that is, marriage between people with similar characteristics.

be done with an eye to the kind of young people their children are likely to meet. Whether or not parents fully recognize the significance of their actions, moving to a "nicer" neighborhood and sending the children to a "better" school makes it more probable that the children will meet, fall in love with, and want to marry someone who will be more acceptable to the parents.

Religions and religious organizations also frequently try to influence mate selection. Young members of most religions are encouraged by religious leaders to marry within their faith. Religious organizations often have rules that prohibit marriage to someone out of the faith, or procedures that must be observed if such a marriage is proposed. The religion's rules may require the nonmember to convert or to take religious instruction or training before the marriage is allowed.

Some impersonal forces in the society also lead to marriages within racial, religious, nationality, and socioeconomic groups. Because of discrimination, unequal opportunities, and economic sorting, people of the same race, religion, nationality, and social class are likely to live in the same neighborhoods, go to the same schools, have the same kinds of jobs, and belong to the same organizations. People who do not come into contact with each other obviously will not marry one another.

Cohabitation as a Premarital Stage

Cohabitation
An unmarried couple living together

In contemporary American society, as well as many other societies, **cohabitation,** that is, unmarried couples living together, has emerged as an expected stage of premarried life. Yet, only two decades ago in the United States, cohabitation was relatively rare, and couples who did cohabit were engaging in behavior that was considered deviant. Often, cohabiting couples in the 1960s and earlier were people from the lower social strata of the society, or people who lived in some kind of Bohemian setting. In a fairly rapid transition, cohabitation became acceptable in the middle classes, and today cohabitation is found in every stratum of society.

In 1970, when the Census Bureau started collecting data on cohabiting couples in the United States, cohabiting households numbered slightly over a half-million. By the end of the 1980s there were over 2.2 million cohabiting couples (U.S. Bureau of the Census, 1987b). The greater social acceptance of cohabitation does not mean that everyone will cohabit or that every couple will live together prior to marriage. A recent survey of United States' young adults, aged 23–24, found that one-third of the women and men had experienced cohabitation by that age. Among those who were married by age 23½, one-third of the women and two-fifths of the men had cohabited first (Thornton, 1988).

A similar pattern has emerged in many other societies. For example, in Australia in 1982 about 17 percent of all single persons aged 25–44 were in cohabiting relationships. This figure is not directly comparable to the United States' figures above, but clearly, cohabitation is frequently found in Australia, just as it is in the United States (Khoo, 1987).

The most widespread pattern of cohabitation is found in the Scandinavian countries of Europe. In Sweden the cohabitation pattern has moved beyond being simply a premarital stage of life. Marriage rates have been going down rapidly in Sweden since the mid-1960s, and the reduced number of marriages is directly related to the increase in long-term cohabitation (Popenoe, 1987). For some, but not all, Swedes, cohabitation has become a substitute for marriage.

Almost all Swedes who do marry, cohabit first—estimates are variously placed at 98 or 99 percent. In Sweden today, becoming pregnant or having a child is no longer a reason for marriage. One Swedish couple described their "marital history" to a researcher in the following manner:

> They met in 1967, moved in together in 1969, exchanged rings in 1973 (this was around the time their first child was born and was for the purpose of "showing others that they were attached"), and married in 1977. When asked what anniversary they celebrated, they responded, "The day we met" (Popenoe, 1987, p. 176).

In contemporary Sweden the customs, rituals, and ceremonies connected with marriage, if there is a marriage, have diminished in significance. Marriage ceremonies in most societies have social significance because they signal to the community, and to other social groups, that a couple is establishing a new relationship. Yet in Sweden the ceremonies and rituals connected with marriage are decreasing in importance. ". . . Swedish young people today are merely drifting away from their families of orientation, usually in stages, and eventually settling down with someone else, all seemingly without any form of public or social recognition" (Popenoe, 1987, p. 176).

When individuals enter into marriage or cohabiting relationships, without the involvement of family members or other social groups, the sociological implications are considerable. The involvement of family and community members in any couple relationship, whether cohabitation or marriage, serves to keep the couple together. When relationships are formed on an individual basis, without the benefit of these social supports, they tend to break up more easily. Again, the case of Sweden is instructive, for even among cohabiting couples who have a child, the rate of breakup is three times as high as the rate for comparable married couples (Popenoe, 1987).

The Early Years of Marriage

A paradox of married life is that newly married couples often consider their first year or so together as the most difficult and yet the happiest. The early years of marriage can be difficult because of the adjustments that new husbands and wives have to make. When a person enters marriage with highly romantic or idealistic notions about married

Newly married couples often consider their first year of married life a difficult time, but it is also the time when they report the greatest satisfaction with their marital relationship.

life, the reality of living day to day with someone can be very upsetting. An interview study of working-class couples revealed that many men and women had unrealistic notions about married life (Rubin, 1976). One woman, a 30-year-old typist and mother of three, married for 11 years, said:

> When I got married, I suppose I must have loved him, but at the time, I was busy planning the wedding and I wasn't thinking about anything else. I was just thinking about this big white wedding and all the trimmings, and how I was going to be a beautiful bride, and how I would finally have my own house. I never thought about problems we might have or anything like that. I don't know even if I ever thought much about him. Oh, I wanted to make a nice home for Glen, but I wasn't thinking about how anybody did that or whether I loved him enough to live with him the rest of my life. I was too busy with my dreams and thinking about how they were finally coming true (Rubin, 1976, p. 69).[2]

When Rubin asked husbands about adjustments after marriage, one answered:

> Was there? Wow! Before I got married, I only had to do for myself. . . . Then, I suddenly found I had to worry about where we'd live and whether we had enough money, and all those things like that. Before, I could always get a job and make enough money to take care of me and give something to the house. Then, after we got married, I suddenly had all those responsibilities. Before, it didn't make a difference if I didn't feel like going to work sometimes. Then, all of a sudden, it made one hell of a difference because the rent might not get paid, or, if it got paid, there might not be enough food money (Rubin, 1976, p. 70).

---

[2] Excerpts from *Worlds of Pain: Life in the Working-Class Family* by Lillian Breslow Rubin. Copyright © 1976 by Lillian Breslow Rubin. Reprinted by permission of Basic Books, Inc., Publishers.

In addition to unrealistic and romantic expectations, some adjustment problems during the early years of marriage stem from the mismatched marital scripts of new husbands and wives.

Marital scripts
The expectations one has when entering marriage about what is proper and appropriate behavior

Marital Scripts. Anyone who enters marriage is going to have some expectations about what is proper and appropriate behavior for husbands and wives. These expectations, which are likely to be unconscious and unspoken, are called **marital scripts** (Broderick, 1989, 1979). During the early stages of marriage, husbands and wives may have arguments and hurt feelings because they have different (or conflicting) marital scripts. Family sociologist Carlfred Broderick, who developed the concept of the marital script, illustrates with a personal example how a married couple with mismatched scripts can experience disappointment and even anger over the resultant misunderstandings. Even though Broderick had known his wife since they were both in kindergarten and they had dated from the time they were in the tenth grade, he learned early in marriage that he and his wife had mismatched scripts regarding what happens when someone gets sick:

> Every right-thinking person knows what you should do when you get sick—you go to bed. That is your part. Then your mother, or whoever loves you, pumps you full of fruit juice.
>
> Well, I married this woman I had known all my life, and in the natural course of events I caught the flu. I knew what to do, of course. I went to bed and waited. But nothing happened. Nothing, I couldn't believe it!
>
> I was so hurt, I would have left if I hadn't been so ill. Finally, I asked about juice and she brought me some—in a little four-ounce glass. Period. Because, as I learned later,

When young people enter marriage, they often have expectations about what is proper and appropriate behavior for husbands and wives. These expectations, called *marital scripts,* can lead to problems in the early stage of a marriage if the scripts of wife and husband are mismatched.

> the only time they drank juice at her house was on alternate Tuesdays, when they graced breakfast with a drop in a thimble-size glass. My family's "juice glasses" held 12 ounces and there was always someone standing by to refill them.
>
> It does not matter that an issue may seem foolish to an outsider, or that it may be solved simply. The point is that mismatched scripts can so easily derail a young couple (Broderick, 1979, p. 154).

Marital scripts, as can be seen from the illustration above, often come from unique family background experiences. Before we marry, the marriage relationship we have observed most closely is usually that of our parents. Whether that marriage was harmonious and idyllic or quarrelsome and stormy, we are likely to have picked up some deep-seated notions about the nature of the husband/wife relationship and of family life in general.

Marital Quality

Marital quality Marital satisfaction or happiness, the degree to which a relationship is positive or satisfying

Marital quality is a general term referring to marital satisfaction or marital happiness, and is an indication of how positive and satisfying a marriage relationship is. Sociologists who study marital quality are likely to ask people to agree or disagree with statements such as: "We have a good marriage," "My marriage with my partner is very stable," or "Our marriage is strong" (Norton, 1983). Other more elaborate measures of marital quality inquire into the degree of consensus about important matters such as philosophy of life, work and careers, or recreational activities. Marital quality can also be ascertained by asking a couple about the amount of affection they display, or how frequently they express their love. Conversely, low marital quality can be identified by asking how frequently they have arguments and fights (Spanier, 1976).

Studies of marital quality have consistently shown that despite the adjustment problems of couples during the early years of marriage, they are likely to see their marriage relationship as good. Couples who are recently married and do not yet have children are especially satisfied with their married lives. Most studies of marital quality have shown that at no time after the first years of marital life do couples express a higher level of satisfaction with marriage (Anderson et al., 1983).

Parenthood and Marital Quality. A marriage changes when couples become parents. Couples with a new baby experience a number of problems that tend to reduce their level of marital satisfaction. A most important factor is that they simply have less time together than they did before the arrival of the baby (White et al., 1986). Most new parents express some surprise about the sheer level of physical demands. One mother wrote in her diary when her daughter was a month old, "A month is only four weeks . . . but it has been an eternity for me. I'm a zombie. Four weeks of night feedings and little sleep. I haven't read a paper. I barely have time to shower and wash my hair" (Lowenstein and Lowenstein, 1983, p. 18). Among most new parents the overwhelming responsibility for caring for their baby falls to the mother. Most studies show that fathers carry less than 20 percent of the load in the routine tasks of infant care.

Naturally, if a new mother is too busy to take a shower and is not getting much sleep, a great many other aspects of married life are also being sacrificed, including a reduction in sexual activity because of decreased opportunities or fatigue (Sollie and Miller, 1980; LaRossa, 1983).

Married couples who have children when they are young and very shortly after they are married are particularly apt to experience feelings of dissatisfaction. A 28-year-old woman with three children describes her feelings:

> One day I woke up and there I was, married and with a baby. And I thought, "I can't stand it! I can't stand to have my life over when I'm so young" (Rubin, 1976, p. 81).

A husband describes how his wife's pregnancy and the baby made him feel resentful and jealous:

> When we were first married, I'd come home from work and she'd be kind of dressed up and fixed up, you know, looking pretty for me. Then she kept getting bigger and bigger, and she'd be tired and complaining all the time. I could hardly wait for her to finish being pregnant. And when that was over, she was too busy and too tired to pay me any mind.
>
> I used to get mad and holler a lot. Or else I'd stay out late at night and get her worried about what I was doing. We had nothing but fights in those days because all she wanted to do was to take care of the baby, and she never had any time for me. It sounds dumb when I talk about it now—a man being jealous of a little kid, but I guess I was (Rubin, 1976, p. 82).

Marital Quality through the Later Stages of Marriage. Marital quality generally continues to decline after the first years of parenthood, especially after children reach school age (Anderson et al., 1983; Rollins and Galligan, 1978). The negative effects of children are especially severe for lower-socioeconomic-status women who are employed (Schumm and Bugaighis, 1986). When children reach adolescence, the relationships they have with their parents are related to the marital relationship between their parents. Mothers who report having difficulties with their oldest daughters, and fathers who report difficulties with their oldest sons, are both more likely to be less satisfied with their marriages than parents who have fewer problems with their children (Steinberg and Silverberg, 1987). Many different studies show consistent evidence that children put a strain on parents and make their marital relationships less satisfying. Supporting evidence comes from the fact that children (along with money) are what husbands and wives argue and fight about most (Scanzoni and Scanzoni, 1981; Straus et al., 1980).

Among older married couples, some studies show that marital quality is somewhat higher than couples who are in the middle years of life. However, this result may in part reflect the breakup of the worst marriages, ones that did not survive the stresses and conflicts of earlier years. Thus the marriages that last over many years are somewhat different from the average marriage, since the poorer quality marriages have been removed from the total. The other possibility is that marriage relationships improve after children have grown up and are on their own. However, one study of long-term married couples has shown that the negative effects of having children extends into the later years of married life. If older married couples (over 55 years) still have children living at home, both husbands and wives are less satisfied with the marriage relationship. But, among the husbands, the negative effects of having had children were still in evidence, even if the children have left home. This study seems to show that the strains of raising children

"Janet, we have to stop meeting like this. It has become a source of increasing friction in my marriage to Elizabeth."

produce a negative effect on the quality of marriage, and this effect extends into the later years of life (Lee, 1988).

Only a few studies have followed the same couples over many years of marriage. One early study of long-term marriages painted a gloomy picture, describing "disenchantment in the later years of marriage" (Pineo, 1961). However, a recent study of 17 couples who had been married for 50 years offered a more encouraging picture. This study confirmed what others have shown, that marital *problems* decrease in long-term marriages. But this study, contrary to some others, also found that love and affection increased in the later years of many long-term marriages (Weishaus and Field, 1988).

Power as a Dimension of Husband and Wife Relations

Power is the ability to impose one's will upon someone else, and the exercise of power is found in the family just as it is in other social groups. In family decision-making, power is partly a function of traditional male and female roles. In chapter 10 we discussed the way women, especially married women, have traditionally been expected to play a subordinate role to men. When married couples accept the traditional gender-role prescription of the wife as a subordinate to her husband, then she clearly has less power than her husband. Most couples today claim to hold an egalitarian view of marriage; they emphasize that family decisions are made jointly and that neither husband nor wife has greater power. Despite these egalitarian ideals, however, other factors influence the exercise of power in marriages, and these factors also tend to give greater power to husbands.

One important theoretical formulation about family power, called **resource theory,** explains the distribution of power in terms of the resources brought into the marriage

Resource theory
In a marriage, power based on resources such as income, education, and occupation

by each of the spouses (Blood and Wolfe, 1960). Resources include income-earning ability, education, and occupational prestige, which are all closely tied to the economic world outside the home, where men have a distinct advantage over women. Of course, there may also be noneconomic resources, such as companionship, emotional support, and social skills—attributes that have been more closely associated with women (Safilios-Rothschild, 1970).

Although noneconomic resources may give some advantage to women, the fact is that in American society greater weight is given to money, status, and occupational prestige. These latter characteristics are exactly what gives husbands in most marriages a distinct advantage over their wives. The larger society, in which all marriages are embedded, gives men distinct advantages in money earnings and occupational status and prestige (Szinovacz, 1987).

Research over the last 25 years on the power relations between husbands and wives has continued to show that husbands have greater power in marriages than their wives (Allen, 1984; Olsen and Cromwell, 1975; Scanzoni, 1979; Szinovacz, 1987). Despite the fact that many husbands and wives seek an egalitarian ideal, they do not always achieve it. In the next section we will see one major manifestation of the continuing marital power of males: despite ever-greater participation of married women in the labor force, they continue to do the greatest proportion of family work, such as cooking, cleaning, and child care.

The Family and Employment

A very important feature of marriage and family life today is the relationship between family and employment. There was a time, not many years ago, when the family and employment were viewed as two separate worlds. That may always have been a myth, but today, in a very real sense, the worlds of family and employment are closely linked.

Prior to the industrial revolution, work and family were closely tied together. In the United States when the economy was largely agricultural and other industries were at the craft level (shoemaking and tailoring, for example), almost all work was done by family units. However, when industries became mechanized and powered by water, coal, and steam, the places of employment moved out of the home. Men went out into the work world—factories and offices—and the concept of the breadwinner emerged. At the same time, women, especially in the middle and upper classes, remained in the home. This situation led to the glorification of women as homemakers, and the breadwinner/homemaker division of labor came into being. In the United States the transition to the breadwinner/homemaker system reached its peak at the beginning of the twentieth century. At that time only about 5 percent of married women were employed outside the home (Davis, 1984).

The nineteenth century movement that separated women from the workplace and kept them in the home as homemakers was supported by a new set of cultural values about women, motherhood, and the home. Historians have called this new cultural image the "cult of true womanhood" (Lerner, 1969; Welter, 1966). This image stressed that women had a moral duty and responsibility to remain in the home and care for

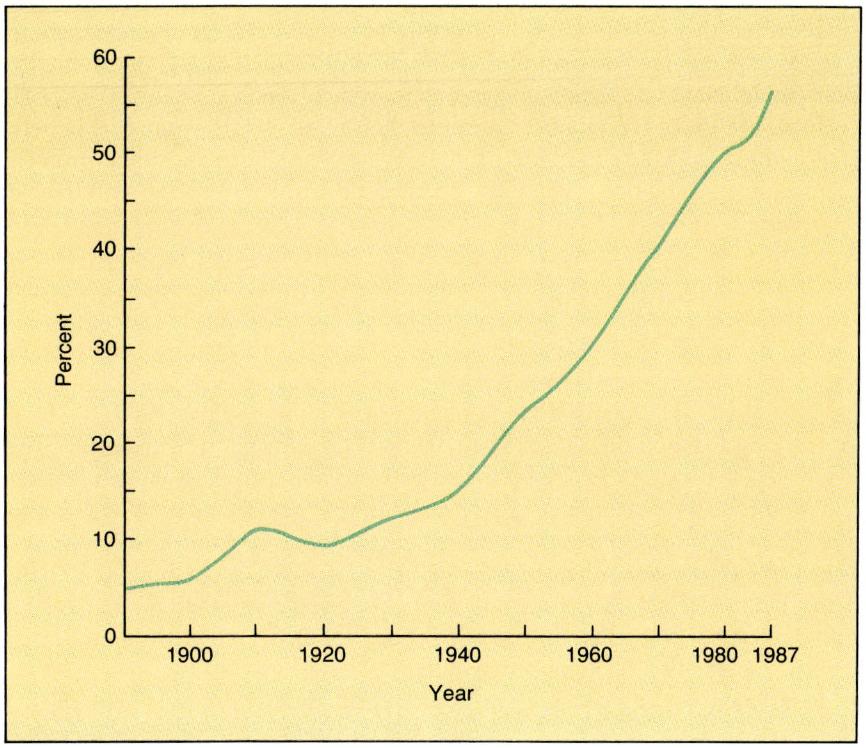

Figure 11–1. Percent of All Married Women Who Are in the Labor Force, 1890–1987. (*Source:* U.S. Bureau of the Census, 1987b.)

their families. The "natural" place for women was the home where they could attend to the physical and moral development of their children and give comfort to their husbands, who were facing the cruel and difficult outside world of work (Piotrkowski et al., 1987).

During the twentieth century the ideal of the breadwinner/homemaker system has remained firmly embedded in American culture, but at the same time an objective reality emerged that deviated from it. The percentage of married women in the labor force started going up at the beginning of the century and continued to increase through each decade up to the present time (see figure 11–1).

At the present time only a minority of married women conform to the homemaker ideal because most are employed in the labor force. In 1987, 56.8 percent of married women with children under six were employed outside the home; more than 70 percent of married women with children between 6 and 17 years were employed. Over 70 percent of divorced women with children (both below 6 years, and from 6 to 17) were also employed (U.S. Bureau of the Census, 1987b).

Even though only a small percentage of American mothers is remaining at home as full-time homemakers, the role expectations embedded in the cultural ideal have not disappeared. Mothers rather than fathers are still expected to take primary responsibility for tasks related to children. Women also are expected to do much of the family work, such as cooking and cleaning (Piotrkowski et al., 1987; Spitze, 1988).

The expectation that women are still primarily responsible for family work is borne out by the research evidence. For example, both men and women today report conflicts between their employment and family obligations; however, men experience the conflict as resulting from the excessive number of hours they work, while women experience the conflict as coming from scheduling difficulties. For women, the scheduling problems reflect their dual responsibilities: their jobs, on the one hand; home and children, on the other (Voydanoff, 1988).

With regard to housework, many studies have been conducted in recent years to see if husbands are taking a larger share of family work. The most consistent conclusion is that women, regardless of whether they are employed, are still doing the great majority of family work. However, after years of finding few significant changes in husbands' contributions, there are indications that husbands are increasing their contributions to family work by a small amount. One study of time use among adults, aged 25–45, in both the United Kingdom and the United States, shows some increases by males. Between the mid-seventies and mid-eighties, slight increases were noted in both the amount and proportion of domestic work (cooking, cleaning, laundry) done by men. Women in the United States are still doing about three times as much domestic work as men, but this represents less of an imbalance than existed in previous decades. In both the United States and the United Kingdom, women have decreased the number of minutes per week they do domestic work, while men in both countries have increased their domestic work somewhat (Gershuny and Robinson, 1988).

Even when men do somewhat more housework, they often see themselves as "helping their wives" do *their* work. Husbands still see household work as "feminine home chores" (Barnett and Baruch, 1987).

Mismatched Work Schedules

When both husbands and wives are working, there is a fairly good chance that their work schedules will not be the same. Only 8½ percent of all working couples have perfectly matched schedules, which leaves over 90 percent with mismatched schedules. A substantial minority of working couples have extremely mismatched schedules because one is working during a "normal" work day, while the other is working **shift work.** Shift work, done at night or on an irregular schedule, is especially characteristic of many service occupations. Frequently, these are occupations filled primarily by women—nurses, waitresses, sales workers, and telephone operators (Presser, 1988).

Shift work
Work done at night or on an irregular schedule

Many couples with children may be making the choice to work at different times of the day so that one of the two parents will be available at all times to care for the children. This work arrangement eliminates taking the children to a babysitter or leaving them with a child-care service. Although there may be child-care advantages when the husband and wife work at different times, serious disadvantages may arise with respect to the marital relationship. One study has shown that 11 percent of employed couples have work schedules that may give them as little as an hour together between the time one spouse returns home and the other leaves for work. In some cases one spouse must leave for work before the other returns home (Nock and Kingston, 1984). When married couples are limited in the amount of time they have together, fewer opportunities are available for resolving problems, for intimacy, and for sexual relations (Piotrkowski and Gornick, 1986; Piotrkowski, 1987).

Conflict and Violence in the Family

The mass media have made most Americans aware of "abused children" and "battered wives." It is now well known that violence occurs in families, although some confusion might still remain about its nature and frequency. Sociologists started examining the nature and extent of family violence in the 1970s, and as a result of their research, we now have a clearer and fuller understanding of this important social problem (Gelles, 1987; Steinmetz, 1987).

One misconception about family violence is that it is associated only with pathological or "sick" individuals. The most extreme and bizarre cases, often leading to serious injury and even death, are most widely reported; and on the basis of these cases, many people conclude that violence is the product of a mentally ill person. However, sociological studies have shown that violence is widely condoned as an acceptable way to deal with family problems, and is used frequently in "normal" or "average" families.

Many Americans accept the idea that it is legitimate to hit family members—under some circumstances. Marital partners, for example, often justify hitting a spouse, or being hit by a spouse, for one of two basic reasons: (1) the spouse is doing (or has done) something wrong in the eyes of the aggressor; or (2) the spouse "won't listen to reason" (Straus, 1980, p. 693). Both of these justifications can be found in interviews with a young married couple named Jennifer and Joe (LaRossa, 1980). Jennifer described herself as a strong-willed person who had been independent for much of her life and wanted to "run things" in her marriage. Her husband concurred in this evaluation, but he had opposing ideas about who should dominate the marriage. When the interviewer asked if Jennifer still wanted to run things, the following interchange occurred:

> INTERVIEWER: Do you think you run things now?
> JENNIFER: No, I tried, though!
> JOE: She tries. One day we had a conflict and she more or less tried to run me and I told her no, and she got hysterical and said, "I could kill you!" And I got rather angry and slapped her in the face three or four times and I said, "Don't you ever say that to me again." And we haven't had any problems since (LaRossa, 1980, p. 160).

Joe analyzed his use of violence in the following way:

> You don't use it until you are forced to. At that point I felt I had to do something physical to stop the bad progression of events. I took my chances with that and it worked (LaRossa, 1980, p. 160).

Later in the interview, Jennifer said:

> Joe doesn't usually use force. That was the first and last time he'll ever do that. It was my fault. I was trying to dominate him, that's for sure (LaRossa, 1980, p. 161).

Joe, in this case, justified his use of violence by implying that Jennifer had gone too far in trying to dominate him. But, in addition, by saying that she was "hysterical," he was justifying what he had done on the grounds that she was beyond reason. For her part, Jennifer made it clear that it would be the last time he would hit her, but then she immediately added that it was her fault.

The case of Jennifer and Joe reveals that both the victim and the aggressor accepted violence under some circumstances. In this regard they are not unlike many other married couples. In a national sample of married couples, approximately one out of three husbands and one out of four wives agreed that it was at least "somewhat necessary," "somewhat normal," or "somewhat good" for couples to "slap each other around" (Straus et al., 1980, p. 47).

One of the most encouraging results coming from these studies is that family violence may have declined since 1975. Two national surveys, conducted ten years apart—the first in 1975, the second in 1985—allow comparisons to be made over that period of time. In these surveys, violence was measured by asking interviewees to think of situations in the last year when they had had a disagreement or were angry with a specified member of the family (e.g., wives might be asked about husbands). Interviewees were then asked if they had engaged in certain acts in that situation; these acts included throwing something at the other person, pushing, grabbing, shoving, slapping, spanking, kicking, biting, hitting with a fist, hitting with something else, beating, threatening with a knife or gun, and using a knife or gun (Straus and Gelles, 1986).

Between 1975 and 1985 *severe* violence (kicking, biting, hitting with fist, and more extreme) by husbands against wives declined from 38 cases per 1,000 to 30 cases per 1,000. As the researchers point out, this reduction may seem small, but when thought of in terms of the total number of United States' couples, this difference could result in 432,000 fewer beaten wives.

These changes at least give some hope that there has been a reduction of violence in the family, perhaps produced in part by women having more options (shelters, support groups), greater police and law enforcement support, and a recognition on the part of males that they cannot use physical violence. It is possible that the reductions in violence, as reported in the national survey, may simply reflect people's greater reluctance to report violent acts to interviewers. While that may be, the researchers take some hope even from this possibility, arguing that the reluctance may reflect a change in public attitudes and may indicate new standards regarding the acceptability of violence in the family (Steinmetz, 1987; Straus and Gelles, 1986).

The 1985 study of family violence shows, as other studies have shown, that wives commit violent acts against their husbands at the same rate that husbands do against wives. This controversial finding must be assessed carefully so that its meaning and consequences are not misinterpreted or overstated. It is far less likely that a wife will severely beat her husband than vice versa. Males are bigger and stronger, and their blows do much more damage than those of females. Often wives are striking back after being hit or they are defending themselves (Saunders, 1986). Even when women are the aggressors (i.e., commit the first act of violence), husbands often respond with more violent acts and are apt to strike the most damaging blows.

Child Abuse and Maltreatment

Before 1960 public awareness of child abuse was low; that does not mean, however, that children were not abused in earlier times, for child abuse has a long and terrible history. One historian has said: ". . . the history of childhood is a nightmare from which we have only recently begun to awaken. The further back in history one goes, the lower the level of childcare, and the more likely children are to be killed, abandoned, beaten, terrorized, and sexually abused" (deMause, 1974, p. 1).

The life of Hedda Nussbaum shocked the nation when the man with whom she had cohabited was convicted of manslaughter in the death of their adopted daughter. Nussbaum's face also bears the marks of years of physical abuse by this man.

Today, child abuse is recognized as being much more widespread than just occasional sensational stories of severe abuse. Child abuse is now understood as covering a range of behaviors, including physical abuse, sexual abuse, and physical neglect. Emotional abuse, which is much more difficult to define and detect, is also recognized for the harm it can do to children. However, even with this increase in public awareness, parents commit a variety of physical and verbal actions against their children in the name of discipline and normal punishment.

In the 1940s Hollywood actress Joan Crawford reared her two children in a severe manner because she believed that, in this way, they would learn how to work and behave properly. When her daughter, as an adult, published an autobiographical account of the way she and her brother had been treated as children, many readers concluded that the children had been mistreated and abused (Crawford, 1978). And yet, it seems that Miss Crawford's colleagues, friends, and visitors saw her only as a strict and demanding mother whose children always behaved perfectly. Even today, some people might discount the daughter's account as exaggerated and, in any case, give the benefit of the doubt to the parent.

The abuse and mistreatment of children in the family has been called a hidden problem because the public generally accepts that parents may use physical methods to punish children. Corporal punishment is defined as an act intended to inflict physical pain on a person. Exactly when this physical pain is excessive is difficult to ascertain. In the range of physical punishments, American legal and informal norms allow parents to spank and slap a child, or to hit a child with an instrument such as a stick, hair brush, or belt. In the 1985 survey of adult Americans, the rate of slapping or spanking children between 3 and 17 was over 549 per 1,000 children. Thus, in any year the likelihood of a parent's hitting a child is more than 50 percent. The rate of hitting or trying to hit a child with some object was 97 per 1,000—one in ten. The rate for very severe violent acts against children, including kicking, hitting with a fist, beating up, or using a knife or gun in some way, was 19 per 1,000. It must be remembered that these figures come from the admissions of parents during telephone interviews, and may therefore understate the extent of violence toward children. However, again, some encouragement may be found in the declining rate between 1975 and 1985 of very severe violence against children. During these years, the rate of very severe violence against children declined 47 percent (Straus and Gelles, 1986).

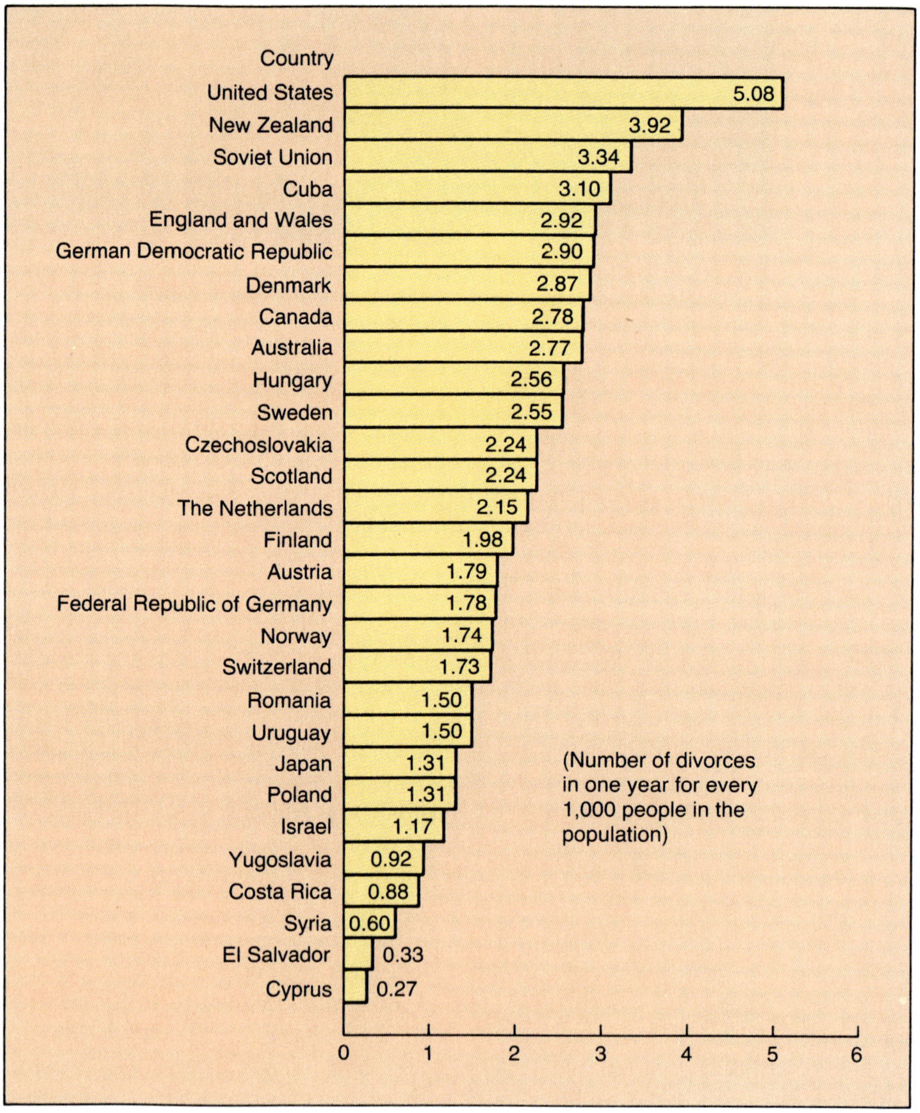

Figure 11–2. Divorce Rates in Selected Countries. (*Source:* United Nations, *Demographic Yearbook: Special Topic Marriage and Divorce Statistics,* 1984.)

Studies of family violence have shown consistently that families have a cycle of violence—violence in one generation is continued in the following generation. When children are treated with violence, they are more apt to become adults who see violence as a way of solving their problems. As adults they are more likely to hit their spouses and their own children. And in a final irony, children who have been struck by their parents are more likely to strike these same parents when they reach old age. Because of the cyclical nature of family violence, the family provides the training ground for violence (Steinmetz, 1987).

Separation and Divorce

Any discussion of contemporary marriage and family life must consider the issue of divorce. The divorce rate in the United States is higher than any other country for which there are acceptable data. New Zealand and the Soviet Union are the next highest—see figure 11–2 for the ranking of selected countries (Reiss and Lee, 1988).

For the United States, statistical projections lead some researchers to conclude that nearly 50 percent of all marriages started in the 1970s could end in divorce (Weed, 1980). An even more extreme conclusion has been reached about marriages started in the 1980s, by two researchers who have concluded that nearly two-thirds of these recent marriages will be disrupted, by *either* separation or divorce[3] (Martin and Bumpass, 1989). This conclusion does not mean that two-thirds of these marriages *will* end in divorce. The researchers have simply projected this outcome because of the amount of separation and divorce that has already occurred in the first years of the early 1980s' marriages. Thus far, the disruption of these marriages seems to be outpacing that of 1970s' marriages, and thus could lead to the very high projected level of marital disruption. One must be very cautious, however, about projecting a number of years into the future because unanticipated events may make these projections invalid. It will be many years before we actually know how many of the marriages of the early 1980s will be disrupted by divorce.

The most realistic way to evaluate trends in divorce is to look at divorce rates, not the projected percentages of marriages that might end in divorce. A useful divorce rate can be obtained by determining the number of divorces in any year per 1,000 marriages existing in the population. It is best to relate divorces to existing marriages because any marriage in the population is "at risk" for a divorce. For the United States this divorce rate is shown in figure 11–3, which covers the years 1925 to the present.

Divorce Rate Trends in the United States

During the twentieth century the overall trend in divorce has obviously been upward, although there have been some notable ups and downs in the divorce rate.

One obvious pattern in figure 11–3 is the high peak of divorce in the middle 1940s. This peak corresponds with the end of World War II and probably reflects the

[3] This study is different from most studies attempting to determine the chances of divorce because it is based on a national sample of the U.S. population (Current Population Survey) rather than divorce statistics from the states. It is also unusual because separation is counted as a marital disruption, the same as an actual divorce.

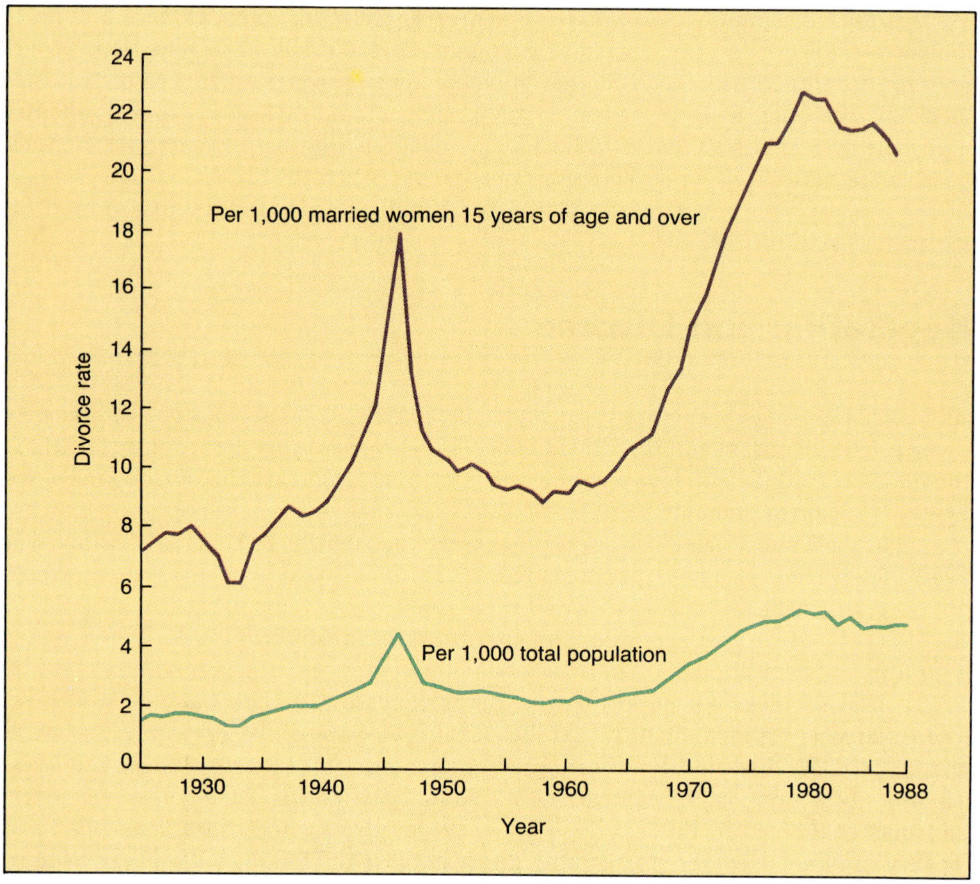

Figure 11–3. Divorce Rates for the United States, 1925–1988. (*Sources:* National Center for Health Statistics, 1981. "Advance Report on Final Divorce Statistics, 1981." National Center for Health Statistics, 1985. "Births, Marriages, Divorces and Deaths for 1981." National Center for Health Statistics, "Advance Report, Final Divorce Statistics, 1986. Vol. 38, Hyattsville, Md.: Public Health Service, 1989. The 1987 rate per 1,000 married women was calculated by the authors from provisional data provided by the National Center for Health Statistics.)

way in which marriages were affected by couples being apart. The instability of marriages that were entered into hastily during the war is undoubtedly a factor here as well.

However, an even more dramatic increase in the divorce rate started in the 1960s and continued through most of the 1970s. During these two decades the divorce rate of the United States more than doubled. Several societal-level explanations for this rapid increase are possible. Since wars have sometimes been associated with increases in divorce, some sociologists have suggested that the Vietnam War might have been a contributing factor (Glick and Lin, 1986). However, that war could not account for the entire period of 20 years since its societal impact was limited to the late sixties and early seventies. Also the proportion of the young population in the military was much smaller than in previous wars. Furthermore, a similar twentieth century war—the Korean conflict—was associated with a *decline* in the divorce rate (South, 1985).

More frequently, explanations for the rising divorce rate of the 1960s and 1970s have centered around the major cultural and societal changes of that period. One notable change was the rise of the women's movement, or feminism, which emphasized, among other things, that women should have equal opportunities for self-realization and personal development. During this period women moved into education and the labor force in greater numbers than ever before, which may have had the effect of freeing them from marriages that were less than satisfactory. Of course, a general liberalization of social and sexual norms also took place during this time that may have freed many married people, both men and women, from traditional constraints and obligations (Raschke, 1987).

Although the United States' divorce rate is still at a high level, it has stabilized and even declined slightly during the 1980s. Some plausible explanations have been offered as to why the divorce rate is no longer climbing (Kammeyer, 1981). One factor may be that the average age of marriage in the United States has been increasing for some years. Viewed in another way, marriages among 18-year-old and 19-year-old women have sharply declined. The marriage rate for women in this age group in 1984 was only 35 percent of what it was in 1960. All available evidence points to the fact that when one marries early, especially in the teenage years, the chance of divorce is much higher (Booth and Edwards, 1985; Glenn and Supancic, 1984). Even during the 1980s, when the divorce rate for all other age groups was going down, the divorce rate among married women under 20 was *still increasing* (Glick and Lin, 1986).

A closely related factor that may account for the slight decline in the divorce rate during the 1980s is the reduction in marriages precipitated by premarital pregnancies. Some studies have shown that premarital pregnancy is related to higher divorce rates (Furstenberg, 1976, 1979a), while other studies have found that only premarital childbearing is related to higher divorce rates (Billy et al., 1986; Teachman, 1983).

Several reasons exist as to why premarital pregnancies and premarital childbearing are not leading to marriages as often as they did in the past. First, although higher percentages of unmarried young people are having sexual intercourse at earlier ages, they are more likely to use contraception than they did in the early 1970s (Zelnik and Kantner, 1980). Second, even when premarital pregnancies do occur, they do not lead to marriage as often as they would have in previous decades. Apparently less stigma is attached to an unmarried woman's having and raising a baby, so there is less pressure for some women to marry. But the more important reason that premarital pregnancy is not leading to marriage is the availability of legal abortion. As we noted in chapter 7, 60 percent of unmarried teenagers who become pregnant have abortions (U.S. Bureau of the Census, 1987). Without abortion, some of these pregnancies would have led to teenage (pregnancy-prompted) marriages, which, as we have noted, have a higher chance of divorce.

Another factor that may be contributing to a decline in the divorce rate is that, for women, the economic consequences of divorce are often severe (Weitzman, 1985). Although men fare quite well economically after divorce, women have substantial declines in their levels of living. Weitzman concluded that divorced women had a 73 percent decline in their standard of living approximately one year after divorce. A reanalysis of her data indicates that the lowered level in income for divorced women may not have been quite as severe—perhaps only a decline of one-third—but the decline is still substantial (Hoffman and Duncan, 1988). Furthermore, when divorce occurs in families where the pre-divorce income is over $40,000, even the reanalysis of Weitzman's data shows declines of over 50 percent. If women can foresee that divorce will lead to substantial declines in level of living, they may choose to remain in less-than-satisfactory marriages. Effectively, then, the divorce rate would be somewhat reduced.

The combined influence of all these factors could produce stability or even a further decline in divorce in the future. And yet, as we noted earlier, early 1980s' marriages have a high level of marital disruption (Martin and Bumpass, 1989). The actual rate of divorce during the 1990s will be the only certain way of determining whether contemporary marriages are more or less stable than they were when the divorce rate was at its peak in 1979.

The Separation and Divorce Experience

Separation and divorce are almost always stressful and disruptive events in people's lives. Even though both parties may agree that divorce is the correct course of action for them, it is nonetheless a wrenching personal experience. Divorce, by all accounts, is a confusing tangle of emotional experiences, uncertain decisions, and difficult actions.

In an attempt to sort out some of the complexities of the experience, Bohannan (1970) has identified six different "stations" of divorce. These are:

1. Emotional divorce—the recognition that the emotional relationship with one's spouse is deteriorating and the marriage is ending.
2. Legal divorce—the process of learning and going through the legal and procedural steps required by the state.
3. Co-parental divorce—the determination of the custody of children, visitation rights, and child support.
4. Economic divorce—the division of money and property, and the establishment of levels of economic support (alimony).
5. Community divorce—the changes necessary, because of the divorce, in relating to friends, relatives, and associates.
6. Psychic divorce—the process of regaining an individual identity and autonomy.

The emotional divorce, which is when individuals conclude that their marriage may actually end and they begin to act on that conclusion, is the most stressful stage of the divorce process. A divorce means the end of a relationship that one has entered into with the expectation that it will last a lifetime. Divorce means a refutation of one's earlier decision, which makes it very hard for most married people, even when the marriage has been unhappy.

The legal divorce has changed greatly since 1970 because since that time almost every state has adopted some form of "no-fault" divorce. When no-fault divorce is possible—or required, as it is in some states—an adversary divorce procedure, in which one spouse charges the other with some wrongdoing (adultery, cruelty, mental cruelty, and others), is no longer necessary. Today couples can usually get a divorce by claiming irreconcilable differences, irretrievable breakdown, or incompatibility. Although divorce is easier to obtain than it was previously, no evidence supports the claim that liberalized divorce laws have been the cause of increasing divorce rates. Evidence does show that the change to no-fault divorce laws has had the positive effect of reducing the legal wrangling and rancor so often found in adversary divorce cases (Bahr, 1983; Raschke, 1987; Weitzman, 1985).

The economic divorce has also changed in recent years. As we noted above, women today fare much worse after divorce than men, for several reasons. If minor children are involved, wives receive custody in about 90 percent of the cases. There are clear economic costs to having children, including the additional costs for food, clothing, and shelter. Child support from fathers is almost always inadequate and frequently not received. Alimony or economic maintenance is rarely awarded to wives today after a divorce. Community property laws often require the sale of a couple's major asset, their home. When the proceeds from the home are divided, husbands, with their typically greater earning power, can usually repurchase a home of comparable value; wives frequently cannot (Weitzman, 1985).

The community divorce is a reversal of the community aspects of marriage. When two people marry, they make a public (community) commitment through the wedding announcement and ceremony. Although norms and rituals exist for most other transitions in marriage and family life, there are no similar rituals for the end of marriage. The announcement of a separation or divorce is typically awkward for the person who makes it and the person who hears it. The confusion is reflected in the words of one man, who responded to the news of his associate's separation by asking: "Do I feel sorry for you or congratulate you?" (Bohannan, 1970).

The psychic divorce is almost always the last stage of a divorce. The process of adjustment that comes after the divorce itself involves the dual tasks of establishing a new life and a new personal identity. This process is often very difficult, especially for people who have been married for a long time. Not atypical is the statement of a woman who is about 35 years old:

> I feel this total lack of any direction. You know, I'm flailing around, "What am I going to do? What am I going to be when I grow up?" You know, one would like to know before one got one foot in the grave (Weiss, 1975, p. 69).

The Effects of Divorce on Children

Because a million children a year in the United States have parents who divorce, there is widespread concern about how the divorce affects these children psychologically, educationally, and socially. The research on this matter has demonstrated what is generally expected. When parents are in the process of separating, a great deal of stress falls on the children except, of course, if they are infants (Hetherington et al., 1978; Longfellow, 1979; Wallerstein and Kelly, 1975, 1976).

Children who are in the later preschool years, between the ages of three and one-half and six, often respond egocentrically about the separation and may blame themselves for what has happened. A child of this age might say, "Daddy left home because I was a bad boy—I didn't put away my toys that day" (Longfellow, 1979, p. 300). Children of school age, especially between 6 and 12, have a wide range of emotional responses to divorcing parents, but they commonly cover up their fears and negative feelings. Eventually, however, anger, fear, loss of identity, and loneliness are likely to emerge (Wallerstein and Kelly, 1976).

Children who are teenagers or older when their parents divorce also have feelings of anger, sadness, and a sense of loss or betrayal. However, at these ages they can also be more detached and analytical about their parents and their relationships with them (Longfellow, 1979).

Many studies have been conducted on the long-range effects of divorce on children, but the results are mixed. A recent study compared third and fourth grade children whose families had *recently been disrupted* with children in situations where disruption had occurred earlier, and with children in intact families. The children who had recently experienced family disruption showed somewhat lower academic achievement and performance than the other two categories of children (Kinard and Reinherz, 1986). A study of 12-year-old to 16-year-old children found more behavioral problems among the youngsters whose families had been disrupted (Peterson and Zill, 1986). Evidence also shows that in adulthood the children of divorced parents (especially females) are somewhat more likely to divorce than the children of parents who did not divorce (Glenn and Kramer, 1987; Keith and Finlay, 1988). Although all of these results are negative for the children of divorce, their severity and depth should not be overstated. Most children of divorce do not show serious long-run impairments, either psychological or social (Kulka and Weingarten, 1979; Kurdek et al., 1981; Raschke, 1987).

Although the effect of divorce on children is complex, widespread agreement exists that conflict between parents during separation and divorce is likely to have negative impacts on children. But parents who remain married and have high levels of conflict are also apt to affect their children adversely. Finally, when divorced husbands and wives continue to have conflicts after divorce, their children will suffer (Demo and Acock, 1988).

Family Relations after Divorce

Binuclear family
Family system made up of the two households of divorced parents

Divorced parents with minor children usually continue to have regular contact. Children often live primarily with the parent who has custody, but they may often be spending some time in the home of the noncustodial parent as well. The concept of the **binuclear family** describes a family system made up of the two households of divorced parents, in which minor children move from one parent's home to the other (Ahrons, 1981). This family system requires a considerable amount of coordination and cooperation between divorced spouses. When the relationship between them is relatively friendly (or not hostile), the task of coordinating activities that involve the children can usually be handled with minimal problems. However, if divorced spouses have unresolved conflicts, a high likelihood exists that children will be used as a way of hurting or gaining advantage over the former spouse (Ahrons and Rodgers, 1987; Weiss, 1979).

Remarriage

Remarried couple household
A household in which one or both of spouses have been previously married

Blended, or reconstituted family
A family into which one or both spouses brings children of previous marriages

About five out of six men and three out of four women remarry after divorce (Glick and Lin, 1986; Thornton and Freedman, 1983). These high rates of remarriage have led to large numbers of remarried couple households. A **remarried couple household** is a household maintained by a married couple, one or both of whom have been previously married (Cherlin and McCarthy, 1985, p. 23). When one or both partners in a remarriage bring children to that marriage, the resulting family is often called a **blended, or reconstituted, family** (Duberman, 1975; Spanier and Furstenberg, 1987).

The families created by remarriage, especially when there are children involved (his, hers, or theirs), are filled with complexity, uncertainty, and problems. One source

Many children of divorced parents learn that they will often be moving back and forth between the homes of their parents. The children are generally able to make the adjustment to a binuclear family. The long-term consequences of such arrangements are the subject of study by sociologists, psychologists, and others.

of problems is the incomplete institutionalization of remarriage (Cherlin, 1978). Remarriage is an incomplete institution because the roles and norms and even the legal aspects of remarriage have not yet evolved enough to give order to this new family form. One illustration of incomplete institutionalization is found in the shortcomings of our language. We do not have terms or names for many people who may be, in a sense, part of one's kin group—what does one call the parents of one's father's new wife?

The most common problem connected with the families of remarriage results from the fact that the boundaries of families have expanded to include many new people for whom there are no clear role relationships. Many complications are introduced into family life by these greater numbers of people for whom there are ambiguous obligations and relationships (Spanier and Furstenberg, 1987).

Summary

The family can be organized in many different ways and still carry out a variety of functions that can be both necessary and useful for the society. Some important functions of the family, found in most societies, are reproduction, care and nurturance of children, socialization, fulfillment of economic needs, provision of intergenerational and kin support, regulation of sexual behavior, and social placement. Many different types of family structures exist, as well as many different norms governing the family life.

The family is an adaptive institution. Historical and contemporary examples support the idea that the family is likely to adapt to changes in other parts of the society, especially the economic system.

In many societies, including contemporary Iran, and to a lesser extent Japan, marriage is arranged by parents. However, in many Western societies the young people themselves choose their mates on the basis of mutual attraction and romantic love. The mate selection system of the United States has, throughout its history, been based primarily on romantic love. But, even when mate selection is left to young people, the family and other social groups can influence the process.

Cohabitation is now a stage of pre-married life for many young people. The trend is more advanced in Scandinavia but is also prominent in the United States and Australia.

The early years of marriage are difficult in terms of adjustment, but these are also the years of high satisfaction with the marital relationship. Marital quality often declines with the arrival of children and continues to be negatively influenced by children throughout the later life stages. Some evidence shows that marital quality improves in the later years of marriage.

The relationship between family and work (both inside and outside the home) is the source of many complications and problems in contemporary family life. When both husband and wife are employed, they often have mismatched work schedules.

Conflict and violence in marriage is more widespread than is often suspected. The major serious forms of violence are spouse abuse and child abuse. Recent studies have shown slight declines in reported levels of both spouse and child abuse.

The divorce rate of the United States is among the highest in the world. Divorces increased gradually after 1920 and more rapidly in the 1960s and 1970s. Since the peak in 1979, the divorce rate has declined somewhat. The slight decline in the 1980s may be due to later marriage and possibly to the serious economic consequences that divorce has for many women.

Separation and divorce are stressful and complicated experiences. Six stations of divorce have been identified: emotional, legal, co-parental, economic, community, and psychic. As a result of divorce and remarriage, family relationships in contemporary society are becoming increasingly complex.

CRITICAL THINKING

1. Explain how the example of the Nayar shows that the family is an adaptive institution. Give examples of the adaptive nature of families in your society.
2. What functions does the institution of the family commonly serve in societies? Explain how each of these needs is met in your society.
3. Describe the various family types mentioned in the chapter.
4. Compare and contrast various methods for mate selection in different societies. To what extent do these methods reflect basic cultural values of the societies in which they are used?
5. How do you explain the emergence of cohabitation as a stage before marriage? What are the sociological implications of a lack of societal support for such a living arrangement?
6. What is marital quality? How might marital scripts and parenthood affect marital quality?
7. What relationship exists between the family and work in contemporary society?
8. Describe the extent to which violence is a part of family life in American society. How do you explain this phenomenon?
9. How does statistical information about divorce and separation prove the family is an adaptive institution?
10. How has divorce complicated the family structure in society? What other institutions in society have been affected by divorce?

C H A P T E R

12

Education

The United States has a long history of educating its citizens. The educational system of the nation was built on the principles of Thomas Jefferson who proclaimed that an educated electorate is necessary for a democratic society. Americans value education and often look to the schools to solve social problems or to straighten out "wayward" youth. The statistics also tell us that educational opportunities are nearly universally available and that the actual percentage of youth enrolled in schools is as high as any other country in the world.

However, almost daily we hear or read criticisms of the schools. Critics say that schools are failing to educate our young people, and because the educational system is not doing its job the United States is falling behind in economic and technical competition with other countries. Still other critics say the schools are teaching the wrong things or are not intellectually rigorous enough. Complaints continue to arise about how the schools are run badly or how the teachers teach poorly. Concerns are voiced about too much violence in the schools, too many drugs, and not enough discipline. The list of concerns and complaints about the school system is never-ending.

The paradox is that in the United States, in a country where education is valued and universally provided, the educational system is often seen as a failure. In this chapter we take a sociological look at educational systems. We will direct most of our attention to the educational system of the United States, but comparisons will be made with other countries, especially Japan and Great Britain. We will see both the problems and the successes of educational systems, but, more important, we will see how educational systems are closely tied to the culture and the structure of the societies in which they exist.

A Brief Look at the History of Education in the United States

In the earliest settlements of colonial America, most youngsters were educated in the "real world" instead of the classroom. In 1647, however, more than a century before the American Revolution, the first mandatory school systems were established in the Massachusetts Bay Colony (Monroe, 1940). Education in the United States initially emphasized the four R's: reading, 'riting, 'rithmetic, *and religion*. Later, schools began to replace the emphasis on religion with a variety of occupational and economic concerns. This change reveals a feature of education that we consider more fully below, namely, the tendency for the educational system to reflect the needs and desires of those who control the society. Early in American history a major purpose of education, as defined by colonial leaders, was to serve religious needs. Later, however, economic leaders and economic interests took priority in defining the objectives of the educational system.

Children in nineteenth century American schools were often tested orally while members of the community looked on. Free public education was an important part of the Jeffersonian ideal of an educated citizenry in a democratic society.

Traditional view (of education)
American education produces the informed and educated electorate necessary for a democratic society

Revisionist view (of education)
American education meets the needs of economic and social elites, not the masses

Between colonial times and the 1870s, elementary education became more democratized—that is, more widely available to all children. Following the principles of universal education advocated by Jefferson, a free public school system emerged by the mid-1800s. The widespread education of girls at the elementary level also became a reality during this era. By the middle of the nineteenth century, the first public high schools had been founded. This description of a universal and democratic American education has been labeled the *traditional view*. The **traditional view** of the *history* of American education is that the United States was founded on democratic political principles, which required an educated and informed electorate. The United States also had a social and economic philosophy that was highly democratic. According to the ideal, every person, regardless of origins or social background, should have an equal opportunity to achieve and succeed. A school system that is available to all the children of the society, i.e., a free and open system of mass education, is the major means by which equality is assured.

The traditional view of the history of American education still prevails today. Politicians, educators, and most citizens see the system of free and mass education as a way of assuring that the society will have an informed citizenry, capable of making decisions in a democratic society. The educational system is seen as the key to success and achievement in the United States. However, among historians of education, this view has been challenged by the revisionist view.

The **revisionist view** of the history of American education emphasizes that the economic and social elites of the society will develop an educational system that meets their needs, not the needs of the masses of people. This view is a more critical, a less idealistic, perspective on education, based on the assumption that a fundamental conflict of interests always exists between the elites and masses of the society (Bowles and Gintis, 1976; Katz, 1968, 1987; Mennerick and Najafizadeh, 1987).

The revisionist historians of education contend that a major goal of mass education in the nineteenth century was to socialize the working-class and immigrant children so that they would be better workers in the nation's factories and businesses. The children were not learning the skills necessary for work as much as they were learning proper work habits. The educational system was teaching future workers the importance of punctuality, regular attendance, submission to authority, cleanliness, and order. Nowhere was the link between the needs of industrialization and those of the educational system more vividly revealed than in the "Lancaster system."

Lancaster system
A 19th century school system organized on the principles of efficiency and order

The **Lancaster system,** named after its founder Joseph Lancaster, was a school system based on the principles of efficiency and order. Although the Lancaster system was found primarily in urban places, near industries and factories, it became the model for centralized and efficient school systems emerging around the country. In the Lancaster system careful attention was devoted to every detail of student behavior and classroom procedures. Teaching in the classrooms of a Lancaster school was always conducted in precisely the same way: the emphasis was on rote memorization of facts and on strict discipline. The way in which students were seated and even the way in which they wore their hats were carefully regulated. The hats were to be attached by strings to shirt collars, slipped off at the proper signal, and left resting on the students' backs (Parelius and Parelius, 1978, p. 60).

As a way of increasing the efficiency of the system, the Lancaster schools made maximum use of a minimum number of teachers; only one teacher was assigned to every 400 to 500 students. To manage such large numbers of students, the system relied heavily on student "monitors" who had previously been taught the lesson by the teacher. The huge classes were divided into groups of ten, each of which was headed by a monitor.

Lancaster schools were like factories, except that their product happened to be students. It is easy to see how students who were often headed for work in factories were well prepared by a school system that was itself a factory. This interpretation is consistent with the revisionist view of education, since it would obviously be in the interests of factory owners to have well-socialized workers.

In some ways, the traditional and revisionist views of the history of education resemble two competing sociological interpretations of education: functional and conflict theory. Functional theory offers an explanation of education that has some of the same elements as the traditional view. Conflict theory picks up key features of the revisionist view.

Functional Theory and Education

One aspect of functional theory emphasizes that societies are made up of separate institutions that are integrated and interdependent. Thus, in an urban, industrial society where families are less able to socialize their children for the work force, the educational system will take over some of the socializing functions. The educational system, according to functional theory, will assure the social, political, and economic stability of the society.

The schools can transform heterogeneous ethnic and religious groups into informed and productive citizens who have common values. Viewed in this way, the educational system contributes to an integrated, stable, and smooth-running society (Mennerick and Najafizadeh, 1987).

Moral function (of education) Teaching the children and young people the norms and values of the society

From a functionalist perspective, the schools perform more than an educational function; they provide a moral function as well. The **moral function** of the educational system is to teach children and young people the norms and values of the society. The norms and values are taught, in part, through the day-to-day activities of classrooms and schools, and, in part, through the content of what is taught to the young people. For example, even at the kindergarten level, children are being taught that they must conform to the expectations of those in authority and respect the rights of others. Kindergarten teachers organize the lives of the children in a way that prepares them for the order and conformity necessary at higher grades (Gracey, 1967).

The content of education, especially at the elementary level but to some degree at the secondary level, often depicts the culture of the society in ideal terms. The ideal culture, as we saw in chapter 3, reflects the cultural norms and values as they are supposed to be, not as they are. The materials presented by the schools, beginning with the earliest reading books and stories, are lessons in the "ideal" way of life. Families in these books and stories usually include a father, mother, probably two children (a boy and a girl, of course), pets, a pleasant house, a car, and so on. Even if a few of the contemporary books and stories show the mother working, or apartment life instead of a house in the suburbs, their depiction of life is far from the realities of life experienced by many children. Rarely will the stories describe divorced families, poverty, poor housing, large families (or, for that matter, married couples without children), illegitimacy, or sibling fights. Such books never show the more negative features of family life such as child or wife abuse or parental neglect. We are not arguing here that they should show this side, but we are emphasizing that education, particularly at the elementary level, tends to offer an idealistic version of the culture in which the students live.

Drawing by M. Stevens; © 1987 The New Yorker Magazine, Inc.

"Put your hands on your hips, like this." Even at the kindergarten level children are taught to conform to the expectations of those in authority.

The same kind of idealized treatment is given to all institutional spheres. Political affairs are typically described in their ideal form—a political system as it is supposed to work, not as it actually works. Courses in government teach about checks and balances, not about bribes, payoffs, corruption, excesses of power, falsification of records, or illegal use of government resources. As the educational process continues at the college and university levels, students are often given more realistic and critical assessments of their society and its culture. However, the early emphasis on the positive and idealized versions often causes these views to become deeply internalized.

Because schools transmit a society's norms and values, the student is likely to internalize and accept as proper most of the values and rules that guide the larger society. For example, competition and achievement are two widely accepted American values. The school is instrumental in conveying the idea that it is fair to give different rewards for different levels of achievement (Parsons, 1959). Children soon learn that those who get their lessons done quickly and accurately will be praised and rewarded with good grades. Furthermore, and this is a very important lesson, the highest achievers will be given additional rewards—being allowed to carry out special errands for the teacher, becoming room monitors, engaging in recreational activities, and receiving honors and recognition. The winners not only get the intrinsic reward of accomplishing their school work but they get the additional external rewards as well.

This familiar classroom experience teaches a variety of lessons that apply again and again throughout life. The lesson that most activities are competitive is reinforced later in dating, making athletic teams, winning college scholarships, being admitted to the best colleges, getting into a professional or graduate school, and getting the best jobs.

Functional theorists view this part of the school's teaching in a positive light because it provides a shared set of values for all the people of the society who have gone through the school system. The moral function of the schools helps to integrate and stabilize the society. Conflict theorists, as we will see below, view this matter somewhat differently.

Functional theory also emphasizes that an educational institution, especially one that rewards students for their ability and the quality of their work, provides an equal opportunity for every individual. The task of the schools is, therefore, to evaluate and sort the students according to their ability and performance (Mennerick and Najafizadeh, 1987).

Conflict Theory and Education

Conflict theory stresses that in any social system or society conflicts of interests will exist between different groups or categories of people. This theory also stresses that some groups will have more power than others and that the most powerful groups will take advantage of their position to maximize their interests. Thus, conflict theorists agree that the schools teach and gain acceptance for the prevailing norms and values of the society, but these are the norms and values that especially serve the needs of the advantaged and powerful people of the society.

When children in the schools learn that competition and achievement are the routes to economic rewards and high status, the positions of those who already have wealth and high status are legitimized. It is in the best interests of those who are already in advantaged and powerful positions to get the largest number of people agreeing that they have a right to be there. It is especially important that people who are in lower-status positions, and are likely to remain there, accept the legitimacy of a system of inequality.

Not only do children learn in school that competition and achievement are the routes to reward but, more important, they also learn to believe in the correctness of this method of obtaining rewards. For nearly everyone the method learned is so right that it seems natural or even instinctive. Even those who do not win the competition and thus do not get the rewards generally believe in and accept the system. Often losers blame themselves for not getting the rewards. Rarely do they question the legitimacy of the norms and values of the system (Sennett and Cobb, 1972).

Conflict theorists also see the educational system as organized to favor the interests of the most powerful members of the society in another way that is similar to the revisionist historical view of education: the educational system will produce the kinds of workers needed by the dominant economic interests of the society (Useem, 1986). The schools often do this, as we have seen, by providing well-socialized workers who have learned to be responsible and to carry out the assignments they have been given.

Another point of dispute between conflict and functional theorists concerns the fairness of the educational system. Conflict theorists see the schools as organized and operated in ways that give the children of the advantaged groups a better chance of succeeding, and thus the schools perpetuate inequalities in the social structure. The sharpest continuing dispute between conflict and functional theorists rests on this last point. Instead of an educational system that gives everyone equal opportunities for

There are often great differences in the quality of classrooms, teachers, and resources between middle-class and lower-class schools. Conflict theorists emphasize that these inequalities keep lower-status youngsters at the bottom of the social structure.

success, conflict theorists argue that the system favors the children of higher-status families and works against the lower-status youngsters (Bowles and Gintis, 1976).

The differences between the views of functional theorists and conflict theorists regarding the educational system may be summarized around three issues:

1. Functionalists view the teaching of cultural norms and values as an integrating function of schools; conflict theorists view these norms and values as favoring the already dominant groups in the society.

2. Functionalists see the educational system as providing the skilled and trained workers needed by the economy; conflict theorists see the educational system as providing a docile work force that will be used by the dominant economic interests.

3. Functionalists view the educational system as fair and equitable—a system that gives everyone a chance at success, based on individual ability, hard work, and diligence; conflict theorists see unfairness and inequity in the educational system—a system that operates to keep lower-status youngsters in their place at the bottom of the social structure and that gives the children of the advantaged groups a greater likelihood of success.

Throughout this chapter, as we examine different aspects of educational systems and schools, we will see these issues reflected at several points: at the elementary, secondary, and college levels, and in educational systems of the United States and other countries of the world.

Education and Educational Systems Worldwide

The worldwide picture with regard to education has improved dramatically since the 1950s. The percentage of young people in primary and secondary schools has increased, and often greatly, in virtually every country of the world for which there are available data. In 1950, some European countries had only about half of their children in schools (Italy, 53 percent; Portugal, 40 percent; Romania, 50 percent; Spain, 53 percent; and Yugoslavia, 55 percent). Today, every European country has at least 75 percent of its children in schools, and in most countries the percentage is over 90. The United States stands out, even in comparison with the European countries, since nearly 100 percent of its children are in primary and secondary schools, and have been since 1950 (Najafizadeh and Mennerick, 1988).

In developing countries the percentage of youth enrolled in schools has also increased since 1950. However, even today only about one-quarter of the children in some African and Asian countries are in primary and secondary schools. The largest of these developing countries with low enrollments are Afghanistan (27 percent), Ethiopia (28 percent), and Pakistan (27 percent). Furthermore, the schools that the children attend in developing countries are often seriously inadequate. For example, the developed countries have an average of one teacher for every 28 students; the developing countries have only one teacher for every 87 students. Yearly per capita expenditures on education in developed countries average $477; in developing countries the average is only $79 (Najafizadeh and Mennerick, 1988).

The money spent on education in many developing countries is often used disproportionately to support higher education, especially for males.

Even the limited amount of money that the developing countries are able to put into education is not equitably distributed. The monies are often concentrated in urban areas, and among the social and economic elites. Subsidies for education are given more to upper-class youth. In a study of ten selected Asian and Latin American countries, youths from the richest 20 percent of the population received from 38 percent to 83 percent of the educational subsidies (World Bank, 1988). Developing countries also use more of their economic resources to support students in higher education than they do for primary and secondary students. This policy, too, benefits the elites of these countries more than people in the lowest socioeconomic classes.

In most countries around the world, females are not enrolled in primary and secondary schools as frequently as males. Again, major differences exist between the developed and the developing countries. In the developed countries of the world, the numbers of males and females enrolled in primary schools are nearly equal (the number of enrolled females is 97 percent of the number of enrolled males). At the secondary level in the developed countries, the number of enrolled females is 78 percent of the enrolled males. However, in the developing countries as a whole, at the primary level, 86 percent of the male children are enrolled compared to only 71 percent of the female children. At the secondary level in the developing countries, 35 percent of the males, but only 29 percent of the females, are enrolled. Although some exceptions do exist, the developing countries are more likely to educate their males than their females (Najafizadeh and Mennerick, 1988).

National Systems of Education

Many differences in the educational systems of different nations can be noted, but one of the most fundamental is the degree to which systems are differentiated and rigid. A **differentiated school system** is one in which different programs, tracks, or streams lead to different educational outcomes (Bidwell and Friedkin, 1988). In the United States a typical high school will have several different programs, usually including vocational, college preparatory, and perhaps a commercial or business curriculum. Obviously, students in the college preparatory program are aimed toward college to earn a degree. Vocational and commercial students are much more likely to go directly into the work force, although they may get additional training at technical or vocational institutes. Differentiation can also be found at the elementary school level, where different tracks are available for students with different ability levels.

Differentiated school system
An educational system with different programs, tracks, and streams

Rigidity (of education)
The difficulty of moving from one educational track or program to another

The **rigidity** of an educational system refers to the ease or difficulty of moving from one educational track or program to another (Bidwell and Friedkin, 1988). For example, the United States is often thought of as a less rigid system than the systems of many other countries. As a cultural ideal, that is true, but in practical terms the United States' system is more rigid than we might suppose. It is certainly possible for a student who has graduated from a vocational or commercial high school program to enter college at some later date. Such a student might be limited initially in the type of college he or she could enter, but it is possible to make a change in educational and career paths. Also, anyone can choose to go on for more education at a later point in life. Moreover, one important value of American society is that everyone has the right to a higher education, at any time in life. For example, it is not uncommon at graduation exercises for elderly graduates to be given special recognition, and news stories delight in describing how an older person has returned to college and earned a degree.

Although the American cultural value supports an open educational system, actual practice is a different matter. Again, this point illustrates the considerable difference between a cultural ideal and reality. Few students probably begin in a vocational track in high school and then later go on to a college or university to earn a degree. Such a student would probably have to find a way to make up courses that are prerequisites for college admission or would have to find a college that would waive them. These and other kinds of barriers make the American system of education more rigid in fact than the cultural ideals would lead us to believe.

Nonetheless, the educational system in the United States is generally less rigid, both in the ideal and in practice, than are educational systems in some other societies. Many Asian and European countries have very rigid educational systems. Great Britain and Japan are examples of more rigid systems, although they are somewhat different in nature. Both, however, place great emphasis on special examinations administered to all students at critical stages in their educational careers. Since these examinations are often given at very young ages, educational careers, and often occupational fates as well, are determined early in life.

The British Educational System. Until about 1970, the British school system had three types of state-supported high schools: grammar schools, technical schools, and secondary modern schools. Since 1970 a new type of school, called the comprehensive high school, has been added (Kerckhoff, 1986).

The most prestigious British high schools have traditionally been the grammar schools. (Of course, Britain has also had very prestigious private secondary schools—called public schools—whose students are almost entirely the children of higher-status parents who can afford the tuition and boarding costs.)

The British technical schools are for talented students who are aiming for technical colleges and, later, technical occupations. The secondary modern schools, in contrast, are attended by students who have shown the lowest level of academic promise. The recently established comprehensive high schools of Britain are similar to American high schools in that all ability groupings attend the same school. However, within the comprehensive high school the children are still put in tracks, or "streams," on the basis of ability levels. The comprehensive school now enrolls about 60 percent of British students and 90 percent of Scottish students (Kerckhoff, 1986).

The introduction of the comprehensive high school in Great Britain may have made their system less rigid but it remains more rigid than the educational system of the United States. British students who have been chosen for either an elite school or a higher ability track are consistently and effectively moved toward better colleges and universities, and later to more prestigious occupations and professions (Kerckhoff, 1986, p. 857).

The Japanese Educational System. In Japan the differentiation of students takes on a special meaning. Japanese children are differentiated by the particular schools they attend, even at the junior and senior high school levels but especially at the college level. The Japanese educational system is built around a series of examinations, each one determining admission for the next level in the system. The culminating examination occurs at the end of high school and is the one that determines admission to Japan's colleges and universities. The Japanese examination system, especially at the end of high school, is so intense it has been labeled "examination hell" or "examination war" (Duke, 1988; Rohlen, 1983).

The process of gaining admission to one of Japan's prestigious universities begins for some parents and children at the kindergarten level. Five-year-old kindergartners will sometimes take entrance examinations for the elementary schools that have the best records for getting their students into the most successful junior high schools. The ranking of junior high schools is determined, in turn, by their success in placing students in the best high schools. The examination hell near the end of high school allows a select few to be admitted to Tokyo University or to one of the major Japanese medical schools (White, 1987).

The Japanese educational system requires that students spend considerably more time in school each year than American students. The school day typically begins at 8:30 A.M. and ends at 3:30 P.M., with a short lunch break. However, elementary school children often remain in school for another hour or more for additional class activities. Japanese children also attend school for a half day on Saturdays. Summer vacation is limited to the month of August, so the Japanese school year is 240 days, compared to the average of 180 days in American schools (Duke, 1986; White, 1987).

In addition to the regular schools, the Japanese have developed a private educational or tutoring system especially designed to prepare students for the next level of entrance examinations. These "examination cram" schools, called ***juko,*** drill the students on subjects that will be on the entrance examinations. Since about 80 percent of entering

Juko
Japanese "examination cram" schools that drill students for entrance examinations

Japanese students at the elementary and high school level go through a rigorous educational program. Their entire education is oriented toward the examinations that may eventually allow some of them to attend the most prestigious Japanese universities.

high school students aspire to a college or university education, almost all students attend *juko* schools after regular school hours. Furthermore, many Japanese students take one, two, or even three years off from their regular schools in order to attend the examination cram schools full time (White, 1987).

After all of this intense preparation, the Japanese students take the critically important university entrance examination. It is one of the ironies of Japanese education that the pace of work at the college and university level is rather leisurely, and very few students fail. Japanese students tend to see their college years as a time to enjoy life and indulge themselves.

Recent Trends in American Education

The schools of a society tend to mirror the characteristics and trends of that society. For example, during periods of war or national crises, the schools are likely to respond in the same way as the nation at large is responding. For example, during World War II in the United States, schools engaged the children in collecting scrap metals and other needed materials, buying war bonds and stamps, and participating in patriotic programs. In a similar way, general societal currents such as periods of political conservatism or radicalism are also reflected in the educational system. In the United States the 1960s and 1970s were periods of general change when many traditional ways were rejected in favor of more liberal ways. The schools, from the elementary level to universities, made parallel liberalizing changes.

It is not surprising, then, that schools also follow broader, more pervasive changes and trends in the society. For example, the increasing level of bureaucratization that has occurred in the United States—and most other societies—has also occurred in the educational system.

Increasing Bureaucratization

The bureaucratization of schools means, among other things, that many different, specialized statuses exist in contemporary schools. Although the early schools were made up mostly of teachers and students, with perhaps a few administrators, modern schools have large and specialized staffs. A large school system today will have, in addition to teachers and students, several layers of administrators, special education teachers of various types, counselors, psychologists, nurses, speech therapists, physical therapists, occupational therapists, nutritionists, and transportation specialists.

The bureaucratization of schools is also reflected in the increasing volume of formal, written communications, and quantitative analyses of the performances of students, teachers, administrators, and entire school systems. Student performances are evaluated with various tests that attempt to place a numerical value on presumed "inherent" abilities, such as intelligence, or on achievement in reading, mathematics, and other skills. Even entire school systems are evaluated on how effectively they are performing based on the average test scores of their students.

One justification for the objective and numerical testing of students is that evaluations are taken out of the subjective realm and made more impartial. The testing of students may have eliminated some biases, such as the cases of students admitted to high-prestige colleges just because their parents are alumni, but serious questions have been raised about the fairness of objective tests such as the Scholastic Aptitude Test (SAT) or American College Testing (ACT) examinations. Such tests might be oriented to the cultural backgrounds of higher-status students and give them an advantage over lower-status students (Crouse and Trusheim, 1988).

The bureaucratization of schooling also places increasing emphasis on formal credentials, especially college and professional degrees. The United States has been described as a society where great significance is attached to credentials with little or no attention paid to people's real qualifications (Collins, 1979). One interesting side effect of the great emphasis on credentials is that it has encouraged many people to fake their degrees, to buy "degrees" from commercial diploma mills, or to obtain "advanced" degrees without attending graduate schools.

The Liberalization of Schools in the 1960s

During the 1960s a variety of social and protest movements emerged in the United States—the civil rights, anti-war, women's, and the student rights movements. These social movements attacked the status quo of many institutions, including the educational system. The student rights movement began at the major universities in the mid-1960s, and within ten years its influence had been felt throughout American education. It criticized the rigidity of the traditional grading system, the mindless bureaucratic requirements and procedures, the inflexible course requirements, the absolute power of teachers, professors, and administrators, and the irrelevance of academic courses to contemporary social problems.

As these criticisms worked their way through the educational system, many changes were made in American schools and colleges. New courses were introduced; grading systems were modified; required courses were reduced; student participation in decision-making was increased; and many rules governing personal behavior, dress, and appearance were relaxed or abandoned. These changes loosened the educational system, making it less narrow and restrictive, but in the process, it might have lowered the intellectual quality of education.

Return to the Basics

With the beginning of the 1980s, many of the changes produced by the "loosening" of education still appeared in one form or another in the American educational system. But the pendulum had clearly started to swing back (Apple, 1986; Ravitch, 1985). Many reasons can be cited for why schools have reverted to a more traditional pattern, but one central explanation is the political trend in the United States during the decade of the 1980s, which was in a more conservative direction. This conservatism was epitomized for many of these years by former Secretary of Education William Bennett, who advocated a comprehensive revamping of American education through a "return to the basics."

The return-to-the-basics slogan may have various meanings, but for many people it suggests a return to teaching the fundamentals of reading, writing, history, science, and mathematics. It also suggests a de-emphasis of many of the social sciences that are seen as intellectually "soft," subjects that tend to undercut absolute moral values and national patriotism. Thus, the advocates of a return to the basics reflect the conservative political agenda of the Reagan and Bush Administrations.

A return to the basics also calls for a more rigorous and intellectually demanding school system in the United States. Many Americans fear that our present educational system is not producing adults who can compete successfully with the graduates of other nations' schools. They are concerned that the American educational system is failing to produce well-qualified people, and thus the United States is not competitive in world economic markets.

One way to evaluate the American educational system is to consider which young people are successfully completing high school and college. In the next sections we will examine who succeeds, especially in acquiring a college education in the United States.

Who Succeeds in the American Educational System?

Functional and conflict theorists disagree about how well the educational system of the United States serves *the entire* population. One way to examine this issue is to look at the educational attainment of Americans. Table 12–1 shows what percentage of Americans—white, black, and Hispanic—aged 25–29, have completed various levels of education. Blacks and whites are apt to graduate from high school in almost equal numbers (83.3 percent and 86.3 percent, respectively), but the Hispanic population has a substantially lower percentage of finishing high school (59.8 percent). At the college level, whites begin to exceed blacks and Hispanics considerably. Whites enroll in college more, and graduate more, than either blacks or Hispanics. Nearly a quarter of white

Table 12–1. Schooling Completed among 25- to 29-Year-Olds: Whites, Blacks, and Hispanics, 1987

	Completed High School	Some College	Completed College
Whites	86.3%	43.9%	23.0%
Blacks	83.3%	35.9%	11.4%
Hispanics	59.8%	26.7%	8.7%
All Categories	86.0%	43.6%	22.0%

Source: U.S. Bureau of the Census, "Educational Attainment in the United States: March 1987 and 1986." *Current Population Report,* Series P-20, No. 428. Washington, D.C.: U.S. Government Printing Office, 1988a.

Americans are now graduating from college (23 percent), while among blacks 11.4 percent, and among Hispanics 8.7 percent, are graduating (U.S. Bureau of the Census, 1988a).

A recent study has examined the educational, occupational, and economic conditions of young American adults, and has identified 20 million 16–24-year-olds as "the forgotten half" (William T. Grant Foundation, 1988). The forgotten half of American young adults are those who have not finished high school and high school graduates who are not college bound. Today, according to this report, even those who have high

In the United States the percentage of whites graduating from college is more than double that of blacks, and nearly triple that of Hispanics.

school degrees are often destined for low-paying jobs with limited chances for future economic advancement.

In the past a high school education was generally adequate for a reasonably well-paying job and an economically secure future. But recent technological and economic changes have altered the prospects for today's young adults who do not have college educations. Their economic futures are not bright, because even with a healthy economy, their opportunities are limited and their vulnerabilities great. In the years between 1973 and 1986 the median income of households headed by persons under 25 declined 26.3 percent. These households are largely made up of the young people who have not gone on to get a college education, but have married and entered the labor force. The drop in income for this group has been greater than that experienced by Americans between 1929 and 1933—critical years of the Great Depression in the United States (William T. Grant Foundation, 1988).

Another way to examine the relationship between education and economic circumstances is to see how educational attainment influences relative incomes. In fact, educational attainment has a greater impact on income today than it had in the 1970s, as is shown in figure 12–1. The relative incomes of civilian males aged 20–24 is shown for the years 1973 and 1986 (in 1986 dollars). In 1973 males in this age group who had not finished high school earned 80 percent of what college graduates were earning.

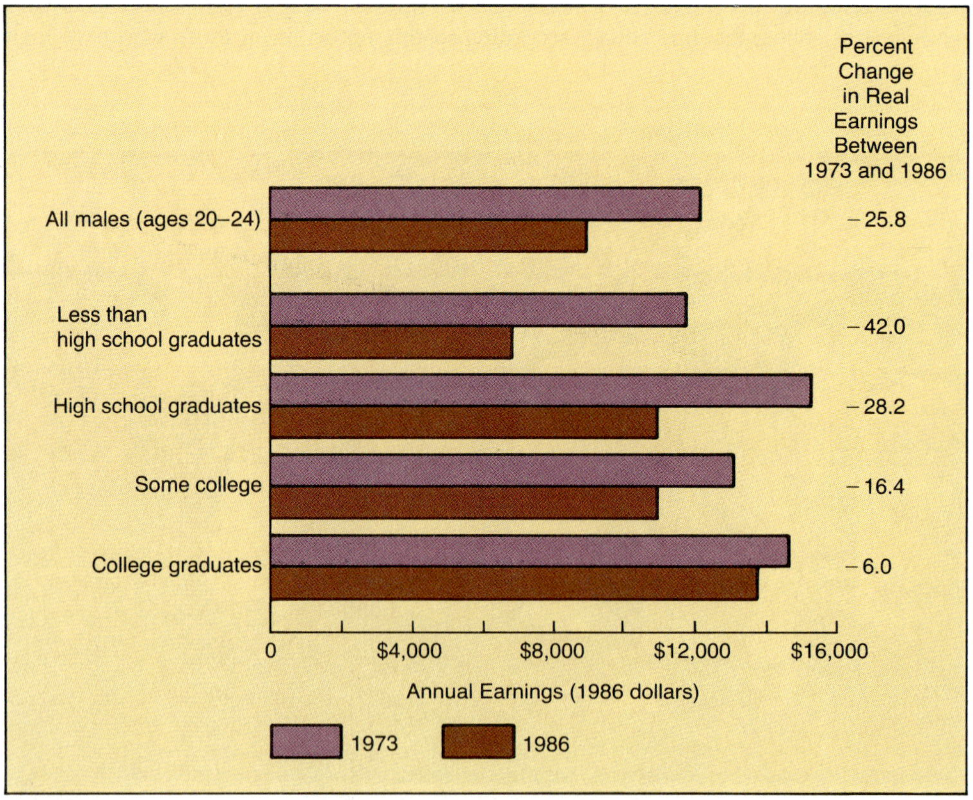

Figure 12–1. Real Average Yearly Earnings of 20- to 24-Year-Old Civilian Males in 1973 and 1986, by Educational Attainment. (*Source: Youth and America's Future.* The W. T. Grant Foundation, 1988.)

In 1986 young males who had not finished high school earned only 50 percent of what college graduates were earning. This advantage in earnings for the college-educated, while already significant before age 25, will only increase at later ages because the incomes of college graduates will generally go up faster than those with less education.

Economic Background and College Attendance

Conflict theorists argue that young people who come from advantaged economic backgrounds will benefit more from the educational system than the children of the poorer classes. Also, the children who belong to racial and ethnic minorities will benefit less often from the educational system than the children of the dominant white population. This contention can be checked by seeing if larger proportions of children from better-off families attend college than do children from poorer families, and if children from minority groups attend college least frequently.

Figure 12–2 shows how the economic, racial, and ethnic characteristics of families are related to having an 18–24-year-old child (or children) in college. The percentages show a general pattern of an increasing likelihood of at least one child, out of any 18–24-year-olds in the family, being in college. Among white families, the college attendance

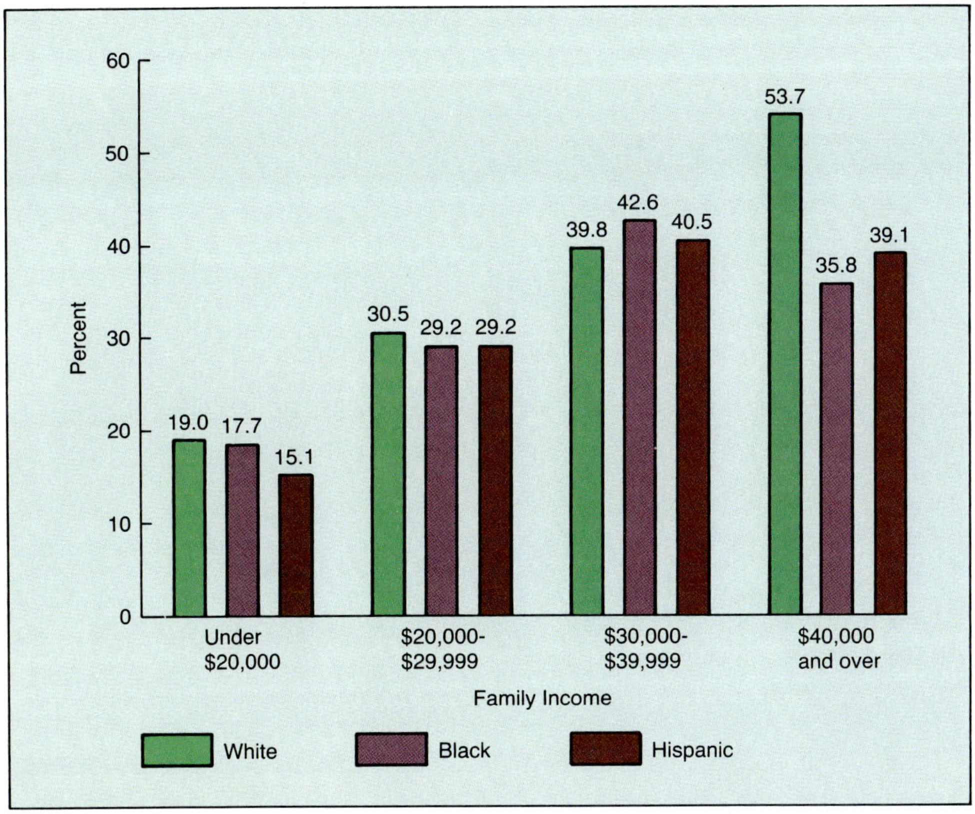

Figure 12–2. Percent of Households with at Least One of Its Primary Family Members, 18–24 Years Old, in College, by Family Income, Race, and Origin. (*Source:* United States Bureau of the Census, *Current Population Reports*, Series P-20, No. 429, 1988g, Table 12.)

of their children goes up very steadily as family income goes up. Among blacks and Hispanics college attendance goes up until family income is in the $30,000 range but does not continue upward as family income goes beyond $40,000. In fact, among black families the percentage is inexplicably less at the higher income level.

These figures on college attendance do support the conflict theory perspective. Young people coming from families making over $30,000 are twice as likely to go to college as young people coming from families making under $20,000. Furthermore, when white families have incomes over $40,000, their children are much more likely than any other group to go to college (53.7 percent).

The Importance of an "Elite" College Education

Today it is nearly a necessity to have a college education if one aspires to a high-status position in any relatively large corporate business in the United States. The same is true of the other developed societies of the world. However, not all colleges are equal because the degrees they grant are not considered equal. Colleges and universities in the United States are hierarchically ordered, with a small set of elite schools at the top that have the best reputations for academic excellence, distinguished faculties, and carefully selected, intellectually talented students. Disagreements may arise about the rank order of particular schools, but a typical list of elite colleges in the United States includes Harvard (also the oldest), Yale, Princeton, Columbia, and Stanford, just to name a few.

A question often asked by the public as well as sociologists is: "Does the college that one attends make a difference in one's career opportunities and occupational ad-

Studies have shown that individuals who graduate from one of the elite schools in the United States, such as the Harvard Business School, will have a better chance of making it to the very top of the corporate and business worlds.

vancement?" The question is more complicated than it first seems, for several reasons. The college one attends is associated with a number of other characteristics that can also influence career opportunities and occupational advancement. These other characteristics include family background, personal ability, academic performance, and motivation to succeed (Alwin, 1974).

One study found that, even when all these factors were controlled, some independent effect of the college attended still prevailed (Alwin, 1974). Furthermore, a study conducted among Japanese males also found that the graduates of the most elite colleges of Japan attained higher lifetime incomes and higher positions in organizations than men who had graduated from less prestigious colleges. Although this study was not able to rule out family background as a contributing factor, the author argues that in Japan the status of the college from which one graduates does make a difference in the occupational careers of males (Miyahara, 1988).

In a study of over 2,729 senior managers and executives of 208 major corporations in the United States, researchers tried to determine if getting a degree from one of the elite schools of the country influenced the chances of attaining the very topmost levels of corporate America (Useem and Karabel, 1986). The researchers were especially interested in whether the social (family) backgrounds of these top corporate leaders could account for their positions, or whether degrees from elite schools were more influential. The researchers considered not just bachelor's degrees but also master's of business administration degrees and law degrees. Thus, they came up with somewhat different lists of elite schools for each type of degree.[1]

This study concluded that the main portion of these 2,729 senior managers and executives who made it to the very top of the corporate and business structure were helped by their educational credentials. Holding a bachelor's degree from a prestigious school made it more likely that a person would be chosen as a chief executive officer (CEO) of one of the major U.S. corporations. A bachelor's degree from an elite school made the chances of becoming a CEO twice as great as a noncollege graduate in this group. (About 15 percent of the 2,729 corporate managers had not gone to college or had not completed college.) Master's degrees in business administration from elite business schools, and especially law degrees from one of the elite law schools, also gave these corporate managers a better chance of being selected for the top corporate positions (Useem and Karabel, 1986).

However, elite social background—coming from a family listed in the *Social Register* or attending one of the nation's exclusive prep schools—also aided in moving up in the higher levels of corporate management. In particular, an upper-class family background led more often to the boards of directors of corporations and to leadership positions in the top-level business associations. Of course, combining a high-status social background with an elite education made it even more likely that these highest levels of corporate management and leadership in the business world would be reached.

Since these managers were almost all middle-aged and older, and thus had received their college and professional degrees many years earlier, it is not clear why the status

---

[1] The elite schools for bachelor's degrees were: Columbia, Cornell, Dartmouth, Harvard, Johns Hopkins, Massachusetts Institute of Technology, Pennsylvania, Princeton, Stanford, Williams, and Yale. Elite schools for master's degrees in business administration were: Columbia, Dartmouth, Harvard, M.I.T., Northwestern, Stanford, California—Berkeley, California—Los Angeles, Chicago, Michigan, and Pennsylvania. Elite schools for law degrees were: Columbia, Harvard, New York University, Stanford, California—Berkeley, Chicago, Michigan, Pennsylvania, and Yale.

of their schools should continue to aid them in their careers. It seems unlikely that what they learned in college would still be an influential factor. It may be that their personalities or styles, which had been developed or cultivated in elite schools, gave them an advantage in the corporate world. It may also be that at the highest level of corporate management a great deal of uncertainty prevails, and trust is a critical factor. Thus, the top level of promotions go to people who are most like those already in power, both educationally and socially (Useem and Karabel, 1986, p. 198).

The Performance of the American School System

The task of the schools is to educate the children and young people of the society, and widespread concern exists about how the school system is performing its primary responsibility. The schools have many critics who have pointed to failures and shortcomings in various areas. In the early 1980s a government report on the educational system was ominously titled *A Nation At Risk* (1983). The crux of this report emphasized that the American educational system was mediocre, and the threat that our schools posed for our national well-being and security was as great as any external threat. Many of the problems identified in *A Nation at Risk* are still in evidence, while others may have been modified. We will review some of the most important of these problems, including functional illiteracy in the United States and achievement levels of American students. We will also consider the problems of teachers in the contemporary school systems.

Functional Illiteracy

To be illiterate is to be totally unable to read and write. Illiteracy in this sense is not a widespread problem in the United States today, at least compared to other countries of the world. But some adults who have gone through the elementary school system and even beyond have not yet learned to read, even though they are capable of doing so. The number of illiterate people is unknown because they often hide their inability to read and write. Also, residents of the United States who have emigrated from other countries may know how to read and write in their native languages, but they are not literate in English. Again, the numbers are not known.

Although the overall illiteracy rate in the United States is low, particular segments of the population have much higher rates. For example, estimates show that 60 percent or more of the prison population of the United States is illiterate. It is possible that illiteracy contributes to being in prison because those who commit crimes may have been unable to read about job openings or may have been afraid to apply for jobs because of the need to fill out application forms. Without legitimate jobs they may have turned to illicit acts and crime (Omang, 1982).

Functional illiteracy Lack of reading, writing, and calculating skills necessary to get along in society

In recent years the concept of functional illiteracy has emerged. **Functional illiteracy** refers to the lack of basic skills needed to get along in society: for example, to read a newspaper, fill out job application forms, follow written directions, calculate prices, write checks, or understand bus schedules. Recent tests have been developed to measure the literacy skills (both reading and quantitative) of the young adult (21–25 years of age) population of the United States. One test measures "prose literacy," the knowledge and skills needed to gain understanding and use information from written

Many Americans go through adulthood, or maybe their entire lifetimes, as functional illiterates. Even though they may have gone through the school system their reading skills are so low they cannot read a newspaper, a bus schedule, or a restaurant menu.

materials such as editorials, news stories, and poems. To have a minimal score of 200, a person must be able to write a simple description of the type of job he or she would like to have. Among the total sample of young adults, including those who attended high school and those who did not, 3.9 percent scored below the 200 level. However, in the black population, 13.8 percent scored below the 200 level; among Hispanics, 6.2 percent scored below 200 (Snyder, 1987).

A second test measured the ability to locate and use information from documents such as indexes, tables, paycheck stubs, and order forms. Specifically, in order to score at a minimal level of 200 on this dimension, a young adult had to be able to match money-saving coupons to a shopping list of several items. On this test of "document literacy," 4.5 percent of the total sample of young adults scored below the 200 level.

A third test, dealing with "quantitative literacy," measured the knowledge and skills needed to apply the arithmetic operations of addition, subtraction, multiplication, and division, either alone or sequentially. A minimal score of 200 indicated an ability to total two entries on a bank deposit slip. Among the total sample of young adults, 3.6 percent could not achieve this level. Among blacks, 12.6 percent scored below 200; among Hispanics, 6.9 percent scored below 200.

Functional illiteracy was most pronounced among students who did not attend high school. Among them, the following percentages of young adults did not score at the minimal levels on the three tests: prose literacy—18.8 percent, document literacy—38.2 percent, quantitative literacy—18.5 percent. Even among students who spent some time in high school before dropping out, the percentages below the minimal literacy levels were 11.9 percent, 16.0 percent, and 14.1 percent, respectively (Snyder, 1987). Many critics of the schools regard these figures on functional illiteracy as a reflection

Cross-National Perspectives

International Competition in Mathematics and Science

The Educational Testing Service has conducted tests for the National Science Foundation to determine the mathematics and science skill levels of 13-year-old students in six countries. The students came from the United States, South Korea, the United Kingdom, Ireland, Spain, and Canada. The students in these countries were given the same 63 mathematics questions and 60 science questions. For example, the students were asked to calculate the average age of five children aged 13, 8, 6, 4, and 4. More complicated questions required the students to know what the radius of a circle is, or how a plant would respond to artificial light.

In comparison with the students of the other countries, the United States' students did not do well. In fact they were near the bottom in both the mathematics and science tests. It was the South Korean students who excelled on these tests. Seventy-eight percent of the Korean students could solve two-step mathematics problems, such as computing an average, compared to only 40 percent of the American students. In science, 73 percent of the South Koreans could design scientific experiments and draw conclusions from them, compared to only 42 percent of the American students.

It wasn't only the Korean students who outperformed the American students in mathematics and science. In mathematics, students in four Canadian provinces performed above the mean, while those in two other Canadian provinces, Spain, the United Kingdom, and Ireland were about average. Only students from one Canadian province (French-speaking Ontario) and the United States scored below the mean. In science, students from British Columbia, Canada, performed about as well as the Korean students. Scoring at about the mean were those from the United Kingdom, Quebec (English-speaking), Ontario (English-speaking), Quebec (French-speaking), New Brunswick (English-speaking), and Spain. Joining students from the United States—well below the mean—were those from Ireland, Ontario (French-speaking), and New Brunswick (French-speaking).

This test is just one of several that has revealed how American students perform poorly in comparison to students in other countries, especially those from Asian countries. While this relatively poor performance is a problem in itself, it is an even greater problem in terms of what it portends for the future. Said one official of the Educational Testing Service: "It's a pretty accurate prophecy of what the 23-year-olds of 1999 will be able to do" (Leff, 1989, p. A16). Said an official of the National Science Foundation: "The lack of preparation for further education and future employment that these teenagers demonstrated is nothing short of frightening" (Leff, 1989, p. A14).

At one level, the fear is that Americans will do less well than those in other countries in college and post-graduate education. This would seem to mean that the world's leading scientists, engineers, and physicians will be less and less likely to come from the United States. Furthermore, most experts believe that the work world is going to require more highly trained personnel in the future. But while the work world is demanding more, America's educational system is turning out students whose ability is declining in comparison to students around the world. Thus, a huge and growing gap is emerging between the demands of American business and the students coming from the American educational system. The educational difficulties experienced by today's teenagers promise to translate into grave economic problems for the society as a whole in the future.

On the other hand, Asian nations like South Korea and Japan, which are already doing quite well both economically and educationally, should do even better in the future as their well-trained teenagers mature into productive adults. Thus, the United States could easily fall behind the Japanese economically and may even find itself threatened in several sectors by South Koreans and other Asians. Because of their ambition and diligence, now being combined with excellent educational training, the South Koreans will be daunting competitors for years to come.

LAPOINTE, ARCHIE E.; MEAD, NANCY A.; and PHILLIPS, GARY W. *A World of Differences: An International Assessment of Mathematics and Science*. Princeton, NJ: Educational Testing Service. 1989.

LEFF, LISA. "Survey of Math, Science Skills Puts U.S. Students at the Bottom." *Washington Post*, February 1, 1989, A14, A16.

of failure on the part of the school system to carry out its basic task of educating the population. This failure is especially serious with minority students.

Despite the fact that some American students go through elementary school, and even through some years of high school, and still do not have the skills in reading and arithmetic that allow them to function in everyday life, the educational field may have some encouraging news. New evidence shows that performances on various standardized IQ and achievement tests are improving after a number of years of decline. We will review these new trends in the next section.

Performance on Achievement Tests

When *A Nation at Risk* was published in 1983, some disturbing trends were noted in the achievement levels of American children, at both the elementary and high school levels. In international comparisons, especially with the Japanese, American students were losing ground. Equally disturbing was the fact that American students as a whole were averaging lower scores in the late 1970s and early 1980s than they had been a decade before. On standard IQ tests the scores of Japanese students had increased by more than ten points in a generation. The average Japanese student had a score of 111 compared to 100 for an average student in the United States. More striking was the fact that over 10 percent of Japanese had IQs above 130, while in the United States only 2 percent of students had IQs that high.

As a result of these concerns and others dating back to the 1960s, the Congress of the United States mandated that periodically the knowledge, skills, and attitudes of American children and youth be assessed. Beginning in 1970–1971, schools initiated periodic assessments of American students through a program called the National Assessment of Educational Progress (NAEP). The NAEP has measured reading achievement of 9-year-old, 13-year-old, and 17-year-old students five times since 1970–1971. The results of these tests indicate that students in these age groups were reading better in 1984 than they were in 1971. The 9-year-old and 13-year-old students started improving in the 1970s; the 17-year-olds, between 1980 and 1984. However, these reading assessments also reveal that 40 percent of 13-year-old students had not acquired "intermediate" reading skills and may therefore have difficulty reading the range of materials they encounter in school (Snyder, 1987).[2]

Changing SAT Scores

The decline in American student performance during the 1970s was also revealed in lower average scores on the Scholastic Aptitude Tests (SAT). Between 1967 and 1980 the average SAT verbal scores dropped more than 40 points, and mathematics scores dropped by 26 points. One possible cause of the decline in average SAT scores may have been that a larger proportion of high school seniors were choosing to take the examinations. Perhaps due to the greater numbers of less-qualified students, the average scores were being depressed.

However, the 15-year decline in average SAT scores started turning around in the early 1980s. Between 1980–1981 and 1985–1986, the SAT combined verbal and mathematics scores rose from 890 to 906. This increase returned the scores to the 1976 level, but the average is still far below the 980 level of 1963. The encouraging news is that the trend is again upward, both in average scores and in the percentage of the college-bound students who are able to score above 600 on the SAT verbal and mathematics tests. In 1986 3.0 percent of students scored above 600 on the verbal test and 6.8 percent scored above 600 on the mathematics test (Stern and Chandler, 1987).

Social Dimensions of Schools and Classrooms

Schools and their classrooms are not just places for teaching and learning; they are also social settings. As with all other social settings there are roles, norms, values, and status hierarchies. From a sociological perspective it is important to see how social factors influence what happens in schools and classrooms—both to the students and to the teachers. We will begin our consideration of social dimensions of schools by examining the most basic of all relationships—the relationship between teachers and students.

Teacher/Student Relationships

Without a doubt, the relationship between a teacher and a student can have a great influence on the student's academic performance and, ultimately, on his or her academic achievements. Many successful people are asked if any teachers influenced them, and usually they can recall one or two who had a significant effect on their lives. This kind of anecdotal evidence showing that teachers "make a difference" is supported by a growing body of research that identifies how teachers' attitudes and behavior can and do influence

[2] The intermediate level of reading is described as "the ability to search for specific information, interrelate ideas, and generalize from relatively lengthy passages dealing with literature, science, and social studies."

the academic performances of children. Sometimes, however, the teachers themselves are unaware of just how much their attitudes and personal values can influence their evaluations of student performances.

For example, as children go through a school system teachers in that system often become aware of the qualities and characteristics of many students even before they are directly responsible for teaching them. Teachers are likely to communicate with each other about particular students and may form judgments on the basis of siblings or other relatives. Teachers may reach conclusions about ability levels and expect corresponding performances in class work or behavior. Thus, if teachers expect a poor academic performance or a good performance from a student, the student may be evaluated in a way consistent with that expectation. This is an example of the self-fulfilling prophecy. A **self-fulfilling prophecy** is an initial expectation that may be based on a *false* definition of the situation; it can actually produce a behavior that makes the original expectation become true (Merton, 1968). A teacher's self-fulfilling prophecy might be illustrated by the following instances. If a boy is told that he is good at arithmetic, he develops ideas about himself (expectations) consistent with the evaluation. These ideas lead him to behave in ways that make the evaluations come true. The boy who believes that he is good at arithmetic, for example, will try hard to do problems in arithmetic. This assumption, of course, is just as likely to operate in the opposite way: students who are expected to perform poorly tend to live up to those expectations.

Self-fulfilling prophecy An initial expectation producing behavior that makes the original expectation become true

In addition to forming expectations for specific children, teachers also develop positive or negative expectations for whole groups of children. One consequence is that members of the group tend to live up to these expectations, whatever a member's individual level of ability is. The following advice was given to a new teacher by a fellow teacher at an all-black California high school:

> "Jim, you ever work with these kids before?"
>
> "No," I admitted.
>
> "I thought so. Well, now, the first thing is, you don't ever push 'em, and you don't expect too much . . . . you take them as they are, not as you and me [sic] would like them to be. That means, you find out what they can do, and you give it to them to do" (cited in Silberman, 1970, p. 84).

Rosenthal and Jacobson (1968) have done the best-known research study on the effect of teacher expectations on the performance of groups of students. At "Oak School," the site for the study, all the students were given IQ tests. At the beginning of the next school year, each of the 18 teachers in grades one through six were given the names of students (about 20 percent of the population) who, researchers told them, could be expected to show dramatic intellectual growth in the coming academic year. These predictions were supposedly based on the students' IQ scores of the previous year. In fact, the names of the 20 percent had actually been drawn at random from the school population as a whole; there were no differences between them and the other students. As Rosenthal and Jacobson (1968, p. 196) put it: "The difference between the special children and the ordinary children, then, was only in the mind of the teachers."

The crucial finding in this research was that teacher expectations made a difference: the IQ's of the "special" children increased much more than the IQ's of the control group (Rosenthal and Jacobson, 1968, p. 176). Rosenthal and Jacobson's research was admittedly limited; it was only one study of a single school. Subsequent efforts to replicate their study at other schools (e.g., Elashoff and Snow, 1971) have failed to produce such dramatic findings. Nevertheless, a variety of additional studies have supported the general notion that teacher expectations have an important effect on student performance (Boocock, 1980, pp. 154–160).

A somewhat different way of seeing the impact of teachers on the performances of their students comes from the study of a large and diverse sample of beginning first graders in the Baltimore, Maryland, public schools. Many of the schools in this study are inner-city schools serving minority (primarily black) populations. This study set out to see if it makes a difference when the teachers and parents of a student have different attitudes about what constitutes "good" and "bad" student behavior (Alexander et al., 1987a). The main hypothesis of the study was that if a student's teacher and parent had the same notion of a good student (or bad student), the student would perform better in the first grade. This hypothesis was *not* supported by the research, but something equally important was found. *The values of the teachers were related to the performances of the students in their classes.*

The researchers were especially interested in the way teachers' values were negatively related to the report card grades of black first graders. The researchers speculate that "Teachers who place a premium on 'proper values' and on 'following the rules' may be especially frustrated when their expectations for how pupils ought to behave are not

Sociological studies have shown that when a teacher's social class background and values are different from those of the students, the teacher's evaluation of student performance is affected.

fulfilled in the context of predominantly black inner-city schools, and they may find themselves, whether consciously or not, grading these students down as a result" (Alexander et al., 1987a, p. 74).

In another analysis with this same sample of Baltimore first graders, the researchers found that minority students performed less well when their teachers were from high socioeconomic backgrounds. The same findings occurred among nonminority students who came from low-socioeconomic-status backgrounds. Both nonminority, low-status students and minority students had their greatest difficulties with teachers when the teachers had high-socioeconomic-status backgrounds. The high-status teachers were more apt to evaluate their students as less mature and to hold lower performance expectations for them. These high-status teachers were also the ones who had especially low scores when asked to evaluate the general climate of their schools. The picture that comes through is one of teachers who are not satisfied with their teaching settings and are, in the process, turning out low-achievement students. The sociological point of considerable significance is that the social origins of teachers can influence student academic achievement (Alexander et al., 1987a; Alexander et al., 1987b).

Long-Term Effects of Elementary School Teachers

The early evaluations that teachers make of particular students may have a long-term impact on academic performance. In a follow-up study of students who had been first, second, and third graders some four to nine years earlier, evidence showed that the early influences of teachers (and parents) were continuing to affect academic performance. When these students were first studied in the early grades, their grades and achievement levels were found to be closely related to the influences of their teachers (for some students) or their parents (for other students). The teachers and parents influenced the performances of the students even when their cognitive or intellectual abilities were the same. Four to nine years later, these effects of "significant others" were still related to the school performances of these youngsters (again, among students with the same levels of cognitive ability).

Different interpretations might be made of these long-term effects of early experiences in school, but one possibility is that children incorporate as a part of their self-image a view given to them by their early teachers or by their parents. Furthermore, in school systems the grades earned one year may influence the grades earned the next year. In the researchers' words, ". . . a 'paper person' is created that follows the child from grade to grade. Cumulative records that follow children through the school could support the children's high performance in later grades by affecting subsequent teachers' expectations" (Entwisle and Hayduk, 1988, p. 158).

Tracking and Later School Performance

One of the hotly debated topics of education is the impact that **tracking** (grouping children by ability level) has on the subsequent academic performances of students. The underlying assumption about tracking is that when students with similar ability levels are placed in classes together, the academic gains for all students will be maximized. High-ability students will not be slowed down by the less competent students, while students with less ability will be taught at a level and pace that will be more appropriate and thus beneficial for them (Kerckhoff, 1986).

Tracking
Grouping children in the schools by ability level

Tracking is used widely in United States and many other countries, sometimes at the elementary school level but especially at the junior and senior high school levels. The system appears to be widely accepted by teachers and administrators, but it has also developed a corps of critics (Oakes, 1985; Rosenbaum, 1976). One basic criticism cites tracking as a system that perpetuates inequality. The argument is that students who are placed in low-ability tracks will come to define themselves as poor students, unable to do academic work, and consequently they will do poorly. In other words, the tracking system also tends to become a self-fulfilling prophecy (Eder, 1981); being placed in a high track tends to elicit high-quality performance, while being placed in a low track tends to produce poor academic performance. The following statement by a student illustrates the negative effects a tracking system can have:

> I felt good when I was with my class, but they went and separated us—that changed us. That changed our ideas, our thinking, the way we thought about each other and turned us into enemies toward each other—because they said I was dumb and they were smart (Schaefer, Olexa, and Polk, 1970, p. 12).

In a participant observation study of "Suburban High School," Finley (1984) examined the ways in which teachers shape and maintain a tracking system. Looking at English courses, Finley found four tracks—gifted, advanced, average, and remedial. Middle-class white children tended to be placed in the two highest tracks, while lower-class children, especially from minority groups, tended to be overrepresented in the lower tracks. The teachers defined high-track classes as desirable places in which to work, while low-track classes were regarded as undesirable. As a result, the teachers competed among themselves to teach the high-track classes and to avoid low-track classes.

Teachers evaluated themselves on the basis of the ratio of high-track to low-track classes they taught; the higher the ratio, the more positive the self-evaluation. This fact led teachers to create more higher-track classes, in which they could teach and thus increase their ratio. The key point is that the dynamics of the status system within the school led teachers to create and maintain a tracking system. In sum, "teachers created ability groupings for their own reasons," and the educational needs and fates of their students were affected by the ambitions of the teachers (Finley, 1984, p. 242).

Other studies of students in different tracks have found that students in lower tracks were likely to be more alienated, distant, and punitive toward each other. Lower-track students also had more negative attitudes about themselves, were less attentive in classes, and were more negative about their futures. Lower-track classes were more apt to be disrupted, which contributed to lower reading levels. Teachers of lower-track students had lower expectations for their students (Oakes, 1982; Eder, 1981; Femlee and Eder, 1983).

The critical question about tracking is whether it does, in fact, improve the academic achievements of *all* students, as its supporters claim. Does it improve the academic performances and achievement levels of the students in the low-ability tracks as well as those in the high-ability tracks? On this question, studies coming from the United States, Great Britain, and Israel all support the same conclusion: students who are in the high-ability track generally improve their academic and intellectual performances over what they would otherwise be, but students in low-ability tracks are more likely to lower their performances (Kerckhoff, 1986; Rowan and Miracle, 1983; Shavit and Featherman, 1988).

In the Israeli study, these effects of tracking were found on cognitive intelligence tests administered to young males when they were tested for military service (Shavit and Featherman, 1988). This study finds that the experience of having been in a high-ability track in high school actually improved a person's cognitive *intelligence* level between ages 13 and 17. Students in high-track classes apparently had certain kinds of intellectual stimulation that raised their intelligence, while students in low-track classes did not. The measured intelligence of students in the low track remained the same at age 17 as it had been at age 13.

The impact of tracking on students in British schools was measured by achievement-test performances in both reading and mathematics. The evidence from this study left little doubt that students in the low-ability tracks lost ground when compared to students who had the same earlier academic performance but who were not placed in ability tracks. The opposite occurred for students in high-ability tracks: they increased their average performance level relative to comparable students in ungrouped schools. Thus, tracking improves the education of only the students who get in the high track, while it lowers the achievement levels of the students in the low track (Kerckhoff, 1986).

At least three possible reasons can be given as to why the different ability tracks produce opposite results for students in the low and high tracks: (1) students in the high-ability track are provided with a different, and better, educational program; (2) teachers assigned to the high-ability track are more competent and more highly motivated; (3) students are influenced by their peers, so that students at each level adopt the standards of their classmates (Kerckhoff, 1986).

Order and Control in the Classroom

Classroom discipline and school violence are viewed by most teachers, as well as much of the public, as a critical problem in the schools. One-third of a sample of teachers said that discipline was the biggest problem in the schools (Dworkin, 1987).

Disruptions in the classroom can be of many different types, but their underlying characteristic is that they distract from the educational task. In the following vignette the student's behavior is not unruly or aggressive, but, nonetheless, it disrupts the class and is the kind of problem that teachers must confront.

> Pauline was in another part of the school picking up her year-book pictures when the bell rang, signalling the beginning of the period. She arrived in her English class late; and placing her books on her desk, immediately left the room. Ten minutes later she returned. . . . Once in class she devoted her attention to trying to close her purse, while her teacher presented a lesson from the textbook. Then she sashayed to the front of the room, casually sharpened a pencil, and returned at the same leisurely pace.
>
> Being a physically attractive young lady in an extremely short skirt, this jaunt captured the attention of everyone in the room, the teacher included. In her seat, she shortly began a whispered conversation with those around her, even though textwork had been given. Pauline started hers, which was to write a business letter, but suddenly decided she needed something from her purse. After a few minutes' search, she dumped its contents onto the desk with a clatter, picked out an eraser, whisked everything else back into her purse, and resumed her work. Five minutes later she began another conversation with one of her neighbors (Stebbins, 1977, pp. 45–46).

Such disruptions are not unusual, and indeed they often take a more serious and dramatic form. Maintaining order in a classroom is, from a teacher's perspective, frequently difficult.

From a teacher's perspective one of the most persistent problems is maintaining order and discipline in the classroom.

In his study of classroom discipline, Wegmann (1976, p. 77) concludes: "Regardless of what may be written in state law or school board regulations, the actual exercise of teacher authority is an uncertain, precarious enterprise."

The problem of maintaining discipline in the classroom, especially at the high school level, has been labeled by one researcher as "defensive teaching" (McNeil, 1986, p. 157). Defensive teaching occurs when teachers reduce the difficulty of academic work in order to keep the support and good will of the students, and thus the harmony and control of their classrooms can be maintained. Another way to describe what happens in many classrooms is to see it as an implicit "bargain" between teachers and students. The teachers, on their side of the bargain, keep the academic demands low, while the students, in return, are reasonably well behaved and passive (Sedlak et al., 1986). By "spoon-feeding" easy academic material, teachers are able to keep peace in their classrooms and avoid behavior problems.

Different explanations may be given as to why defensive teaching is necessary in today's schools. One reason already given is that life for the teacher can be easier by striking a bargain with the students. If the material is simple and can be evaluated as right or wrong through objective examinations and quizzes, classroom teaching is easier. But probably a more important reason, one that most teachers quickly learn, is that if discipline is not maintained in one's classroom, the repercussions are serious. School superintendents and principals judge classroom performance largely on the absence of problems. As one observer has noted:

> A teacher will rarely, if ever, be called on the carpet or denied tenure because his [or her] students have not learned anything; he [she] will certainly be rebuked if his [her]

> students are talking or moving about the classroom, or—even worse—found outside the room . . . (Silberman, 1970, p. 140).

The obvious result of defensive teaching and the classroom bargain is that educational quality is lowered. Knowledge is sacrificed for control, and the students are sold short in their educations (McNeil, 1986; Sedlak et al., 1986).

Summary

Government-supported education on the American continent had its beginnings in 1647. The first formal schools were influenced by religious interests, but later occupational and economic factors became predominant influences. In the 1800s a universal education system emerged, a system, which, from a traditional view, was important for a democratic society and provided equal opportunities for all children. An alternative historical view, labeled revisionist, emphasizes that the economic and social elites of the society develop an educational system that meets their needs. The Lancaster system of education is an example of a system that produced workers suited for the industrial workplace.

Functionalist theory, paralleling the traditional view of education, emphasizes how education is an integrating institution. Education helps to socialize children coming from diverse backgrounds, presenting them with an ideal version of the society and culture. Functional theory takes a positive view of education, emphasizing how students are rewarded for their ability and hard work.

Conflict theory, recognizing the conflicts of interest among different groups and categories of people, stresses that powerful interest groups in the society will control the educational system for their own ends. The educational system serves the powerful by providing the workers needed by the economic interests of the society. Conflict theorists also see the educational system as favoring the children of the advantaged groups over the disadvantaged.

The worldwide picture with respect to education has improved dramatically since the 1950s. Although great advances have been made, some areas of the world, notably in Africa and parts of Asia, still provide education for only about one-fourth of their children. Throughout many countries, especially the less developed ones, females receive less education than males.

School systems of nations vary in their differentiation and rigidity. Differentiation refers to different schools, tracks, or streams for different students, and rigidity refers to the ease of moving from one to another. The United States' educational system, especially from the perspective of cultural values, is less rigid than many European and Asian countries. Great Britain and Japan provide illustrations of more rigid systems in which universal examinations are key determinants of educational and occupational opportunities.

Changes in education tend to mirror trends in the larger society. These changes include the increasing bureaucratization of school systems, with a greater emphasis on quantification and formal credentials. In the 1960s in the United States, the schools underwent a liberalization process, which has more recently been reversed by a return to the basics.

The educational system does not serve different groups in the population equally. Blacks, Hispanics, and students from lower socioeconomic backgrounds tend to succeed less often in the educational system than those from the dominant white population. A college education today gives a great advantage in the occupational world, and therefore the economic world. An education from one of the elite colleges or universities is a key to top corporate management in both the United States and Japan.

In recent decades, many people have been critical of the performance of the American educational system. A substantial number of Americans continue to be functionally illiterate. However, reading levels have increased in the last 20 years, and SAT scores, after declining in the 1970s, have now started to increase.

A key social aspect of the educational system is the relationship between teachers and students. The evaluations that teachers make of students, even if based on false assumptions, can influence how they grade students. The values and social class origins of teachers also are related to how teachers grade students. The influence of teachers at elementary grade levels tends to be long-lasting.

Tracking students according to ability level is supposed to maximize the academic performances of all students, but the evidence shows that it has a positive effect on the high-track students and a negative effect on the low-track students.

Order and control in schools and in the classrooms is an important problem in American education. Many teachers lower their educational standards as a way of maintaining control of the students in their classrooms.

CRITICAL THINKING

1. Compare and contrast the traditional view of the history of American education with that of the revisionists. Which theory does the Lancaster example support?
2. Give examples from your own education of the idealization of culture at the elementary level. Why would or should colleges teach more realistic and critical assessments of society?
3. Assume, as the functionalists do, that the education system serves a moral function. Give examples of norms and values you have learned in school.
4. Compare and contrast the conflict and functional sociological interpretations of educational systems.
5. To what extent is American education differentiated and rigid? Compare your conclusions with the educational systems found in Japan and England.
6. In what ways are American schools becoming increasingly bureaucratized? Do you consider this to be a positive or negative trend?
7. Does our educational system provide equal opportunity for all individuals in society? Use information from the chapter to support your conclusion.
8. In what ways might schools serve the needs of the advantaged and powerful people in society?
9. Does tracking perpetuate inequality? Use evidence from the chapter to support your conclusion.
10. What effect does defensive teaching have on the quality of education? What suggestions can you make to reverse this situation?

CHAPTER 13

The Economy and Work

In the past, the economy of the United States was able to cash in on its own technological innovations. For example, the automobile assembly line technology created by Henry Ford in the early 1900s was used nationwide to help build an exceptionally profitable automobile industry as well as hugely successful industries of various types. In more recent years, however, although the United States has continued to introduce a large number of important technological innovations, it has been left to the economies of other societies to implement them, realize their mass market potential, and reap the resulting huge economic rewards. For example, the video recorder was invented in the United States in the 1960s, but it was mass produced by the Japanese who, until recently, had virtually the entire world market for this enormously successful and profitable technology.

The issue facing us today, and in the near future, is whether the United States has learned economic lessons from the past and will be able to exploit its own technological breakthroughs. At the moment, the race is on for the development of commercial applications of advances in superconductivity that were largely made by Americans. Who, for example, will be the first to develop trains that travel, by magnetic levitation, *above* rails rather than on them? Obviously, the stakes are high, and the United States and its economy can ill-afford many more failures. Although the outcome is far from clear, the initial signs are that, despite outspending the Japanese by a wide margin, the United States is behind in the race to commercialize superconductivity (Burgess, 1988).

The **economy** is the social institution involved in the production and exchange of a wide range of goods and services. These activities are accomplished by various economic elements, including businesses, industries, corporations, markets for goods, labor markets, the banking system, labor unions, relevant government agencies, and occupations.

Economy
Social institution involved in production and exchange of goods and services

In this chapter we look at economic systems, as well as many of their elements. We begin with an examination of broad changes in the economy including the Industrial Revolution, the changing nature of capitalism and socialism, as well as the rise of industrial democracy in Sweden. Then we turn more specifically to the changing nature of the American economy, focusing on such issues as changes in the labor force, the decline of labor unions, deindustrialization, the growing strength of America's foreign competitors, projections on the future of the American economy, and the post-industrial society.

Historical Changes in Economic Systems

Revolutionary changes in economic systems have occurred during the last century, and the next century promises many more to come. Because much of the future of the American economy will be shaped by past changes, we need to understand the major developments of the past as well as the dynamics of the present (Hearn, 1988).

The Industrial Revolution

Industrial Revolution
In the nineteenth century, a rapid major social and economic change marked by the use of power-driven machinery

To understand modern economies and the nature of work in America today, we must go back to the nineteenth century and the **Industrial Revolution,** which introduced the factory system of production. In this system, machines replaced hand tools, and steam and other sources of energy replaced human or animal power. The many workers who operated the machines ranged from the highly skilled to the almost totally unskilled. Because much of the needed skill was already built into the machine, skilled workers could be replaced by adults and children with little or no training, who worked long hours for low pay. The transformation of workers into machine tenders led to a decline in the use of skilled workers and a rise in the use of unskilled workers.

Another defining characteristic of this age was the elaborate division of labor whereby a single product went through the hands of a number of workers, each of whom performed a small step in the entire production process. Adam Smith depicted this development in his famous description of the new method of producing pins. Under the old system a single person producing a whole pin could produce only a few each day, but in the new division of labor a group of ten workers could produce almost 5,000 pins each per day. He describes the division of labor:

> One man draws out the wire; another straights it, a third cuts it; a fourth points it; a fifth grinds it at the top for receiving the head; to make the head requires two or three distinct operations; to put it on is a peculiar business; to whiten the pin is another; it is even a trade by itself to put them into the paper; and the important business of making a pin is in this manner divided into about eighteen distinct operations, which in some manufactories are all performed by distinct hands (Smith, 1937, pp. 4–5).

Mass production
Production system with standardized products, interchangeable parts, high volume, and continuous process

The first factories were primitive affairs, but they gave way over the years to larger and more efficient entities geared to mass production. **Mass production** had a variety of characteristics: products were standardized; parts were made interchangeable; precision tools were used so that parts could be made to fit universally; the production process was mechanized to yield high volume; the flow of materials to the machine and products from the machine were synchronized; and the entire process was made as continuous as possible. This, of course, is the assembly-line type of production that continues today in such industries as automobile manufacturing. These systems reached their fullest application in the United States in the mid-twentieth century and spread throughout the world.

Types of Economies

Economic systems can be organized in different ways to accomplish the fundamental tasks of producing and exchanging goods and services. The two major economic systems world-wide are capitalism and socialism, although most countries today are neither purely capitalist nor purely socialist. As we shall see in the pages ahead, the philosophies of both capitalism and socialism are moderated greatly in the actual workings of economies, including that of the United States.

Capitalist Economic Systems

Capitalism is an economic system that emphasizes the private ownership of property and the means of production. The owners of property and especially the means of production are expected to strive for economic gains called *profits*. Capitalism is the guiding economic philosophy in many societies, including most prominently the United States.

Karl Marx on Capitalism. As we saw in chapter 8, social theorist Karl Marx offered a critical analysis and description of capitalist systems. He saw capitalist societies as divided into two social classes, one of which exploited the other. One class, the capitalist, owned the means of production, which included land, raw materials such as mines and forests, and factories with all their tools and machinery. The other class, the proletariat, was forced to sell its labor time to the capitalist class in order to have access to the commodities produced by the economic system. The capitalists pay the workers for their labor time, but, as Marx emphasized, the workers are paid *less* than the value of what they produce for the capitalist. The gap between the costs of labor and production and the worth of what is produced is called the profit.

Marx saw the capitalist system as exploitive of the proletariat because the workers were paid only enough for survival for themselves and their families. The capitalists, by contrast, could reinvest their profits and expand their businesses. The general success of the capitalist class is therefore derived from exploiting the work of the proletariat.

Writing in the mid-1800s, Marx was describing capitalism in its heyday. Over the years capitalism has changed tremendously, and many neo-Marxian scholars have attempted to adapt Marx's ideas to the changing realities of capitalist society. For example, the capitalism of Marx's day can be described as **competitive capitalism.** No one capitalist, or small group of capitalists, could gain complete and uncontested control over a market. Although it was Marx who foresaw the growth of monopolies, Baran and Sweezy (1966) designated modern capitalist society as **monopoly capitalism.** In this updated type of capitalism, one or a few capitalists control a given sector of the economy. Monopoly capitalism weakens competition and introduces changes in the control structure of capitalist enterprises. In competitive capitalism an enterprise tended to be controlled by a single capitalist-entrepreneur. In monopoly capitalism, however, the modern corporation is owned by a large number of stockholders, although often a few large stockholders own most of the shares in a given company. Although stockholders "own" the company, managers exercise the actual day-to-day control. Managers are crucial in monopoly capitalism, whereas the entrepreneurs were central in competitive capitalism. One byproduct of this distinction is that Marx's simple model of opposition between capitalist and proletariat no longer applies. Who are the capitalists? Are the millions of people who own a few shares of stock in General Motors capitalists? Are the managers of modern enterprises capitalists? Or are they members of the proletariat since they are employees of the organization? These are just a few of the questions raised by changes in the capitalist system during the last century.

Competitive capitalism No single capitalist, or small group of capitalists, controlling the market

Monopoly capitalism Modern capitalism in which one or a few capitalists control the market

Another significant change in capitalism has been the growth of white-collar and service workers and the decline of the blue-collar workers whom Marx saw as the proletariat. Can Marx's theory of exploitation be extended to white-collar and service occupations? Making such an extension, Braverman (1974) argued that the concept of

The early factories were often cramped, dark, and dangerous. Critics of such a factory system were often drawn to the anti-capitalistic ideas of Karl Marx.

the proletariat describes not a specific group of people or occupations but a process of buying and selling labor power. Like blue-collar workers, white-collar and service workers are forced to sell their labor time to capitalists, although the impact of this exploitation and control is not yet as great as it has been on blue-collar occupations.

The Changing Nature of Worker Control. Braverman recognized economic exploitation, which was Marx's focus, but he concentrated on the issue of managerial control over workers. Edwards (1979) sees control at the heart of the transformation of the workplace in the twentieth century. Following Marx, Edwards sees the workplace, both past and present, as an arena of class conflict—in his terms, a "contested terrain." Within this arena, dramatic changes have taken place in the way in which those at the top control those at the bottom. In nineteenth century competitive capitalism, simple control was used. The "bosses exercised power personally, intervening in the labor process often to exhort workers, bully and threaten them, reward good performance, hire and fire on the spot, favor loyal workers, and generally act as despots, benevolent or otherwise" (Edwards, 1979, p. 19). Although this system continues to survive in small businesses, it has generally been undermined by the growth of large organizations. Simple *personal control* has been replaced by *impersonal technical* and *bureaucratic control*.

Technology is often used today as a way of controlling workers. The classic example is the assembly line found, for example, in the production of automobiles or farm machines, or in the processing of meat and other food. When workers are on an assembly line, their actions are controlled by the incessant demands of the moving line.

In today's industries and businesses many kinds of electronic automated equipment are used by management to increase control over workers. For example, telephone operators today do not have to be carefully watched and controlled by human supervisors because every operator's work is monitored by electronic equipment that records the exact amount of time an operator spends on each customer call. Operators know how long they should be spending to process each request, so there is no time for a friendly word before moving on quickly to the next caller. Technological control also diminishes the quality of the work experience (it is more boring, stressful, etc.) and demeans the lives of workers. Many kinds of jobs do not take advantage of the distinctive human ability to think, create, and be inventive (Shaiken, 1986).

The major direction in which capitalism has changed and modified is toward state capitalism. In **state capitalism,** capitalistic enterprises continue to exist, but there are also an array of state-owned branches of production and the state regulates and manages the economy. The best contemporary example of this is Sweden where state ownership and regulation coexist with capitalistic enterprises.

State capitalism
Capitalist system in which the state is deeply involved

Socialist Economic Systems

Socialism is an economic system in which the means of producing goods and services are publicly or collectively owned. Sometimes socialist economies are found among small groups of people who share in the ownership of property and benefit equally from the production of their work. Many times small religious sects are organized along socialist lines. However, the typical socialist economy today is state socialism in which the economy is controlled by the government. Under **state socialism,** the government—through its political leaders, officials, and bureaucrats—establishes what will be produced, manages how it will be produced, and controls the distribution of goods and services. The most familiar systems of state socialism today are the Soviet Union and its Eastern European allies (Edwards et al., 1986).

Socialism
Economic system in which the means of producing goods and services are publicly or collectively owned

State socialism
An economic system that lacks capitalistic enterprises and in which the state owns and runs the economy

The socialist ideology holds that socialism is a democratic system in which the people have a voice in the economic decisions that affect them. With no private ownership of property, wealth is supposed to be redistributed so that everyone has the resources they need for living. According to the ideology of socialism, workers are not supposed to be alienated from their work or from any other aspects of their society. Individuals should be able to express their distinctive abilities and capacities. These principles might be called the theory of socialism, but in practice, especially under state socialist systems, the reality often differs from the theory.

The state socialism of the Soviet Union, Poland, and other East European states has obviously not succeeded in all of these objectives. In chapter 8, we saw that the Soviet Union has a stratification system leading to the unequal distribution of material goods and other economic advantages. In the Soviet Union decisions about production have not been made by the people, but have been handed down from the top by government officials and bureaucrats. Soviet workers have a high rate of alcoholism, a fact that is now acknowledged by the Soviet leadership. Both low productivity and the poor quality of products have been attributed to the excessive use of alcohol. Unrest and dissatisfaction among Polish workers have been obvious, and have led to frequent strikes and clashes with the police and military. Societies like the Soviet Union, then, while using the name socialism, fall far short of the socialist ideology.

The gap between socialist theory and reality is undoubtedly responsible for the remarkable changes taking place in the Soviet Union and other socialist societies today. There is a broad movement in socialist societies away from centralized state control and toward more free enterprise. Interest is also increasing in democratizing previously authoritarian socialist societies. Mikhail Gorbachev, in his appeals for *glasnost* and *perestroika*, is clearly calling for a more open, restructured Soviet Union. In other words, he wants closer correspondence between the theory of socialism and the reality of life in the Soviet Union. The 1990s will be a particularly momentous time for the Soviet Union and its allies. We will learn whether they will succeed in moving away from state socialism and in the direction of the socialist ideal.

The Industrial Democracy Movement

Industrial democracy System in which workers control what they do

An interesting development in both capitalist and socialist economies is the effort to democratize work settings. Broadly defined, **industrial democracy** means that the workers themselves gain control over what they do. Industrial democracy has occurred in both state capitalist (for example, Sweden) and state socialist (Yugoslavia) societies, and can be seen as an effort to bring some of the ideals of socialism into the workplace. Democratization can occur either at the level of the shop floor, with autonomous groups of workers deciding how their own work should be done, or at the level of the organization, with workers (or their representatives) coming to play a role in directing the organization as a whole.

Sweden. Sweden has led the way in democratizing the workplace. In the late 1960s and early 1970s, Sweden experienced rising worker unhappiness as educated and sophisticated workers rebelled against their routine and boring jobs. This unrest was manifested in large numbers of strikes and high levels of absenteeism and turnover. Sweden has had a long tradition of liberal and humane thinking, and concern about these signs of social unrest and dissatisfaction was widespread. A more practical consideration was that, with a small population and almost no unemployment, Sweden had only a handful of reserve workers available if the unhappy members of the workforce should quit their jobs. (Quitting would be possible for many workers because Sweden has a government welfare system that provides for the unemployed.) As a result, Swedish industries took the lead in trying to deal with these problems by democratizing work at the shop-floor level. The expectation was that workers would be happier if they controlled the workplace and made important decisions about how the work was to be done. More satisfied workers would be less likely to quit, go on strike, or be absent (Ritzer, 1977b).

In the early 1970s a new automobile assembly plant was opened in Kalmar, Sweden, by the Volvo company. This plant was built with the idea of fostering greater democracy among plant employees. Instead of the familiar assembly line, the Kalmar plant was built in a kind of hexagonal shape, which allowed for well-defined assembly areas in which clearly structured groups of workers performed a specific production task, such as assembling the engine. The group members could decide for themselves how their task would be completed and who was to perform specific tasks. The major external requirement was that each group keep the next work group in line provided with enough products so that the performance of their work would not be interrupted. The key feature of this system was that control of the work was largely in the hands of the employees in their autonomous groups.

This plan for a more democratized workplace did not succeed as well as expected. Despite the new organizational form there was still a great deal of external control over workers. Much of what autonomous work groups did was still controlled by the technology, and management continued to shape worker choices through the fixing of goals. Although some shift in power occurred among workers and from foremen (first-line supervisors) to workers, there was no overall change in workers' control over their environment (van Houten, 1987).

Swedish management officials also lost some of their enthusiasm for this effort at democratizing the workplace. Their reasons, however, were related to some changes in the larger society. An economic downturn in Sweden led to an increase in unemployment; in fact, in 1982 Sweden had its highest unemployment rate since the Depression. Given a high unemployment rate, workers are less likely to express dissatisfaction with their work by being absent, striking, or quitting. Thus, the main pressure for democratization was removed, and Swedish industry moved in other directions, including the use of robots. The robotization of many industries eliminated jobs as well as the need to deal with "problem" workers (van Houten, 1987).

The Changing State of the American Economy

Among the most important changes in the American economy are changes in the labor force, the changing nature of labor unions, deindustrialization, the rise in America's foreign competitors, the development of some hopeful signs for the economy in the coming years, and the arrival of the post-industrial society.

Changes in the Labor Force

Enormous shifts in the occupational structure of the United States have occurred since the turn of the century. (See table 13–1.) The most dramatic decline has been seen in the number of people who work on the farms or perform farm-related activities. In 1900 about 38 percent of the labor force was found on the farm, but by 1986 that figure had declined to slightly over 3 percent. We have not yet reached the end of this decline: projections show that by 1995 farmers will represent less than 2 percent of the labor force (Silvestri, Lukasiewicz, and Einstein, 1983). A major factor here has been an array of technological changes that have allowed fewer and fewer people to produce ever-greater quantities of food. Today the independent farmer, being replaced by huge agribusinesses, is on the verge of extinction.

A second major change in the labor force has been the rise in the percentage of people in the professions, which almost quadrupled between 1900 and 1986. Growth in this category has now stabilized and in 1995 the percentage of the labor force in the professions will be about the same as it was in 1986. Major factors responsible for the rise include increasingly sophisticated knowledge, technologies that require more highly trained people, and increasing wealth and sophistication that allow us to want and afford a wide array of professional services.

Table 13-1. Changes in Labor Force by Occupational Group

Occupational Level	Percentage of the Labor Force					
	1900	1930	1960	1970	1982	1995*
White-collar	17.6	29.4	40.8	45.6	53.7	52.5
Professionals	4.3	6.8	10.8	14.0	17.0	17.1
Managers	5.9	7.4	8.7	7.9	11.5	9.6
Clerical workers	3.0	8.9	14.1	16.9	18.5	18.9
Sales	4.5	6.3	7.2	6.8	6.6	6.9
Service	9.1	9.8	11.6	11.8	13.8	16.3
Manual	35.8	39.6	36.4	33.4	29.7	29.3
Farm	37.5	21.1	6.2	2.9	2.7	1.9
Not reported	—	—	5.0	6.3	—	—
Total	100.0	100.0	100.0	100.0	99.9	100.0

* The figures for 1995 are projections.

Source: Data for 1900 and 1930 adapted from Philip M. Hauser, "Labor Force," in Robert E. L. Faris, ed., *Handbook of Modern Sociology* (Chicago: Rand-McNally, 1964), p. 183. Data for 1960 and 1970 adapted from Constance Bogh DiCesare, "Change in the Occupational Structure of U.S. Jobs," *Monthly Labor Review* (1975), p. 24. Data for 1982 from *Employment and Earnings* (30) 1 (Washington, D.C.: U.S. Department of Labor, 1983), p. 157. Data for 1995 from George T. Silvestri, John M. Lukasiewicz, and Marcus E. Einstein, "Occupational Employment Projections Through 1995," *Monthly Labor Review* 106 (1983), pp. 37–49. Totals are rounded.

The demands of large bureaucracies and modern technologies such as the computer have helped fuel a massive increase in clerical workers.

Third, something has occurred that could be labelled the *clerical revolution*. Clerical workers and those in related occupations constituted only 3 percent of the labor force in 1900, but by 1982 that percentage had multiplied sixfold to 18.5 percent. Projections indicate that by 1995 clerical workers will increase to 24 million, or nearly 19 percent of the entire labor force. The major cause of this increase is the rise of bureaucracies with their seemingly insatiable need for white-collar workers of all types. Another key factor is technological change: the rise of the computer has created an "information society" that needs workers to manage the computer's tremendous generation of information.

Finally, blue-collar or manual work has declined substantially. In 1930 the blue-collar workers were, by a wide margin, the largest occupational category, comprising almost 40 percent of the labor force. By 1956, however, the number of people in white-collar occupations exceeded the number in blue-collar occupations for the first time, and since then the gap between them has steadily widened. The forecast is for a further modest decline of people in blue-collar occupations through the mid-1990s. The decline in American industry, technological changes that have eliminated the need for many blue-collar jobs, and the general shift to services all help to account for the decline in blue-collar occupations.

Fastest Growing Occupations. The fastest growing occupation between now and the year 2000 will be paralegals, whose number is expected to more than double by the year 2000. This trend is part of a growth pattern for various occupations (medical assistants, dental assistants, etc.) that assist people in higher-status occupations. This, in turn, corresponds to substantial growth in a wide range of health-related occupations such as physical therapists, home health aides, radiologic technologists, and occupational therapists. Still another cluster of occupations that is likely to grow substantially includes occupations linked to computers—data processing equipment repairers, systems analysts, programmers, and equipment operators. Therefore, the fastest growing occupations are tied to basic changes in society in general and the workworld in particular—increases in services, greater attention to health matters, and the boom in computer technology (Silvestri and Lukasiewicz, 1987).

Increasing Importance of Women in the Labor Force. One of the most dramatic changes in the last few decades has been the increasing number of women in the labor force (Shank, 1988). In 1890 only slightly more than 17 percent of the labor force was female, but by 1987 women constituted 56.2 percent of the labor force. Between 1972 and 1986, the number of women in the labor force grew by 57 percent, compared to a 22 percent growth rate for males. Between 1986 and 2000 the growth rate for women will continue to double that for men (25 percent to 12 percent), although growth rates for both will be down as a result of the overall decline in the birth rate. As far as the net change in the labor force is concerned, two-thirds of it has come, and will continue to come, from women. Not only are women more apt to be in the labor force but increasingly they are in high-status and high-paying occupations (Blum and Smith, 1988).

Although women appear to be doing quite well in the workworld, many problems remain. For example, a stubborn pay gap (the percentage of male income earned by female workers) exists between female and male earnings, and women have a long way

This day-care center at a Stride Rite factory is atypical because relatively few American work settings offer such centers. It is also noteworthy that the father is visiting the children.

to go before achieving pay parity with men (Hodson and England, 1986). Another continuing problem for women is the lack of adequate corporate child-care facilities (Fernandez, 1986). This need has become particularly pressing in the 1980s since 60 percent of women are working by the time their children are four years of age. Approximately 25 million children are living in households in which the mother works for at least part of the day on a regular basis (Hayghe, 1986). These difficult problems are among many others that remain for women despite their significant gains in the labor force.

Changing Labor Unions

In 1900 only 3 percent of the labor force of the United States belonged to unions, but the percentage grew to 23 percent by the end of World War II. By the mid-1980s, however, the percentage had dropped to 18 percent (Flaim, 1985). An expected continuation of this decline leads to estimates that by the year 2000 union membership could drop to 13 percent of the labor force (Lipset, 1987).

Not only have unions lost members but they have shown evidence of decline in other ways as well. Although in the past many unions could often negotiate large wage increases for their members, in recent years wage increases have generally been small. In addition, in order to get contracts with management, unions have been giving up rights and benefits they had won in previous contract negotiations (Katz, 1985). In a variety of ways, unions are weaker overall, including in their ability to negotiate with management. In numbers and in power, the American labor movement is the weakest in the Western world.

Factors Involved in Union Decline. Four key factors help to explain the decline in union membership: lack of competition among unions, worker resistance to unionization, management opposition to unions, and technological change. First, the union movement itself lost some of its dynamism because the internal competition between union organizations was reduced. The most notable case of reducing union competitiveness came when the two major unions, the AFL (American Federation of Labor) and the CIO (Congress of Industrial Organizations), combined to form the AFL-CIO, a single union organization.

Second, by the early 1950s, unions had already organized a large proportion of the group most receptive to unionization—blue-collar factory workers. When they had to look elsewhere for members, they found that other occupations proved resistant to union membership drives.

As one example, unions have not succeeded in organizing white-collar workers. Many white-collar workers are women, and females have historically been less likely to join unions, partly because of negative attitudes toward unions and partly because of their structural position in the workworld. Among the structural factors is the fact that women are more apt to be in sectors of the economy (for example, bureaucracies rather than industries) where unionization is less common (Freeman and Medoff, 1984).

Unions have also failed to attract young people. As with the underrepresentation of women, the reason is not primarily a lack of desire to join unions but the result of a series of structural factors (Freeman and Medoff, 1984). For example, young people are often in temporary jobs, and temporary workers are clearly less interested in unions and more difficult to unionize than permanent employees.

The third factor in the decline of unions is management opposition. Management in the United States has never been favorably disposed to the union movement. (In other societies, especially in Western Europe, management has been much more accepting of unions.) In the earlier part of this century management hired thugs and killers to keep unions out. More recently, most companies came to accept unions, even though grudgingly. But in the 1980s management opposition to unions rose again. One successful move has been for companies to discontinue operations, or restructure the company, and thus break union contracts. Later the operations may be reestablished under a new name or different management, but the newly hired workers are nonunion. Also, many company managers have stepped up their efforts to avoid unionization (Lawler and West, 1985).

The fourth factor in the decline of unions has been technological change that reduces jobs. Often the jobs eliminated are blue-collar jobs, which were most likely to have been unionized. A good example of this trend is in the printing industry, once one of the bastions of union strength. In the old days when type was set by skilled hands, a large proportion of the workers was unionized. However, manual typesetting has been replaced by computer technology, and virtually all of the skilled manual jobs have disappeared. With the disappearance of those jobs came a decline in union membership, and consequently the decline and disappearance of unions in the typesetting industry (Scott, 1987). More generally, new technologies such as computers and robots often cost jobs, and these lost jobs often translate into declines in union membership and union power.

Union Responses to Declines in Numbers. Unions have tried to adapt to their new, reduced situation by concentrating on new groups of workers like government employees, health workers, and professional athletes. They have also tried to develop a series of new goals such as job guarantees for members, the prevention of the loss of American jobs to other countries, and new benefits for members.

In addition to the four factors discussed in this section, union decline is also linked to the decline in American heavy industry where many unionized workers have been employed. As these industries have laid off workers, shut plants down, and "downsized," unions have lost large numbers of members. We turn now to a detailed discussion of this industrial decline, one that is often called **"deindustrialization."**

Deindustrialization The decline of American industry through plant shutdowns, layoffs, and downsizing

Deindustrialization

While American industry continues to dominate the capitalist world, it is not the powerful force it once was. Many American industries, especially steel and automobiles, have declined—a process Bluestone and Harrison (1982) call "the deindustrialization of America."

A major manifestation of deindustrialization is the dramatic drop in employment in such key "smokestack" industries as steel where the number of employees declined from more than 400,000 in 1980 to 155,000 in 1987 (Ignatius, 1988). Many workers have been "dislocated," which in most cases means they have lost their jobs forever. They not only lose their jobs but they also may forfeit their benefits (health insurance, retirement, etc.). They are apt to be laid off with few skills and with few opportunities for the training needed for many of the high-tech occupations now being created by our economy. For many, their only options are jobs such as selling hamburgers in fast-food restaurants. Many companies have been downsized or restructured. For example, USX (formerly the once-mighty U.S. Steel) went from about 100,000 employees in 1980 to less than 20,000 in 1987 (Ignatius, 1987). As a result of downsizing, many blue-collar workers have lost their jobs, but managers and professionals are not immune to major reductions in force (*Fortune*, 1988a).

As a result of deindustrialization, the standard of living in the United States has not risen nearly as rapidly as it has in other countries. The standard of living in the United States was surpassed by West Germany in 1977, and the gap has widened over the ensuing years. Japan, once near the bottom of industrialized nations in terms of standard of living, has been making rapid strides and is poised to pass the United States (Auerbach, 1988)

Disinvestment, Mergers, and Takeovers. Another aspect of the deindustrialization of America is the fact that many American companies have stopped reinvesting substantial sums of money in their own growth and development (Bluestone and Harrison, 1982, p. 6). To maintain productivity as well as to stimulate growth, industries must invest in basic plants and equipment. This kind of industrial investment made the United States the world's greatest economic power. However, in recent years, money has been diverted from such productive investment. For example, instead of investing in new plants and equipment in the United States, corporations are investing in similar facilities in other countries.

Another major source of disinvestment is the merger and takeover mania that has swept through the American corporate world in recent years. Mergers between corporations cost money and, in themselves, produce no new factories, technologies, or jobs. Even more threatening are the huge multibillion dollar takeover efforts that have become commonplace in American industry. In such efforts, one organization may borrow billions of dollars to take over another organization. Since the money is borrowed, it adds nothing to the productivity of the economy. In fact, in the case of takeovers, the economy may actually lose productive capacity as corporations that are taken over are dismantled and sold off in pieces in order to finance the takeover.

Economic Competitors of the United States

Foreign manufacturers have become formidable competitors in the international marketplace. The products of Western Europe and Japan are marketed throughout the world in competition with United States' products. Furthermore, for many years Americans have purchased more goods from other countries than other countries have purchased from us, which leads to the often-reported negative "balance of payments" for the U.S. economy. There is no question that Asian economies, and especially the Japanese, have proved to be our most serious economic competitors. (See figure 13–1.)

The Growing Power of Asian Economies. The success of the Japanese automobile and electronics industries is the most dramatic example of the growing power of America's foreign competitors. After World War II Japan had to rebuild its factories,

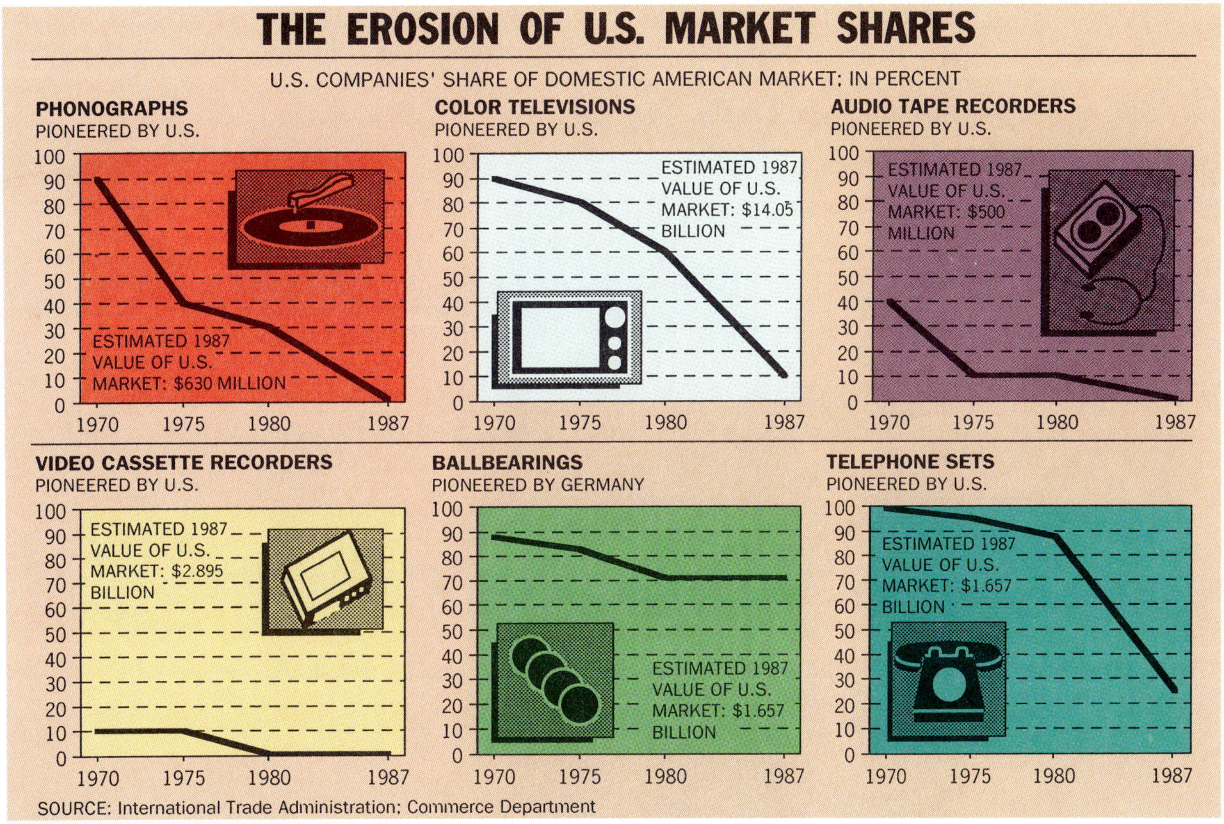

Figure 13–1. The Decline of United States Companies' Share of the Domestic American Market, in Percent. © *The Washington Post*, Sept. 8, 1988.

In recent years, the American economy has been rocked by the closing of many factories, often due to the penetration of United States' markets by foreign competitors.

and those new factories proved to be a big advantage over the aged factories already functioning in the United States. However, much of the success of the Japanese is traceable to the hard work and dedication of their managers and workers. Japanese workers are generally very loyal to their companies and are proud of the products they make. This pride and hard work makes Japanese products highly valued in the markets of the world (Halberstam, 1986).

Asian manufacturers, like Hyundai and its automobile assembly-line depicted here, have become daunting competitors to U.S. manufacturers. Part of the reason is the willingness of Asian employees to work diligently for long hours for comparatively little pay.

However, the Japanese are now experiencing an economic threat from their Asian neighbors—the "four tigers" of Taiwan, Hong Kong, Singapore, and South Korea. South Korea has already made important inroads into the world market for small automobiles (Hyundai) and consumer electronics (Samsung), and they are likely to become significant players in the world economy in other areas as well. The industriousness of the Koreans is revealed in their attitudes toward the Japanese, who are viewed as the "lazy Asians" (Halberstam, 1986). As if to support such a view, the Japanese passed a new law that lowered the maximum work week from 48 to 46 hours, and further reductions will lower the maximum work week to 40 hours by the early 1990s (Shapiro, 1988). Therefore, the United States must compete not only with Japan but also with newer and more vigorous producers like South Korea and other countries on the "Asian Rim."

The Changing Soviet Economy. Another important economic change on the world scene is currently under way in the Soviet Union. Soviet leader Mikhail Gorbachev has used the term *perestroika* to describe this program for restructuring the society. Centralized economic planning and government control over every facet of the economy has defined the Soviet economy since the Communist revolution of 1917. Low productivity and goods of shoddy quality have been characteristic. Thus, for example, it has been claimed that "the most exciting thing about watching Soviet television was that the set was liable to catch fire" (*Fortune*, 1988b, p. 11).

Perestroika aims at increasing productivity and the quality of goods by moving toward more local control by factories, farms, and other economic enterprises. Instead of having centralized agencies make decisions, local units will make those decisions; and those judgments will be shaped, at least to some degree, by market forces. What

The Soviet economy is manifesting a new openness as reflected in the presence of Pepsi Cola signs. However, inadequacies in the economy make it necessary for Soviet citizens to wait in long lines for even the most basic consumer goods.

is produced, how much is produced, and how much the goods will cost will be determined more by the market for the goods and less by fiat from Moscow.

The goal is to produce a system in which incentive exists for high levels of productivity and high quality products. This means that some workers will need to be paid more than others and that consumer goods will be available to workers who are economically successful. Gorbachev has said that it is time that productive workers be rewarded "even if, Marx forbid, some of them get rich at it" (Ford, 1988, p. 74).

The current Soviet view is that workers need to be more motivated, more ambitious, more interested in earning money, and more concerned with accumulating material possessions. Workers will also be given more voice in running their organizations and in the selection of management. Organizations, too, will be motivated by allowing them to earn profits and to be free to decide what to do with those profits (expansion, higher pay, etc.). More entrepreneurship will be encouraged as people are allowed to go into various kinds of businesses for themselves or as members of a group. This program is obviously very revolutionary and ambitious, and it is unclear how far Gorbachev will succeed with *perestroika*. In the short run, much economic disruption and substantial price increases are forecast. But if Gorbachev is successful in weathering the early storms, a radically altered Soviet economy might emerge.

The American Economy in the Coming Years

Although the recent history of American industry has been somewhat negative, there are some hopeful signs. Many believe that manufacturing continues to be the key to America's economic prosperity; signs of expansion are emerging in American manufacturing, and greater success has been reported in the international marketplace (*Fortune*, 1988c). Even the smokestack industries have some bright spots, such as the revival of Ford and its record-high profits, although that revival has come, to some degree, from downsizing the company, which results in a far smaller payroll. Outside of traditional areas of strength, other bright spots in American industry include pharmaceuticals (for example, the drug t-PA that saves lives by dissolving clots that cause heart attacks [*Fortune*, 1988d]), biotechnology, "cosmeceuticals" (for example, Retin-A to remove wrinkles and Rogaine to stimulate hair growth in people with male-type baldness [*Business Week*, 1988a]), semi-conductors, as well as the superconductors mentioned at the beginning of the chapter. All these examples demonstrate the strength of American industries in terms of technological innovation. Finally, the changing relations with China and the Soviet Union may lead to huge new markets that American industry might be able to supply with a wide range of goods.

The Post-Industrial Economy

Many observers see the economy of the United States as moving beyond industrial capitalism into a stage called a "post-industrial society" (Bell, 1973). As we noted in chapter 4, a post-industrial society is one defined more by service industries than goods-producing industries. In 1940, 51.4 percent of the workforce was in goods-producing areas like agriculture, mining, construction, and manufacturing. In 1986 about 22 percent of the workforce was in those areas. On the other hand, in 1940, 48.6 percent of the workforce was in service areas, but by 1986 the percentage had increased to 67 percent (Kutscher, 1987).

The projections for the year 2000 are even more striking. Between now and 2000 the number of workers in goods-producing areas is likely to remain exactly the same, while the number of people in service-producing areas is likely to increase by 20 million people! In the year 2000, only 19 percent of the labor force will be in goods production, while 71 percent will be in services (Kutscher, 1987).

In addition to the growth in well-known service areas in recent years, a number of new service arenas have emerged. Many organizations now provide services to other businesses. For example, accounting, computing, and security services have boomed (Tschetter, 1987). Also in this category are the organizations that provide temporary help to business. Processing knowledge and information and providing it to those who need it have become major sectors of the service area. Some have argued that instead of calling it a "service society," it should be called an "information society" (Lyon, 1986).

The Declining Economic Fortunes of the Younger Generation

With all of the changes occurring in the American economy, many people in the younger generation will have a difficult economic future. Between 1945 and 1973, the wages of American workers, adjusted for inflation, increased between 2.5 and 3.0 percent per year. But since 1973 wages have stagnated or even declined. Americans who were participating in the economy during the earlier time period were able to develop quite comfortable lifestyles, which they continue today. They have job security through sen-

"Eventually I'd like to have a business where the money rolls in and I wouldn't have to be there much."

Cross-National Perspectives

"Quality Circles" in Japanese and American Industries

As we saw in chapter 4, the successes of Japanese industry have caused the leaders of American industry to rethink many of their management practices. One specific innovation that many American companies have copied from the Japanese is the "quality circle." A quality circle is a small group of 6 to 12 workers that meets on a regular basis to solve problems that arise in its particular work area.

The members of quality circles first receive training in problem solving, statistical control over quality, and how to interact as a group. With these skills, the group is able to decide on ways to improve the quality of the production process and the final product. A facilitator from management is present, whose job is to train the group and make sure that everything runs smoothly. The group meets for several hours each month, sometimes on company time, sometimes on personal time, to discuss work-related problems. The goal is to offer suggestions for improving the quality of products, increase productivity, and enhance employee involvement in Japanese corporate activities.

While improvement in the quality of products is the primary goal of quality circles, these groups are also important because they demonstrate to the workers that they are being treated as human beings and that their ideas are being taken seriously. Such groups have come up with innumerable suggestions that have greatly helped Japanese industry. Furthermore, they have played a central role in maintaining the morale of Japanese workers and helping them to become some of the most productive workers in the world.

A quality circle usually operates in the following way: One or more members of the circle may come to recognize a problem that is serious and important enough to involve the whole group (such as too many defects in the production of automobile bumpers). These group members may then bring the problem to the attention of the quality circle, and, if the group agrees to focus on the problem, it will begin to study it systematically. A typical course of action is to collect statistics on the exact number of bumper defects, and especially the number that appear at each stage of the production process. After the study is completed, perhaps taking a few months, the quality circle meets to analyze the data. The goal is to identify the source of the problem. Is it a defective design from engineering? Bad parts from suppliers? An improperly functioning machine? Poor coordination among work team members? An incompetent operator? Once the group feels that it has identified the source of the problem, it then makes recommendations as to how it can be corrected. If the suggestions can be implemented within the team, the group itself can decide to accept them. Otherwise, upper levels of management must be involved in the ultimate decision. In any case, it is likely that a solution will be found and put into practice. The results of the quality circle's study may be published in the company newsletter, and the group is often recognized by the company if the suggestion is a good one. It is even possible for the group to receive a national award. In addition, the company reports to the employees the results of suggested procedures, which shows workers that their ideas have been important. They can thereby see the relationship between their efforts and company profits, which may mean pay increases (Ouchi, 1981).

While quality circles are usually associated with manufacturing industries such as automobiles, the possible settings are almost limitless. The Japanese now use quality circles among white-collar workers in offices, among sales workers, in warehouses, banks, and insurance companies.

Prior to the Japanese industrial invasion, Americans had nothing to parallel the quality circle. The closest thing was the "suggestion box" into which workers were urged to put slips indicating how work-related matters could be improved. However, it was often suspected that management paid little attention to these suggestions. Many American companies have now tried to implement quality circles, but it remains to be seen how well they will work and how long they will survive. A method may work in one society, but because of cultural differences, it may not be possible to transfer the method directly to another. Just to note one difficulty: many American workers may be unwilling to devote unpaid personal time to group meetings designed to help management.

Lawler, Edward E., and Mohrman, Susan A. "Quality Circles After the Fad." *Harvard Business Review* January/February, 1985.
Ouchi, William G. *Theory Z.* New York: Avon Books, 1982.

iority, their housing costs remain stable because of fixed mortgages, and they have savings that grew dramatically during periods of high interest rates. In contrast, the generation coming into adulthood after 1973 has had a much more difficult time achieving the same life style as their predecessors, and many are struggling economically. In order to achieve economic success, they will have to make many more sacrifices than the preceding generation. Many young American couples today have both spouses working, and even so, they find it impossible to achieve what their parents did. Frequently they are unable to accumulate the capital necessary to purchase a home, and many incur great amounts of consumer debt. In addition, although many young couples want families, they must postpone or curtail having children because of economic considerations (Levy, 1987).

Experiences in the World of Work

Sociologists have studied the world of work in many different settings and occupations (Ritzer and Walczak, 1986). While many people enjoy their work and get fulfillment from their jobs or careers, many other people experience stresses and conflict through their work. Conflict is a major factor in occupational life and is often built into the work role.

Role Conflict

Role conflict
When a person in a position is confronted with mutually exclusive expectations

Role conflict refers to a situation in which a person who holds a position is confronted with conflicting or contradictory expectations so that compliance with one makes compliance with the other difficult. We will consider three of the major forms of role conflict: role overload, inter-role conflict, and inter-sender role conflict.

Role overload
When a person is in a role in which too many expectations must be satisfied in a given time

Role Overload.

Role overload occurs when an individual in a role is confronted with a large number of expectations and finds it difficult, if not impossible, to satisfy all of them in a given time period. Because of the nature of their position at the top of organizations, executives are prone to virtually every form of role conflict and are particularly likely to be confronted with role overload.

The president of a broadcasting company describes his day and his role overload, which, incidentally, he seemed to enjoy.[1]

> My day starts between four-thirty and five in the morning. . . . I dictate in my library until about seven-thirty. Then I have breakfast. The driver gets here about eight o'clock and often times I continue dictating in the car on the way to the office. . . . I will probably have as many as 150 letters dictated by seven-thirty in the morning. I have five full-time secretaries, who do nothing but work for (me) . . . (seven more) work for me part-time. This does not include my secretaries in New York, Los Angeles, Washington, and San Francisco. They get dictabelts from me every day. . . . I get home around six-thirty, seven at night. After dinner with the family I spend a minimum of two and a half hours each night going over the mail and dictating. I should have a secretary at home just to handle the mail that comes there. . . . Although I don't go to the office on Saturday or Sunday, I do have mail brought out to my home for the weekend. I dictate on Saturday and Sunday. When I do this on holidays, like Christmas, New Year's and Thanksgiving, I have to sneak a little bit, so the family doesn't know what I'm doing (Terkel, 1974, pp. 390–391).

Role overload is also illustrated by this school superintendent's comments: "There are times when I feel like I have about 15 balls in the air at one time, like a juggler. It's *so* many things. A committee working on this, a committee working on that, a dozen things going. Trying to keep abreast of all of them" (Blumberg and Blumberg, 1985, p. 151). Very often, as these two examples reveal, role overload is associated with the heavy time demands of high-status occupations and professions.

Inter-role conflict
When expectations of one role are in conflict with expectations of another

Inter-Role Conflict.

Inter-role conflict occurs when the expectations attached to one role are in conflict with the expectations of another role. Women in the labor force are especially apt to experience inter-role conflict because the demands of their jobs are in conflict with the expectations their family members have about their family responsibilities. The inter-role conflict comes between the job and family roles. Their bosses and fellow workers expect dedication to the job, while family members expect time and attention to their needs. Much has been written in the media about the "superwoman" who holds a high-prestige professional job and also fulfills relatively traditional family roles. However, as sociologist Myra Ferree (1987) points out, most women do not have

---

[1] Excerpts from *Working: People Talk About What They Do All Day and How They Feel About What They Do*, by Studs Terkel.

jobs that conform to the media superwoman. The majority of employed women are employed as clerical workers, service workers, factory workers, or the relatively low-status professions of nursing and teaching. Despite the status level of these jobs, married women, especially those who have children, frequently experience inter-role conflict between their employment and family roles.

Inter-sender role conflict
When two or more people have conflicting expectations of a person in a given role

Inter-Sender Role Conflict. **Inter-sender role conflict** occurs when two or more people have conflicting expectations of a person in a given role. As one illustration, college professors often experience inter-sender role conflict because two important groups, students on the one hand and fellow professors on the other, place conflicting demands on them. These two groups have radically different expectations of the professor, who is literally caught in a crossfire between them. Students expect their professors to do a good job of teaching: they should remain up to date on relevant material, prepare carefully for class, and work hard at communicating what they know in an interesting and informative manner. Furthermore, professors are expected to prepare and grade exams carefully, being sure to give students feedback on their performance and to comment on how they could improve in the future. Professors should also be available to students during office hours and at other times of mutual convenience. This all seems quite reasonable from the students' perspective. It clearly takes a lot of the professor's time, but, after all, isn't that what professors are supposed to do with their time?

From the point of view of professional colleagues, that is *not* what professors are supposed to do with their time. Fellow professors generally expect their colleagues to put in a minimum amount of time teaching. The majority of their time is expected to be devoted to research, writing, giving papers at professional meetings, and engaging in an array of other professional activities. Professors expect their colleagues to contribute to their discipline, primarily through research and writing. Increases in salary and promotions generally go to professors who do the most high-quality research.

The conflict between the expectations of students and colleagues often forces individual professors to make a choice. Does the professor conform to the expectations of students and carefully prepare a lecture? Or does he or she conform to the expectations of colleagues and work on a research project? This is the inter-sender role conflict experienced by professors on a day-to-day basis.

Another example of inter-sender role conflict is found in many work settings in which a lower-level supervisor is caught between the demands of management and the demands of workers (Sasser and Leonard, 1980; Grimm and Dunn, 1986). In a typical factory setting, a foreman is the supervisor who stands between management and blue-collar, manual workers. Foremen have been the subject of much social research, and most of it has portrayed the occupation as subject to the kind of inter-sender role conflict described above. It is possible for a foreman to avoid, or at least decrease, inter-sender role conflict, as a recent study has shown. This study of foremen in a modern automobile assembly plant found that most foremen did not experience role conflict because they identified with management rather than with the workers. As a result, these foremen reported higher levels of job satisfaction than is usually assumed to be the case for this occupation. Identifying with management, these foremen were more troubled by difficulties in moving up the managerial hierarchy than by role conflict.

Grimm and Dunn explain their findings in terms of the changing nature of industrial life. The complexities of contemporary industry require that modern foremen be able to handle complex technical problems rather than being close to, and being able to deal with, workers. In other words, foremen now need technological skills far more than they require human relations skills needed to deal with blue-collar subordinates. Furthermore, modern foremen are more apt to be recruited from outside the organization, even from college graduates, than from the ranks of blue-collar workers, as has been the case in the past. Such modern foremen are far more likely to identify with management than their predecessors. Finally, modern organizations stress a team approach to managerial decision making, further creating ties between foremen and higher level managers. These and other contemporary realities have tended to mitigate, but *not* eliminate, intersender role conflict among foremen (Grimm and Dunn, 1986).

Conflict with Customers and Clients

People in service occupations often experience conflict with customers or clients (Peterson, Schmidman, and Elifson, 1982). Service occupations include, among many others, automobile salespersons, taxi drivers, airline flight attendants, male and female prostitutes, and physicians in private practice. Direct and spontaneous conflict is always possible in occupations that serve customers, as is illustrated by the following examples of waitresses and salespeople.

Waitresses. Customers create all sorts of problems for waitresses, including complaints about service, belligerence, and drunkenness. Much conflict surrounds the waitresses' desire to be respected and the customers' propensity to act superior to them. Finally, the tip is significant to the waitress (as it is to the taxi driver), both as a symbol of success and as a source of income. The customer controls the size of the tip and, indeed, whether a tip is left. This is a continuing source of stress, as revealed by the following statement of a cocktail waitress:

> Tips? I feel like Carmen. It's like holding out a tambourine and they throw the coin. (Laughs) There might be occasions when the customers might make it demeaning—the man about town, the conventioneer. When the time comes to pay the check, he would do little things, "How much should I give you?" He might make an issue about it. I did say to one, "Don't play God with me. Do what you want." Then it really didn't matter whether I got a tip or not. I would spit it out, my resentment—that he dares make me feel I'm operating only for a tip. He'd ask for his check. Maybe he's going to sign it. He'd take a very long time and he'd make me stand there, "Let's see now, what do you think I ought to give you?" He would not let go of that moment. And you know it. You know he means to demean you. He's holding the change in his hand, or if he'd sign, he'd flourish the pen and wait. These are the times I really get angry. I'm not reticent. Something would come out. Then I really didn't care, "God-damn, keep your money!" (quoted in Terkel, 1974, p. 295).

Salespeople. The livelihood of all salespeople depends on their ability to make sales, and, as in all relationships between worker and client/customer, the situation produces a struggle for control. Salespeople seek to persuade the customer to make a purchase, while customers try to resist these efforts and retain control of the situation by not agreeing to a deal. In almost all cases, the resolution of the conflict involves the use of **dramaturgy** (Goffman, 1959b): performances by individuals (in this case, salespeople) aimed at manipulating situations in ways favorable to themselves.

Dramaturgy Theater-like performances aimed at manipulating situations in one's favor

The used car salesperson is the classic example of an occupation that uses dramaturgical techniques in order to achieve its goals (in this case, selling used automobiles).

A good example of the use of dramaturgy to resolve conflict between customer and client appears in Miller's (1964) study of people who sold used cars. The heart of the drama is the "pitch," which begins when customers have made it clear that they really are interested in buying a car. The pitch involves a social drama in which the salesperson tries to understand the customer and modify sales tactics to fit the customer's character. In discussing a trade-in, taking a test drive, and seeing the customer's old car, the salesperson is able to discover things about the customer that help in selling the car. The salesperson tries to find out what the customer is thinking at all times. He or she accomplishes this by taking the role of the customer, as well as by keeping the customer talking. At all times, the salesperson "desires to keep control, in fact, achieve mastery of his relationship with the customer" (Miller, 1964, p. 19).

Alienation

The concept of alienation continues to be an important and powerful idea for understanding occupational experiences. **Alienation** is a Marxian concept that refers to a breakdown of the natural connections between people and their work, other people, and the natural world. A number of sociologists have expanded upon this basic meaning in various ways (Blauner, 1964; Schwalbe, 1986; Silver, 1986). For example, from a social-psychological perspective, alienation has four components. The first is **powerlessness,** or the domination of individuals by other persons or objects and the inability of individuals to reduce or eliminate that control. **Meaninglessness,** the second aspect of alienation, results from the inability of people to see their role in relation to other roles and to the purpose of their work. Third, alienated individuals suffer from **isolation:** they lack a feeling of belonging to the work situation and have little identification with the workplace. Alienation also involves a feeling of **self-estrangement,** which manifests itself in a lack of involvement in one's work. Self-estranged workers are unable to express their unique abilities, potentialities, or personality (Blauner, 1964).

Alienation
Breakdown between people and their work, other people, and the natural world

Powerlessness
Condition of being dominated by another individual or by circumstances

Meaninglessness
Condition in which one cannot see one's place and significance in the broader scheme of things

Isolation
Condition resulting from a feeling of not belonging to one's workplace

Self-estrangement
Condition of not being able to express one's abilities, potentialities, and personality in one's work

We usually think of automobiles when we think of assembly lines, but many other products are produced on an assembly-line basis. Wherever they are found, assembly lines usually lead to boredom and hardship for workers.

Alienation on the Assembly Line. One occupation that epitomizes the characteristics of alienation is assembly-line work, where the major source of alienation is the relentless line itself. Assembly-line workers perform their assigned tasks at set intervals for eight hours every work day, with almost no variation allowed. In an automobile plant, a worker may tighten the same one or two bolts hour after hour. In a poultry processing plant, a worker may stuff a package of giblets into turkey after turkey as they pass by on a conveyor belt. Respite only comes when the line breaks down, an event many workers hope for and sometimes contribute to by sabotaging the machinery.

Many assembly-line workers are almost totally powerless; they are unable to control the pace of the line, their superiors, or top management. This inability to control their own work pace is perhaps the most demoralizing aspect of the job. What distinguishes their work from virtually all other occupations is that both the rate of work and the kind of work are invariable and uncontrollable. Some degree of powerlessness exists in all occupations, but most workers can generally vary their own work pace and make their work more interesting by changing the tasks they perform.

Typically, assembly-line workers are unable to see what their specialized task has to do with the work of others on the line or at other levels in the organization. They are also unable to see what tightening a bolt has to do with the finished product (and, in many cases, they do not even know what the finished product is). The nature of the job contributes to a feeling of meaninglessness because it is so specialized, uninteresting, and unimportant that it is difficult for anyone to derive any satisfaction from the work.

The assembly-line workers' problems are compounded by their isolation. The noise and the demands of the line prevent interaction with co-workers on the job, making it difficult for an informal work group to develop. An assembly-line worker describes this phenomenon:

> You can work next to a guy for months without even knowing his name. One thing, you're too busy to talk. Can't hear. (Laughs) You have to holler in his ear. They got these little guys comin' around in white shirts and if they see you runnin' your mouth, they say, "This guy needs more work." Man, he's got no time to talk (quoted in Terkel, 1974, p. 165).

Workers are also isolated from all levels of management because of the nature of their work and the desire of management to maintain what it considers to be proper distance. Assembly-line work is usually found in large plants, and their size also serves to inhibit the development of personal relationships.

Workers on the assembly line are particularly prone to self-estrangement. The work is so boring and anonymous that they derive little personal good feeling from it. Hence, workers spend a good part of their time daydreaming: "You dream, you think of things you've done. I drift back continuously to when I was a kid and what me and my brothers did. The things you love most are the things you drift back into" (quoted in Terkel, 1974, p. 160). Because no real skills or abilities are needed, assembly-line workers are unable to express themselves in their work.

Efforts to Cope with Alienation on the Job. One device often used by workers in alienating occupations is "working the system." In a participant observer study of a machine shop, Roy (1954) reports how the workers sought "to beat the system." "We machine operators did 'figure the angles,' we developed an impressive repertoire of angles to play and devoted ourselves to crossing the expectations of the formal organization with perseverance, artistry, and organizing ability of our own" (Roy, 1954, p. 257). For example, when a time study was being conducted to set piece-work rates, the workers would take longer to do a job than they ordinarily would. They would run the machines at slower speeds or utilize extra movements such as "little reachings, liftings, adjustings, dustings, and other special attentions of conscientious machine operation and good housekeeping that could be dropped instantly with the departure of the time-study man" (Roy, 1954, p. 257). When the time-study man made a job difficult, the workers revised it to make it easier, even though the change might be harder on tools or reduce the quality of the product.

In another study, Roy (1959–1960) examined informal group practices that were not aimed against management but served to make work life more meaningful. Roy was interested in how machine operators prevented themselves from "going nuts." He was again a participant observer in a group of machine operators engaged in work that was repetitious and very simple and that required long hours and a six-day week. The following is Roy's description of the work:

> Standing all day in one spot beside three old codgers in a dingy room looking out through barred windows at the bare walls of a brick warehouse, leg movements largely restricted to the shifting of the body weight from one foot to the other, hand and arm movement confined, for the most part, to a simple repetitive sequence of place the die, punch the clicker, place the die, punch the clicker, and intellectual activity reduced to computing the hours to quitting time (Roy, 1959–1960, p. 160).

Roy focused on the social devices that machine operators used to find some meaning in an essentially meaningless occupation. First, the machine operators made a little game out of their work: they varied their activities by changing the colors of the material or the die shapes used. Informal group activities made the work day more interesting and pleasant. During the morning "peach time" was announced, and one worker took out two peaches and divided them among the four workers. Then there was "banana time." The same man who brought the peaches also brought a banana, which was for his own consumption. Regularly each morning one of the workers would steal the banana and consume it gleefully while yelling "banana time!" The person who brought the banana would regularly protest, and just as regularly another worker would admonish him for protesting so vociferously. As the day progressed, there was "window time," "lunch time," "pickup time," "fish time," and "Coke time." Through these contrived activities, workers in an essentially meaningless job endeavored to make their work life more meaningful.

Runcie (1980) and Houbolt (1982) describe other coping devices among assembly-line workers. For example, workers can withdraw by being absent. In fact, Runcie (1980, p. 109) found that "on many mornings the line could not start due to the shortage of workers. Often we would stand around waiting for the company to find people to fill the holes in the line." Both Runcie and Houbolt found that workers use drugs as a means of coping with alienation. Said one worker: "If I smoke [marijuana], I can stare at a spot on the floor all day long and not get bored" (Runcie, 1980, p. 109).

Problems of Safety and Health in the Workworld

In addition to the conflicts and problems we have already considered, which tend to be connected with the psychological well-being of the worker, there are also physical problems. For larger numbers of workers than might be expected, work is hazardous. The National Safe Workplace Institute estimates that over 60,000 Americans a year die because of their work. About one-sixth of them die as a result of traumatic injuries associated with their work, while the other five-sixths die as a result of diseases, usually cancer, that come from prior exposure to some disease-causing agent on the job (Litke, 1988).

The hazards associated with the workworld take a number of forms. For one thing, various types of work can be unsafe and have the possibility of causing the worker physical harm. A machine operator can lose a limb because of a careless move, or a lumberjack can suffer serious injuries falling from a tree. Steel workers can be scalded, or crushed by equipment. A construction worker can fall from a scaffold or from a building, and a truck driver can die in a fiery crash. Firefighters have died as a result of using defective protective equipment while putting out fires. Hazards also exist for many people who have threatening forms of interaction on the job: the most obvious examples are military personnel and the police, but there are many others. The shopkeeper or the gas station attendant must deal with holdups, while the social worker faces the danger of forays into "tough" neighborhoods (Mayer and Rosenblatt, 1975).

Some workers confront a variety of unhealthy conditions that can bring on debilitating, and in some cases fatal, illnesses. Diseases are much more likely to kill or cripple people than on-the-job accidents. The best known example is Black Lung disease among coal miners; out of the 100,000 cases of this disease in the country today, approximately 4,000 people die from it each year. People who work with uranium run a risk of contracting cancer due to their exposure to radioactivity. Over 80,000 workers were exposed to radiation in 1980. This constitutes an increase in the number of people exposed and in the amount of radiation to which each worker was exposed; the exposure rate has nearly quadrupled since 1969 (Omang, 1981). Another major occupational health hazard is asbestos (McCulloch, 1986). A large number of the one-half million people who have worked with asbestos can expect to contract cancer and other diseases (Stellman and Daum, 1973).

In addition to the danger to employees, we must also mention the danger to the population as a whole from economic undertakings. For example, the widespread production and use of chlorofluorocarbons is now known to reduce the ozone layer in the atmosphere, which can lead to dramatic increases in skin cancer.

Finally, a word about another health hazard—job stress. Many jobs are highly stressful, and prolonged stress can cause an array of physical and psychological problems. Certainly mine workers find their work, especially the threat of cave-ins, highly stressful. Similarly, being a firefighter, a police officer, or a paramedic can be highly stressful (Spitzer, 1988).

Many assume that high-status occupations produce the greatest amount of stress. According to a major study of the relationship between occupations and heart disease, that assumption is probably true, but it is not the entire story. The Framingham (Massachusetts) heart study found that males in professional and white-collar jobs—lawyers, doctors, dentists, and business managers—had the highest rate of coronary heart disease. Blue-collar men had the next highest rate, while male clerical workers had the lowest rate.

Among the women in the Framingham heart study, however, one group of employed women had a particularly high risk of coronary heart disease. Women who had clerical occupations, husbands in blue-collar occupations, and children living at home were far more likely to have coronary heart disease than any other working women or housewives. The researchers concluded that these women had heightened stress from the combined responsibilities and frustrations of their work and home lives (Haynes and Feinlieb, 1980).

Unemployment

Unemployment has been a persistent reality in the American economy. During the last 30 years the unemployment rate has rarely been below 5 percent of the labor force. During the early 1980s the unemployment rate was near 10 percent for several years. Five or 10 percent of the labor force translates into many millions of people out of work, many of whom are likely to be struggling economically and socially to survive. Traditionally, unemployment has plagued those in blue-collar, semi-skilled, and unskilled occupations. Although deindustrialization, downsizing, and restructuring have all served to increase the unemployment rate for white-collar and managerial workers, the rate for blue-collar workers still far outstrips that for white-collar workers. Other factors are highly related to unemployment. For example, those with less than a high school education have a far higher unemployment rate than college graduates. Race is also highly related to unemployment. Blacks since World War II have consistently had an unemployment rate that is double (or more) the rate for whites.

Unemployment is more than statistics; it involves highly personal effects on the people who are out of work (Burman, 1988). The most obvious problems for the unemployed person are the loss of income and the absence of a job in a society in

Unemployment and unemployment lines are persistent aspects of the American economy. Being unemployed is not only economically disastrous, but it causes many other personal problems as well.

which one is usually judged by one's occupation. But, as we saw in chapter 5, the unemployed person must learn how to structure the hours of the day that would normally be taken up by a job.

As symbolic interaction theory would suggest, an unemployed person is also likely to have some problems with his or her self-concept. Without work to think about, many of the unemployed have little to occupy their thoughts other than themselves: *"The only thing I have on my mind on those days is me. Nothing else"* (Burman, 1988, p. 188). More important, unemployment has a negative effect on self-esteem: *"On a bad day . . . I'll take it personally. Those are the days I feel incompetent, very unsure of myself"* (Burman, 1988, p. 200).

Obviously, structuring time and maintaining self-esteem are only two of the many difficulties facing those who are unemployed. The list is long, but the key point is that unemployment has a powerful impact on people. The unemployed are left to "kill time," and as a result end up in an endless process of "losing ground" occupationally, economically, and in a variety of other ways.

Satisfaction from Work

Many Americans go about their work each day without a feeling of personal gratification from what they do. The expansion of impersonal bureaucracies, factory-like offices, and assembly lines have all made it increasingly difficult for people to find satisfaction in their work. Yet many Americans do find satisfaction and even pride in their work.

The garbage collectors ("scavengers") of San Francisco (Perry, 1978) offer an interesting example. Collecting garbage is considered one of the dirty jobs of society; it is low in prestige and often low in pay. Garbage collectors have their problems with

CHAPTER 14

Health and Medicine

The twentieth century has brought dramatic changes in types of illnesses, causes of death, and the nature of health care. The illnesses and diseases that caused most deaths at the beginning of this century are no longer the scourges they once were. In 1900 half of the leading causes of death were infectious diseases, with tuberculosis ranking first and pneumonia second. Influenza was another major killer. These are diseases caused by bacterial and viral agents, and their victims at the turn of the century were often children and young adults. By 1985 tuberculosis was far down the list as a cause of death; in fact, it was largely eradicated, accounting for only 1,700 of the 2 million deaths yearly in the United States. In 1985 pneumonia was the *only* infectious disease in the top ten, having dropped from second to sixth. Today, infectious diseases cause death primarily among the elderly, not among children as was the case at the beginning of this century.

Now, noninfectious diseases such as heart disease, cancer, and cerebrovascular disease (for example, stroke) have become the leading causes of death. These three diseases accounted for about 60 percent of all deaths in 1985. In contrast to the infectious diseases, noninfectious diseases are related in large part to lifestyle and the aging process. Among young people, injuries from accidents, suicides, and homicides are now the leading causes of death. Because all of today's major causes of death are connected to lifestyles and personal choices—in other words, social factors—sociologists have a keen interest in both health and medicine, as well as the medical profession itself.

Sociology of Health and Medicine

We may not be accustomed to thinking of sociology as a field concerned with health-related issues; these matters seem to fall within the exclusive province of physicians, biologists, and other health professionals. Yet the sociology of health and medicine, often called *medical sociology,* is one of the most popular specialties among sociologists.

The sociological study of health considers how human behavior contributes to disease and illness or detracts from good health. The sociological view is that both health and illness are not defined simply by physiological factors. Many social and cultural factors are involved, by serving as causes of illness, by influencing the course of an illness, or by affecting whether and how a person recovers from an illness. In addition, a powerful relationship exists between a person's health status and the social and cultural milieu in which the individual lives.

For example, consider how the food and dietary habits of the people in a society can influence their health. The Japanese prefer to eat fish, which has low levels of cholesterol, and they have very low rates of heart disease. In contrast, Americans have

The poster tells these African women that "To destroy filth is to kill cholera." Even though infectious diseases are not a major cause of death in the United States, some, like cholera, are still major killers in many African nations and other developing countries.

traditionally preferred red meat in their diet, which has a high level of cholesterol. Americans have a relatively high rate of heart disease.

Social epidemiology
Study of the frequency and pattern of a disease within a population

This comparison between the Japanese and American dietary habits, and their apparently related heart-disease rates, illustrates an important aspect of medical sociology called social epidemiology. **Social epidemiology** is the study of the frequency and pattern of a disease within a particular population (Wolinsky, 1988). Epidemiologists focus on the prevalence of specific diseases or illnesses in different populations and then try to determine if a distinguishing social or behavioral factor can be isolated that could account for the differences. One of the early, classic examples of social epidemiology occurred in the late 1700s when Sir Percival Potts discovered that chimney sweeps had a higher rate of scrotum cancer than other groups in the population. It seemed probable that something in the nature of their work caused chimney sweeps to suffer more from this form of cancer, and ultimately the cause was found to be the excessive amounts of soot to which they were exposed.

Social Epidemiology and AIDS

Social epidemiology was a major tool in identifying how the AIDS virus was being transmitted. AIDS (Acquired Immune Deficiency Syndrome) was first reported in 1981, and it quickly became clear that the group in which AIDS was most prevalent was the homosexual male population. Early studies of gay men indicated that those who got the disease had engaged in sexual relations with a large number of partners. Therefore, it appeared that the sexual behaviors of these men were implicated in their contracting AIDS.

American consumers have traditionally included much red meat in their diets, especially when compared to the Japanese, who consume more fish. These dietary differences apparently help account for the lower heart disease rates among the Japanese.

In 1982 further research revealed other high-risk groups in the population, indicating that the means of transmission could be other than sexual. People who had received blood transfusions, especially hemophiliacs who need transfusions regularly, also had a high prevalence of AIDS. In addition, drug addicts who were taking their drugs intravenously appeared as a high-risk group. This evidence indicated that the virus was being transmitted by either infected blood or semen, and that victims were infected when the virus somehow entered the blood stream. These facts were further confirmed when infants were born with the AIDS virus, which they were obviously getting from the infected blood of their mothers.

After these early facts were uncovered, it was clear that AIDS was not exclusively a disease of the gay population but could be contracted by anyone who had direct contact with the blood or semen of a person carrying the virus. The direct contact that most frequently transmitted the virus, however, involved the sexual practices of gay/bisexual males and intravenous drug use (apparently because users were sharing dirty hypodermic needles). In 1988 gay and bisexual men and intravenous drug users still accounted for over 80 percent of new cases of diagnosed AIDS.

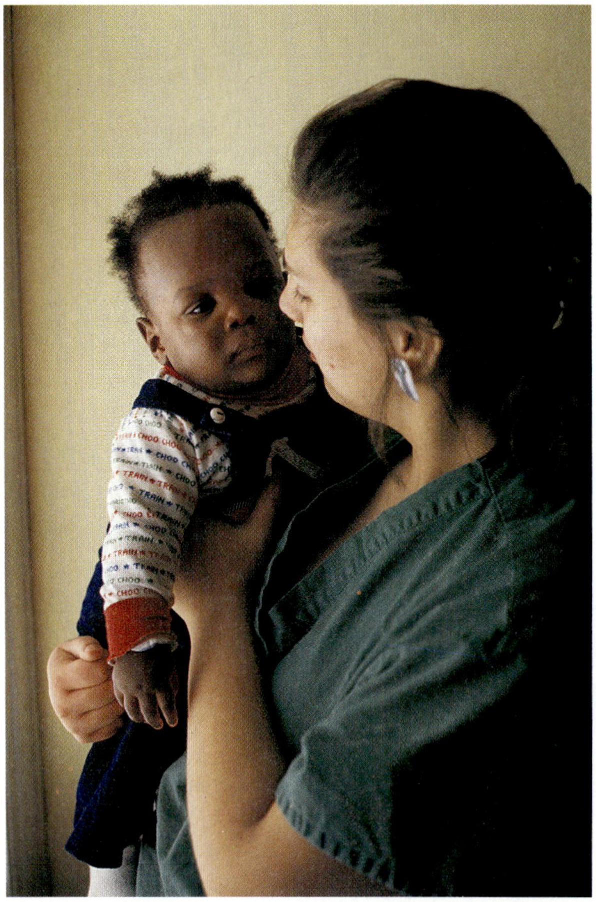

AIDS is being found more and more in babies born to mothers who have the disease. They get the virus from the blood of their mothers while they are in the uterus.

Other Interests of Medical Sociology

Medical sociology involves much more than studies of social epidemiology, however. Sociologists are interested in how different sociocultural backgrounds affect peoples' "attitudes, beliefs and behavior concerning health, illness, and death" (Wolinsky, 1988, p. 39). Medical sociologists are also concerned with the nature of the relationship between physicians and patients and the changes that have taken place over the years in that relationship. Some sociologists direct their attention to the study of hospitals as bureaucratic organizations. Others focus on medical and health occupations (ambulance personnel, laboratory technicians) and professions (physicians, nurses, and pharmacists). A growing concern of sociologists is the overall organization of health care in society and the changes taking place within the health-care system. This brief description provides only a glimpse of the field of medical sociology, but many of these issues will receive fuller treatment throughout this chapter.

The Changing Nature of Health and Medicine

The infectious diseases that were the major killers at the beginning of the century are called communicable diseases. **Communicable diseases** are diseases that can be transmitted to people in a variety of ways—by other people, by animals or other organisms, or from contaminated food or water that is ingested. Since, at the beginning of the twentieth century, there were few effective medicines or other techniques to combat these diseases, life expectancy was comparatively short (47 years in 1900 compared to almost 75 years in 1985); the infant mortality rate was high (the 1900 rate was almost three times as high as the 1985 rate); and there was an ever-present likelihood of epidemics that could take massive numbers of lives in short periods of time. In many cases, contracting one of these infectious diseases had little to do with anything that people did or did not do. If a person happened to come into contact with the bacteria or virus, chances were that he or she would become ill. This point was proved most clearly in the case of the epidemics that swept through entire populations, often causing millions of deaths. People feared epidemic diseases in the earlier part of the century, but they had little fear of cancer. Cancer aroused less dread than tuberculosis, the greatest killer of that time (Patterson, 1987).

Communicable diseases Diseases that can be contracted from other people, animals, organisms, food, and water

For an individual who lived at the turn of the century, contracting a disease and dying from it must have seemed largely a matter of chance or fate. Matters are quite different today. Most of the major diseases now prevalent can be traced to "problems of living" (for example, life style, stress, environmental problems) rather than bacteria or viruses. In other words, diseases such as heart disease and cancer involve multiple causes, many of which are more closely related to the way people live than to strictly biological factors. To take just a few examples, eating high cholesterol foods increases the likelihood of heart disease, smoking cigarettes is linked to lung cancer and emphysema, living in a community where pesticides are used heavily may contribute to a higher risk of cancer, and spending long hours sunbathing may lead to increased risk of contracting melanoma and other, less deadly, skin cancers. Diseases and illnesses today are apt to be tied to the actions we choose to take or not take. To a considerable

We now know that burning the skin through long hours of sunbathing increases the risk of contracting melanoma and other skin cancers. This woman either believes a deep tan is worth the risk, or she somehow has not been informed of the sun's dangers.

degree, our individual chances of healthful living are much more in our own hands now than they were at the turn of the century.

In this context it is interesting to consider again the spread of AIDS. Like many of the infectious diseases that killed people at the turn of the century, AIDS is caused by a virus. Because the AIDS virus is not easily transmitted from one person to another, however, contracting the disease is closely linked to the choices people make in their actions and behavior. For example, people are more likely to get AIDS if they engage in male homosexual behavior, use drugs intravenously, and engage in heterosexual sex with high-risk partners. In addition, AIDS is tied to actions people fail to take, such as using condoms with a sex partner of whom they are uncertain, or using clean hypodermic needles when taking drugs intravenously. Thus, although AIDS is infectious, it is difficult to catch; the chances of being stricken with it are heightened by things that people do or don't do. People have much more control over this epidemic than they did over the epidemics that occurred in earlier times.

Individuals do not have complete control in all matters relating to their health, however, because illnesses are also influenced by the actions of other people and by societal conditions. For example, widespread use of chlorofluorocarbons in refrigerants, and in aerosol spray cans in many countries, is reducing the protective ozone layer in the atmosphere. This thinning of the ozone layer is linked to increases in skin cancer, including melanoma. Another example of an external threat to health is the use of pesticides and chemicals in the production and processing of foods. Most grains, fruits, vegetables, and meats today carry some residues of these chemicals, and are adversely affecting the health of entire societies.

Historical Causes of Declining Death Rates

Many people assume that advances in medical practices and medical discoveries are responsible for the victory over the infectious diseases that historically plagued humankind. However, historical studies of disease and death have shown that declines in the major infectious diseases cannot be attributed to medical discoveries, treatments, and practices (McKeown, 1976, 1979). Studies have shown that death rates for most infectious diseases were on the decline long before the most effective medical intervention was discovered or developed. For example, studies of England have shown that the death rate due to tuberculosis was declining at least 30 years before the tubercle bacteria was discovered in 1882. These declines were not produced by the medical treatments of that day since they were generally ineffective. In some cases medical treatment may even have been harmful to the patient, as it probably was in the case of President Andrew Jackson's wife, who was advised by her doctor to start smoking as a treatment for her tuberculosis (Remini, 1984). Not until 1947, with the introduction of streptomycin, was an effective chemotherapy for tuberculosis available. By that time, the death rate due to tuberculosis was only one-sixth of what it had been a century earlier (McKeown, 1976).

The reduction in deaths from most other infectious diseases have followed a similar pattern. In the United States in the nineteenth and twentieth centuries, McKinlay and McKinlay (1977) discovered that, for nine infectious diseases, the death rate was declining for eight of them *before* vaccines were created or treatment developed. (Polio was the exception.) What did bring the death rates down in these cases? *Death rates for infectious diseases declined because of changes in social and environmental factors, rather than medical factors.* Such changes included better sanitation, housing, and nutrition—in other words, an overall improvement in the standard of living (McKeown, 1971, 1979).

None of this discussion is intended to argue that medical care does no good or that medical discoveries are not important. The development of inoculation procedures and vaccines have certainly had a long-term impact on the health of people around the world. In fact, when the medical discoveries of the Western world have been applied to much of the developing world during the last half of the twentieth century, they have been highly effective. These more recent medical successes should not, however, obscure the historical fact that declines in infectious disease did not result primarily from improved medical practices and treatments. In both Europe and the United States, social and environmental factors were more important in reducing death rates (McKinlay and McKinlay, 1977).

The Medicalization of Society

In this century we have witnessed an increase in the power of the medical profession, and the increasing dominance of the medical approach to health and illness. One manifestation of this dominance is the **medicalization of society,** defined as the tendency to exaggerate the importance of medicine and to "medicalize", or treat as an illness, things that are not normally considered ilnesses (Conrad and Schneider, 1980; Conrad, 1986). The process of medicalization has been obvious in the area of deviance, where people who exhibit behavior that is considered deviant have come to be labelled as sick and therefore in need of medical help. The most notable example is the way in

Medicalization of society
Treating things as illnesses that have not normally been considered illnesses

Cross-National Perspectives

An International View of AIDS

AIDS is an international problem. No major area of the world is free of the disease. Furthermore, the leaders and citizens of virtually every country in the world have expressed concern about AIDS, and often have taken stringent actions to keep the disease out of their countries. The Chinese, for example, insist that any student coming from another country be tested and found free of the disease.

Although AIDS is a global disease, there are important differences in the prevalence of the disease from one country or continent to another. The two areas that have the greatest prevalence, or rate, of the disease are North America and Africa, especially Zaire and Uganda. In many countries of the world, however, the number of cases is small. Sweden, for example, which has a very active program of testing for and identifying AIDS cases, has found only 125 cases in its 8 million population.

At the present time most of the attention with regard to AIDS is directed toward the United States and parts of Africa where the disease is most common. Both social and economic factors are related to AIDS in these two areas and have produced important differences in the AIDS populations.

In general terms, AIDS is transmitted through sexual activity, blood, and prenatal contact. However, people in the United States and Africa get the disease in very different ways, which means that the distribution in the population also differs. In the United States the disease afflicts primarily homosexual men, and to a lesser, but increasingly important degree, intravenous drug users. Since intravenous drug users are also more likely to be male, over 91 percent of the identified AIDS victims have been male. In Africa, by contrast, AIDS is widespread among heterosexuals and thus there is a roughly 50-50 split between male and female cases. These differences are traceable, in part, to differences in the sexual practices of the United States and Africa, but many more Africans than Americans acquire AIDS through blood transfusions. In the United States blood donors are now screened for the AIDS virus, but this is rarely the case in Africa due to the lack of resources available for such procedures.

In the United States, between March, 1988, and February, 1989, one-third of the new AIDS victims were either intravenous drug users, or persons who had had sex with intravenous drug users. By contrast, Africans are much less likely to get the disease through intravenous drug use because such drug use is virtually absent there. The intravenous drug users in the United States typically get AIDS by sharing contaminated needles with someone who has the disease, but Africans are likely to contract AIDS from other kinds of contaminated needles. For example, because of improper sterilization, AIDS is transmitted in Africa through medical injections for diseases such as malaria and diarrhea. In one study of AIDS patients in Kinshasa, the capital of Zaire, 80 percent reported that they had received medical injections before the symptoms of the disease appeared (Mann et al., 1986).

Also, because of the prevalence of heterosexual transmission of AIDS in Africa, African mothers are more likely to carry the virus than American mothers. This means that there is a greater likelihood of newborn children getting the disease before, during, or shortly after birth in Africa.

Of course, there are important differences between the United States and Africa in the ability to deal with the disease. While it is a burden, the United States has the resources to care for its AIDS patients and to see that they receive the latest treatments. In Africa, there is little money to treat AIDS patients given the continent's limited resources and its many other problems. Furthermore, although the United States and other nations such as Great Britain have gone to great lengths to inform and educate their populations about AIDS, such programs are likely to lag in Africa because of a lack of funds.

An interesting aspect of cross-national comparisons of AIDS is that, in different societies, different groups have come to be stigmatized as carriers of the disease. In the United States, homosexuals and intravenous drug users are most likely to be stigmatized. In Africa, female prostitutes have come to be stigmatized because they have an unusually high rate of the disease. In other nations, it is sometimes Americans and other times Africans who are stigmatized because of the prevalence of the disease in their countries.

MANN, JONATHAN. "The Global AIDS Situation." *World Health* June, 1987.
MANN, J.; FRANCIS, J.M.; QUINN, T.; et al. "Surveillance for AIDS in a Central African City: Kinshasa, Zaire." *Journal of the American Medical Association* 255, June 20, 1986.

which alcoholism is now nearly universally defined as a disease. In the past the excessive use of alcohol was generally viewed as a result of a person's lack of willpower. Now most people regard this form of substance abuse as stemming from a chemical imbalance in the body, genetically transmitted, in many cases. Other compulsive behaviors and disorders have been similarly reanalyzed. A recent example is the medicalization of compulsive gambling. Described in the past as a personal weakness—a failure of will—compulsive gambling today is increasingly defined as a disease (Rosecrance, 1985).

A more controversial example of medicalization is the argument that hyperactivity in children is a medical problem (Conrad, 1975). In the past, children who were overly active, impulsive, and aggressive would simply have been seen as disruptive youngsters who needed to be controlled or perhaps punished. Today, children who have these characteristics are labeled as hyperactive and viewed as having a medical problem. The problem must then be treated by physicians, often with the use of mind-altering drugs (Conrad, 1975).

The medicalization process is not restricted to deviant behavior. For example, medicine has come to define childbirth as a medical problem that must be handled by physicians in a hospital context (Arney, 1982). What was once a natural process dominated by family and midwives came to be seen as at least a potential medical problem (Wertz and Wertz, 1986). Of course, one factor that contributed to the medicalization of childbearing was the extremely high rate of death associated with the birth process. Recent years have brought a resurgence of midwives as a reaction against the medicalization of childbirth (Weitz and Sullivan, 1985). A greater interest has also arisen in natural childbirth, and a few people are choosing to have babies at home rather than in hospitals. Despite these trends, medicine continues to control the childbirth process as reflected in the extraordinarily high rate of births by Caesarian section, a technique dominated by physicians.

Nor is the medicalization process restricted to the United States. For example, in Japan a number of extraordinary "diseases" have come to be defined as medical problems. For example, two diseases that now "strike" Japanese women are "kitchen syndrome" and "moving-day depression." A woman with kitchen syndrome might go on wild shopping sprees, while someone suffering from moving-day depression might complain that the water in their new home does not agree with them. Japanese doctors have come to define these afflictions as diseases and treat them by counseling the "victims" as well as by prescribing medicines (Lock, 1987).

Variations in Health among Different Populations

In this section we will compare the health status of a number of populations or subpopulations in the United States, including differences between men and women, among races, and social classes. As we proceed through the various comparisons between groups, we will rely heavily on the work of social epidemiologists, as described earlier.

Men and Women

Historically, there have been significant differences between men and women in patterns of health, illness, and death. Although some of these differences persist, indications are that greater similarities in the lives of men and women in the United States are producing more similarities in their mortality patterns.

Sex differences for some major causes of death have either stabilized, decreased, or are only slowly increasing (Verbrugge, 1985). Considerable speculation exists about the possible effects on female health of their increased participation in the labor force and changes in life style, but it will be several years before these effects can be fully determined.

Gender, Smoking, and Lung Cancer. One important explanation for some equalization in death rates is the growing number of female smokers. As a former Secretary of Health, Education, and Welfare bluntly pointed out: "Women who smoke like men, die like men." In the 1980s we are already seeing increased lung cancer among women because greater numbers of women began smoking cigarettes after World War II. Lung cancer has almost overtaken breast cancer as the leading cause of cancer deaths among women.

The link between smoking and lung cancer is well established, and there is considerable evidence that living or working in a smoke-filled environment (passive smoking) can be harmful to health.

The relationship between the rise in smoking by females and increased likelihood of death from lung cancer is quite clear. Estimates show that smoking accounts for at least three-quarters of lung cancer deaths among females and slightly more (80 percent) among males (National Center for Health Statistics, 1988, p. 16). In figure 14–1 we see a comparison between males and females in terms of the percent of people who have ever smoked cigarettes. Although males started with a much higher level of smoking, the increase for males was much less rapid than the increase for females. More striking is the fact that for males there was a decline in the percentage who had ever smoked from the cohort born between 1931 and 1940 as compared to the preceding cohort born between 1921 and 1930. On the other hand, females born between 1931 and 1940 were *more* likely to have smoked than the preceding cohort. In short, smoking among males has begun to decline, while smoking among females continues to increase (National Center for Health Statistics, 1988).

What is striking is that changes in smoking are directly related to changes in death from lung cancer. As figure 14–2 makes clear, male cohorts demonstrated the same

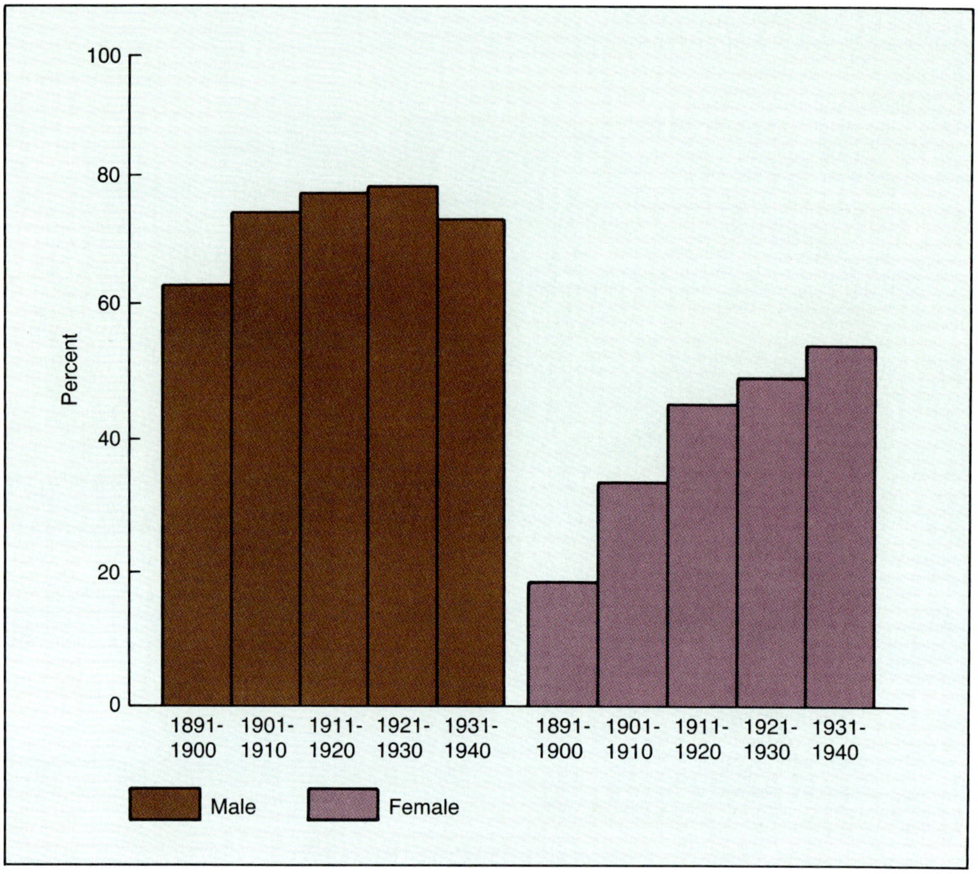

Figure 14–1. Percent of Persons Who Have Ever Smoked Cigarettes, According to Sex: United States, Selected Birth Cohorts, 1891–1940. (*Source:* National Center for Health Statistics, Division of Vital Statistics, National Vital Statistics System.)

kind of increase in death rates from lung cancer as they did in smoking rates; and the same decline is shown in the death rate for lung cancer in the 1931–1940 cohort as is shown in the smoking rate for that cohort. Similarly, death rates for lung cancer for women have shown the same kind of steady increase as in the numbers of women who have ever smoked.

Other Health Differences Between Men and Women. In spite of the increase in death rates due to lung cancer, women still have a higher life expectancy than men. Life expectancy for females born in 1985 was 78.2 years; for males, it was 71.2 years (National Center for Health Statistics, 1988, p. 44). Male death rates generally exceed female deaths at all ages.

With respect to the two major causes of death, the male death rates due to heart disease and cancer are greater than the rates for women (at all ages). Women, on the other hand, tend to be sick more often, but their health problems are usually not as serious or as life threatening as those encountered by men. Women, for example, are

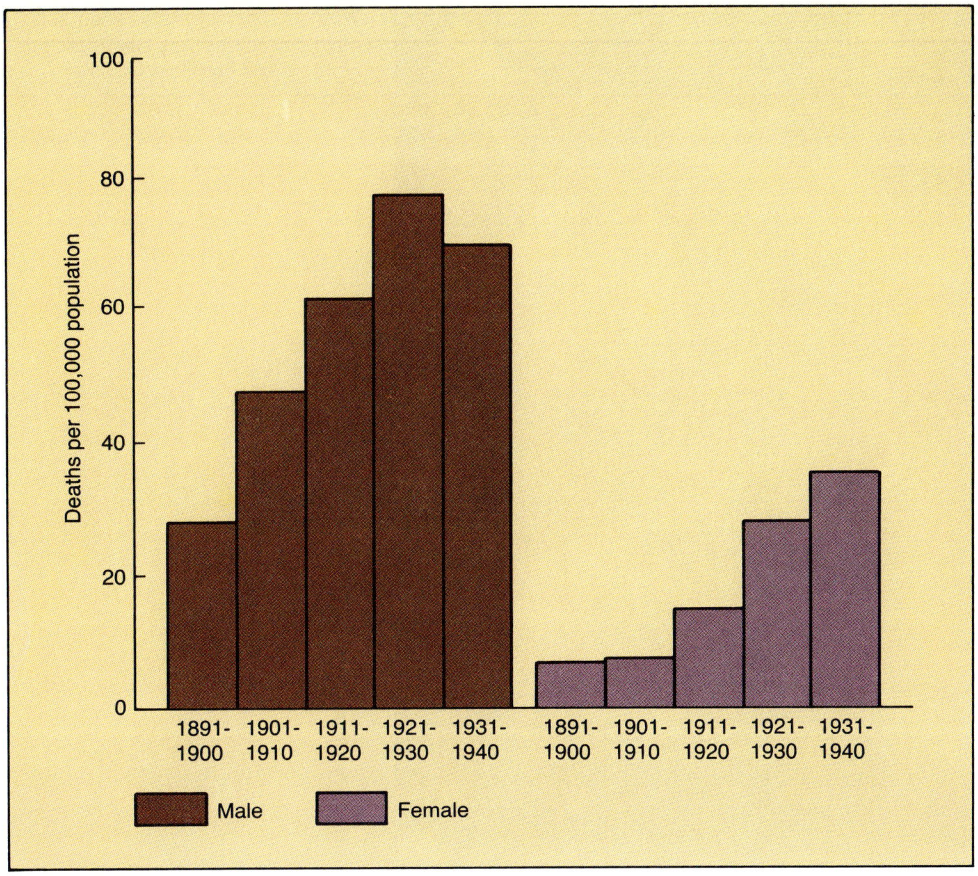

Figure 14–2. Death Rates for Lung Cancer among Persons 45–54 Years of Age, According to Sex: United States, Selected Birth Cohorts, 1891–1940. (*Source:* National Center for Health Statistics, Division of Vital Statistics, National Vital Statistics System.)

11 times more likely than men to have acute or short-term illnesses, such as infectious and parasitic diseases and digestive and respiratory conditions. But women, especially in later life, tend to die from the same causes as men. The difference is that men tend to develop these more serious illnesses much earlier in life and die from them at an earlier age (National Center for Health Statistics, 1988).

Some scholars suggest that women do not have more illnesses but are simply more sensitive to their bodily discomforts and more willing to report their symptoms. The best evidence indicates, however, that the differences in sickness are indeed real (Waldron, 1983). Verbrugge (1976, p. 401) observes: ". . . females experience a less comfortable and satisfying life with regard to a cherished attribute"—feeling healthy. To summarize, women are sick more often but live longer. Men are sick less often but die sooner.

The longevity of men is less than that of women because of both biological and social-psychological factors. The lesser biological durability of males is evident in mortality rates from the prenatal and newborn stages of life onward. The chances of male fetuses dying before birth are about 10 percent higher than for female fetuses (McMillen, 1979). In the newborn stage, males continue to have higher death rates because a variety of

Women generally outlive men and often find themselves late in life primarily in the company of other women.

respiratory, circulatory, and other disorders are more common among male babies (Cockerham, 1986). Females are less likely to get childhood leukemia, and they have a better chance of survival when they do. When they are adults, their female sex hormones may protect them to some degree from heart disease up to the time of menopause.

For adults, social psychological effects on life expectancy appear more important than biological differences (Verbrugge, 1985). These effects are seen in the health risks associated with various social roles, occupations, and life styles. Males use more alcohol, illegal drugs, and cigarettes (despite the significant decline in male smokers), and they often have greater job-related stress. The life style of the male business executive or professional, with its emphasis upon "career" and "success," is believed to contribute strongly to high rates of coronary heart disease. Among lower-class men, high levels of obesity and smoking, along with less leisure-time exercise and poor diet, join with the stress that accompanies a life of poverty to produce especially high rates of heart disease. The risk of dying from cancer is also higher than average for unemployed or underemployed men who live alone in poor, overcrowded, urban neighborhoods. They have less chance of early detection of cancer, and they are exposed to health conditions that make death more likely once cancer occurs (Jenkins, 1983).

The fact that accidents are also a major cause of death for males but not for females strongly suggests a difference in gender roles. Men are generally expected to be more aggressive than women in both work and leisure activities. High accident rates among males may be attributed to exposure to more dangerous activities, including jobs where the risk of death or injury is higher. Automobile accidents, too, kill or maim significantly more men than women, especially young adult males. Driving at high speeds is more common for males, as is participating in violent sports. Therefore, it would seem that the social psychology of the male gender role and male competitiveness are significant factors adversely affecting male longevity.

Women seem to take better care of themselves. They more readily admit that they are sick and more often consult with physicians. Whether women will assume the behavioral traits associated with the male role as they increasingly enter the same occupations as men is a question that sociologists will study with great interest in the years to come.

Health and Quality of Life in Old Age. Women live longer than men, but the quality of their lives in old age appears to be lower than men in old age. On a variety of dimensions women aged 74 and over are *worse off* than their male counterparts. Women at this age are more likely to live alone than men are. Beyond age 74 about 70 percent of men are married, but only about one-fourth of women are married after that age. Since traditional gender roles are likely to prevail in this age group, males are apt to benefit from having wives who take care of them. Another factor is that older women are less likely to have adequate incomes. On medical issues, older women have higher cognitive impairment, and their health tends to be poorer than males of the same age. Finally, older women have less ability to perform the basic activities of daily living (Haug and Folmar, 1986).

Race and Health

The health of racial minority groups, as measured by life expectancy and infant mortality, has improved significantly during the twentieth century. Between 1900 and 1985, the life expectancy of black females increased from 33.5 years to 73.5 years; for black males, the increase for this period was from 32.5 to 65.3 years. Although the life expectancy of blacks has risen dramatically in the United States since 1900, blacks still lag behind their white counterparts. On the average, white females outlive black females by 5.2 years, and white males outlive black males by 6.6 years. In terms of infant mortality, for blacks the rate has declined from 43.9 in 1950 to 18.2 in 1985, while for whites it declined from 26.8 to 9.3. Despite the substantial decline in the rates for both races, the black infant mortality rate in 1985 was still double the rate for whites.

Although some diseases that are especially prevalent among blacks (such as hypertension and sickle cell anemia) appear to have a genetic basis, differences in life expectancy between the races for many other health problems can be attributed to the fact that racial minorities are also most likely to be poor. Low-income groups living in poverty show high rates of influenza and pneumonia, lead poisoning, rat-bite fever, ear infections, murder, alcoholism, drug addiction, and lung cancer.

Social Class and Health

Membership in the lower class is closely associated with health disadvantages. The poor suffer more, not only from the infectious diseases that have been so devastating in the past, like influenza and tuberculosis, but also from the so-called "modern ills" like heart disease. In recent years the death rates from coronary heart disease have declined for all Americans, but more for the middle and upper classes than for the lower classes (Susser et al., 1983).

A study by the state of Maine further highlights the less favorable health situation of the poor. This study found that children from low-income families had higher death rates than children from more affluent families. Low-income children were ten times more likely to drown, 12 times more likely to die in fires, 16 times more likely to be murder victims, eight times more likely to die of disease, and four times more likely to be killed in automobile accidents (Cockerham, 1986).

Not only are the poor more apt to suffer ill health but they are also less able to afford to pay for needed health care. For example, the poor are much less likely to have health insurance (Davis and Rowland, 1986). Cutbacks in support of welfare programs by the federal government in the 1980s may increase further the inability of the poor to pay for health services, and some hospitals have limited the number of Medicaid patients they will accept. The poor receive fewer health services in relation to actual need, they cope with more bureaucratic agencies, and they receive lower-quality medical care. Although Medicaid has not met all the needs of the poor, it has provided health services where such services were not previously available.

Because the poor are less likely to go to doctors, they are more likely than affluent people to come to hospitals for treatment of preventable conditions such as diabetes and bronchitis (Abramowitz, 1988). Even when they do go to doctors, the poor are apt to receive service that is inferior to that of their middle-class peers. This lower quality care is related, in part, to the fact that middle-class patients are more actively involved in consultations with doctors, while lower-class patients tend to be more passive (Boulton et al., 1986).

The most important relationship between social class and health is the manner in which social class has an impact on the opportunities that a person has for a generally healthy life. Crowded living conditions, poor diet, inferior housing, low levels of income and education, exposure to violence, and alcohol and drug abuse combine to decrease the chances of a healthy life for the poor.

Policy Changes in Health Care in the United States

The Problem of Escalating Costs

Health expenditures for Americans increased an average of 12 percent annually between 1965 and 1986. In 1965, Americans spent a total of $41.9 billion on health needs, as compared to 1986 expenditures of $458.2 billion. Also, in 1966 an average of $201 per person was spent on health, but by 1982 this figure had risen to $1,220. Between 1980 and 1986, the rise in spending for health was particularly dramatic—from $248.1 billion to $458.2 billion.

Two major factors contributing to higher costs of health care are inflation and increased labor costs. *Inflation* means increases in the cost of medical equipment, supplies, and new construction, and it also serves to intensify the demands of hospital employees for higher salaries. *Labor* represents about 60 percent of a hospital's total expenses; therefore, increased labor costs are a highly significant component of rising hospital expenses. Inflation and the higher costs of operation have resulted in a more than 450 percent increase in semi-private hospital room rates since 1967. Doctors' fees have more than doubled during this period (Cockerham, 1986). Furthermore, the number of physicians in the United States has risen substantially, and this increase in numbers has contributed in some measure to national increases in health expenditures (Rushing, 1985).

Technology and Transplants. Another factor in the explosion of medical costs is the development and increasing use of new, highly expensive technologies such as CT (computerized tomography) and MRI (magnetic resonance imaging). CT scanners cost about $1 million, and MRI machines, which are increasingly preferred over CT scanners, cost between $2 and $3 million (Gladwell, 1988).

Also very costly are the many new medical procedures, especially the increasing frequency of organ transplants, of the heart and kidney, for instance. The cost of a heart transplant is well over $100,000, and a liver transplant costs even more. The drugs that patients need to prevent them from rejecting the new organs are also expensive. Furthermore, attempts by the body to reject a new organ are not uncommon, which requires further hospitalization and additional expense (Kutner, 1987). Even though transplants are still comparatively rare, they do contribute disproportionately to the explosion in health-care costs.

With the cost of health care continuing to rise, government measures have been aimed at controlling health-care expenditures. In the early 1980s came the establishment of Diagnostic Related Groups by the federal government that placed a ceiling on how much the government would pay for specific services rendered by hospitals and doctors to Medicare patients. This action was bitterly contested by hospitals and the American Medical Association. The cost of health care continues to be one of our most serious societal problems and is a source of considerable public dissatisfaction.

Organization of Health-Care Systems in the United States

American doctors in the eighteenth and early nineteenth centuries did not enjoy high social status (Starr, 1982). Few physicians were trained in either university settings or medical schools. Anyone who wanted to practice medicine usually could do so and could claim the title of "doctor." Many early doctors in the United States were trained as clergymen, pharmacists, or even barbers.

After 1800, the number of medical schools increased significantly, but their quality was not high. Several medical schools were organized for the primary purpose of making money from student fees. It was easy to be admitted and not difficult to graduate—provided that one's fees were paid. Doctors, in general, did not have a good reputation, and sometimes their procedures (such as "bleeding" patients) were more dangerous than the diseases they treated.

But this situation changed for the better with impressive developments in medical technology and increased control over medical education exercised by the medical profession. The Flexner Report, issued in 1910, which described the conditions in U.S. medical schools (some schools were called "plague spots" and "utterly wretched"), resulted in an overhaul of these schools. The better schools improved their training, while lesser schools eventually closed, as state licensing boards established quality standards for the training of doctors. The twentieth century has been characterized by significantly improved medical training.

The Autonomy of Physicians

As of 1985, 512,900 medical doctors and 21,900 doctors of osteopathy actively practiced medicine in the United States—22.0 doctors for every 10,000 Americans. There were also 1,531,000 registered nurses providing nursing services. Altogether, over 8 million people are employed in the health-care industry in the United States (National Center for Health Statistics, 1988). Although medical doctors constitute much less than 10 percent of the industry's total workforce, at present the entire health-care delivery system is subordinate to their professional authority. Physicians usually control not only the conditions of their own work but also the working conditions of other members of the health profession as well. Consequently, the status and prestige awarded to the physician by the general public is recognition of the physician's monopoly of one of society's essential needs: health care.

Even though many changes in health care have occurred in recent decades, such as the increasing employment of physicians in for-profit hospitals, medical doctors continue to subscribe to a pattern of professional behavior that, in many ways, is based on an image of medical practice as it was around 1950. It is an image of the physician as an independent, fee-for-service, private practitioner. This image is of an entrepreneur completely free of lay control and totally in command of providing medical care. Medicine's autonomy rests on its supposed orientation of serving the public, its strong system of ethics, peer regulation, and professional expertise.

In practice, these bases of medical autonomy have not worked as well as they should. Peer regulation by physicians has generally been weak and ineffectual except in circumstances where errors and offenses have been blatant (Freidson, 1975; Millman, 1977; Bosk, 1979; Paget, 1988). Confronting a medical colleague is considered distasteful, even in private, and would be unthinkable in public. Freidson (1975) observes that rules of etiquette have restricted the evaluation of work and discouraged the expression of criticism. Millman (1977) contends that a "gentleman's agreement" exists among physicians, an unspoken agreement to overlook each other's mistakes, which grows out of a fear of reprisal and a recognition of common interests.

The American Medical Association has typically placed the self-interest of the medical profession over changes in public policy—especially when it comes to protecting the fee-for-service pattern of payment (Stevens, 1971). The medical profession in the United States has a consistent record of resisting social legislation that in any way reduces the authority, privilege, and income of physicians. As a group, the profession has opposed workmen's compensation, Social Security, voluntary health insurance, and health maintenance organizations (HMOs) in their initial stages. It has also opposed professional standards review organizations (intended to review the quality of medical work in

THE FAR SIDE By GARY LARSON

Street physicians

federally funded programs), national health insurance, Medicare, Medicaid, and the Diagnostic Related Groups program. This has reduced societal confidence in medicine, since physicians in general are often viewed as placing the desire for financial profit ahead of the desire to help people.

A final example of the medical profession's self-serving position can be seen in the ways in which other health occupations have suffered because of the profession's manipulation. Chiropractors were at one time labeled *quacks* by the AMA, which continued its official efforts to discredit chiropractors until 1980. In 1987 a federal court decided that the AMA was guilty of unlawfully eroding the credibility of chiropractors (Shell, 1988). Physicians have also opposed acupuncturists; after they successfully drew acupuncture into the realm of medicine, they drastically limited its use (Wolpe, 1985).

The Dominance of Physicians in Germany. The United States is not the only society in which physicians have gained considerable power, nor is it the only society in which questions have been raised about that dominance. In Germany a long history of dominance by doctors exists as evidenced, often negatively, by their long-running efforts in opposition to programs of "socialized medicine." As a matter of historical fact, the German government approved the world's first national health insurance plan in 1883. Programs derived from this legislation employed large numbers of German doctors.

Other progressive programs flourished (for example, prototypes of what are now health maintenance organizations) toward the end of the nineteenth century and into the early twentieth century, in part because the medical profession in Germany was not as powerful then as it became later. Some physicians, a very large proportion of whom were Jewish, were actively involved in furthering socialized medicine. By 1900 an organization opposed to socialized medicine was formed with the title "Union of German Physicians for the Defense of Their Economic Interests." By 1919, 90 percent of all physicians belonged to this organization, and professional opposition to progressive forms of medicine solidified. Many changes were made in these programs as a result of pressure brought to bear by the evolving medical profession.

When the Nazis came to power in the 1930s, large numbers of physicians joined the party, in part as a reaction against socialized medicine and in part out of hostility to Jews, especially the Jewish doctors who were heavily committed to socialized medicine. More physicians were in the Nazi party than any other profession; its membership rate was three times that of the general population. The Nazi party moved against the various socialized medicine programs and gained control over them through the party physicians. Furthermore, the Nazis rewarded doctors by passing laws that gave physicians monopoly power over medical practice; non-physician practitioners could no longer practice medicine. In return, physicians carried out the medical programs of the Third Reich. World War II ended in the defeat of the Nazis, but physicians in West Germany continued their drive for professional dominance by "eliminating institutions of social medicine that threatened its markets and autonomy" (Light, Liebfried, and Tennstedt, 1986, p. 82). Like their colleagues in the United States, German physicians fought for a dominant position in medicine and were largely able to achieve it.

The Changing Status of Nurses

Nursing is a major occupation in the health field. As physicians became the dominant profession in the United States, nurses have had great difficulty achieving full professional recognition and, in fact, are usually considered by sociologists as semi-professionals. They have never achieved anything close to the power, prestige, and income level attained by physicians. Because physicians have most of the formal, official power over patients in hospital settings, nurses' power is limited, although they may find ways of exercising informal power within this system. Nurses certainly enjoy less prestige than physicians, and there is no comparison between the incomes of the two occupations: the average income for a physician in the United States is almost $120,000 per year, while the average nurse earns under $30,000.

How do we account for the failure of nurses to win full professional recognition? First, the overwhelming power of physicians within the health field makes it difficult for nurses to demonstrate their distinctive capabilities. Second, physicians have overtly opposed nurses' efforts to win professional recognition. Third, since nursing tends to be dominated by females (about 95 percent), males in general have opposed professional recognition for nursing. In fact, in male-dominated American society, at least in the past, female-dominated occupations have found it impossible to win professional recognition. Finally, while physicians have generally assumed the high-status tasks (e.g., brain surgery, open-heart surgery) for themselves, they have relegated nurses to the "dirty work" in hospitals (changing linen, emptying bed pans, etc.). Occupations that do dirty work are obviously hard-pressed to win professional recognition.

Changes in Contemporary Nursing. Dramatic changes are occurring in nursing today. The most visible one is a widespread shortage of nurses. Every day, newspapers run advertisements by hospitals and other agencies trying to recruit nurses. A recent government report found almost 120,000 vacant nursing positions in hospitals and more than 20,000 open positions in nursing homes (Rich, 1988). The problem is not the supply of nurses, which, since 1977, has increased by nearly 35 percent. Rather, the problem is whether the supply of graduating nurses can meet the needs of an ever-expanding health-care system and of the demands made on it. In addition, victims of severe diseases (such as AIDS) require intense nursing supervision, as do the rising numbers of elderly people with serious illnesses. More sophisticated technologies require great time and attention that, along with government and health insurance efforts at cost-containment, make the relatively poorly paid nurse a bargain to hospitals and other employers.

Complicating the problem of accelerating demand is the fact that a number of factors are forcing people out of nursing or are causing young people to rethink nursing as a possible career choice. (Nursing school enrollments are down dramatically.) One inhibiting factor is that, although starting pay (about $21,000) is competitive, the maximum that can be earned by a nurse is comparatively low—an average of about $29,000. (By way of comparison, an accountant is also likely to start at $21,000, but the average maximum is about $61,000.)

A third factor is nurses' lack of power, as noted above. Trained as professionals, they expect to command respect and to make autonomous decisions. However, nurses quickly confront the harsh reality that they must take orders, primarily from physicians. They are also realizing that their professional status involves doing society's dirty work—dealing with people (alcoholics, drug abusers, AIDS victims, schizophrenics) that no one else wants to handle. More and more, nurses are showing signs of unwillingness to tolerate the difficult working conditions, the relatively low pay, and demeaned status of their profession. Therefore, in the near future the United States may be facing an increasing demand for nurses at the same time that their numbers are diminishing. As one nurse put it: "The old attitude toward nurses—'work long, work late, work hard'—is just not going to attract people. . . . Nurses aren't content to be the housewives of the hospital anymore" (*Time*, 1988, p. 78). Said another: "Unless you have this dying need to take care of sick people and clean up a lot of ——, why do it?" (*Washington Post*, 1988a, p. 13).

Doctor/Nurse Relationships

Traditionally, the work in medicine has been divided along gender lines. As mentioned earlier, doctors have been males and nurses have been females, and the authority of doctors has generally been unquestioned. Doctors make their medical decisions on the basis of medical histories, physical examinations, laboratory findings, and, sometimes, on the recommendations of other physicians who have been called in as consultants. Because nurses are often in close day-to-day contact with patients, they too, can give doctors useful information for making medical decisions. However, because doctors are supposed to be the medical authorities and decision makers, the advice given by nurses must be offered very carefully (Stein, 1974). When nurses advise doctors on appropriate medical treatments, they must do so without seeming to do so. For their part, doctors

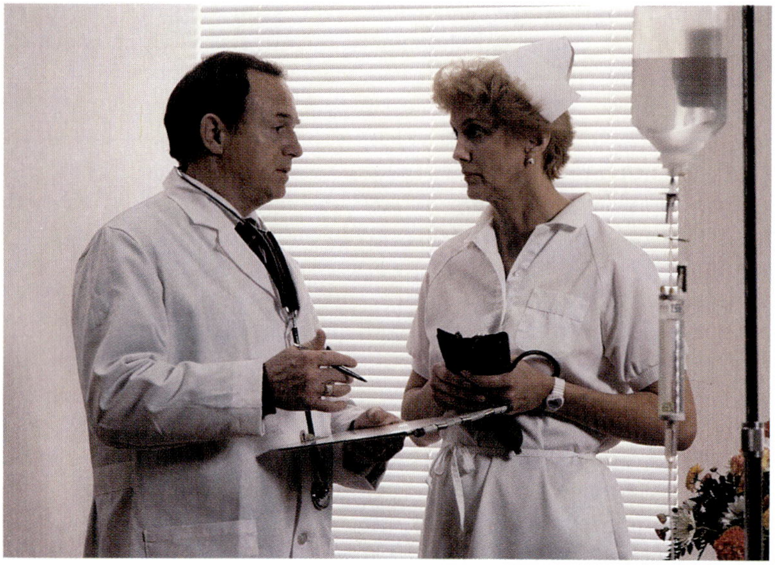

Even though nurses are in closer contact with patients, and thus may have information that could be useful to doctors, a nurse must be very careful about offering advice to the higher-status doctor.

sometimes have to ask for the recommendations of nurses, but again without seeming to do so. This process has been called the "doctor-nurse game" (Stein, 1974, p. 202).

Hughes (1988) accepts Stein's views on the doctor/nurse game, but argues that it does not apply in all settings. Specifically, Hughes studied a casualty department in a British hospital. Although the formal authority for the sorting and initial diagnosis of acutely ill patients lies with doctors, in reality the need to make rapid decisions under great pressure falls mostly to nurses. The authority of the nurse is particularly clear in dealing with new doctors or with doctors recently returning to hospital work. Nurses in this setting often give doctors suggestions; they also reprimand doctors (especially young ones) and even question their competence.

Female Doctors

Although, as we have seen, medicine has often been divided along gender lines, changes are occurring. A particularly important development is the dramatic increase in female doctors. (It continues to be the case that relatively few males are entering nursing.) The increase in the number of women in medical schools is impressive: in 1971–1972, women made up only 10.9 percent of medical school students, but by 1985–1986 that percentage had virtually tripled to 32.5 percent (National Center for Health Statistics, 1988, p. 134). Less dramatic, but still indicative of a trend, is the fact that the percentage of female physicians increased from 10.8 percent in 1979 to 17.4 percent in 1986. (Figure 14–3 shows the increase in medical degrees granted to women.)

Several accounts of women medical students and physicians detail the problems women have in gaining recognition as equal colleagues by male physicians and as "real" doctors by patients (Hammond, 1980; Lorber, 1984; West, 1984). But the trend is clear:

women physicians will be commonplace in the future, and the impact should be significant. As more women enter the medical profession, there is the potential for a change in the relationship between doctors and nurses and, more important, between doctors and patients. With more women as doctors, improved communication is possible, along with a greater willingness to relate to patients as people. Lorber (1984) found that when male doctors assessed their accomplishments during their careers, they tended to talk of their skills and choices of appropriate treatment. The personal side of the physician/patient relationship was rarely mentioned. Women doctors, on the other hand, stressed their value to patients and did so using words like "help" and "care." As one woman physician put it: "I think the best thing that I do is simply taking care of patients and being a warm and caring physician" (Lorber, 1984, p. 106).

As women doctors in increasing numbers choose to work in specialties like internal medicine, family practice, and even surgery, instead of the usual choices of psychiatry, pediatrics, and pathology, they will be treating a wider range of patients and extending their influence. With a somewhat higher percentage of women doctors (soon one-third), sexist attitudes on the part of male physicians will likely diminish, since these doctors will have had exposure to competent and professional female counterparts in medical school and later in clinical practice (Halpern, 1988).

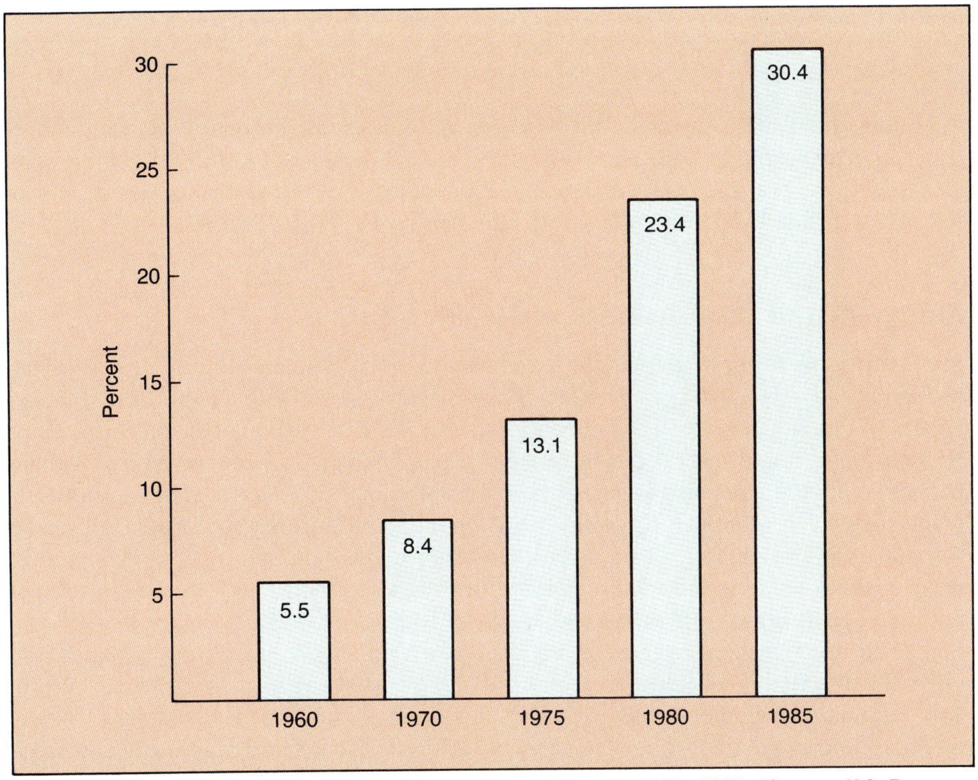

Figure 14–3. Percent of Medical Degrees Granted to Women, 1960–1985. (*Source:* U.S. Bureau of the Census, *Statistical Abstract of the United States.*)

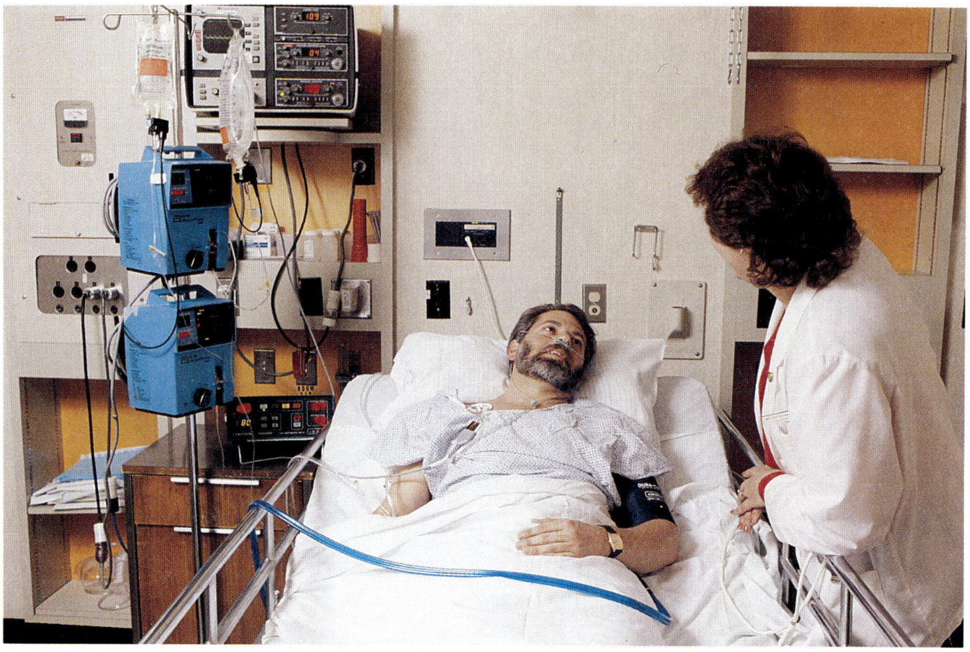

The number of female doctors has increased in the United States in recent years, and, based on medical school enrollments, the numbers will increase even more rapidly in the future. However, at present, female doctors have an average yearly income that is $45,000 less than male doctors.

In spite of the gains being made by female physicians, however, they continue to lag behind male physicians in several ways. Most notable is the fact that while male physicians earn, on the average, almost $120,000 per year, the average yearly income for a female physician is less than $75,000 (*Washington Post*, 1988b).

Emergence of the Business of Health Care

Important signs are now emerging that the professional dominance of the physician may be significantly reduced in the future. According to Cockerham (1986), three factors appear to account for this development. One is greater government involvement. Government intervention in health-care delivery remains limited at present, yet the evolving pattern is one of increased government regulation of medical practice. The second factor is the rise of consumerism in health care. More affluent and better educated people are attempting to take greater control over their health by making their own decisions about what medical services and health practices are best for them, and thereby interacting with physicians on a more equal basis.

The third challenge to the dominance of doctors is coming from a particularly powerful direction. A significant portion of the health market is being taken over by large business conglomerates (Starr, 1982; Ritzer and Walczak, 1988). Massive government funding of programs like Medicare and Medicaid have made health care a lucrative business. This fact has caused people to invest their money in private hospitals and nursing homes. Observing this trend, corporate chains began purchasing these facilities.

This has been followed by a wave of mergers, acquisitions, and diversifications involving not only hospitals and nursing homes but a variety of enterprises such as hospital restaurants and supply companies, medical office buildings, emergency care centers, HMOs, health spas, and hospital management systems. The profit-making corporations expanded into markets that were underserved or into areas where they could compete successfully with nonprofit institutions by providing more attractive rooms, better food, a friendlier staff, and more efficient services.

In the context of corporate health care, the physician becomes an employee rather than an independent practitioner. The doctor is bound to the rules, regulations, and procedures for practices established by the corporation, which, in all probability, is managed by people trained in business, not medicine. Hence, doctors who do corporate practice are not as likely to play the decisive role in decision making about policy, hospital budgets, capital investments, salaries, promotions, and personnel appointments. Work routines will undoubtedly be more regulated. Standards of performance will be developed, and the salaries of the doctors will be based on how well they perform. Physicians who do not meet these standards are apt to lose their jobs. Mistakes will also be closely scrutinized, not only to ensure quality care but also to avoid corporate liability for malpractice. In sum, the control of corporate medicine tends to be outside the immediate health-care facility and in the hands of a management system that is primarily business oriented. Within this system, the doctor's autonomy will be significantly reduced. And as the twenty-first century approaches, the definition of medicine as a "sovereign profession" shows signs of being increasingly less accurate.

As a result of the changes discussed in this section, medicine is losing some of its luster. For example, applicants to medical school peaked in the mid-1970s at about three applicants for every medical slot, and by 1987–1988 the number of applicants had dropped to less than two applicants for every position. Physicians themselves may be steering young people away from medical careers. As one physician said: "The realities of the new medicine are intruding on that relationship [between doctor and patient] and, for me and many others, are bringing this unique experience to an end" (Colburn, 1988, p. 9).

Patients and the Medical System

The Sick Role

The most influential theory explaining the behavior of sick persons in Western society is Talcott Parson's (1951) concept of the sick role. It is based upon the assumption that being sick is undesirable, and the sick person wants to get well. However, because the sick are seen as unable to take care of themselves, they must seek medical treatment and cooperate with care providers. Therefore, sick persons have, in Parson's view, a "duty to get well."

The **sick role** consists of four basic components: the sick person (1) is exempt from "normal" social roles, (2) is not responsible for his or her condition, (3) should try to get well, and (4) should seek technically competent help. Exemption from normal social roles because of illness is a temporary condition and is based upon the premise

Sick role
Social expectations of those who are ill

that the sick person will try to get well. Therefore, the person who is excused from normal duties assumes an obligation to get well. This includes a further obligation to seek help from a technically competent practitioner, typically a physician. The physician, on the other hand, has an obligation to return the sick person to as normal a state as possible.

The merit of this analysis is that it describes a patterned set of expectations that defines the norms and values appropriate to being sick, both for the sick individual and for others who interact with that person. This pattern allows us to predict the behavior of the ill in certain circumstances, such as situations where people are excused from school or work to try to improve their condition, including a visit to a doctor if necessary. Consequently, Parsons' concept of the sick role describes the behavioral norms appropriate to being sick in Western society.

Situations do exist, however, where the sick role concept has limited value for explaining illness behavior. Not everyone behaves in the manner the sick role suggests. Some people deny being sick when they have symptoms of illness; others refuse to go to the doctor even when they know they should. Some do not cooperate with doctors when they receive medical advice; and others may not feel any particular obligation to get well—especially if they can benefit from illness by avoiding responsibilities such as work. The sick role applies best to illnesses that are temporary and can be overcome by a physician's help. But some diseases cannot be cured and are not temporary, and in this case becoming "well" is impossible. In addition, the sick role described by Parsons incorporates the middle-class assumptions that rational problem solving (seeking medical assistance for illness) is the most effective behavior possible, and effort will result in positive gain (health). The concept fails to take into account attitudes typical of an environment of poverty where success is the exception.

Yet the sick role does provide a reasonably good explanation of the patient/physician relationship in terms of mutual obligations and expectations. (Both are expected to cooperate in improving the patient's health.) The concept also helps us understand the role of medicine in controlling deviant behavior. Taking a structural-functionalist approach, Parsons suggests that illness is a form of deviance, since it is abnormal to be sick. Illness is not only deviant but it is also dysfunctional for society as a whole because it interferes with the smooth functioning of a social system. If too many people were sick and not functioning properly, social systems would become unstable. This could lead to social breakdown because essential functions like growing food and educating the young could not be carried out.

The medical profession thus functions to offset the dysfunctional aspects of illness by curing, controlling, or preventing disease. Hence, medical practice becomes a mechanism by which a social system seeks to control the illnesses of its deviant sick by returning them to as normal a state as possible. Consequently, implicit in the concept of the sick role is the idea that medicine is an institution for the social control of deviant behavior and represents society in maintaining social stability. Whether medical procedures should be used to control a wide range of human behavior is a debatable topic, but the trend in modern society is to have medicine assume more and more responsibility for behavioral problems. (See our earlier discussion of the medicalization of society.) It has been argued, for instance, that there are few problems today that some group does not think of as a medical problem. Parsons helps us to see how medical practice operates as a form of social control.

Patients as Consumers

In contemporary times, health care has expanded beyond caring for the sick to the prevention of illness. Again, social class differences appear. The middle and upper classes feel more responsible for maintaining their health. The more affluent tend to visit doctors for preventive care, while the poor visit physicians primarily for the treatment of overt symptoms of illness (Dutton, 1978). Furthermore, there is widespread interest among college-educated persons in health-protective activities like dieting and exercise (e.g., jogging, aerobic dancing). All of this points toward a consumer orientation toward health among the middle and upper classes. The power of the health consumer lies in having the freedom to choose one's source and type of health care.

According to Reeder (1972), the concept of a person as a "health consumer" rather than a "patient" became established in the United States during the 1960s. In this context, physicians were defined as "health providers." In an age of consumerism, the traditional physician/patient relationship is significantly modified. The patient exerts more control and assumes a more equal footing with the doctor in terms of status, decision making, and responsibility for outcomes. The trend toward consumerism in medicine is similar to consumerism in other aspects of American life in which people make informed choices about the services available to them. This activity is usually more characteristic of the middle and upper classes who have the resources to support it (Cockerham et al., 1986).

Lower-class persons, in turn, may have a more passive orientation toward life and less willingness to take responsibility for their problems (Arluke et al., 1979). When it comes to health, the lower class may place greater responsibility upon the health-care system to keep them healthy than the other classes do. Several studies have shown, for instance, that persons with low incomes are the most likely to agree that people should not be held responsible for their own illnesses (Wolinsky and Wolinsky, 1981). According to this view, if someone is sick (and poor), it is not his or her fault.

An important counter-influence on health consumerism, however, is medical technology. The development of a complex array of medical equipment and procedures has increasingly taken away the self-management of health from all patients, but especially from those at the bottom of society with their more limited levels of education and experience with technology. Although all patients are dependent upon physicians as experts, better educated persons are likely to be less in awe of medical "wonders."

Seeking Medical Care

Not everyone responds to the symptoms of illness in the same way, as mentioned earlier. Some people will consult with a doctor as soon as they feel sick, while others with similar symptoms will try self-treatment, ignore the symptoms, or perhaps simply wait to see what develops from them. Only about one-third of all symptoms that a person experiences will eventually be brought to the attention of a physician. The more uncertain someone is about the meaning of his or her symptoms, the more likely that person is to visit a doctor.

Typically, older people and females will see a physician about their health more readily than younger people and males. The aged visit doctors more often because, as a person becomes old, his or her bodily afflictions, even minor ones, tend to be more serious. Women visit physicians more often because they have more health problems. Even after subtracting doctor visits for conditions associated with pregnancy, women still show more visits to the doctor than men. Men visit doctors about four times a year, while women average over five visits annually (Cockerham, 1986).

Prior to the late 1960s, the poor in American society were significantly less likely than the more affluent to utilize a doctor's services. However, because of Medicare and Medicaid public health insurance programs, the elderly and the poor have obtained more equitable access to professional health care. Although serious problems remain with respect to quality of care, research shows that people who are less able to pay for health care are still able to obtain it (Dutton, 1978; Rundall and Wheeler, 1979). The poor are visiting physicians more often than ever before, while the more affluent, in contrast, showed no change in the rate of physician utilization between 1983 and 1986 (National Center for Health Statistics, 1988).

The pattern of physician utilization in the United States is clear: middle-class and upper-socioeconomic groups continue to maintain the highest levels of health and participate more in preventive care. Preventive care is intended to keep healthy people healthy and consists of regular physical examinations and the like. The lower class has more illness and disability, and visits physicians more for treatment of symptoms. However, when the affluent really have need of doctors, they have the financial resources to seek the services of the best doctors whenever they want. (Rock Hudson, the movie star, who was afflicted with AIDS, chartered a jet liner to fly to Paris for the best available treatment for his condition.)

Doctor/Patient Communications

The concept of the sick role details the obligations of patients and physicians toward each other. Patients cooperate with doctors, and doctors attempt to return patients to a state of good health and as normal a level of functioning as possible. When people visit physicians for treatment and medical advice, doctors usually (but not always) take some type of action to satisfy the patient's expectations. Scheff (1966), for example, describes the medical decision role as the guiding principle behind everyday medical practice: the work of the physician is for the good of the patient, so it is better for physicians to impute illness to their patients than to deny it and risk overlooking or missing it. This perspective may promote "overprescribing" and is intended to satisfy the demands of patients. As Freidson (1970, p. 258) points out: "While the physician's job is to make decisions, including the decision not to do anything, the fact seems to be that the everyday practitioner feels impelled to do something, if only to satisfy patients who urge him to do something when they are in distress."

The interaction that takes place between doctor and patient is an exercise in communication. As is the case in any other face-to-face situation, the effectiveness of this exercise depends upon the ability of the participants to understand each other. A major barrier to effective communication, however, rests in the differences between patients and physicians with respect to status, education, professional training, and authority. Some doctors are very effective communicators, while others do poorly when it comes to communication with patients (Waitzkin, 1985).

Two groups in society, those with a poor education and women, have been identified as having the most communication problems with physicians. It has been found, for example, that poorly educated persons are the most likely to have their questions ignored and to be treated impersonally as a disease entity instead of an individual to be respected (Ross and Duff, 1982). Other studies show that physicians prefer upper-class and upper-middle-class patients and give them more personalized service (Link, 1983). A major reason is that doctors find these patients to be more like themselves; that is, higher strata patients reflect values, norms, and attitudes similar to those held by the doctor. Thus, doctors can be more comfortable in working with them. In contrast, Roth (1969) describes the way many physicians regard lower-class patients:

> They are considered the least desirable patients. The doctor has probably dealt with "their kind" during his years as a student and resident in outpatient and emergency clinics, and he has concluded that they are often dirty and smelly, follow poor health practices, fail to observe directions or meet appointments, and live in a situation which makes it impossible to establish appropriate health regimes (Roth, 1969, p. 227).

As for women, Fisher (1984) studied doctor/patient communication in a family practice clinic and found that many women patients were not satisfied with the explanations given them. Sometimes they did not believe they were being given the information needed to understand their health situation. "The women who called were often well educated and articulate, yet they did not feel they had enough information with which to make reasonable decisions or they felt they did not understand or could not trust

The communication between a doctor and patient can be a critical aspect of health care. Patients who question doctors and act as knowledgeable consumers of medical services are apt to get better treatment.

the recommendation their physician made" (Fisher, 1984, p. 2). Their feelings were intensified when their medical problems were related to reproduction and their questions were always the same: How could they determine whether the treatment being recommended was in their best interest?

In one example cited by Fisher, her friend Andrea, a fellow graduate student, telephoned her to ask whether she should have a hysterectomy. The woman had developed a pelvic inflammatory disease, and treatment by antibiotics was unsuccessful. The doctor then recommended a hysterectomy, which meant she could never have children. Fisher suggested that she tell the doctor she was engaged to be married to another doctor who wanted a family and ask if there was any other way to treat her problem. Fisher states:

> Several weeks later my phone again rang. Andrea had followed my advice. Once the doctor learned of her impending marriage his attitude changed. He assured her that there were alternative treatments available and they would work hard to avoid a hysterectomy. She was treated with another course of antibiotics, her infection cleared up, avoiding unnecessary surgery (Fisher, 1984, p. 2).

Fisher found that Andrea's distressing experience was not an isolated case. Typically, the women patients in her study unquestioningly accepted the recommendations of the doctors in the clinic, and those recommendations were not always in the best interests of the women. Women tend to visit physicians not only more often than men but also for more intimate conditions. Yet medicine remains a male-dominated profession, and research like Fisher's calls for more insight on the part of doctors in dealing with female patients.

Decisions to visit doctors, even for complaints that may be trivial, make such visits significant for a patient. Routine ailments may be boring to some physicians, but the outcome of the visit may involve significant changes in the patient's life and self-concept. According to Strong (1977, p. 44): "For me I am not just another case, I am *the* case." So even in routine visits, patients have strong concerns that they trust will be addressed satisfactorily. Underlying the patient's concern is the possibility that the situation may be more serious than believed.

We can see an example of this situation in the experience of British sociologist Ann Holohan (1977), who visited a physician to receive treatment for what she thought was an infection in her breast resulting from an injury a few months previously. She recognized she had a health problem but saw no particular danger from it. The physician discovered a lump in her breast and asked her to report to a hospital for a biopsy. The effect of this request was "shattering" because she had not even considered the possibility that she might have cancer. The discovery of the lump had come as a complete surprise, and knowledge of its existence left her reeling with dismay. She suddenly had difficulty hearing her physician as he quoted the odds for and against the possibility of the tumor being malignant. She reports:

> His voice seemed to be coming from a distance, and I could only pick up stray words. Physically, he appeared to become smaller and smaller, his voice fainter and fainter, while a jumble of thoughts about my family and survival pressed in on me. Inwardly I protested "it cannot be me." I got up, struggled to preserve normality (this seemed enormously important) and was astonished to hear myself asking mundane questions about admission procedures for tomorrow. He opened the door and, still in a state of utter turmoil, I walked into the street. I sat in my car, and with the conventional constraints

> removed, immense waves of panic engulfed me. I drove blindly home and recall very little of the actual journey. I felt this alien, pathological change was inexorable, gone was the reassuring external cause of my symptoms. Yet clearly I was no "sicker" than before my consultation. All that had changed was the possibility of a medical label for my symptom (Holohan, 1977, pp. 87–88).

Upon her return home, Holohan did some housework as a form of denial. She reasoned that if she could still perform household chores she could not be seriously ill. She considered not going to the hospital for the biopsy, but she was unsure about what might happen if she declined to go. The thought of even touching the lump in her breast was repulsive to her. Her course was set. The potential danger was too strong to ignore. She felt she had to have the biopsy because the situation could be very serious. She entered the hospital and the results of the biopsy indicated that she did not have a malignant tumor. While she was leaving the hospital, however, another woman who was being discharged for the same reason remarked to her, "I wonder what would have happened if it had been the other way. It's like asking what's on the other side" (Holohan, 1977, p. 96).

A recent study casts light on what happens when it turns out the other way. Taylor (1988) studied 118 cases in which doctors had to tell female patients that their biopsies indicated that they had breast cancer. Because doctors considered this task a thankless and unpleasant part of their job, they sought to deal with it by routinely using four basic techniques. The first step involves an effort to use medical knowledge to come up with a definite prognosis and communicate it in a way that is understandable to the patient. In the second technique doctors communicate the idea that prognosis is uncertain, and they are not sure which treatment is best. Third, the doctors may distort reality by offering a diagnosis and prognosis that the facts do not substantiate. The fourth and most frequently used technique (accounting for 45 percent of all the cases) is evasion. It was most often used when a truthful response would indicate that the woman had a poor chance of long-term survival. Overall, doctors are apt to use techniques that make the situation less uncomfortable to *them* rather than using methods that are well suited to the needs of the patient.

Because the potential outcome for patients can be a significantly altered self-concept and style of life, the patient/physician relationship remains an important area of study by medical sociologists.

Summary

In contemporary urban-industrial societies the major illnesses are no longer the infectious communicable diseases; instead they are chronic disorders. The major chronic diseases, heart disease and cancer, are importantly influenced by life styles.

The sociological specialty called *medical sociology* focuses on many different aspects of health and illness. Among the important parts of medical sociology is social epidemiology, which is the study of the frequency and pattern of disease within a particular population.

It is often assumed that medical discoveries and practices were responsible for the victory over infectious diseases, but social and environmental changes were far more important than developments in medicine.

The medicalization of society is a pattern of defining a variety of behaviors, often deviant behaviors, as medical problems. Alcoholism, compulsive gambling, and the treatment of hyperactive children are examples.

Males and females differ in their health problems and their responses to them. Women are sick more often, but live longer; men are sick less often, but die sooner. There are both biological and social psychological reasons for the earlier deaths of men. Smoking is increasing among females, however, which is bringing the female death rate for lung cancer closer to that of males.

The aging of the United States' population is an increasingly important factor in the health problems of the country, even though the health of people reaching old age is better than it was in the past.

Black Americans have generally poorer health and higher mortality than the white population. The lower social classes of the society have higher rates of infectious disease, as well as higher rates of the "modern ills" like heart disease. The life styles, economic limitations, and social environmental conditions of the poor contribute to their higher illness rates.

Health costs have escalated greatly in the last 20 years, primarily because of increased labor costs, new and expensive technologies, and inflation. Attempts to control costs have had only limited success.

In the eighteenth and early nineteenth centuries, the training of doctors was limited and poor. The twentieth century has seen a great improvement in medical training. The health field has traditionally been dominated by the doctors, both individually and through their professional organizations. This dominance is not restricted to the United States; in Germany a notable example is provided of the power of physicians and their relationship to the Nazi party.

Nurses are another important part of the health field, but they have failed to win the power, status, and wealth accorded to physicians. There is currently a major shortage of nurses as demand has increased and, with nursing school enrollments down, supply beginning to fall.

In doctor/nurse relationships, doctors maintain a dominant position, even when they must rely on the greater knowledge of nurses. More and more women are becoming doctors, and their presence is likely to bring changes in the relationship between doctors and their patients.

Several changes are likely to reduce the dominance of physicians, including greater government involvement, increased consumerism among patients, and the rise of corporate health care.

The sick role is an undesirable role that carries with it both exemptions and expectations. The most important expectation is that patients will cooperate with medical practitioners in order to leave the sick role. People today are often thought of as "health consumers," who are expected to take an active responsibility for their health. Seeking medical care is one such responsibility that the more affluent, in the past, have been more likely to do. Those with greater economic resources could afford to get medical care because it caused them less financial hardship.

Communication between doctors and patients is largely controlled by the doctors. Some doctors communicate well and others, poorly. The quality of communication between doctor and patient is an important element in the treatment of disease.

CRITICAL THINKING

1. Explain how social epidemiology has been a useful tool in understanding the AIDS crisis in the United States.
2. How have the major causes of death in the United States changed since the beginning of this century? How do these changes move health even further into the realm of sociology?
3. How is the contraction of disease closely linked to people's actions and behaviors?
4. Give examples of the medicalization of American society. Is this a positive or negative trend?
5. Compare and contrast the health status of various subpopulations in the United States. How important are gender, social class, age, and race in determining the quality of a person's health?
6. What accounts for the escalating costs of health care in American society? Which groups in society will be most affected by rising costs? Do changes in medical technology necessarily benefit all of society or only a select few?
7. Describe the traditional pattern of physician behavior in the United States. Upon what has physician status and prestige been based? What forces in the medical community may change this pattern?
8. Contrast the status of nurses and doctors in American society. What accounts for the differences you see? How might the impending nursing shortage force change in this profession?
9. How is doctor behavior affected by patient expectations? Which groups in society have trouble communicating with doctors? Why?

CHAPTER 15

Religion

One of the most striking developments of the past decade has been the revival of the importance of religion throughout the world. Religion has been an integral factor in bloody clashes between Hindus and Sikhs in India, Jews and Arabs in the Middle East, Catholics and Protestants in Northern Ireland, Shiite Muslims in Iran and Sunni Muslims in Iraq, and Buddhists and Hindus in Sri Lanka. The religious resurgence has also been felt in the United States, where Protestant fundamentalism has become a powerful force in American political and cultural life. Thus, despite earlier predictions of its gradual decline, religion remains of vital importance in the modern world (see table 15–1).

Table 15–1. Estimated Memberships of the Principal Religions of the World

Religionists	World	%
Christians	1,669,520,440	32.9
Roman Catholics	951,843,360	(18.8)
Protestants	337,480,980	(6.6)
Orthodox	161,774,350	(3.2)
Anglicans	70,340,940	(1.4)
Other Christians	148,080,810	(2.9)
Muslims	880,555,210	17.4
Non-religious	866,759,660	17.1
Hindus	663,495,450	13.1
Buddhists	311,836,170	6.1
Atheists	229,711,410	4.5
Chinese folk religionists	172,278,230	3.4
New religionists	111,911,560	2.2
Tribal religionists	92,040,570	1.8
Jews	18,169,340	0.3
Sikhs	17,187,390	0.3
Shamanists	12,381,640	0.2
Confucians	6,188,160	0.1
Baha'is	4,691,890	0.1
Jains	3,555,690	0.1
Shintoists	3,379,030	0.1
Other religionists	8,221,480	0.2
World population	5,071,883,320	100.0%

Source: Barrett, David B. "Adherents of All Religions by Eight Continental Areas, 1988." *1989 Britannica Book of the Year*. Chicago: Encyclopedia Britannica, 1989, p. 299.

Religion, a universal feature of human existence, is one of the most dynamic, fascinating, varied, and complex of all human phenomena. Wallace (1966) estimated that, from the earliest human history to the present day, humans have practiced about 100,000 different religions. Religions are intimately involved with the working of societies. On the one hand, religions often provide social stability and inhibit social change. On the other hand, religious inspiration has been a dynamic source of social change. Therefore, to comprehend fully the nature of human life, it is essential to understand the intimate relationship between religion and the functioning of human societies.

Religion has been a social institution of great interest to sociologists. Almost all of the classical social theorists—Marx, Weber, Durkheim, Simmel—and many of the most prominent sociologists today have been interested in the role of religion in human societies and, especially, in the emergence of modern society.

For example, in *The Protestant Ethic and the Spirit of Capitalism*, a study that has become one of the classics of sociological theory, Max Weber suggested that the development of the emphases on acquisitiveness, systematic calculation, and the work ethic that characterize the economic system of modern capitalism was closely linked to the spread of Protestantism throughout Western society. This relationship was especially pronounced among sects that had adopted the doctrines of John Calvin, a sixteenth century Swiss theologian. Chief among Calvin's tenets was the idea of predestination, the doctrine that held that the fate of all people—whether they would be going to heaven or condemned to eternal hell when they died—was predetermined by God.

Calvinist religious doctrine eliminated the Catholic sacraments that guaranteed being saved, and ruled out good works and feelings as ways of determining whether God had selected them to go to heaven. Therefore, Calvinists could never know their fate with certainty. They were perpetually insecure and had to look elsewhere for signs that would indicate whether they might be among the "elect," those who were in God's favor and would escape the fires of hell. Having accepted Luther's view that all earthly callings serve God, Calvinists came to believe that economic success in this life was a sign of salvation in the next. As a consequence, they struggled to accumulate wealth beyond their needs, and, in the process, they developed the character traits of hard work, self-discipline, and industriousness to achieve worldly success.

The Calvinist drive to achieve economic success was not simply a matter of personal greed but was rather an expression of a profoundly religious impulse. However, because Calvinists rejected worldly pleasures, they could not enjoy the fruits of their labors—the wealth that their hard work had enabled them to accumulate. Moreover, because they could never quite be sure whether they were saved, they could never relax. Instead, by reinvesting their profits and expanding their businesses, they were able to achieve additional worldly assurances of their other-worldly fate.

Protestant ethic
A system of beliefs and action involving a moral commitment to hard work, frugality, self-denial, acquisitiveness, and systematic calculation

Eventually the religious basis of this constant quest for wealth was lost, and people came to seek the accumulation of profits, not as a sign of success in the next world but as a measure of success in this world. However, the accumulation of profits was made legitimate by what Weber called the **Protestant ethic**—a system of beliefs and action involving a commitment to hard work, frugality, self-denial, and acquisitiveness. According to Weber, it was this legitimation (or justification) of the profit motive that contributed to the development of the values and personality traits that characterized the spirit of capitalism in the Western world and led ultimately to the development of the capitalist economic system (Weber, 1904–1905/1958).

The Sociological Perspective—Religion as a Social Phenomenon

A sociologist's perspective on religion differs from a theologian's or an adherent's. On the surface, a sociology of religion may seem to be a contradiction in terms. If sociologists are committed to an empirical and scientific analysis of social phenomena, how can they study something that is intimately related to the supernatural, which cannot be examined empirically?

Although we cannot scientifically study the supernatural, we can analyze the social phenomena that are related to the experience of the supernatural and expressed as religious feelings. These phenomena include religious behaviors, such as praying, missionary work, and preaching, and religious beliefs—for instance, in an all-powerful God, a vengeful God, an uninvolved God, or a benevolent God. In addition, the social roles (such as the clergy) connected with religion and the social organizations of religion (such as churches, sects, and denominations) are also frequent subjects of sociological investigation.

The **sociology of religion** examines the behaviors, beliefs, roles, and organizational structures of the world's major religions, such as Islam, Christianity, Hinduism, Judaism, Buddhism, and Confucianism, as well as newly emergent religious movements such as Rastafarianism, Cargo cults, and the Hare Krishnas.

Sociology of religion
Study of religions, including experiences, behaviors, beliefs, social roles, and organizational structures

However, the sociology of religion is also concerned with a variety of social activities and symbol systems that many people might not normally define as religious. For example, Communism has become for many people a kind of religion that provides a set of doctrines for explaining and giving meaning to human existence; it provides policies for achieving a "heaven on earth"; and it has developed ceremonial rituals that unite its followers into a community of believers.

Besides identifying political ideologies that assume a religious quality, some writers have suggested that for many people psychoanalysis and other therapeutic techniques have become religions that are based on a rational and scientific approach to "soul-building" (Glazer and Moynihan, 1963, p. 175; Dinges, 1988, p. 173). Finally, some commentators have argued that organized sport in contemporary society has taken on many of the characteristics of religion (Rudin, 1972; Novak, 1976; Prebish, 1984; Hoffman, 1985).

The essential element uniting these diverse phenomena in the category of religion is that, to some extent, each has developed a sacred quality. In his classic study of religion, *The Elementary Forms of Religious Life*, Emile Durkheim (1912/1965) argued that at the heart of religion is the idea of the sacred, as contrasted with the profane. The **profane** refers to the ordinary, the everyday, the commonplace, the utilitarian, the mundane aspects of life. The sacred, on the other hand, elicits an attitude of reverence, respect, mystery, awe, and sometimes fear. The respect accorded to certain objects transforms them from the profane to the sacred. Although societies differ in what they define as sacred and profane, all societies make such distinctions. Often nonmaterial entities such as gods and spirits are defined as sacred, but "a rock, a tree, a spring, a piece of wood, a house—in a word, anything—can be sacred" (Durkheim, 1912/1965, p. 52). The **sacred** are those objects that people define and act toward with respect

Profane
Everyday, commonplace, utilitarian, and ordinary

The sacred
Those things treated with reverence, respect, mystery, awe, and honor

At the heart of every religion there are sacred objects that are treated with respect and reverence. In the Hindu religion the cow is considered sacred, the mother of life, and is tolerated in both the countryside and in cities.

Clergymen of the Christian Ethiopian Orthodox Church conduct a Christmas service under a traditional ceremonial canopy. The long prayer sticks are among the sacred objects used in the ceremony.

and reverence. Churches or temples are not merely buildings where religious meetings are held; they are also sacred places. They and their contents are treated with reverence and respect.

Above all, religion is a *social* phenomenon. First, religion involves aspects of human existence that are socially defined as sacred; what comprises the sacred varies among religious systems. Therefore, all religious systems are human phenomena, defined and constructed by people. Second, religion is fundamentally a shared, communal activity; it is expressed in communities of people who share common creeds, moral and ethical codes, and rituals. Thus religion is rooted in social processes, and its expression is shaped by the same factors—social class, ethnicity, technology, and language—that affect other social institutions. Sociologists are especially interested in examining how social conditions affect the expression of religious patterns.

Religion is a social phenomenon in still another sense; it is a socially defined way of interpreting and comprehending the realities of human existence, and of making them understandable. Religion provides a system of meaning, a definition and interpretation of life. **Religion,** then, involves those things that a society holds sacred; it comprises an institutionalized system of symbols, beliefs, values, and practices that deal with questions of ultimate meaning.

Religion
An institutionalized, sacred system of symbols, beliefs, values, and practices that deals with ultimate meaning

A Buddhist monk sits among the sacred objects of his religion in Rangoon, Burma.

The Social Functions of Religion

Society and religion are closely interrelated. Neither can exist without the other. A useful way of viewing this interrelationship is to examine the functions and dysfunctions of religion for individuals and for the larger society. Such an examination underscores the social character of religion.

Meaning, Social Solidarity, and Social Control

Religion is a source of personal comfort and consolation. A religious system offers emotional support for people that enables them to endure very difficult circumstances. Human existence, after all, is precarious and uncertain. Religion enables people to accept the unacceptable and the inevitable—the disappointments, frustrations, sufferings, tragedies, and inevitable death—that are inherent in human existence. Religion provides a source of strength and meaning in the face of the ever-present possibility of the unanticipated, unexpected, and unanswerable.

One of the objectives of Durkheim's classic study of suicide was to demonstrate the role of religion in providing the individual with strength in the face of adversity (Durkheim, 1893/1951). In the 1980s Stack (1983) examined the relationship between religiosity and suicide rates in the United States. Using church attendance as his primary measure of religiosity, he found that the lower the rates of church attendance, the higher the rates of suicide. Indeed, the religious factor was more important than the unemployment rate in explaining suicide rates. He concluded that a decline in institutionalized religion will lead to a situation in which the individual is not integrated into a moral community and thus will be more vulnerable to suicide.

A recent study by Pescosolido and Georgianna (1989) of differences among American religious denominations confirmed the general proposition that religion influences the suicide rate. However, they found that suicide rates are influenced by the denominations found in a specific geographic area, and that some denominations exert a stronger "protective" influence (that is, have lower suicide rates) than others. Counties with higher percentages of Catholics and evangelical Protestants (Nazarenes, Evangelical Baptists, Seventh-Day Adventists, Churches of God) had lower suicide rates than counties where mainstream Protestant denominations (Episcopalian, Presbyterian, United Methodist, United Church of Christ, Lutheran) predominated. The authors' explanation for these denominational differences lies in the nature of the social bonds and the sense of community that each of these denominations creates. Catholics and evangelical Protestants are much more likely to have their religious membership result in ties that bind people to a religious community and create a sense of belonging. Thus, by integrating individuals into a moral community, religion provides a source of strength, security, and emotional support that sustains people during difficult times.

Social Control. One of the basic problems for any society is to keep order and maintain social control. Society must deal with deviance and prevent those who have deviated from becoming fully alienated and thereby disrupting society. Religious ceremonies provide a source of social cohesion and unity for a society. Moreover, through various rites and ceremonies, such as the Catholic confessional or the Protestant communion, religion supplies ritualized ways in which those who have deviated from societal norms and values can rid themselves of their guilt. Religion provides an emotional release for the individual that also maintains the cohesion of the society. Religion thus serves as a means of social control, by which members of society accept and conform to dominant norms and values.

Religion not only provides psychological support for individuals; it also maintains the existing social order. Religions tend to support and to justify a society's norms and values, and to maintain the established and dominant groups within a society. Religion thus often functions to legitimate, that is, to provide ideological support, or justification, for the status quo. Berger (1967) has argued that this legitimating function is the primary and defining characteristic of religion.

An excellent example of the use of religious authority to support the traditional social order involves the widespread religious opposition to certain aspects of the Women's Movement. Pope John Paul II, for example, has said that motherhood is at the center of Christian beliefs and should be promoted. "I want to remind young women that motherhood is the vocation of women. It was that way in the past. It is that way now and it will always be that way. It is a woman's eternal vocation" (*Washington Post*, 1979).

By interpreting the existing social order as ordained by God, religion can mask the fact that all societies are constructed by people; it can make a society's norms, values, and social arrangements appear to be fixed, permanent, and immutable—beyond human control. In the process, religion may obscure the humanly constructed nature of society and social problems, especially for those at the bottom of the social hierarchy. By acting as a conservative force in supporting the status quo, religion can undermine and retard reform and change. This was the essence of Karl Marx's critique of religion. Marx argued that because religion deflects attention from the humanly created inequalities in a society, it serves as the "opiate of the masses."

From this perspective, religion offers temporary relief for the poor and the dispossessed, but it prevents them from acting to change the structure of society and thus dealing with the basic source of their problems. It leads the poor to reject earthly rewards—which they cannot achieve—as valueless when compared with the rewards promised by their religious belief system. Individuals may not be a "success" in this earthly existence, but because they have accepted the "other-worldly" values of a religious system, their ultimate salvation is ensured.

Critical, or Prophetic, Function

Even though religion often legitimizes an existing social order, it can also challenge and change it. Therefore, religion can also perform a critical, or prophetic, function. Religion performs a **prophetic function** when it provides the standards for critically examining, challenging, and changing the existing social order. This prophetic function has occurred throughout the history of Judaism and Christianity, and it exists in constant tension with religion's tendency to support the status quo.

Prophetic function
When religion provides standards for critically examining, challenging, and changing the existing social order

Many radical social movements have been grounded in religion. One of the most visible in the world today has been the development of "liberation theology" that has emerged as a force for radical change, especially in Latin America. Liberation theology is committed to social justice for the poor and the dispossessed and to the elimination of the injustices created by systems of extreme social inequality (Brown, 1986).

While religions are often conservative forces in society, they can also serve a critical or radical function. This Nicaraguan priest, a staunch supporter of the Sandinista revolution, preaches the doctrine of "liberation theology," which has attacked the social inequalities found in many Latin American countries.

For example, throughout Latin America, Roman Catholic priests, nuns, and lay preachers have abandoned their traditional support of the social, economic, and political elites, and have come to defend the poor and to support militant peasant movements. Many have been murdered in the process. "Everything was peaceful before the Jesuits arrived here," complained the owner of a sugar plantation in El Salvador. "Then they began to agitate, to sow hate among the peasants" (*New York Times*, 1980b, p. A10).

Group Identity and Adaptation

In addition to performing a prophetic function, religion can also provide a sense of identity. Participation in a religious group or institution provides a source of meaning, belonging, and group identity and helps to provide answers to the question, Who am I? Herberg (1955) has argued that the need to find a socially acceptable means of maintaining ethnic identity has contributed to the vitality of American religion. Religion was especially important to European immigrants, whose primary identity was often tied to the religious community of which they were a part in Europe. For many immigrants, migration to the United States did not lessen, but rather heightened, their religiosity. However, in their desire to become fully Americanized, second-generation immigrants frequently abandoned many of their parents' cultural traits, including religion. Members of the third generation (the immigrants' grandchildren) were not as insecure about their

Cross-National Perspectives

Population Growth in Islamic Nations

Sociologists have long been fascinated by the influence of religion on social life. For example, in his classic study of suicide, Durkheim compared suicide rates among Jews, Catholics, and Protestants. Similarly, Weber's classic, *The Protestant Ethic and the Spirit of Capitalism*, examined how the doctrines of Calvinism influenced the development of modern capitalism.

Many sociological studies have noted that religious affiliation tends to be associated with a variety of demographic factors, including fertility levels. In the United States, for example, Catholics have generally had higher fertility rates than Protestants and Jews, although these historic differences have recently become less pronounced. Because Muslim nations are among the world's most rapidly growing, we will examine whether Islam, today the world's second largest religion with nearly a billion adherents, influences population growth.

Islam was founded in the seventh century by the Prophet Muhammad in what is today Saudi Arabia, and it is characterized by considerable continuity with Jewish and Christian traditions. Muslims share with Christians and Jews a belief in the same God and in the Old Testament prophets, and they acknowledge Jesus as a prophet. However, they believe that the Prophet Muhammad was the messenger through whom God's final revelation was communicated and transcribed in Islam's sacred book, the *Qur'an*.

From its Middle Eastern Arab origins, Islam quickly spread to Europe, Africa, and Asia. Today Muslims live in every nation of the world, although Islam's primary strength is found in the Middle East, Southern and Southeastern Asia, and Northern and sub-Saharan Africa. Muslims are a majority of the population in 40 nations, and in 7 others they represent a significant minority (25 to 49 percent).

Like most major religions, Islam is characterized by considerable diversity. The major sectarian division in Islam—between the Sunnis and the Shi'is (Shiites)—emerged in a dispute over who should lead Islam after the death of the Prophet Muhammad. Although a majority of Muslims in the world today are Sunnis, Shiites represent a powerful minority that has become most visible to the West in Iran, where post-revolution social change led by the Ayatollah Khomeini reestablished religious authority over many aspects of life that had become increasingly secularized under the monarchy headed by the Shah. In addition to sectarian divisions, there is substantial ethnic, regional, economic, and other religious diversity among nations that have large proportions of Muslim citizens. These various factors must be considered when assessing the social impact of the "religious" factor.

The primary source of Islam's dramatic population growth, which is expected to reach nearly 2 billion by the year 2020, is the extremely high fertility rates in Islamic countries, which average 6 children per woman, in contrast to a figure of 1.7 for developed countries. However, this average obscures considerable regional variations, from an average of 3.6 in Islamic nations of Southeast Asia (Indonesia,

Malaysia, Brunei) to 6.6 for nations in sub-Saharan Africa (Somalia, Senegal, Gambia, Niger, Mali, Guinea, Sierra Leone).

These very high rates of childbearing are not a result of religious objections to contraception; "Islam itself prescribes no special barriers to the use of contraception" (Weeks, 1988). The frequency of contraceptive use among married Muslim women ranges from 45 percent in Southeast Asia to 5 percent in sub-Saharan Africa, but in each case contraceptive use is lower in Islamic nations than in non-Islamic nations in the same region. Regional differences are also pronounced in the frequency with which women marry at a young age in Islamic countries, thereby increasing the probable number of pregnancies. As many as 47 percent of women under age 19 are married in South Asia (Pakistan, Bangladesh, Afghanistan) compared to only 18 percent in Southeast Asia. Early marriage, like resistance to contraceptive use, is a practice prescribed by tradition, not by Islam. Therefore, as the variations in fertility rates among Islamic nations indicate, current and future fertility trends among Muslim peoples are not influenced by Islam but rather by broader social, economic, and political factors.

KELLY, MARJORIE. *Islam: The Religious and Political Life of a World Community*. New York: Praeger, 1984.
MUNSON, HENRY, JR. *Islam and the Revolution in the Middle East*. New Haven: Yale University Press, 1988.
WEEKS, JOHN R. "The Demography of Islamic Nations." *Population Bulletin* 43, December, 1988.

status as Americans. Instead they desired a way of asserting and maintaining their ethnic identity in an impersonal urban society. According to Herberg (1955), membership in one of the "three religions of democracy"—Protestantism, Catholicism, or Judaism—provides a socially acceptable means of self-identification and thereby contributes to the integration and stability of the entire society. Thus religion is "an important part of the social cement that holds American social structure in place" (Hout and Greeley, 1987, p. 342).

Religion, therefore, is a complex and multifaceted phenomenon. It can have a variety of positive and negative consequences for individuals, social groups, and society as a whole. It can contribute to the integration of society and support the status quo. Or it can serve as a source of social conflict and challenge the existing social order.

The Changing Nature of Religion in the United States

Religion in America has been characterized both by relatively unchanging, stable features and by constant change. Religious organizations come and go; patterns of participation change; prevailing religious ideas vary from one generation to the next. At the same time, the basic patterns of commitment and participation are much as they were a century ago, and, despite evidence of a restructuring of American religion, the same broad religious communities (Protestant, Catholic, and Jewish) continue to be prominent features of American religious life. Here we examine three basic characteristics of American religion—its pervasiveness, its secularism, and its denominational pluralism—in light of its tradition of simultaneous continuity and change.

Pervasiveness of Religion

Religion has always been a conspicuous part of American life. From the earliest European settlements, religious factors have been uniquely prominent in this society; the dominant trends in American religion have been "profoundly different" from those in Europe (Caplow, 1985, p. 101). Almost all available data indicate that since colonial days, "the United States has been among the most religious countries in the Christian world" (Lipset, 1963a, p. 150).

The extraordinarily religious character of the American people persists even today. Numerous surveys have shown that, among industrial nations, Americans are the most religious people in the world. Public opinion surveys conducted over the past 40 years indicate that the vast majority of Americans (between 94 and 99 percent) believe in God or a universal spirit, a percentage greater than in any other Western industrial society. In addition, when asked to rate, on a scale of 1 to 10, how important God is in their lives, the average rating of Americans is exceeded only by South Africans, with the highest rating reported by black Americans (see figure 15–1).

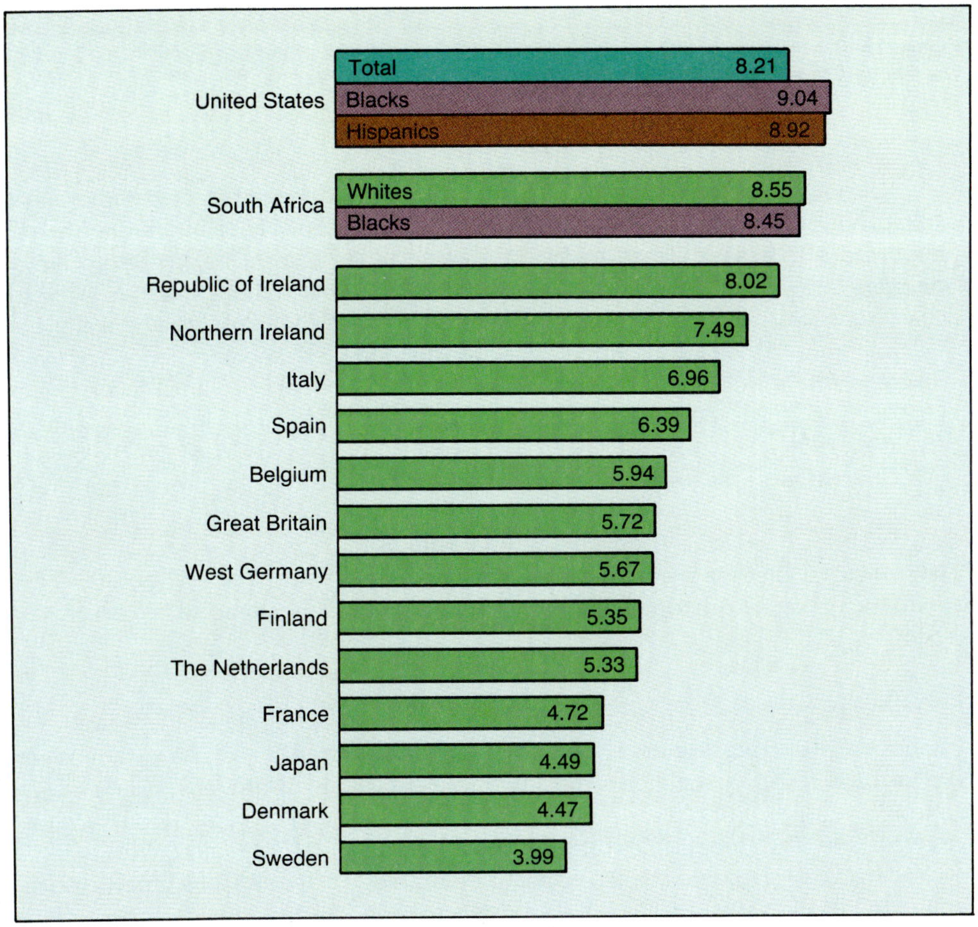

Figure 15–1. Importance of God in Life (1981) (average ratings on ten-point scale). (*Source:* Gallup Opinion Index, "Religion in America: 50 Years: 1935–1985," Report No. 236, 1985, p. 50.)

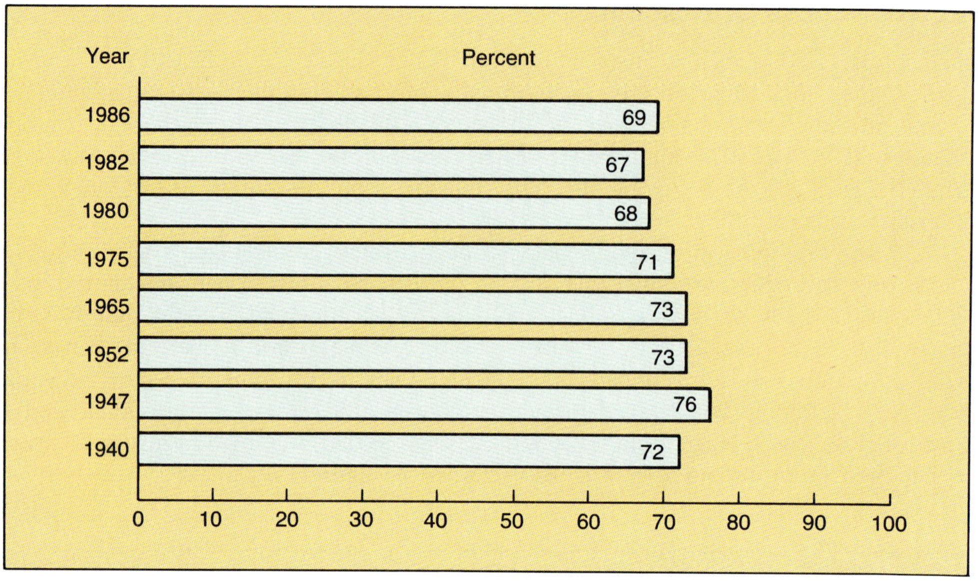

Figure 15–2. Church and Synagogue Membership as a Percent of the U.S. Population. (*Source: The Gallup Report,* "Religion in America," Report No. 259, April, 1987, p. 35.)

Religious behavior among the American people—as measured by membership or participation in a religious community—has remained relatively stable during the past four decades. As figure 15–2 indicates, church and synagogue membership among Americans has remained relatively unchanged since 1965, although, as we will note below, shifts have occurred in the religious groups with which people have been affiliated. The proportion of American adults who say that they are members of a church or synagogue rose to a peak of 76 percent in 1947 and gradually declined to 67 percent in 1972. Since then, church or synagogue membership has risen slightly, reaching 69 percent in 1986.

Church and synagogue attendance also declined during the post-World War II period (see figure 15–3), especially during the 1960s among Roman Catholics who disagreed with Pope Paul VI's encyclical on "artificial birth control" (Hout and Greeley, 1987). Since 1975, however, religious participation has been relatively constant, with about 40 percent of Americans indicating that they regularly attend religious services.

Secularization

Secularization
A decline in the authority of religious beliefs, values, and practices

Paradoxically, another feature of American religion has been its secular quality. **Secularization** refers to a decline in the authority of religious institutions, beliefs, values, and practices. Secularization is the process by which religious institutions and symbols cease to legitimate, support, and justify various aspects of society and culture.

Berger (1967) contends that secularization has occurred on three levels: societal, cultural, and individual. At the societal level, religious institutions no longer exercise substantial control or influence over the state or other important aspects of society, such as the educational system. Or, to put it another way, secularization involves the separation of other institutions from organized religion and religious ideas. To illustrate, we can point to the degree to which functions such as education and social welfare, once the responsibility of religious institutions, have become the responsibility of the government. In this sense, religion has been relegated to a subordinate position in which its influence over the larger society has diminished.

Patterns of secularization have also influenced various aspects of cultural life. As secularization proceeds, the arts, literature, and philosophy less frequently draw on religious sources for inspiration.

Finally, secularization also has a subjective, psychological aspect, involving the secularization of consciousness. "Put simply, this means that the modern West has produced an increasing number of individuals who look upon the world and their own

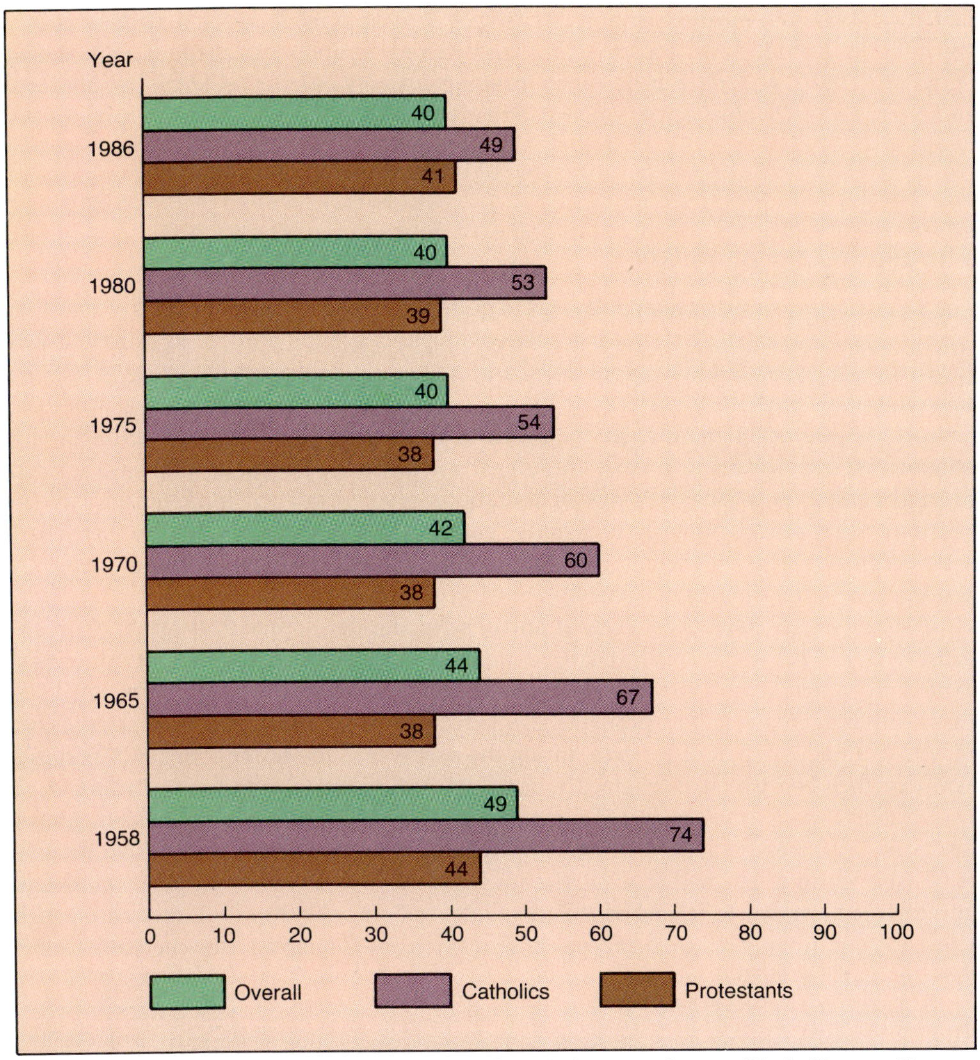

Figure 15–3. Percent of Americans Attending Church during an Average Week. (*Source: The Gallup Report*, "Religion in America," Report No. 259, April, 1987, p. 38.)

lives without the benefit of religious interpretations" (Berger, 1967, p. 107). In a presecular era, religious ideas were accepted as fundamental truths and were difficult, if not impossible, to change. Today many people are no longer sure of traditional religion because its authority has been undermined.

Secularization is one aspect of the massive transformation of Western society that has included industrialization, urbanization, bureaucratization, and rationalization. Yet, despite the dramatic and pervasive impact of secular trends in the modern world, religion remains a vital force in most societies today.

However, today's society differs from earlier societies in which supernatural religion provided the dominant system of meaning, or meaning system. The first point of departure is that American society permits competition among a number of different religious systems. Second, in addition to competing among themselves, supernatural religions must also compete with a variety of other forms of religious consciousness, sacred symbols, and meaning systems. These new conceptions of the sacred are especially apparent in the religious consciousness and sacred symbols attached to nationalism (Crippen, 1988), and offered by other meaning systems, such as science, psychology, and Marxism, each of which provides alternative ways of defining and interpreting the world.

The Marketing of Religion

The necessity of competing for followers requires that traditional organized religion be "marketed." To compete in a secular society, religious groups are forced to tone down their religious message and to adopt the characteristics of secular organizations in making their appeals. Therefore, modern supernatural religions, like other modern organizations, compete in the open market. In their drives to sell their product—their distinctive religious message—and to finance the organizations and enterprises they have created to market their messages, religious organizations often resort to "hucksterism." When religious organizations adopt nonreligious characteristics in order to survive, their character becomes increasingly secularized, often to the point where religious and nonreligious phenomena become indistinguishable.

These trends have become most apparent in the development of television evangelism, which has dramatically changed the manner in which millions of Americans experience religion. In 1987 about half (49 percent) of American adults reported occasionally watching religious programs—a percentage greater than those reporting that they had attended religious services during the past week; about one-fourth (25 percent) said that they had watched religious programs on television during the preceding week (*The Gallup Report*, 1987, p. 60). Televangelists such as Jim and Tammy Bakker, Jimmy Swaggart, Oral Roberts, Pat Robertson, Jerry Falwell, and Robert Schuller have become national celebrities. The personal indiscretions of some of them have been sensationalized, and the scandals that have rocked the huge financial empires they have created through television contributions have been closely scrutinized by the media, the Internal Revenue Service, and the United States Congress.

Today the "electric church" has adopted the formats of the most successful commercial television shows and the most sophisticated marketing techniques to become a highly rationalized multibillion-dollar enterprise. As a consequence, televangelism has become one of the most important political and cultural forces in modern American life

"Are these microphones, O Lord, on?"

(Frankl, 1987). Hadden and Shupe contend that the near-monopoly of television evangelism by evangelical and fundamentalist Christians has enabled them to mobilize very effectively religious and political conservatives into a powerful social movement. Not only has American religion been reshaped by television but televangelists have had a substantial impact on the conservative movement of the 1980s in American culture in general and American politics in particular, producing the "most profound social and cultural upheaval in twentieth century America" (Hadden and Shupe, 1988, p. 40).

Civil Religion

Americans have historically regarded religion as a "good thing" and important for national well-being. Because of a strong tradition of separation of church and state, a national church has never been established in the United States. The common thread uniting Americans of diverse denominational affiliations is what Herberg (1955) has characterized as its underlying "culture-religion"—a secular, nonsectarian religion that unifies Americans around a cluster of sacred beliefs, symbols, and rituals that are a prominent part of America's civil religion, a public religious expression that reflects America's secular religiosity and serves as a source of cultural and social cohesion (Bellah, 1967).

Civil religion refers to the set of symbols, beliefs, values, and practices about the ultimate meaning of life in a nation, including patriotic and political phenomena not typically associated with religion. Civil religion is an important part of almost all American political events. God is mentioned in the pledge of allegiance to the flag; the motto "In God We Trust" is engraved on the nation's currency. Political events of all kinds, from political party conventions to sessions of Congress, begin with invocations, frequently by members of the clergy. The existence and blessings of God have been explicitly invoked in the Inaugural Address of nearly every president. George Bush's first act as President was a prayer offered during his 1989 Inaugural Address that demonstrates the religious legitimation of political authority by the nonsectarian God of civil religion:

Civil religion
Symbols, beliefs, values, and practices that give sacred meaning to a nation and a people

> Heavenly Father, we bow our heads and thank You for Your love. Accept our thanks for the peace that yields this day and the shared faith that makes its continuance likely.

> Make us strong to do Your will, and write on our hearts these words: "Use power to help people." For we are given power not to advance our own purposes nor to make a great show in the world, nor a name. There is but one just use of power, and it is to serve people. Help us to remember, Lord. Amen (*New York Times*, 1989, p. B1).

Civil religion in America is more than belief in a nonsectarian God who is deemed to have a particular interest in the destiny of the United States. Its pantheon of saints includes George Washington and Thomas Jefferson, the revered "founding fathers." Among its martyred saints are Abraham Lincoln and John F. Kennedy. Like other religious systems, American civil religion has developed elaborate rituals, sacred symbols, and a sacred literature. The Declaration of Independence and the Constitution are the religion's sacred scriptures. Its holy days include the Fourth of July, Memorial Day, Veterans Day, and, especially, Thanksgiving, each of which involves ritual celebrations that invoke the name and support of God for the nation. During its religious ceremonies sacred hymns such as the "Star-Spangled Banner," "America the Beautiful," and "God Bless America" are played and sung. Finally, among the religion's sacred symbols are the American flag and monuments such as the Statue of Liberty, the Lincoln Memorial, the Vietnam Veterans Memorial, and Arlington National Cemetery, each of which has acquired a sacred quality that is perceived to embody the nation's basic values.

The Vietnam Veterans Memorial has become a sacred place in the civil religion of the United States, eliciting feelings of awe, respect, and reverence. Ritual behaviors include placing flags, flowers, and many other objects at the wall where the names of the war dead are engraved.

The notion of an American civil religion has generated considerable research since Bellah's formulation in 1967 (Richey and Jones, 1974; Gehrig, 1979; Bellah and Hammond, 1980; Demerath and Williams, 1985). Empirical studies have demonstrated widespread belief among the American people in an American civil religion. However, some writers (including Bellah, who has been most closely identified with developing the concept) have questioned whether its assumption of a cultural consensus, or unifying ideology embraced by most Americans, can be accurately applied today to an American society that has become increasingly "fragmented, polarized, and fractured" (Demerath and Williams, 1985).

Denominational Pluralism

A civil religion is nonsectarian; it transcends denominational differences. Its symbols are uniquely American. It can be embraced by persons of all faiths and by people who have no formal religious affiliation. Civil religion is therefore consistent with one of the most distinctive features of religion in America—its **denominational pluralism.** Religious diversity has long been a feature of American life, but it is more apparent today than ever before. Melton (1987) has identified more than 1,200 different religious organizations in the contemporary United States.

Denominational pluralism
Different religious groups coexisting in society, with no single group dominating

The pluralistic character of American religion was established during the colonial era, when marked denominational differences existed among the colonies. Puritans were concentrated in New England; the Dutch Reformed, in New York; Quakers and German Moravians, Mennonites, and Lutherans, in Pennsylvania; Scotch-Irish Presbyterians, along the western frontier; Swedish Lutherans, along the Delaware River; Roman Catholics, in Maryland; Anglicans, in Virginia; and French Huguenots, in South Carolina—to name only some of the colonial religious groups. Despite this diversity, in only four of the 13 colonies—Rhode Island, New Jersey, Delaware, and Pennsylvania—were there genuine religious liberty and toleration of religious dissent. Not until the 1830s was full religious liberty available in all the states (Hudson, 1973; Marty, 1985).

Religious diversity in the United States, which at its founding was overwhelmingly Protestant, became more pronounced during the nineteenth century. Rapid population growth, westward expansion, the dramatic growth of towns and cities, and massive European immigration provided the dynamic conditions in which diverse religious groups developed and flourished. Niebuhr (1929) has shown the important role that class, ethnic, and regional factors have played in creating and maintaining American religious diversity.

Social Class, Ethnicity, and Religious Affiliation. Claiming more than 77 million members, Protestant churches comprise the largest religious category in the United States today (Jacquet, 1988a). The two largest Protestant groups—Baptists and Methodists—increased their numbers dramatically during the nineteenth century, primarily because they were what Niebuhr termed "the churches of the disinherited." Neither emphasized ritual nor a highly intellectualized theology. They also did not require an ordained, educated clergy. Consequently, they appealed to the common people both on the Western frontier and in the towns and rural areas of the East. Another major source of growth among Protestant churches was immigration. Most immigrant groups brought distinctive religious traditions with them. For example, different strains of Lutheranism were imported by Scandinavians and by Germans, who were the largest immigrant groups in the nineteenth century.

However, the most striking impact of nineteenth century immigration upon the structure of American religion was the growth of the Roman Catholic church, which drew adherents from a great variety of ethnic backgrounds, including Irish, German, Italian, Polish, Czech, French, and Hungarian. Germans and especially Irish Catholics were prominent in the development of American Catholicism during the nineteenth century. By 1900 membership in the Catholic church exceeded 12 million, and an elaborate Catholic institutional system of churches, schools, hospitals, and charities had been established. The "new" immigration from southern and eastern Europe and the later influx of Spanish-speaking immigrants from Mexico, Puerto Rico, Cuba, and Latin America further swelled the ranks of Catholics during the late nineteenth and twentieth centuries. By 1988 the American Roman Catholic church claimed a membership of 53 million, making it the largest single religious denomination in the country and the "wealthiest, most stable branch of world Catholicism" (Duff, 1971, p. 73; Jacquet, 1988a).

The growth of Judaism in the United States was also primarily a product of nineteenth and early twentieth century immigration. By 1880 there were about 250,000 Jews here, most of them German Jews who emigrated in the mid-nineteenth century. The predominant influence on contemporary Judaism, however, was the wave of more than 2 million Eastern European Jews who entered the country between 1880 and 1924. Today there are nearly 6 million Jews in the United States (Jacquet, 1988a).

Another major source of America's religious pluralism has been the creation of new religious groups. Religious movements have frequently emerged during periods of intense religious enthusiasm. This was especially true during the Second Great Awakening, which took place in the first three decades of the nineteenth century. During this period of religious ferment several new religious movements appeared, emphasizing utopian ideals of community and religious brotherhood. Many utopian communes, such as the Oneida Community, were relatively short-lived. Other religious innovations, such as Christian Science, the Millerites (later known as Seventh-Day Adventists), the Campbellites (which later included both the Disciples of Christ and the Church of Christ), survived. Most dramatic and vigorous of the movements that endured from that period is the Church of Jesus Christ of Latter-Day Saints (the Mormons), which grew from an impoverished and persecuted cult in the 1840s into one of the most distinctive and firmly established religious groups in the United States today. The Mormons now claim a membership of 4 million as well as the distinction of having their religious doctrine and ideals provide the basis for a unique cultural region in Utah and in many communities in surrounding states (O'Dea, 1957; Shepherd and Shepherd, 1984).

Recent Trends in Religion in the United States

During the 1950s several sociologists argued that the United States was undergoing a religious revival, a "surge of piety." Church attendance and membership reached all-time highs, and public professions of religious faith became fashionable. The religiosity of the 1950s ended dramatically during the 1960s, when church attendance, particularly among Roman Catholics and the young, dropped sharply. Public opinion polls indicated a substantial decrease in the importance that Americans attributed to religion. During the 1960s, the authority of many traditional institutions, including the government, the family, schools, and religion, was challenged. Churches became deeply divided over political and social controversies, particularly over the civil rights of minorities and the Vietnam War. The counterculture that challenged the prevailing cultural values of the Protestant work ethic, materialism, and conventional sexual mores also threatened traditional religion. These issues produced a crisis in American religion that led not only to tension and division within and a defection from established religious organizations but also to spiritual experimentation and to the creation of new religious movements (Pritchard, 1976; Roof and McKinney, 1987; Wuthnow, 1988b).

Neither the political movements nor the counterculture itself extended much beyond the 1960s, but the impact of that period on American religion today has been substantial. Religion in American society has undergone several critical changes during the 1970s and 1980s.

Decline of Mainstream Protestantism

The Protestant majority—the "religious establishment"—has declined substantially. Protestants comprised 69 percent of the American population in 1947 but only 59 percent in 1986 (see table 15–2). This decline has occurred primarily among mainstream Protestant denominations (Episcopal, United Methodist, Evangelical Lutheran, United Presbyterian, United Church of Christ). Since 1965 mainstream Protestant churches have stopped growing or experienced substantial membership losses, and have experienced declines in participation and institutional support, resulting mostly from a scarcity of new members (Roof and McKinney, 1987).

Not all Protestant churches were declining, however. During the 1970s and 1980s a new wave of religiosity has been especially pronounced among evangelical and conservative Protestant groups, such as the Assemblies of God, the Church of Christ, Pentecostal and Holiness groups, the Mormons, Seventh-Day Adventists, Jehovah's Witnesses, and Southern Baptists (Kelly, 1972; Hoge and Roozen, 1979; Roof and McKinney,

Table 15–2. Religious Preference in the United States, 1947–1986 (by percent)

Religion	1947	1957	1967	1977–1978	1986
Protestant	69	66	67	60	59
Baptist	*	*	21	19	20
Methodist	*	*	14	11	9
Lutheran	*	*	7	6	5
Presbyterian	*	*	6	4	2
Episcopalian	*	*	3	2	2
Roman Catholic	20	26	25	29	27
Jewish	5	3	3	2	2
All others	1	1	3	1	4
No religious preference	6	3	2	8	8

Source: The Gallup Report, 1987.

* Data not available.

1987). Similarly, Roman Catholicism has experienced a conservative movement (Dinges, 1988), and Orthodox Judaism has grown more rapidly than either of Judaism's two more liberal branches—Reform and Conservative. Not only has membership in such conservative religious bodies been rapidly increasing but these groups have become particularly adept at using the electronic media—television, in particular—to spread their doctrines. The most substantial impact of religious conservatism has been seen on American political life, where the "New Christian Right" has had a powerful influence on the debates over such issues as school prayer, abortion, gay rights, women's rights, and pornography (Liebman and Wuthnow, 1983; Hadden and Shupe, 1988).

Growth of the Roman Catholic Church

The Roman Catholic church has grown in numbers and influence, increasing from 20 percent of the American people in 1947 to 27 percent in 1986, making it the largest single religious denomination in the United States. Moreover, Catholics have increasingly become part of the social, cultural, political, and religious mainstream of American life. Today, more affluent and better educated than ever before in American history, they have become virtually indistinguishable from other Americans in their social and cultural characteristics (Berger, 1987).

Proliferation of New Faiths

A wide array of new religious bodies, both Christian and non-Christian, has emerged. For the first time in American history, groups drawn from Eastern religions (especially Islam, Buddhism, and Hinduism) have attracted substantial numbers of American devotees. As a consequence of increased spiritual experimentation with "foreign" religious faiths and changing patterns of immigration to the United States since 1968, the number of adherents of Eastern religions has increased. Some of these, such as the International Society of Krishna Consciousness (Hare Krishnas), the Divine Light Mission (followers of the Guru Maharaji), or the Rajneesh movement (followers of the Bhagwan Shree Rajneesh), were highly visible and gained national notoriety. By 1986, 4 percent of the population (more than 9 million) indicated identification with a faith outside of the three major religious categories of Protestantism, Catholicism, and Judaism. By the end of the 1970s Islam had supplanted Judaism as the second largest American religious tradition (after Christianity); by 1989 there were about 6 million Muslims in the United States, and their numbers were rapidly increasing (Melton, 1987, p. 147; Goldman, 1989, p. 1).

Included among the new Christian groups are those with a fundamentalist Christian basis: the Children of God, Marantha Christian Ministries, the Way International, the Calvary Chapel Movement, and a host of local groups with no national relationship. Moreover, a number of religious innovations have had a substantial appeal. Like some religious groups drawn from Eastern religious traditions, some of these have proved to be widely publicized and highly controversial: the Church of Scientology, which combines elements of popular psychology, folk wisdom, and spiritualism; and the Unification Church, founded by Reverend Sun Myung Moon, who claims to be the prophet of a religion that fulfills traditional Christianity.

Rise of Privatized Religion

Religion has increasingly become a private, individualistic, and personal affair. Many people today fashion their own individual religious belief systems without communal support and without participation in traditional institutionalized religious bodies. Many of those embracing a private faith are apt to be non-affiliates, people indicating no religious preference, whose number rose from 2 percent of Americans in 1967 to 8 percent in 1986 (see table 15–2). The primary goal of privatized religion is self-fulfillment, and the focus of such religious forms is therefore on the techniques—mystical, magical, psychotherapeutic, and technological—whereby fulfillment can be achieved. This focus has been the common denominator of what has been termed the "New Age" movement, which includes a great number of consciousness-raising groups (such as est, Transcendental Meditation, Silva Mind Control, biofeedback, Gestalt Awareness Training, and Lifespring), designed to heighten an individual's physical, social-psychological, and spiritual awareness, and to enhance individual self-discipline and personal effectiveness. What these diverse New Age groups hold in common is their "belief in a cosmic destiny for [humankind], which individuals pursue mainly through mystical examination of the self; and in a 'new age' of existence that will be peopled by superior beings who have undergone a process of inner 'transformation'" (Bordewich, 1988, p. 38).

Changing Role of Women in Religion

One of the major issues that grew out of the "equality revolution" of the 1960s and has since become more pronounced in American religion concerns the role of women. Although women have traditionally been more active participants than men and played very crucial support roles in most religious organizations in the United States, they have until recently been virtually excluded from positions of authority and leadership. Today women cannot be ordained in the Roman Catholic church, the Eastern Orthodox church, many conservative Protestant denominations, and Orthodox Jewish congregations. However, reflecting the impact of the feminist movement, since the 1970s significant challenges have been brought to the traditional definitions of male and female roles within several religious organizations. Although overall seminary enrollments in recent years have been declining, between 1972 and 1987 female enrollments in Protestant seminaries increased 450 percent; in 1972 only one-tenth (10 percent) of the country's Protestant seminary students were women, but by 1987 that figure stood at more than one-fourth (27 percent) (Jacquet, 1988a, pp. 274–275). Moreover, as table 15–3 indicates, the number of female Protestant clergy nearly doubled between 1977 and 1986. Women were most prominent in certain theologically conservative denominations (e.g., Assemblies of God, Salvation Army, Foursquare Gospel Church) and in some theologically liberal denominations (e.g., United Methodist, Presbyterian Church, USA, United Church of Christ, Disciples of Christ) (Jacquet, 1988b). The feminist impact was also reflected in movements within the Roman Catholic church seeking the ordination of women and within Conservative Judaism to permit women to participate more fully in religious observances and in policy-making bodies (Wuthnow, 1988b, p. 229).

The increasing presence of women in the clergy and in policy-making positions—primarily in mainstream Protestant denominations—also sparked controversies over other issues related to the status of women. Illustrative of these controversies has been

Table 15–3. Ten Protestant Denominations with Largest Number of Women Clergy, 1986

Denomination	Number of Women Clergy	Women Clergy as Percentage of Total
Assemblies of God	3,718	13.9
Salvation Army	3,220	62.0
United Methodist	1,891	5.0
Presbyterian Church, USA	1,519	7.8
United Church of Christ	1,460	14.5
Episcopal	796	4.5
Christian Church (Disciples of Christ)	743	10.9
International Church of the Foursquare Gospel	666	19.1
Lutheran Church in America	484	5.6
American Baptist Church	429	5.6

Source: Jacquet, Constant H., Jr. *Women Ministers in 1986 and 1977: A Ten Year View.* New York: National Council of Churches, 1988b.

The consecration of Barbara Harris as an Episcopal bishop in 1989 typifies the increasing prominence of women in positions of authority and leadership in religious organizations.

the movement for "inclusive language"—the effort to alter the terminology in which conceptions of the sacred are communicated. Critics of traditional religious discourse argue that the very symbols and language that have been used to describe God in Judaism and Christianity—King, Lord, Master, and Father—not only reflect a tradition of male domination, power, and authority but also limit and circumscribe conceptions of what is virtually impossible to describe in human terms. The movement for inclusive language seeks to "minimize the male bias reflected in its language about human beings and language about Christ and God," and reflects one of the major issues in contemporary American religious life (National Council of Churches, 1983, p. 6).

Personal Religious Experience

Religious experiences vary widely in form and intensity. For many whose lives have been secularized, religious interpretations have little meaning. For many others, religion is a purely formal and social obligation that may involve activities such as attending religious services, but it has little other effect on their lives. However, a substantial number of Americans claim to have had one or more dramatic and intensely personal religious experiences. In 1984, 40 percent of adults questioned indicated that they had had a "born-again" Christian experience (Gallup Opinion Index, 1985, p. 38).

On the basis of extensive research on the diversity of religious experience in American society, Glock and Stark (1965) have developed a typology of religious experience, which we examine in the order of the frequency with which each type of experience occurs. The four types of religious experience are *confirming, responsive, ecstatic,* and *revelational.*

Confirming Religious Experience

The most frequently reported form of religious experience in contemporary American society is a confirming experience, "a sudden feeling, knowing, or intuition that the beliefs one holds are true" (Glock and Stark, 1965, p. 43). The individual becomes aware of the existence or presence of the sacred. A confirming experience is not a spectacular, overwhelming, or particularly dramatic event. However, it has deep personal meaning and significance to the individual. The sudden intensification of feeling that occurs may take a general form in which the individual experiences a sense of reverence, awe, solemnity, or calmness. Or the individual may have a distinct awareness of the closeness of a divine being, such as may be elicited by the wonders of nature (Hay, 1979). During the mid-nineteenth century Henry David Thoreau described such an experience during his solitude at Walden Pond.

> Once, . . . in the midst of a gentle rain, . . . I was suddenly sensible of such sweet and beneficent society in nature, in the very patterning of the drops, and in every sight and sound around my house, and infinite and unaccountable friendliness all at once, like an atmosphere, sustaining me, as made the fancied advantages of human neighborhood insignificant. . . . Every little pine-needle expanded and swelled with sympathy and befriended me. I was so distinctly made aware of the presence of something kindred to me, that I thought no place could ever be strange to me again (Thoreau, 1854, p. 116).

Responsive Religious Experience

The confirming experience is passive; the individual merely feels aware of the presence of the divine. The responsive experience, on the other hand, is marked by reciprocity; the individual feels that the divine is responding to him or her as well. Rather than merely being made aware of the presence of the divine, individuals sense that the divine has taken special notice of them.

The responsive experience can take a variety of forms. It frequently involves an awareness of an external power controlling and guiding the individual. It can also produce a sense of peace, serenity, and joy, a feeling that the divine has chosen the individual (Hay, 1979). A responsive experience is frequently reported among those who pronounce themselves "born-again Christians." Responsive religious experiences frequently occur during periods of stress (Hay, 1979, p. 176), as when individuals perceive the divine to have helped them out in a time of crisis, such as an illness, a miraculous escape or rescue from danger, or a positive turn in one's economic fortune.

Ecstatic Religious Experience

The ecstatic religious experience involves not only awareness of the presence and responsiveness of the divine but also a feeling of an intense and intimate emotional relationship with the sacred. So powerful is the intensity of the ecstatic experience that one of the most prominent features reported about them is the imagery of light or the physical sensation of being electrified. Probably the most famous conversion in Christian tradition was that of the Apostle Paul, whose experience is described in the New Testament: "Now as he journeyed he approached Damascus, and suddenly a light from heaven flashed about him. And he fell to the ground and heard a voice saying to him, 'Saul, Saul, why do you persecute me?' " (Acts 9:3–4).

In his analysis of religious experiences among British graduate students, Hay (1979), within the category of ecstatic religious experiences, has found extrasensory perceptions, out-of-body experiences (in which an individual's soul or mind is reported to have left the body and observed the body from outside), and visions. He reports the following visionary experience.

> A week after I met __________, we were sitting looking at each other's eyes in a bedroom and there began to be a beam passing between our eyes and also a third eye in the middle of our foreheads. This lasted for about two hours and we didn't say a word to each other. Towards the end of the two hours . . . [it] came and went in waves, and we began to know that we had known each other in a previous life. Because we had known each other, we *knew* each other (Hay, 1979, p. 171).

Revelational Religious Experience

Orthodoxy
Religious revelation or doctrine that supports the existing religious and social order

Heterodoxy
Religious revelation or doctrine that is critical and disruptive of the existing religious and social order

The least common type of religious experience, but perhaps the one that receives the most publicity, is the revelational. While other types of religious experiences may involve a sense of the divine speaking, the distinctive characteristic of the revelational experience is that the individual receives "confidential information about the future, divine nature, or plan" (Glock and Stark, 1965, p. 55). Such relevations may be **orthodox**—that is, supportive of the existing religious and social order—or **heterodox**—that is, critical and potentially disruptive of the status quo.

An example of an orthodox revelation is the reported appearance or apparition of the Virgin Mary, a religious experience with a long tradition in Christianity. Although such appearances or apparitions reached a peak during the Middle Ages, between 1928 and 1973 more than 200 such encounters were reported to Roman Catholic authorities, and in recent years apparitions have been reported by devout Roman Catholics in Ireland, France, Yugoslavia, Italy, and the United States (Zimdars-Swartz, 1988, 1989a). Reports of such experiences have frequently had a substantial public impact. Some have been memorialized by the establishment of sacred shrines, such as the shrine in Lourdes, France. Reports of appearances by the Virgin Mary have often drawn great crowds of people. In 1950 an estimated 100,000 people traveled to the Wisconsin farm of Mary Ann Van Hoof to hear messages that were transmitted through her from the Virgin Mary (Zimdars-Swartz, 1989b). In 1988 over 13,000 people from all over the United States gathered in Lubbock, Texas, after three people reported that they were receiving messages of peace and hope from Mary (Pratt, 1988, p. 1).

These experiences of encounters with the Virgin Mary are orthodox in the sense that they usually encourage people to become more devout in their adherence to established religious practices and authority. Heterodox revelations, on the other hand, are important sources of social change, for they provide visions of a new social order and a basis for rejecting and challenging established authority.

Many examples of revelational experiences have been recorded among the world's religions. The Islamic and Christian faiths, as well as many sects in both religions, originated with their founder's claims of having received divine revelation.

One of the most dramatic revelational experiences in American religious history was that of Joseph Smith, from whose experiences the Latter-Day Saints (Mormon) churches have developed. As an adolescent, Smith, who had been deeply troubled by the competing claims of truth offered by various denominations, had a striking revelational experience.

> After I had retired . . . I kneeled down and began to offer up the desires of my heart to God. I had scarcely done so, when immediately I was seized upon by some power which entirely overcame me, and had such an astonishing influence over me as to bind my tongue so that I could not speak. Thick darkness gathered around me, and it seemed to me for a time as if I were doomed to sudden destruction. . . . just at this moment of great alarm, I saw a pillar of light exactly over my head, above the brightness of the sun, which descended gradually until it fell upon me. . . . When the light rested upon me I saw two personages, whose brightness and glory defy all description, standing above me in the air. One of them spake unto me, calling me by name, and said—pointing to the other—THIS IS MY BELOVED SON, HEAR HIM (*History of the Church of Latter-Day Saints*, 1902, pp. 5–6).

Revelational experiences have frequently provided the inspiration and source of authority for new social movements. Weber called the authority derived from such experience *charismatic*. As noted in chapter 4, *charisma* refers to qualities of an individual personality that are believed to be exceptional and sometimes of supernatural origin that give the individual authority over others.

Persons with charismatic qualities frequently become the leaders of **revitalization movements:** "deliberate, organized efforts by members of a society to create a more satisfying culture" (Wallace, 1966, p. 626). A revitalization movement provides a new belief system for interpreting and explaining the universe. Faith in a charismatic leader elicits a total commitment among movement followers, which accounts for the extremely

Revitalization movements
Social movements organized to provide a new belief system for explaining life and the universe

well-disciplined nature of many such groups. Throughout the American experience many revitalization movements have developed into organized religions. Among the more successful and enduring are the Mormons, Christian Scientists, and the Black Muslims. More recently, sensational publicity has been directed toward such revitalization movements as the Unification Church, the Children of God, and the International Society for Krishna Consciousness (Hare Krishnas), among others.

Leaving Religion

Most of our discussion of religious experience has focused on processes whereby people affiliate or identify with a religious tradition. However, people may also become disillusioned with and reject or disaffiliate from religion. Therefore, it is necessary to consider the experience of leaving religion.

We noted above that a substantial minority (40 percent) of American adults reported having had some form of personal religious experience. However, an almost equal proportion report being relatively uninvolved in religious activities. In 1978, 41 percent of American adults sampled in a national survey were "unchurched," that is, they had not participated in a formal religious service during the previous six months (Princeton Religious Research Center, 1978). The vast majority of the unchurched are people who report a religious preference but who seldom attend religious services. Only a small proportion of the American people—about 7 percent—report no religious preference. Among these are people who never had a religious identity and those who once had a religious identity but rejected it later in life.

Religion is always a dynamic, changing phenomenon, and many people change their religious identities during their lifetimes. Many people at some point leave the religion in which they were reared (Bromley, 1988). Many of these will switch to another religious affiliation (Roof and Hadaway, 1979; Nelson and Bromley, 1988).

Apostates
People who have a religious identity early in their lives which they later reject

Hadaway and Roof (1988) focused on **apostates**—those who earlier in their lives had had a religious identity but who later came to reject any religious identity. They found that apostates are most likely to be young, single, male, highly educated, politically independent, geographically mobile, more involved socially with friends than with family, urban and suburban residents, and much more accepting of the "new morality" on issues such as drug use and sexual behavior. The peak period of rejection of religion in the post-World War II period occurred during the 1960s and early 1970s, when many young Americans questioned traditional institutions. However, since the early 1970s religious apostasy appears to have declined (Hadaway and Roof, 1988).

Leaving religion can be a gradual, drawn-out process of increasing uninvolvement, or it can be the result of a profound intellectual and emotional crisis. A university graduate student describes his experience:

> I was deeply involved in church activities all the time I was growing up. It even evolved to the point where, when I was in high school, I preached a sermon on Youth Sunday and, as a freshman in junior college, I taught a high school Sunday school class. . . . However, I became increasingly disenchanted with religion because I didn't see my church working on issues I thought it should address. One day I went to my minister to ask him to sign a newspaper ad opposing the Vietnam War. Instead of supporting me, he ranted and raved about my lack of patriotism. He really symbolized the inaction of the church on social issues. That was it. I left. I bolted. I vowed when I was sitting

> there listening to him tell me how un-American I was for wanting to bring about a world of peace that I would never darken the doorstep of that church again—that I would have nothing to do with it. And I didn't—ever. . . . The church has simply become irrelevant to my life. . . . I've written it off. It may serve certain functions for some people, but not for this boy (personal communication).

The Institutionalization of Religious Experience

The origins of many religious organizations, beliefs, and forms of worship can be located in the religious experiences of a religion's founder, frequently a charismatic leader claiming to speak for the divine. Whenever a new religious movement is founded and dominated by a charismatic leader, the death of that leader threatens the religion's continued existence. Members must adapt to new circumstances if they want to continue the practice of their religion. If charismatic leaders want to ensure the success of the group beyond their lifetimes, some means for governing the religious organization must be created. The authority of the charismatic leader may be transferred to relatives, to trusted colleagues, or to impersonal positions in the organization itself.

The crisis of continuity for a religious organization on the death of a charismatic leader is resolved by the institutionalization of religious experience. Many religious rituals are methods developed to continue the religious experiences of a movement's earliest participants. Thus, a relatively spontaneous and subjective experience becomes institutionalized, patterned, and routine. Institutionalized behaviors and structures then become the ways of eliciting, creating, or maintaining religious experience. O'Dea and Aviad (1983) have identified three aspects of the process of institutionalization in a religious movement: cultic activity, religious behavior that involves patterns of worship or ritual; beliefs, which are a religious movement's pattern of ideas; and organization, that is, the social organization, or social structure, of a religious group.

Religious Behaviors

Rituals are complex, communally shared, ceremonial forms of religious behavior. They symbolically express spontaneous religious values and experiences that have become standardized and institutionalized over time. Rituals occur during worship services and around events, such as christenings, weddings, and funerals, that mark important stages in the life cycle. In Christianity, for instance, the Mass or Liturgy "became both the re-presentation of the original experience and the way in which the worshippers expressed their relationship to the sacred" (O'Dea and Aviad, 1983, p. 42). Similarly, a Jewish seder at Passover is characterized by a prescribed series of prayers, the recitation of sacred literature, a huge feast, and a congregational gathering that both commemorates the historic experiences of the Jewish people and unites them in a community. As time passes, proper performance of a ritual becomes increasingly important, and any effort to change it is upsetting.

Ritual
Complex, communally shared, ceremonial expression of religious experience

Religiosity can be expressed in a variety of rituals. It would be difficult to describe all religious behaviors because many that are not usually defined as religious actually are manifestations of religious sentiments. For example, for the strongly patriotic who perceive their particular brand of nationalism as deriving from God, standing at attention

Among Muslims, daily prayers are performed separately by men and women. These Muslim women are engaged in a prayer ritual in the holy city of Mecca, which all Muslims are expected to visit during their lifetimes.

for the raising of the flag or the playing of the national anthem is a religious behavior. On the other hand, some behaviors commonly defined as religious (for example, attending church) may involve nonreligious motivations, such as making social contacts, impressing business associates, or finding a suitable marriage mate for one's child.

Prayer, a form of addressing the sacred, is one of the most widespread forms of religious behavior and is found in virtually all religions. A prayer can take the form of asking the sacred for a favor or giving thanks to the sacred force for a past blessing. It can also serve as an affirmation of faith in the religious system itself.

Another basic religious behavior involves some form of physical exercise. Guttman (1978, p. 16) has pointed out that many societies have "incorporated running, jumping, throwing, wrestling, and even ball playing in their religious rituals and ceremonies." The ancient Olympic games, conducted in honor of the god Zeus, were sacred festivals, an integral part of ancient Greek life. In Iran's national religion, Shiism, a branch of Islam, religious activities among the most devout adherents involve an exhausting and arduous athletic ritual designed to purify the minds of participants ("The Sport of Religion," 1972). Sufism, a mystical Islamic tradition that has recently gained increasing numbers of American adherents, uses physical exercises, including breath control, body movement, and dance, to gain control over the senses and achieve a mystical experience (Awn, 1987, p. 119). Similarly, sumo wrestling, Japan's most popular spectator sport, has its roots in Shinto, the national religion. Early sumo contests were part of Shinto religious festivals (Halloran, 1974, p. 10:1). For the Shakers, a communal religious group that flourished in eighteenth century and nineteenth century America, physical exercise in the form of an elaborate communal dance was an integral part of their religious ritual (Nordoff, 1875/1971).

Drugs may be used as a means of producing physiological changes in the individual that could induce a spiritual state. Although many religious leaders deny the religious authenticity of a drug-induced experience, drugs have been used for sacramental purposes in many societies. The ancient Greeks, for example, chewed the intoxicating leaves of ivy to induce an ecstatic state. In the Native American Church, a religion that has become popular among North American Indians since the turn of the twentieth century, an elaborate ritual surrounding the use of peyote has developed. A participant in the peyote rites recalled:

> For three days and for three nights I had been eating the peyote and not slept at all. Now I [suddenly] realized that throughout all the years that I had lived, I had never once known a truly holy thing. Now, for the first time, I knew it (Radin, 1926, p. 182).

Drugs or physical exercise are not the only methods by which religious experiences can be elicited. Other methods of physiological inducement of religious feeling include the mortification of the flesh by pain, sleeplessness, or going without food or water. All these methods were employed among the Plains Indians, for whom fasting and self-torture were a necessary prelude to a young male's acquiring a vision or communication with a "guardian spirit," which served as a ritual transition from adolescence to maturity (Benedict, 1922; Powers, 1987).

Religious behavior often involves notions of mana and taboo. **Mana** refers to the power inherent in sacred objects. To a believer, touching sacred objects will cause the powerful qualities of those objects to be transmitted to them or will bring them good

Mana
The force or power believed to be inherent in a sacred object

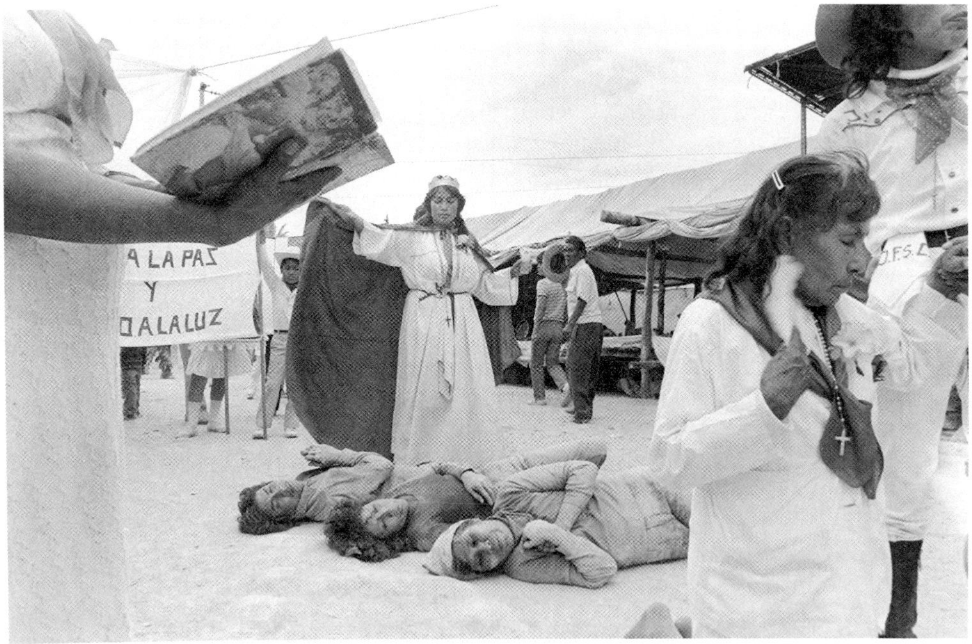

Religious commitments often elicit extraordinary demonstrations of devotion, including the inducement of physical pain or even self-sacrifice. These Mexican women are participating in a dramatic penitential ritual, rolling in the dust to the tomb of Niño Fidencio.

fortune. Touching the Western Wall in Jerusalem is a sacred rite for Jews. Many Christians claim miraculous cures by visiting sacred shrines, such as the one in Lourdes, France. On a more mundane level, mana is exemplified in the belief that luck follows from carrying a rabbit's foot or kissing the Blarney Stone.

Taboo
Religious proscription against physical contact with objects that may affect a person

The converse of the notion of mana is a **taboo,** a religious proscription against having physical contact with certain objects in order to prevent the power embodied by these objects from affecting a person. The Polynesians, for example,

> . . . maintained an elaborate set of taboos on contacts of one kind or another between status groups, particularly between royalty and commoners. The chief's body could not be touched by the body of a commoner; even if the contact were accidental, death would be the result for the commoner. The commoner could not look down upon his chief from a higher elevation (looking is, in a sense, like touching), and so the chief had to sit upon a raised platform and be carried on a raised litter above the shoulders of his subjects (Wallace, 1966, pp. 61–62).

Taboos are often related to food, drink, or other substances that may be taken into the body. Among Orthodox Jews a wide variety of foods are taboo. Similarly, several contemporary religious sects, such as the Hare Krishnas, forbid the use of drugs. Mormons proscribe the use of tobacco, alcoholic beverages, and drinks containing caffeine, such as coffee and tea.

Another type of religious behavior involves the creation and use of various forms of religious symbols or icons. These symbols represent either sacred entities, or the values, relationships, processes, or events associated with the sacred. Examples of religious symbols include the Christian cross or fish, the Jewish Star of David or menorah, and (in civil religion) the flag of the United States.

Religious Belief Systems

Myth
A sacred story that communicates the moral prescriptions of divine beings

Religious belief systems include both myth and theology. A **myth** is a sacred story, a parable, or a graphic way of communicating a basic idea concerning the activities and moral prescriptions of divine beings. It provides a concrete and emotionally charged explanation of the historically significant events in a religious system. To a sociologist, the importance of a myth is not its truth or accuracy, but its ability to bind believers into a common community and to reinforce belief in a society's basic values and social institutions. The Christmas stories of the shepherds, the angels, and the three kings are part of Christian mythology. Their historical accuracy or inaccuracy are irrelevant; their importance lies in uniting Christians into a sacred community for the celebration of Christmas.

Of particular importance are "origin" or "creation" myths, found in many different societies. Creation myths describe the origins of the universe and humans' place in it. They usually include descriptions of the origins of societal norms and values, family organization, law, and government. They are kept alive by periodic recitation. Although such myths persist in contemporary society, recitation today most often takes the form of reading or repeating aloud the basic truths as they are recorded in sacred documents, such as the Old and New Testaments in the Christian tradition.

The belief system of a new religion is born in the experience or inspiration of the religion's founders. The rational and logical development and extension of these ideas

Every religion has a sacred oral or written literature that is often read or recited to keep the important ideas alive. The Jewish boy at his Bar Mitzvah in Jerusalem is reading from the sacred text of the Talmud.

is the task of theology. **Theology** applies the process of rationalization to a religious belief system. A theology usually develops when a priestly class is differentiated from lay members of a religion. The more clear the distinctions between clergy and laity become, the more specialized the clergy's functions become, and the more likely it will be that a system of religious ideas, a theology, will become elaborated and rationalized.

Theology
The rational and logical development of religious belief systems

Religious Organizations

The process of institutionalization is clearly apparent in the organization or structure of religious groups. An important distinction in religious organization appears in the two ideal types that the German sociologist Ernest Troeltsch (1931) called *sect* and *church*. A further distinction is made between these two forms of religious organization and cults.

Sect. A **sect** is a small, voluntary group of members who join the group of their own conscious choice. A sect is the type of organization that characterizes a religion in the first stage of a revitalization movement. Primary emphasis in a sect is placed on a personal religious experience, and its leadership is usually composed of laypeople with no specialized training. The primary source of guidance for the sect's members is the sacred scriptures or personal inspiration. Rather than accepting the existing society, sect

Sect
A small, voluntary, religious group that has broken away from an existing religion

members tend to reject or feel alienated from it. Consequently, membership is often drawn from the lower classes—the "disinherited," who have no vested interests in maintaining the status quo.

Sect members withdraw into their own community, which develops its own rigorous standards of perfection (such as a conversion experience, renunciation of all worldly possessions, or renunciation of "vices," such as smoking, drinking, or gambling). Sects are exclusive religious organizations; they do not admit people who do not conform to their rigorous norms. Membership in a sect is total; the group's code of ethics is uncompromising and absolute, demanding full conformity. This characteristic is reflected in the group's limited interaction with outsiders and its refusal to participate in many societal activities (such as military service, saluting the flag, or medical treatment). Frequently, sects set themselves apart by such things as peculiar dress or dietary restrictions. Sect members may live in territorial isolation from the world, as the Amish do, or within the general society but with limited social interaction with nonmembers, as Hasidic Jews do. (See chapter 3.)

Church
A large, socially acceptable, institutionalized religious group

Church. Distinct from a sect, a **church** is a large, socially acceptable, institutionalized religious group into which one usually is born, rather than converted. No special requirements are prescribed for membership; some members join only for secular or social reasons. While the sect is exclusive, a church is inclusive and often national in scope. It tries to extend its spiritual influence to as many people as possible. A church is characterized by a bureaucratic structure made up of a professional clergy within an established hierarchy. Ritual and belief systems tend to be elaborate and highly prescribed. Because most members are born into a church and do not actively choose membership, a strong emphasis is placed upon education as a means of perpetuating the faith.

One further distinction between a sect and a church is that a church accommodates itself to the secular world, while a sect resists such accommodation. Churches tend to be relatively larger and more socially inclusive than sects, but sects make stronger demands on and elicit greater commitment from their members. "Churches attempt to regulate or fulfill a few of the activities or needs of large numbers of people; sects attempt to regulate or fill many of the activities or needs of small numbers of people" (Wuthnow, 1988a, p. 495). That sects elicit greater commitments from their members is reflected by the differences in levels of financial contributions among American Protestant denominations. The ten Protestant denominations with over a million adherents average $304 per capita in annual contributions. However, as table 15–4 indicates, the Protestant groups with highest per capita giving tend to be relatively small in membership. Of the ten groups with the highest per capita contributions, seven had memberships of less than 100,000, and only one—the Seventh-Day Adventists—had a membership exceeding 200,000 (Jacquet, 1988a, p. 264).

Because their appeal is oriented primarily to the middle and upper classes, churches are frequently alien to the lower classes in decorum and social composition. Sects emerge from the dissatisfaction felt toward these established expressions of religiosity. However, the sectarian character of a religious group is almost always short-lived. It is either modified over time, or it ceases to exist.

The transition of an organization from sect to church illustrates the process of routinization or institutionalization, which is a common characteristic of religious move-

Table 15–4. Differences in Annual per Capita Contributions among American Protestant Churches: The Ten Largest Denominations and the Ten Denominations with the Highest Contributions

	Membership	Per Capita Contributions
Ten largest denominations		
Presbyterian Church (USA)	3,007,000	$521.00
Episcopal Church	2,505,000	453.00
Christian (Disc. of Christ)	1,107,000	298.00
United Church of Christ	1,676,000	294.00
Southern Baptist Convention	14,614,000	282.00
Lutheran Church—Mo. Synod	2,631,000	272.00
United Methodist Church	9,192,000	254.00
Lutheran Church in America*	2,896,000	235.00
American Lutheran Church*	2,319,000	228.00
American Baptist Church	1,576,000	200.00
Average	4,152,300	$304.00
Ten highest in contributions		
Reformed Episcopal Church	5,733	1,289.00
Evangelical Mennonite Church	3,841	953.00
The Wesleyan Church	109,196	845.00
Evangelical Covenant Church	86,079	836.00
Seventh-Day Adventists	666,199	793.00
Brethren in Christ Church	16,693	779.00
The Missionary Church	26,869	779.00
Free Methodist Church	71,682	776.00
Presbyterian Church in America	188,083	765.00
International Pentecostal Church of Christ	2,743	742.00
Average	117,712	$856.00

Source: Jacquet, Constant H., ed. *Yearbook of American and Canadian Churches, 1988*. Nashville: Abingdon Press, 1988a, p. 264.

* Since these data were compiled, the American Lutheran Church and the Lutheran Church in America have merged (with the Association of Evangelical Lutheran Churches) to form the Evangelical Lutheran Church in America.

ments. As Niebuhr has pointed out, "by its very nature the sectarian type of organization is valid only for one generation" (Niebuhr, 1929, p. 19). Numerous Christian denominations that began as sects appealing to the disinherited, such as Baptists, Methodists, and Quakers, gained social respectability and became churches. Although an individual may join a sect by choice, his or her children are born into the group and do not necessarily share the enthusiasm and fervor that prompted the parent's participation. To convince a new generation, the sect must modify entrance requirements, usually by making them less stringent, and it must emphasize the role of education. If a sect is successful and attracts increasing numbers, an organizational apparatus becomes necessary.

As the organization expands, it begins to develop a life of its own. Those who work within the religious organization develop the need to expand their own power bases, to advertise the good deeds of the organization, and to develop educational techniques to ensure the support of the succeeding generations. All of these needs lead to an ever-expanding bureaucratic structure. In addition, the organization develops an interest in its own survival that leads to the support of the status quo. If the group is prospering in its environment, it will resist efforts to change it. Religious routines tend to become less dynamic and spontaneous and more routine. All of these developments signal the loss of characteristics that initially marked the sect. Once the organization becomes institutionalized, it tends to become rigid and formal. Inevitably some people find that its prescribed formulas do not meet their religious needs. Sectarian groups that respond to this dissatisfaction are apt to develop. Thus a religious organization may be subject to the same kinds of disaffection, change, and revitalization that originally led to its own formation.

Cults. The basic distinction between a church and a sect is that a church accepts the status quo while a sect rejects it. However, Stark and Bainbridge (1979) have argued that sects should be distinguished from cults, even though both stand in tension with their surrounding socio-cultural environment. **Cults** are small, voluntary, and exclusive religious groups that have created new religious systems. These two types of religious organizations are distinguished primarily by their origins—the manner in which they begin.

Cult
A small, voluntary, and exclusive religious group that has created a new religious system

The International Society of Krishna Consciousness (Hare Krishnas), a religious movement drawn from the Hindu tradition, has been among the more visible cults that have been established in American society in the past two decades.

Sects are the result of schisms; they break off from existing religious organizations. Founders of a sect do not seek to create a new religious body but to realize what they perceive as the "original" beliefs and practices of the organization from which they have split. They begin as internal factions of a religious body. They are religious conservatives, seeking to reestablish the "true faith," which they claim the established religious body has abandoned. For example, many Protestant denominations in the United States were organized not as efforts to establish new religious faiths but as attempts to realize more fully the essence of the Christian church.

Cults, on the other hand, are not schismatic; they are not splinter groups breaking away from an established religious tradition. With no previous organizational attachment to an existing religious body, they represent a new religious tradition altogether. Because they introduce new religious beliefs or practices that may be completely alien to an established religious tradition; founders of cults are religious radicals. Cults may take the form of either religious innovations, which are based on new revelations or insights, or importations, which involve acceptance of a tradition or faith well established in another society but new and different in the receiving society. Examples of innovative cults include the early Mormons and the Unification Church of the Reverend Sun Myung Moon, the founders of which both claimed to be introducing new doctrines that fulfilled traditional Christianity. Among recent imported cults are several groups drawn from Eastern religions, such as various Muslim and Buddhist sects.

Summary

Religion is one of the most pervasive and complex of all human activities. The sociology of religion is concerned with understanding the role that religion plays in society and the influence of social factors upon religious activity. Religion is what is socially defined as sacred, encompassing entities that evoke a sense of awe, mystery, respect, and honor. For many people the sacred involves supernatural entities. It can also include a variety of other phenomena, such as political ideologies or even scientific systems, that provide a system of ultimate meaning.

Religion has several social consequences, both positive and negative, depending upon one's individual perspective. By providing an explanation and interpretation of the universe, religion deals with the problems of meaning that are inherent in the precariousness of human existence. It serves as a source of strength, comfort, and consolation for the individual, a means of warding off uncertainty. It provides a sense of individual and group identity. Religion also often functions to legitimate the existing social order. By interpreting society as something other than a human creation that is difficult, if not impossible, to change, religion reinforces the status quo. However, religion also frequently performs a critical function by providing a basis from which to criticize and challenge society. Many revitalization movements, which are efforts to create a more satisfying society, have their origins in a religious impulse.

Religion in American society has been characterized by three basic features: pervasiveness, secularism, and denominational pluralism. From colonial times to the present, religion has been a prominent feature of American life. Yet, despite this pervasive attachment to religion, the authority of religious beliefs, values, and practices has declined.

Religious diversity, or denominational pluralism, has characterized religion in America. It is a result of social class, racial, and ethnic factors, and the spontaneous creation of new religious groups within American society.

Religion involves several different but related features: personal experiences, behaviors, beliefs, and organizations. Personal religious experience takes many forms. New religions or religious revitalization movements often are based on a charismatic leader's claim of having had a revelational experience. New religious movements can take the form of sects or cults. Sects are offshoots of existing religious organizations, while cults represent religious innovations or importations. Once new religious movements are founded, they attempt to institutionalize the religious experience of their founders. This involves the development of rituals, beliefs, and organizational structures. As a group's organizational structure becomes established, new movements, with different social bases, may emerge to start the process again. Thus, change in religious organizations is a dynamic and recurring process.

CRITICAL THINKING

1. Is religion a source of social stability or social change? Give examples to support each viewpoint.
2. Why are sociologists so interested in the role of religion in society? Use Max Weber's study on the Protestant ethic to show how religion and economics might be intertwined.
3. How can sociologists who believe in the scientific method study a subject that is associated with "faith" rather than "facts"?
4. What is religion? Why is it considered by sociologists to be a social phenomenon?
5. What aspects of religious behavior in America are relatively unchanging?
6. What is "liberation theology"? With which part of the world is it most commonly associated? How does the existence of liberation theology show that religion is a social phenomenon that affects other parts of society?
7. Describe the major social functions of religion and give examples to illustrate each function. Does religion provide social stability or promote social change?
8. What is secularization? How is secularization related to other major trends in American society such as industrialization, urbanization, bureaucratization, and rationalization?
9. In what ways is religion "marketed" in American society? How does this trend show religion to be social behavior related to other aspects of society? Is this a positive or negative trend?
10. Describe civil religion in the United States. Speculate as to the nature of civil religion in the "atheist" society of the Soviet Union.
11. What is privatized religion and why is it on the rise in the United States? In what ways does such religion circumvent the traditional functions ascribed to religious behavior?
12. Compare and contrast the various types of religious organizations mentioned in the chapter. What function might each serve in society?

CHAPTER

16

Political Life

The political system of the United States was designed to give people a strong voice in determining what their government should do. Voting for political leaders is an important way for people to express their will. In contrast to many democracies, however, especially those in Western Europe, a comparatively small percentage of the population participates in the voting process. For example, in the 1988 presidential election only about half of those eligible to vote bothered to cast a ballot. The youngest eligible voters in the population are least likely to vote—those between 18 and 29 years of age. The paradox is that young people have the greatest stake in political elections. If elected leaders get the country into a war or undertake other military adventures, young people will most likely do the fighting and dying. Young people have the longest time to live, and political decisions made now (for example, increasing the national debt) are apt to have a great effect on them for many years.

Even among older age groups, from one-third to one-half of Americans are non-voters in presidential and congressional elections. Although Americans give great lip-service to democracy, their voting behavior is very low compared to other democratic nations (Piven and Cloward, 1988). Americans think of their government as the most democratic in the world, but large numbers of them do not participate, even in the simple act of voting.

Power, the State, and Government

The central concern of the political institution, or polity, is power—the ability to control other people's behavior and carry out one's will despite resistance. Obviously there are some situations in which people comply more willingly to the imposition of power than others. As we saw in chapter 4 in our discussion of bureaucracy, the German sociologist Max Weber (1918/1946) distinguished between legitimate and illegitimate power. Legitimate power, or *authority,* is power exercised by leaders that is generally approved or accepted as appropriate by members of a group or society. Although they may strongly disagree with laws that their elected officials enact, most Americans accept the right of those officials to pass such laws and hence accept them as legitimate.

On the other hand, there are circumstances in which people do not recognize as legitimate the power exerted over them and do not comply willingly to its exercise; they comply only because they are forced to do so. **Coercion** is power based on the threat or use of force, and is therefore considered illegitimate by the people who are forced to act against their will.

Coercion
Illegitimate power based on threat or use of force

The State and Government

State
Sole source of legitimate physical force

The state is the dominant political institution in modern societies (Lehman, 1988). The **state** is the sole source of legitimate physical force (Weber 1918/1946); it is the only institution that can impose taxes, declare war, and imprison law violators.

The enormous power of the state appears in the variety of functions it performs (Weber, 1921/1978, p. 905):

1. The enactment of law (legislative function).
2. The protection of personal safety and public order (police).
3. The protection of vested rights (administration of justice).
4. The cultivation of hygienic, educational, social-welfare, and other cultural interests (the various branches of administration).
5. The armed protection against outside attack (military administration).

Nation-state
State that has power over people living in a distinct geographical area

Sociologists sometimes use the term **nation-state** when referring to a state that has power over people living in a distinct geographical area known as a nation. The nation-state developed in Europe only about 500 years ago, and it has emerged in most Asian and African societies during this century. However, the nation is not found in all societies. Some pre-industrial societies in Africa and Asia exist without clearly defined state structures.

The principal organization of the state is the government. Governments can be organized in a number of different ways and can take different forms. Governments typically take one of three major forms: autocracy, totalitarianism, or democracy.

Autocracy
Government in which ultimate authority is vested in a single person

Autocracy.

In an **autocracy,** ultimate power is held by a single person. An autocrat may gain the position through heredity (an absolute monarch) or by rule of force (a dictator). Among the most recognizable autocratic rulers in the world today are Urgarte Pinochet of Chile, Manuel Noriega of Panama, and Roh Tae Woo of North Korea. Autocrats rely on their ability to control the military and police systems of their countries, and to maintain the unquestioning loyalty of large numbers of their subjects. Criticism of the government and the autocrat is usually prohibited. The government often censors the media and sometimes uses terror to stifle public dissent. However, an autocracy tends to separate the private and public lives of its subjects, allowing individuals some degree of freedom in private matters of family and religion.

Totalitarianism
Government involving state control over all major institutions

Totalitarianism.

Totalitarianism is a form of government involving state control and regulation of all major institutions in a society. The state is represented by a small ruling clique that relies on physical force and terror to maintain social order. A totalitarian government exerts total control over a nation and makes little distinction between public and private concerns. A totalitarian regime seeks to control family life as well as economic and political institutions. Friedrich and Brzezinski (1965) have suggested six elements of totalitarian rule:

1. *A single political party.* Totalitarian states are one-party governments led by dictators or by a ruling clique. The one political party is the only legal party in the state.

2. *Control of the economy.* Totalitarian states exercise control over virtually all portions of the economy. The state may set goals for economic production, establish prices and supplies for goods, and dissolve private ownership of either industry or farms.

General Manuel Noriega of Panama has continued to exercise autocratic rule over his country, even though the people voted for a change in a recent election. Like most autocratic leaders, Noriega has relied heavily on his military and police forces to maintain his power.

3. *Control of media*. Totalitarian states control television, radio, newspapers, and magazines. They deny a public forum to dissenting opinions so that only the official party position is communicated to the people.
4. *Control of weapons*. Totalitarian states monopolize the use of weapons, denying the individual the right to own arms.
5. *Ideology*. Totalitarian states use an elaborate ideology to explain virtually every aspect of social life. Social goals and values are described in simple terms, and distortions are often made about the state's enemies.
6. *Terror*. Totalitarian states rely on terror to maintain social control. Secret police, torture, and punishment without trial are common in totalitarian states.

Nazi Germany is a major example of totalitarian rule in this century. Anti-Semitic ideology, concentration camps for Jews and others, and the terror of the Gestapo (Hitler's secret police) were key elements of Nazi Germany's totalitarian power. Many of these features have also characterized the Soviet Union and its client states in Eastern Europe.

Democracy. The word democracy is derived from the Greek roots *demos,* which means people, and *kratia,* which means rule. Literally, then, democracy means rule by the people.

Democracy
Government where there are periodic opportunities to retain or replace officials

In everyday conversation the political system of the United States is usually referred to as a democracy. A **democracy** is a form of government in which there are periodic opportunities for the people being governed to retain or replace governing officials. A country is democratic when a large part of the population is able to "influence major decisions by choosing among contenders for political office" (Lipset, 1963a, p. 28). By this criterion it appears that the United States is a democratic society. We do have periodic elections to select the president, senators, representatives, governors, mayors, and other elected officials. In choosing among aspirants to political office, voters are presumably able thereby to influence the programs and policies of the government.

Three Views of the Political System of the United States

Considerable controversy exists among sociologists concerning the extent to which the American political system is actually democratic. There are three different views of the American political system: pluralist, neo-Marxian, and elitist. Of these three views, only the pluralist is consistent with characteristics of a democratic system. The neo-Marxian perspective emphasizes how power is held by those who control the economic system. The elitist view also contends that power is held by a relatively small group, but that group is not limited to capitalists controlling the economic system.

The Pluralist View

Pluralism describes a society that is made up of a number of competing interest groups (Rose, 1967). These competing groups serve to disperse power in a pluralistic society (Wasburn, 1982, p. 299). Such groups may represent the interests of business, labor, education, medicine, sports, or others. Each group has power within its own realm, and exerts power and influence over the federal government. Although the government is not a pawn in the hands of various interest groups, it is seen as directed and influenced by each of these powerful interests. Which interest group, or coalition of interest groups, wins out on a particular issue depends upon which one is most powerful at a given time in a particular sphere. Since each group can exert greater power on some issues than on others, no single interest group ever fully realizes its goals and dominates other groups. In a pluralistic society the political process is not run by a single powerful elite but is characterized by shifting patterns of interest-group influence. In fact, in the pluralist view, the balance of power among interest groups makes the United States a democratic society (Dahl, 1967).

An ideal pluralistic system operates under four basic conditions (Gamson, 1975). First, everyone must accept the norms and values of constitutional democracy. Second, there must be a set of groups whose interests overlap so that individuals are linked to a variety of groups in which they encounter people with different orientations. This prevents people from developing a single image of what should be done in society. Thus, a given individual is likely to be a member of a wide array of very different groups, including family, community, work, religion, ethnic, and social class. Third, in a pluralistic political system, access to the political arena should be open so that any group has the opportunity to receive a fair hearing for its point of view. Fourth, a balance of power must exist among competing groups so that no one group can dominate on all issues and so that coalitions among groups can shift, depending on the issue.

A Theory of Power Based on a Pluralist View. The sociologist David Riesman (1961) has advanced a pluralist view of power based on the notion of veto groups. A **veto group** is a special interest group that attempts to protect itself by blocking the actions of other groups. Riesman suggests that American society has two levels of power—an upper level of competing veto groups, and a lower level of the unorganized public. Veto groups compete for dominance on particular issues and they seek public support in their efforts. An example of veto group competition is the fight over handgun regulation between the National Rifle Association (opposed) and Handgun Control, Inc. (in favor). In Riesman's view, power is diversified among the plurality of veto groups, and no single group dominates political decision making. The emergence of veto groups has been an important political development. Indeed, Riesman suggests that the "only leaders of national scope left in the United States today are those who can placate the veto groups" (Riesman, 1961, p. 213).

Veto group
Special interest group that defends itself by blocking actions of other groups

Political Action Committees. In recent years political action committees, usually simply called PACs, have emerged as influential veto groups (Stern, 1988; Sabato, 1985). PACs are political organizations that operate independently of political parties, channeling money from special interest groups into the election campaigns of political candidates. The special interest groups are sometimes representatives of some part of the political spectrum, such as conservatives or liberals, but more often they represent some special economic or demographic group (the elderly, for example). The number of PACs grew from 113 in 1972 to 4,211 in 1987. Between 1972 and 1986 total PAC gifts to congressional candidates grew from $12.5 million to $132.2 million (Stern, 1988, p. 24). PAC contributions have become an important means of funding political campaigns. Although individual contributions to federal candidates are limited to $25,000 in a given election, the total amount that a PAC can contribute has no legal limit. For example, in 1985–1986 NCPAC (National Conservative PAC) spent over $9 million on political activities (E. Zuckerman, 1988).

PACs vary greatly in size, strength, and political ideology. The Peanut Butter and Nut Processors Association has its NUTPAC, the beer distributors have their PAC (once called SIXPAC), and the snack food industry has its SNACKPAC (Carlson, 1988). The objective of a PAC is to gain influence over, and access to, members of the House and the Senate in order to advance its interests and/or adversely affect the interests of other groups. Given the large amounts of money at their disposal and the fact that there are no legal limits on their total contributions, PACs are growing in influence; many (e.g., Stern, 1988) would say that their influence is excessive and dangerous.

PACs were originally founded by labor unions and were heavy contributors to the Democratic Party. Within a few years businesses moved in to form PACs that were largely oriented to supporting the Republican Party. Since 1980, the new PACs that have been formed show a marked preference for Democratic candidates (Wilcox, 1988). In the 1988 election PAC support for Democratic candidates for the House of Representatives and the Senate far outstripped support for Republican candidates. (This is, in part, due to the fact that PACs give almost 90 percent of their contributions to incumbents.) In fact, one official attributed much of the Democrats' success in the 1988 House elections, despite the overwhelming vote in favor of the Republican candidate for president, to the Democrats' big advantage in PAC support. One interesting point here is that in the late 1970s Democrats opposed PACs, but, with the success of pro-Democratic PACs in the 1980s, some Republicans are now calling for legislation outlawing PACs. However, one expert concluded that it is unlikely that PACs would be made illegal: "Believe me, the genie's out of the bottle" (Berke, 1988a, p. B17).

The Neo-Marxian View

Neo-Marxian theory
Legal and political systems are seen as reflecting an economic base

Neo-Marxian theory is derived from Karl Marx's idea that the legal and political systems are built upon, and are a reflection of, the economic base of the society. Neo-Marxians generally accept this idea but have often modified it to correspond with contemporary realities in capitalist countries. Some neo-Marxists have taken an even more extreme view of these matters than Marx did. They have seen the state as *wholly* determined by economic forces. Lenin, for example, saw the state as simply a tool used by one social class to oppress another. Thus, he felt that if economic inequality were ended, it would lead to a withering away of the state, at least as an instrument of oppression. Of course, the history of the Soviet Union since the Revolution of 1917 indicates anything but a withering away of the state. The Soviet state has become huge, powerful, and often oppressive, capable of murdering millions in what Solzhenitsyn (1973) called the "Gulag Archipelago."

Most modern neo-Marxists no longer accept this simplistic view of the relationship between the state and the economy. At one time, neo-Marxists argued that in American society the state was simply a tool of the capitalist class, but such a view is no longer considered tenable. A moderated neo-Marxist view is that the state is not dominated by economic interests, but it still usually protects the interests of the capitalists (Poulantzas, 1973).

The Military-Industrial Complex. A good example of the continued applicability of the neo-Marxian perspective is found in the idea of a military-industrial complex. The **military-industrial complex** refers to the close alliance between the military establishment and the industries that make a major share of their profits from producing military equipment (Dye, 1983).

Military-industrial complex
Close alliance between the military and the defense industry

The two sectors—the military and industrial—tend to foster the interests of each other. It is in the economic self-interest of the military-weapons industry to support the military; conversely, it is in the interest of the military to support industries that enhance its power and ensure its existence. Critics of the military-industrial complex charge that it adversely affects the military, industry, and the society as a whole.

Although the idea of a military-industrial connection had been recognized some years before by sociologist C. Wright Mills (1956), public awareness was increased greatly when President Dwight D. Eisenhower, in his farewell address, warned of the dangers of this connection. Eisenhower told the nation that the combined influence of the military establishment and the industries that benefitted from producing weapons could become too powerful. With too much power the military-industrial complex could "endanger our liberties and democratic processes" (Eisenhower, 1972, pp. 31–32).

In the years since Eisenhower's warning, both the military and the industries supplying the military have grown immensely. Weapons systems and defense systems have been created, only to be abandoned when they became obsolete, leading to the expenditure of billions of dollars. The military budget is now approaching $300 billion a year. Serious questions have been raised about many costs within the military system, especially because of repeated scandals that revealed waste, corruption, and crime.

The most obvious examples of a large and uncontrolled military-industrial complex have involved industries overcharging the government for military materials. For example, in late 1985 several executives of General Dynamics, the third largest military contractor, were indicted for improperly billing the government for $7.5 million. This incorrect billing was, however, only a small part of a larger scandal. The billing was related to DIVAD, the name of a prototype for a General Dynamics gun (later known as the Sergeant York) that was supposed to protect troops from air attack. A contract for its production had been awarded in 1981. By 1985, following the expenditure of almost $2 billion, the DIVAD project was scrapped because this anti-aircraft gun had repeatedly failed to perform satisfactorily. It was the close connection between the military establishment and defense contractors that explains how such a vast amount of money could have been spent on a failed weapons system (Rasor, 1985). Investigations have now revealed that for many years the Pentagon withheld information from Congress that

The Bradley infantry combat vehicle is an example of a piece of military equipment that was designed, developed, and produced at a cost of billions of dollars. Yet when it was tested operationally, a variety of problems were uncovered and there are still some uncertainties about its military usefulness.

would have revealed the ineffectiveness of the gun under combat conditions. It seems that within the military the program managers for any weapons system have a vested interest in keeping the procurement process going once it has been started. Of course, the latter is clearly in the interests of the weapons makers. A Pentagon watchdog describes the situation this way:

> Because of the high stakes created each year by a $100 billion procurement budget, the system puts tremendous pressure on each individual [military program manager] to not rock the boat and then places him in a position to become very cozy with the contractor (Rasor, 1985, p. 137).

Military officers who are in charge of procuring weapons for the Defense Department are often well rewarded if they remain "cozy" with defense contractors. Upon retirement from military duty, many high-ranking officers join the same corporations whose products they have been purchasing and approving (Rasor, 1985). This practice is so widespread that it has been called the "revolving door." It is good business for the defense contractors to hire former military officers because the knowledge they bring to the company can greatly aid in retaining present contracts and gaining new ones.

This close connection between military people and industrialists enhances the possibilities for corruption and crime. With billions of dollars to be made from Defense Department contracts, defense industry executives and military officials can be tempted. For example, in 1989 a former top executive with the Unisys Corporation (a major electronics firm) pleaded guilty to bribing an assistant secretary of the Navy. During the same period that the bribes were made, the Unisys Corporation received two Navy contracts totaling over $300 million. This incident is only one in a series of corrupt and illegal actions described as the military procurement scandal (Murphy, 1989).

When military purchases are influenced by bribes, corruption, and various levels of collusion, it is not surprising that many purchases made by the military are outrageously priced. Some widely publicized examples of overcharging include:

- A rechargeable flashlight that costs the commercial airlines $35. Cost to the Air Force was $181.
- A flight engineer seat priced at $5,065 for the private airlines. Cost to the Air Force was $13,905.
- A coffee brewer for a private airline that costs $2,125. Air Force cost was $7,622 (Rasor, 1985).

Among other examples of exorbitant prices paid by the military, it is difficult to find a case that exceeds the boxes of tools the Gould Corporation sold to the Navy for $10,168.56 each. When Congressman Berkley Bedell's staff went to a hardware store and bought the same tools, the cost was $119.23 (Rasor, 1985, p. 164). The Navy audit system found the tools overpriced but concluded that the costs were "legal." The Navy then negotiated with the Gould Corporation, which returned 10 percent of the overcharge. The Navy held a press conference when the refund check was received from Gould, apparently feeling that this represented "a big victory" (Rasor, 1985, p. 166).

The military-industrial complex constitutes a huge economic bloc that wields substantial power and strongly influences American policies and actions. This exceptional power lends support to the neo-Marxian view that the political and social aspects of a society will be shaped by its most powerful economic interests.

The Elitist View

The third approach to the state emphasizes the existence of a political **elite,** or a small group of people who come to power and dominate the population. Proponents of this approach also dispute the pluralist idea that American society is democratic. Elite theorists developed their orientation in direct opposition to the Marxian belief that it is possible under communism to develop a society characterized by political, social, and economic equality. In their view, an elite evolves to govern any and every form of society.

Elite
Small group of people who come to power and dominate the population

Elite theorists believe that political systems are run by a small elite. One elite theorist describes the United States this way: "Great power in America is concentrated in a tiny handful of people" (Dye, 1983, p. 3). However, elite theorists sometimes differ in their evaluation of this condition. Some favor the concentration of power in the hands of the elite rather than in the hands of the masses (Ortega y Gasset, 1932). This group of elite theorists is fearful of democratic rule and favorably disposed toward control by a small elite. Others who subscribe to elitist political theory tend to be critical of elites and to see them as having a negative effect on society.

The Power Elite. C. Wright Mills (1956) suggested such a negative elitist model of power, which he called the "power elite." The **power elite** is a small group of influential persons who occupy key positions in large corporations, the executive branch of government, and the military. Members of the power elite share common interests and goals; many have attended the same colleges, and many know one another personally. The members of the power elite are powerful not because of extraordinary personal skills and abilities but because they occupy important bureaucratic positions:

Power elite
Small group in key positions in corporations, the executive branch, and the military

> No one, accordingly, can be truly powerful unless he has access to the command of major institutions, for it is over these institutional means of power that the truly powerful are, in the first instance, powerful. Higher politicians and key officials of government command such institutional power; so do admirals and generals, and so do the major owners and executives of the larger corporations (Mills, 1956, p. 9).

Mills suggests three basic levels of power in the United States. At the top, of course, is the power elite. Interest group leaders, legislators, and local opinion leaders compose the middle level. The bottom level consists of the mass of unorganized citizens who are controlled by the "higher-ups" and are often unaware of how important political decisions have been made.

G. William Domhoff (1967, 1978, 1983) presents an elitist model of power based on the idea of a "ruling class":

> . . . the ruling class is socially cohesive, has its basis in the large corporations and banks, plays a major role in shaping the social and political climate, and dominates the federal government through a variety of organizations and methods (Domhoff, 1983, p. 1).

Membership in the governing class is based on an individual's being listed in the *Social Register*, attending a prestigious preparatory school, belonging to an exclusive men's club, or being a millionaire. Domhoff estimates that the governing class consists of not more than 0.5 percent of the population, or about 1 out of every 200 people. This uppermost social class is extremely wealthy and exerts control over the executive branch of government, major corporations, the military, the mass media, major regulatory agencies, and boards of trustees of major universities. Through their control of these organizations and institutions, the ruling elite is able to formulate American political and economic policies that will be of greatest benefit to their interests. This policy-planning process begins in the boardrooms of America's largest corporations, and it extends into policy-discussion organizations where the issues of the day, such as "foreign aid, tariffs, taxes and welfare policies," are discussed (Domhoff, 1983, p. 84).

Another useful mechanism of the ruling class for establishing policy is the non-profit foundation. Foundations are tax-free institutions that are "an upper-class adaptation to inheritance and property taxes. They provide a means by which wealthy people and corporations can in effect decide how their tax payments will be spent, for they are based on money that otherwise would go to the government in taxes" (Domhoff, 1983, p. 84). The most famous and influential of the "old money" foundations are those created by the Ford, Rockefeller, and Carnegie fortunes.

After the ruling elite has established which political and economic policies are most advantageous, the next step is to get them implemented. This goal is accomplished, in part, by shaping public opinion through the public schools, churches, and voluntary associations. Opinions, beliefs, and attitudes of the people are also shaped through ". . . movies, television programs, books, pamphlets, speakers, advice and financial support" (Domhoff, 1983, p. 99).

However, the ruling elite, according to Domhoff, need not rely heavily on shaping public opinion because policy objectives can be attained much more effectively by affecting the operations of the government directly. One method for doing this is to influence the candidate selection process of the major political parties. The method of the ruling elite is simple and direct: ". . . large campaign donations that far outweigh what other classes and groups can muster" (Domhoff, 1983, p. 117). But even this method can be unstable and unreliable as a way of influencing policy. A more direct approach is to influence the elected officials after they are in office, regardless of who they may be. This effort is accomplished through a variety of lobbying and influence groups.

Influence groups include specially created presidential commissions that deal with specific problems, and quasi-governmental groups such as the Business Council (Domhoff, 1983). The Business Council is composed primarily of the chairmen or presidents of the largest corporations in the country. Members of the Business Council invite government officials to attend friendly, relaxed, and semi-social meetings, often at exclusive resorts near Washington, D.C., with all expenses paid by the Business Council. Through speeches, panel discussions, and reports, as well as informal conversations, the policies favored by the Business Council are conveyed to governmental leaders.

The Business Council prefers to work in the background or behind the scenes, but it also has a more public counterpart called the Business Roundtable. The Business Roundtable is an active and direct advocacy organization that sends representatives to lobby members of Congress, as well as the president and cabinet members (Domhoff, 1983).

Domhoff's notion of a ruling class closely parallels Mills's "power elite" model. Both views see the masses as unorganized and powerless. Both models suggest that Congress has relatively little power compared to the executive branch, and, most important, both argue that power resides with a small and cohesive group of individuals who share similar social backgrounds. The major difference in the models is that Mills considers the military leadership and the executive branch more or less co-equals with the corporate rich, while Domhoff views the upper social class as completely dominant; it controls the power elite.

There is no certain way of judging whether the pluralist, the neo-Marxian, or the elitist view of politics is the best description of the American political system or any other political system. All three views provide insights into the workings of political systems, and thus they help us to understand the political process, both in our own country and elsewhere. As each new political issue arises, we can observe whether the pluralist, the neo-Marxian, or the elitist view provides the best explanation of the outcomes.

The American Presidency

The framers of the Constitution tried to prevent any occupant of the presidency, or any other branch of government, from acquiring inordinate and arbitrary powers. In so doing they tried to create a balance of power among the three branches of government—the presidency, the legislature, and the judiciary. This balance of power is consistent with the pluralist image of democracy in the United States. But political systems, like all other humanly created systems, do not always work exactly as planned. In recent years several views of the American presidency have been expressed, especially views on the power that the holder of that office can wield.

Since the presidency of Franklin D. Roosevelt in the 1930s, the power of the president has been widely perceived to have increased, especially relative to the Congress and the judiciary. This presumed power has seemed to decline only during terms of office when the president did not want to exercise it. Dwight Eisenhower, for example, is generally viewed as a president who did not strive to demonstrate or expand the power of the presidency. Among more recent presidents, Gerald Ford and Jimmy Carter are also seen as relatively passive.

However, the presidents who occupied the White House between Eisenhower and Ford are viewed as active. John Kennedy, Lyndon Johnson, and Richard Nixon are regarded as presidents who tried and succeeded in various ways to exercise and strengthen the power of their office. Ronald Reagan was likewise considered a strong leader who increased the power of the presidency. Clearly, it is too early in George Bush's administration to render a judgment on its exercise of power.

Among the many indications of the growth of presidential power in the United States in the last 50 years, the single most visible sign is the power to involve the nation in wars, military actions, and foreign adventures. According to the Constitution, the power to declare war is expressly given to Congress. But presidents can and often have taken actions leading to war or the equivalent of war (even though undeclared). Since World War II the United States has been involved in numerous military actions around the world, but in no instance has Congress declared war.

Although presidential power may rise and decline with the incumbent of the office, the underlying question still remains of how much basic power resides in the presidency. The answer may be seen best by dividing presidential power into different spheres: foreign-policy power, domestic-policy power, and "personal power."

Foreign-Policy Power

Aaron Wildavsky (1969) has noted that, in general, American presidents have had much greater success in controlling the nation's military and foreign policies than in dominating its domestic policies (Fleisher and Bond, 1988). Presidential acts, such as Reagan's invasion of Grenada, support this argument. The president, as Commander-in-Chief of the Armed Forces, can engage in many foreign-policy actions without the consent of the Congress or the people (Prados, 1986).

The foreign-policy actions of presidents may also include efforts to reduce military confrontations. For example, the several summit meetings between Reagan and Soviet leader Mikhail Gorbachev led to a 1987 agreement to eliminate intermediate range nuclear weapons in Europe and provided the basis for future summit meetings where efforts will be made to reduce nuclear and conventional armaments further. An illustration of just how powerful the president is in this area occurred in the 1986 summit in Reykjavik, Iceland. To his complete surprise, Reagan found himself confronted by a proposal by Gorbachev to ban all nuclear weapons. Although such a proposal had never been analyzed or discussed by his advisers, to say nothing of the Congress, reports indicated that Reagan came very close to unilaterally accepting Gorbachev's proposal. Foreign policy thus offers presidents an arena for a considerable exercise of political power.

The invasion of Grenada by American military forces was ordered by the President, as Commander-in-Chief of the military. Even though this was a war-like action, the Congress was not consulted in advance.

Domestic-Policy Power

Recent presidents have often found it difficult to extend their power to domestic issues. Even presidents who have been perceived as most powerful have often failed to attain their objectives in the realm of domestic policy. In a short period after John Kennedy's assassination, Lyndon Johnson was remarkably successful in getting several significant pieces of domestic legislation through the Congress. Among others, the Economic Opportunity Act (the War on Poverty program), Medicare, the Civil Rights Act of 1964, and the Voting Rights Act of 1965 were all passed during a two-year period. Several of these had been on the agenda for years but had previously failed to be enacted. Despite the dramatic success with domestic legislation early in his presidency, Johnson found it increasingly difficult to get domestic policies passed later in his tenure as president.

Richard Nixon and Jimmy Carter both faced serious political crises that weakened their support in Congress. The Watergate affair made it difficult for Nixon to get much of his domestic legislation through Congress during his last two years in office. Similarly, the capture of American embassy personnel in Tehran, Iran, seriously weakened the Carter presidency, and portions of his domestic legislation failed to be passed by Congress. Especially during his first term, Ronald Reagan succeeded in getting much of his domestic legislation through Congress. As M.B. Oglesby, Jr., chief White House lobbyist, commented about 1984 congressional voting: "We won more than we lost" (*Congressional Quarterly Almanac*, 1985, p. 19-C). Reagan's fortunes with Congress declined, however, and in 1987 he lost far more votes than he won (*Congressional Quarterly Almanac*, 1987).

The Iron Triangle. Not only is the president often blocked by Congress but presidential policies (particularly at the domestic level) often are effectively blocked by what Hodgson (1980) calls the **Iron Triangle**—three points of power limiting presidential action. One point is the part of the existing bureaucracy that will be affected; the second is the interest group that has an economic stake in the outcome, and the third is the members of Congress who are on the relevant congressional committees and act on behalf of the special interest groups. Sometimes presidents discover that even the power of the White House cannot overcome the resistance of the Iron Triangle.

Iron Triangle
Power points in government bureaucracy, interest groups, and Congress that limit the president

The effectiveness of an Iron Triangle is illustrated by the workings of the triangle that supports American agriculture. During his candidacy, Ronald Reagan made it clear that he did not favor federal farm subsidies and price support programs for agricultural products. Nonetheless, in the first four years of his presidency, "farm income stabilization" costs were approximately $47 billion.

Personal Power

One of the most fascinating aspects of the power political leaders have is the control they exercise over the people around them in their everyday lives. This type of power is called *personal power,* and it allows presidents and other heads of state to command the people who serve them to do virtually anything. The recently released memoranda of President Nixon reveal that he once asked his chief of staff to do something about the birds that were crashing into his oval office window at the White House (Oudes, 1988).

Often personal power is used for actions that are questionable and that border on being illegal. A retired director of the White House Military Office, Bill Gulley (1980), has described many of the things that he did at the request of four American presidents: Lyndon Johnson, Richard Nixon, Gerald Ford, and Jimmy Carter. Gulley says that the Military Office allows presidents the greatest freedom because the costs of things done under the cover of military secrecy can be hidden from public view. The amount of money available for such presidential projects seems unlimited; for example:

- Johnson had an airplane hangar on his ranch converted into a comfortable, completely air-conditioned movie theater. It was built ostensibly to show training films to "military personnel," but in fact only two Army baggage handlers were there periodically. Johnson's daughters did enjoy movies in the theater, however (Gulley, 1980, p. 92).
- Richard Nixon had millions spent on his two personal homes in Key Biscayne, Florida, and San Clemente, California. Nixon also provided his millionaire friend Bebe Rebozo with a military phone system that gave him free world-wide phone service (Gulley, 1980, p. 158).

A mini-scandal that arose at both the beginning and end of the Reagan years involved the clothes and jewelry worn by the president's wife, Nancy Reagan. In 1981

Nancy Reagan, as the wife of the president of the United States, often borrowed expensive designer clothing and jewelry. This is just one example of the personal power and privilege connected with the office of the presidency.

Mrs. Reagan announced that she had been accepting clothing as loans (which she sometimes kept) from designers, including a $25,000 creation worn at the 1981 Inauguration. Told that she must disclose such loans and gifts and that they might be taxable, Mrs. Reagan announced that she would no longer accept them. No such loans were disclosed, or appeared, on Reagan tax forms between 1982 and 1987. However, in 1988 it was disclosed that Mrs. Reagan had continued to borrow large numbers of expensive dresses (valued at well over $1 million) and jewelry during that period. One designer said that Mrs. Reagan had borrowed between 60 and 80 creations and had kept a large number of them. A jeweler told of loaning the First Lady "a pair of diamond earrings that are $800,000 with ten-carat drops" (Magnuson, 1988, p. 29). When it came to light that Mrs. Reagan had resumed the practice of borrowing clothes and jewelry, her press secretary dismissed the matter by saying, "She made a little rule, and she broke it."

The Personal Power of Prime Minister Margaret Thatcher. Great Britain's Prime Minister Thatcher has been the leader of her country's government since 1979. Her social and economic policies have been significant aspects of her political success, but her personal style is also an important element of her stay in power.

Many observers agree that her most striking characteristic is an unshakeable certainty that she is right about everything. One of her colleagues has said, "I don't think I ever heard [her] say, 'I wonder whether . . .'" (Newhouse, 1986, p. 77).

As a child, Margaret Thatcher learned the principle of seeing things through to the end. She recalls:

> . . . there is the little rhyme that I was taught as a child: "It is easy to be a starter, but are you a sticker, too? It is easy enough to begin a job. It is harder to see it through" (Newhouse, 1986, p. 75).

Mrs. Thatcher is a tireless worker. She arises at 6:00 A.M. and, after a full day of meetings, usually has a modest supper (that she herself has prepared) at about 10:00 P.M. After that she usually reads official papers until about 2:30 A.M. "She thrives on three and a half hours of sleep, and has little patience with those who cannot keep pace" (Newhouse, 1986, p. 79).

As Prime Minister, Margaret Thatcher demands much from those who work for her and with her. She dominates her Cabinet meetings, in part because she is usually better prepared than anyone else, but also because she treats every issue as a battle, which she must win. To a Cabinet minister who is submitting a report, she may say: "Who wrote this?" . . . "Well, I should have known. What can you expect? That's why it's so awful" (Newhouse, 1986, p. 83).

This style of leadership may not always win her friends, but she has already remained in power longer than most previous prime ministers of Great Britain.

Changes in American Politics

American politics has changed dramatically in recent years. These changes are especially clear in elections for the presidency and presidential politics, but some of the same changes have occurred at other political levels as well.

Money and Presidential Elections

One outcome of the Watergate scandal was the revelation that Richard Nixon, in his 1972 election campaign, had received huge, illegal, corporate contributions. In addition, large sums had come from individuals, some of whom were later rewarded with ambassadorships. The result was a 1974 law limiting individual and corporate contributions to presidential (and congressional) campaigns, and establishing public financing of presidential campaigns. Once nominated by his or her party, a candidate gets a set sum from the government and is not allowed to take private contributions. As a result of this dictum, the two parties waged the 1976 presidential campaign on roughly equal economic footing. A Commission on National Elections concluded that the reforms had worked and that public financing had "clearly proved its worth in opening up the process, reducing undue influence of individuals and groups and virtually ending corruption in presidential election finance" (Ignatius, 1988, p. D5). However, Congress soon made some changes in the law that subverted its effectiveness.

The 1979 changes to the law re-created the potential for imbalances in future elections. For example, state and local party organizations were allowed to spend unlimited sums for voter registration and efforts to get out the vote. An individual or corporation could give enormous sums (now called "soft money") to state or local drives aimed at helping elect a presidential candidate. In terms of its effect, this money worked in a way similar to giving it directly to the presidential candidates. Thus, the 1974 law was circumvented; huge contributions could again be made, albeit indirectly, to presidential campaigns (Drew, 1983).

That is, in fact, what occurred in the 1988 presidential election. Federal law allowed each party to spend $46.1 million in public funds and $8.3 million raised by the parties on the 1988 presidential race. But the election laws also allowed each party to raise an additional $50 million, much of it going directly or indirectly to the presidential election campaign. There were more $100,000 donors in 1988 than in 1972, when the excessive number of large contributions led to the 1974 law. Said the president of Common Cause, a public interest group: "We now face the potential of once again seeing the presidency out there on the auction block. It is incumbent on everyone to watch very closely any decisions made by the incoming Bush administration to give government benefits, appointments or financial advantage to these large donors" (Babcock, 1988, p. A20).

The Increasing Role of Television

Television is clearly playing a key role in politics, especially at the presidential level. The political candidate who controls the news broadcasts is almost certain to win the election. In recent years, President Ronald Reagan was able to dominate the news media (Hertsgaard, 1988). Through television, Reagan overrode the stars of network news (Dan Rather, Tom Brokaw, etc.). "He stepped right past these stars and took his place alongside the Americans in their living rooms, and together they paid no great mind to what these media were saying" (Schram, 1987, p. 27). The key to Reagan's success was an emphasis on visual rather than verbal impact. Writer Martin Schram calls this "The Great American Video Game." Presidential advisers were able to create great visual scenes (e.g., Reagan with World War II veterans on the beach in Normandy) with the president in the forefront in order to manipulate the electronic media into building stories around the photo opportunities. Because television by its nature is a visual medium, the visual image tends to create a more powerful impression than verbal communication. The candidate who can control visual imagery has the significant advantage in a campaign.

The 1988 Presidential Elections. This emphasis on how the president, as well as candidates for the presidency, are covered by television news was particularly clear in the 1988 presidential elections. In fact, it has been claimed that "1988 is the year that television *was* the campaign" (L. Zuckerman, 1988, p. 66). As an example of the lengths to which politicians will go to manipulate television images, "one party, at its convention, deliberately muted the colors of the flag so they would televise better" (L. Zuckerman, 1988, p. 66).

Of central importance is how candidates are covered on the evening news broadcasts. Said one expert: "TV producers are like nymphomaniacs when it comes to visuals. . . . Television's insatiable need for pretty pictures has cheapened the campaign" (L. Zuckerman, 1988, p. 66). Said another: "Television news has been co-opted by the image makers and the media managers. . . . The manipulators learned that by controlling the pictures you end up controlling the content" (L. Zuckerman, 1988, p. 66). In the 1988 campaign George Bush stuck to choreographed scenes that played well on the news, while Michael Dukakis, following the older model, held almost daily news conferences. Although these press conferences were laudable in terms of Dukakis's accessibility to the press, they provided little in the way of visuals that could be used on the evening news. Bush's advisers didn't even mind when newscasters commented critically on the staged quality of Bush's appearances. Said one, "If we get the visual that we want . . . it doesn't matter as much what words the networks use in commenting on it" (L. Zuckerman, 1988, pp. 66, 71).

Increasing Attention to Campaign Advertising

Intimately related to the accelerating importance of television imagery is the increasing significance of campaign advertising, especially television ads, which, of course, depend heavily on their visual component (Jamieson, 1984). Television ads are important for several reasons. First, they build name recognition for the candidate. Second, they allow the candidates to frame precisely, in whatever way they want, the issues that they consider central to the election. Third, they allow the candidates to expose themselves, their temperaments, and their talents in the most favorable light. Fourth, they are short (usually a minute) and therefore are in line with the limited attention devoted to such matters by most television viewers. (The 60-second spot ad has now replaced the 30-minute speech that was the norm in the 1952 presidential election.)

Many argue that television advertising played a central role in the victory of George Bush and the defeat of Michael Dukakis. On the one hand, Bush ran an aggressive—some said even vicious—television campaign in which he sought to tie the Massachusetts governor to pollution in Boston Harbor and the rape of a woman by a furloughed Massachusetts prisoner. Jamieson (1988a, p. C1), who saw the 1988 campaign as unprecedented in terms of fabrications, argues that Bush's (and to a lesser extent, Dukakis')

Cross-National Perspectives

Elections in the Soviet Union

On March 26, 1989, the Soviet Union held its freest elections since the Communists came to power in 1917. Indeed, since there was no history of free elections in pre-Revolution Russia, it might be said that these were the freest elections in Russian history. Before 1917 Russia was ruled by a royal family (the czars) and since 1917 the Soviet Union has been ruled by a series of autocratic leaders. However, when the present Soviet leader, Michael Gorbachev, came to power, he almost immediately moved in the direction of greater openness (*glasnost*) and initiated a restructuring of Soviet society (*perestroika*). The elections held in March, 1989, certainly reflect greater openness in Soviet society and appear to be a part of, and a contributor to, that restructuring.

In terms of greater openness, it is estimated that about 80 percent of the 184 million eligible Soviet voters participated in the election. They voted for members of the Congress of People's Deputies. There are 2,250 seats in the Congress, but only 1,500 were openly contested. The rest were reserved for members of various organizations and the Communist Party (which is guaranteed 100 seats). About three-fourths of the 1,500 seats were contested by two or more candidates. The

In 1989 the Soviet Union conducted one of the first elections in its history where there was competition among candidates. These elections were part of the new policies of *glasnost* (greater openness) and *perestroika* (a restructuring of the society).

election was preceded by a heated political campaign (by Soviet standards) with rallies, demonstrations, and speeches. Some of these speeches expressed opposition to the Communist establishment. Such opposition was previously impossible.

To the great surprise of many observers, a number of leading Communist officials who were seen as unenthusiastic about the current reforms were defeated for office by politicians who wanted to hasten reform. The most notable victor, and by a landslide, was Boris Yeltsin in Moscow. Yeltsin had previously been chief of the Communist Party in Moscow, but was deposed in 1987 because he favored a more rapid change than that undertaken by Gorbachev. Among other things, Yeltsin ran on a platform that urged the abolition of special privileges for elite members of the Communist Party.

Regarding restructuring, or *perestroika,* the Congress of People's Deputies will meet once a year to decide on important issues. It will also elect by secret ballot the Supreme Soviet, which will be composed of two houses with a total of 542 members. The Supreme Soviet will meet twice a year and intends to be more responsive to the public than previous legislatures. The Congress will also elect the head of state, or the president. The expectation is that the first president elected in this way will be Gorbachev, since he was the architect of this new system. This more democratic and open election of a head of state will replace the closed and secret system used in the past by the leaders of the Communist Party. It is widely believed that Gorbachev will attempt to transfer many day-to-day powers from the Communist Party to the Supreme Soviet. If he is successful, a substantial decline in the power of the Communist party will result. However, it should be remembered that most of the members of the legislature will be members of the Party.

Since open elections are new to the Soviet Union, and the legislative and executive systems are also new, it will take a considerable amount of time to see how this all works out in practice. Many things could happen, such as rebellions in various territories, and worsening economic distress to upset these political reforms as well as the broader programs of *glasnost* and *perestroika.* However, the political reforms have gone so far that it is unlikely that the Soviet Union will slide back to its former political ways in the near future.

KELLER, BILL. "Soviets Savor Vote in Freest Election Since '17 Revolution." *New York Times*, March 27, 1989, pp. A1, A6.

KELLER, BILL. "Soviet Voters Deal a Mortifying Blow to Party Officials." *New York Times*, March 28, 1989, pp. A1, A10.

advertisements were sometimes outright lies. "Take, for example, this ad from the Bush campaign: The picture shows a pool of sludge and pollutants near a sign reading, 'Danger/Radiation Hazard/No Swimming.' The text indicts Dukakis for failing to clean up Boston Harbor. But the sign shown has, in fact, nothing to do with the Massachusetts governor or his record. Instead, it warns Navy personnel not to swim in waters that had once harbored nuclear submarines under repair." On the other hand, Dukakis failed to come up with either an adequate television response to such criticisms or a positive message of his own. In addition, some of his attempts at television imagery, such as a helmeted Dukakis riding in a tank, backfired as the public refused to accept the intellectual Dukakis in such a setting. Concern is increasing that the nature of television images, not ideas and issues, are decisive in presidential (and other) elections.

What is worrisome about the negative and distorted campaign advertisements is that they seemed to work (Edsall, 1988). Because of advertisements such as those mentioned above, many voters came to view Dukakis as weak on crime, ineffective in cleaning up the environment, unpatriotic, and left-wing, a politician who was out of step with the mainstream of the American electorate. In addition, advertisements focused public attention *away* from Bush's weaknesses. Bush was put on the offensive, which forced Dukakis into the position of responding to Bush's initiatives. The success of Bush's negative campaign makes it highly likely that we will see more of such campaigns in the future.

The Changing Nature of Political Speeches

In *Eloquence in an Electronic Age*, Kathleen Jamieson (1988b) has related the impact of television to the transformation of political speechmaking. Jamieson writes that the increasing role of television is reducing the importance of memorable words and speeches. Instead, as mentioned earlier, the visual image matters most. "Television has changed public discourse dramatically. Increasingly, eloquence is visual, not verbal" (Jamieson, 1988b, p. 44). Even when television does report on the speeches themselves, the emphasis in newscasts is on the so-called "15-second sound bite." Jamieson (1988b, p. 9) reports a study that found that the average number of seconds a candidate for president was shown speaking on a network news segment in the 1984 campaign was slightly less than 15 seconds. By the 1988 campaign reports indicated that speaking time had been reduced to nine seconds (Kalb, 1988). Because political campaign speeches are tailored for television coverage and *not* the immediate audience, they have grown shorter, less than 20 minutes on the average, including time for applause. The focus in candidates' speeches and campaign appearances is on the limited, 15-second portion that is apt to be picked up by the national television networks. Since this 15 seconds will be seen by many times more than the number of people witnessing the speech or appearance, most of the attention of presidential advisors is lavished on producing just the right snippet for the TV news.

In addition to the decline of televised reports of speeches, televised speeches have undergone a similar decline. Prior to the advent of television, political speeches on radio were at first usually an hour in length, but by the 1940s the norm had dropped to 30 minutes. In the early years of television, speeches were that same length, but they rapidly decreased to five minutes, and by the 1970s the speech itself had been replaced by the 60-second advertisement. A tremendous decline in information transfer has occurred in this historical process, and complex ideas have given way to simple assertions. In addition, the brevity of contemporary speeches leads to increased use of hyperbole to catch the audience's attention.

Similar developments have affected debates between candidates for elected office. In contemporary televised debates, if they can really be called that, candidates have a minute or two to offer their position on a given issue. "By contrast, in each of their seven senatorial debates of 1858, Lincoln and Douglas spoke for ninety minutes each on a single topic: the future of slavery in the territories" (Jamieson, 1988b, p. 11).

Another development has been the increasing differentiation between speech writer and speech giver. Instead of writing their own speeches or daring to speak extemporaneously, today's politicians rely on texts written for them by professional speech writers. Hence, the successful modern politician needs to be good only at reading speeches and not at creating artful prose. In the political party conventions in 1988 it was generally agreed that both Bush and Dukakis gave extraordinary speeches. In both cases the speeches were written by batteries of speech writers.

The Rise of Political Consultants

Another reality of contemporary presidential politics is the increasing use of a wide array of political consultants. Several types of consultants are employed. Polling consultants are experts brought in to conduct various polls to tell the candidates how they are doing, what is working, what is not, how the opposition is doing, and so on (Barone, 1988). Media consultants are hired to help candidates get more media exposure and to be sure that the correct message comes across. The importance of media consultants was underscored when President-elect Jimmy Carter wrote to his media consultant, Gerald Rafshoon: "I'll always be grateful that I was able to contribute in a small way to the victory of the Rafshoon agency" (Sabato, 1981, p. 112). In addition, direct-mail fund-raising consultants are needed whose expertise lies in the techniques necessary to raise the huge amount of money needed to finance a national political campaign. The danger in all these high-powered, high-priced consultants is that they are anxious to mold a candidate into an image that will win; the candidate may go along with these efforts, even if the image runs counter to who he/she "really" is (Sabato, 1981).

"Let's run through this once more—and, remember, you choke up at Paragraph Three and brush away the tear at Paragraph Five."

The Voters in Democratic Societies

The Apathy of American Voters

As we noted at the beginning of this chapter, American elections in the twentieth century have had relatively low voter turnouts. During the nineteenth century, American voter participation was much higher, with a peak of approximately 85 percent of those eligible to vote casting ballots during the presidential election of 1876. During the early years of the twentieth century, however, voter participation substantially declined: the rate of voter participation (43 percent) in 1920 was about half of what it had been in 1876. Since 1920, the high point of voter participation occurred in the Kennedy-Nixon contest of 1960, in which 63 percent of those eligible to vote cast ballots. Voter participation consistently declined until 1984 when the Reagan-Mondale contest attracted slightly more than half (53 percent) of those eligible to vote and ended a 20-year decline in the presidential-year voter-turnout rate (see table 16–1).

In the 1988 Bush-Dukakis election, the decline continued, and quite dramatically, as only 50.2 percent of eligible voters cast ballots (U.S. Bureau of the Census, 1988h). Furthermore, the total number of people voting was several million less than in 1984—the first time since 1944 that the total number of voters declined from one presidential election to the next.

This relatively low rate of voter participation contrasts sharply with the situation in other modern democracies. Since World War II, voter participation in Italy and Belgium has exceeded 90 percent. In Portugal, West Germany, and Norway, from 80 to 85 percent of those eligible actually vote, and from 70 to 80 percent of Canadians, Greeks, and Japanese vote (Glass, Squire, and Wolfinger, 1984). Overall, the average turnout in other industrialized countries is 80 percent of the eligible electorate (Powell, 1986, p. 16).

In contrast to the low voter turnout, however, there is one sense in which Americans appear to be more politically involved than the citizens of other democracies (Powell, 1986). In comparison with seven other industrial nations, Americans are most likely to feel that they have a say in what the government does, and that they have at least some interest in politics. These views of Americans are borne out by some of their political activities: Americans are most apt to discuss politics with others and to have worked for a party or candidate during an election. Thus, on a variety of attitudinal and behavioral measures, Americans are highly involved in the political process. If this is the case, then why the low voter turnout in American elections?

Some important structural and institutional conditions in the United States make the average voter turnout relatively low. First, some industrialized nations invoke legal penalties if a citizen does not vote, but the United States does not mandate voter participation. Second, in many nations the government takes the initiative to get people to register to vote, but in the United States registration is left largely to the individual. Other aspects of the registration process inhibit voting in the United States such as the absence in most states of day-of-voting registration. Often it is inconvenient to get to registration sites during their hours of operation. If a person moves, he/she must re-register. Since almost half the population might move in a five-year period, a large portion of the electorate must make the *double effort* of registering *and* voting. In fact, a post-1988 election survey indicated that 37 percent of nonvoters did not vote because they were not registered. Two-thirds of these people indicated that they would have voted if they could simply have shown up on election day without prior registration. Three-quarters of these people think the election laws should be changed to allow easier registration (Dionne, 1988b).

Another factor inhibiting voting in the United States is the electoral college system, which gives all of a state's votes to the winning candidate. With this system, neither

Table 16-1. Percentage of Persons Eligible to Vote Who Voted in Presidential and Congressional Elections, 1920–1988

	Percentage of Those Eligible to Vote Who Voted	
Year	**President**	**Representatives**
1920	43	...
1922	...	32
1924	44	...
1926	...	30
1928	52	...
1930	...	34
1932	52	...
1934	...	41
1936	57	...
1938	...	44
1940	59	...
1942	...	33
1944	56	...
1946	...	37
1948	51	...
1950	...	41
1952	62	...
1954	...	42
1956	60	...
1958	...	43
1960	63	...
1962	...	45
1964	62	...
1966	...	45
1968	61	...
1970	...	44
1972	56	...
1974	...	36
1976	54	...
1978	...	35
1980	52.6	...
1982	...	38
1984	53.3	...
1986	...	33.4
1988	50.2	...

Source: Data from U.S. Bureau of the Census, *Statistical Abstract of the United States,* 93rd ed. Washington, D.C.: U.S. Government Printing Office, 1972; and 105th ed. Washington, D.C.: U.S. Government Printing Office, 1985; 109th ed. Washington, D.C.: U.S. Government Printing Office, 1988h.

Even though Americans have one of the lowest voter rates of any industrial country, they participate actively in election campaigns.

political party will make an effort to get out the vote in states where the outcome appears to be a foregone conclusion.

Finally, voting in the United States is hampered by the fact that, unlike many European countries, there is no strong tie between belonging to certain groups (occupational, religious) and partisan political activity. Such a strong linkage between one's social group and one's political party seems to lead to a higher voter turnout.

Even in light of these structural and institutional barriers, a large number of Americans still choose not to vote in presidential and congressional elections. In contrast, there have been some state and local elections recently in which the turnout has been very high (C. Gans, 1988). Perhaps the issues of national elections are too remote for most people. Or it may be that citizens are "turned off" by excessively long political campaigns and the self-serving actions of the political candidates. With presidential campaigns now extending over a two-year or three-year period, many people often say that they are tired of the candidates' charges and counter-charges.

Beyond barriers to voting and legitimate reasons for not voting, people in a democratic society still have a responsibility to exercise their vote. Primarily through their votes they can shape and influence governmental policy and action. Yet substantial evidence shows that many Americans, particularly the young, simply do not care enough and are not interested enough to participate in elections.

Alternative Forms of Democratic Government

The political system of the United States was created by the framers of the Constitution. These early leaders wanted to form a government that would not repeat the evils that they saw in other governments of their time. In particular, they wanted an elected president, but one whose power would be balanced by a legislative and judicial system. Although different points of view existed among these political leaders of the various states, no political parties were clearly defined.

In contrast to the political system of the United States, which was created by a constitutional convention, the governments of many nations have simply evolved over hundreds of years. European governments, such as that of Great Britain, moved toward democratic government in a series of gradual steps. The end result is a parliamentary system similar in some ways to the legislative system of the United States, but distinctly different in some ways as well.

Because of Great Britain's colonial influence, the democratic governments of many of the newer nations of the world are more like the British parliamentary system than the American system. To illustrate how these alternative democratic systems work, we will examine the political system of Israel.

The Israeli Political System

The state of Israel was created in 1948 when the United Nations divided Palestine into a Jewish state and an Arab state. The Israeli political system was then formed and modelled after the British parliamentary system. Among other things, this means that national leaders are determined by the votes received by the various political parties, and not by the votes received by individual candidates as in the United States. Thus, in Israel the leader of the party that wins a majority of seats in the Knesset (the Israeli national assembly), becomes the premier, the most powerful elective office in Israel. The premier's party then forms a national government. If no single party has a majority of the 120 seats in the Knesset, however, two or more parties must join to form a coalition government. As in the United States, Israel held an election in 1988. While the U.S. election led to a decisive victory for George Bush, the Israeli election, as its recent predecessors, was indecisive. In both the 1983 and 1988 elections neither major political party, Likud or Labor, was able to win a clear majority. The result in 1983 was what was called a "National Unity" government formed jointly by the two major parties. Under an agreement reached by the two parties, the leader of the Labor party, Shimon Peres, would serve as premier for 25 months, while the leader of the Likud party, Yitzhak Shamir, would be the foreign minister. After 25 months, the two men would change positions.

Both Israel and the United States have often had divided governments, especially in recent years. These divided governments, produced in very different ways in the two countries, have led to internal conflicts and stalemates. In Israel, the divided government has been at the leadership (premier) level, when no party could gain control of the Knesset. In the United States the division comes from the election of a president from one party and the majority of Congress from the other. The 1988 U.S. election is a prime example of a divided government, with a Republican president and both the House of Representatives and the Senate controlled by the Democrats.

Conflict theory is most useful for analyzing the current political situation in Israel and the United States. Rather than have consensual governments as predicted by structural functionalism, both societies have produced conflict-riddled governments. The situation in Israel is far more severe than in the United States, but even in the United States the election of a Republican president and a Democratic Congress virtually guarantees conflict.

War and Peace

As noted at the beginning of this chapter, the state not only has a monopoly of the use of physical force in a given territory but it also has the ability to declare war on other states (Weber, 1946). In the words of a famous military dictum, "War is the continuation of politics by different means." Our concerns about war (and peace) move us out of a discussion of politics within specific nations and into a discussion of political relationships between and among nations. We will return again to structural functionalism and conflict

The Berlin wall, dividing East and West Berlin, became a symbol of the cold war between the Soviet Union and the United States.

In Nicaragua in the 1980s, the United States supported and supplied the *Contras* while the Soviet Union did the same for the *Sandinista* government. This was just one of many areas where the two major powers confronted each other through surrogates in third countries.

theory to demonstrate how these theoretical perspectives can help us to understand the global realm of war and peace.

The United States and the Soviet Union: The Cold War

The issue of war and peace at an international level has been dominated for several decades by the relationship between the United States and the Soviet Union. Although these two nations have not directly entered into a shooting war with one another, they have been engaged in a "cold war" since the close of World War II. From the U.S. viewpoint, the Soviet Union has been expansionistic, seeking to pull more and more countries into the communist camp. From the Soviet Union's viewpoint, the United States has been imperialistic, trying to make the world safe for capitalism. Thus, in a seemingly never-ending series of confrontations, the two nations squared off against each other in a number of different regions of the world. After World War II, for example, the Soviet Union actively supported East Germany while the United States allied itself with West Germany. More recently, the Soviet Union has supported the *Sandinista* government in Nicaragua while the United States supported the rebels, the *Contras*. In these cases, and in innumerable others, the United States and the Soviet Union confronted each other in a cold war—that is, a non-shooting war—although fighting and dying did occur among the surrogates of the two countries (e.g., the *Sandinistas* and the *Contras*).

In addition to facing one another in a series of national showdowns, the United States and the Soviet Union sought superiority over one another in the realms of

When the Soviet troops left Afghanistan after trying for many years to eliminate the Afghan rebels, it was clear that they had not achieved their objectives, and there was some doubt about whether the costs in lives and material had been justified.

conventional and nuclear arms. The resulting arms race led to a buildup of military weapons on both sides that was extremely threatening. There was a constant danger that these weapons, especially nuclear missiles, would be used by one side or the other, either by accident or as a first strike. Regardless of the reason for launching the first missiles, the other side was almost sure to make a massive retaliation. Thus, for many decades, the world has been threatened with the possibility of destruction.

Conflict theory offers a useful sociological perspective on the cold war between the United States and the Soviet Union. An inherent conflict of interest has prevailed between the two nations. The United States sought to protect and extend capitalist (or at least non-socialist) economic systems around the world, while the Soviet Union held the view that socialist economic systems should be protected, and new socialist economies should be encouraged and supported. Each side had a corresponding ideology to support its actions. The ideologies differed in some respects, but both emphasized that their economic (and political) systems were in the best interests of the people of the world.

By the late 1980s, both the Soviet Union and the United States had experienced some setbacks in their efforts to protect and expand their interests. The United States had been unsuccessful in keeping Vietnam out of Communist control and had suffered a great deal of social upheaval in the process. The Soviet Union had engaged in a similar effort in Afghanistan and had also not achieved its goal. The Afghanistan experience may have caused a reassessment of what the best interests of the Soviet Union were.

Thus, as the conflict of interest between the two countries became less severe, the cold war tensions also began to ease.

Among other things, in 1988, the Soviet Union and the United States negotiated a treaty eliminating intermediate nuclear weapons in Europe, and the Soviet Union unilaterally announced its intention to reduce its military force by half a million men, to make corresponding cuts in conventional arms, and to alter its military deployment patterns in Europe so that they were clearly in a defensive posture. While it is probably premature to say that the cold war has ended, the United States and the Soviet Union seem to have embarked on a course that, if it continues, could make the world a much safer and harmonious place.

This reduction of the possibility of war, and a corresponding increase in peace, was brought about under the leadership of Ronald Reagan in the United States and Mikhail Gorbachev in the Soviet Union. Reagan's interest in reaching an accord with the Soviet Union was surprising given his reputation as a staunch anti-Communist and his well-known view that the Soviet Union was an "evil empire." However, it was probably this position that allowed him to reach a series of understandings with the Soviets. That is, because he was such a strong anti-Communist, the American people trusted the fact that if he were able to reach an understanding with the Soviet Union, it would be advantageous to the United States. To put it another way, a liberal Democratic president who was perceived to be "soft on Communism" would have had a much more difficult time gaining national political support for an agreement with the Soviets.

In his early years in office, Reagan found it difficult to deal with the Russians because of the instability in their leadership. Brezhnev had come to power in 1964, but by the early 1980s he was ill and enfeebled, and he died in late 1982. Andropov succeeded Brezhnev and, despite some promising beginnings, he, too, soon became ill and died in early 1984. His successor, Chernenko, was ill almost from the beginning, and he died in early 1985. Beginning in March, 1985, Reagan found himself faced with a relatively young and healthy Soviet leader, Mikhail Gorbachev, who was very different from his often belligerent predecessors. Gorbachev was a new kind of Soviet leader who was faced with a series of internal realities that required immediate and dramatic attention. His country's political and economic systems were not working well, and Gorbachev launched an effort to restructure Soviet society (*perestroika*). In order to create a climate for internal reform and to generate the money necessary for those reforms, Gorbachev needed to ease the tensions with the United States and to reduce nuclear and conventional military expenditures.

Gorbachev's efforts to ease the cold war can be analyzed from the point of view of structural functionalism. A major structure in the Soviet Union, the economic system, had not been functioning well and was rapidly deteriorating. Gorbachev needed to democratize the political structure and reduce the economic drain of the military in order to turn his attention to the faltering economy. Structural functionalism makes us aware of the interrelationship of societal structures; the recent history of the Soviet Union shows us that in order to change one structure (the economic system), other structures (political system, military) must also be transformed.

For decades, the success of the Soviet military had been tied to the weakness of the economy. As Bialer (1986, p. 280) puts it: "until recently the Soviet military sector could be modern precisely because the civilian economy remained backward. . . . simply put, the entire economy works for the military forces." The Soviet economy suffers, among other things, from extraordinary overcentralization, poor technology, declining

The new policy of openness in the Soviet Union has encouraged many of the ethnic and nationality groups of the Soviet Union to press for greater autonomy, or national independence. These Armenians are conducting a protest demonstration to signal their demands.

production and productivity, and managers and workers who are unresponsive to the needs of the economy. The tangible results of these inadequacies include abominable service, waste, long lines, empty shelves, and notoriously poor quality goods. In order to begin modernizing the economy, Gorbachev had to cut back the amount of his country's gross national product (GNP) devoted to military expenditures.

The money to be saved by military cutbacks, and the money to be gained from investments from the West, presumed because of the improved international climate, could help begin financing economic (and political) reforms at home. The view here, then, is that, in the last few years, the Soviet Union has led the way toward reducing the possibility of nuclear war and increasing the likelihood of long-term peace; its array of internal economic problems that required money and attention brought it to this point. However, while we bask in the glow of a more peaceful world, we cannot rule out the possibility of a return to the cold war or even the development of a "hot" war between the superpowers. Gorbachev has embarked on an ambitious and dangerous program that could disintegrate at any moment. Old-line opponents remain entrenched in the Soviet political system, waiting for dramatic signs of failure on Gorbachev's part. A failure to improve the economic system through military cutbacks, escalation of protests in ethnic areas within the Soviet Union, or signs of significant independence among the satellite nations of the Warsaw Pact could dramatically weaken Gorbachev's position and increase the likelihood of his political defeat. If that occurs, the next leader of the Soviet

Union would undoubtedly be less enamored of reform and be more apt to return to some version of the cold war (Bialer, 1986; Galbraith and Menshikov, 1988; Hough, 1988; Frankland, 1987; Medvedev, 1986).

Summary

Political sociology is primarily concerned with the distribution and exercise of power, which is the ability to control other people's behavior and to carry out one's will. Legitimate power, or authority, involves acceptance of the exercise of power by members of a society or group, while illegitimate power, or coercion, is power that relies solely on force to achieve its objectives. The dominant political institution in modern societies is the state, which claims a monopoly over the legitimate use of force.

The United States is nominally a democracy, but three different views exist about the degree to which the nation is, in fact, democratic. The pluralist view emphasizes the existence of many competing interest groups. The give-and-take among these groups produces a relatively democratic system because no one group gains control. The neo-Marxist perspective stresses the way in which the dominant economic groups in the society hold the most political power. One major special interest group predominates in American society: the military-industrial complex. This huge economic interest group can exert extraordinary influence on government policies. The dominance of this coalition supports a neo-Marxist view of political power in the United States. The elitist view also perceives that power is held by a relatively small group but sees this group as not limited to the economic elite.

The presidency is a key feature of the American political system. Beginning in the 1930s, American presidents started to increase their power relative to Congress and the judiciary. However, recent American presidents have had less power to define policy, especially in domestic affairs. Presidents retain considerable power in shaping foreign policy. Major political leaders in every society, including presidents of the United States, have great personal power, which is the control they exercise over the people around them and in their every-day lives.

American politics in general, and more specifically presidential politics, are changing dramatically. In spite of laws designed to limit individual contributions to presidential campaigns, ways have been found to funnel huge sums of money into them. This puts the presidency on the "auction block" and opens the possibility that huge contributors will be rewarded by the victor in various ways. Television news is playing an increasingly central role in presidential campaigns, with the emphasis more and more on visual images rather than substance. In a related area, advertising, especially on TV, is key to a presidential victory. Political speeches are growing shorter and less substantive, with emphasis shifting to the generation of the "correct" 10-second or 15-second "sound bite" for the evening news. Political consultants (e.g., media advisors) are more and more important to presidential campaigns. While evidence shows increasing voter apathy in presidential elections, Americans continue to be involved in various ways in political activities.

There are alternative ways of organizing democratic governments, including the parliamentary systems found in many European countries. Israel is an instructive example of one alternative. While in recent years the American system has been stalemated by the election of Republican presidents and Democratic congresses, the recent stalemate in the Israel system has stemmed from the inability of any party to win a majority of seats in the Knesset.

Concerns about war and peace dominate the international political scene. Conflicts of interest sparked the cold war between the Soviet Union and the United States for many decades, but these conflicts seem to have diminished somewhat, and tensions have decreased. A few tentative steps have been made toward a more peaceful world.

CRITICAL THINKING

1. In what ways does a state wield power over its citizens? What means might be used to assure the continuation of power? What is the basis of governmental power in the United States?
2. Describe the three major forms of government listed in the chapter and give a contemporary example of each.
3. What explanations would you offer for why the youngest voters in the United States have the lowest percentage voting in elections?
4. What is the military-industrial complex? In what ways does this interest group exert influence on government policy? What does this example teach you about the nature of power in our political system?
5. Is the American political system truly democratic? Compare and contrast the three major sociological views of the American political system: the pluralist, the neo-Marxist, and the elitist. What evidence can you muster to support each viewpoint?
6. In what ways has presidential power in the United States increased since the term of F.D.R.? How has the Iron Triangle limited presidential action? What role does personal power play in determining the effectiveness of a president?
7. Assess the impact of campaign finances, television, campaign advertising, political speeches, and PACS on presidential elections. Does the picture presented conform to society's notion of the ideal democracy?
8. Democracy in the United States is based on the notion that an informed electorate will participate in the selection of the nation's leaders. What evidence in this chapter contradicts this notion? What steps might be taken to make reality match the ideal? What might be the consequences of such action?
9. The United States is stereotyped as the greatest democracy in the world. How does American voting behavior contradict this stereotype? Compare American voting behavior with that in other Western democracies.
10. Compare and contrast the democratic governmental systems in Israel and the United States. What accounts for the divided governments in each? How is conflict theory useful in analyzing these situations?
11. Use conflict theory to analyze the cold war between the United States and the Soviet Union. What incentives does each country have in eliminating tensions between the nations?

CONNECTIONS

Working Parents and Latchkey Children

Introduction

In a suburb of a large metropolitan city, 5-year-old Mark gets off his school bus and patiently waits on his doorstep for two hours until his mother gets home from work. "The child just started kindergarten this year," protested his teacher. "Beginning school is a big step in itself. But having to wait without adult supervision for such a long time puts even more stress and responsibility on this child that youngsters his age are not developmentally prepared to handle" (Robinson, Rowland, and Coleman, 1986).

Mark is a "latchkey" child, one of about 2 million children who are left unsupervised in their homes while their parents are working (Cole and Rodman, 1987). The heart-rending picture painted of Mark is similar to those routinely offered by the mass media—of children with their house keys hanging on dirty strings around their necks, going home to empty houses, where they are scared and lonely. Hardly a television station or a magazine hasn't devoted some time or space to the "problem" of latchkey children. Indeed, the mass media have played a significant part in making latchkey children a national *social problem*.

From a sociological perspective, as we have seen, social problems are best understood as phenomena that the people in a given society define as a problem at any given time. The "social problem" of latchkey children deserves a more careful and systematic examination. Here we will consider the issues associated with latchkey children from a sociological perspective.

Some Background Issues

Often the people who express concern about latchkey children imply that it is a very recent phenomenon. But latchkey children are not new in the United States. The term itself is derived from the eighteenth century when doors were opened by lifting a latch. At the turn of this century, children who returned to unsupervised homes were called "dorks." This label was derived from the words *door key,* and should not be confused with the contemporary meaning and usage of "dork." During the Depression of the 1930s and during World War II, when fathers and mothers were either employed or at war, latchkey children were common.

Throughout our history a negative connotation has usually been associated with latchkey children; they have typically been viewed as neglected, as having to eat cold meals, and as not having their mothers' full-time attention and affection (Robinson, Rowland, and Coleman, 1986).

A common bias in discussions of latchkey children is to consider the employment of mothers as a primary cause of the problem. Yet, most children have two parents, even when their parents are divorced, and thus an unsupervised child is one who has *neither* parent available for childcare. The implicit assumption by those concerned about latchkey children, and one they often state explicitly, is that mothers have the primary responsibility for childcare. This is, of course, a continuing reflection of the traditional gender role expectations for women, as discussed in chapter 10.

It is often taken for granted that there will be negative social and emotional consequences for children who are left alone and unsupervised. There are claims that these children will do poorly in school, have poor self-concepts, be more insecure, and be fearful. All of these claims or concerns about the negative consequences of unsupervised children can be called *latchkeyphobia*. But is latchkeyphobia based on fact or on stereotypes and myths? Do working parents inflict irreparable damage on their children by not being at home after school to offer chocolate chip cookies and milk? Was June Cleaver, of the 1950s' "Leave it to Beaver" show, a better mother than Roseanne, a current television working mother?

The answers to these questions are important because economic conditions in today's society often necessitate that both parents work. And in the case of single mothers, there may be no choice at all about working; it is an absolute necessity. As a result, parents must make important decisions about how their children will be cared for when they are not at home. Therefore, the issues created by having children and holding jobs are likely to touch most families' lives. Two issues are of interest here: (1) What insights about latchkey children can be derived from the major sociological theories? (2) What research has been done (or should be done) to enhance our understanding of latchkey children? We will begin by seeing how the major sociological theories can add to our understanding of the issues.

Structural-Functional Theory

Writing in the 1950s, functionalist theorists, especially Talcott Parsons and his associates (Parsons and Bales, 1955), described a family system in which the roles of males and females (as well as children) were clearly defined and differentiated. This functional view was in conformity with the prevailing societal views of that time, which stressed that in the ideal family a woman should be in the home as a full-time homemaker to care for her family. If a woman were to be employed, her work should not interfere with her primary role responsibilities, especially the responsibility of caring for the children (Renzetti and Curran, 1989). Functional theory and popular opinion were in agreement—a woman who left her children unsupervised was neglecting her duty.

From the perspective of the 1950s' functionalists, the family as an institution functioned both as the primary socializating agent of children and as a stabilizing force for adults in the family setting. Family roles that were separate and distinct for males and females provided a balance and a stability that made the family a smoothly working social unit that contributed positively to the society.

Among sociologists today, this overly simple functional view of the family has very few, if any, supporters. The 1950s' functionalist view has been criticized on a number of grounds, but the most frequent complaint is that it gave a kind of scientific endorsement to the traditional gender roles of women and men that prevailed at the time. A closely related criticism is that this functional view of the family endorsed a particular family form as best for the participants and best for the society. As we have seen throughout the preceding chapters, both gender roles and family forms vary greatly from society to society and from one time to another. A scientific theory that simply supports one society's view at one time in its history is inadequate as a theory.

An equally important criticism of the traditional functional view of employed mothers is that it was inconsistent with the reality of the 1950s, because many mothers *were* employed, even then. The idea of mothers remaining in the home has grown increasingly out of touch with the contemporary reality of women and employment. Many mothers work because they are not in husband-wife households; they work because as single mothers they must. Even in households with both parents present, it is often necessary to have two earners.

It is simply not possible today to describe the ideal family as one in which the husband is employed while the wife remains in the home to care for the children.

Contemporary functional theorists continue to be interested in the way societal structures influence the functioning of the society. With respect to the issue of work and the family, a functionalist today would focus on how the economic institution, or other institutions of the society, produce conditions to which the family must adapt and make adjustments. In the case of women and employment, the interest is likely to be on how being employed creates problems, stresses, and frictions in the family unit. The arrangements that parents have to make in caring for their children, including having children care for themselves when neither parent is available, is one such problem.

Conflict Theory

Conflict theory, because of its inherent concerns, seems to be even better suited than functional theory to the study of parents who, because of their work, may leave their children unsupervised in the home. Conflict theory emphasizes that conflict exists at all levels of social organization and in all social units. Conflict theorists at the macroscopic level expect to find conflict between social institutions, as, for example, conflict between the economy and the family. Conflict theorists at the microscopic level expect that there will be conflict in the family as a social unit. Conflict is expected and normal in social relationships. From a conflict perspective, for example, when parents work they will have to make decisions about child care that reveal competing or conflicting interests among family members.

Conflict theory, especially in its Marxian beginnings (chapters 1 and 13), emphasized how those who dominate the economic system will be in conflict with those who do the work. Furthermore, again as Marx emphasized, the capitalists will exploit the relative powerlessness of the workers in order to maximize their profits. One example of this conflict between workers and employers is in the area of childcare services for employees in the United States. Very few American employers provide any kind of childcare services at the place of employment, or even make any accommodations to the childcare concerns of their employees. Employers resist because childcare services would be costly and would reduce their profits. Parents and single mothers have been unable to exert enough pressure on the government to provide childcare, again because dominant economic interests oppose the higher taxes (and thus lower profits) that would result.

Conflict theory sensitizes us to the conflict of interest between working parents and their employers. Thus far, parents, both married couples and single mothers, have proved to be relatively powerless in getting employers or the state to help them with their childcare needs. Since adequate and affordable childcare is often not available, many working parents, and especially single mothers, may leave their children unsupervised while the parents are at work (Mason, 1988).

Symbolic Interactionism

The sociological theory called symbolic interactionism offers another, and very different, view of latchkey children. This theory stresses the importance of symbols and their meanings. The meanings of symbols define situations for people and influence their responses to those situations. We saw earlier that the phrase *latchkey child* has a long and mostly negative history. When television, radio, and the print media consider the issue of working parents leaving their children without supervision, they invariably connect the label *latchkey children* to images of lonely, scared, and sometimes endangered youngsters. A more neutral, though still somewhat negative, label is *unsupervised children*. But some sociologists have pointed out that the term *self-care children* is even more neutral, and thus encourages a more objective approach (Cole and Rodman, 1987).

The major point to be made from a symbolic interaction viewpoint is that social problems are often created or diminished by the successful application of a label. Instead of thinking in terms of the negative images of latchkey children, if we were to think about self-care, the way would be opened to consider important questions in a more unemotional and objective way. For example, under what conditions is self-care by a child relatively safe and appropriate? At what age can a child be entrusted to care for himself or herself? In what kinds of communities, neighborhoods, and home settings is self-care more appropriate? At what time of the day, and for how much time, may children be left in a self-care situation? The main point from a symbolic interaction perspective is that the label we use to define a situation can strongly influence our response to it.

Social Exchange Theory

Since exchange theory focuses primarily on the interaction between individuals, we can expect it to be most important in the relationship between latchkey children and their parents. When parents ask children to care for themselves, they are asking their children to assume responsibility, but in return the parents are showing that they have trust and confidence in the child. Trust and confidence are likely to translate, in a general way, into more freedom for the child. This is consistent with social exchange theory since the cost of more responsibility (as well as loneliness, and perhaps fear), are repaid with parental trust and greater personal freedom for the child.

This pattern of parent-child relations has been documented in the case of children who live with a single custodial parent after divorce. Such children are often given greater home and family responsibilities. Indeed, divorced mothers are often the parents who must ask their children to take care of themselves while they are at work. These children of divorce have been described as children who "grow up a little faster" (Weiss, 1979). In return these mothers often treat their children more as equals, rather than as subordinates. Again, this is an example of social exchange theory in action.

Looking at the Research

Definitions. Research on any subject requires precise and unambiguous definitions of key terms. While journalists and television broadcasters can use a term like *latchkey children* quite loosely, and thus imprecisely, a researcher cannot. To compare latchkey, or self-care, children with children who have adult care, a researcher must specify exactly what criteria must be met to qualify a child as a *latchkey child.* For example, does a latchkey child have to be the child of working parents? Not necessarily, since

parents may be engaged in many different activities (shopping, recreation, medical appointments) that take them away from home, while their children are left to care for themselves (Cole and Rodman, 1987).

At what ages is an unsupervised child considered a latchkey child? Would a 15-year-old be considered a latchkey child? Generally an adolescent at this age is thought to be able to care for himself or herself. How young can a child be and still be thought of as a self-care child? Most people would agree that leaving a three- or four-year-old child alone would constitute a form of child neglect, and thus would be qualitatively different from self-care.

Other definitional questions deal with whether siblings are present in the home, and if so, what their ages are. An older sibling in the house, say a 19-year-old, can be seen as a surrogate parent for a younger child.

But a younger sibling simply means more responsibility for the child. There is also the question of how much time the child spends alone, and how frequently. A child who must be at home five hours every day before a parent arrives home is in a different situation from the child who must occasionally wait alone for a half-hour because heavy traffic conditions detain a parent.

After considering all of these factors, one group of researchers concluded that a latchkey, or self-care, child should be defined as ". . . one between the ages of approximately 6 and 13 who spends time at home alone or with a younger sibling on a periodic basis" (Cole and Rodman, 1987, p. 93).

Studies. Even though the media has shown a flurry of interest in latchkey children, relatively few studies have been conducted by sociologists and other social scientists. Cole and Rodman (1987) reviewed the studies that have been published, and found only five that studied the consequences of self-care for the functioning and development of children.

A study conducted by Rodman and his associates may be taken as an example of this research (Rodman, Pratto, and Nelson, 1985). In this study, 96 children in the fourth and seventh grades were studied; half were self-care children, the other half had adult care. Pairs of these children (one self-care, the other adult care) were matched on age, sex, race, family composition, and family status. No statistically significant differences were found in their self-esteem, or in their feelings of having personal control over the events in their lives. Their teachers did not see significant differences between the self-care and adult-care children on social adjustment or interpersonal relations.

Some studies have found differences between self-care and adult-care children. For example, a study conducted in the 1970s found self-care girls to have some shortcomings in school social relations (Woods, 1972). Other studies, however, have found no differences between self-care and adult-care children. At best, the research results are mixed, but there is certainly no overwhelming evidence that children who care for themselves suffer serious negative consequences as a result of the experience (Cole and Rodman, 1987).

There is, however, some evidence that latchkey children show more independence, self-reliance, responsibility, resourcefulness, and maturity than their peers who are supervised. As Robinson, Rowland, and Coleman have concluded, "Whatever the reason, research to date suggests that many latchkey kids are doing well and appear to be growing and developing similarly to their nonlatchkey contemporaries" (1986, p. 33).

A need certainly exists for more research, especially research that asks more refined questions about the effects of self-care under different circumstances and varying conditions. But we already know that much of the sensationalism about latchkey children, and the more extreme examples of latchkeyphobia, are not supported by the available research.

In contrast to the pathetic description of the latchkey child Mark, waiting desolately on his front steps (one wonders why he didn't use his key), we have the case of Heather.

> Ten-year-old Heather comes home from school, unlocks her front door, and secures it behind her. She calls her mother at work to inform her that she is home safe and sound and spends the next two hours completing homework until her mother gets home. "We have strict rules that Heather must follow when she's home alone," her mother says with ambivalence. "She knows that she is not to allow strangers or friends inside when I'm not home. She has a routine that she follows every afternoon so I feel pretty secure about that. I think being alone for a few hours a day makes her more self-reliant and responsible" (Robinson, Rowland, and Coleman, 1986).

But her mother then voices a concern that is apt to be expressed by all parents, whenever their children are not under their close supervision: "But I must admit that I worry about her constantly" (Robinson, Rowland, and Coleman, 1986). This parental attitude is apt to be a key distinguishing factor between self-care that is appropriate, perhaps even beneficial, and self-care that is inappropriate and potentially harmful to the child. Responsible parents must carefully consider the circumstances and conditions under which they ask their children to care for themselves.

References

COLE, CYNTHIA, and RODMAN, HYMAN. "When School-Age Children Care for Themselves: Issues for Family Life Educators and Parents." *Family Relations* 36, 1987.

MASON, MARY ANN. *The Equality Trap*. New York: Simon and Shuster, 1988.

PARSONS, TALCOTT, and BALES, ROBERT F. *Family, Socialization and Interaction Process*. New York: The Free Press, 1955.

RENZETTI, CLAIRE M., and CURRAN, DANIEL J. *Women, Men, and Society: The Sociology of Gender*. Boston: Allyn and Bacon, 1989.

ROBINSON, BRYAN E.; ROWLAND, BOBBIE A.; and COLEMAN, MICK. *Latchkey Kids: Unlocking Doors For Children and Their Families*. Lexington, Mass.: Lexington Books, 1986.

RODMAN, HYMAN. "Forget the Horror Stories About Latchkey Children." *Los Angeles Times*, September 5, 1985.

RODMAN, HYMAN; PRATTO, DAVID J.; and NELSON, ROSEMARY SMITH. "Child Care Arrangements and Children's Functioning: A Comparison of Self-Care and Adult-Care Children." *Developmental Psychology* 21, 1985.

WEISS, ROBERT S. *Going it Alone: The Family Life and Social Situation of the Single Parent*. New York: Basic Books, 1979.

WOODS, M.B. "The Unsupervised Child of the Working Mother." *Developmental Psychology* 6, 1972.

CHAPTER

17

Population and Urbanization

• More people were *added to* the world's population in the last 12 years (1 billion) than existed in the entire world when the United States became a nation.

• This rapid growth in population is contributing to dramatic increases in the growth of the world's cities. In 1950 only 78 cities had more than a million residents. By the year 2010 over 500 cities will have a million or more residents.

Societies around the world have been deeply influenced, and continue to be shaped, by two unprecedented trends of the twentieth century: (1) population growth, in both individual societies and the world as a whole; (2) ever-increasing numbers of people living in urban rather than rural places.

The scientific study of population is called **demography.** Demographers study why and how populations grow and decline by examining the three basic processes that determine population size. The first process is **fertility,** a term used by demographers to indicate the actual childbearing behavior of people. The second is **mortality,** which refers to deaths and death rates of a specific population. The third is **migration,** which is the permanent (or semi-permanent) change of one's place of residence. In addition to studying these dynamic features of populations, demographers also consider the characteristics of populations (called **population composition**). The most frequently considered characteristics of a population are age and sex.

Demography
The scientific study of population

Fertility
Demographic term for childbearing

Mortality
Demographic term for deaths and death rates

Migration
The permanent (or semi-permanent) change of one's residence

Population composition
Demographic term for characteristics of a population—especially age and sex

Fertility

Having children is fundamentally a social behavior since it is profoundly influenced by the social contexts in which people live. These contexts may be as large scale as the economic or political times or as small scale as the particular couples who are making decisions about whether to have a baby. Even if, as some people believe, there is a human "instinct" or genetic "drive" to have children, this explanation would not reveal why some people have many children, others have only a few, and some have none.

Just as individuals (or couples) vary greatly in the number of children they have, so do groups or categories of people. As an extreme example, the Hutterites, a fundamentalist religious group living in the plains states of the northern Midwest and southern Canada, have the record for the highest fertility ever reliably recorded for any population. As recently as the 1950s, Hutterite women had an *average* of nearly 11 children. The Hutterites oppose any methods of controlling childbearing, they marry in their late teens or early twenties, and they do not allow divorce. Among the Hutterites all property is owned in common and children are cared for communally. Because of these particular social arrangements and cultural values the Hutterites have what population scientists believe to be the maximum level of fertility (Stockwell and Groat, 1984). This maximum level of uncontrolled childbearing is called **natural fertility** (Bongaarts, 1987).

Natural fertility
The maximum level of uncontrolled childbearing

Both population and urbanization are evident on Takeshita shopping street in Tokyo, Japan.

As an interesting contrast to the Hutterites, there were two American religious groups of the nineteenth century for which fertility was almost non-existent. The Shakers and the Rappites, both located in the eastern United States, prohibited sexual intercourse for most of their members. The only way these religious groups could grow in size was to recruit new members and to adopt children. Today the Rappites have completely disappeared, and only a handful of Shaker women survive (Kephart, 1976; Muncy, 1973).

The fertility extremes of the Hutterites, on the one hand, and the Shakers and Rappites, on the other, illustrate very well how social contexts influence childbearing. In contemporary American society differences in fertility still exist between some societal groups and categories, but the differences are not great, and they are less pronounced today than they were in the past. Some differences in fertility among religious, racial, and socioeconomic groups will be considered after we examine some general trends in American fertility.

Childbearing in the United States today is at the lowest rate in history. At the time of the founding of the country the average woman had just under eight births. Today the number of births per woman is less than two (1.8 average). The birth rate went down steadily through the entire nineteenth century and for nearly half of the twentieth. Then, after World War II, the birth rate went up substantially and remained high during the 1950s. This period between 1946 and 1960 is called the "baby boom."

By the late 1980s the birth rate had again fallen to a level that reflects the long, generally steady decline in United States' childbearing (Westoff, 1986).

Since the baby-boom generation continues to affect the U.S. population and will continue to do so until past the middle of the twenty-first century, it qualifies as a demographic phenomenon of some importance. The "causes" of the baby boom are still not completely understood, but demographers do offer some explanations. Much of the increase in childbearing during the 1950s can be attributed to the high percentage of Americans marrying (over 90 percent), and marrying at an early age. Throughout the entire twentieth century, Americans married youngest during the middle of the baby boom, in 1956. Although the ideal family size for many Americans in the 1950s was three or four children, exceptionally large families did not produce the baby boom. Most of the increase in birth rates came from early and near-universal marriage, and rapid childbearing (Westoff, 1986).

The increase in birth rates during the baby-boom years came as a surprise to almost all demographers. The trend of declining childbearing had persisted for more than a century, and it was expected to continue. Since it did not, it raises the question of whether the birth rate could rise again, producing a new baby boom. For the near future, that possibility appears unlikely, primarily because the trends for age of first marriage and age of having a first child have been going up for the last two decades. These trends are exactly the opposite of what occurred to produce the baby boom.

Social Factors Related to Fertility Rates

The influence of social factors on childbearing can be easily demonstrated by comparing the birth rates of various groups or categories in the society. For example, a century ago farm people in the United States had higher birth rates than the urban people. Today the differences in fertility between farm and urban people are not important, primarily because only 2 percent of the national population now lives on farms (U.S. Bureau of the Census, 1987). However, various religious, racial, and socioeconomic groups are of significant size in the United States' population so their differences in fertility could be important.

Religion. Because the Roman Catholic church disapproves of the use of mechanical and chemical methods of contraception (including sterilization), it might be assumed that Catholic birth rate would be much higher than the birth rates of other religious groups. Such is not the case, however; Catholic family size in the United States today is nearly the same as Protestant family size (1.96 children compared to 1.92 children, respectively). In fact, with regard to contraception, Catholics in the United States use various birth control methods at about the same level as non-Catholics (Westoff, 1986). American Jewish women have somewhat lower fertility than either Protestants or Catholics (1.72 children), but the lowest levels of fertility are generally found among members of the population who claim no religion.

Race and Ethnicity. Differences still exist in the fertility levels of different racial and ethnic groups in the United States. A comparison between whites and blacks finds that black American women have, on average, about one-half child more than white women. Hispanic women in the United States have more children than either blacks or whites, although there are significant differences among Hispanics. Cubans have the lowest fertility among Hispanics, while Mexicans have the highest. Asian-Americans generally have lower fertility than other Americans, although again there are important differences: Japanese-Americans have lower fertility than whites, while Vietnamese in the United States have higher fertility than whites (Westoff, 1986).

Socioeconomic Status. Most people accept the precept that socioeconomic status is related to fertility. In sociological terms, "lower socioeconomic status is associated with higher fertility." This is consistent with the old cliche that ends, ". . . and the poor get children." Although these statements are somewhat true, qualifications are necessary. For example, the opposite is the case in traditional peasant societies where wealthier land-owning couples may have more children than those less well off. Studies from India, Bangladesh, Iran, Nepal, the Philippines, and Thailand show some tendency for higher-status landowners to have higher fertility than other farm families. In these societies, owning land increases the demand for children and provides greater security for old age (World Bank, 1984).

In Western societies during the twentieth century, however, the relationship between socioeconomic status and fertility has usually been negative. But this negative relationship was strongest in the early part of the twentieth century, as the middle and upper middle classes started using family limitation methods that were not yet available to the lower classes.

In present-day American society, regardless of whether socioeconomic status is measured by educational level, occupational status, or income, higher-status women have fewer children. Of these three indicators of socioeconomic status, the educational attainment of a woman is the strongest variable. Among married women aged 25 to 34 years, those with less than a high school education have an average of 2.3 children, while women of the same age with four years of college have an average of 1.1 children. Of course, some of these college-educated women who are still in their twenties are likely to have more children before they complete childbearing years. Figure 17–1 shows

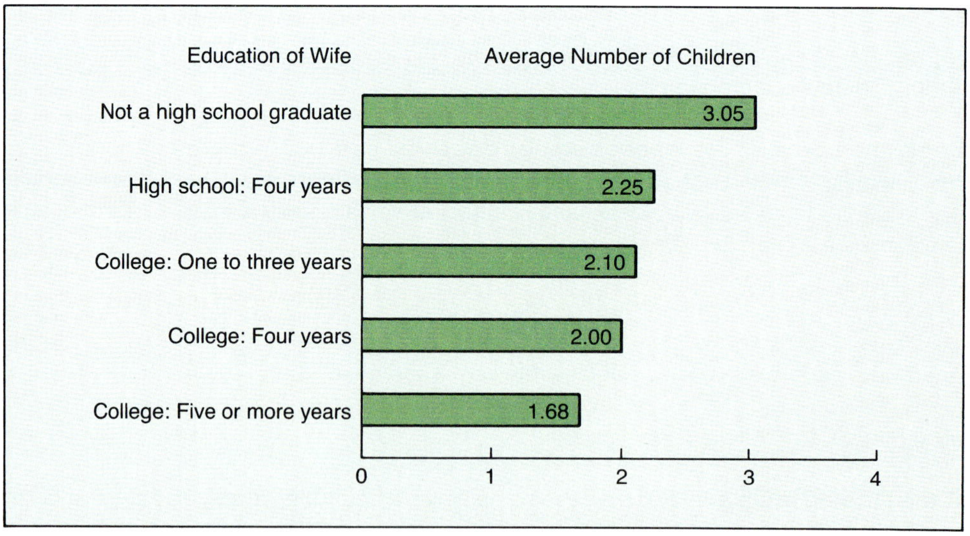

Figure 17–1. Average Number of Children Born to Wives Aged 35–44 Years in Married-Couple Families, by Education of Wife, 1987. (*Source:* U.S. Bureau of Census, *Fertility of American Women: June 1987*, Current Population Reports, P-20, No. 427, Table 3, 1988b.)

the average number of children per woman aged 35 to 44 years (an age group that has probably completed most of its childbearing) at various educational levels. For this age group in 1987, there is still a one-child difference between women who did not complete high school and women who completed college. Although this figure does show the expected relationship with socioeconomic status, the difference is not much more than one child between the lowest education group and college-educated women.

Mortality

Death is obviously a biological event, since every death is ultimately due to a biological cause. Nonetheless, social factors do contribute to differences in death rates among different groups and categories in society. Two distinctive aspects of social life are related to mortality differences: (1) the positions that people have in the social structure and (2) life styles.

Position in the social structure refers to the way some groups or categories have lower (or higher) places in some ranking system of the society. Life style refers to the choices people make in the conduct of their daily lives. This includes how they eat, use alcohol or drugs, exercise, and so on. Life style is not a precise scientific concept, but a number of causes of death are clearly associated with the choices people make about their lives. We begin our examination of the way in which these social factors influence mortality by considering some examples of how position in the social structure influences death rates and longevity.

Position in the Social Structure

In chapter 8 we saw how the position one has in the stratification structure of a society can influence length of life. People in the lower socioeconomic classes have higher death rates and a shorter life expectancy. As a general principle we may say that people who are in lower or disadvantaged positions in a society (or social structure) will have higher death rates and shorter lives.

This principle is also illustrated by comparing the life expectancies of black and white Americans. At birth a black female has a life expectancy that is five years less than a white female (73.5 years versus 78.8 years). Black males are even more disadvantaged compared to white males since white males can expect to live almost seven years longer. The difference between black and white life expectancy has been decreasing since the beginning of the twentieth century, when life expectancy for whites was about 16 years longer than for blacks (National Center for Health Statistics, 1988).

A distressing recent trend occurred in 1985 and 1986 when, for two years in a row, life expectancy for blacks in the United States declined. During these same two years, life expectancy among whites increased slightly. During the twentieth century there has rarely been a year when life expectancy has declined, and when it did (as in 1979), the decline was related to a general cause of death (such as an influenza epidemic) that affected the death rates of all races. Several reasons are possible for the lowered life expectancy among black Americans, including increases in death rates due to homicide, accidents, tuberculosis, pneumonia, AIDS, and possibly to drug-related deaths (Hilts, 1988).

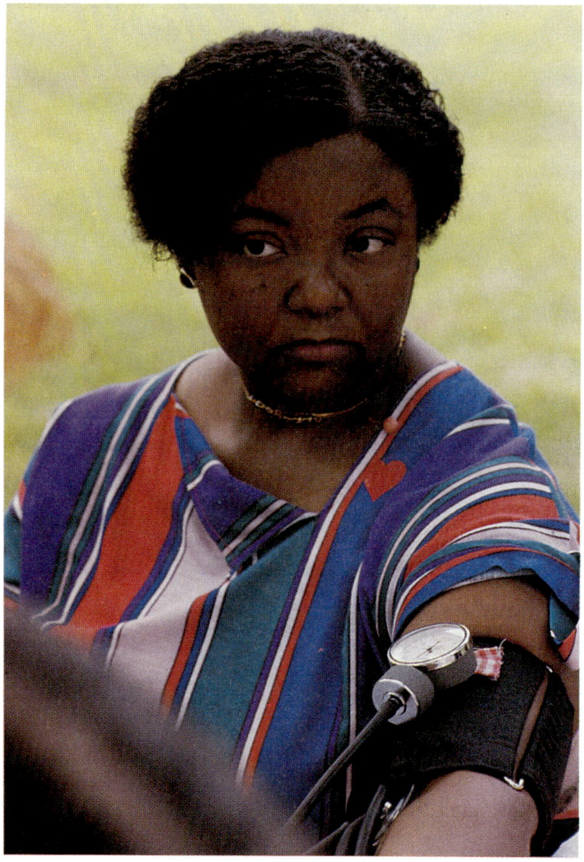

A city-sponsored Health Fair provides an opportunity for this woman to have her blood pressure checked. Hypertension is found more frequently among black Americans than among white Americans, and may contribute to the higher death rates of blacks.

Gender Roles and Mortality. In chapter 10 we saw that the feminine gender role, especially in traditional, patriarchal societies, places women in positions subordinate to men. It follows, therefore, that females should have higher death rates or lower life expectancy than males. In fact, females in the contemporary world generally have a longer life expectancy than males, but that may be due to a biological advantage of females over males. We know, for example, that the death rate among male fetuses is higher than female fetuses during pregnancy, and that males have a higher death rate than females during the first four weeks of life. Both of these facts suggest that the female organism is more viable than the male organism, since social and cultural factors could not account for the lower death rates of females.

Yet societies do exist in which females do not survive as long as males, or they have only a slight advantage over males; these are often the same societies in which males have distinctly dominant positions in the social structure. For example, infanticide has been practiced in some societies, and in those cases, almost invariably, female infants are the ones who are killed or allowed to die. (See the Cross-Cultural Perspectives box: "Infanticide and the Preference for Male Children.") Today, for example, there are indications that some female infanticide is occurring in contemporary China as an outgrowth of the family limitation policies of the central government (Arnold and Zhaoxiang, 1986).

In the Punjab state of India, where parents often do not want female children, the childhood mortality rate of females is twice as high as that of males (Das Gupta, 1987).

As another example of how women's subordinate status may affect their longevity, a World Bank report shows only three countries of the world (India, Pakistan, and Bhutan) in which female life expectancy is less than male life expectancy (World Bank, 1984). In the two large Asian countries, females generally hold a status subordinate to that of males (Miller, 1981; Preston, 1982).

Another interesting case of how the gender-role position of women lowers their life expectancy is found in nineteenth century Ireland, where there was a pronounced difference between the rights and duties of males and females. Females were required to work very hard, having complete responsibility for the home, for the livestock (almost all families were rural people), and for helping with the planting and harvesting of crops. Life was hard on the small Irish farm; resources, which were limited, were given to the males of the family first. This was true especially with food; females ate only after the men were satisfied. "Women and children did not eat their meals until after the men and older boys had had their fill, a practice which systematically made the more nutritious food and larger helpings available to the favored sex" (Kennedy, 1973, p. 52). The gender roles that prevailed in Ireland, and still remain to a lesser degree today, gave males a dominant and advantageous position relative to females.

Kennedy found that between 1871 and 1962 Irish females had much less of a life expectancy advantage over males than did their female counterparts in England and the United States. Even as recently as the 1970–1972 period, Irish females had only a 4.75 years' advantage over males, while females in England and Wales had a 6.2 years'

There are some societies—India, Pakistan, and Bhutan—where the life expectancy of women is less than that of men. This likely reflects the subordinate status of women in those societies.

Cross-Cultural Perspectives

Infanticide and the Preference for Male Children

In societies around the world there is a preference for male babies over female babies. Parents in virtually every society candidly admit that they prefer their first child to be a male, and, in general, they prefer a larger number of sons than daughters (Williamson, 1978). This widespread cultural preference has often led to female infanticide, in which female babies are killed, or allowed to die, after they are born. While most examples of infanticide are historical, there is evidence that even in the contemporary world female babies are sometimes allowed to die because they are not wanted by their parents. Contemporary India, China, and Japan all provide illustrations of female infanticide.

In Japan the year 1966 was called the year of the Fiery Horse. According to traditional Japanese beliefs, a girl born in the year of the Fiery Horse was ill fated. Some Japanese parents apparently accepted this belief, because in 1966 a larger proportion of female babies died in the first month of life than would have been expected from the records of previous, or subsequent, years. While this could be a confirmation of the validity of the folklore, a more likely possibility is female infanticide (Kaku, 1975).

There is also much evidence of infanticide in India's history. Before the British outlawed the practice in 1870 with the passage of the Infanticide Act, female infanticide was openly practiced. In the nineteenth century the following dialogue occurred between a British official and an Indian landholder:

> 'It is the general belief among us, Sir, that those who preserve their daughters never prosper; and, that the families into which we marry them are equally unfortunate.'
>
> 'Then you think that it is a duty imposed upon you from above, to destroy your infant daughters; and that the neglect and disregard of that duty brings misfortunes upon you?'
>
> 'We think it must be so, Sir, with regard to our own families or clan!' (Miller, 1981).

In fact, the practice of female infanticide in some areas of India was so common that visitors noticed, and later censuses confirmed, that there was a shortage of females.

Why was female infanticide practiced so often in certain parts of India prior to 1870? Pride and money appear to be important factors. Fathers wanted to marry their daughters into families of equal or higher status, and a prestigious marriage required the payment of a large dowry. In addition, it was considered shameful to have unmarried daughters at home. Thus, if parents had many daughters or few resources, economics and pride would lead them to consider killing some as infants.

While open infanticide is no longer condoned in India, it may still be practiced in a more subtle manner. One researcher found that, in families where mothers expressed a preference for no more children, there was a higher rate of female infant deaths. Male infant deaths were also higher in such families, but not to the same degree as females (Simmons et al., 1982).

One observer of contemporary India has said:

> The actual murder of little girls has in great measure ceased, but it has been replaced . . . by a degree of carelessness hardly less criminal. (Miller, 1961)

In modern China, also, there is circumstantial evidence of some female infanticide. When China's one-child policy is rigidly enforced, a higher percentage of female first-children die than would normally occur.

Even in contemporary England, the fourth or fifth child of a family has a 25 percent greater chance of dying in infancy than a child who is the first born (Weeks, 1989). Although not indicating a preference for male children, or female infanticide, such evidence suggests that infanticide may be occurring, even in developed countries with modern medical systems.

KAKU, KANAE. "Were Girl Babies Sacrificed to Folk Superstition in 1966 in Japan?" *Annals of Human Biology* 2, 1975.

MILLER, BARBARA D. *The Endangered Sex: Neglect of Female Children in Rural North India.* Ithaca, N.Y.: Cornell University Press, 1981.

SIMMONS, G.; SMUCKER, C.; BERNSTEIN, S.; and JENSEN, E. "Post-neonatal Mortality in Rural India: Implications of an Economic Model." *Demography* 19, 1982.

WEEKS, JOHN R. *Population: An Introduction to Concepts and Issues*, 4th ed. Belmont, Calif.: Wadsworth Publishing Co., 1989.

WILLIAMSON, NANCY E. "Boys or Girls? Parents' Preferences and Sex Control." *Population Bulletin* 33, 1978.

advantage and females in the United States had a 7.4 years' advantage. The explanation for this difference may lie in the relative social statuses of the two sexes in Ireland, which put Irish females at a disadvantage compared to English and American females (Kennedy, 1973).

Life Styles and Mortality

Life style, as we noted earlier, refers to the choices people make in the conduct of their daily lives. Today, in a country like the United States, heart disease, cancer, and accidents are major causes of death, and all appear to be greatly influenced by the choices we make in our daily lives. The significance of life style is vividly illustrated by the recent trends in heart disease and stroke death rates in the United States and the Soviet Union.

Since 1970 the heart disease death rate in the United States has gone down by more than 28 percent (when adjusted for the older age of the population). Although some part of this decline may have come as a result of the early detection and treatment of high blood pressure, most medical experts agree that much of it came from the changes that Americans have made in their life styles. They were smoking less, consuming less fatty and high-cholesterol food, and exercising more. All these changes probably helped reduce deaths due to heart disease and stroke (Byington et al., 1979; Havlik and Feinleib, 1979).

Heart Disease and Stroke—the Soviet Union. The decline in heart disease deaths in the United States stands in stark contrast to conditions in the Soviet Union (Cooper, 1981; Dutton, 1979). In that country, since the mid-1960s the overall death rate for both men and women has gone up steadily. Middle-aged men in particular have had marked increases in their death rates, which appears to be almost totally accounted for by increases in heart disease deaths.

The reasons for the increase in heart disease deaths in the Soviet Union have been the cause of much discussion, both within and outside that country. Soviet officials have said that the increase is due to the stresses and difficult living conditions experienced during World War II. This explanation has been rejected by other authorities, who doubt that stresses and difficulties experienced 30 years earlier would have such long-lasting effects (Cooper, 1981). Some observers attribute the increase in Soviet heart disease deaths to the high rate of alcohol consumption (Dutton, 1979). Although the causal relationship is circumstantial, it is a fact that compared to other countries, the Soviet Union is near the top in the consumption of distilled spirits—only Poland and Peru have higher rates of consumption (Dutton, 1979).

While acknowledging that alcohol may have been a contributing factor, other experts have pointed to tobacco usage, especially cigarette smoking, as a likely cause of high rates of heart disease in the Soviet Union (Cooper, 1981). It is reported that more than 70 percent of Russian men living in Moscow are smokers. An additional piece of evidence regarding smoking is the great increase in cancers of the respiratory system and larynx in the Soviet Union. Between 1960 and 1977, the death rate from these cancers rose more than 70 percent (Dutton, 1979).

Death Rates among Mormons and Seventh-Day Adventists. The contrast between what has happened to heart disease death rates in the Soviet Union and the United States is a significant piece of evidence supporting the importance of life style. Similar evidence comes from differences in death rates among various religious groups in American society. Particularly interesting are the Mormons and Seventh-Day Adventists, who have religious restrictions on the use of both alcohol and tobacco products. The Mormons also restrict the use of coffee, tea, and addictive drugs, while the Seventh-Day Adventists are urged to abstain from coffee, tea, other caffeine beverages, and meat (Enstrom, 1978; Phillips et al., 1980).

In an eight-year study of cancer death rates, Seventh-Day Adventists in California were compared with the general California population. With regard to cancers that are strongly related to smoking (such as cancer of the lungs, mouth, pharynx, and esophagus), the Seventh-Day Adventists had a risk of death that was only 20 to 30 percent of the general population of similar age and sex (Phillips et al., 1980). Even in the case of cancers that are not known to be smoking-related, the risk of death among Seventh-Day Adventists was only 65 to 75 percent of that for the general population (Phillips et al., 1980).

Studies of Mormons in both California and Utah have shown similar results. In a study by Enstrom (1978), comparisons were made between Mormon males who were active in the church and U.S. males in general. The death rates for the Mormon men (aged 35–64) were only 35 percent of the death rates of U.S. white males of the same age category (Enstrom, 1978). Seen in a somewhat different way, active Mormon males at age 35 could expect to live about eight years longer than U.S. males as a whole at the same age.

Migration

Migration is the movement of individuals or groups from one place of residence to another when they have the intention of remaining in the new place for some substantial amount of time. By this definition it is not migration if someone simply travels someplace for a visit and returns. Even temporarily living in another place, as one might do at a summer vacation home, is not migration. The key to migration is that a new residence is being established. Sometimes that new residence may be a different house in the same neighborhood or community, but at the opposite extreme, the new residence may be in a different country. The term *immigration,* which we discussed in chapter 9, refers to migration from one nation or country to another.

Migration in the United States

Throughout the history of the United States, migration from one state, or one region, to another has been an important factor in determining the growth and development of the country. Historically the two major migration trends in the United States have been from rural to urban places, and from east to west. (Later in this chapter we will focus on migration from rural to urban places and, in particular, on the continuing growth of metropolitan areas.)

The Calle Ocho Festival in Miami, Florida. The "sun belt" states, especially Florida, Texas, and California, have received large numbers of new migrant residents predominantly from the northern industrial states in the last decade, and the trend is expected to continue into the twenty-first century.

Migration to the Sun Belt. A general westward migration has characterized much of American history, and it continues, but in recent decades that trend has been modified by a southward movement as well. The new migration pattern is toward the "Sun Belt"—the states in the southern and western parts of the United States that have mild climates. Although poorer economic conditions during the 1980s did slow migration to some of the oil-producing states on the Gulf Coast, Sun Belt states are still growing. In looking to the future, it is estimated that until the year 2010 the states of California, Texas, and Florida will experience more than half of the increases in the United States' population. Some of that growth will be due to the migrants coming from other states, and another part will be due to immigration. Among these three states, Florida's growth will come primarily from internal migration, while Texas, and especially California, will add more population due to immigration (U.S. Bureau of the Census, 1988f).

Some states are expected to lose population in the next two decades, in part because of out-migration. These states are located primarily in the upper Midwest but also include some western, eastern, and border states. Specifically, the states expected to lose population in the next two decades include Montana, Wyoming, North Dakota, Nebraska, Iowa, Wisconsin, Illinois, Michigan, Indiana, Kentucky, Ohio, West Virginia, and Pennsylvania (U.S. Bureau of the Census, 1988f).

World Population Growth

Population explosion The rapid growth of the world's population in the twentieth century

The term **population explosion** has been widely used to describe the rapid growth of the world's population in the twentieth century. Although this is not a technical demographic term, it is an apt description of how much the population of the world has grown in the last 50 years. In comparison with the rest of human history, there has been an explosion in the number of the earth's inhabitants.

In the long history of human life on earth, which some archaeologists and anthropologists estimate to be as much as 2 million years, the human population did not grow very rapidly. It is estimated that even after the world was well into the Christian era, 1000 A.D., there were fewer than 300 million people (Durand, 1977). It took all the preceding thousands of years for the population of the earth to reach 300 million people, but in our time it takes less than four years to add that many people to the world's population.

In all likelihood, the world first achieved a population of 1 billion people in the early part of the 1800s. By 1930 the size of the population had reached 2 billion; the third billion was added in just 30 years, by 1960. The fourth billion was added in about 13 years, in 1973. Since then, the rate of growth has slowed down a little, but with a larger population base, it now takes only about 12 years to add a thousand-million people (a billion). Every four days a million more people are added to the earth's population.

Let us be clear on this point. A million people are added to the world's population every four days, despite the high death rates that prevail in many countries, despite high rates of infant mortality, despite deaths caused by wars, starvation, natural disasters, and disease. In other words, the number of births occurring each year exceeds the number of deaths, and thus the world's population grows by more than 85 million people each year.

Some people say that there is no population explosion, or that talk about a population explosion is an exaggeration or scare tactic. Since the term has no precise definition, these charges are difficult to evaluate. However, two things can be said with certainty. First, the number of people being added to the earth's population each year is many times greater than ever before in human history. Second, since a 1.7 percent growth rate doubles the earth's population every 40 years, such growth cannot go on indefinitely. These facts have led most people to conclude that steps must be taken to slow down or stop the rate of population growth. As we will see below, not everyone agrees with this view, but in order to address the question of what should be done about world population growth, we must first understand why the earth's population, after hundreds of thousands of years of relative stability, started growing in the seventeenth century and has been growing especially fast in the last 50 years. It will help us if we first consider an important idea of demography called the Modern Demographic Transition.

The Modern Demographic Transition

The **Modern Demographic Transition** can be defined as a three-stage pattern of population change that occurs as a society is transformed from an agricultural to a fully industrialized, urban economy. The agricultural stage has a balanced population with a high death rate and a high birth rate. The transition stage has a growing population with a high birth rate and a decreasing death rate. And the final stage of the transition has a much lower population growth rate because the birth rate has dropped to a level roughly equal to that of the death rate. The three stages of the Modern Demographic Transition and the levels of population growth are shown in table 17–1.

Modern Demographic Transition
A three-stage pattern of population change occurring as societies industrialize and urbanize

Modern Demographic Transition theory helps to explain why the world's population is currently growing so fast. One point it makes clearly is that recent dramatic increases in population growth are caused by *changes in the death rate* and not by changes in the birth rate. Many people erroneously believe that the birth rate has been rising rapidly in many countries, thus producing rapid population growth. This is not true; the population has "exploded" because of the decline in the death rate.

The demographic transition occurred first in the countries of northern and western Europe. By the beginning of the eighteenth century, as the countries of this region began the process of modernizing and industrializing, their death rates started to decline. The birth rates in these countries, which had traditionally been high, remained at that level

Table 17–1. The Three Stages of the Modern Demographic Transition

Stage	Death Rate	Birth Rate	Population Growth Rate
1. Agricultural	High	High	Low
2. Transition	Low	High	High
3. Final	Low	Low	Low

As Japan rebuilt its economy after World War II, its modernization was accompanied by a decline in family size. Like the people of Europe and the United States, many Japanese couples have only two children.

for some time. The result, of course, was population growth during the transition period. Although exceptions to this pattern were found in some European countries, they do not outweigh the far greater number of cases where mortality started declining at the beginnings of modernization, to be followed considerably later by declines in fertility (Beaver, 1975).

According to transition theory, modernization also brings about a decline in birth rates, but this decline comes much later than the decline in death rates. One reason why birth rates go down after death rates is that the characteristics of childbearing are very different from the characteristics of mortality. This is especially the case with respect to the positive value that most societies place on life (both producing it and keeping it going). Whereas lowering the death rate is completely consistent with the positive value placed on life, lowering the birth rate is not. Producing new life by having children, in society after society, is an act that is praised and greeted with joy. If fertility is to go down, it is necessary to some degree for individual couples to act contrary to this valued act. Even when it might be advantageous for an individual couple to refrain from having children, the prevailing values, supported by customs and norms, act as strong pressures for them to have children anyway.

Nonetheless, as the modernization process continues, and especially as societies become primarily urban instead of rural, the birth rates do go down. This is the final stage of the demographic transition, and usually means that population growth slows down greatly or stops completely. Today almost all European countries (as well as the United States, Canada, Australia, and New Zealand) have stopped growing at a rapid rate because their birth rates have declined to levels almost as low as their death rates. In some European countries, the birth rates are now equal to, or slightly lower than, the death rates, so their growth has stopped, at least for the moment. Currently, Austria, Denmark, East Germany, Italy, Hungary, and West Germany have birth rates as low as, or lower than, their death rates (Population Reference Bureau, 1988).

For European countries, the transition from high birth and death rates to low birth and death rates took about 200 years. The declines in the death rates came about because of changes and advances that evolved gradually. The entire demographic transition, as experienced in Europe, is shown in figure 17–2.

The demographic experience of the developing countries in the past 35 or 40 years has been similar to the European experiences in the transition stage, although one part of the process has been much more rapid. In the developing countries, representing 75 to 80 percent of the world's population, the decline in the death rate has been very fast. It has taken only a few decades for the death rates in these countries to drop because of the importation of medical, technical, and scientific advances from the developed countries. Since the birth rates have remained high, the gap between births and deaths is great, and the resulting growth rate is extraordinary. In some areas of the

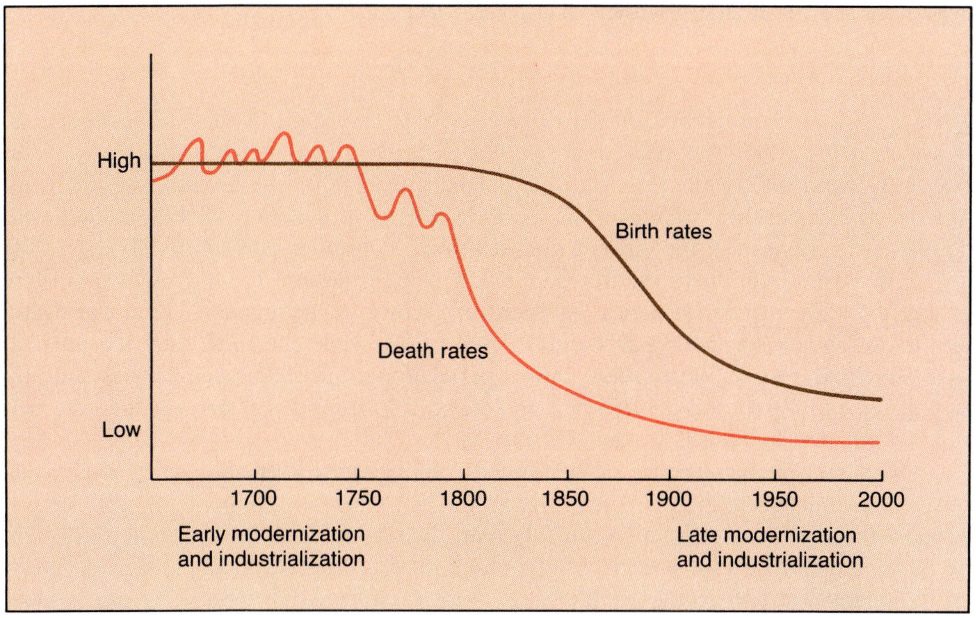

Figure 17–2. The Modern Demographic Transition (as modeled on the Western European experience).

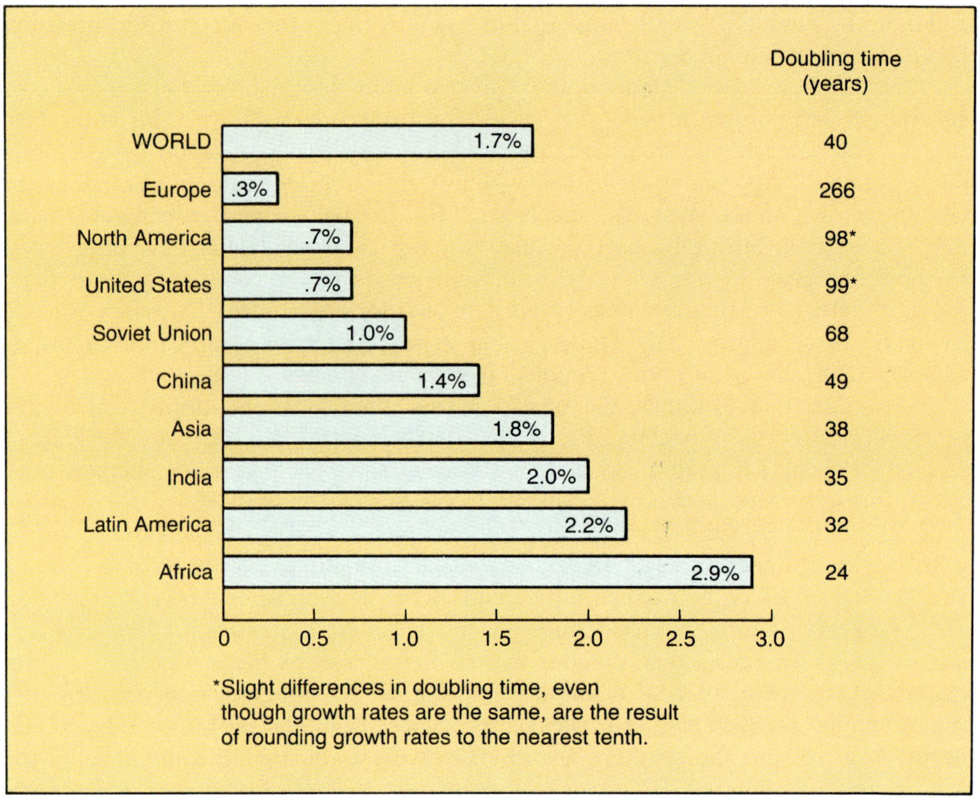

Figure 17–3. Growth Rates and Doubling Times for the World, the Five Continents, and Major Countries. (*Source:* Population Reference Bureau, 1988, *World Population Data Sheet* (Washington, D.C.: Population Reference Bureau, Inc., 1988).)

world with huge populations, the birth rate remains very high, while the death rate is as low as that in the developed countries. For example, all of Latin America has a birth rate of 29 per 1,000, while the death rate is eight per 1,000. The growth rate for Latin America is 2.2 percent, which means that the present population of 429 million will double every 32 years if the current rate of growth continues (see figure 17–3).

The African continent, with a population of 623 million, has a growth rate even greater than that of Latin America (2.9 percent). However, in much of Africa the death rate is not as low, remaining at about 15 per 1,000, while the birth rate is estimated at a very high 44 per 1,000. Asia, with a population of 3 billion people, has a death rate of ten per 1,000 and a birth rate of 28 per 1,000, for a 1.8 percent increase per year (Population Reference Bureau, 1988).

Seen from the perspective of the Modern Demographic Transition, the current rate of world population growth is largely due to the fact that the developing countries have reduced their death rates far more quickly than their birth rates. Birth rates remain high because of the value that societies place on producing life. Death rates have declined fairly quickly because people are likely to adopt the means for controlling death soon after they become available. Lowering birth rates, however, runs counter to the value placed on producing life, so methods of controlling birth are not so quickly adopted. Many, many individual couples have to modify their orientations toward childbearing before the birth rate begins to go down. Generally, this takes a considerable period of time, during which the population grows very rapidly.

This point raises the question about whether decreases in fertility can be brought about more quickly so that population growth will be less rapid. Much of the debate about population growth centers around the question of how fertility can be lowered in populations where it remains high. We consider some major points of view about this question next.

Approaches to Reducing Fertility

Some experts on population have argued that it is not necessary to make any special efforts to lower fertility levels and slow population growth (Simon, 1981). However, this view is clearly in a minority; the broad consensus is that it would be better for individual countries and the world in general if the growth of population could be slowed. Three different views about reducing fertility can be identified: economic development, voluntary family-planning programs, and societal change.

Economic Development. The following slogan is often heard from the advocates of this view: *Economic development is the best contraceptive.* The assumption is that developing countries, which are now experiencing the highest growth rates, will experience a lowering of fertility when their economies become more urban, industrialized, and modernized. Economic development in these countries is expected to have the same effects on fertility as it did in Europe, the United States, and other developed countries. This view reflects a faith that the modern demographic transition will take its course, just as it did in the societies that modernized in the nineteenth and early twentieth centuries.

Some advocates of the economic development view urge developing countries to adopt free-enterprise, capitalist economies as a way of hastening economic development. Others take a Marxist view of economic development and urge developing countries to adopt socialist economic principles as a way of achieving economic development. Both economic views, while otherwise diametrically opposed, believe that economic development is the easy way to bring fertility rates down and thus slow population growth. Critics of this view point out that economic development is impeded by high birth rates that produce large numbers of children who are not economically productive.

Voluntary Family Planning. *Family-planning programs* have three basic elements: providing knowledge and information about reproductive physiology and contraceptive techniques; (2) providing contraceptive techniques; and (3) conducting a propaganda campaign that supports the small family ideal and the acceptability of contraception.

This approach is voluntary because the aim is not to coerce or force people to use contraception or limit their family size. In fact, in some countries, there is evidence that a substantial number of couples want fewer children than they have. Family planners

Family-planning programs typically include a propaganda campaign supporting the small-family ideal. This Indian billboard contrasts the happy mother who has two children with the distraught mother of four children.

generally believe that with a well-run, comprehensive family-planning program, the reduction in fertility rates will come from fewer births of unwanted children (Mauldin, 1983).

Societal Change. A number of demographers have pointed to the limitations of family-planning programs alone, arguing that without some basic societal changes, it will be difficult or impossible to reduce fertility. These advocates point out that most societies, especially many of the developing ones, have social institutions and cultural values that make large families both advantageous and desirable (Davis, 1967; Demerath, 1976).

The social institutions of many societies are arranged in such a way that children have economic value for parents. In many societies, even young children are able to contribute to the economic well-being of the family. This is especially true of children who live in rural areas who work in the fields, tend livestock, and take care of smaller children while their parents are working. Even in the urban areas of many Third World countries children begin working beside their parents at an early age. Later in life, children are economically beneficial because they will care for their elderly parents (Caldwell, 1982; Nugent, 1985).

Advocates of societal change argue that, in addition to family-planning programs, there must be reductions in these economic motivations for having children. For example, if compulsory education laws are passed, or if child-labor laws prohibit children from working, parents will have fewer economic motivations for large families. Similarly, if governments initiate some form of economic support in old age, such as a Social Security system, parents will be less motivated to have large families to care for them in old age.

Changes in the role of women in society can also be a factor that will reduce fertility levels. When women are isolated from participating in activities outside the home, their status (or worth) rests largely on their ability to bear and rear children. Under these societal and cultural conditions, where the primary role for women is motherhood, fertility is likely to remain high. To decrease fertility, societal changes can be made that will improve the status of women. Studies have shown that when women are given greater educational and employment opportunities, fertility declines (World Bank, 1984; Youssef, 1974).

Can Population Growth Be Slowed or Stopped?

Demographers have identified key ways of reducing fertility—through economic development, family-planning programs, and societal change—but the question still remains as to whether these solutions can be made to work in the real world. Many observers doubt that deeply embedded social institutions and cultural values can be changed among people who live in poverty, who are poorly educated, and who are bound by custom, superstition, and tradition. Although the efforts required to reduce fertility in many developing countries are difficult, accumulating evidence shows that when family-planning programs are combined with strategic societal changes, reduction can be accomplished.

Several countries that had high fertility rates 30 or 40 years ago, and were then considered less-developed countries, now have fertility levels similar to those of the United States and some European countries. Taiwan, South Korea, and Singapore are examples of countries that have lowered fertility through a combination of family-planning programs, some societal changes, and economic development. But the most important example is China, which, in the space of 40 years, has lowered its fertility to a level that would not have been anticipated in 1949. In 1984 and 1985 the crude birth rate of China (about 17.5) was at a level just slightly above that of the United States (16.0) (Hardee-Cleveland and Banister, 1988).

The Chinese reduction of fertility occurred, in part, because the government undertook extensive family-planning programs. The first program was started in 1954, and although it produced some decline in the birth rate, the most important family-planning program has been the well-publicized one-child program of the 1980s. But in addition, again going back to the 1950s, the Chinese made some societal changes that had the potential for reducing fertility. These included efforts to improve the status of women and laws to raise the age of marriage.

The one-child policy of China has often had a near-mandatory family-planning component, with close supervision of the contraceptive practices of couples and some penalties for disregarding the regulations. However, the one-child policy also includes some rewards, and these are consistent with what we have described as societal changes.

Couples who agree to have only one child are given greater monthly stipends, better housing, preferred status for their children in schools, and supplemental pensions when parents reach old age (Chen and Kols, 1982). These rewards, in combination with the family-planning program, have been most effective in the major cities of China and somewhat less effective in the rural areas (Hardee-Cleveland and Banister, 1988; Whyte and Gu, 1987).

Since 1983 the Chinese government has sometimes modified its enforcement of the one-child program, but the government still has the aim of keeping its growth rate at less than 1.5 percent until at least the year 2000. The important point to be drawn from the Chinese experience is that fertility can be lowered to the levels of Western societies, even before a substantial amount of economic development has been achieved (Whyte and Gu, 1987).

The Chinese experience, combined with those of a number of other developing countries, show that the present rate of population growth in the world can be reduced in a relatively short period of time. But it can only be done with family-planning efforts, societal changes to reduce motivations for fertility, and, to the extent possible, economic development. All of these efforts are most easily and successfully undertaken in cities and urban environments, as we have seen in the Chinese case. In the remainder of this chapter we examine the urbanization process, both in the United States and in other countries of the world.

Urbanization

The rise of cities has been one of the most dramatic and momentous developments in human history. Most of the classic European sociological theorists discussed in this book (Durkheim, Marx, Weber, and others) focused much of their attention on efforts to understand the changes transforming Western civilization during the nineteenth and early twentieth centuries. One of the central concerns was to analyze the unprecedented social changes accompanying the process of urbanization.

Key Concepts in Urbanization

Several key terms and concepts help to develop a sociological understanding of our increasingly urban society. First, we need to identify what we mean by the term *urban*. Often people consider the adjective *urban* to carry the same meaning as the noun *city*. However, the two terms need to be distinguished. A **city** can be defined as a relatively large, permanent, and spatially concentrated human settlement with a population far more economically interdependent and occupationally diverse than in agriculturally oriented rural areas.

City
A relatively large, densely populated, and diverse settlement of people

There are several bases for classifying a geographically defined area and its population as urban. The definitions developed by national census agencies generally focus solely on the numbers of persons living in a specified area. In the United States, any town, municipality, or other politically defined place with a population of 2,500 or more residents is classified as **urban** by the U.S. Census Bureau. However, this number differs substantially in other nations. For example, in Greece only areas with populations exceeding 10,000 are defined as urban; in Denmark, villages with only 250 residents are defined as urban; in Canada, the official definition of an urban place is one with 1,000 or more residents. In light of the confusion generated by such different standards, the United Nations has recommended a standard of 20,000 residents as the level of population necessary to characterize an area as urban. Sociologically this number makes sense because an urban place is one that has a complex array of social, economic, political, and cultural characteristics that are unlikely to emerge in places with only a few hundred or few thousand residents.

Urban
A place in which population exceeds a specific number of residents

A third concept—**urbanization**—refers primarily to the process by which an increasing percentage of a society's population comes to be located in urban areas. Thus, at any given time the extent of urbanization in a society is reflected by the proportion of the total population living in urban places. Urbanization occurs largely as a result of migration of formerly rural residents within a society to urban areas, or as a result of urban settlement patterns among immigrants from other societies. The resulting concentration of population in urban centers, in turn, contributes to an expansion of the scope of urban influence in modern societies. Indeed, the term *urbanization* is also used to refer to the concentration of economic activity, political administrative organization, communication networks, and political power in urban centers.

Urbanization
The process by which the population of a society becomes concentrated in cities

Urbanism refers to the "way of life" associated with urban residence. Much of the field of urban sociology has focused on ways in which living in urban places may affect the life styles, attitudes, and social relationships exhibited by urban dwellers. As noted later in this chapter, sociologists continue to debate whether urban life is characterized by negative or positive features. However, there is little doubt that the unique experiences associated with the urban environment do contribute to ways of life that are very different from those in rural areas and small towns.

Urbanism
The ways of life found in cities

World Urbanization

The first cities appear to have been established during the period of 3000 to 5000 B.C. Until very recently, however, only a small proportion of the world's people were city dwellers. As late as 1850 only 2 percent of the world's population lived in cities of more than 100,000 persons. Today, about 40 percent of the world population resides in urban places, and that number is expected to increase to more than one-half by the year 2,000 (Van der Tak, Haub, and Murphy, 1980).

The emergence of early urban settlement patterns seems to have depended upon two developments. The first was the existence of a surplus supply of food and other staples. The cultivation of grain, domestication of animals, and development of rudimentary agricultural technologies combined to create the **Agricultural Revolution.** These developments contributed to a shift from nomadic living patterns to residential stability, and allowed a family to produce more than it needed for its own survival. The

Agricultural Revolution
The shift to subsistence based on the cultivation of grains and domestication of animals

São Paulo, Brazil, and a number of other Third World cities (Mexico City, Rio de Janeiro, Shanghai, Beijing, Bombay, and Calcutta) are expected to be the fastest growing cities in the world during the next decade.

second development, related to the first, was the emergence of forms of social organization other than those based solely on family and kinship ties.

Until recently, most cities were very small by modern standards. Cities of more than 100,000 people were extremely rare, although some, such as Rome in the second century A.D., were substantially larger.

A major factor underlying the development of an urban world occurred in the late 1700s and early 1800s with the Industrial Revolution. As we noted in chapter 13, the Industrial Revolution occurred when machines were substituted for hand tools, and when inanimate sources of energy (water, steam, coal, oil) were used for power instead of humans or animals. The development of machines for production and the use of new energy sources greatly increased productivity and gave rise to the factory system. Large numbers of workers were needed to work in the factories, as well as to distribute and sell the manufactured products. At the same time, improvements in agricultural technology made it possible for fewer farmers to supply the needs of an expanding population.

World urban growth has been especially rapid since World War II. The world's urban population grew from 724 million in 1950 to 1½ billion in 1975, and it is projected to exceed 3 billion by 2000. The number of cities with over 1 million inhabitants has tripled in the last 35 years; in 1950 only 78 urban centers had more than 1 million inhabitants, but by 1985 more than 258 metropolises exceeded this size (Dogan and Kasarda, 1988, p. 13). By 1980 there were 28 metropolitan areas in the world with over 5 million people; ten, with over 10 million; and three, with over 15 million (Hall, 1984, p. 3). Thus the last half of the twentieth century has witnessed "the greatest flowering of cities and urban life in world history" (Hall, 1984).

As table 17–2 shows, the world's largest cities are found today on every continent except Australia. They are located in both developed countries, such as the United States, France, and Japan, and in developing countries, such as Indonesia (Jakarta), India (Calcutta and Bombay), and Iraq (Baghdad). By the year 2000 two-thirds of the world's urban population will be located in developing countries (Dogan and Kasarda, 1988).

Mexico City is an important illustrative case of a major and growing city in a developing country. This city had a population of about 3 million in 1950, which grew to 15 million in 1980. It is estimated that its population will reach nearly 26 million by 2000, making it the largest city in human history. Similar dramatic increases in growth are projected for other Third World cities such as São Paulo and Rio de Janeiro, Brazil; Shanghai and Beijing, China; and Bombay and Calcutta, India (Hall, 1984) (see table 17–2).

Table 17–2. World's Ten Largest Urban Areas, 1985 and 2000

1985

Urban Area	Population (in millions)
Tokyo-Yokohama, Japan	18.8
Mexico City, Mexico	17.3
São Paulo, Brazil	15.9
New York, United States	15.6
Shanghai, China	12.0
Calcutta, India	11.0
Buenos Aires, Argentina	10.9
Rio de Janeiro, Brazil	10.4
London, United Kingdom	10.4
Seoul, Republic of Korea	10.3

2000

Urban Area	Population (in millions)
Mexico City, Mexico	25.8
São Paulo, Brazil	24.0
Tokyo-Yokohama, Japan	20.2
Calcutta, India	16.5
Bombay, India	16.0
New York, United States	15.8
Shanghai, China	14.3
Seoul, Republic of Korea	13.8
Tehran, Iran	13.6
Rio de Janeiro, Brazil	13.3

Source: United Nations. "World Population Trends and Policies, 1987." *Population Studies* No. 103, New York, United Nations, 1988, p. 184.

Urban Development in the United States

In 1790, when the first U.S. Census was taken, only one in 20 Americans (5 percent) was an urban resident. Since that time, the urban proportion of the population has increased in every decade except one (1810–1820). By 1980 nearly three-fourths (73.7 percent) of the U.S. population was urban (see figure 17–4). The American population has become so concentrated that by 1980 the nation's urban residents occupied less than 2 percent of the land in the United States.

Preindustrial Cities

The urban proportion of the American population remained quite low until well into the nineteenth century. Preindustrial cities were usually quite small, and they were predominantly commercial and shipping centers. The largest cities were East Coast seaports; Boston, for example, led the country in size and importance in 1743 with a population of slightly more than 16,000. In 1775, just before the American Revolution, Philadelphia's population of 40,000 made it the nation's largest city. In 1800, only six

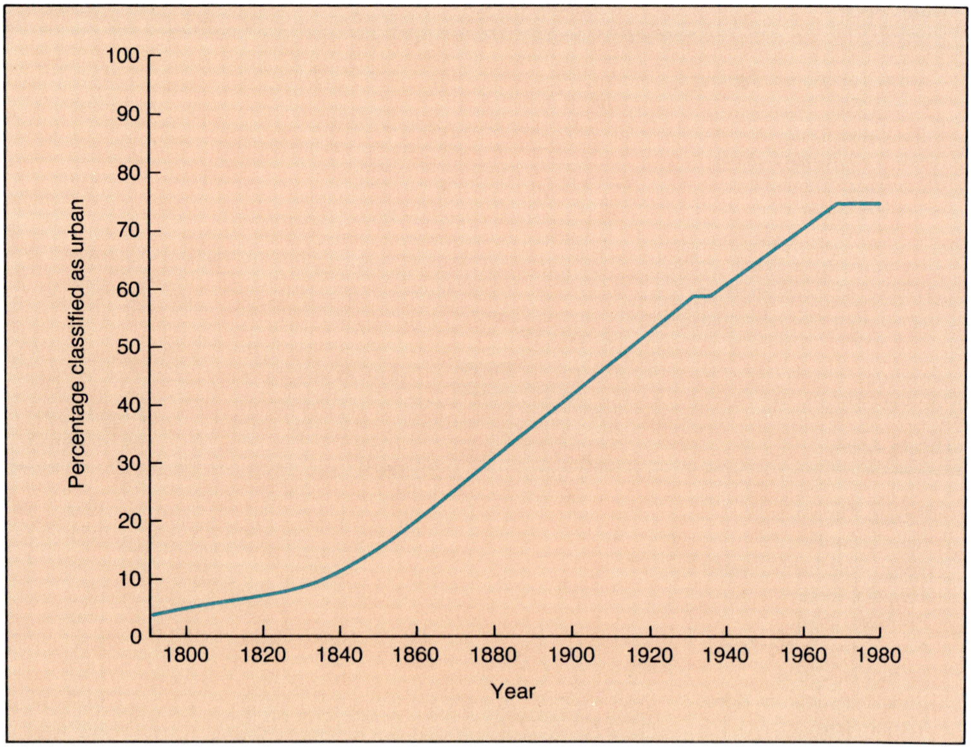

Figure 17–4. Urban Population of the United States: 1790–1980. (*Sources:* U.S. Bureau of the Census, *Statistical Abstract of the United States, 1961 and 1972*, pp. 14, 16; U.S. Bureau of the Census, *U.S. Commerce Dept. News*, August 13, 1981.)

cities in the United States had more than 8,000 residents (Bridenbaugh, 1938; Gist and Fava, 1974, p. 63).

Industrial Cities

By the beginning of the twentieth century the United States had become the foremost industrial nation in the world, and the rapid urbanization of the country paralleled its increasing industrialization. The urban-industrial period between 1850 and 1920 marked the era of America's most dramatic urban growth. The urban portion of the total population rose from less than one-sixth (15 percent) in 1850 to over half (51.2 percent) by 1920. By 1920 New York City had more than 5.5 million inhabitants, and Philadelphia, nearly 2 million. Chicago grew from less than 4,000 in 1830 to over 2 million in 1910.

Several factors contributed to this dramatic spurt in American urbanization. First, transportation improvements such as the construction of extensive inland canal systems and the building of transcontinental railroads made it easier to ship both raw materials and agricultural products. Second, manufacturing grew as the basis of urban economies. Unlike handicrafts and other home-based economic activities of the preindustrial city, manufacturing required the employment of large numbers of people in factories. The demand for unskilled factory labor attracted many residents from rural areas into the major industrial cities. By 1910 at least one-third of the total urban population consisted of native-born Americans who had migrated from rural America.

As industrial growth continued, factory operators turned to European immigrants to provide an abundant and cheap labor supply. During the first decade of the twentieth century about 1 million immigrants entered the United States each year. The influx of foreign-born residents created in most American cities a mosaic of immigrant neighborhoods, located in distinct areas where cheap housing was within walking distance of work.

Newcomers of each immigrant wave moved from one urban neighborhood to another as their social and economic status changed. Areas deserted by one ethnic group were often quickly taken over by members of another. For example, in the years following the Civil War, the Irish and Germans of New York moved from the Lower East Side to areas of north Manhattan and Brooklyn. Italians moved into the old Irish neighborhoods, while Russian and Polish Jews occupied the formerly German districts (Glaab and Brown, 1967, p. 139). **Invasion-succession** is the term used by sociologists to identify the process whereby one group moves to a different area and is replaced by another.

Invasion-succession The process whereby one group moves out and is replaced by another group

Although the immigrant neighborhoods usually contained a high proportion of one particular ethnic group, they were never entirely homogeneous. In contrast, urban black neighborhoods, which grew rapidly in the twentieth century, tended to be much more homogeneous and permanent. Social restrictions on geographical and social mobility for blacks contributed to the emergence of racially distinct cities within cities, where proportions of black population reached as high as 95 percent. By 1920 the enduring black ghetto had become firmly established in most American cities.

Urban Differentiation. As cities grew in size and diversity, areas within them became increasingly specialized and differentiated. Rather than locating residential and commercial properties in the same neighborhood, cities came to be characterized by a distinct business district, a wholesale district, a manufacturing district, and so on.

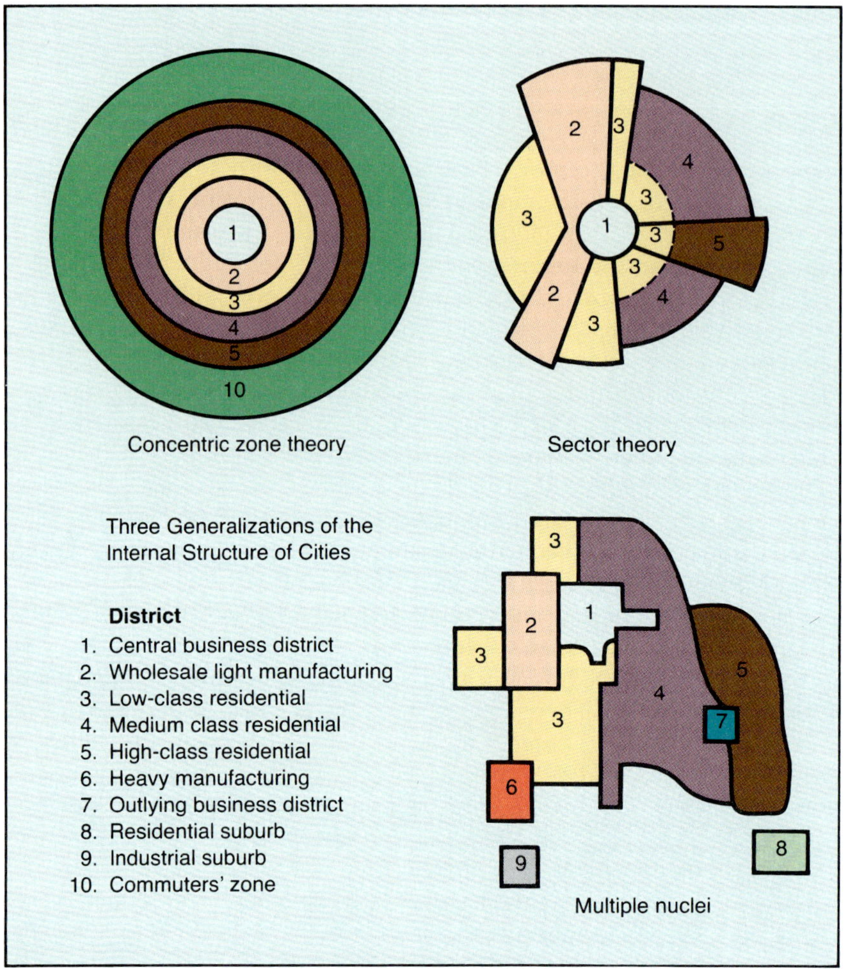

Figure 17–5. Patterns of Urban Spatial Differentiation. (*Source:* Chauncy Harris and Edward Ullman, "The Nature of Cities," *Annals of the American Academy of Political and Social Sciences* 242, November 1945, p. 13.)

Concentric zone model
A model of urban development involving a series of successive rings surrounding a central business district

During the first four decades of the twentieth century, numerous sociologists worked to develop general theories to explain the patterns of urban spatial differentiation. The **concentric zone model** (Park et al., 1925) suggested that urban differentiation occurred through the development of unique zones of land-use types, organized in successive rings around the city center. As indicated in figure 17–5, this approach identified a central business district at the core of the city, representing the economic center in which retail stores, theaters, hotels, banks, and office buildings were concentrated. Adjacent to this was the "zone of transition," an area of older warehouses, factories, and the deteriorating residential neighborhoods in which immigrant populations were initially concentrated. Next came the "zone of workingmen's homes," an area characterized by neighborhoods often populated by second-generation and third-generation immigrant families. The fourth zone, called the "residential zone," was characterized primarily by middle-class residential neighborhoods. Finally, at the outer edge of the city were the upper-class residential areas and the "commuter zone," representing the earliest suburbs, in which upper-middle-class and upper-class populations resided.

Although the concentric zone model appeared to provide a fairly accurate depiction of urban differentiation in Chicago during the early twentieth century, sociologists who focused on other urban settings discovered that in many instances urban development patterns exhibited different characteristics. One attempt to account for such differences was the **sector model** (Hoyt, 1939), which focused on the importance of major transportation arteries such as streets and trolley lines as key determinants of development patterns, resulting in the appearance of wedge-shaped areas of unique land uses (see figure 17–5). A third approach, the **multiple nuclei model** (Harris and Ullman, 1945), suggested that in many cities a number of distinct centers of activity and land use may develop. As figure 17–5 illustrates, this approach focused on the importance of several different "nuclei" rather than one main urban core as the center for development patterns.

Sector model
A model of urban development reflecting the influence of transportation paths

Multiple nuclei model
A model of urban development characterized by several distinct centers of activity

The Metropolis

As American cities expanded and became differentiated, they also became increasingly intertwined with the outlying areas that surrounded them. In the process, urban areas became decentralized—that is, spread over a much broader geographic area. The **metropolis**—a large urban area containing a central city and surrounding communities that are economically and socially linked to the central city—is an urban form that has emerged in American society since approximately 1920. During the metropolitan period cities have been restructured and have become increasingly decentralized as both people and many of the cities' basic activities have been relocated.

Metropolis
An urban area containing a central city and surrounding communities economically and politically linked to it

Recognizing that many central cities and their adjacent communities have become integrated economically and socially, the United States Bureau of the Census has adopted a measure called a Metropolitan Statistical Area. A **Metropolitan Statistical Area (MSA)** is a geographic area (usually a county or series of counties) of at least 100,000 residents that includes a center city of 50,000 or more people. Presently, more than three-fourths of the United States' population lives in the nation's 281 MSAs (U.S. Bureau of the Census, 1987b, p. 872–873).

Metropolitan Statistical Area (MSA)
A U.S. Census Bureau measure of a metropolitan area

In several parts of the country, MSAs have grown so large that the outer ring of one MSA area expands and ultimately overlaps with the outer ring of a neighboring one. The result is an unbroken chain of urban and suburban development, sometimes stretching for hundreds of miles. Urban scholars have referred to this continuous urban sprawl as a **megalopolis** (Gottman, 1961). As of 1986, the United States Bureau of the Census had identified 21 megalopolitan areas. The largest megalopolis in the United States today—familiarly known as the "Boston-Washington corridor"—stretches along the northeastern seaboard and encompasses more than 53,000 square miles from southern New Hampshire to northern Virginia. The trend toward contiguous urban development has also been pronounced in California and Florida and, to a lesser degree, around the Great Lakes and the Northwest coastline. Although sociologists or urban planners find it difficult to predict accurately future urban patterns, they have projected that by the year 2000, the United States will have at least 25 megalopolitan areas (see figure 17–6).

Megalopolis
Continuous urban sprawl formed when the outer rings of adjacent metropolitan areas merge

Figure 17–6. Megalopolis in the Year 2000. (*Source:* Presidential Commission on Population Growth and the American Future, *Population Growth and the American Future* (Washington, D.C.: United States Government Printing Office, 1972), p. 33.)

Suburbanization

Suburbs
Urban areas adjacent to but beyond the political boundaries of a city

Decentralization—of population, business, and industry—has, therefore, been the distinguishing feature of metropolitan America. This decentralization has usually been associated with the growth of **suburbs,** which are the urban areas adjacent to, but beyond, the political boundaries of a city. Although suburbs began to emerge in some areas before the turn of the twentieth century, suburban growth has been most pronounced since World War II. Since then the suburban population has grown much more rapidly than the population of central cities. In 1940 only about 17 percent of

Americans lived in suburbs; by 1980 almost one-half (46 percent) of the American population resided in suburban areas.

A prominent feature of the residential expansion into areas formerly at the periphery of central cities has been the selectivity of the suburbanization process: it has been primarily a middle-class phenomenon. Prompted by problems of urban decay and pollution, increasing concern over urban violence, and conflicts and tensions between minority groups and the white majority, many urban dwellers have fled to suburbia in search of cleaner air, lower crime rates, better schools, and affordable single-family housing (Fischer, 1984).

However, the rapid post-World War II suburbanization of the United States was greatly aided by both private enterprise and government programs. For example, use of the automobile, which sparked the suburbanization of modern America, as the primary means of transportation (instead of mass transit systems) reflected the impact of certain interest groups on public policy (Gottdiener and Feagin, 1988, p. 181). Other factors influencing metropolitan expansion included cheap energy, the investments of billions of federal dollars in massive urban expressways and interstate highway systems, and the provision of federally supported, low-interest mortgage programs that encouraged new suburban housing developments.

Policies that facilitated suburbanization also increased racial and class polarization. As a result of "white flight" from the central cities, suburbs have generally been overwhelmingly white and middle class, while the central cities have been left to racial minorities and the poor. Despite laws that should ensure fair housing practices, racial minorities—especially blacks—have been prevented from entering the suburbs by deliberate exclusionary housing practices, exclusionary zoning ordinances, and the persistence of a stratification system that blocks social mobility for the poor and minorities.

The rapid growth of suburbs over the last fifty years has been overwhelmingly white and middle class, as the people in these categories sought to escape a variety of urban problems. This pattern has been described as "white flight" from the central cities.

In 1980 about 75 percent of American blacks lived in urban central city areas. In contrast, only 25 percent of white Americans lived in central cities (Logan and Schneider, 1984).

Although suburbs have frequently been portrayed simply as places where people live, business and industry have also moved out of the central city. The past three decades have seen the decline of central-city manufacturing, retail, and wholesale enterprises, especially in the North. In the process, central cities have been transformed from goods-producing and -processing centers to information-producing and -processing centers. As a result, blue-collar and relatively unskilled jobs have declined significantly, while white-collar, information-processing jobs requiring substantial education have increased.

Between 1948 and 1977 the country's 12 largest Northern cities lost more than 2 million jobs, most of them in manufacturing. During the same period the suburbs of these cities added nearly 4 million private sector jobs (Kasarda, 1985). Because of the movement of both population and business to the urban fringe, many central city manufacturing districts have become virtual wastelands of empty buildings and closed stores.

Today the majority of people who live in suburbs also work there. Facilitated especially by interlocking expressways and advances in communications technology, twice as many workers in 1982 commuted *between* suburbs than commuted from suburbs to central cities (Leinberger and Lockwood, 1986). Industrial parks, real estate developments, shopping malls, and business offices have spread over the landscape of suburban and even outlying non-metropolitan areas.

Some of the decentralization of urban populations has seen residents moving into small towns beyond metropolitan areas. During the decade of the 1970s and for much of the 1980s areas outside of existing metropolitan areas grew more rapidly than either central cities or suburbs (Kasarda, 1980; Kowinski, 1980). Most rural workers are employed in urban-type occupations. Indeed, agricultural employment today represents less than 10 percent of all non-metropolitan jobs (Frisbee and Kasarda, 1988).

Recent Counter-trends. As manufacturing has fled the central city, however, a recent counter-trend of growth has developed in highly skilled, information-processing service occupations. For example, by 1980 the cities of New York and Boston had more people employed in knowledge-intensive, information-processing occupations than in manufacturing, construction, retail, and wholesale industries combined, a dramatic change from 30 years earlier when the traditional urban industries outnumbered information-processing occupations by three to one (Kasarda, 1985).

Some observers interpret these trends as indications that the fortunes of the city will soon improve. Massive urban redevelopment projects, including large hotels, offices, civic centers, entertainment areas, restaurants, and retail shopping areas, sometimes within one "megastructure," have appeared in a number of cities. Boston's Quincy Market, Baltimore's Inner Harbor, San Francisco's Ghirardelli Square, Detroit's Renaissance Center, and Chicago's Water Tower Palace illustrate such urban revitalization.

The growth of high-rise administrative buildings constructed during the 1970s and 1980s symbolizes the recent growth in information-processing service occupations. Manufacturing, wholesale trade, and retail activities, which provided the economic base for cities in an earlier period, required large areas for the work of their employees. These space requirements could only be met with buildings spread horizontally over large areas. Information-processing enterprises, on the other hand, can be carried out efficiently in small spaces. "Thus people who process information can be stacked, layer after layer, in downtown office towers with resulting proximity actually increasing the productivity of those whose activities require an extensive amount of nonroutine, face-to-face interaction" (Frisbee and Kasarda, 1988, p. 636).

In addition to the development of some massive, urban, commercial complexes, other factors have contributed to changes in the social composition of American cities. First, the social composition of the suburbs is changing. The most rapid period of suburban development coincided with the post-World War II baby boom. Young couples moved to the suburbs to raise their children in a more "wholesome" and socially homogeneous environment. Moreover, the suburban life style strongly emphasized traditional male and female gender roles. Today, however, more young women are rejecting the traditional role of housewife in favor of white-collar and professional occupations. Declines in the birth rate and in household size make large suburban homes both impractical and unattractive for many people. Increasing numbers of young adults are choosing to live in high-density settings such as condominiums and central city apartments, rather than in single-family dwellings.

People working in professional, managerial, administrative, and information-processing jobs in central city office complexes often seek housing close to their work. Moreover, such people are particularly attracted to the way of life offered by the city. The amenities of urban life, including its restaurants, clubs, parks, zoos, theaters, cultural activities, and sporting events, provide a stimulating and exciting range of opportunities often unavailable in the suburbs. Seeking to capitalize on these amenities, an "urban gentry" of young, affluent, business and professional people have, in some instances, moved into declining urban neighborhoods and restored their deteriorating stock of housing. This process of urban residential revitalization of older neighborhoods is known as **gentrification** (Zukin, 1987).

Gentrification
The process of residential revitalization of older urban neighborhoods

However, many central city residents, especially minorities, have not benefited from these changes in American cities. First, although service sector jobs have grown, many central city residents lack the educational qualifications to take advantage of them. Instead, a mismatch has developed between the educational qualifications required for the knowledge-intensive jobs being created in the service sector and the educational skills of the minorities who make up an increasing proportion of the population of central cities. The situation in today's central cities is much different from that in central cities in the industrial period when widespread opportunities existed for those with little education and few skills. This mismatch between increasing educational requirements for urban employment and the educational attainments of central city residents represents one of the major dilemmas for urban social policy today (Kasarda, 1989).

Second, despite highly publicized revitalization efforts, the prospects for an urban renaissance are at best uncertain. Between 1968 and 1979 gentrification affected only a small fraction—less than 1 percent—of central city housing units. Nearly three-fourths of those who moved into restored housing units were intracity movers, not suburbanites who had moved to the city (Kasarda, 1980).

Third, urban redevelopment efforts, including the creation of urban megastructures and gentrification, have contributed to the displacement of substantial numbers of urban elderly and low-income residents (LeGates and Murphy, 1984; LeGates and Hartman, 1986). The result has been the disruption of long-established and socially integrated neighborhoods, forcing many residents to experience financial distress as they look for

Young, affluent business and professional people often find the amenities of the central city attractive. They have buildings and houses in deteriorating areas refurbished and made into attractive homes; this process is called gentrification.

new homes in housing markets characterized by an increasingly short supply of low-income housing (Hopkins, 1985). In a study of the effects of gentrification in ten major American cities, Nelson (1988) found that in most cities poor residents were displaced from gentrifying areas into lower class areas, contributing to new concentrations of poverty.

The Impact of Urban Life

Negative Views

Earlier we discussed the changes accompanying the rapid urbanization of Western society, in particular of the United States during the late nineteenth and early twentieth centuries. We noted that modern sociology emerged from the work of people who tried to understand and explain these changes. Most sociologists who considered the impact of increasing urbanization did not respond to it merely as disinterested social scientists. They themselves were products of societies being rapidly transformed, and in many instances they tended to view the passing of traditional society with nostalgia. The negative view of urban life, which for many years dominated sociological perspectives on the city, reflected in many respects the preference for a rural society that the early sociologists saw being undermined by the forces of modernization—by industrialization, bureaucratization, and urbanization.

As we noted in chapter 4, Ferdinand Toennies used the terms *gemeinschaft* and *gesellschaft* to distinguish the social relations characteristic of rural, traditional societies and modern, urban societies. *Gemeinschaft* communities are characterized by personalized, face-to-face relationships such as those in the family, the rural village, and the small town. *Gesellschaft* societies, in contrast, are associated with impersonal and distant relationships, the kind we associate with urban life. In *gemeinschaft* communities, social relationships are valued as ends in themselves. In *gesellschaft* communities, social relationships are little more than means to other ends; e.g., people associate only with those who reward them with money, goods, or services (Toennies, 1857/1957).

One of the earliest and most influential sociological analyses of the city was made by the German sociologist Georg Simmel (1903/1971). Primarily concerned with the psychological effects of urban society on individuals, Simmel observed that life in cities (as contrasted with life in small towns and rural areas) exposes people to a greater variety and intensity of stimuli. He argued that the more hectic pace and intensity of city life produce more psychological stress than the slower, less hectic, and more relaxed pace of rural life.

Simmel concluded that the greater psychic stress of urban life affects the emotional and intellectual character of urban residents. In attempting to adapt to and protect themselves from stresses created by the profusion of people and environmental stimuli about them, urban residents may suppress their emotions and follow only their intellect in deciding how to act. As a consequence, urban dwellers develop an emotional restraint or insensitivity in their dealings with others. They develop rational standards of calculation, punctuality, and exactness so that some semblance of order can be maintained within a chaotic array of events and social contacts. In Simmel's view, the more leisurely pace and more intimate nature of social life in rural areas enable people to be more spontaneous and less calculating in their personal relations than is characteristic of

Drawing by M. Stevens; © 1987 The New Yorker Magazine, Inc.

"Could you walk a little faster, buddy? This is New York."

urbanites. Moreover, as urbanites are subjected to a barrage of stimuli, events, and individual differences, they become less likely to be shocked or excited by new, unusual, and bizarre events.

Simmel also recognized that cities allow a greater expression of personal freedom than do rural communities. Rural communities are apt to have restrictive social norms and conservative attitudes about social diversity, and may severely restrict the expression of individual differences and insure that those people who do not conform to the norms will feel social isolation from those who do. However, Simmel did not feel that this increased freedom necessarily enhanced the quality of human life. On the contrary, he contended that increased individual freedom tends to heighten the urbanite's feelings of social isolation and loneliness in the midst of a social milieu characterized by impersonality and anonymity, rather than intimacy and primary group ties.

Challenges to the Negative View

Simmel's negative perspective of urban life has been shared by several prominent American sociologists. In recent years, however, an increasing number of sociologists have argued for a more balanced assessment of the effects of urban life. Two closely related perspectives—the compositional and the subcultural approaches to urbanism—have challenged the idea that cities inevitably produce psychological distress and other dehumanizing effects.

Compositional theory of urbanism
A model that emphasizes the importance of social class, ethnicity, and life cycle stage in determining urban social relationships

The **compositional theory of urbanism** emphasizes the positive aspects of the cosmopolitanism and diversity that characterize city life. Compositionalists view the city as a mosaic of different social worlds based on kinship, neighborhood, ethnicity, occupation, common interests, and life style. The presence of these social worlds allows intimate, primary group relations to exist independently of the broader urban environment, affording protection against the city's anonymity and the psychological stresses emphasized by Simmel.

From the compositional perspective, behaviors and experiences of urbanites are shaped not so much by the size, density, or social diversity of the urban population as by the characteristics—including social class position, stage in the life cycle, and ethnic identity—of those who live there.

Even in the largest cities people create and live within communities—"urban villages"—that prevent them from feeling socially isolated. The traditional negative perspective of urbanism fails to distinguish how people act in public settings and how they act in more private contexts. Claude Fischer (1981) has suggested that in the "public world," urbanites are confronted by numerous others who are strangers and who are often perceived as "strange" because of the cultural diversity of the urban milieu. Therefore, in public contexts, most urban dwellers do tend to feel and act like anonymous, detached individuals.

In the "private world" of interactions among family and friends, however, social relations characterized by primary associations and mutual support and assistance tend to flourish. Indeed, the "personal communities" provided by the networks of association among urban dwellers appear to provide a majority of urbanites with greater opportunities for social attachments than may exist among small-town and rural dwellers (Fischer, 1982; Wellman, 1979).

Subcultural theory of urbanism
A model that emphasizes how the city's size, density, and diversity create a variety of subcultures

The **subcultural theory of urbanism** argues that a city's size, density, and diversity do affect the urban experience, but in a positive way. Intimate social worlds

Arts and crafts fairs that exhibit the work of local artists and artisans thrive in an urban environment. For many people, the city has many positive features that make it a desirable place to live.

are *created* and *enhanced* in an urban milieu, not broken down, as the critics of urban life argue. The urban environment provides opportunities to create a variety of meaningful subcultures (for example, ethnic, artistic, religious, homosexual, literary, intellectual) that could not develop in smaller communities because there would not be a sufficient number—a critical mass—of similarly interested individuals. Urbanism can thus foster unconventional and deviant behavior, not because an impersonal city produces anomie and undermines social control but because it provides an environment in which subcultures identified as deviant by the larger society can be created and thrive. The subcultural and compositional perspectives differ slightly in their focus but both demonstrate ways in which personal relationships are sustained and fostered in an urban environment.

In conclusion, the negative view of the city reflects a general tendency among both the American public and social scientists to exaggerate and romanticize the virtues of a rural existence, to which cities are often contrasted. Urban life certainly has its problems, but so do suburban and rural life. To assess accurately the effects of urbanism, we must examine them carefully and systematically.

Summary

Demography is the scientific study of population. The three basic processes of population are fertility (childbearing), mortality (death), and migration (change of residence). Age and sex are the two major demographic characteristics of population.

Fertility is a socially motivated behavior, as the extremes in childbearing behavior (the Hutterites, the Shakers, and the Rappites) illustrate. Childbearing in the United

States today is at its lowest rate in history. Differences in fertility can still be found between religious, racial, ethnic, and socioeconomic status groups.

Mortality is influenced by one's social position and personal life style. Migration shapes the growth and development of different parts of the country, and has generally been from rural to urban places, and from east to west in the United States.

The most far-reaching population issue today is the rapid growth of the world's population. The "population explosion" is a recent phenomenon in demographic history, having begun with the modernization and industrialization of various European states in the seventeenth and eighteenth centuries and accelerated greatly in the twentieth century. The theory of the Modern Demographic Transition holds that populations grow rapidly during the early stages of modernization because the death rate declines while the birth rate remains high. The rapid rate of the world's population growth today stems from the fact that the death rates in many of the developing countries have dropped while the birth rates remain high or very high.

Responses to the rapid growth of the world's population are varied. One view is that "economic development is the best contraceptive," so emphasis should be placed on development, and fertility declines will follow. A second view is the family-planning approach, which emphasizes contraception, education, and propaganda as ways of reducing fertility. A third view would combine the family-planning approach with societal changes to reduce motivations for childbearing. Contemporary China is an exemplar of the latter approach to reducing fertility.

Cities are a relatively recent form of human organization, although some did appear soon after the Agricultural Revolution. In more recent times the Industrial Revolution sparked the growth of cities. The pace of urban growth has been especially pronounced since World War II. Recent urban growth has been most rapid in Third World countries.

In the United States, industrialization in the nineteenth and early twentieth centuries led to urbanization. The process of suburbanization has seen the growth of primarily white suburbs and the abandonment of the central cities to minority residents and the poor. Business and industry have also been part of the flight to the suburbs, creating severe economic problems for the central cities. As suburban metropolitan fringes have moved farther away from central cities, they have overlapped with the fringes of other metropolitan areas, creating a continuous metropolitan complex known as a megalopolis.

Recently, counter-trends to the decentralization of American urban areas have been noted. Urban redevelopment projects in many cities have produced massive office buildings in which to conduct the growing number of central-city service jobs. Some cities have also experienced gentrification, but this process has not benefited all city residents, especially minorities and the poor.

The long-standing negative perception of urban life is being challenged today. Sociologists who emphasize a more balanced portrait of the city argue that the city's anonymity has not led to social anarchy and personal isolation. Instead, the city offers a "mosaic of social worlds," opportunities for the creation of intimate associations and communities based on kinship, neighborhood, ethnicity, occupation, or life style.

CRITICAL THINKING

1. Explain how a demographic phenomenon, such as the baby boom, can have a drastic effect on a variety of factors in a society.
2. What general trends in fertility are evident in the United States? The developed world? The developing world?
3. What factors might influence the rate of fertility in a given society? Give examples to support your ideas.
4. What three basic processes determine population size? Explain how each is affected by social influences.
5. What is the population explosion? Explain how this phenomenon is unprecedented in human history. Why should it concern you?
6. Speculate on the social effect of population measures such as the one-child policy in China. How would such measures affect social institutions, such as the family, education, and the economy?
7. Distinguish among the terms *urban, urbanization,* and *urbanism.*
8. Why is the Industrial Revolution considered to be a major factor in the development of urbanization?
9. Where are the ten largest urban areas in the world concentrated? In your opinion, is this a positive or negative phenomenon?
10. Describe the general history of urbanization in the United States. What general theories exist to explain the patterns of urban spatial differentiation? Which best describes the urban area closest to you?

CHAPTER 18

Social Change, Collective Behavior, and Social Movements

"You can't teach an old dog new tricks." "Can a leopard change its spots?" "The more things change, the more they stay the same." Such folk sayings suggest that change is difficult and relatively rare. But, as we have seen throughout this book, change is pervasive. Indeed, our experience of the world teaches us that we live in the midst of ongoing change.

We have only to ask our parents or grandparents to describe life when they were growing up. Their descriptions of work, education, entertainment, and technology are apt to be very different from what we experience today. We can also compare a current map of Africa with one published in 1950, where we will see that many of today's countries were not in existence 40 years ago. As we saw in chapter 16, relations between the United States and the Soviet Union have undergone dramatic changes in the last decade. Some observers are even saying that the "cold war," which has threatened our existence over the last 40 years, is over. The pace of change in East-West relations is, at the moment, almost dizzying (Goldman, 1987). Rather than living in a relatively changeless world, it appears at times that we live in an age in which everything that had been nailed down is coming loose.

In this chapter—building on prior discussions of social theory, bureaucracy, and culture—we look more closely at the nature of social change, at social movements, and at people's experiences of change.

The Meaning of Change

Social Change Defined

We define **social change** as variations over time in the relationships among individuals, groups, cultures, and societies. Social change is pervasive; all "of social life is continually changing" (Lauer, 1982, p. 4; Harper, 1989). In the family, for example, recent changes include the surge of married women and mothers into the labor force, and the increasing proportion of nontraditional living arrangements (such as an unmarried couple's living together). At the societal level, crime rates, population statistics, distribution of income, and level of technological development register measurable shifts. At the global level, trade patterns, political alliances, and the distribution of wealth take new shapes over time.

Social change
Variations over time in the relationships among individuals, groups, cultures, and societies

Patterns of Change

Change is not a purely haphazard process, but rarely are its patterns represented by smooth lines or curves. Patterns of change fall into three broad categories: a general trend (upward or downward), cyclic variations, and irregular or random variations. A general trend designates a long-term tendency to increase or decrease. Cyclic variations may occur around seasons or over periods of years or even centuries. Irregular variations are often tied to particular events, such as natural disasters, wars, or inventions. The American economy, for example, has grown over the past century (an upward trend), has had a series of booms and recessions (cyclic variations), and has also had some short-term reversals and sudden surges (irregular and random variations).

At every level of human life (family, society, and the world), then, trends, cycles, and variations help us to identify changes that have occurred, changes that are currently occurring, and changes likely to occur in the future. Change is pervasive.

Theories of Change

In Aldous Huxley's *Brave New World*, one of the leaders of the Western world calls change a "menace." In the novel, the rulers of the society did not want any change. Wary of any invention or innovation, they cherished stability above all else. They believed that maintaining the social order as it was would keep them secure and happy. Had Huxley's characters understood history, they would have known that they could never bring human society into a state of changeless stability. Societies change as inexorably as the ocean tide comes in.

How do we account for the multitude of changes at the various levels of social life? Sociologists as well as other social scientists try to answer this question. Economists, political scientists, anthropologists, and psychologists tend to focus on a particular segment of society—the economy, political institutions, culture, or individual personalities. Sociologists try to understand the totality—how the social structure and culture change over time. They tend to look at change in terms of the social factors involved. They explore such factors as internal systemic strains and contradictions, interpersonal and intergroup processes such as conflict, technological developments, and institutional arrangements.

To begin to understand social change, some theorists have looked at the broad sweep of history. Others have focused on structure and process in the social order. In chapter 1 we discussed the Marxist perspective that identifies inherent contradictions in the social order as the driving mechanism of change throughout human history. We also looked at structural-functionalism, that posited more stability than change in social systems. Functionalists acknowledge that social systems change, but generally they argue that the forces tending toward stability are stronger than the forces tending toward change. In addition to these two perspectives, three other theories of change have been influential in sociology—cyclic theory, evolutionary theory, and conflict theory. We examine each type through a representative theorist.

Cyclic Theory

Cyclic theory
Change seen as an ongoing series of recurring cultural emphases

Cyclic theory conceptualizes change as an ongoing series of cycles rather than as a process with some kind of direction. The Greeks, Romans, and Chinese, among others, viewed history in terms of great cycles rather than in terms of progress or decline.

Pitirim Sorokin, a sociologist who formulated a cyclic theory of change, investigated the whole field of human culture, including art, science, literature, technology, philosophy, and law. He concluded that culture is composed of a series of parts that are unified around a fundamental principle and a basic value (Sorokin, 1941, p. 17). In any given age, more than one society can exhibit the same principle or basic value. The United States, Canada, and Western Europe could be one "culture" in Sorokin's terms because all of these societies are essentially materialistic. In a materialistic culture, science, art, literature, and all other cultural areas will be materialistic. Sorokin called the materialistic culture *sensate*. A **sensate culture** is one pervaded by the principle that the material or sensory world is the true reality and value. A second type is the **ideational culture,** pervaded by the principle that a supersensory or nonmaterial world is the true reality and the highest value. The third type, the **idealistic culture,** combines the other two in an integrated blend of the supersensory and the sensory (nonmaterial and material). Sorokin argued that medieval Europe, with its belief that the sensory world is only a transitional step on the way to the eternal City of God, typified an ideational culture, while the modern West typifies the sensate culture.

Sensate culture
Culture dominated by the principle that the sensory (material) world is the only true reality

Ideational culture
Culture dominated by the principle that supersensory (nonmaterial) world is the only true reality

Idealistic culture
Culture that blends supersensory and sensory (nonmaterial and material)

All of history, according to Sorokin, is a cyclic variation among the three types of cultures. Cultures grow and decline, and give way to one of the other types of culture. Our own Western system, he insisted, is not only sensate but an "overripe" sensate culture, ready to give way to an ideational or idealistic type. In the late 1930s, Sorokin (1957, pp. 699–701) forecast a number of dire developments that would signal the downfall of our sensate culture. Among them were an increasing loss of moral sensitivity, a mechanistic view of humans, the use of force and deception to maintain social order, the disintegration of the family, an obsession with quantity rather than quality, and an increase in such things as suicide, mental illness, and crime. In his analysis, these lamentable developments do not mean the demise of civilization but merely the transition to an ideational or idealistic culture, and a new period of growth and development in a more spiritual world.

Cyclic theory contributes to our understanding of change by identifying one important pattern of change in social life. Cyclic variations occur at every level of life, from the individual to the global. At the individual level, for example, cyclic variations appear in physiological functions, such as diurnal variations in body temperature and blood pressure. A great variety of social phenomena have been charted and shown to vary cyclically over time, including wars, crime, marriage and birth rates, and religious and scientific activity.

Cyclic theory, however, does not account for all of the important factors in charge. Sorokin, in particular, fails to consider social-psychological factors. His theory casts people as virtual pawns of the massive sociocultural cycles in human history. Moreover, broad descriptions of cycles in social life fail to capture qualitative differences in different phases of the cycles. For example, to describe both the modern West and the Greco-Roman world at the birth of Christ as sensate cultures may be accurate, but it does not illuminate essential differences in the two cultures. There is more to change than cyclic variations.

Evolutionary Theory

In contrast to the cyclic theory, **evolutionary theory** gives direction to change. Gerhard and Jean Lenski (1982) have developed one of the more influential discussions of evolutionary change. Not all change, they argue, is evolutionary; some is cyclic, and some is unpatterned and random. But evolutionary change is the predominant pattern

Evolutionary theory
Change seen as directional, a process of cumulative change

and differs from the others because it is a "process of cumulative change" (Lenski and Lenski, 1982, p. 56). Organic and sociocultural evolution are similar in some ways, including the fundamental fact that both are cumulative change based on systems of encoded information. Organic evolution is based in part on the information encoded in the DNA molecule. Sociocultural evolution is based on symbol systems, or language.

Thus, the Lenskis define sociocultural evolution as "the process of change and development in human societies that results from cumulative change in their stores of cultural information" (Lenski and Lenski, 1982, p. 60). Cumulative change occurs through the twin processes of innovation and selection. Innovation produces new variations, and selection produces decisions about which variations to retain and which to reject.

Inventions, discoveries, alterations of existing cultural elements, and diffusion from one society to another constitute the basic forms of innovation. More than anything else, however, technological developments provide the driving mechanism of change. New technologies help satisfy human needs more completely or more efficiently. "Needs" here refers to socially and culturally derived needs as well as to subsistence needs. We *need* to have esthetic satisfaction and to find self-fulfillment as well as to obtain food, clothing, and shelter. In the course of seeking satisfaction of such needs, people continually develop new technologies. Those technologies, in turn, alter social life by opening up new options for people. The dramatic changes in the shifts from simple hunting-and-gathering societies through agricultural and industrial societies to today's world highlight the impact of technological developments upon the social order. The store of cultural information in a computer society is vastly different from that in the stone-tool, plow, or steam-engine societies.

According to the Lenskis, the processes of innovation and selection occur at two different levels: in individual societies and in the world system. At the level of the individual society, the variations produced are cultural elements, some of which are retained while others are rejected. Those retained shape the character of the evolving social order. At the level of the world system, the variations produce entire societies. Those with the greater amount of technological information will survive and shape the character of the evolving world system. The world system has evolved from one in which the dominant social order was hunting and gathering, through systems dominated by the horticultural and the agrarian society, to a system dominated by an industrial society.

And where is evolution leading us? The Lenskis assert that human culture has been highly successful as an adaptive mechanism, for the human race has not only survived but has flourished in terms of sheer numbers. If we go beyond numbers and ask about progress toward such values as freedom, justice, and happiness, however, we find a complex situation. Technological developments have certainly raised the upper level of freedom, in the sense that those in the upper strata in industrial societies have a far greater range of options than those who had the most options in agrarian societies. The freedom of the average person is more debatable; industrial societies offer fewer physical and biological restraints but more social restraints. People in advanced societies today, for example, have far fewer problems with health than in former years, but they have more governmental restrictions.

Dealing with justice, the Lenskis point out that the amount of inequality in societies changes as we move from one type of society to another. Inequality increases in the shift from a hunting-and-gathering to a horticultural and agrarian society. The surplus of goods increases, but that surplus is invariably distributed unequally among the population. Industrial societies initially maintain this trend toward increasing inequality, but the trend finally reverses as industrialization continues.

The Lenskis raise important issues about equality, justice, and happiness that we cannot resolve here. Generally, they portray the course of evolution as one of progress for the human race. Evolutionary theory also underscores the fact that certain factors, such as technology, are far more crucial to the process of change than other factors. On the other hand, although evolutionary theory may be useful in explaining large-scale, long-term trends, it is not useful in accounting for the smaller-scale, shorter-term alterations in social life, such as alterations in social institutions or public attitudes. Nor is evolutionary theory useful for explaining the significant differences in societies at the same level of evolutionary development. In fact, some older evolutionists argued that the process of evolution demands that all societies evolve along the same lines toward the same kind of social order. Clearly, that has not happened. What else, then, is going on in social life that is crucial to our understanding of social change? For some theorists, the answer is conflict.

Conflict Theory

Conflict theory of change, as we have seen throughout, views change as the inevitable result of inherent conflicts between groups with diverse interests. In a statement representative of conflict theory, Dahrendorf (1959, p. 208) comments: "I would suggest . . . that all that is creativity, innovation, and development in the life of the individual, his group, and his society is due, to no small extent, to the operation of conflicts between group and group, individual and individual, emotion and emotion within one individual." The origin of social conflict, according to Dahrendorf, is the dominance relations that prevail in societies. Conflict is generally a struggle over the legitimacy of authority relations.

Conflict theory of change
Change seen as a result of conflicting interests between groups

Dahrendorf develops four propositions to highlight the nature of conflict and its role in social change:

1. Every society is at every point subject to processes of change; social change is ubiquitous.
2. Every society displays at every point dissensus and conflict; social conflict is ubiquitous.
3. Every element in a society makes a contribution to its disintegration and change.
4. Every society is based on the coercion of some of its members by others (Dahrendorf, 1959, p. 162).

Change is inevitable because authority relationships are pervasive, and there will always be conflict over authority relationships.

The analysis of bureaucracy (chapter 4) provided specific illustrations of conflict as a force for change in industrial organizations. Many case studies have documented struggles between employees and management. In Dahrendorf's analysis, conflict will occur regardless of the nature of management, whether management is composed of owners, stockholders, or the government. Whether managers try to fashion a participatory system or a restrictive bureaucracy, conflict will still exist because it is rooted in the contradictory interests embedded in authority relationships. Conflict and its outcome—social change—are inevitable.

Conflict, like technology, is an important part of social change. Nevertheless, conflict does not explain all change, and it can sometimes impede change. In some Third World nations, such as Burma and the Sudan, intergroup conflict has been so intense that progress toward a modern, constitutional state has been stifled. Furthermore, some change occurs without conflict. As James G. March (1981, p. 563) points out, organizations may change "routinely, easily, and responsively." Many businesses have changed their internal structure and processes in an effort to enhance productivity or to adapt to a changed environment, and they have implemented the changes without conflict.

Terrorism
Systematic threat or use of violence to achieve a political end

Conflict and Terrorism. In contemporary world conflicts, we find many militant groups that engage in terrorism. **Terrorism** can take many forms, but it can be defined as the systematic or threatened use of murder, injury, or destruction in order to achieve some political end (Laqueur, 1987, p. 72). By their actions, terrorists seek to create tensions that can ultimately lead to the changes they desire.

Over the years we have all heard of terrorist acts committed by such groups as the Irish Republican Army (IRA), Fatah, the major terrorist group within the Palestinian Liberation Organization (PLO), the Red Brigades (Italy), and others. Terrorists engage in a wide range of activities, including plane hijacking, kidnapping, embassy bombings, car bombings, and other violent acts.

Terrorist attacks in heavily populated areas, such as this bombing on a Paris street, are among the most frightening acts of political violence.

Terrorists do not always achieve their aims. The objective of the IRA, for instance, is to free Northern Ireland from British control. As of this writing, however, Northern Ireland continues under British domination, and there is little sign that control will be relinquished in the near future. Changes have not occurred in spite of many terrorist activities undertaken by the IRA over a period of many years. The high point for IRA activities was 1972 when 467 people were killed, including 103 members of the British military. Occasionally, the IRA has taken even more extreme steps, such as their effort in the early 1980s to assassinate Prime Minister Thatcher when she attended a political convention in the resort city of Brighton, England. Despite these extreme steps, IRA actions have failed to bring about the desired changes.

The same could be said about Fatah and the Palestine Liberation Organization. This organization has sought to regain land from the Israelis in order to create a Palestinian homeland and, if possible, to eliminate Israel completely. Although conflict has certainly existed between the PLO and Israel, Israel remains firmly in place, and there is little immediate prospect of a homeland for Palestinians.

In spite of the failures of the IRA and the Fatah/PLO, it would be wrong to conclude that terrorist groups inevitably fail. For example, in the 1940s, terrorist groups like Irgun and the Stern Gang contributed to the ouster of the British from Palestine. Even in this case, however, the activities of the terrorists were not the decisive factor in achieving the desired objective. In summary, terrorism is a reflection of conflict and is being used as an instrument of conflicting groups, but its successes in bringing about social change have been limited.

Although all the types of theory are useful, no one adequately explains all change. Perhaps a future theorist will utilize elements of the various theories to fashion a more complete explanation of social change than is now available.

Sources of Change

Various change theories stress differing sources of change. Sorokin saw change as a normal outcome of the functioning of the social system. Marx pointed to inherent contradictions in the larger society, while conflict theorists stress the role of the struggle between groups with opposed interests. Functionalists identify many sources of change, both internal (such as strain in the system) and external (such as changes in the physical environment or war with another society). The functionalists correctly point out the multiple sources of change. All of the factors noted by the theorists, in fact, are part of the process of social change. We now discuss three of the more important factors: technology, ideologies, and competition/conflict.

Technology

Our earlier discussion of culture pointed to the importance of technology—materials, tools, machines, skills, and procedures—in a society. An examination of Ogburn's (1964) view of *cultural lag* established that change occurs first in material culture and that rapid technological change causes maladjustment because the old norms, roles, and, in some cases, values no longer seem to apply to the situation created by the new technology. The maladjustment, in turn, stimulates people to address the resulting problems. Thus

"Someday man will find a peaceful use for my machines."

change is ongoing as people must continually seek to adapt their nonmaterial culture to the material.

As an example of cultural lag, we saw in chapter 3 how the development of nuclear armaments has made it irrational for nations to wage wars with these weapons in order to achieve political goals. And yet national leaders often talk about potential wars, or they even threaten wars, as if we were in a pre-nuclear-missile age.

How Technology Causes Change. Ogburn identified one of the ways in which technology causes change—by creating social problems that require people's action. But technology also leads to change in a second way—by increasing our alternatives. Consider, for example, the options opened up by the computer (Turkle, 1984). In many cases, the computer has radically altered the nature of the workplace, changing the kind and number of workers needed and the kind and amount of information that can be kept and used. The computerization of an office may mean that fewer workers are required, and that those who are needed will have to possess different skills (e.g., the ability to work at the computer terminal) than those who previously worked there. On the other hand, that office force can handle much more information (facts about inventory, production and clients, and forecasts about the future) than could the noncomputerized group. Largely because of the computer, the number of workers in the information field—those engaged in collecting and analyzing various kinds of data pertinent to an operation—has dramatically increased in modern nations. The computer's impact can be seen in virtually every human endeavor. New methods of education, such as computer-assisted instruction, are available. Health care can be individualized in a way not possible before; a hospital patient can be hooked up to a computer that will continually monitor his or her physical status or make analyses to facilitate an accurate diagnosis and treatment. Computers allow people to shop from their homes. Of course, the options are not all desirable. Computers can also be used to commit crime and to wage war. Criminals have learned to use the computer to "break in" to the operations of a company and steal information or materials. The military has used the computer to create frightening new weapons that can kill more people with greater accuracy at longer distances. The options opened up by the computer are enormously varied, but not all are conducive to human well-being.

The third way in which technology leads to change is by altering interaction patterns—new technologies frequently lead to new interaction patterns. For instance, one study has shown that a robot installed in a machine plant drastically altered the workplace (Goleman, 1983, pp. 40–41). In essence, the robot did the work previously done by a human, and the human ran the robot. Workers agreed that the robot had eliminated physical stress, but they noted other stresses that were added because the robot required the full attention of the worker. The joking and bantering of pre-robot days were gone. As one worker put it, "I don't have time to talk with anyone. I don't want them breaking my concentration." The robot changed interaction patterns in the factory. In other cases, a new technology does not demand, but may result in, changed patterns. The automobile and television are examples of technologies that an individual can use to change his or her interaction patterns, though neither requires those changes. That is, one need not break off friendships or cut down on interaction with family members in order to use an automobile or television. In fact, the automobile can help one to maintain existing interaction patterns even after a move to a different location; television can be a shared experience with friends or family members. Most technologies do not require us to alter interaction patterns, but they give us the option to do so.

Ideology: Impediment or Facilitator of Change?

As we saw in chapter 8 on stratification, an *ideology* is a set of ideas that explains reality, provides directives for behavior, and expresses the interests of particular groups. An ideology may be elaborate, such as the ideologies of Marxism, capitalism, or Catholicism.

Or the ideology may be focused on a specific issue, such as the ideologies of the pro-choice and anti-abortion groups. In either case, the ideologies fulfill several functions. For instance, groups in this controversy each have an ideology that explains their position on abortion; among other things, the ideologies take a position on whether the fetus is a living human. Anti-abortionists argue that the fertilized egg is a human. From a biological point of view, they say, the fertilized egg is a unique, genetic entity. The Catholic church agrees, and adds that the fertilized egg must be considered a human because it has human potential, because "if you are conceived by human parents, you are human" (*Time*, 1981, p. 23). On the other hand, those who favor a woman's right to abortion argue that human life does not technically begin until some time after conception. For example, one biologist argues that fertilization is not the beginning of human life, but a "highly significant step in its continuity," since the egg and sperm are both living human cells. The fertilized egg lacks some of the important characteristics we attribute to people, including a nervous system and the ability to respond to stimuli. One may also consider a human as someone with self-awareness. But during the first three months, the fetus "lacks an adequate neural foundation for minimal subjective experience, let alone self-awareness" (Grobstein, 1982, p. 14).

For those opposed to abortion, however, the act is one of killing a human being, regardless of how soon the abortion occurs after conception. As a legislative aide put it, "We must do everything we can under our constitutional system to stop the killing of unborn children. We're talking about life and death" (*Time*, 1981, p. 20). For those who favor women's choice in the matter, the issue is one of a woman's right to have control of her body and her general well-being. A woman's right to self-determination is threatened, they say, by anti-abortion efforts.

These ideologies also provide directives for behavior; each group actively lobbies and propagandizes in an effort to win public and governmental support. Each group tries to marshal support for political candidates who support their position. Anti-abortionists mobilize supporters to picket (or disrupt) abortion clinics. And the ideologies clearly reflect the interests of the two groups; those who argue for choice in the matter feel that such choice is important to maintain the rights of women, while those who argue against abortion feel that the sanctity of human life generally, and of their quality of life in particular, is being threatened. In addition to serving the various functions for groups holding them, ideologies affect change in a number of ways.

Ideology as an Impediment to Change. Although change is inevitable, some people who benefit enough from the existing order will always vigorously resist change. In some cases, people use ideologies to impede or block change. During the Middle Ages, the clergy used religious ideology to gain more power for themselves and to impede certain economic developments. For instance, they inhibited the development of economic surplus by defining usury as sinful. They diverted whatever surplus wealth there was from economic enterprises by stressing the insignificance of worldly gain and the crucial importance of spiritual works. Consequently, people tended to use their energies and resources to build religious monuments and secure greater favor with God. The large number of religious holidays and festivals similarly consumed people's time and energies, and diverted them from such things as economic development.

Nonreligious ideologies can also inhibit change. In the United States, people have used the ideology of equality of opportunity to resist changes that would benefit mi-

"Pro-life" and "pro-choice" activists engaged in the controversy over abortion use very different ideologies to support their positions.

norities. After all, they argue, if every American truly has the same opportunity as every other American, why do we need such things as affirmative action laws?

The ideology of equal opportunity also inhibits the development of class consciousness and class antagonisms. Even the poorer among us may accept the ideology. In a survey of 105 rural people of Appalachia, 71 percent agreed with the statement: "Regardless of social class, anyone willing and able to work has an equal chance to earn a good income in this country" (Smith and Bylund, 1983, p. 259). To the extent that people accept the ideology, they will attribute their success or blame their failure on their own efforts and abilities rather than on the social structure in which they function. As a garbage man put it: "Look, I know it's nobody's fault but mine that I got stuck here where I am. . . . if I'd applied myself, I know I got it in me to be different, can't say anyone did it to me" (Sennett and Cobb, 1972, p. 96).

Ideology as a Facilitator of Change. If ideology impedes change, it can also be used to facilitate change. Many changes in American society are related to the ideology that technology will resolve all of our problems. For example, some Americans hold to the idea that we can resolve the problem of war by developing a superior military technology. In particular, in 1983 President Reagan proposed a system of defense that would defend against the missiles of any enemy. The system—dubbed "Star Wars"—would use laser beams and other technology to destroy incoming enemy missiles from space stations. "Let's use the wonders of technology not to make war, but to protect the peace" was President Reagan's argument (*San Diego Tribune*, 1986, p. A3). Of course, experts disagree about the feasibility and effectiveness of a Star Wars system. Some agreed with the President that such a system would be not only practical but effective in preventing war. Others, such as Nobel-Prize-winning physicist Hans Bethe (1985, p. 83), argue that the system is impractical "until there are technical breakthroughs that have not yet been conceived of." Other critics have argued that if a system such as this were to be developed, it would increase, not decrease, the likelihood of nuclear war.

Ideology has also facilitated action in social movements. In the women's movement, the ideology of female/male equality has led to the demand for female participation in areas formerly believed to be appropriate only for males. Women have entered the military academies, become a part of construction crews, and opted for careers in engineering—all considered unsuitable for women only a few years ago. Similarly, homosexuals have "come out" in large numbers and have begun to win such rights as marriage and adoption of children in some states. The pursuit of these rights was stimulated by the ideology that gays and lesbians are as normal as anyone else and deserve, therefore, the same rights as heterosexuals.

The Role of Competition and Conflict in Change

Competition and conflict have stimulated so much change that some sociologists would argue that all change is the result of these two forms of interaction. Although this view overstates the case, it is true that they are fundamental and pervasive aspects of social change.

Competition. The importance of competition in change is well illustrated by the progress of science. While science is supposed to be governed by the norms of sharing, cooperation, and openness, in reality, fierce competition is more typical. For instance, three researchers won the 1977 Nobel Prize in Physiology or Medicine for their research on the role of hormones in the chemistry of the body. Two of the men—Roger Guillemin and Andrew Schally—were bitter enemies (Wade, 1981). At one time they were colleagues, but each formed his own team and set out to win the prize. In the course of the race, the two scientists often ignored the norms that supposedly govern science. For instance, they tried to avoid acknowledging each other's work. Guillemin left out Schally's work when he wrote review articles. Schally told members of his team not to talk to "the enemy." The two researchers even refused to report some of their advances at scientific meetings for fear that the other might pick up on the information and jump ahead in the race. Ultimately, they had to share the prize for discovering and characterizing the hormones that the brain uses to control various bodily functions. Their rivalry was intense, leading them to work fiercely toward the goal. For our analysis, the important point is that the goal was achieved, and that the competition facilitated the achievement by impelling the scientists to intensive work.

Conflict. Conflict is a potent factor in change at all levels of life, including in organizations, communities, and whole societies. The conflict between workers and management, between ideological factions in communities and the nation, between individuals who dislike each other in an organization, between representatives of various social institutions such as religion and government—all are examples of the multitude of different conflicts that pervade societies.

The changes resulting from the conflict between students and college and university administrators in the 1960s illustrates the kind of shifts that can occur in organizations as a result of conflict (Kriesberg, 1982, pp. 248–249). The conflicts were ideologically based and centered on diverse goals. One conflict, for instance, focused on the role of the schools in national and local matters. Liberal and left-wing students protested such things as the contribution of university research to war generally and to the war in Vietnam in particular; the investments made by colleges and universities in corporations that students defined as exploiting the poor or contributing to international tensions and exploitation of Third World nations; and the expansion of school property that resulted in a displacement of the poor. Students and administrators also had conflict over such academic matters as the relevance of certain subjects for study and over such practical matters as dormitory rules.

The conflicts produced significant changes in a number of areas of college life. Rules about dormitory living were liberalized throughout the country, including the broadening or elimination of rules about curfews, drinking, and entertaining members of the opposite sex in dormitory rooms. There were curriculum changes, with many schools instituting programs of black studies and women's studies. Grade inflation occurred, and many schools gave students more pass/fail options for courses in lieu of grades. Some schools even ended their research affiliation with the military. Finally, as noted above, administrators in many schools agreed to student participation in the decision-making process. By the end of the 1970s, a survey of colleges and universities showed that students participated on the boards of trustees for 20 percent of the schools, and on faculty curriculum committees in 58 percent of the schools (Kriesberg, 1982, pp. 248).

Many of those changes have been reversed as a new generation of students showed less interest in participating in the administration of their schools, and administrators did nothing to encourage continued participation. By the late 1980s, students may have realized what they had lost, for conflict re-emerged as students on campuses around the nation sought to convince their trustees and administrators to withdraw investments in South African enterprises. Many students felt morally outraged by the fact that they attended schools that supported apartheid through investments, but they often discovered that they had little or no official influence.

In many instances, conflict and change become a self-sustaining process as the conflict leads to change that generates more conflict, leading to still more change. For example, the "green revolution" in India involved the use of new grains, irrigation, fertilizer, and pesticides (Lauer, 1982). Double and even triple crop yields resulted. The result was supposed to be an alleviation of the ever-critical food shortage in the nation as well as a boon to the financial well-being of small farmers. But because the new methods required substantial investment, large farmers benefited more than the small farmers. The investment was more than repaid in profits from the increased yields, but small farmers lacked the resources to make such investments. Moreover, many small tenant farmers found their rent raised as large land owners attempted to capitalize on the increased value of the land by forcing the tenant farmers off and using their own workers. Eventually, a number of land reform movements arose, as small farmers demanded consideration for their plight. The land reform movements have resulted in some gains for the small farmers in the form of redistribution of land, but the inequality and the conflict continue, which means that the pressure for change continues. The initial change generated conflict that created pressure for a different kind of change.

Collective Behavior and Social Change

Collective behavior
Behavior of a collectivity in a situation of change, conflict, or uncertainty

Collective behavior is behavior expressed as part of a collectivity (such as a crowd), focused on a particular phenomenon or event (such as a concert or fight), in a situation of relative change, conflict, or uncertainty. Below we look at four types of collective behavior—crowds, rumors, disasters, and social movements.

Crowds

Acting crowd
A large number of people trying to change some aspect of their immediate environment

Turner and Killian (1972) distinguish among acting, expressive, diffuse, and conventionalized crowds. An **acting crowd** is a large number of people who are attempting to change something in their environment. A riot is an example. In 1980, blacks in Miami rioted for three days after an all-white jury acquitted four white policemen in the beating death of a black businessman (Ladner, Schwartz, Roker, and Titterud, 1981). Over two-thirds of the participants who were surveyed said that they believed the riots would get people to pay more attention to the needs of the black community, and nearly half said that the riots would somehow make things better for the community. The rioters hoped to change their economic and political situation by dramatizing the extent of their grievances.

Expressive crowd
People displaying intense feelings, emotions, and exuberant physical behavior

An **expressive crowd** is one in which there are intense displays of feelings and emotions, often accompanied by some kind of exuberant physical behavior. A religious revival meeting may become an expressive crowd when the members of a congregation engage in spontaneous singing, shouting, speaking in tongues, waving arms, and moving

The gathering of thousands of Muslims for the funeral procession of the Ayatollah Khomeini in Iran in 1989 is an example of a conventionalized crowd.

the body rhythmically. The fans at concerts often become expressive crowds when the music brings them to their feet in a frenzy of dancing, clapping, and singing.

A **diffuse crowd** is composed of dispersed individuals who follow a particular kind of behavior or experience a particular sentiment. Fads and crazes are forms of the diffuse crowd. Numerous fads and crazes of all kinds dot American history, including an infatuation with certain games (Trivial Pursuit), with celebrities (the "mania" over the Beatles and some contemporary rock stars such as Michael Jackson and Madonna), with physical activities (piano-wrecking or running), with magical schemes (chain letters), and with daredevil activities (skateboarding). Fads occur in the arts and sciences as well as in every-day affairs. Experts in childrearing at times have extolled the virtues of breastfeeding infants and at other times have lauded the superiority of bottle-feeding.

Diffuse crowd
A large number of dispersed individuals who follow particular behaviors or sentiments, e.g., fads and crazes

Finally, the **conventionalized crowd** is a collectivity gathered for a particular purpose and acting in accord with established norms. The people in the conventionalized crowd expect to experience mutual influence; they are not merely an assemblage of isolated individuals. A theater audience and fans at a sporting event are examples of conventionalized crowds. The fact that they are not merely a gathering of isolated individuals is underscored by such things as rhythmic clapping and chanting.

Conventionalized crowd
Collectivity gathered for a particular purpose and conforming to established norms

Emergent norm theory suggests that, when collective behavior such as a crowd occurs, new norms, social relationships, communications patterns, and values often emerge, especially in response to unforeseen events. In other words, collective behavior is not just random, uncontrolled behavior; instead, it has some degree of social organization (Aguirre, Quarantelli, and Mendoza, 1988).

Emergent norm theory
In collective behavior, new norms, communications patterns, and values often emerge

One tragedy involving a conventionalized crowd that panicked provides support for the emergent norm theory. In 1979, 11 people were killed as they tried to enter a rock concert. The British rock group The Who was scheduled to perform at a stadium in Cincinnati. As crowds massed outside the gates, attempting entry, many people closest to the entry points were crushed. In contrast to widespread interpretations by the mass media that this event was the result of unregulated, callous competition by young "barbarians" for good seats, Johnson (1987a, 1987b) found little evidence to support this interpretation. Instead, Johnson's study found many reports of people trying to help others endangered by the crush. They were not indifferent; they were physically unable to help. In addition, the study found that traditional gender-role behavior remained in effect as men took the lead in trying to help those in danger. Johnson's study also found that most members of the crowd were part of small, primary groups following established norms and values. Thus, Johnson concludes that, as emergent norm theory suggests, the social structure did not break down in Cincinnati.

Rumors

Rumor
Unverified information that diffuses through a collectivity seeking some understanding

A **rumor** is unverified information that diffuses through a collectivity as a result of people attempting to understand something. People need to make sense of their world. But many aspects of life are ambiguous, and the evidence is not clearly available for a meaningful interpretation. Rumors provide the information necessary for understanding. Thus, a rumor is a form of problem solving.

Rumors are likely to appear, then, whenever people lack the information necessary to make sense out of something. For instance, why would a young man not be interested in dating? If nothing about him suggests an answer, a rumor could solve the problem—he is gay. Why does a young woman at work suddenly appear so cheerful? If nothing about her life circumstances suggests an answer, a rumor could resolve the issue—she knows that she is getting the job for which two other people in the office have applied. Or, to take an incident from the news, what is the meaning of the well-known Procter & Gamble logo, the human face in the quarter moon looking out at 13 stars? Why would a soap company select such a logo? In 1980, a rumor began to circulate that answered the question—the symbol is satanic. Moreover, the rumor claimed that Procter & Gamble executives had admitted on television programs that they supported devil worship. Fundamentalist religious groups began to call for a boycott of all Procter & Gamble products. The company took the rumor and the boycott threats seriously, publicly denying any connection with Satan worship and filing defamation suits against three people known to have helped spread the rumor. Actually, there never were any executives on television discussing the logo, and the logo itself dates back to 1852. The 13 stars symbolized the original 13 colonies, and the face in the moon was simply a popular image at the time. Lacking such information, many people accepted the rumor as truth.

Thus, one of the important functions of a rumor is to reduce ambiguity, to make sense out of the world or some part of the world. As such, rumors can reduce anxiety because a world that cannot be understood is a threatening world. Rumors also legitimate and motivate certain kinds of behavior. The Procter & Gamble rumor led some fundamentalists to boycott the products. Race riots in the United States have frequently crystallized around, or been fanned by, rumors (Rosnow and Fine, 1976). When leaders of a movement are jailed, rumors of mistreatment may lead people to take action of various kinds. In an organization, rumors may circulate of an impending "shake-up," leading people to act to protect their own positions. Such rumors may be true or false. In either case, they help people make sense out of their situation and lead them to act accordingly.

Disasters

Much of the research on collective behavior in recent decades has focused on disasters. A disaster may be a natural phenomenon, such as a flood or earthquake, or the result of human action and activity, such as a fire or an airplane crash. Research has shown that there are some common misconceptions about disasters (Wenger, Dykes, Sebok, and Neff, 1975). First, many people believe that disasters almost always create panic and flight. Actually, such behavior is rare. Disasters are more likely to involve convergence behavior—people converge toward the disaster. Some are residents who fled when the disaster first occurred, some are anxious friends or relatives, some are curious or desirous of helping, and some want to exploit the situation.

A second false belief is that looting typically occurs. Frequently rumors of looting spread widely, and police and national guard often are called on to prevent looting (again, the rumor leads to the behavior). But verified cases of actual looting are limited.

Third, most people believe that citizens will readily evacuate an area when warned about an impending disaster (such as a flood or hurricane). The people most likely to

The Armenian earthquake of 1989 was one of the worst natural disasters in recent history. Research on disasters has shown that victims do not generally respond with panic and flight. Rather, a phenomenon called *convergent behavior* in which people converge toward the disaster occurs.

leave, however, are transients and visitors. Residents tend to stay, and some refuse to leave until they are forced by authorities.

Finally, most people believe that victims are in a state of shock, unable to fend for themselves immediately after the disaster occurs. But with a few exceptions, various needs are cared for and services provided by the victims themselves with some assistance from others in the immediate vicinity.

What are the consequences of disasters? They may bring about both short-term and long-term change. The short-term change is likely to be disruption of various kinds. Long-term consequences may be either positive or negative. Research into the effects of a 1974 tornado that killed 33 and injured 1,200 in Xenia, Ohio, reported that some of the survivors discovered that they had more internal resources than they realized (Taylor, 1977). They handled the crisis well, and their self-esteem was enhanced. On the other hand, a study of those caught in a 1972 flood in a Pennsylvania town showed that after five years the disaster victims, compared to people in nearby towns that had not flooded, had a greater incidence of various kinds of physical illness and more problems of emotional health (Logue, Hansen, and Struening, 1981).

Social Movements

Social movements
Collective efforts to resist or bring about change

Social movements are a key type of collective behavior. By definition, they are integrally tied to change because they are collective efforts to resist or to bring about some kind of change. We focus here on the way social movements intersect with social change.

Why are social movements important? As individuals, we are limited in our ability to make the societal changes we would like. There are massive social forces that make change difficult; these forces include the government, large and powerful organizations, and the prevailing values, norms, and attitudes. As individuals going to the voting booth, we have minimal power. As individuals protesting to officials, we have minimal power. As individuals standing against the tide of public opinion, we have little hope of exerting influence. As individuals confronting a corporate structure, we are doomed to frustration and failure. But if we combine with others who share our convictions, organize ourselves, and map out a course of action, we may be able to bring about numerous and significant changes in the social order. Through participation in a social movement, we can break through the social constraints that overwhelm us as individuals.

Revolutionary movement
Social movement aimed at creating a new social order

Types of Social Movements. Sociologists have classified four different types of social movements according to their relationship to social change: *revolutionary, regressive, reform,* and *expressive* (Rush and Denisoff, 1971). A **revolutionary movement** is an attempt to create a new social order. It aims at radical change, though not always by radical methods. Some Marxist groups see the violent overthrow of the government as the only realistic way to bring about the changes they desire. American libertarians, on the other hand, advocate laissez-faire capitalism and stress the efficacy of educating people to accept their ideology. Once the ideology is accepted, they argue, people will act on it to change the society accordingly (Lauer, 1976). In any case, a revolutionary movement always seeks to alter the power structure of the society.

Many examples of revolutionary movements exist, but one of the most recent took place in the Philippines in the early and middle 1980s. The Philippines had been led for almost two decades by the dictator Ferdinand Marcos. The immediate precipitant of the revolution was the assassination, probably planned by Marcos supporters, of opposition leader Benigno Aquino when he returned from exile in 1983. His funeral procession turned into a demonstration—the first of many demonstrations, some peaceful, some violent. In 1984 Marcos decided to call for a quick election which, because of its short lead-time, would give him an enormous advantage over any opposition candidates. However, the key opposition candidate turned out to be Corazon Aquino, the wife of Benigno Aquino. Corazon Aquino proved to be a very popular candidate, but she lost the election amid charges that the vote had been rigged by Marcos.

In the ensuing days and weeks, there were acts of civil disobedience as well as boycotts against businesses owned by Marcos's cronies. A coup attempt soon followed, and the people rallied around the dissident military officers leading the coup. Hordes of people positioned themselves between the rebel soldiers and troops loyal to Marcos, preventing the latter from attacking the rebels. Soon government soldiers began defecting to the side of the rebels. Not long after, Marcos fled the country in an aircraft provided by the United States, and Corazon Aquino became president of the Philippines (Simons, 1987).

Why do people get involved in revolutionary activities? On the surface, it would appear more rational for people to sit on the sidelines, to be "free riders," and wait to see how the revolution comes out. An individual who takes this position stands to gain

The people of the Philippines carried out a successful revolutionary movement when they ousted autocratic dictator Ferdinand Marcos and supported the democratic government of Corazon Aquino.

the collective benefits of a revolution without incurring the private costs (e.g., risking injury or death). However, history shows that people do get involved in revolutions, often in large numbers. Such people might appear to be behaving irrationally, deviating from their personal interests. Although this may be true, individuals also adopt a collectively rational point of view, realizing that without their participation in revolutionary activities, revolutions will fail. Thus, some individuals are willing to risk the private costs, accepting the fact that their individual effect on the revolution will be minimal, in order to aid the collectivity (Muller and Opp, 1986).

Regressive movement Social movement aimed at restoring a past or a passing social order

A **regressive movement** attempts to restore a past or passing social order on the grounds that the past order is preferable to any other. For example, the long-standing battle over the teaching of evolution in the schools took on new intensity in the 1980s. The battle arrays those who stand for "scientific creationism" against those who affirm evolution. The former argue that the Book of Genesis gives an adequate account of the beginning of the world, that the universe is no more than roughly 7,000 to 10,000 years old, and that the action of God rather than some impersonal evolutionary process is responsible for the existence of the world as we know it. Those who support current evolutionary theory, itself diverse, accept the idea of a slow process of change requiring billions of years for the world to reach its present stage. The evolutionary process involved the gradual emergence of humans from lower forms of life. Creationists want textbooks to reflect their view, or at least to give it equal weight with evolutionary theory.

In 1980, creationists were able to influence 11 state legislatures to consider bills that would require the teaching of scientific creationism in any biology class where evolution was taught. Texas had already established laws in 1974 that set guidelines for the content of textbooks, which made the teaching of evolution difficult. In 1981, Arkansas passed a law that required equal time for the two perspectives. Creationists also were able to persuade some textbook publishers to modify the way their books treated evolution and the age of the earth. But a series of court cases defeated the anti-evolutionists. A 1981 California court ruling held that the teaching of evolution without giving any attention to creationism did not infringe on the right of freedom of religion. The Arkansas law was ruled unconstitutional in 1982. In 1984, Texas repealed its anti-evolution textbook selection rules. In 1985, an appeals court upheld a ruling against Louisiana's "balanced treatment" approach to the issue. The creationist movement has been soundly defeated, but its members will undoubtedly continue their efforts to bring back a past social order.

Reform movement Social movement aimed at making the existing social order more acceptable

Reform movements aim at alterations in the existing order to make it more acceptable. Typically, reform movements seek to make the existing order more effective or more equitable for more people. That may mean extending certain rights to people for whom they have been denied (such as occupational opportunities for women or equal housing and job opportunities for minorities). New legislation, rather than a radically altered power structure, may suffice to bring about such changes.

Expressive movement Social movement aimed at changing individuals who will then change the social order, or adapt to it

Expressive movements seek to change individuals, who will then either change the social order or adapt better to the existing order. Religious movements exemplify the expressive social movement. One of the most rapidly growing movements of recent decades is the charismatic or pentecostal movement, stressing the experience of "speaking in tongues." Those who have the experience, according to the ideology or the movement, have a supreme spiritual experience as well as concrete evidence of the presence of the Holy Spirit. The movement tends to operate independently of established churches, but has secured the commitment of many members of those churches.

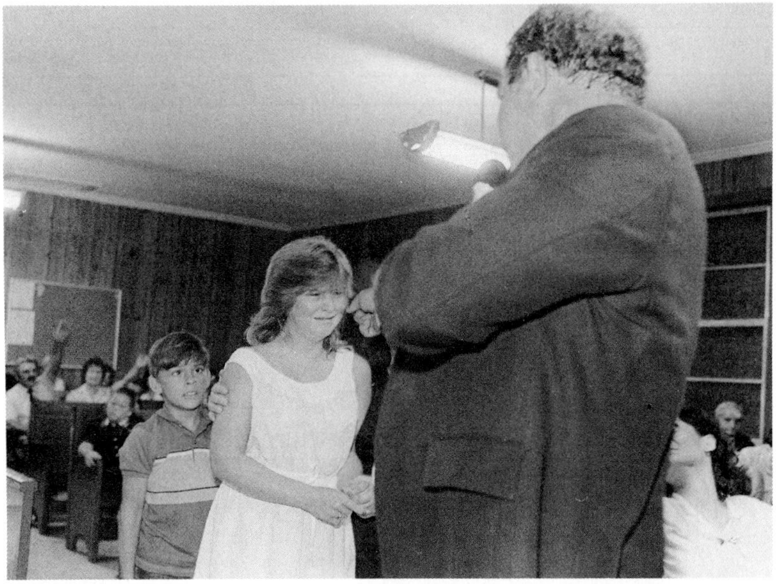

The charismatic religious movement has been one of the most rapidly growing expressive social movements in the United States. The people in this movement report a variety of religious experiences such as speaking in tongues, walking after being crippled, and encountering God directly.

Movements and Mobilization of Resources. Although there are various theoretical perspectives on collective behavior generally and social movements in particular, the newest approach to understanding movements uses the concept of resource mobilization (Jenkins, 1983). **Resource mobilization** refers to the idea that protest movements form not so much because of deprivation among people as in response to available resources and the effective mobilization of those resources. The level of grievances and extent of deprivation in a society are generally sufficient among some groups to justify protest. However, for a movement to arise, adequate resources must be available, as well as an organization and leadership to exploit those resources.

Resource mobilization
Protest movements arise as a result of the existence and use of available resources

Three resources are particularly worthy of note—*members*, a *communication network*, and *leaders* (McAdam, McCarthy, and Zald, 1988). All social movements need members and usually recruit them through established lines of interaction. Second, social movements need a communication network to succeed. For example, the women's movement was aided by a communications network consisting of women involved in the Presidential and State Commissions on the Status of Women, established under President John F. Kennedy, and feminists working within the Equal Employment Opportunity Commission (Freeman, 1983). Well aware of the inequities that they and other women faced, these women had contact with each other through their participation in the governmental organizations. Third, the leaders are usually drawn from pre-existing groups. Other resources may also be important, such as support from well-to-do people, and institutional resources obtained from government agencies, private foundations, the mass media, and corporations (McCarthy and Zald, 1977). Resources may also be mobilized through the actions of professionals who, as part of their mobilization efforts, may aim

Cross-National Perspectives

Successful Social Movements: The Case of Islamic Fundamentalism in Iran

Many social movements fail to achieve their objectives, but some movements do succeed. Even when they succeed, however, the problems of maintaining, continuing, or expanding the objectives of the movement remain. What happens to a successful social movement is an interesting sociological question. Although it is not possible to generalize from a single case, the analysis of one example can be interesting and instructive. The social movement led by the Ayatollah Ruhollah Khomeini in Iran—usually referred to as the Islamic fundamentalist movement—provides such an opportunity for analysis.

In the 1970s, Khomeini was exiled to France, but he emerged as the leader of the Islamic fundamentalist movement that sprang up in Iran later in that decade. Muslim religious fundamentalists in Iran opposed the rule of the Shah. Agitation by this group led to Khomeini's return to Iran on February 1, 1979. Ten days later the Shah was deposed. The fundamentalists viewed the United States as the "Great Satan" and took control of the American embassy, where they held 52 hostages from November 4, 1979 to January 20, 1981. Khomeini, and then, subsequently, his followers, have controlled the Iranian government since 1979. It is a social movement that succeeded.

However, since taking power, this revolutionary social movement has run into a long series of problems. For one thing, Iran engaged in an eight-year war with Iraq that led to many deaths, huge costs, and no real gains, before a truce was signed in 1988. Iran's president has said that the war "robbed the revolution of its best years" (Tyler, 1989). In spite of Iran's oil wealth, the country now faces severe economic problems. Electricity is rationed and homes are sometimes blacked out for as many as six hours a day. Inflation ran at 100 percent in 1988, and numerous necessities are priced beyond the reach of many families. Many staples (for example, meat, sugar, eggs, soap powder) are rationed, and people wait in long lines to get the needed coupons. Said one European envoy: "For ordinary people . . . life is quite hard" (Tyler, 1989). The population's birth rate is one of the highest in the world, a fact that can only add to the economic burdens of the country.

Another problem in contemporary Iran is its lack of political freedom. In May 1988 the leader of the political opposition wrote Khomeini a letter criticizing the continuation of the war against Iraq. Shortly thereafter, police stormed the headquarters of the opposition, arrested several members, and sealed the building. The building is sealed to this day, and three of the movement's leaders remain in solitary confinement.

Did Khomeini's social movement succeed after all? In one sense it certainly did. That is, it achieved its goal of overthrowing the Shah and setting up a new government that it controlled. But in many other senses it did not. In many ways, Iran is far worse off today than it was before Khomeini took power. The issue, of course, is, now that the war with Iraq is over, can the social movement run the country and develop it politically, economically, and socially? It will be difficult to do so, especially with Khomeini's death in 1989.

However, it may be that we are using a Western standard to evaluate the success of the Iranian revolution. That is, the main objectives of Khomeini's revolution may not be political, economic, and social development. Rather, the main objective may be the religious revitalization of the Iranian population and the exportation of fundamentalism to other Muslim countries. In these terms, the success of the Iranian revolution needs to be judged on the growth of religious practice in Iran and the growth of Islamic fundamentalism in other countries. Approached from this point of view, the Iranian revolution appears to have been successful, at least for the time being.

The Islamic fundamentalist movement faces the same problem as every movement led by a dominating, charismatic personality: how does the movement carry on now that Khomeini is dead? Although he held no administrative post in the government, he was its constitutionally recognized spiritual leader. Ali Khamenei has been selected as Khomeini's successor, but he is seen as lacking the charisma and personal power to hold the government and the country together as Khomeini did. The possibility exists for dramatic conflict between religious and political leaders for control of Iran (Smolowe, 1989).

SMOLOWE, JILL. "A Frenzied Farewell." *Time*, June 19, 1989.
TYLER, PATRICK E. "Ten Years Later, Iran Struggles to Rebuild." *Washington Post*, January 29, 1989.

to raise the consciousness of people to develop a clientele. The environmental and consumer rights movements, for example, were developed largely by professional organizers who educated people on the necessity of the movements.

A Successful Social Movement: Stopping the Export of Baby Formula. In the 1970s, a social movement all but stopped the selling of Nestle's baby-food formula in the developing countries of the world. Although the formula is nutritious, problems arose in selling it in less developed countries. In many countries a high illiteracy rate prevented parents from reading the directions for using the formula, and, because the parents were often poor, they tried to stretch the formula by adding additional water, which, in some cases, led to malnutrition and even death. In addition, drinking water was often contaminated, and infants were exposed to bacteria in their formula. Perhaps most important, babies who were fed infant formula instead of breast milk were deprived of the natural immunities derived from their mothers' milk.

Nestle began producing baby formula in the 1920s, but it was not until the 1960s that its products and practices came under attack. One criticism centered on Nestle's marketing techniques. For example, the company employed salespeople who dressed as nurses and "advised" people on the need to use formula. Free samples of formula distributed to mothers were often used up after a point when breastfeeding could not be resumed. Nestle was also attacked for making unreasonable claims about its product (e.g., saying that it was "*better* than mother's milk").

In the 1960s the United Nations became involved in the issue. It urged the promotion of breastfeeding and the limitation of the use of formula. Other organizations soon joined the fray. One Swiss group published a pamphlet titled, "Nestle Kills Babies." Rather than giving in to the pressure, Nestle fought back through counter-publicity campaigns and lawsuits against organizations opposing it. By 1977, since Nestle was still unresponsive, a boycott of all its products was organized. This boycott, as well as an active publicity campaign against Nestle, eventually took the form of an international social movement.

In 1984, when Nestle finally agreed to accept international guidelines on the marketing of its formula, the boycott was lifted. The social movement aimed against Nestle's baby formula had succeeded in achieving its goals. However, why did it take Nestle over two decades to respond adequately to its critics? This question is particularly important since, during that period, large numbers of children became ill and died because of that company's practices (Gerber and Short, 1986).

Modernization and Development

Modernization
Degree to which developing countries follow the model of the West

Over the years sociologists have devoted much attention to the issue of the changing nature of developing countries (LDCs). For a time, that work was dominated by modernization theory. **Modernization** essentially meant the degree to which developing countries followed the model of the West—the degree to which they "Westernized." This mainly translated into economic growth, primarily the degree of industrialization (especially growth in manufacturing), but it also meant adopting Western social and cultural developments (Harper, 1989). In recent years, modernization theory has come under attack, primarily because of its ethnocentric bias that Western practices ought to be followed by the rest of the world.

Development
General process of economic growth, not necessarily emphasizing manufacturing

Modernization theory has generally been replaced by development theory. **Development** may be defined as a general process of economic growth (in production, consumption, per capita income, etc.), but it does not necessarily mean that manufacturing industries must be emphasized. Economic development can be spearheaded by advances in mining, fishing, or agriculture. Emphasis lies not just on improvement in material well-being but also in the quality of people's lives. Societies can grow larger and more complex without copying the Western model. Saudi Arabia is a good example of a country that has developed substantially *without* following the West.

Dependency theory
View that developed countries caused underdevelopment of other countries

Among the earliest critics of modernization theory were those who accepted dependency theory (Frank, 1969). According to **dependency theory,** the developed countries did not represent the salvation of developing countries but were instead the *cause* of their underdevelopment. The West had grown rich on the basis of its exploitation of poor nations; its development required the underdevelopment of other nations. Modernization theory led developing countries to seek internal changes (e.g., develop manufacturing), but the real changes, according to dependency theory, had to be made in the relationships between developing and developed nations. Dependency theory was a forerunner to an orientation that has come to be the dominant approach to understanding development—world-system theory.

Saudi Arabia has been able to develop its economy through income derived from its vast oil reserves. However, in its architecture, as well as in many other cultural features, such as religious practices and the status of women, the Saudis have not followed the Western model.

The World-System Approach to Development

World-system theory is an attempt to comprehend contemporary processes of development and underdevelopment (Wallerstein, 1974, 1979, 1980). Using the entire world as the unit of analysis, the **world-system theory** stresses the economic and power inequalities of the present international order. The world is viewed as a stratified system shaped by the world economy. In a geographical division of labor within the world economy, certain nations exploit the labor of others. In the core (richer) nations, free labor engages largely in skilled labor. In the peripheral (poorer) nations, there exists a preponderance of coerced and unskilled labor. Since the core nations are the major benefactors of the cheap goods and materials produced by the laborers in the poor nations, the situation is essentially one of exploitation.

World-system theory Stresses the economic and power inequalities of the international order

World-system theorists argue that the gap between the rich and the poor nations is growing. A minority of the world's people are living well at the expense of the majority. How can such a system be maintained? Wallerstein identifies three mechanisms. The superior military power of the core nations minimizes the probability of a forceful alteration of the system by the poorer nations. Moreover, leaders of both rich and poor nations have an ideological commitment to the system; most leaders try to convince their people that progress can be made by working within the system rather than by rebelling against it and trying to establish a different system. Finally, a group of nations is midway in terms of affluence between the core and the periphery—the semi-periphery. The semi-periphery has a function similar to the middle class within a nation—symbolizing to the poorer nations the possibility of progress. It appears to demonstrate that the world situation is not simply one of an impervious core and a relatively powerless and exploited periphery. The existence of such a middle group, therefore, keeps the world from being polarized into two camps which could, ultimately, lead to the rebellion of the periphery and a world-wide war that would force alterations in the system.

A substantial amount of research supports world-system theory. The research underscores the significance of such things as world trade patterns and multinational corporations in constraining the development of the poorer nations. Essentially, the development of the poorer nations is tied up with processes in advanced capitalist societies. Changes have occurred in the economies of the developing nations like Venezuela over time, but those changes can only be understood in terms of the nation's linkage with the world capitalist economy (Roseberry, 1983).

Not only are the economies of the poorer nations dependent upon policies and practices of the rich nations but the latter frequently work to the detriment of the former. For example, one factor that inhibits development in poorer countries is overurbanization—too heavy a concentration of the population in the urban areas and too much employment in service rather than manufacturing occupations. Both agriculture and industry suffer when there is overurbanization. Studies of the problem suggest that overurbanization is not simply the outcome of internal processes of a nation but is related to the nation's dependence on foreign capital (Timberlake and Kentor, 1983). The more a nation's economy depends on foreign capital, the more the nation tends to suffer from overurbanization. And as overurbanization increases, per capita economic growth tends to decline.

Even foreign aid has done little to change the advantage of the developed nations. In fact, both investments and aid have frequently resulted in worsening some aspects of the situation in developing nations. Bornschier et al. (1978, p. 652) summarized the results of a number of studies based on data from 1950 to 1970 by saying that "foreign investment and aid have the long-term effect of decreasing the rate of economic growth and of increasing inequality."

World-system theory has recently been used to help explain the decline of the American economy on the world scene. The world system has two long-term characteristics. First, periods of economic boom are followed by periods of economic stagnation. Second, a cycle of the rise and fall of a core nation comes to dominate the world system. From this point of view, the problems of the American economy are traceable to the fact that these two cycles are currently intersecting. That is, the world economy is stagnating *and* the United States is simultaneously losing its dominant position in the world economy to Japan and other nations (Boswell and Bergeson, 1987).

World-system theory is derived from Marxian theory, but it has been criticized by Marxists for failing to emphasize the importance of social classes. To most Marxists the key issue is not the relationship between the core and the periphery but rather the relationship between social classes within given societies. A compromise position would be that *both* relationships between core and periphery *and* class relationships within society are of great importance (Bergeson, 1984). Others have criticized world-system theory for its oversimplification: reducing a complex world into a simplistic core/semi-periphery/periphery model.

A horse-drawn cart and a modern bus approach high-rise apartments in Beijing, China. While modernization is occurring in China, there is still much that remains of a traditional, pre-industrial society.

The Paths to Development

Developing nations tend to follow some similar and some divergent paths as they develop. Among other things, the population tends to grow, the middle class expands, status depends more upon achievement than upon ascription, nationalism (as opposed to localism) is emphasized, functions of the state are expanded, emphasis on universal education is increased, and some functions of the family (such as education and health care) are lost. In the occupational structure, a shift is seen toward the white-collar and more skilled kinds of jobs. Other similarities include the tendencies toward urbanization, secularization, and bureaucratization. All three processes can facilitate the development process. Urbanization can provide a nation with centralized political control, opportunities for education, and coordination of activities, and can help break down the local loyalties that may impede national development. Secularization frequently involves not the demise of religion, but a change of religion and a new emphasis on reason, a prime requisite of a modern nation. Bureaucratization can give a nation the organizational structure necessary for efficient development.

On the other hand, the similarities do not mean that all developing nations become alike. Even in the same country, two urban areas or two bureaucratic organizations can be quite different from each other. To say that the developing nations are becoming urbanized, secularized, and bureaucratic, therefore, is not to say that they are becoming exactly like the West. Two important reasons account for the differences. The first is the point mentioned above—the different contexts in which nations develop today. And second, what a nation becomes depends in part upon the traditions on which it builds. Development does not obliterate all traditions; it modifies some, and builds on some.

India offers a good example of the importance of tradition. In the city of Madras, a process of adaptation between traditions and development exists (Singer, 1972). Many scholars have argued that the Hindu religion has impeded change in India because of its emphasis on such things as otherworldliness. They based their arguments, however, largely on teachings in Hindu scriptures rather than on the actual practice of religion in India. When orthodox Hindus learned of the Western interpretation of their religion, they were astounded and asked how India could have achieved so much historically if Hinduism precluded rational action, as Westerners claimed. In fact, Singer found that about half of the industrial leaders in Madras were Brahmans, high-caste Hindus who would be the most careful of all Hindus to observe the religious traditions. The leaders did not find an inherent conflict of interest between their faith and their careers. Rather, they adapted each to the other. For example, Westerners read the Hindu scriptures and looked at traditional practices and believed that members of different castes should not eat together under any circumstances. While at their businesses, leaders would work and eat with members of other castes, although they would not do so outside the business settings. The leaders did not define this act as a violation of their devout commitment to Hinduism. Furthermore, rather than giving four to six hours a day to rituals, in accord with orthodox teaching, the Hindu leaders would take 15 to 30 minutes. Some performed their rituals early in the morning, others prayed while they shaved and washed, and still others said they would perform their obligations when they were older. Thus, the Indian business leaders retained a modified form of their traditional practices while engaging in the process of development.

The flexibility of tradition has also been shown in a study of the kinship structure (the *Hamula*) in an Arab community in Israel (Al-Haj, 1988). Although some changes in attitudes in response to development were found, actual behavior did not change in a parallel fashion. The traditional kinship structure did not break down in the face of development. It retained much of its customary form, but it also reorganized in an effective manner and became well integrated into the modern system. Thus Westernization is *not* the inevitable result of development.

The Consequences of Change

The consequences of change include those defined by people as both desirable and undesirable. Any particular change can have manifold consequences for human life, but not all of those consequences will be welcome to people.

Negative Consequences

Some observers argue that rapid change is always a traumatic experience for humans. For instance, Toffler's (1970) "future shock" thesis asserts that rapid change overwhelms the individual's capacity for adaptation, resulting in physical and psychological distress. According to Toffler, modern society is changing rapidly in every area—norms, values, institutions, and technology. An individual might handle rapid change in one area as long as he or she has stable anchors elsewhere. When we are forced to confront a world that requires us to continually adapt and readapt in all areas of our lives, our capacity for adaptation simply cannot handle the challenge, and we fall prey to various physical and mental problems.

In developed nations (and, increasingly, in developing nations) computers have moved into every area of contemporary life, influencing both the ways things are done and the way we think about ourselves.

But despite the pervasiveness of change, the future shock thesis overstates the case. People who perceive the world to be changing very rapidly around them do have higher levels of stress than others, but the stress is moderated if they define the changes as desirable (Lauer, 1974). In other words, the same change can have very different impacts upon people depending upon whether they define the change as desirable or undesirable. For one person, the computerization of the workplace poses a threat, while another finds it an exciting challenge. For one person, a new housing code causes financial strain, while another finds it desirable because it enhances property values. Any change will be defined as desirable by some and as undesirable by others; the consequences for physical and emotional well-being will therefore also differ.

Changes associated with development also have a number of deleterious effects on individuals. Industrialization and modernization tend to bring an increase in certain diseases or higher rates of illness generally (such as higher rates of tuberculosis in nations during the early stages of industrialization, and an increased incidence of diarrhea, ulcerative colitis, and asthma among Westernized people). High rates of tuberculosis during early industrialization result from lack of sanitation and crowding in growing urban areas. The rate of diabetes in urbanized areas of Africa and Asia increased in part because of increased sugar consumption and lower expenditure of energy (Eaton, 1977). Development also tends to break down traditional interpersonal ties. Many people in developing nations feel isolated after they migrate to the cities. The consequences might be a variety of psychosomatic complaints. Finally, as a result of the various strains and stresses associated with the changes in the developing society, some increase in mental illness, anxiety, alcohol consumption, and crime and violence is also noted (Lauer, 1982).

In addition, development can ravage and deplete the natural environment, which could eventually lead to declines in a country's economic development. For example, it

Whole regions of the Amazon rain forest in Brazil have been destroyed for economic development. This portion was leveled to exploit an oil deposit. Development efforts in many different countries have led to the rapid disappearance of the world's forests and may have serious consequences for the earth's environment.

is argued that the deforestation of the Amazon has had negative economic effects on Brazil (Bunker, 1984; Katzman, 1987). Technological advances in communication (e.g., television) can adversely affect the culture and make political repression more possible. Involvement in the international market by less developed countries may lead them to export workers to more developed countries, thereby weakening their internal labor force (Evans and Stephens, 1988).

Thus, although development continues to have allure for many developing countries, those nations are increasingly sensitive to the problems involved in development as well.

Positive Consequences

If change brings about a certain amount of trauma, it also yields much that is desired. Many things that we value—affluence, enhanced health, opportunities for advancement, diminished inequality—have come (for developed countries) through the changing of old sociocultural systems. With all of the problems attendant upon modern civilization, few people would care to lead a regressive movement and return to a premodern form of life.

Some positive consequences of change appear in development. The people of such recently developed countries as Japan and Korea have clearly enjoyed unprecedented leaps in their standard of living. Many people in these countries, as well as in still-developing nations, not only are better off economically but experience a life of greater happiness with fewer physical and mental ailments. Those who benefit financially and interpersonally from development report a deeper satisfaction with life. However, we should remember that not all nations, or all people in those nations, benefit from development. Some people remain impoverished while others are succeeding; some endure severed relationships while others are building new, more meaningful ties (Assael and German, 1970).

The East Asian Success Story. Economic development in East Asia in recent years has been remarkable (Balassa, 1988). Everyone is familiar with the startling growth in the Japanese economy, but in many ways more startling has been the development of the "Four Tigers"—Hong Kong, South Korea, Singapore, and Taiwan. Even less developed East Asian countries like Thailand and the Philippines have demonstrated strong growth, stronger than a nation like India. How do we account for this remarkable set of success stories?

The key factor in the development of these countries appears to be their active involvement in the export of an array of products including electronics of varying types, clothing, and—in the case of South Korea—automobiles. Exports fuel economic expansion for several reasons. First, exports lead countries to invest in industries that make use of a given nation's specific advantages (e.g., natural resources, personnel). Second, these countries are able to overcome the limitations of their domestic markets, which may be too poor and or too small to fuel economic expansion. Large export markets allow them to take advantage of economies of scale (e.g., mass production). Third, export competition among companies leads them to refine their organizations, develop new technologies, and so on. Fourth, the governments of these nations have tended to modernize (e.g., develop up-to-date communications facilities), to create stable systems of economic exchange, and to create a government bureaucracy that will help rather than hinder exports. In other parts of the world, government bureaucracies have developed regulations and controls that have stifled economic development. Thus, a variety of factors help us to understand economic development in East Asia and its positive consequences.

The Domino Effect

The **domino effect** refers to the tendency for any technological development to set off a chain of other developments. As a result, the process of change is self-perpetuating. The effect occurs, in part, because any particular innovation tends to have a variety of applications—a "technological convergence" (Rosenberg, 1976). For example, there was no machine-tool or machinery-producing sector of the American economy in the first part of the nineteenth century. Factories produced their own machines for their own use. Between 1840 and 1880, however, some firms began manufacturing machinery for the use of other firms. Although at first a factory would make a particular kind of machine for a particular use, firms found that the skills needed for any particular machine could be applied to making others. Thus, firms that initially only made machines for textile factories began to make locomotives; the technology for making firearms was used to make sewing machines; and skills used for producing sewing machines and bicycles were applied later to the manufacture of automobiles.

Domino effect
Tendency of technological development to set off chain of other developments

A second reason for the domino effect is **serendipity,** the accidental discovery of something while looking for something else. Here "looking for something else" means

Serendipity
Accidental discovery of something while looking for something else

looking for a different solution or working on a different problem. Numerous incidents of serendipity mark the history of science and technology, including Galvani's discovery of electric current, Roentgen's discovery of x-rays, Fleming's discovery of the antibiotic effect of penicillin, and Goodyear's discovery of the vulcanization of rubber. Researchers frequently find not only what they are directly looking for but other things as well—so the process of technological change is self-perpetuating.

Summary

Social change refers to variations over time in the relationships among individuals, groups, cultures, and societies. Because social change is patterned, we can distinguish trends, cyclic variations, and irregular or random variations.

A variety of theories attempt to explain change. Cyclic theorists, exemplified by Sorokin, view change as an ongoing series of cycles rather than as a process with direction. Evolutionary theorists view change as a directional process; Lenski and Lenski, key exponents of this approach, see technological developments as the major determinant of change. Conflict theorists, exemplified by Dahrendorf, view change as the inevitable result of inherent conflicts between groups with diverse interests.

Technology, one of the most important sources of change, brings about change by increasing our alternatives, altering interaction patterns, and generating social problems. Ideologies affect change in diverse ways, sometimes acting as impediments or barriers, sometimes as facilitators. Competition and conflict have stimulated much change, especially in scientific developments.

Collective behavior frequently arises from change, or it may produce change. Crowds may have the specific purpose of bringing about some kind of change in their immediate environment. Rumors help people resolve ambiguity in their situations and may be used to legitimate certain behavior, such as rioting. Disasters may result in both short-term and long-term changes.

Social movements, collective efforts to promote or resist change, can be classified as revolutionary, regressive, reform, or expressive. One explanation for movements is the resource mobilization perspective, which stresses the importance of mobilizing sufficient resources to redress the grievances always present in a population.

Modernization and development are general processes that include economic growth in less developed countries. Although development is a pervasive pattern in the contemporary world, influences such as world trade patterns and multinational corporations make the process very different from that experienced earlier by the West. Development generally includes urbanization, secularization, bureaucratization, and a changed stratification system, but the process does not necessarily obliterate all traditions.

Change has both positive and negative consequences, and any particular instance has both gainers and losers. Technological change tends to set off a domino effect, a chain of other developments that make the process self-perpetuating.

CRITICAL THINKING

1. In general, how successful is terrorism in promoting social change? Think of recent examples of terrorist incidents described in the newspapers or on television. To what degree were these efforts at change successful?
2. How do sociologists account for the multitude of changes at various levels of life? Give a brief explanation of the perspectives of the following schools of thought: cyclic, evolutionary, and conflict theory. Compare and contrast the theories in terms of their usefulness in explaining various types of social change.
3. In what ways does the introduction of new technology in society cause change? Are these changes positive or negative? What happens when a society's old norms, roles, or values no longer apply to the situation created by new technology?
4. In what ways does ideology facilitate or impede change in society? Give specific examples to support your ideas.
5. Many people view conflict in a negative light. In what ways is conflict useful in promoting social change? In what ways has competition been useful in promoting social change?
6. What stereotypes exist about people's behavior during disasters? Are these stereotypes supported by the evidence presented in this chapter?
7. Compare and contrast the different types of social movements presented in the chapter. Which have been evident in American history? How important is resource mobilization in determining the success of a social movement?
8. Compare and contrast modernization and development theory. Why has development theory proved to be more useful in explaining changes in less developed countries? What are the advantages and disadvantages of development? Is Westernization an unavoidable aspect of development?
9. Describe the world-system theory of development. What evidence supports this viewpoint?

CONNECTIONS

Reproductive Technology

Introduction

Todd is four years old and has just asked his mom the question, "Where do babies come from?" His mother is prepared for his question and takes a book from the bookcase and reads to him.

> Human babies begin just like chicks and puppies. A sperm from the father must join with an egg from the mother. The sperm, which come from the father's testicles, are sent into the mother through his penis. To do this, the father and mother lie down facing each other and the father places his penis in the mother's vagina. Unlike plants and animals, when human mothers and fathers create a new baby they are sharing a very personal and special relationship.

Written for three- to ten-year-olds, this description of conception is found in the book *How Babies Are Made* (Andry and Schepp, 1979). Unlike Todd's mother, some parents today may not wish to choose this book, and instead will create new ways of explaining conception to their children. These are parents who have conceived or received their children through some means other than the "natural" process of mothers and fathers having sexual intercourse, as described in Andry and Schepp's book. They will have used some of the current-day reproductive technology to have children. Reproductive technology refers to the use of scientific innovations and procedures for the conception and production of children.

Reproductive technology is used primarily by couples or individuals who cannot have children due to physical or medical problems. For married couples who have experienced infertility, there are now procedures that allow them options other than adoption. Of course, reasons other than infertility cause some couples, or individuals, to use the new reproductive technology. All of these methods, and the motivations for using them, represent significant social changes. These changes often raise an array of legal, moral, social, economic, and health issues (Kammeyer, 1987; Fromer, 1983). Before we consider these issues and the sociological analysis of them, we will take a brief look at the major kinds of reproductive technology in use today.

1. *Artificial insemination and sperm banks.* Artificial insemination involves the implantation of sperm into a woman's uterus. This method is often used by couples when the man is sterile and sperm are taken from a donor. But, of course, this method can be used by any woman who wishes to become pregnant, whether she is married or not. Sperm banks now exist in which donor sperm are stored in a frozen state. There are even some specialized sperm banks for those who are selective about the donor. The most well-publicized is located in California and is popularly called the "Nobel sperm bank." This enterprise specializes in storing the sperm of famous and successful scientists, including three who are Nobel prize winners (Matthews, 1982).

2. *Test-tube babies or in vitro fertilization.* A test-tube baby, or the use of in vitro fertilization, is different from artificial insemination because an ovum is taken from a woman and combined with sperm from a husband or a donor, then fertilized in a laboratory. The baby does not actually grow inside a glass test tube, but the egg and sperm are brought together in a special medium that has been placed in a glass dish. The resultant fertilized egg is later implanted into the woman's uterus (Hartley, 1981; Zimmerman, 1982).

3. *Surrogate motherhood.* Surrogate mothers are childbearing women used by other women who are physiologically incapable of carrying a baby to full term. In this type of reproductive technology the husband's sperm are generally used to impregnate the surrogate mother who has agreed, through legal contract, to give the baby to the couple at the time of birth (Volpe, 1987).

4. *Gender selection.* At the present time there is only one certain way of selecting the gender of one's child before birth, but there are a number of techniques that purport to change the probability of having a male or female baby. The only certain way is by combining a technique called amniocentesis with abortion. Amniocentesis involves withdrawing and analyzing a small amount of amniotic fluid from the uterus of a pregnant woman. This method is used most commonly to determine if there are any fetal abnormalities (such as Down's syndrome), but it can also be used to determine the gender of the fetus. Thus, it is possible to abort the pregnancy if the fetus were not of the desired gender.

Obviously, many people object to gender selection simply because it involves abortion, since they object to abortion for any reason. However, abortion is not the issue here, for gender selection is likely to be possible by other means. Gender selection is now accomplished in farm animals by separating sperm bearing the (XY) chromosome (male) from those bearing the (XX) chromosome (female). Then through artificial insemination the gender of choice can be produced. In the future, there are apt to be other technologies that will allow gender selection without either abortion or artificial insemination. The interesting sociological question is whether couples and individuals will select the gender of their children, and what the social implications will be if they do.

All of these types of reproductive technology are so recent that it is difficult to see all their social ramifications. In the remainder of this discussion we will see how sociological theories and research can help us to understand the implications of these technological innovations in reproduction. We will begin by seeing what some of the major sociological theories can add to our understanding of the issues.

Structural-Functional Theory

Structural-functional theory focuses attention on the functions or purposes of social structures, including the institutions of a society. In chapter 11 we saw that the family institution normally carries out a number of crucial functions that aid in the survival of a society. Among those functions, and especially important for our consideration of reproductive technology, are *reproduction* and the *regulation of sexual behavior*. The new reproductive technologies are generally consistent with the reproductive function of the family. It is now possible for virtually all married couples to have children, if they are willing, and have the economic resources, to use the methods of artificial insemination, in vitro fertilization, or, in some cases, surrogate mothering. By using these methods, couples who would otherwise be childless can now have children, thus continuing the family lineage, and supplying new members for the society.

The family function of controlling sexual behavior is, however, differently affected by the new reproductive technologies. Societies often control sexual behavior through the institution of marriage. This is illustrated most vividly in the case of lesbian or gay couples who have often been deprived of having children because of their sexual preferences. These restrictions acted as a societal control on individuals whose sexual preferences did not accord with those of the majority. Individuals who insisted on homosexual relationships were deprived of children and families. It is still not possible for gay or lesbian couples to marry in the United States, but by using the new reproductive technology they are having children. Today, many lesbian couples are using artificial insemination, often with a male friend as a donor, to have children of their own. From this example we see that the new reproductive technologies are changing the way in which the family system has traditionally functioned to control sexual behavior.

Conflict Theory

We have seen throughout this book that conflict theorists, and particularly followers of Marx, often focus on the economic inequalities that exist in societies. Some people simply have greater access to the goods, services, and benefits of the society than others do. Indeed, people at the bottom of the socioeconomic structure may be exploited so that those at the top may enjoy the greater benefits.

Two of the new reproductive technologies illustrate vividly how benefits are unequally accessible, and may be exploitative of the poor. Both in vitro fertilization and surrogate mothering are very costly and thus are practically available only to the relatively well-off. In vitro fertilization is extremely expensive—each fertilization attempt may cost up to $7,000 (Lemonick, 1989). Since not every attempt will be successful, the total cost is prohibitive for couples or individuals with modest or low incomes. Even more costly is the expense associated with surrogate mothering. In most cases the woman who becomes impregnated and carries the baby to the time of its birth is paid between $10,000 and $15,000 (*The Kansas City Times*, 1989). In addition, the hospital delivery costs, associated medical bills, legal fees, and a variety of incidental costs are paid by the couple receiving the baby. All told, the cost of having a baby through a surrogate mother is likely to run into tens of thousands of dollars. Obviously, only the highest socioeconomic-status couples will be able to spend this amount of money.

Conflict theorists emphasize that in addition to economic inequalities in the availability of reproductive technology, there is also frequently exploitation of the poorer classes. While $10,000 to $15,000 may be a considerable expense for a couple "purchasing" a baby, it is not an exceptionally large amount to pay a woman who agrees to use her body to produce a baby. In general, women who agree to be surrogate mothers are apt to be lower income women.

The most famous surrogate mother case—the "Baby M" case—is a prime illustration of the inequities and exploitation that can often be found when women agree to produce a baby for money. In this case, William and Elizabeth Stern, both professionals, contracted with Mary Beth Whitehead (shown opposite) to bear a baby for them. Ms. Whitehead was not employed, and her husband at the time was a garbage collector. This case gained national notoriety when Ms. Whitehead decided late in the pregnancy that she wanted to keep the baby. In this case she was the biological mother because she both provided the ovum and carried the baby to the time of its birth. Mr. Stern was the biological father because his sperm was used to impregnate Ms. Whitehead. The two sides fought for the custody of the child and, after a long and unpleasant legal battle, the Sterns won. Ms. Whitehead was, however, granted limited visitation rights.

Many observers of this case believe that the decision reflected the unequal economic (and social) positions of the two opposing sides. While it is true that Ms. Whitehead had made a contractual agreement to turn the baby over to the Sterns, it is also true that part of the court's decision was based on the Sterns' ability to provide Baby M with more economic advantages. This case is consistent with what conflict theory would predict—namely, that people in higher economic positions will be able to win out over, and even exploit, people with lower economic positions.

Symbolic Interactionism

As we have seen throughout this text, symbolic interactionists believe the development of a child's self-concept is a crucial aspect of the socialization process. Through the early years of their lives, children begin to see themselves as distinct from others, but their views about themselves are received from significant others, especially parents. They look toward parents for judgments about their own behaviors.

As we noted in the introduction, when parents use various forms of reproductive technology, they may have to use very different ways of explaining to their children the circumstances of their births. This raises some serious symbolic interactionist questions about how such explanations will affect the self-esteem of children who were conceived and brought to life by unconventional means. What will it mean to the child of a surrogate who is told that their birth mother gave them up at birth for a large fee?

We noted in chapter 3 that in the United States, as well as many other societies, a great significance is attached to the concept of *biological father*. The same is, of course, true for the biological mother. Will the children of surrogate mothers experience the same problems as adopted children, some of whom feel a need to learn the identity of their biological parents? Symbolic interactionists would predict that in American society they would.

Social Exchange Theory

Social exchange theorists, as we have seen, are concerned with the rewards and costs that people experience in their interaction with others. This theory, then, will direct our attention to the costs and rewards involved in the new reproductive technologies we have been discussing. Furthermore, the theory emphasizes that costs and rewards must be balanced, or reciprocal.

In the case of surrogate mothering, and specifically the Baby M case that we have just considered, the contractual arrangement made between the Sterns and Mary Beth Whitehead was obviously an attempt at reciprocity. The Sterns agreed to pay Ms. Whitehead a specified amount of money, for which she agreed to bear a child and turn it over to them. As Ms. Whitehead neared the end of her pregnancy, however, she decided that the costs of losing the baby were no longer reasonable for the rewards ($10,000) she was to receive. This example also reminds us that exchange theory is not limited to issues of money, but can involve the exchange of anything of value. There have been some surrogate mothers who have reported that part of their reward, in addition to the money they received, was the satisfaction they received from providing a baby for a couple that would not otherwise be able to have a child of their own.

Artificial insemination involves a different set of costs and rewards. When a sperm bank is used, the costs and rewards are again primarily economic. Donors of sperm are usually paid for their sperm, and the recipients pay a fee for the sperm and the service. Often donors are medical students who earn extra money (about $30) for contributing to the sperm bank, an action which for them is a straightforward economic reward. Many lesbian couples report that they receive sperm from a male friend, rather than the more impersonal sperm bank. In these cases the male donors apparently receive as their reward the friendship of the couple, since they almost never expect any rights to the child.

Looking at the Research

Since the reproductive technology we have been discussing is so new, relatively little research has been completed (McKinney, 1989). For example, the first "test-tube" baby was born in 1978, and to date somewhat over 500 babies have been born by this method. That number is likely to increase greatly in the years ahead, since there are 138 medical centers that do in vitro fertilization, and many couples are on their waiting lists (*American Demographics*, 1987). About 500 babies have been born to surrogate mothers (Leslie and Korman, 1989). Artificial insemination has been much more widely used, with more than 250,000 babies conceived in this way. Gender selection has been used in an indeterminate number of cases, but it is not likely that many couples have aborted their pregnancies in order to have a child of a selected gender. This judgment is based on the research that has been done on how Americans feel about selecting the gender of their children—by any means.

National surveys of the U.S. adult population have shown that a little over one-third of adult women approved of the idea of being able to predetermine the sex of their children, and a substantial majority (59.1 percent) disapproved (Pebley and Westoff, 1982). The question asked in this survey was general and abstract, since no method was identified and no conditions were specified. In a different survey, many more people approved when they were asked about selecting the gender of a child if it were used to avoid a gender-linked hereditary defect (Chico and Hartley, 1981). There was also greater approval for gender selection in the case of a couple who already had two or more children of the same sex and wanted their last child to be of the opposite sex.

One of the outcomes of gender selection that has frequently been predicted is an excess of males in the resulting population if couples could (and would) easily choose the gender of their children (Etzioni, 1973; Williamson, 1978). If American women who have not yet had children were to satisfy their gender preferences, among their firstborn they would have 189 boys for every 100 girls (Williamson, 1976a). The preference for boys over girls is worldwide, found in almost every country. Only five societies have been found that preferred girls over boys. All were very small, and only two still exist as they were described in the anthropological literature (Williamson, 1976b). With these minor exceptions, it can be said that the vast populations of the world—India, China, the Middle East, Latin America, and Africa, as well as Europeans and North Americans—all have a strong preference for males.

Some interesting additional evidence for male preference is found in the folk-sayings of widely different cultures:

> A German adage goes: "A house full of daughters is like a cellar full of sour beer."
>
> A Chinese proverb: "Eighteen goddesslike daughters are not equal to one son with a hump."
>
> The Talmud states: "When a girl is born, the walls are crying" (Corea, 1985, p. 190).

Since most methods of reproductive technology are such recent innovations, we have only begun to see the societal and cultural changes that may occur as they are used more extensively. For it is almost certain that these and other reproductive technologies will be used increasingly in the future, and will provide countless exciting opportunities for sociological analysis and research.

References

American Demographics 9, 1987.

ANDRY, ANDREW, and SCHEPP, STEVEN. *How Babies Are Made*. Boston: Little, Brown and Company, 1979.

CHICO, NAN PAULSEN, and HARTLEY, SHIRLEY FOSTER. "Widening Choices of Motherhood of the Future." *Psychology of Women Quarterly*, 1981.

COREA, GENA. *The Mother Machine: Reproductive Technologies From Artificial Insemination to Artificial Wombs*. New York: Harper and Row, 1985.

ETZIONI, AMATAI. *Genetic Fix*. New York: Macmillan, 1973.

FROMER, MARGOT J. *Ethical Issues in Sexuality and Reproduction*. St. Louis: The C.V. Mosby Co., 1983.

HARTLEY, SHIRLEY FOSTER. "Attitudes Toward Reproductive Engineering: An Overview." *Journal of Family Issues* 2, 1981.

KAMMEYER, KENNETH C.W. *Marriage and Family: A Foundation for Personal Decisions*. Boston: Allyn and Bacon, 1987.

LEMONICK, MICHAEL D. "Trying to Fool the Infertile." *Time*, March 13, 1989.

LESLIE, GERALD R., and KORMAN, SHEILA K. *The Family in Social Context*, 7th ed. New York: Oxford University Press, 1989.

MATTHEWS, JAY. "Surrogate Motherhood Becoming an American Growth Industry." *Washington Post*, January 25, 1983.

MCKINNEY, KATHLEEN. *Human Sexuality: The Societal and Interpersonal Context of Reproduction*. 1989.

PEBLEY, ANNE R., and WESTOFF, CHARLES F. "Sex Preferences in the United States: 1970 to 1975." *Demography* 19, 1982.

ROWLAND, ROBYN. "Technology and Motherhood: Reproductive Choice Reconsidered." *Signs: Journal of Women in Culture and Society* 12, 1987.

The Kansas City Times. "New Issues Surround Test-Tube Surrogacy," April 8, 1989.

VOLPE, E. PETER. *Test-Tube Conception: A Blend of Love and Science*. Macon, Ga.: Mercer University Press, 1987.

WILLIAMSON, NANCY E. "Sex Preferences, Sex Control, and the Status of Women." *Signs: Journal of Women in Culture and Society* 1, 1976a.

WILLIAMSON, NANCY E. *Sons or Daughters: A Cross-Cultural Survey of Parental Preferences*, Vol. 31. Sage Library of Social Research. Beverly Hills: Sage, 1976b.

WILLIAMSON, NANCY E. "Boys or Girls? Parents' Preferences and Sex Control." *Population Bulletin*, 1978.

ZIMMERMAN, SHIRLEY L. "Alternatives in Human Reproduction for Involuntary Childless Couples." *Family Relations* 31, 1982.

GLOSSARY

Acculturation *See* Cultural assimilation.

Achieved status A status that people acquire through their own efforts.

Acting crowd A large number of people trying to change some aspect of their immediate environment.

Adult socialization Those occasions in life when adults learn the new behaviors expected of them as they enter new occupations, professions, work settings, institutions, or life stages.

Agricultural revolution The shift from hunting-and-gathering subsistence patterns to the cultivation of grains and domestication of animals.

Alienation Breakdown of the natural connections between people and their work, other people, and the natural world.

Anglo-conformity The American concept of assimilation that assumes that minorities should adopt traits of the dominant group.

Anomie A state of normlessness; situations in which individuals are uncertain about the norms of society.

Anticipatory socialization The process of learning what will be expected of one in a status before entering that status.

Apartheid The South African legal system of "separate development" that perpetuates white power and privilege.

Apostates People who early in their lives have a religious identity but later come to renounce or reject it.

Applied research Research designed and conducted to answer a specific practical question or solve a particular social problem.

Ascribed status A status into which individuals move, or are placed, irrespective of their efforts or capacities.

Assimilation The integration or incorporation of a minority into the mainstream of a society.

Attitudinal discrimination Discrimination that stems from prejudicial attitudes and usually involves direct and overt forms of behavior.

Attitudinal objectivity Scientists maintaining an attitude of fairness and honesty when planning and conducting their research.

Authority Legitimate power; the exercise of power that is accepted by those over whom it is exerted.

Autocracy A form of government in which ultimate authority is vested in a single person.

Basic research Research designed and conducted to test hypotheses derived from theories.

Bureaucracy An organization that has division of labor, hierarchical authority, rules and procedures, impersonality in relations among members, and selection and promotion based on competence and expertise.

Bureaucratic personality The tendency of bureaucrats to conform slavishly to organizational rules, with the result that the rules are more important than the task or objective of the organization.

Capitalism Economic system that emphasizes the private ownership of property and the means of production (raw materials, factories, machines, and equipment).

Capitalists Marx's term for the owners of the means of production in a capitalist economic system.

Caste system The most rigid and closed of stratification systems in which one's status is inherited and fixed, and people are prohibited from marrying members of other strata.

Catch-22 A situation in which the rules of a bureaucracy are in conflict in such a way as to block action.

Charisma Extraordinary qualities, often believed to be supernatural, that give a leader authority over others.

Church A large, socially acceptable, institutionalized religious group.

City A relatively large, densely populated, and diverse settlement of people.

Civil religion The system of symbols, beliefs, values, and practices that have sacred meaning for a nation and a people.

Class Social ranking in a stratification system based on one's relationship to the means of production; more commonly, social ranking based on economic factors such as income and wealth.

Closed class system A system of stratification in which people's positions are fixed and there is little possibility of social mobility.

Coercion Power that is based on the threat or use of force and is therefore considered illegitimate by the people who are forced to do what they do not wish to do.

Coercive organization An organization that uses force to control those at the bottom of the structure.

Collective behavior Behavior that is expressed as part of a collectivity, focused on a particular phenomenon or event, involves a situation of change, conflict, uncertainty, or ambiguity, and is relatively unconstrained by well-established social patterns.

Communicable disease Disease that can be transmitted to people in a variety of ways, including other people, animals, other organisms, food, and water.

Competitive capitalism Capitalist system in which no one capitalist, or small group of capitalists, can gain complete or uncontested control over the market.

Compositional theory of urbanism A model of urban life that emphasizes the importance of social class, ethnicity, and life cycle stage in determining urban social relationships.

Computer abuse Unauthorized entry into someone else's computer data and altering, stealing, or sabotaging it.

Concentric zone model A model of urban development emphasizing differences in urban land use involving a series of successive rings surrounding a central business district.

Concept A word or phrase that summarizes some meaningful part of the social world.

Conflict theory A view of society as constantly in a state of imbalance and conflict; in which social groups or societies are composed of units that are often engaged in a struggle for power.

Conflict theory of change Change seen as a result of conflicting interests between groups.

Conformists People who accept cultural goals and conventional means to them.

Conspicuous consumption Acquiring things simply to display them and to show that one can afford them.

Control group Subjects in an experiment who are not exposed to the experimental variable.

Convenience sample Research subjects who are conveniently available to complete questionnaires or to be interviewed.

Conventionalized crowd	A collectivity gathered for a particular purpose and acting in accord with established norms.
Correlation	A measure of how much two variables are co-related or associated; indicated by a correlation coefficient, expressed as a decimal fraction from -1.00 to $+1.00$, that summarizes the degree and direction of the relationship between the variables.
Counterculture	A societal group that is consciously in opposition to the widely held norms and values of the dominant culture.
Crime	Deviant behavior that violates the law and is subject to formally sanctioned punishment by the larger society.
Crimes against people (violent crime)	Crimes involving the threat of injury, or threat (or use) of force, against victims.
Criminology	The subfield of sociology devoted to the study of crime, criminal behavior and the treatment of criminals.
Cross-cultural studies	Often anthropological reports and descriptions of other (often small) non-literate, societies and their cultures.
Cross-national research	The collection of similar types of data in two or more societies so that results can be compared.
Cross-national studies	Studies that examine sociological dimensions of two or more contemporary nations.
Cult	A small, voluntary, and exclusive religious group that has created a new religious system.
Cultural assimilation	A process by which members of subcultures and minorities acquire cultural characteristics (including values, beliefs, language, and behaviors) of the dominant group.
Cultural diffusion	The spread of a cultural trait from one society to another.
Cultural lag	Social and cultural practices that are no longer appropriate when technological change occurs faster than social systems can adapt.
Cultural relativism	An approach that evaluates the behavior of the people of other societies, not on the basis of the evaluator's own culture, but in terms of the culture under consideration.
Cultural values	A key component of culture, the standards of desirability, of rightness, and of importance in a society.
Culture	The entire complex of ideas and material objects that people of a society (or group) have created and adopted for carrying out the necessary tasks of collective life.
Cyclic theory	The theory of social change in which change is seen as an ongoing series of recurring cultural emphases rather than as a process with some kind of direction.
Deindustrialization	The decline of American industry through plant shutdowns, layoffs, and downsizing.
Delabelling	A process by which a deviant label is shed and replaced by a socially acceptable label.
Democracy	A form of government in which there are periodic opportunities for the people being governed to retain or replace governing officials.
Denominational pluralism	A situation in which different religious groups coexist in a society, with no single group dominating.
Dependency theory	A theory that argues that the developed countries are not the salvation of developing countries, but the cause of their underdevelopment.
Dependent variable	A variable that is changed or influenced by an independent variable.
Descriptive statistics	Statistics used to communicate information about numerical data.

Descriptive survey A survey designed to obtain some basic information about a population, e.g., surveys of attitudes and behavior, opinion polls, and market surveys.

Development The general process of economic growth, not necessarily emphasizing manufacturing.

Deviance Any behavior that most members of a society or social group consider a violation of group norms.

Differential association theory A sociological theory that sees deviance as learned by individuals being socialized by a group of people who engage in and accept deviant behavior.

Diffuse crowd A large number of dispersed individuals who follow particular kinds of behavior or who experience a particular sentiment, e.g., fads and crazes.

Direct expulsion Use of laws and government policies to expel minorities.

Discreditable stigma A negative characteristic of a person that is neither known about by those present, nor immediately perceived by them.

Discredited stigma A negative characteristic of a person that is known about already or is evident to any observer.

Discrimination Unfavorable treatment of people because of their group membership.

Dominant group *See* majority group.

Domino effect The tendency of any technological development to set off a chain of other developments.

Dramaturgy Performances by individuals aimed at manipulating situations in ways favorable to themselves.

Dyad Two people engaged in interaction.

Dysfunction A detrimental consequence of some social structure for a society.

Economy The social institution involved in the production and exchange of a wide range of goods and services.

Elite deviance Deviant or criminal acts committed by the wealthy and powerful members of society.

Elite A small group of people who come to power and dominate the population.

Emergent norm theory In collective behavior, a theory that emphasizes the similarity between collective behavior and institutionalized social life. When some form of collective behavior is occurring, new norms, social relationships, communication patterns, and values emerge.

Empiricism The act of experiencing something with one's senses, in contrast to imagination and speculation.

Ethnic group A group that is socially defined on the basis of its cultural characteristics. Members of an ethnic group consider themselves, and are considered by others, to be part of a distinct culture or subculture.

Ethnicity The sense of belonging to and identifying with a particular ethnic group.

Ethnocentrism The view held by the people of a society that they are of central importance in the universe and therefore their ways of doing things are the right ways.

Evolutionary theory A theory of social change in which change is seen as directional, a process of cumulative change.

Exclusion Policies and practices that seek to maintain a society's cultural homogeneity by refusing to admit culturally different groups.

Experimental treatment Exposure to the independent variable in an experiment.

Experimental group Subjects in an experiment who are exposed to the experimental variable.

Experiments Research method in which the independent variable is under the control of the researcher so that its impact on a dependent variable can be observed directly.

Explanatory surveys Surveys attempting to find independent variables that relate to or account for differences in behaviors or attitudes.

Expressive crowd A group of people displaying intense feelings, emotions, and exuberant physical behavior.

Expressive movements A social movement aimed at changing individuals, who will then either change the social order or adapt better to the existing order.

Expulsion Practices and policies that seek to move minorities from areas controlled by the dominant group.

Extermination Practices and policies that seek to reduce, destroy, or eliminate a minority population.

Felonies Serious crimes, punishable by a year or more in prison.

Feral children Wild children—children who have allegedly been reared in the wild by animals.

Field experiments Experiments conducted in settings that are natural and involve activities that are relatively normal.

Folkways Rules that generally govern everyday conduct, such as the rules for eating.

Function According to structural-functional theory, a positive purpose or consequence necessary for the continued existence of a society (or some other social system).

Functional theory *See* Structural-functionalism.

Functional theory of stratification An application of structural-functional theory stressing how social inequality and differential rewards are necessary to motivate the most able people to fill a society's most important tasks; the stratification system is seen as beneficial to the individual and the society.

Game stage Mead's final stage of a child's social development in which the child simultaneously assumes the roles of a number of other people and responds to the expectations made of them by these people.

***Gemeinschaft* societies** Toennies's term for societies characterized by personal, face-to-face relationships, such as those in families, rural villages, and perhaps small towns.

General deterrence The threat of punishment having the intention that people will not commit crimes because they fear they will be caught and punished (*see* **Specific deterrence**).

Generalized other The internalization of the norms of the larger social group or society by an individual.

Genocide *See* Extermination.

Gentrification The process in which affluent people move into and restore previously declining older urban neighborhoods.

***Gesellschaft* societies** Toennies's term for a society characterized by impersonal and distant social relationships; people interact with each other, but in very limited ways, and for what the relationship may provide in terms of calculated self-interest. Associated with urban life.

Group A relatively small number of people who interact with one another over time and thereby establish patterns of interaction, group identity, and rules or norms governing behavior.

Heterodox revelation A religious experience or doctrine that is critical and disruptive of the existing religious and social order.

Historical-comparative method The examination and comparison of the events and histories of whole societies, or of the events and histories of major components of societies (e.g., religious systems).

Horizontal mobility Movement from one social position to another of equal rank.

Hypothesis A statement about how various phenomena are expected to be related to each other.

Ideal culture Values and norms that most people are aware of and accept, but do not necessarily live up to.

Ideal type A logical, exaggerated, and "pure" model of some phenomenon one is studying or wishes to analyze.

Idealistic culture Culture that blends the supersensory and sensory (nonmaterial and material) worlds.

Ideational culture Culture dominated by the principle that a supersensory or nonmaterial world is the only true reality and the highest value.

Ideology A set of ideas used to legitimate and justify the existing social order; also a set of ideas that explains reality, provides directives for behavior, and expresses the interests of particular groups.

In-group A group with whom members are involved and with whom they identify.

Income The economic resources that people receive or obtain during a specified period of time.

Income sufficiency The amount of money needed to purchase the basic necessities of life.

Independent variable A variable that is thought to produce a change in some other variable.

Index offenses (street crimes) Crimes against people and property crimes.

Indicators Observable phenomena that indicate the presence or absence, or level, of a concept.

Indirect expulsion Use of harassment, discrimination, and persecution to force minorities to leave an area or nation.

Individualism The importance placed on the rights, freedoms, and responsibilities of every person.

Industrial democracy System in which workers gain control over the work that they do.

Industrial Revolution In the nineteenth century, a rapid major social and economic change marked by the use of power-driven machinery; the rise of the factory system.

Inferential statistics Techniques that assist in making statements about a population from a sample.

Innovators People who accept cultural goals but reject conventional means.

Institution A set of groups and organizations, with norms and values, that attend to the basic needs of a society.

Institutional discrimination Practices or policies that appear to be neutral but have the effect of excluding minorities from positions of power and prestige.

Intergenerational mobility Differences between the social class position of children and the social class position of their parents.

Inter-sender role conflict Situation in which two or more people have conflicting expectations of a person in a given role.

Inter-role conflict Situation in which expectations attached to one role are in conflict with expectations of another role.

Interview Questions asked by an interviewer or researcher, in person or by telephone.

Intragenerational (or career) mobility Movement in the class structure by individuals during their lifetimes.

Invasion-succession The process whereby one identifiable group moves to a different part of an urban area and is replaced by another group.

Iron Triangle Three points of power in the government—bureaucracy, interest groups, and Congress—that limit presidential action.

Isolation A condition resulting from a feeling of not belonging to one's workplace or other settings; a dimension of alienation.

Juvenile delinquency Illegal or antisocial behavior on the part of a minor.

Knowledge and beliefs A body of information created and accepted by the people of a society that influences their behavior.

Labeling theory A sociological theory that focuses on the process by which some people in society are able to label other individuals as deviant.

Laboratory experiments Experiments conducted in specially designed rooms that are equipped with one-way mirrors, audio systems, and video recording equipment.

Latent function A less obvious, unanticipated, or unexpected consequence of a social structure.

Laws The norms that are written and enforced by the government.

Liberation theology A contemporary Christian religious doctrine emphasizing social justice for the poor and dispossessed.

Life expectancy The average number of years that people in a social or demographic category will live.

Life chances The likelihood of realizing a certain standard of living or quality of life as it is affected by one's position in a stratification system.

Looking-glass self The image of oneself that is a reflection of how others respond to one.

Macroscopic sociology The sociological study of the larger social units—groups, organizations, cultures, and societies.

Majority group A group that occupies a position of superior power, prestige, and privilege, and is able to realize its goals and interests even in the face of resistance.

Mana The force or power believed to be inherent in a sacred object.

Manifest function The intended and well-recognized purpose or consequence of a social structure.

Mass production Production system in which products are standardized, parts are interchangeable, the production process yields high volume, the flow of materials is synchronized, and the entire process is as continuous as possible.

Master status A position so important that it dominates or overrides all other statuses, both for the person and for all other people.

Material culture The artifacts, objects, and tools used by the members of a particular society.

Materialism A preoccupation with acquiring more and more possessions and property.

Mean A numerical average of a set of numbers, obtained by adding all the numbers in a set and dividing the sum by the total number of cases in the set; a measure of central tendency.

Meaninglessness A condition in which one cannot see one's place and significance in the broader scheme of things; a dimension of alienation.

Median The middle number of a distribution of numbers arranged from lowest to highest; a measure of central tendency.

Medicalization of society The tendency to exaggerate the importance of medicine and to call something an illness that was not previously thought of in this way.

Megalopolis An area of continuous urban and suburban settlement formed when the outer rings of adjacent metropolitan areas merge.

Melting pot A description of assimilation as many different ethnic groups contribute to the creation of a new and different culture.

Meritocracy An ideology that justifies social inequality by emphasizing equality of opportunity.

Metropolis A large urban area containing a central city and the surrounding communities that are economically and politically linked to the central city.

Metropolitan Statistical Area (MSA) A term used by the United States Census Bureau to refer to a geographic area (usually a county or series of counties) of at least 100,000 residents that includes a center city of at least 50,000 inhabitants.

Microscopic sociology The sociological study of the smallest social units—individuals, their thoughts, and actions.

Military-industrial complex The informal but closely knit cooperation between military and industrial sectors that tends to foster the mutual interests of each.

Minority group A group that occupies an inferior or subordinate position of prestige, power, and privilege; is excluded from full participation in the life of the society; and is the object of discrimination by the majority group.

Misdemeanors Minor crimes punishable by less than a year in prison.

Mode The most frequently observed number in a set of numbers; a measure of central tendency.

Modern Demographic Transition A three-stage pattern of population change occurring as societies industrialize and urbanize.

Modernization The degree to which less developed countries follow the model of the developed countries of the West.

Monopoly capitalism Modern capitalist system in which one or a few capitalists control a given sector of the economy.

Mores Rules relating to serious behaviors and moral standards, such as stealing, robbing, killing, espionage.

Multiple nuclei model A model of urban development emphasizing that cities have several distinct centers of activity.

Myth A sacred story that communicates the moral prescriptions of divine beings and binds believers into a community and a belief system.

Nation-state A state that has power over people living in a distinct geographical area known as a nation.

Natural selection A theory that states that the fittest members of any species will be allowed to survive and to spread their traits throughout the population.

Neo-Marxian theory A sociological theory in which legal and political systems are seen as being built upon, and are a reflection of, a society's economic base.

Net financial assets Household wealth after equity in homes and vehicles has been deducted.

Net worth Household wealth based on the difference between assets and liabilities.

New class The stratum of managers, executives, scientists, intellectuals, and other professionals who have gained positions of power in bureaucratically dominated societies.

"New" immigration Immigrants of the late nineteenth and early twentieth century who were drawn primarily from southern and eastern Europe (e.g., Poland, Italy, Greece, Russia).

Nonverbal symbol A physical display that has social meaning.

Norm of reciprocity A standard that calls for two interacting people to give one another things of equal or almost equal value.

Normative, or voluntary, organization An organization that controls participants by its norms and values.

Norms Rules for what should and should not be done in given situations.

Objectivity In science, conducting research in a way that personal, subjective views do not influence research results.

"Old" immigration The wave of immigrants from northern and western Europe (e.g., Great Britain, Germany, Ireland, and Scandinavia) who immigrated to the United States primarily between 1820 and 1895.

Oligarchy A small, powerful, controlling group at the top of an organization having almost all of the control and power.

Open class system A system of stratification in which there are few obstacles to people moving up or down in the system.

Organization A deliberately constituted collectivity aimed at achieving specified goals, with clearly delineated statuses, roles, and rules.

Organized crime Self-perpetuating, structured, and disciplined associations in which profits are obtained wholly or in part through illegal means.

Orthodox revelation A religious experience or doctrine that supports the existing religious and social order.

Out-group From the point of view of in-group members, a group to which outsiders belong.

Participant observation A research method that typically involves the researcher directly in the lives and events of the people being studied; the researcher is both a participant and an observer.

Personal control The idea that individuals cannot be made to do things that they do not want to do by social, political, or economic forces.

Personal values The values individuals use to make decisions about their personal lives and how they will respond to public issues.

Play stage Mead's second stage of a child's social development in which the child evaluates himself or herself from the point of view of significant others.

Pluralism (1) A system in which different ethnic or racial groups can coexist equally and be preserved. (2) A political situation in which a number of competing interest groups exert power, with no single group able to control all situations.

Political crime Misconduct and crime committed within or against a political system.

Postindustrial society A society that was formerly industrial, but is now primarily producing services and information, rather than manufactured goods.

Posttest measurement Measurement of the dependent variable after the experimental treatment has been introduced.

Poverty index The federal government's estimate of the annual income necessary to meet minimal living costs in the United States.

Poverty rate The percentage of the population below the poverty line.

Power The ability of an individual or group to realize its interests and to impose its will upon others, despite resistance.

Power elite Small group of nationally influential persons who occupy key positions in large corporations, the executive branch of government, and the military.

Powerlessness A condition of being dominated by another individual or by circumstance; a dimension of alienation.

Prejudice A set of rigidly held negative attitudes, beliefs, and feelings toward members of another group.

Preparatory stage Mead's first stage of a child's social development in which the young child engages in imitation of those around him or her.

Prestige The esteem, honor, and social approval accorded to an individual or a social status.

Pretest measurement Measurement of the dependent variable before the introduction of the experimental variable.

Primary deviance Early, non-patterned acts of deviance.

Primary socialization Socialization by parents (or caregivers) that lays the foundation for personality development.

Primary groups Groups characterized by intimate face-to-face association and cooperation, typically small and close-knit.

Procedural objectivity Performing and reporting all research tasks so that any interested person will know how the research was conducted.

Profane Those things socially defined as everyday, commonplace, utilitarian, and ordinary; contrasts with the sacred.

Proletariat As used by Marx, the masses of workers, the subordinate, propertyless members of a capitalist society who must sell their labor to capitalists in order to survive.

Property crime Crimes aimed at gaining or destroying property unlawfully.

Prophetic function Those circumstances in which religion provides standards for critically examining, challenging, and changing the existing social order.

Protestant ethic A system of beliefs and actions involving a moral commitment to hard work, frugality, self-denial, acquisitiveness, and systematic calculation.

Qualitative research Sociological studies that use verbal descriptions and analysis, often done by those who claim that the subject matter of sociology cannot be reduced to mathematical formulae and statistical techniques.

Quantitative research Sociological studies that use numerical measurement and statistical analysis as a way of conducting research.

Questionnaire Written set of self-administered questions delivered to respondents by hand or mail.

Race A group that is socially defined on the basis of physical characteristics.

Racism Belief in the inherent superiority of one racial group and the inherent inferiority of others.

Random sample A sampling procedure giving every person in a population an equal chance of being selected in the sample.

Rational-legal authority Legitimization of authority by the rule of law; authority derived from the rules and regulations of the system rather than from personal qualities of individuals or tradition.

Rationality A form of human action based primarily on efficiency; goals and objectives set and achieved in the most efficient way possible.

Real culture The everyday conduct of people, which may differ from the ideal culture.

Rebels People who reject both cultural goals and means and substitute new goals and means.

Recidivism Reimprisonment for new crimes committed after having previously served time in prison.

Reciprocity The socially accepted idea that if you give something to someone, he or she must give you something of equal or near equal value in return.

Reference groups Groups that a person takes into account when evaluating his or her actions or characteristics.

Reform movement A social movement aimed at altering the existing social order to make it more acceptable.

Regressive movement A social movement aimed at restoring a past or a passing social order on the grounds that the past order is preferable to any other.

Religion An institutionalized system of symbols, beliefs, values, and practices dealing with those things believed to be sacred and with questions of ultimate meaning.

Resocialization The process of unlearning old norms, roles, and values, and learning new ones required by a new social environment.

Resource mobilization The idea that protest movements arise as a result of the existence of available resources and the effective mobilization of those resources.

Retreatists People who reject both cultural goals and conventional means of conduct.

Reverse socialization When people who are normally the ones being socialized are instead doing the socializing.

Revolutionary movement A social movement aimed at creating a new social order.

Ritual Complex, communally shared, ceremonial expressions of religious experience that have become institutionalized.

Ritualists People who cannot achieve cultural goals but continue to adhere strictly to conventional means of conduct.

Role Behavior generally expected of one who occupies a particular status.

Role conflict Situation in which a person who holds a position is confronted with conflicting or contrary expectations so that compliance to one makes compliance to the other difficult.

Role making The ability of individuals to modify their roles, at least to some degree.

Role orientation An individual's emphasis on specific aspects of a role.

Role overload Situation in which an individual in a role is confronted with a large number of expectations and finds it difficult, if not impossible, to satisfy all of them in a given time period.

Routinization of charisma The process of passing on the qualities associated with an individual leader and incorporating them into the characteristics of a group or organization.

Rule creators Those who devise society's rules, norms, and laws.

Rule enforcers Those who attempt to maintain social control and order through the threat or actual application of undesirable labels.

Rumor Unverified information that diffuses through a collectivity as a result of people's attempting to understand something.

Sanctions Punishments for violation of mores.

Sapir-Whorf hypothesis The idea that perceptions of reality are shaped by words and language.

Secondary analysis The reanalysis of survey data sets collected by other researchers.

Secondary deviance Forms of deviance that persist in individuals and that cause them to organize their lives and personal identities around their deviant status.

Secondary groups Groups that are typically large and impersonal; members do not know each other as intimately or completely as do the members of a primary group.

Sect A small, voluntary, and exclusive religious group that has broken away from an existing religious organization.

Sector model A model of urban development that emphasizes the influence of transportation paths (waterways, railways, and highways) in determining patterns of urban land use.

Secularization A decline in the authority of religious beliefs, values, and practices.

Self concept An individual's thoughts about and evaluations of himself or herself.

Self esteem The degree to which people have positive views of themselves.

Self estrangement A condition of not being able to express one's abilities, potentialities, and personality in one's work or other settings; a dimension of alienation.

Sensate culture Culture dominated by the principle that the sensory or material world is the only true reality and the highest value.

Separatism A system in which minorities choose to be isolated from the majority group.

Serendipity The accidental discovery of something while looking for something else.

Sexual coercion Sex through force or rape.

Sick role The role of sick people in society with respect to how they are supposed to act when ill.

Significant other People close to an individual whose views shape an individual's self and provide definitions of other social objects; most common examples are parents, family members, friends, marriage partners, fellow workers, etc.

Social change Variations over time in the relationships among individuals, groups, cultures, and societies.

Social control Process by which a group or society enforces conformity to its demands and expectations.

Social epidemiology The study of the frequency and pattern of a disease within a particular population.

Social exchange theory A theory emphasizing that motivations for human behavior are found in its costs and rewards; that a person will repeat behaviors that have been rewarded and will stop behaviors that have been costly.

Social integration Belonging to, or being part of, social groups or society.

Social mobility Movement of people from one position in a system of stratification to another.

Social movements Collective efforts to resist or bring about some kind of social change.

Social stratification The hierarchical structure of social inequalities that are institutionalized; the manner in which scarce resources and social rewards are distributed among different social categories.

Social structure A regular pattern of social interaction and persistent social relationships, e.g., the socioeconomic status system.

Social survey Collecting information from a sample of people through questionnaires or interviews.

Socialism Economic system in which the means of producing goods and services are publicly or collectively owned.

Socialization The process by which a person learns and generally accepts the ways of a particular social group or society.

Society A population of people living in a given territory, who share a culture and have a system of patterned interaction—a social structure.

Sociobiology A theory that posits that human behavior reflects genetically inherited traits that have been acquired through the evolutionary process of natural selection.

Sociological theories Theories that explain a wide range of human behavior and a variety of social and societal events.

Sociology of religion The study of the social manifestations of religions, including experiences, behaviors, beliefs, social roles, and organizational structures.

Specific deterrence The threat of actual punishment of an individual is supposed to deter him/her from committing other crimes in the future (*see* **General deterrence**).

State The dominant political institution in modern societies and the sole source of legitimate physical force.

State capitalism Capitalist system in which capitalist enterprises continue to exist, but where there are also state-owned enterprises and the state regulates and manages the economy.

Statistics Techniques used to process numbers produced by research and measurement.

Status A position or place within a set of social relationships; also used in stratification to denote social ranking on the basis of prestige.

Strain theory A sociological theory that sees deviance as being caused by lack of congruence between institutional means and cultural goals.

Structural assimilation The integration of minorities into primary and secondary social relations with the dominant group.

Structural-functional theory A theory emphasizing that every societal pattern (structure) makes some positive or negative contribution to the society.

Structural mobility Social mobility resulting from changes in a society's occupational structure.

Subcultural groups (*or* subcultures) Societal groups that differ significantly from the dominant culture.

Subcultural theory A sociological theory that sees deviant behavior as conformity to the norms and values of a subculture that are different from those of the larger society.

Subcultural theory of urbanism An interpretation of urban life that emphasizes how the city's size, density, and diversity create a variety of subcultures that provide meaningful social settings for its inhabitants.

Subordinate group *See* Minority group.

Suburbs Urban areas adjacent to but beyond the political boundaries of a city.

Symbolic interactionism A theory that views social phenomena primarily through interaction among individuals at the symbolic level.

Symbols Words, gestures, and objects that communicate meaning because people agree on and recognize what they represent.

Taboo A religious proscription against physical contact with objects.

Technology The complex interplay of machines, equipment, tools, skills, and procedures for carrying out tasks.

Terrorism Systematic, or threatened, use of murder, injury, or destruction in order to achieve some political end.

Theology The rational and logical development of religious belief systems.

Theory A set of ideas that provide explanations for a broad range of phenomena.

Total institution A closed organization that is set apart from the rest of society, forms an all-encompassing social environment, and serves as the only source of meeting the needs of its members.

Totalitarianism A form of government involving state control and regulation of all major institutions in a society.

Tradition The ways things have been done for a long time in a society or social group; as a source of authority it comes primarily from the position into which one is born.

Triad Three people engaged in interaction.

Underclass The most impoverished segment of American society for whom poverty is relatively permanent.

Urban A place in which population exceeds a specific number of residents. The United States Bureau of the Census identifies as urban all towns and municipalities having more than 2,500 residents.

Urbanism The ways of life characteristic of urban residents.

Urbanization The process by which the population of a society becomes concentrated in cities; also refers to the concentration of economic activity, political-administrative organization, communication networks, and political power in urban centers.

Utilitarian organization An organization that uses money to control those at the bottom of the structure.

Variables Objects or phenomena that can change from one size, state, or degree to another.

Verbal symbols Verbal utterances that are part of the spoken or written language of a society.

Vertical mobility Movement upward or downward in social rank.

Veto group A special interest group that attempts to defend itself by blocking the actions of other groups.

Victimless crime Crimes in which it is difficult to identify a victim; participants choose to be involved in the activities.

Wealth The accumulated economic resources that people possess or have acquired over time.

White ethnics Contemporary descendants of the "new" immigrants.

White-collar crime Crime committed by upper-status people in the course of their occupations.

Working poor Working people whose incomes fall below the poverty line.

World-system theory A theory that stresses the economic and power inequalities of the present international order.

REFERENCES

Abrahamson, Mark. *Functionalism*. Englewood Cliffs, N.J.: Prentice-Hall, 1978.

Abramowitz, Michael. "Primary Health Care Lacking for D.C.'s Poor, Study Shows." *Washington Post*, August 3, 1988.

Acker, Joan R. "Women and Stratification: A Review of the Literature." *Contemporary Sociology* 9, 1980.

Aguirre, B.E.; Quarantelli, E.L.; and Mendoza, Jorge L. "The Collective Behavior of Fads: The Characteristics, Effects, and Career of Streaking." *American Sociological Review* 53, 1988.

Ahrons, Constance R. "The Continuing Coparental Relationship Between Divorced Spouses." *American Journal of Orthopsychiatry* 51, 1981.

Ahrons, Constance R., and Rodgers, Roy H. *Divorced Families: A Multidisciplinary Development View*. New York: W.W. Norton & Company, 1987.

Akers, Ronald L., and Cochran, John K. "Adolescent Marijuana Use: A Test of Three Theories of Deviant Behavior." *Deviant Behavior* 6, 1985.

Aldous, Joan. "Birth Control Socialization: How to Avoid Discussing the Subject." *Population and Environment* 6, 1983.

Alexander, Jeffrey C., and Colomy, Paul. "Toward Neo-Functionalism." *Sociological Theory* 3, 1985.

Alexander, Karl L.; Entwisle, Doris R.; Cadigan, Doris; and Pallas, Aaron. "Getting Ready for First Grade: Standards of Deportment in Home and School." *Social Forces* 66, 1987a.

Alexander, Karl L.; Entwisle, Doris R.; and Thompson, Maxine S. "School Performance, Status Relations, and the Structure of Sentiment: Bringing the Teacher Back In." *American Sociological Review* 52, 1987b.

Al-Haj, Majid. "The Changing Arab Kinship Structure: The Effect of Modernization in an Urban Community." *Economic Development and Cultural Change* 36, 1988.

Allen, Craig M. "On the Validity of Relative Validity Studies of 'Final Say' Measures of Marital Power." *Journal of Marriage and the Family* 46, 1984.

Alic, John A., and Jones, Martha Caldwell. "Employment Lessons from the Electronics Industry." *Monthly Labor Review*, 109, 1986.

Alwin, Duane F. "College Effects on Educational and Occupational Attainments." *American Sociological Review* 39, 1974.

Alwin, Duane F. "Trends in Parental Socialization Values: Detroit, 1958–1983." *American Journal of Sociology* 90, 1984.

American Council on Education. *One Third of a Nation*. Washington, D.C.: American Council on Education, 1988.

Anderson, Stephen A.; Russell, Candyce S.; and Schumm, Walter R. "Perceived Marital Quality and Family Life Cycle Categories: A Further Analysis." *Journal of Marriage and the Family* 45, 1983.

Antonovsky, Aaron. "Social Class, Life Expectancy and Overall Mortality." *Milbank Memorial Fund Quarterly* 45, 1967.

Apgar, William C., Jr., and Brown, H. James. *The State of the Nation's Housing*. Cambridge, Mass.: Joint Center for Housing Studies of Harvard University, 1988.

Apple, Michael W. *Teachers and Texts: A Political Economy of Class and Gender Relations in Education*. New York: Routledge & Kegan Paul, 1986.

Ariés, Phillipe. *Centuries of Childhood*. New York: Random House, 1962.

Arluke, Arnold; Kennedy, Louanne; and Kessler, Ronald C. "Reexamining the Sick-Role Concept: An Empirical Assessment." *Journal of Health and Social Behavior* 20, 1979.

Arney, William Ray. *Power and the Profession of Obstetrics*. Chicago: University of Chicago Press, 1982.

Arnold, Fred, and Zhaoxiang, Liu. "Sex Preference, Fertility, and Family Planning in China." *Population and Development Review* 12, 1986.

Asch, Solomon. *Social Psychology*. Englewood Cliffs, N.J.: Prentice-Hall, 1952.

Assael, M., and German, G.A. "Changing Society and Mental Health in Eastern Africa." *The Israel Annals of Psychiatry and Related Disciplines* 8, 1970.

Auerbach, Stuart. "New Index Shows U.S. Losing Ground." *Washington Post*, June 3, 1988.

Avery, Robert B., and Elliehausen, Gregory E. "Financial Characteristics of High-Income Families." *Federal Reserve Bulletin* 72, 1986.

Awn, Peter J. "Sufism." In Mircea Eliade (ed.), *The Encyclopedia of Religion*. New York: Macmillan, 1987.

Babcock, Charles R. "Big Donations Again a Campaign Staple." *Washington Post*, November 17, 1988.

Bachman, Jerald G.; Johnston, Lloyd D.; and O'Malley, Patrick M. *Monitoring the Future: Questionnaire Responses from the Nation's High School Seniors 1986*. Ann Arbor: University of Michigan Press, 1987.

Bahr, Stephen J. "Marital Dissolution Laws: Impact of Recent Changes for Women." *Journal of Family Issues* 4, 1983.

Baker, Ray Stannard. *Following the Color Line: American Negro Citizenship in the Progressive Era*. New York: Harper Torchbooks, 1964.

Balassa, Bela. "The Lessons of East Asian Development: An Overview." *Economic Development and Cultural Change* 36, 1988.

Baran, Paul A., and Sweezy, Paul M. *Monopoly Capital: An Essay on the American Economic and Social Order*. New York: Modern Reader Paperbacks, 1966.

Barker-Benfield, G.J. *The Horrors of the Half-Known Life: Male Attitudes Toward Women and Sexuality in Nineteenth-Century America*. New York: Harper & Row, 1976.

Barker, Irwin R., and Currie, Raymond F. "Do Converts Always Make the Most Committed Christians?" *Journal for the Scientific Study of Religion* 24, 1985.

Barnett, Rosalind C., and Baruch, Grace K. "Determinants of Fathers' Participation in Family Work." *Journal of Marriage and the Family* 49, 1987.

Baron, James N., and Bielby, William T. "Organizational Barriers to Gender Equality: Sex Segregation of Jobs and Opportunities." In Alice S. Rossi (ed.), *Gender and the Life Course*. New York: Aldine, 1985.

Barone, Michael. "The Power of the President's Pollsters." *Public Opinion*, September/October, 1988.

Barrett, David B. "Adherents of All Religions by Eight Continental Areas, 1988." *1989 Encyclopedia Britannica Book of the Year*. Chicago: Encyclopedia Britannica, 1989.

Bazemore, Gordon. "Delinquent Reform and the Labeling Perspective." *Criminal Justice and Behavior* 12, 1985.

Beach, Frank A., ed. *Human Sexuality in Four Perspectives*. Baltimore: The Johns Hopkins University Press, 1977.

Beaver, Steven E. *Demographic Transition Theory Reinterpreted*. Lexington, Mass.: Lexington Books, 1975.

Becker, Howard S. *Outsiders: Studies in the Sociology of Deviance*. New York: The Free Press, 1963.

Beckwith, Carol. "Niger's Wodaabe: People of the Taboo." *National Geographic*, October, 1983.

Bell, Daniel. *The Coming of the Post-Industrial Society: A Venture in Social Forecasting*. New York: Basic Books, 1973.

Bellah, Robert N. "Civil Religion in America." *Daedalus*, Winter, 1967.

Bellah, Robert N., and Hammond, Phillip E., eds. *Varieties of Civil Religion*. New York: Harper & Row, 1980.

Bellah, Robert; Madsen, Richard; Sullivan, William M.; Swidler, Anne; and Tipton, Steven M. *Habits of the Heart*. New York: Harper & Row, 1985.

Benedict, Ruth. "The Vision in Plains Culture." *American Anthropologist* 24, 1922.

Benet, Sula. *Abkhasians: The Long Living People of the Caucasus*. New York: Holt, Rinehart & Winston, 1974.

Berger, Arthur A. "Introduction." In Arthur A. Berger (ed.), *Television in Society*. New Brunswick, N.J.: Transaction Books, 1987.

Berger, Joseph. "Being Catholic in America." *New York Times Magazine*, August 23, 1987.

Berger, Peter. *The Sacred Canopy: Elements of a Sociological Theory of Religion*. Garden City, N.Y.: Doubleday, 1967.

Berger, Peter, and Luckmann, Thomas. *The Social Construction of Reality*. Garden City, N.Y.: Anchor Books, 1967.

Bergeson, Albert. "The Critique of World-System Theory: Class Relations or Division of Labor?" In Randall Collins (ed.), *Sociological Theory—1984*. San Francisco: Jossey-Bass, 1984.

Berk, Richard A.; Lenihan, Kenneth J.; and Rossi, Peter H. "Crime and Poverty: Some Experimental Evidence from Ex-Offenders." *American Sociological Review* 45, 1980.

Berke, Richard L. "PAC's Hear, and Make, Calls for Their Abolition." *New York Times*, November 21, 1988a.

Berke, Richard L. "Experts Say Low 1988 Turnout May be Repeated." *New York Times*, November 13, 1988b.

Bernard, Jessie. *The Female World from a Global Perspective*. Bloomington, Ind.: Indiana University Press, 1987.

Berryman, Phillip. *The Religious Roots of Rebellion: Christians in Central American Revolutions*. Maryknoll, New York: Orbis Books, 1984.

Bethe, Hans A. "Can Star Wars Make Us Safe?" *Science Digest*, September, 1985.

BETTELHEIM, BRUNO. "Punishment vs. Discipline." *The Atlantic* 256, 1985.
BIALER, SEWERYN. *The Soviet Paradox*. New York: Knopf, 1986.
BIDWELL, CHARLES E., and FRIEDKIN, NOAH E. "The Sociology of Education." In Neil J. Smelser (ed.), *Handbook of Sociology*. New York: Sage, 1988.
BIELBY, WILLIAM T., and BARON, JAMES N. "Men and Women at Work: Sex Segregation and Statistical Discrimination." *American Journal of Sociology* 91, 1986.
BILLY, JOHN O.G., and UDRY, J. RICHARD. "The Influence of Male and Female Best Friends on Adolescent Sexual Behavior." *Adolescence* 20, 1985.
BILLY, JOHN O.G.; LANDALE, NANCY S.; and MCLAUGHLIN, STEVEN D. "The Effect of Marital Status at First Birth on Marital Dissolution Among Adolescent Mothers." *Demography* 23, 1986.
BIRD, GLORIA W.; BIRD, GERALD A.; and SCRUGGS, MARGUERITE. "Determinants of Family Task Sharing: A Study of Husbands and Wives." *Journal of Marriage and the Family* 46, 1984.
BIRENBAUM, ARNOLD, and SAGARIN, EDWARD. *Norms and Human Behavior*. New York: Praeger, 1976.
BLACK, MERLE, and REED, JOHN SHELTON. "Perspectives on the American South." In *Annual Review of Society, Politics and Culture* 2. New York: Gordon & Breach, Science Publishers, 1984.
BLAU, PETER. *The Dynamics of Bureaucracy*. Chicago: University of Chicago Press, 1963.
BLAU, PETER. *Exchange and Power in Social Life*. New York: John Wiley, 1964.
BLAU, PETER M., and MEYER, MARSHALL W. *Bureaucracy in Modern Society*, 3d ed. New York: Random House, 1987.
BLAUNER, ROBERT. *Alienation and Freedom*. Chicago: University of Chicago Press, 1964.
BLOOD, ROBERT O., and WOLFE, DONALD M. *Husbands and Wives: The Dynamics of Married Living*. New York: The Free Press, 1960.
BLUESTONE, BARRY, and HARRISON, BENNETT. *The Deindustrialization of America*. New York: Basic Books, 1982.
BLUESTONE, BARRY, and HARRISON, BENNETT. "The Great American Job Machine: The Proliferation of Low Wage Employment in the U.S. Economy." Study Prepared for the Joint Economic Committee of the Congress. Washington, D.C., 1986.
BLUM, LINDA, and SMITH, VICKI. "Women's Mobility in the Corporation: A Critique of the Politics of Optimism." *Gender and Society* 13, 1988.
BLUMBERG, ARTHUR, and BLUMBERG, PHYLLIS. *The School Superintendent: Living with Conflict*. New York: Teachers College Press, 1985.
BLUMBERG, RAE LESSER. "A General Theory of Gender Stratification." In Randall Collins (ed.), *Sociological Theory—1984*. San Francisco: Jossey-Bass, 1984.
BLUMSTEIN, PHILIP, and SCHWARTZ, PEPPER. *American Couples: Money, Work, Sex*. New York: William Morrow and Company, 1983.
BOAS, FRANZ. *Handbook of American Indian Languages*. Washington, D.C.: U.S. Government Printing Office, 1911.
BOCK, E. WILBUR; BEEGHLEY, LEONARD; and MIXON, ANTHONY J. "Religion, Socioeconomic Status, and Sexual Morality: An Application of Reference Group Theory." *The Sociological Quarterly* 24, 1983.
BOCK, KENNETH. *Human Nature and History: A Response to Sociobiology*. New York: Columbia University Press, 1980.
BOHANNAN, PAUL. "The Six Stations of Divorce." In Paul Bohannan (ed.), *Divorce and After*. New York: Doubleday, 1970.
BOLTON, CHARLES D., and KAMMEYER, KENNETH C.W. *The University Student*. New Haven, Conn.: College & University Press, 1967.
BONACICH, EDNA. "A Theory of Ethnic Antagonism: The Split Labor Market." *American Sociological Review* 37, 1972.
BONGAARTS, JOHN. "Why High Birth Rates Are So Low." In Scott W. Menard and Elizabeth W. Moen (eds.), *Perspectives on Population: An Introduction to Concepts and Issues*. New York: Oxford University Press, 1987.
BOOCOCK, SARANE SPENCE. *Sociology of Education*, 2d ed. Boston: Houghton Mifflin, 1980.
BOONE, LOUIS E.; KURTZ, DAVID L.; and FLEENOR, C. PATRICK. "The Road to the Top." *American Demographics* 10, 1988.
BOOTH, ALAN, and EDWARDS, JOHN N. "Age at Marriage and Marital Stability." *Journal of Marriage and the Family* 47, 1985.
BORDEWICH, FERGUS M. "Colorado's Thriving Cults." *New York Times Magazine*, May 1, 1988.
BORNSCHIER, VOLKER; CHASE-DUNN, CHRISTOPHER; and RUBINSON, RICHARD. "Cross-National Evidence of the Effects of Foreign Investment and Aid on Economic Growth and Inequality: A Survey of Findings and a

Reanalysis." *American Journal of Sociology* 84, 1978.
BOSE, CHRISTINE E., and ROSSI, PETER H. "Gender and Jobs: Prestige Standings of Occupations as Affected by Gender." *American Sociological Review* 48, 1983.
BOSK, CHARLES L. *Forgive and Remember: Managing Medical Failure*. Chicago: University of Chicago Press, 1979.
BOSWELL, TERRY, and BERGESON, ALBERT. "American Prospects in a Period of Hegemonic Decline and Economic Crisis." In Terry Boswell and Albert Bergeson (eds.), *America's Changing Role in the World-System*. New York: Praeger, 1987.
BOTTOMORE, T.B. *Classes in Modern Society*. New York: Pantheon Books, 1966.
BOULTON, MARY, et al. "Social Class and General Practice Consultation." *Sociology of Health and Illness* 8, 1986.
BOUVIER, LEON F. "Immigration at the Crossroads." *American Demographics* 3, 1981.
BOUVIER, LEON F., and GARDNER, ROBERT W. "Immigration to the U.S.: The Unfinished Story." *Population Bulletin* 41, 1986.
BOWLES, SAMUEL, and GINTIS, HERBERT. *Schooling in Capitalist America: Educational Reform and the Contradictions of Economic Life*. New York: Basic Books, 1976.
BREAULT, K.D. "Suicide in America: A Test of Durkheim's Theory of Religious and Family Integration, 1933–1980." *American Journal of Sociology* 92, 1986.
BRAITHWAITE, JOHN. "The Myth of Social Class and Criminality Reconsidered." *American Sociological Review* 46, 1981.
BRAITHWAITE, JOHN. "White Collar Crime." In Ralph H. Turner and James F. Short, Jr. (eds.), *Annual Review of Sociology*, 11. Palo Alto, Calif.: Annual Reviews, Inc., 1985.
BRAVERMAN, HARRY. *Labor and Monopoly Capital: The Degradation of Work in the Twentieth Century*. New York: Monthly Review Press, 1974.
BRIDENBAUGH, CARL. *Cities in the Wilderness: The First Century of Urban Life in America*. New York: Ronald Press, 1938.
BRODERICK, CARLFRED B. "How to Rewrite Your Marriage Script So It Works." *Redbook*, February, 1979.
BRODERICK, CARLFRED B. *Marriage and the Family*, 3d ed. Englewood Cliffs, N.J.: Prentice-Hall, 1989.
BROMLEY, DAVID G. *Falling From the Earth: Causes and Consequences of Religious Apostasy*. Beverly Hills, Calif.: Sage, 1988.
BROWN, ROBERT MCAFEE. "Recent Titles in Liberation Theology." *Quarterly Review* 159, 1986.
BROWNING, GENIA K. *Women and Politics in the USSR: Consciousness Raising and Soviet Women's Groups*. New York: St. Martin's Press, 1987.
BROWNMILLER, SUSAN. *Against Our Will: Men, Women and Rape*. New York: Simon and Schuster, 1975.
BRUBAKER, ROGERS. *The Limits of Rationality: An Essay on the Social and Moral Thought of Max Weber*. London: George Allen & Unwin, 1984.
BRYANT, CLIFTON D. *Sexual Deviancy and Social Proscription: The Social Context of Carnal Behavior*. New York: Human Sciences Press, 1982.
BUNKER, STEPHEN G. *Underdeveloping the Amazon: Extraction, Unequal Exchange, and the Failure of the Modern State*. Urbana: University of Illinois Press, 1984.
BURGESS, JOHN. "Study Says U.S. May be Behind Japan in Commercializing Superconductors." *Washington Post*, June 29, 1988.
BURGESS, ROBERT G. *In the Field: An Introduction to Field Research*. London: George Allen & Unwin, 1984.
BURMAN, PATRICK. *Killing Time, Losing Ground: Experiences of Unemployment*. Toronto: Wall and Thompson, 1988.
BURRIDGE, KENELM O.L. "A Tangu Game." *Man*, 1957.
Business Week. "Delivering What Makeup Only Promises." February 8, 1988.
BYINGTON, ROBERT; DYER, ALAN R.; GARSIDE, DAN; LIU, KIANG; and MOSS, DOROTHY. "Recent Trends of Major Coronary Risk Factors and CHD Mortality in the United States and Other Industrialized Countries." In Richard J. Havlik and Manning Feinleib (eds.), *Proceedings of the Conference on the Decline in Coronary Heart Disease Mortality*. Bethesda, Md.: National Institutes of Health, 1979.
CAHAN, ABRAHAM. *The Rise of David Levinsky*. New York: Harper Torchbooks. 1966. Originally published 1917.
CALDWELL, JOHN C. *Theory of Fertility Decline*. New York: Academic Press, 1982.
CALIFORNIA ASSEMBLY OFFICE OF RESEARCH. *California 2000: A People in Transition*. Sacramento: Assembly Office of Research, 1986.
CAMPBELL, ANNE. "Self Definition by Rejection: The Case of Gang Girls." *Social Problems* 34, 1987.
CAMPBELL, ERNEST Q. *Socialization: Culture and Personality*. Dubuque, Iowa: William C. Brown, 1975.
CAPLOW, TED. "Contrasting Trends in European and American Religion." *Sociological Analysis* 46, 1985.
CARLSON, BONNIE E. "Wife Battering: A Social Deviance Analysis." In Josefina Figueira-McDonough and Rosemary Sarri (eds.), *The Trapped Woman: Catch-22 in Deviance and Control*. Beverly Hills, Calif.: Sage, 1987.

CARLSON, PETER. "Leader of the Snack PAC." *Washington Post Magazine*, November 13, 1988.

CARROLL, LEO. "Concern with AIDS and the Sexual Behavior of College Students." *Journal of Marriage and the Family* 50, 1988.

CHAGNON, NAPOLEON A. *Yanomano: The Fierce People*. New York: Holt, Rinehart & Winston, 1968.

CHAGNON, NAPOLEON A. "Life Histories, Blood Revenge, and Warfare in a Tribal Population." *Science* 239, 1988.

CHAMBLISS, WILLIAM J. "A Sociological Analysis of the Law of Vagrancy." *Social Problems*, 1964, *12*.

CHARON, JOEL M. *Symbolic Interactionism: An Introduction, An Interpretation, An Integration*, 3d ed. Englewood Cliffs, N.J.: Prentice Hall, 1988.

CHEN, P.C., and KOLS, A. "Population and Birth Planning in the People's Republic of China." *Population Reports*, Series J, No. 25. Baltimore, Md.: Johns Hopkins University, 1982.

CHERLIN, ANDREW J. "Remarriage as an Incomplete Institution." *American Journal of Sociology* 84, 1978.

CHERLIN, ANDREW J., and MCCARTHY, JAMES. "Remarried Couple Households: Data from the June 1980 Current Population Survey." *Journal of Marriage and the Family* 47, 1985.

CHIROT, DANIEL. "The Rise of the West." *American Sociological Review* 50, 1985.

CHRISTIE, ROBERT. *Empire in Wood*. Ithaca: New York State School of Industrial and Labor Relations, 1956.

CIARDI, JOHN. *A Browser's Dictionary and Native's Guide to the Unknown American Language*. New York: Harper & Row, 1980.

CLARK, JOHN. "Presidential Address on the Importance of Our Understanding of Organizational Conflict." *The Sociological Quarterly* 29, 1988.

CLOWARD, RICHARD, and OHLIN, LLOYD. *Delinquency and Opportunity: A Theory of Delinquent Gangs*. New York: The Free Press, 1960.

COCHRAN, JOHN K.; BEEGHLEY, LEONARD; and BOCK, E. WILBUR. "Religiosity and Alcohol Behavior: An Exploration of Reference Group Theory." *Sociological Forum* 3, 1988.

COCKERHAM, WILLIAM C. *Medical Sociology*, 3d ed. Englewood Cliffs, N.J.: Prentice-Hall, 1986.

COCKERHAM, WILLIAM, et al. "Social Stratification and Self-Management of Health." *Journal of Health and Social Behavior* 27, 1986.

COHEN, ALBERT K. *Delinquent Boys: The Culture of the Gang*. Glencoe, Ill.: The Free Press, 1955.

COHEN, ARTHUR M., and BRAWER, FLORENCE. *The American Community College*. San Francisco: Jossey-Bass, 1982.

COHEN, ROBIN. *Endgame in South Africa?* Paris: Unesco Press, 1986.

COLBURN, DON. "Medicine, Losing Its Appeal." *Washington Post-Health*, August 30, 1988.

COLE, STEWART G., and COLE, MILDRED WISE. *Minorities and the American Promise*. New York: Harper & Row, 1954.

COLLINS, RANDALL. "A Conflict Theory of Sexual Stratification." *Social Problems* 19, 1971.

COLLINS, RANDALL. *The Credential Society: An Historical Sociology of Education and Stratification*. New York: Academic Press, 1979.

COLLINS, RANDALL. *Sociology of Marriage and the Family: Gender, Home and Property*, 2d ed. Chicago: Nelson-Hall, 1988.

CONGRESSIONAL BUDGET OFFICE. *The Changing Distribution of Federal Taxes: 1975–1990*. Washington, D.C., 1987.

Congressional Quarterly Almanac, vol. XL, 19-C. Washington, D.C.: Congressional Quarterly Press, 1985.

Congressional Quarterly Almanac. "Reagan Took a Beating on Key Votes in 1987." Washington, D.C.: Congressional Quarterly, Inc., 1987.

CONRAD, PETER. "The Discovery of Hyperkinesis: Notes on the Medicalization of Deviant Behavior." *Social Problems* 23, 1975.

CONRAD, PETER. "Problems in Health Care." In George Ritzer (ed.), *Social Problems*. New York: Random House, 1986.

CONRAD, PETER, and SCHNEIDER, JOSEPH W. *Deviance and Medicalization: From Badness to Sickness*. St. Louis: Mosby, 1980.

CONVERSE, JEAN M., and PRESSER, STANLEY. *Survey Questions: Handcrafting the Standardized Questionnaire*. Beverly Hills, Calif.: Sage Publications, 1986.

COOK, KAREN S.; O'BRIEN, JODI; and KOLLOCK, PETER. "Exchange Theory: A Blueprint for Structure and Process." In George Ritzer (ed.), *Frontiers of Social Theory*. New York: Columbia University Press, 1990.

COOK, T.D., and CAMPBELL, D.T. *Quasi-Experimentation: Design and Analysis Issues for Field Settings*. Chicago: Rand-McNally, 1979.

COOLEY, CHARLES HORTON. *Human Nature and the Social Order*. New York: Charles Scribner's, 1902.

COOLEY, CHARLES HORTON. *Social Organization: A Study of the Larger Mind*. New York: Charles Scribner's, 1909.

COOPER, RICHARD. "Rising Death Rates in the Soviet Union." *New England Journal of Medicine* 304, 1981.

COSER, LEWIS A. *The Functions of Social Conflict*. Glencoe, Ill.: The Free Press, 1956.

COX, GARY W. "Closeness and Turnout: A Methodological Note." *Journal of Politics* 50, 1988.
CRAWFORD, CHRISTINE. *Mommie Dearest.* New York: William Morrow, 1978.
CRIPPEN, TIMOTHY. "Old and New Gods in the Modern World: Toward a Theory of Religious Transformation." *Social Forces* 67, 1988.
CROUSE, JAMES, and TRUSHEIM, DALE. *The Case Against the SAT.* Chicago: The University of Chicago Press, 1988.
CURRIE, ELLIOTT; DUNN, ROBERT; and FOGARTY, DAVID. "The Fading Dream: Economic Crisis and the New Inequality." In Jerome H. Skolnick and Elliott Currie (eds.), *Crisis in American Institutions.* Glenview, Ill.: Scott Foresman and Company, 1988.
CURTISS, SUSAN. *Genie: A Psycholinguistic Study of a Modern-Day "Wild Child."* New York: Academic Press, 1977.
DAHL, ROBERT. *Pluralist Democracy in the United States: Conflict and Consent.* Chicago: Rand McNally, 1967.
DAHRENDORF, RALF. *Class and Class Conflict in Industrial Society.* Stanford, Calif.: Stanford University Press, 1959.
DAS GUPTA, MONICA. "Selective Discrimination Against Female Children in Rural Punjab, India." *Population and Development Review* 13, 1987.
DAUNER, JOHN T. "Man Gets Prison for Racial Attack." *Kansas City Times*, February 3, 1987.
DAVENPORT, WILLIAM H. "Sex in Cross-Cultural Perspective." In Frank A. Beach (ed.), *Human Sexuality in Four Perspectives.* Baltimore: The Johns Hopkins University Press, 1977.
DAVIS, CARY; HAUB, CARL; and WILLETTE, JOANNE. "U.S. Hispanics: Changing the Face of America." In Norman R. Yetman (ed.), *Majority and Minority: The Dynamics of Race and Ethnicity in American Life.* Boston: Allyn and Bacon, 1985.
DAVIS, KAREN, and ROWLAND, DIANE. "Uninsured and Underserved: Inequities in Health Care in the United States." In Peter Conrad and Rochelle Kern (eds.), *The Sociology of Health and Illness: Critical Perspectives 1986.* New York: St. Martin's Press, 1986.
DAVIS, KINGSLEY. "Extreme Isolation of a Child." *American Journal of Sociology* 45, 1940.
DAVIS, KINGSLEY. "Final Note on a Case of Extreme Isolation." *American Journal of Sociology* 50, 1947.
DAVIS, KINGSLEY. "Population Policy: Will Current Programs Succeed?" *Science* 158, 1967.
DAVIS, KINGSLEY. "Wives and Work: Consequences of the Sex Revolution." *Population and Development Review* 10, 1984.
DAVIS, KINGSLEY, and MOORE, WILBERT E. "Some Principles of Stratification." *American Sociological Review* 10, 1945.
DE CREVECOEUR, J. HECTOR ST. JOHN. *Letters from an American Farmer.* New York: Penguin Books, 1782/1981.
DEDMAN, BILL. "Blacks Turned Down for Home Loans from S&Ls Twice as Often as Whites." *Atlanta Constitution*, January 22, 1989.
DELAMATER, JOHN, and MACCORQUODALE, PATRICIA. *Premarital Sexuality.* Madison, Wisc.: University of Wisconsin Press, 1979.
DELAMATER, JOHN. "Gender Differences in Sexual Scenarios." In Kathryn Kelley (ed.), *Females, Males, and Sexuality.* Albany, N.Y.: State University of New York Press, 1987.
DEMAUSE, LLOYD, ed. *The History of Childhood.* New York: The Psychohistory Press, 1974.
DEMERATH, NICHOLAS J. *Birth Control and Foreign Policy: The Alternatives to Family Planning.* New York: Harper & Row, 1976.
DEMERATH, N.J., III, and WILLIAMS, RHYS H. "Civil Religion in an Uncivil Society." *The Annals of the American Academy of Political and Social Science* 480, 1985.
DEMO, DAVID H., and ACOCK, ALAN C. "The Impact of Divorce on Children." *Journal of Marriage and the Family* 50, 1988.
DENTLER, ROBERT A., and ERIKSON, KAI T. "The Functions of Deviance in Groups," *Social Problems* 7, 1959.
DENZIN, NORMAN K. *The Recovering Alcoholic.* Beverly Hills, Calif.: Sage, 1986.
DENZIN, NORMAN K. *The Alcoholic Self.* Beverly Hills, Calif.: Sage, 1987.
DE TOCQUEVILLE, ALEXIS. *Democracy in America*, Vol. 1 & 2. New York: Schocken Books, 1961.
DINGES, WILLIAM D. "Catholic Traditionalism." In Joseph H. Fichter (ed.), *Alternatives to American Mainline Churches.* New York: Rose of Sharon Press, 1983.
DINGES, WILLIAM D. "Quo Vadis, Lefebvre?" *America*, June 18, 1988.
DINNERSTEIN, LEONARD, and REIMERS, DAVID M. *Ethnic Americans: A History of Immigration and Assimilation.* 3rd edition. New York: Harper & Row, 1987.
DIONNE, E.J., JR. "'Solid South' Again, but Republican." *New York Times*, November 13, 1988a.
DIONNE, E.J., JR. "If Nonvoters Had Voted: Same Winner, but Bigger." *New York Times*, November 21, 1988b.
DIPRETE, THOMAS A., and SOULE, WHITMAN T. "Gender and Promotion in Segmented Job Ladder Systems." *American Sociological Review* 53, 1988.
DOBSON, RICHARD B. "Mobility and Stratification in the Soviet Union." In Alex Inkeles, James Coleman, and

Neil Smelser (eds.), *Annual Review of Sociology*, 3. Palo Alto, Calif.: Annual Reviews, Inc., 1977.

DOGAN, MATTEI, and KASARDA, JOHN D. *The Metropolis Era*. Newberry Park, Calif.: Sage, 1988.

DOMHOFF, G. WILLIAM. *Who Rules America Now?* Englewood Cliffs, N.J.: Prentice-Hall, 1983.

DORRIS, MICHAEL A. "The Grass Still Grows, the Rivers Still Flow: Contemporary Native Americans." *Daedalus* 110, 1981.

DOTTER, DANIEL L., and ROEBUCK, JULIAN B. "The Labeling Approach Re-examined: Interactionism and the Components of Deviance." *Deviant Behavior* 9, 1988.

DRAPER, PATRICIA. "!Kung Women: Contrasts in Sexual Egalitarianism in Foraging and Sedentary Contexts." In R. Reiter (ed.), *Toward an Anthropology of Women*. New York: Monthly Review Press, 1975.

DREW, ELIZABETH. *Politics and Money: The New Road to Corruption*. New York: Macmillan, 1983.

DUBERMAN, LUCILE. *The Reconstituted Family: A Study of Remarried Couples and Their Children*. Chicago: Nelson-Hall, 1975.

DUFF, JOHN B. *The Irish in the United States*. Belmont, Calif.: Wadsworth, 1971.

DUKE, BENJAMIN. *The Japanese School: Lessons for Industrial America*. New York: Praeger, 1986.

DUNCAN, GREG, J., et al. *Years of Poverty, Years of Plenty: The Changing Economic Fortunes of American Workers and Families*. Ann Arbor, Mich.: Institute for Social Research, 1984.

DUNNING, ERIC; MURPHY, PATRICK; and WILLIAMS, JOHN. "Spectator Violence at Football Matches: Towards a Sociological Explanation." *The British Journal of Sociology* 37, 1986.

DURAND, JOHN D. "Historical Estimates of World Population." *Population and Development Review* 3, 1977.

DURKHEIM, EMILE. *Suicide*. New York: The Free Press, 1951. Originally published 1897.

DURKHEIM, EMILE. *The Division of Labor in Society*. New York: The Free Press, 1964. Originally published 1895.

DURKHEIM, EMILE. *The Elementary Forms of Religious Life*. New York: The Free Press, 1965. Originally published 1912.

DUTTON, DIANA B. "Explaining the Low Use of Health Services by the Poor: Costs, Attitudes, or Delivery Systems." *American Sociological Review* 43, 1978.

DUTTON, JOHN, JR. "Changes in Soviet Mortality Patterns, 1959–1977." *Population and Development Review* 5, 1979.

DWORKIN, ANDREA. *Intercourse*. New York: The Free Press, 1987.

DWORKIN, ANTHONY GARY. *Teacher Burnout In Public Schools*. Albany, N.Y.: State University of New York Press, 1987.

DYE, THOMAS R. *Who's Running America? The Reagan Years*, 3d ed. Englewood Cliffs, N.J.: Prentice-Hall, 1983.

EATON, CYNTHIA. "Diabetes, Culture Change, and Acculturation: A Biocultural Analysis." *Medical Anthropology* 1, 1977.

Economic Report of the President. Washington, D.C.: U.S. Government Printing Office, 1983.

EDER, DONNA. "Ability Grouping as a Self-Fulfilling Prophecy: A Micro-Analysis of Teacher-Student Interaction." *Sociology of Education* 54, 1981.

EDSALL, THOMAS B. "Poll Shows GOP Attacks Worked Against Dukakis." *Washington Post*, November 16, 1988.

EDWARDS, RICHARD. *Contested Terrain: The Transformation of the Workplace in the Twentieth Century*. New York: Basic Books, 1979.

EDWARDS, RICHARD C.; REICH, MICHAEL; and WEISSKOPF, THOMAS. *The Capitalist System*, 3d ed. Englewood Cliffs, N.J.: Prentice-Hall, 1986.

EISENHOWER, DWIGHT D. "Liberty Is at Stake." In Herbert I. Schiller and Joseph D. Phillips (eds.), *Super-State: Readings in the Military-Industrial Complex*. Urbana: University of Illinois Press, 1972.

EKEH, PETER. *Social Exchange Theory: The Two Traditions*. Cambridge, Mass.: Harvard University Press, 1974.

ELASHOFF, J.D., and SNOW, R.E. *Pygmalion Reconsidered*. Worthington, Ohio: Charles A. Jones, 1971.

ENGELS, FRIEDRICH. *The Origin of the Family, Private Property and the State*. New York: International Publishers, 1972. Originally published 1884.

ENGLAND, PAULA, and MCCREARY, LORI. "Gender Inequality in Paid Employment." In Beth B. Hess and Myra Marx Ferree (eds.), *Analyzing Gender: A Handbook of Social Science Research*. Beverly Hills, Calif.: Sage, 1987.

ENGLAND, PAULA; FARKAS, GEORGE; KILBOURNE, BARBARA; and DOU, THOMAS. "Explaining Occupational Sex Segregation and Wages: Findings from a Model with Fixed Effects." *American Sociological Review* 53, 1988.

ENSTROM, JAMES E. "Cancer and Total Mortality Among Active Mormons." *Cancer* 42, 1978.

ENTWISLE, DORIS R., and HAYDUK, LESLIE ALEC. "Lasting Effects of Elementary School." *Sociology of Education* 61, 1988.

ERDRICH, LOUISE, and DORRIS, MICHAEL. "Who Owns the Land?" *New York Times Magazine*, September 4, 1988.

ERIKSON, KAI. "Notes on the Sociology of Deviance." In Howard S. Becker (ed.), *The Other Side: Perspectives on Deviance*. New York: The Free Press, 1964.

ETZIONI, AMITAI. *A Comparative Analysis of Complex Organizations*. New York: The Free Press, 1961.

EVANS, PETER B., and STEPHENS, JOHN D. "Development and the World Economy." In Neil Smelser (ed.), *Handbook of Sociology*. Newbury Park, Calif.: Sage, 1988.

EVANS-PRICHARD, E.E. "Sexual Inversion Among the Azande." *American Anthropologist* 72, 1970.

FANTE, JOHN. "The Odyssey of a Wop." In Oscar Handlin (ed.), *Children of the Uprooted*. New York: George Braziller, 1966.

FARLEY, REYNOLDS, and ALLEN, WALTER R. *The Color Line and the Quality of Life in America*. New York: Russell Sage Foundation, 1987.

FARNSWORTH, MARGARET, and LEIBER, MICHAEL J. "Strain Theory Revisited: Economic Goals, Educational Means, and Delinquency." *American Sociological Review* 54, 1989.

FARSON, RICHARD. *Birthrights*. New York: Macmillan, 1974.

FAUPEL, CHARLES E. "Heroin Use, Street Crime, and the 'Main Hustle': Implications for the Validity of Official Crime Data." *Deviant Behavior* 7, 1986.

FEIN, ESTER B. "Glasnost Is Opening the Door on Poverty." *New York Times*, January 29, 1989.

FELMLEE, DIANE, and EDER, DONNA. "Contextual Effects in the Classroom: The Impact of Ability Groups on Student Attention." *Sociology of Education* 56, 1983.

FERNANDEZ, JOHN P. *Child Care and Corporate Productivity: Resolving Family/Work Conflicts*. Lexington, Mass.: Lexington Books, 1986.

FERREE, MYRA MARX. "The View from Below: Women's Employment and Gender Equality in Working Class Families." *Marriage and Family Review* 7, 1984.

FERREE, MYRA MARX. "She Works Hard for a Living: Gender and Class on the Job." In Beth B. Hess and Myra Marx Ferree (eds.), *Analyzing Gender: A Handbook of Social Science Research*. Beverly Hills, Calif.: Sage, 1987.

FIELDS, GEORGE. *From Bonsai to Levi's: When West Meets East: An Insider's Surprising Account of How the Japanese Live*. New York: Macmillan, 1983.

FINE, GARY A. "Symbolic Interactionism in the Post-Blumerian Age." In George Ritzer (ed.), *Frontiers in Social Theory*. New York: Columbia University Press, 1990.

FINE, GARY A. *With the Boys: Little League Baseball and Preadolescent Culture*. Chicago: University of Chicago Press, 1987.

FINEBERG, HARVEY V. "The Social Dimensions of AIDS." *Scientific American* 259, 1988.

FINKELHOR, DAVID. *Sexually Victimized Children*. New York: The Free Press, 1979.

FINLEY, MERRILEE K. "Teachers and Tracking in a Comprehensive High School." *Sociology of Education* 57, 1984.

FIREBAUGH, GLENN, and DAVIS, KENNETH E. "Trends in Antiblack Prejudice 1972–1984: Region and Cohort Effects." *American Journal of Sociology* 94, 1988.

FISCHER, CLAUDE S. "The Public and Private Worlds of City Life." *American Sociological Review* 46, 1981.

FISCHER, CLAUDE S. *To Dwell Among Friends: Personal Networks in Town and City*. Chicago: University of Chicago Press, 1982.

FISCHER, CLAUDE S. *The Urban Experience*, 2d ed. New York: Harcourt Brace Jovanovich, 1984.

FISHER, SUE. "Doctor–Patient Communication: A Social and Micro-Political Performance." *Sociology of Health and Illness* 6, 1984.

FISHER, SUE, and GROCE, STEPHEN B. "Doctor–Patient Negotiation of Cultural Assumptions." *Sociology of Health and Illness* 7, 1985.

FLAIM, PAUL O. "New Data on Union Members and Their Earnings." *Employment and Earnings* 32, 1985.

FLEISHER, RICHARD, and BOND, JON R. "Are There Two Presidencies? Yes, But Only for Republicans." *Journal of Politics* 50, 1988.

FORD, DANIEL. "Rebirth of a Nation." *The New Yorker*, March 28, 1988.

FORISHA, BARBARA LUSK. *Sex Roles and Personal Awareness*. Glenview, Ill.: Scott, Foresman, 1978.

Fortune. "The Downside of Downsizing." May 23, 1988a.

Fortune. "The Soviet Economy." April 9, 1988b.

Fortune. "America's Competitive Revival." January 4, 1988c.

Fortune. "Genentech Has a Golden Goose." May 9, 1988d.

FOX, A.J., and ADELSTEIN, A.M. "Occupational Mortality: Work or Way of Life." *Journal of Epidemiology and Community Health* 32, 1978.

FOX, GREER LITTON. "The Mother–Adolescent Daughter Relationship as a Sexual Socialization Structure: A Research Review." *Family Relations* 29, 1980.

FOX, GREER LITTON, and INAZU, JUDITH K. "Patterns and Outcomes of Mother–Daughter Communications About

Sexuality." *Journal of Social Issues* 36, 1980.

FRANCE, ANATOLE. *Crainqueville*. Freeport, N.Y.: Books for Libraries, 1922.

FRANK, ANDRE GUNDER. *Capitalism and Underdevelopment in Latin America: Historical Studies of Chile and Brazil*. New York: Monthly Labor Review Press, 1969.

FRANKL, RAZELLE. *Televangelism: The Marketing of Popular Religion*. Carbondale and Edwardsville: Southern Illinois University Press, 1987.

FRANKLAND, MARK. *The Sixth Continent: Mikhail Gorbachev and the Soviet Union*. New York: Harper and Row, 1987.

FREEMAN, JO. "On the Origins of Social Movements." In Jo Freeman (ed.), *Social Movements of the Sixties and Seventies*. New York: Longman, 1983.

FREEMAN, RICHARD B., and MEDOFF, JAMES L. *What Do Unions Do?* New York: Basic Books, 1984.

FREIDSON, ELIOT. *Profession of Medicine*. New York: Dodd, Mead, 1970.

FREIDSON, ELIOT. *Doctoring Together*. New York: Elsevier, 1975.

FRIEDMAN, THOMAS L. "Kahane Appeal to Oust Arabs Gains in Israel." *New York Times*, August 5, 1985.

FRIEDRICH, CARL J., and BRZEZINSKI, ZBIGNIEW. *Totalitarian Dictatorship and Autocracy*, vol. 2. Cambridge, Mass.: Harvard University Press, 1965.

FRISBIE, W. PARKER, and KASARDA, JOHN D. "Spatial Processes." In Neil J. Smelser (ed.), *Handbook of Sociology*. Beverly Hills, Calif.: Sage, 1988.

FURSTENBERG, FRANK F., JR. *Unplanned Parenthood: The Social Consequences of Teenage Childbearing*. New York: The Free Press, 1976.

FURSTENBERG, FRANK F., JR. "Premarital Pregnancy and Marital Instability." In George Levinger and Oliver C. Moles (eds.), *Divorce and Separation: Context, Causes, and Consequences*. New York: Basic Books, 1979.

FURSTENBERG, FRANK F., JR. "The Social Consequences of Teenage Parenthood." In Frank F. Furstenberg, Jr., Richard Lincoln, and Jane Menken (eds.), *Teenage Sexuality, Pregnancy and Childbearing*. Philadelphia: University of Pennsylvania Press, 1981.

GAGNON, JOHN H. *Human Sexualities*. Glenview, Ill.: Scott, Foresman and Company, 1977.

GAGNON, JOHN H., and SIMON, WILLIAM. *Sexual Conduct*. Chicago: Aldine, 1973.

GALBRAITH, JOHN KENNETH, and MENSHIKOV, STANISLAV. *Capitalism, Communism and Coexistence*. Boston: Houghton Mifflin, 1988.

Gallup Opinion Index. "Religion in America: 50 Years: 1935–1985." Report No. 236, 1985.

The Gallup Report. "Religion in America." Report No. 259, 1987.

GAMSON, WILLIAM A. *The Strategy of Social Protest*. Homewood, Ill.: The Dorsey Press, 1975.

GANS, CURTIS. "No Wonder Turnout Was Low." *Washington Post*, November 11, 1988.

GANS, HERBERT J. *Middle American Individualism*, New York: The Free Press, 1988.

GARBARINO, JAMES, and SHERMAN, DEBORAH. "High-Risk Neighborhoods and High-Risk Families: The Human Ecology of Child Maltreatment." *Child Development* 51, 1980.

GARDNER, ROBERT W.; ROBEY, BRYANT; and SMITH, PETER C. "Asian Americans: Growth, Change, and Diversity." *Population Bulletin* 40, 1985.

GECAS, VIKTOR. "The Influence of Social Class on Socialization." In Wesley R. Burr, Reuben Hill, F. Ivan Nye, and Ira L. Reiss (eds.), *Contemporary Theories About the Family: Research-based Theories*, Vol. I. New York: The Free Press, 1979.

GECAS, VIKTOR. "Contexts of Socialization." In Morris Rosenberg and Ralph Turner (eds.), *Sociological Perspectives in Social Psychology*. New York: Basic Books, 1981.

GECAS, VIKTOR, and SCHWALBE, MICHAEL L. "Beyond the Looking-Glass Self: Social Structure and Efficacy-Based Self-Esteem." *Social Psychology Quarterly* 46, 1983.

GEHRIG, GAIL. *American Civil Religion: An Assessment*. Monograph Series, 3. Storrs, Conn.: Society for the Scientific Study of Religion, 1979.

GELLES, RICHARD J. *Family Violence*, 2d ed. Beverly Hills, Calif.: Sage, 1987.

GERBER, JURG, and SHORT, JAMES F., JR. "Publicity and the Control of Corporate Behavior: The Case of Infant Formula." *Deviant Behavior* 7, 1986.

GERSHUNY, JONATHAN, and ROBINSON, JOHN P. "Historical Changes in the Household Division of Labor." *Demography* 25, 1988.

GERTH, HANS, and MILLS, C. WRIGHT. *Character and Social Structure*. New York: Harcourt, Brace, 1953.

GERTH, HANS, and MILLS, C. WRIGHT, eds. *From Max Weber: Essays in Sociology*. New York: Oxford University Press, 1958.

GIALLOMBARDO, ROSE. *The Social World of Imprisoned Girls: A Comparative Study of Institutions for Juvenile Delinquents*. New York: John Wiley, 1974.

GIBBS, JACK P. "Testing the Theory of Status Integration and Suicide Rates." *American Sociological Review* 47, 1982.

GIBBS, JACK P., and MARTIN, WALTER T. *Status Integration and Suicide*. Eugene: University of Oregon Press, 1964.

GIBNEY, FRANK. "The Strange Ways of Staphorst." *Life*, September 27, 1948.

GIELE, JANET Z. "Introduction: The Status of Women in Comparative Perspective." In Janet Z. Giele and A.C. Smock (eds.), *Women: Roles and Status in Eight Countries*. New York: Wiley-Interscience, 1977.

GIELE, JANET Z. "Gender and Sex Roles." In Neil J. Smelser (ed.), *Handbook of Sociology*. Beverly Hills, Calif.: Sage, 1988.

GIST, NOEL P., and FAVA, SYLVIA FLEIS. *Urban Society*, 6th ed. New York: Thomas Y. Crowell, 1974.

GLAAB, CHARLES N., and BROWN, THEODORE A. *A History of Urban America*. New York: Macmillan, 1967.

GLADWELL, MALCOLM. "City, Suburbs Battle for Scanning Device." *Washington Post-Health*, August 23, 1988.

GLASS, DAVID; SQUIRE, PEVEREILL; and WOLFINGER, RAYMOND. "Voter Turnout: An International Comparison." *Public Opinion*, December/January 1984.

GLAZER, NATHAN, and MOYNIHAN, DANIEL P. *Beyond the Melting Pot: The Negroes, Puerto Ricans, Jews, Italians, and Irish of New York City*. Cambridge, Mass.: The MIT Press, 1963.

GLENN, NORVAL D., and KRAMER, KATHRYN B. "The Marriage and Divorces of the Children of Divorce." *Journal of Marriage and the Family* 49, 1987.

GLENN, NORVAL D., and SHELTON, BETH ANN. "Regional Differences in Divorce in the United States." *Journal of Marriage and the Family* 47, 1985.

GLENN, NORVAL D., and SUPANCIC, MICHAEL. "The Social and Demographic Correlates of Divorce and Separation in the United States: An Update and Reconsideration." *Journal of Marriage and the Family* 46, 1984.

GLICK, PAUL, and LIN, SUNG-LING. "Recent Changes in Divorce and Remarriage." *Journal of Marriage and the Family* 48, 1986.

GLOCK, CHARLES V., and STARK, RODNEY. *Religion and Society in Tension*. Chicago: Rand McNally, 1965.

GOFFMAN, ERVING. "The Moral Career of the Mental Patient." *Psychiatry* 22, 1959a.

GOFFMAN, ERVING. *The Presentation of Self in Everyday Life*. Garden City, N.Y.: Anchor Books, 1959b.

GOFFMAN, ERVING. *Asylums: Essays on the Social Situation of Mental Patients and Other Inmates*. Garden City, N.Y.: Anchor Books, 1961.

GOFFMAN, ERVING. *Stigma: Notes on the Management of Spoiled Identity*. Englewood Cliffs, N.J.: Prentice-Hall, 1963.

GOFFMAN, ERVING. "Where the Action Is." In Erving Goffman (ed.), *Interaction Ritual*. Garden City, N.Y.: Anchor Books, 1967.

GOLDBERG, STEVEN. *The Inevitability of Patriarchy*. New York: William Morrow, 1973.

GOLDMAN, MARSHALL I. *Gorbachev's Challenge: Economic Reform in the Age of High Technology*. New York: W.W. Norton and Co., 1987.

GOLEMAN, DANIEL. "The Electronic Rorschach." *Psychology Today*, February 1983.

GOODE, ERICH, ed. *Marijuana*. Chicago: Aldine, 1969.

GOODE, WILLIAM J. "The Theoretical Importance of Love." *American Sociological Review* 24, 1959.

GOODE, WILLIAM J. "Why Men Resist." In Barrie Thorne, with Marilyn Yalom (eds.), *Rethinking the Family: Some Feminist Questions*. New York: Longman, 1982.

GORDON, DAVID M. "Class and Economics of Crime." *Review of Radical Political Economies* 3, 1981.

GORDON, MICHAEL, and SHANKWEILER, PENELOPE. "Different Equals Less: Female Sexuality in Recent Marriage Manuals." *Journal of Marriage and the Family* 33, 1971.

GORDON, MILTON M. *Assimilation in American Life: The Role of Race, Religion and National Origins*. New York: Oxford University Press, 1964.

GOTTDIENER, M., and FEAGIN, JOE R. "The Paradigm Shift in Urban Sociology." *Urban Affairs Quarterly* 24, 1988.

GOTTMAN, JEAN. *Megalopolis: The Urbanized Northeastern Seaboard of the United States*. New York: Twentieth Century Fund, 1961.

GOULDNER, ALVIN W. *Patterns of Industrial Democracy*. Glencoe, Ill.: The Free Press, 1954.

GOULDNER, ALVIN W. "The Norm of Reciprocity." *American Sociological Review* 25, 1960.

GOUGH, E. KATHLEEN. "The Nayars and the Definition of Marriage." *The Journal of the Royal Anthropological Institute of Great Britain* 89, 1959.

GOUGH, KATHLEEN E. "Is the Family Universal: The Nayar Case." In Norman Bell and Ezra Vogel (eds.), *A Modern Introduction to the Family*. New York: The Free Press, 1960.

GOULD, STEPHEN JAY. *Ever Since Darwin*. New York: W.W. Norton & Co., 1977.

GOVE, WALTER, ed. *The Labelling of Deviance: Evaluating a Perspective*, 2d ed. Beverly Hills, Calif.: Sage, 1980.

GRACEY, HAROLD. "Learning the Student Role: Kindergarten as Academic Boot Camp." In Dennis Wrong and Harold Gracey (eds.), *Readings in Introductory Sociology*. New York: Macmillan, 1967.

GREELEY, ANDREW M. *Ethnicity in the United States: A Preliminary Reconnaissance*. New York: John Wiley, 1974.

GREELEY, ANDREW M. "The Ethnic Miracle." *The Public Interest* 45, 1976.

GREENBERG, DANIEL S. "Finding Time to Produce." *Washington Post*, March 6, 1979.

GRIMM, JAMES W., and DUNN, THOMAS P. "The Contemporary Foreman Status: Illustrative Evidence from an Automobile Assembly Plant." *Work and Occupations* 13, 1986.

GROBSTEIN, CLIFFORD. "When Does Human Life Begin?" *Science* 82, 1982.

GRUSKY, DAVID B., and HAUSER, ROBERT M. "Comparative Social Mobility Revisited: Models of Convergence and Divergence in 16 Countries." *American Sociological Review* 49, 1984.

GULLEY, BILL (WITH REESE, MARY ELLEN). *Breaking Cover*. New York: Simon and Schuster, 1980.

GUNTER, B. G., and GUNTER, NANCY C. "Leisure Styles: A Conceptual Framework for Modern Leisure." *Sociological Quarterly* 21, 1980.

GUSFIELD, JOSEPH R., and MICHALOWICZ, JERZY. "Secular Symbolism: Studies of Ritual, Ceremony, and the Symbolic Order of Modern Life." In Ralph H. Turner and James F. Short, Jr. (eds.), *Annual Review of Sociology* 10. Palo Alto, Calif.: Annual Reviews, 1984.

GUTTMAN, ALLEN. *From Ritual to Record: The Nature of Modern Sports*. New York: Columbia University Press, 1978.

HADAWAY, C. KIRK, and ROOF, WADE CLARK. "Apostasy in American Churches: Evidence From National Survey Data." In David G. Bromley (ed.), *Falling From the Faith*. Beverly Hills, Calif.: Sage, 1988.

HADDEN, JEFFREY K., and SHUPE, ANSON. *Televangelism: Power and Politics on God's Frontier*. New York: Henry Holt & Company, 1988.

HAGE, JERALD (ed.). *Futures of Organizations: Innovating to Adapt Strategy and Human Resources to Rapid Technological Change*. Lexington, Mass.: Lexington Books, 1988.

HALBERSTAM, DAVID. *The Reckoning*. New York: William Morrow and Co., 1986.

HALL, PETER. *The World Cities*, 3d ed. London: Weidenfeld and Nicolson, 1984.

HALLORAN, RICHARD. "Notes of a Sumo Wrestling Fan." *New York Times*, January 6, 1974.

HALPERN, SYDNEY. *American Pediatrics: The Social Dynamics of Professionalism, 1880–1980*. Berkeley: University of California Press, 1988.

HAMILL, PETE. "Facing Up to Drugs: Is Legalization the Solution?" *New York*, August 15, 1988.

HAMMOND, JUDITH. "Biography Building to Insure the Future: Women's Negotiation of Gender Relevancy in Medical School." *Symbolic Interaction* 3, 1980.

HARDEE-CLEVELAND, KAREN, and BANISTER, JUDITH. "Fertility Policy and Implementation in China, 1986–88." *Population and Development Review* 14, 1988.

HARPER, CHARLES L. *Exploring Social Change*. Englewood Cliffs, N.J.: Prentice-Hall, 1989.

HARRINGTON, MICHAEL. *The New American Poverty*. New York: Penguin Books, 1984.

HARRIS, CHAUNCEY, and ULLMAN, EDWARD. "The Nature of Cities." *Annals of the American Academy of Political and Social Science* 242, 1945.

HARRIS, JEAN. *Stranger in Two Worlds*. New York: Macmillan Publishing Company, 1986.

HARRIS, LIS. "Holy Days—I." *The New Yorker*, September 16, 1985.

HARRIS, LIS. *Holy Days: The World of a Hasidic Family*. New York: Summit, 1986.

HARRIS, MARVIN. *Cows, Pigs, Wars, and Witches: The Riddles of Culture*. New York: Vintage Books, 1974.

HARRIS, MARVIN. *America Now: The Anthropology of A Changing Culture*. New York: Simon and Schuster, 1981.

HARTWIG, M.C. "Aborigines and Racism: An Historical Perspective." In F.S. Stevens (ed.), *Racism: The Australian Experience*, vol. 2. New York: Taplinger, 1972.

HAUG, MARIE R., and FOLMAR, STEVEN J. "Longevity, Gender and Life Quality." *Journal of Health and Social Behavior* 27, 1986.

HAVLIK, RICHARD J., and FEINLEIB, MANNING, eds. *Proceedings of the Conference on the Decline in Coronary Heart Disease Mortality*. Bethesda, Md.: National Institutes of Health, 1979.

HAY, DAVID. "Religious Experience Amongst a Group of Post-Graduate Students—A Qualitative Study." *Journal for the Scientific Study of Religion* 18, 1979.

HAYES, C.D. (ed.). *Risking the Future: Adolescent Sexuality, Pregnancy and Childbearing*, vol. 1. Washington, D.C.: National Academy Press, 1987.

HAYGHE, HOWARD. "Rise In Mothers Labor Force Activity Includes Those With Infants." *Monthly Labor Review* 109, 1986.

HAYNES, SUZANNE C., and FEINLEIB, MANNING. "Women, Work and Coronary Disease: Prospective Findings From the Framingham Heart Study." *American Journal of Public Health* 70, 1980.

HAZANI, MOSHE. "A Path to Deviance: A Multi-Stage Process." *Deviant Behavior* 7, 1986.
HEARN, FRANK (ed.). *The Transformation of Industrial Organization*. Belmont, Calif.: Wadsworth, 1988.
HEFFERNAN, ESTHER. *Making It in Prison: The Square, the Cool, and the Life*. New York: Wiley-Interscience, 1972.
HELLER, JOSEPH. *Catch-22*. New York: Dell, 1955.
HENDRY, JOY. "Japan: Culture Versus Industrialization as Determinant of Marital Patterns." In Kingsley Davis (ed.), *Contemporary Marriage*. New York: Russell Sage Foundation, 1985.
HENLEY, NANCY M. *Body Politics: Power, Sex and Non-Verbal Communication*. Englewood Cliffs, N.J.: Prentice-Hall, 1977.
HENLEY, NANCY M., and THORNE, BARRIE. "Womanspeak and Manspeak: Sex Differences and Sexism in Communications, Verbal and Nonverbal." In Alice G. Sargent (ed.), *Beyond Sex Roles*. St. Paul, Minn.: West, 1977.
HERBERG, WILL. *Protestant, Catholic, and Jew*. Garden City, N.Y.: Anchor Books, 1955.
HERTSGAARD, MARK. *On Bended Knee: The Press and the Reagan Presidency*. New York: Farrar Straus Giroux, 1988.
HESS, BETH B., and FERREE, MYRA MARX. "Introduction." In Beth B. Hess and Myra Marx Ferree (eds.), *Analyzing Gender: A Handbook of Social Science Research*. Beverly Hills, Calif.: Sage, 1987.
HESS, STEPHEN. "Why Great Men Are Not Chosen Presidents." *Society*, July/August, 1988.
HETHERINGTON, MAVIS E.; COX, MARTHA; and COX, ROGER. "The Aftermath of Divorce." In J.H. Stevens, Jr., and M. Matthew (eds.), *Mother-Child, Father-Child Relations*. Washington, D.C.: National Association for the Education of Young Children, 1978.
HEWITT, JOHN P. *Self and Society: A Symbolic Interactionist Social Psychology*, 3d ed. Boston: Allyn and Bacon, 1984.
HEYDEBRAND, WOLF V. "New Organizational Forms." *Work and Occupations* 16, 1989.
HILTS, PHILIP J. "Blacks' Life Expectancy Drops." *Washington Post*, December 15, 1988.
HIRSCHMAN, CHARLES, and WONG, MORRISON G. "Trends in Socioeconomic Achievement Among Immigrant and Native-Born Asian-Americans, 1960–1976." *Sociological Quarterly* 22, 1981.
HIRSCHMAN, CHARLES, and WONG, MORRISON G. "The Extraordinary Educational Attainment of Asian-Americans: A Search for Historical Evidence and Explanations." *Social Forces* 65, 1986.
History of the Church of Latter-Day Saints. Salt Lake City: Deseret News Press, 1902.
HOCHSCHILD, ARLIE R. *The Managed Heart: Commercialization of Human Feeling*. Berkeley: University of California Press, 1983.
HODGSON, GODFREY. *All Things to All Men*. New York: Simon and Schuster, 1980.
HODSON, RANDY, and ENGLAND, PAULA. "Industrial Structure and Sex Differences in Earnings." *Industrial Relations* 25, 1986.
HOFFERTH, SANDRA L., and HAYES, CHERYL D. *Risking the Future: Adolescent Sexuality, Pregnancy, and Childbearing, Working Papers*, vol. II. Washington, D.C.: U.S. Government Printing Office, 1987.
HOFFERTH, SANDRA L.; KAHN, JOAN R.; and BALDWIN, WENDY. "Premarital Sexual Activity Among Teenage Women Over the Last Three Decades." *Family Planning Perspectives* 19, 1987.
HOFFMAN, SAUL D., and DUNCAN, GREG J. "What *Are* the Economic Consequences of Divorce?" *Demography* 25, 1988.
HOFFMAN, SHIRL J. "Evangelicalism and the Revitalization of Religious Ritual in Sport." *Arete* 2, 1985.
HOGE, DEAN R., and ROOZEN, DAVID A. *Understanding Church Growth and Decline: 1950–1978*. New York: Pilgrim Press, 1979.
HOLLINGER, RICHARD C., and LANZA-KADUCE, LONN. "The Process of Criminalization: The Case of Computer Crime Laws." *Criminology* 26, 1988.
HOLLINGSHEAD, AUGUST B., and REDLICH, FREDERICK C. *Social Class and Mental Illness*. New York: John Wiley, 1958.
HOLOHAN, ANN. "Diagnosis: The End of Transition." In A. Davis and G. Horobin (eds.), *Medical Encounters: The Experience of Illness and Treatment*. New York: St. Martin's Press, 1977.
HOMANS, GEORGE. *Social Behavior: Its Elementary Forms*, 2d ed. New York: Harcourt Brace Jovanovich, 1973.
HOOYMAN, NANCY R., and KIYAK, H. ASUMAN. *Social Gerontology: A Multidisciplinary Perspective*. Boston: Allyn and Bacon, 1988.
HOPKINS, ELLEN. "The Dispossessed." *New York*, May 13, 1985.
HOPKINS, KEITH. "Brother–Sister Marriage in Roman Egypt." *Journal for Comparative Study of Society and History* 22, 1980.
HOUBOLT, JAN. "An Empirical Critique of Blauner's Concept of Powerlessness on the Automobile Assembly Line." Paper presented at the 53rd Annual Meeting of the Eastern Sociological Society, Philadelphia, Pa., 1982.

HOUGH, JERRY. *Russia and the West: Gorbachev and the Politics of Reform.* New York: Simon and Schuster, 1988.

HOUT, MICHAEL. "More Universalism, Less Structural Mobility: The American Occupational Structure in the 1980s." *American Journal of Sociology* 93, 1988.

HOUT, MICHAEL, and GREELEY, ANDREW M. "The Center Doesn't Hold: Church Attendance in the United States, 1940–1984." *American Sociological Review* 52, 1987.

HOYT, HOMER. *The Structure and Growth of Residential Neighborhoods in American Cities.* U.S. Federal Housing Administration. Washington, D.C.: U.S. Government Printing Office, 1939.

HUBER, JOAN. "Trends in Gender Stratification, 1970–1985." *Sociological Forum* 1, 1986.

HUBER, JOAN, and FORM, WILLIAM H. *Income and Ideology.* New York: The Free Press, 1973.

HUDSON, WINTHROP. *Religion in America.* New York: Charles Scribner's, 1973.

HUGHES, CHARLES C., ed. *Custom-Made: Introductory Readings for Cultural Anthropology.* Chicago: Rand McNally, 1976.

HUGHES, DAVID. "When Nurse Knows Best: Some Aspects of Nurse/Doctor Interaction in a Casualty Department." *Sociology of Health and Illness* 10, 1988.

HUMMEL, RALPH P. *The Bureaucratic Experience.* New York: St. Martin's Press, 1977.

HUMMEL, RALPH P. *The Bureaucratic Experience*, 3d ed. New York: St. Martin's Press, 1987.

HUMPHREYS, LAUD. *Tearoom Trade: Impersonal Sex in Public Places*, enlarged ed. Chicago: Aldine, 1975.

HUNT, JENNIFER. "The Development of Rapport through the Negotiation of Gender in Field Work Among Police." *Human Organization* 43, 1984.

HUNT, JENNIFER. "Police Accounts of Normal Force." *Urban Life* 13, 1985.

HURYN, JEAN SCHERZ. "Giftedness as Deviance: A Test of Interaction Theories." *Deviant Behavior* 7, 1986.

HYER, MARJORIE. "'Sin' of Gender Discrimination Denounced." *Washington Post*, December 8, 1985.

IGNATIUS, DAVID. "What's Left of Big Steel?" *Washington Post-Outlook*, March 20, 1988a.

IGNATIUS, DAVID. "Return of the 'Fat Cats.'" *Washington Post-Outlook*, November 20, 1988b.

INKELES, ALEX. "Social Stratification and Mobility in the Soviet Union." In Reinhard Bendix and Seymour Martin Lipset (eds.), *Class, Status, and Power.* Glencoe, Ill.: The Free Press, 1968.

JACQUET, CONSTANT H., JR., ed. *Yearbook of American and Canadian Churches.* Nashville: Abington Press, 1988a.

JACQUET, CONSTANT H., JR. *Women Ministers in 1986 and 1977: A Ten Year View.* New York: National Council of Churches, 1988b.

JAMIESON, KATHLEEN HALL. *Packaging the Presidency: A History of Presidential Campaign Advertising.* New York: Oxford University Press, 1984.

JAMIESON, KATHLEEN HALL. "For Televised Mendacity: This Year is the Worst Ever." *Washington Post-Outlook*, October 30, 1988a.

JAMIESON, KATHLEEN HALL. *Eloquence in an Electronic Age: The Transformation of Political Speechmaking.* New York: Oxford University Press, 1988b.

JEFFRIES, VINCENT, and RANSFORD, EDWARD. *Social Stratification: A Multiple Hierarchy Approach.* Boston: Allyn and Bacon, 1980.

JENKINS, C. DAVID. "Social Environment and Cancer Mortality in Men." *New England Journal of Medicine* 308, 1983.

JENSEN, GARY F. "Functional Research on Deviance: A Critical Analysis and Guide for the Future." *Deviant Behavior* 9, 1988.

JOHNSON, NORRIS R. "Panic at 'The Who Concert Stampede': An Empirical Assessment." *Social Problems* 34, 1987a.

JOHNSON, NORRIS R. "Panic and the Breakdown of Social Order: Popular Myth, Social Theory, Empirical Evidence." *Sociological Focus* 20, 1987b.

JOINT ECONOMIC COMMITTEE OF THE CONGRESS OF THE UNITED STATES. "Poverty, Income Distribution, The Family and Public Policy." 99th Congress, 2nd Session. Washington, D.C.: U.S. Government Printing Office, 1986.

JONES, A.E., and PLACEK, PAUL. "Teenage Women in the USA: Sex, Contraception, Pregnancy, Fertility and Maternal and Infant Health." In Theodora Ooms (ed.), *Teenage Pregnancy and Family Impact: New Perspectives on Policy.* Philadelphia: Temple University Press, 1981.

JONES, FAUSTINE C. "External Crosscurrents and Internal Diversity: An Assessment of Black Progress, 1960–1980." *Daedalus* 110, 1981.

JOSEPH, NATHAN. *Uniforms and Nonuniforms: Communication Through Clothing.* Westport, Conn.: Greenwood Press, 1986.

JOY, LESLEY A.; KIMBALL, MEREDITH M.; and ZABRACK, MERLE L. "Television and Children's Aggressive Behavior." In T.M. Williams (ed.), *The Impact of Television: A Natural Experiment in Three Communities.* Orlando, Fla.: Academic Press, 1986.

KAHN, JOAN R.; KALSBEEK, WILLIAM D.; and HOFFERTH, SANDRA L. "National Estimates of Teenage Sexual Activity: Evaluating the Comparability of Three National Surveys." *Demography* 25, 1988.

KAHN, ROBERT L.; WOLFE, DONALD M.; QUINN, ROBERT P.; SNOEK, J. DIEDRICK; in collaboration with ROSENTHAL, ROBERT A. *Organizational Stress: Studies in Role Conflict and Ambiguity*. New York: John Wiley, 1964.

KALB, MARVIN. "TV, Election Spoiler." *New York Times*, November 28, 1988.

KALBERG, STEPHEN. "Max Weber's Types of Rationality: Cornerstones for the Analysis of Rationalization Processes in History." *American Journal of Sociology* 85, 1980.

KAMMEYER, KENNETH C.W. "The Feminine Role: An Analysis of Attitude Consistency." *Journal of Marriage and the Family* 26, 1964.

KAMMEYER, KENNETH C.W. "The Dynamics of Population." In Harold Orel (ed.), *Irish History and Culture: Aspects of a People's Heritage*. Lawrence, Kans.: The University of Kansas Press, 1976.

KAMMEYER, KENNETH C.W. "The Decline of Divorce in America." Paper presented at the annual meeting of the Midwest Sociological Society, Minneapolis, Minn., 1981.

KAMMEYER, KENNETH C.W. *Marriage and Family: A Foundation for Personal Decisions*. Boston: Allyn and Bacon, 1987.

KAMMEYER, KENNETH C.W., and GINN, HELEN L. *An Introduction to Population*. Chicago: The Dorsey Press, 1986.

KANDO, THOMAS M. *Leisure and Popular Culture in Transition*, 2d ed. St. Louis: C.V. Mosby, 1980.

Kansas City Star. "Infant Mortality Rate Leveling Off." October 18, 1984.

KANTER, ROSABETH MOSS. *Men and Women of the Corporation*. New York: Basic Books, 1977.

KASARDA, JOHN D. "The Implications of Contemporary Distribution Trends for National Urban Policy." *Social Science Quarterly* 61, 1980.

KASARDA, JOHN D. "Urban Change and Minority Opportunities." In P. Peterson (ed.), *The New Urban Realities*. Washington, D.C.: Brookings Institution, 1985.

KASARDA, JOHN D. "Urban Industrial Transition and the Underclass." *Annals of the American Academy of Political and Social Science* 501, 1989.

KATZ, HARRY C. *Shifting Gears: Changing Labor Relations in the U.S. Automobile Industry*. Cambridge, Mass.: The MIT Press, 1985.

KATZ, MICHAEL B. *The Irony of Early School Reform*. Cambridge, Mass.: Harvard University Press, 1968.

KATZ, MICHAEL B. *Class, Bureaucracy and Schools: The Illusion of Educational Change in America*. New York: Praeger, 1971.

KATZ, MICHAEL B. *Reconstructing American Education*. Cambridge, Mass.: Harvard University Press, 1987.

KATZMAN, MARTIN T. "Ecology, Natural Resources, and Economic Growth: Underdeveloping the Amazon." *Economic Development and Cultural Change* 35, 1987.

KEITH, VERNA M., and FINLAY, BARBARA. "The Impact of Parental Divorce on Children's Educational Attainment, Marital Timing, and the Likelihood of Divorce." *Journal of Marriage and the Family* 50, 1988.

KELLY, DEAN M. *Why Conservative Churches Are Growing*. New York: Harper & Row, 1972.

KELLY, WILLIAM. "Japanology Bashing." *American Ethnologist* 15, 1988.

KENNEDY, ROBERT E., JR. *The Irish: Emigration, Marriage, and Fertility*. Berkeley: University of California Press, 1973.

KEPHART, WILLIAM M. *Extraordinary Groups: The Sociology of Unconventional Life-Styles*. New York: St. Martin's Press, 1976.

KEPHART, WILLIAM M. *The Family, Society and the Individual*, 5th ed. Boston: Houghton Mifflin, 1981.

KERBO, HAROLD R. *Social Stratification and Inequality*. New York: McGraw-Hill, 1983.

KERCKHOFF, ALAN C. "Effects of Ability Grouping in British Secondary Schools." *American Sociological Review* 51, 1986.

KERCKHOFF, ALAN C.; CAMPBELL, RICHARD T.; and WINFIELD-LAIRD, IDEE. "Social Mobility in Great Britain and the United States." *American Journal of Sociology* 91, 1985.

KHOO, SIEW-EAN. "Living Together as Married: A Profile of De Facto Couples in Australia." *Journal of Marriage and the Family* 49, 1987.

KIMBALL, MEREDITH M. "Television and Sex-Role Attitudes." In Tannis M. Williams (ed.), *The Impact of Television: A Natural Experiment in Three Communities*. Orlando, Fla.: Academic Press, 1986.

KINARD, E. MILLING, and REINHERZ, HELEN. "Effects of Marital Disruption on Children's School Aptitude and Achievement." *Journal of Marriage and the Family* 48, 1986.

KING, MARTIN LUTHER, JR. *Why We Can't Wait*. New York: Harper & Row, 1963.

KINGSNORTH, RODNEY, and JUNGSTEN, MICHAEL. "Driving Under the Influence: The Impact of Legislative Reform on Court Sentencing Practices." *Crime and Delinquency* 34, 1988.

KINSEY, ALFRED C.; POMEROY, WARDELL B.; and MARTIN, CLYDE E. *Sexual Behavior in the Human Male*. Philadelphia: W.B. Saunders, 1948.

KINSEY, ALFRED C.; POMEROY, WARDELL B.; MARTIN, CLYDE E.; and GEBHARD, PAUL H. *Sexual Behavior in the Human Female.* Philadelphia: W.B. Saunders, 1953.

KITAGAWA, EVELYN, and HAUSER, PHILIP M. "Education Differentials in Mortality by Cause of Death, United States 1960." *Demography* 5, 1968.

KLEIN, MALCOLM W. "Labeling Theory and Delinquency Policy: An Experimental Test." *Criminal Justice and Behavior* 13, 1986.

KOHLBERG, L. "A Cognitive-Development Analysis of Sex-Role Concepts and Attitudes." In Eleanor Maccoby (ed.), *The Development of Sex Differences.* Stanford, Calif.: Stanford University Press, 1966.

KOHN, MELVIN L. *Class and Conformity: A Study of Values*, 2d ed., with a reassessment. Chicago: University of Chicago Press, 1977.

KOHN, MELVIN L. "Cross-National Research as an Analytic Strategy." *American Sociological Review* 52, 1987.

KOHN, MELVIN L., with MILLER, JOANNE; MILLER, KAREN A.; SCHOENBACH, CARRIE; and SCHOENBERG, RONALD. *Work and Personality: An Inquiry into the Impact of Social Stratification.* Norwood, N.J., Ablex, 1983.

KOHN, MELVIN L., and SCHOOLER, CARMI. "Occupational Experience and Psychological Functioning." *American Sociological Review* 38, 1973.

KOMAROVSKY, MIRRA. *Dilemmas of Masculinity: A Study of College Youth.* New York: W.W. Norton, 1976.

KOWINSKI, WILLIAM S. "Suburbia: End of the Golden Age." *New York Times Magazine*, March 16, 1980.

KRIESBERG, LOUIS. *Social Conflicts*, 2d ed. Englewood Cliffs, N.J.: Prentice-Hall, 1982.

KULKA, R.A., and WEINGARTEN, H. "The Long-Term Effects of Parental Divorce in Childhood on Adult Adjustment." *Journal of Social Issues* 35, 1979.

KURDEK, L.A.; BLISK, D.; and SIESKY, A.E. "Correlates of Children's Long-Term Adjustment to Their Parents' Divorce." *Developmental Psychology* 17, 1981.

KUTNER, NANCY G. "Issues in the Application of High Cost Medical Technology: The Case of Organ Transplantation." *Journal of Health and Social Behavior* 28, 1987.

KUTSCHER, RONALD E. "Overview and Implications of the Projections to 2000." *Monthly Labor Review* 110, 1987.

LADNER, ROBERT A.; SCHWARTZ, BARRY J.; ROKER, SANDRA J.; and TITTERUD, LORETTA S. "The Miami Riots of 1980: Antecedent Conditions, Community Responses and Participant Characteristics." In L. Kriesberg (ed.), *Research in Social Movements, Conflicts and Change*, vol. 4. Greenwich, Conn.: JAI Press, 1981.

LAQUEUR, WALTER. *The Age of Terrorism.* Boston: Little, Brown, 1987.

LAROSSA, RALPH. "And We Haven't Had Any Problems Since: Conjugal Violence and the Politics of Marriage." In Murray A. Straus and Gerald T. Hotaling (eds.), *The Social Causes of Husband–Wife Violence.* Minneapolis: University of Minnesota Press, 1980.

LAROSSA, RALPH. "The Transition to Parenthood and the Social Reality of Time." *Journal of Marriage and the Family* 45, 1983.

LAUER, ROBERT H. "Ideology and Strategies of Change: The Case of American Libertarians." In Robert H. Lauer (ed.), *Social Movements and Social Change.* Carbondale: Southern Illinois University Press, 1976.

LAUER, ROBERT H. *Perspectives On Social Change*, 3d ed. Boston: Allyn and Bacon, 1982.

LAWLER, JOHN J., and WEST, ROBIN. "Impact of Union-Avoidance Strategy in Representation Elections." *Industrial Relations* 24, 1985.

LAZARSFELD, PAUL. "Notes on the History of Quantification in Sociology—Trends, Sources, and Problems." In Harry Woolf (ed.), *Quantification: A History of the Meaning of Measurement in the Natural and Social Sciences.* New York: Bobbs-Merrill, 1961.

LEE, GARY R. "Marital Satisfaction in Later Life: The Effects of Nonmarital Roles." *Journal of Marriage and the Family* 50, 1988.

LEGATES, RICHARD T., and HARTMAN, CHESTER. "The Anatomy of Displacement in the United States." In Neil Smith and Peter Williams (eds.), *Gentrification of the City.* Boston: George Allen & Unwin, 1986.

LEGATES, RICHARD T., and MURPHY, KAREN. "Austerity, Shelter, and Social Conflict in the United States." In William K. Tabb and Larry Sawers (eds.), *Marxism and the Metropolis.* New York: Oxford University Press, 1984.

LEHMAN, EDWARD W. "The Theory of the State Versus the State of Theory." *American Sociological Review* 53, 1988.

LEINBERGER, CHRISTOPHER B., and LOCKWOOD, CHARLES. "How Business is Reshaping America." *The Atlantic Monthly*, October, 1986.

LEMERT, EDWIN. *Human Deviance, Social Problems, and Social Control.* Englewood Cliffs, N.J.: Prentice-Hall, 1967.

LEMERT, EDWIN. *Human Deviance, Social Problems, and Social Control*, 2d ed. Englewood Cliffs, N.J.: Prentice-Hall, 1972.

LENSKI, GERHARD. "Marxist Experiments in Destratification: An Appraisal." *Social Forces* 57, 1978.

LENSKI, GERHARD, and LENSKI, JEAN. *Human Societies*, 4th ed. New York: McGraw-Hill, 1982.

LERNER, GERDA. "The Lady and the Mill Girl: Changes in the Status of Women in the Age of Jackson." *Midcontinent American Studies Journal*, Spring 1969.

LEVY, FRANK. *Dollars and Dreams: The Changing American Income Distribution*. New York: Russell Sage Foundation, 1987.

LEWIS, ROBERT A., ed. *Men in Difficult Times: Masculinity Today and Tomorrow*. Englewood Cliffs, N.J.: Prentice-Hall, 1981.

LIEBMAN, ROBERT C., and WUTHNOW, ROBERT. *The New Christian Right*. New York: Aldine, 1983.

LIEBERT, ROBERT M., and SPRAFKIN, JOYCE. *The Early Window: Effects of Television on Children and Youth*, 3rd ed. New York: Pergamon Press, 1988.

LIGHT, DONALD W.; LIEBFRIED, STEPHAN; and TENNSTEDT, FLORIAN. "Social Medicine vs Professional Dominance: The German Experience." *American Journal of Public Health* 76, 1986.

LIN, NAN, and XIE, WEN. "Occupational Prestige in Urban China." *American Journal of Sociology*, 1988.

LINK, BRUCE. "Reward System of Psychotherapy: Implications for Inequities in Service Delivery." *Journal of Health and Social Behavior* 24, 1983.

LIPSET, SEYMOUR MARTIN. *The First New Nation*. New York: Basic Books, 1963.

LIPSET, SEYMOUR MARTIN. "Comparing Canadian and American Unions." *Society*, January/February, 1987.

LIPSET, SEYMOUR MARTIN; TROW, MARTIN; and COLEMAN, JAMES. *Union Democracy*. Garden City, N.Y.: Anchor Books, 1962.

LITKE, JAMES. "Study Hits Federal Efforts on Work-Place Safety." *Washington Post*, July 16, 1988.

LITTLE, ROGER. "Buddy Relations and Combat Performance." In Oscar Grusky and George A. Miller (eds.), *The Sociology of Organizations*. New York: The Free Press, 1970.

LOCK, MARGARET. "Protests of Good Wife and Wise Mother." In Edward Norbeck and Margaret Lock (eds.), *Health, Illness, and Medical Care in Japan*. Honolulu: University of Hawaii Press, 1987.

LOGAN, JOHN R., and SCHNEIDER, MARK. "Racial Segregation and Racial Change in American Suburbs, 1970–1980." *American Journal of Sociology* 89, 1984.

LOGUE, JAMES N.; HANSEN, HOLGER; and STRUENING, ELMER. "Some Indicators of the Long-Term Health Effects of a Natural Disaster." *Public Health Reports* 96, 1981.

LONGFELLOW, CYNTHIA. "Divorce in Context: Its Impact on Children." In George Levinger and Oliver C. Moles (eds.), *Divorce and Separation: Context, Causes, and Consequences*. New York: Basic Books, 1979.

LORBER, JUDITH. "Deviance as Performance: The Case of Illness." *Social Problems* 14, 1967.

LORBER, JUDITH. *Women Physicians*. New York: Tavistock, 1984.

LORD, WALTER. *A Night to Remember*. New York: Henry Holt, 1955.

LOSH-HESSELBART, SUSAN. "Development of Gender Roles." In Marvin B. Sussman and Suzanne K. Steinmetz (eds.), *Handbook of Marriage and the Family*. New York: Plenum Press, 1987.

LOWENSTEIN, DOUGLAS, and LOWENSTEIN, ROCHELLE. "The Baby and Us." *The Washington Post Magazine*, October 16, 1983.

LUEPNITZ, DEBORAH ANNA. *Child Custody*. Lexington, Mass.: D.C. Heath, 1982.

LUMSDEN, C.J., and WILSON, E.O. *Promethean Fire*. Cambridge, Mass.: Harvard University Press, 1983.

LUXENBERG, STAN. *Roadside Empires: How the Chains Franchised America*. New York: Viking, 1985.

LYON, DAVID. "From 'Post-Industrialism' to 'Information Society': A New Social Transformation?" *Sociology* 20, 1986.

MACCOBY, E.E., and JACKLIN, C.N. *The Psychology of Sex Differences*. Stanford, Calif.: Stanford University Press, 1974.

MACCORQUODALE, PATRICIA, and DELAMATER, JOHN. "Self-Image and Premarital Sexuality." *Journal of Marriage and the Family* 41, 1979.

MADGE, JOHN. *The Origins of Scientific Sociology*. Glencoe, Ill.: The Free Press, 1962.

MAGNUSON, ED. "Why Mrs. Reagan Still Looks Like a Million." *Time*, October 24, 1988.

MALINOWSKI, BRONISLAW. *Magic, Science, and Religion and Other Essays*. New York: Anchor Books, 1955. Originally published 1925.

MALCOLM X. *The Autobiography of Malcolm X*. New York: Grove Press, 1966.

MANTON, KENNETH G., and MYERS, GEORGE C. "Recent Trends in Multiple-Caused Mortality, 1968–1982: Age and Cohort Comparisons." *Population Research and Policy Review* 6, 1987.

MARCH, JAMES G. "Footnotes to Organizational Change." *Administrative Science Quarterly* 26, 1981.

MARSHALL, VICTOR W. *Last Chances: A Sociology of Aging and Dying*. Monterey, Calif.: Brooks/Cole, 1980.

MARTIN, SUSAN EHRLICH. *Breaking and Entering: Policewomen on Patrol*. Berkeley: University of California Press, 1982.

MARTIN, TERESA CASTRO, and BUMPASS, LARRY L. "Recent Trends in Marital Disruption." *Demography* 26, 1989.
MARTY, MARTIN E. "Transpositions: American Religion in the 1980s." *The Annals of the American Academy of Political and Social Science* 480, 1985.
MARX, KARL. *The Economic and Philosophic Manuscripts of 1884.* Dirk J. Struik, ed. New York: International Publishers, 1964. Originally published 1932.
MARX, KARL. *Capital: A Critical Analysis of Capitalist Production*, vol. 1. New York: International Publishers, 1967. Originally published 1867.
MASON, KAREN OPPENHEIM, and LU, YU-HSIA. "Attitudes Toward Women's Familial Roles: Changes in the United States, 1977–1985." *Gender & Society* 2, 1988.
MASSEY, DOUGLAS S., and DENTON, NANCY A. "Trends in the Residential Segregation of Blacks, Hispanics, and Asians: 1970–1980." *American Sociological Review* 52, 1987.
MASSEY, DOUGLAS S., and DENTON, NANCY A. "Suburbanization and Segregation in U.S. Metropolitan Areas." *American Journal of Sociology* 94, 1988.
MASSING, HERTA H. "Decoding 'Dallas': Comparing American and German Viewers." In Arthur A. Berger (ed.), *Television in Society*. New Brunswick, N.J.: Transaction Books, 1987.
MATHEWS, LINDA. "When Being Best Isn't Good Enough." *Los Angeles Times Magazine*, July 19, 1987.
MATTHEWS, MERVYN. *Privilege in the Soviet Union.* London: George Allen & Unwin, 1978.
MATTHEWS, MERVYN. *Poverty in the Soviet Union: The Life-Styles of the Underprivileged in Recent Years.* London: Cambridge University Press, 1986.
MAULDIN, W. PARKER. "Population Programs and Fertility Regulation." In Rodolfo A. Bulatao and Ronald D. Lee (eds.), *Determinants of Fertility in Developing Countries*, vol. 2. New York: Academic Press, 1983.
MAUSS, ARMAND L. "Sociological Perspectives on the Mormon Subculture." In Ralph H. Turner and James F. Short, Jr. (eds.), *Annual Review of Sociology*, 10. Palo Alto, Calif.: Annual Reviews, Inc., 1984.
MAYER, JOHN E., and ROSENBLATT, AARON. "Encounters with Danger: Social Workers in the Ghetto." *Sociology of Work and Occupations* 2, 1975.
MAYER, KURT B., and BUCKLEY, WALTER. *Class and Society*, 3d ed. New York: Random House, 1970.
MCADAM, DOUG; MCCARTHY, JOHN D.; and ZALD, MAYER N. "Social Movements." In Neil J. Smelser (ed.), *Handbook of Sociology.* Beverly Hills, Calif.: Sage, 1988.
MCCARTHY, JOHN D., and ZALD, MAYER N. "Resource Mobilization and Social Movements: A Partial Theory." *American Journal of Sociology* 82, 1977.
MCCULLOCH, JOCK. *Asbestos: Its Human Cost.* St Lucia: University of Queensland Press, 1986.
MCCURDY, DAVID W., and SPRADLEY, JAMES P., eds. *Issues in Cultural Anthropology: Selected Readings.* Boston: Little, Brown, 1979.
MCKEOWN, THOMAS. "A Historical Appraisal of the Medical Task." In G. McLachlan and T. McKeown (eds.), *Medical History and Medical Care: A Symposium of Perspectives.* New York: Oxford University Press, 1971.
MCKEOWN, THOMAS. *The Modern Rise in Population.* London: Edward Arnold, 1976.
MCKEOWN, THOMAS. *The Role of Medicine: Dream, Mirage, or Nemesis?* Princeton, N.J.: Princeton University Press, 1979.
MCKINLAY, JOHN, and MCKINLAY, SONJA. "The Questionable Contribution of Medical Measures to the Decline of Mortality in the United States in the Twentieth Century." *Milbank Memorial Quarterly/Health and Society* 55, 1977.
MCMILLEN, MARILYN M. "Differential Mortality by Sex in Fetal and Neonatal Deaths." *Science* 204, 1979.
MCNEIL, LINDA M. *Contradictions of Control: School Structure and School Knowledge.* New York: Routledge & Kegan Paul, 1986.
MEAD, GEORGE H. *Mind, Self and Society.* Chicago: University of Chicago Press, 1962. Originally published 1934.
MEAD, MARGARET. *Sex and Temperament in Three Primitive Societies.* New York: Mentor Books, 1935.
MEAD, MARGARET. *Culture and Commitment: A Study of the Generation Gap.* Garden City, N.Y.: Natural History Press/Doubleday, 1970.
MEAD, MARGARET. *Blackberry Winter.* New York: William Morrow, 1972.
MEDVEDEV, ZHORES A. *Gorbachev.* New York: W.W. Norton, 1986.
MELLEN, S.L. *The Evolution of Love.* San Francisco: W.H. Freeman, 1981.
MELTON, J. GORDON. *The Encyclopedia of American Religions*, 2d ed. Detroit: Gale Research Company, 1987.
MELTZER, BERNARD N. "Mead's Social Psychology." In Jerome Manis and Bernard N. Meltzer (eds.), *Symbolic Interaction: A Reader in Social Psychology*, 3d ed. Boston: Allyn and Bacon, 1978.
MENNERICK, LEWIS A., and NAJAFIZADEH, MEHRANGIZ. "Observations on the Missing Linkage Between Theories of Historical Expansion of Schooling and Planning for Future Educational Development." *International*

Review of Education 33, 1987.
MERNISSI, FATIMA. *Beyond the Veil: Male-Female Dynamics in Modern Muslim Society*. Bloomington, Ind.: Indiana University Press, 1987.
MERTON, ROBERT "Social Structure and Anomie." *American Sociological Review* 3, 1938.
MERTON, ROBERT. *Social Theory and Social Structure*, rev. ed. New York: The Free Press, 1957.
MERTON, ROBERT. *Social Theory and Social Structure*, 3d ed. New York: The Free Press, 1968.
MESSENGER, JOHN C. *Inis Beag: Isle of Ireland*. New York: Holt, Rinehart & Winston, 1969.
MEYER, LAWRENCE. *Israel Now: Portrait of a Troubled Land*. New York: Delacorte Press, 1982.
MEYER, MARSHALL W.; STEVENSON, WILLIAM; and WEBSTER, STEPHEN. *Limits To Bureaucratic Growth*. New York: de Gruyter, 1985.
MICHELS, ROBERT. *Political Parties: A Sociological Study of the Oligarchical Tendencies of Modern Democracy*. New York: The Free Press, 1962. Originally published 1915.
MIDDLETON, RUSSELL. "Brother-Sister and Father-Daughter Marriage in Ancient Egypt." *American Sociological Review* 27, 1962.
MILGRAM, STANLEY. *Obedience to Authority*. New York: Harper & Row, 1974.
MILLER, B.D. *The Endangered Sex*. Ithaca, N.Y.: Cornell University Press, 1981.
MILLER, STEPHEN. "The Social Base of Sales Behavior." *Social Problems* 12, 1964.
MILLING, KINARD E., and REINHERZ, HELEN. "Effects of Marital Disruption on Children's School Aptitude and Achievement." *Journal of Marriage and the Family* 48, 1986.
MILLMAN, MARCIA. *The Unkindest Cut: Life in the Backrooms of Medicine*. New York: William Morrow, 1977.
MILLMAN, MARCIA. *Such a Pretty Face: Being Fat in America*. New York: W.W. Norton, 1980.
MILLS, C. WRIGHT. *The Power Elite*. New York: Oxford University Press, 1956.
MILLS, C. WRIGHT. *The Sociological Imagination*. New York: Oxford University Press, 1959.
MIRANDE, ALFREDO. *Gringo Justice*. South Bend, Ind.: Notre Dame University Press, 1987.
MIRANNE, ALFRED C., III, and GRAY, LOUIS N. "Deterrence: A Laboratory Experiment." *Deviant Behavior* 8, 1987.
MIROWSKY, JOHN, and ROSS, CATHERINE. "Belief in Innate Sex Roles: Sex Stratification Versus Interpersonal Influence in Marriage." *Journal of Marriage and the Family* 49, 1987.
MITOFSKY, WARREN J., and PLISSNER, MARTIN. "Low Voter Turnout? Don't Believe It." *New York Times*, November 10, 1988.
MITZMAN, ARTHUR. *The Iron Cage: An Historical Interpretation of Max Weber*. New York: Grosset & Dunlap, 1969.
MIYAHARA, KOJIRO. "Inter-College Stratification: The Case of Male College Graduates in Japan." *Sociological Forum* 3, 1988.
MONROE, PAUL. *Founding of the American Public School System*. New York: Macmillan, 1940.
MOONEY, ELIZABETH C. "A Widow's World: Growing Up Alone in Middle Age." *Washington Post*, July 26, 1981.
MOORE, CHARLES A. "Taming the Giant Corporation? Some Cautionary Remarks on the Deterrability of Corporate Crime." *Crime and Delinquency* 33, 1987.
MOORE, JOAN. "Isolation and Stigmatization in the Development of an Underclass: The Case of Chicano Gangs in East Los Angeles." *Social Problems* 33, 1985.
MORGAN, EDMUND. *Visible Saints: The History of a Puritan Idea*. Ithaca, N.Y.: Cornell University Press, 1963.
MORGAN, S. PHILIP; LYE, DIANE N.; and CONDRAN, GRETCHEN A. "Sons, Daughters, and the Risk of Marital Disruption." *American Journal of Sociology* 94, 1988.
MORGAN, S. PHILIP, and RINDFUSS, RONALD R. "Marital Disruption: Structural and Temporal Dimensions." *American Journal of Sociology* 90, 1985.
MOTT, FRANK L., and HAURIN, R. JEAN. "Linkages Between Sexual Activity and Alcohol Use Among American Adolescents." *Family Planning Perspectives* 20, 1988.
MULLER, EDWARD N., and OPP, KARL-DIETER. "Rational Choice and Rebellious Collective Action." *American Political Science Review* 80, 1986.
MULLER, THOMAS, and ESPENSHADE, THOMAS J. *The Fourth Wave: California's Newest Immigrants*. Washington, D.C.: The Urban Institute Press. 1985.
MUNCY, RAYMOND L. *Sex and Marriage in Utopian Communities: 19th Century America*. Bloomington, Ind.: University of Indiana Press, 1973.
MURDOCK, GEORGE P. "Comparative Data on the Division of Labor by Sex." *Social Forces* 15, 1937.
MURDOCK, GEORGE P., and PROVOST, CATRINA. "Factors in the Division of Labor by Sex: A Cross-Cultural Analysis." *Ethnology* 12, 1973.
MURPHY, CARYLE. "Former Executive, 2 Others in Defense Probe Plead Guilty." *Washington Post*, March 10, 1989.

MURRAY, CHARLES. *Losing Ground: American Social Policy 1950–1980*. New York: Basic Books, 1984.

NAJAFIZADEH, MEHRANGIZ, and MENNERICK, LEWIS A. "Worldwide Educational Expansion from 1950 to 1980: The Failure of the Expansion of Schooling in Developing Countries." *The Journal of Developing Areas* 22, 1988.

NAOI, ATSUSHI, and SCHOOLER, CARMI. "Occupational Conditions and Psychological Functioning in Japan." *American Journal of Sociology* 90, 1981.

A Nation at Risk: The Imperative for Educational Reform. Washington, D.C.: The National Commission on Excellence in Education, 1983.

NATIONAL CENTER FOR HEALTH STATISTICS. *Health, United States, 1987*. DHHS Pub. No. (PHS) 88-1232, Public Health Service. Washington, D.C.: U.S. Government Printing Office, March 1988.

NATIONAL CENTER FOR HEALTH STATISTICS. *Vital Statistics of the United States, 1986, Vol. II, Sec. 6, Life Tables*. Washington, D.C.: U.S. Government Printing Office, 1988.

NATIONAL COUNCIL OF CHURCHES. *An Inclusive Language Lectionary*. Philadelphia: Westminster Press, 1983.

NAUGHTON, JIM. "The Devil and Duffy Strode." *The Washington Post*, August 29, 1988.

NELSON, KATHRYN P. *Gentrification and Distressed Cities: An Assessment of Trends in Intrametropolitan Migration*. Madison, Wisc.: University of Wisconsin Press, 1988.

NELSON, LYNN D., and BROMLEY, DAVID G. "Another Look at Conversion and Defection in Conservative Churches." In David G. Bromley (ed.), *Falling From the Faith*. Beverly Hills, Calif.: Sage, 1988.

New York Times. "Life Term Is Upheld in Theft of $120.75." March 19, 1980a.

New York Times. "A Radical Church Pays a Price in Lives." July 7, 1980b.

New York Times, January 21, 1989.

NEW YORK TIMES/CBS NEWS POLL. "Portrait of the Electorate." *New York Times*, November 10, 1988.

NEWACHECK, PAUL W., et al., "Income and Illness." *Medical Care* 18, 1980.

NEWHOUSE, JOHN. "Profiles (Margaret Thatcher) The Gamefish." *The New Yorker*, February 10, 1986.

NEWMAN, WILLIAM M. *American Pluralism: A Study of Minority Groups and Social Theory*. New York: Harper & Row, 1973.

NEWTON, GERALD. *The Netherlands: A Historical and Cultural Analysis*. Boulder, Colo.: Westview, 1978.

NIEBUHR, H. RICHARD. *The Social Sources of Denominationalism*. New York: Henry Holt, 1929.

NIMMO, DAN. "Elections as Ritual Drama." *Society*, May/June 1985.

NOCK, STEVEN L., and KINGSTON, PAUL WILLIAM. "The Family Work Day." *Journal of Marriage and the Family* 46, 1984.

NORDOFF, CHARLES. *The Communistic Societies of the United States*. New York: Schocken Books, 1971. Originally published 1875.

NORTON, ROBERT. "Measuring Marital Quality: A Critical Look at the Dependent Variable." *Journal of Marriage and the Family* 45, 1983.

NOVAK, MICHAEL. *The Joy of Sports*. New York: Basic Books, 1976.

NUGENT, JEFFREY B. "The Old-age Security Motive For Fertility." *Population and Development Review* 13, 1985.

OAKES, JEANNIE. "Classroom Social Relationships: Exploring the Bowles and Gintis Hypothesis." *Sociology of Education* 55, 1982.

OAKES, JEANNIE. *Keeping Track: How Schools Structure Inequality*. New Haven, Conn.: Yale University Press, 1985.

O'BRIEN, WILLIAM V. "International Crimes." In David L. Sills (ed.), *International Encyclopedia of the Social Sciences*. New York: Macmillan, 1968.

O'DEA, THOMAS F. *The Mormons*. Chicago: University of Chicago Press, 1957.

O'DEA, THOMAS F., and AVIAD, JANET O'DEA. *The Sociology of Religion*, 2d ed. Englewood Cliffs, N.J.: Prentice-Hall, 1983.

OGBURN, WILLIAM F. *Social Change*. New York: The Viking Press, 1964. Originally published 1922.

O'HARE, WILLIAM P. "Poverty in America: Trends and New Patterns." *Population Bulletin* 40, 1985.

O'HARE, WILLIAM P. "America's Welfare Population: Who Gets What?" *Population Trends and Public Policy*. Washington, D.C.: Population Reference Bureau, 1987.

OKONJO, KAMENE. "The Dual-Sex Political System in Operation: Igbo Women and Community Politics in Midwestern Nigeria." In N.J. Hafkin and E.G. Bay (eds.), *Women in Africa*. Stanford, Calif.: Stanford University Press, 1976.

OLIVER, MELVIN L., and SHAPIRO, THOMAS M. "Wealth of a Nation: A Reassessment of Asset Inequality in America." *American Journal of Economics and Sociology* 48, 1989.

OLSON, DAVID H., and CROMWELL, RONALD E., eds. *Power in Families*. New York: John Wiley, 1975.

OLSON, PHILIP. "Modernization in the People's Republic of China: The Politicization of the Elderly." *The*

Sociological Quarterly 29, 1988.
OMANG, JOANNE. "A-Worker Exposure Soars, Group Says." *Washington Post*, September 5, 1981.
OMANG, JOANNE. "The Secret Handicap: Millions of American Adults Can't Read." *Washington Post*, November 25, 1982.
ORCUTT, JAMES D. "Differential Association and Marijuana Use: A Closer Look at Sutherland (With a Little Help from Becker)." *Criminology* 25, 1987.
ORTEGA Y GASSET, JOSÉ. *The Revolt of the Masses*. New York: W.W. Norton, 1932.
OUCHI, WILLIAM G. *Theory Z: How American Business Can Meet the Japanese Challenge*. New York: Avon, 1982.
OUDES, BRUCE, ed. *From: The President Richard Nixon's Secret Files*. New York: Harper & Row, 1988.
OUTLER, ALBERT. *Library of Protestant Thought: John Wesley*. New York: Oxford University Press, 1964.
PAGET, MARIANNE A. *The Unity of Mistakes: A Phenomenological Interpretation of Medical Work*. Philadelphia: Temple University Press, 1988.
PARSONS, TALCOTT. *The Social System*. Glencoe, Ill.: The Free Press, 1951.
PARSONS, TALCOTT. "The School Class as a Social System: Some of Its Functions in American Society." *Harvard Educational Review* 29, 1959.
PARELIUS, ANN PARKER, and PARELIUS, ROBERT J. *The Sociology of Education*. Englewood Cliffs, N.J.: Prentice-Hall, 1978.
PARK, ROBERT E.; BURGESS, E.W.; and MCKENZIE, RODERICK D., eds. *The City*. Chicago: University of Chicago Press, 1925.
PATTERSON, JAMES T. *The Dread Disease: Cancer and Modern American Culture*. Cambridge, Mass.: Harvard University Press, 1987.
PEAR, ROBERT. "Millions Bypassed as Economy Soars." *New York Times*, March 16, 1986.
PEPLAU, LETITIA; RUBIN, ZICK; and HILL, CHARLES T. "Sexual Intimacy in Dating Relationships." *Journal of Social Issues* 33, 1977.
PERL, PETER. "Lower Pay for Women Blamed on Job Barriers." *Washington Post*, December 15, 1985.
PERROW, CHARLES. *Complex Organizations: A Critical Essay*, 3d ed. New York: Random House, 1986.
PERRY, STEWART E. *San Francisco Scavengers: Dirty Work and the Pride of Ownership*. Berkeley: University of California Press, 1978.
PERSELL, CAROLINE HODGES. *Education and Inequality: A Theoretical and Empirical Synthesis*. New York: The Free Press, 1977.
PESCOSOLIDO, BERNICE A., and GEORGIANNA, SHARON. "Durkheim, Suicide, and Religion: Toward a Network Theory of Suicide." *American Sociological Review* 54, 1989.
PETERS, JOHN F. "Adolescents as Socialization Agents to Parents." *Adolescence* 20, 1985.
PETERS, THOMAS J., and WATERMAN, ROBERT H. *In Search of Excellence: Lessons from America's Best-Run Companies*. New York: Harper & Row, 1982.
PETERSON, GARY W., and ROLLINS, BOYD C. "Parent-Child Socialization." In Marvin B. Sussman and Suzanne K. Steinmetz (eds.), *Handbook of Marriage and the Family*. New York: Plenum Press, 1987.
PETERSON, JAMES L., and ZILL, NICHOLAS. "Marital Disruption, Parent-Child Relationships, and Behavior Problems of Children." *Journal of Marriage and the Family* 48, 1986.
PETERSON, RICHARD A.; SCHMIDMAN, JOHN T.; and ELIFSON, KIRK W. "Entrepreneurship or Autonomy? Truckers and Cabbies." In Phyllis L. Stewart and Muriel G. Cantor (eds.), *Varieties of Work*. Beverly Hills, Calif.: Sage, 1982.
PFEIFFER, JOHN. "Girl Talk—Boy Talk." *Science* 85 January/February, 1985.
PHILLIPS, ROLAND L.; KUZMA, J.W.; BEESON, W. LAWRENCE; and LOTZ, TERRY. "Influence of Selection Versus Lifestyle on Risk of Fatal Cancer and Cardiovascular Disease Among Seventh-Day Adventists." *American Journal of Epidemiology* 112, 1980.
PIFER, ALAN, and BRONTE, D. LYDIA. "Introduction: Squaring the Pyramid." *Daedalus* 115, 1986.
PIKE, E. ROYSTON. "The Natural History of the Kiss." In Charles C. Hughes (ed.), *Custom-Made: Introductory Readings for Cultural Anthropology*, 2d ed. Chicago: Rand McNally, 1976.
PINEO, PETER C. "Disenchantment in the Later Years of Marriage." *Marriage and Family Living* 23, 1961.
PIOTRKOWSKI, CHAYA S., and GORNICK, L. "The Impact of Work-Related Separations on Children and Families." In J. Bloom-Feshbeck and S. Bloom-Feshback (eds.), *The Psychology of Separation*. San Francisco: Jossey-Bass, 1986.
PIOTRKOWSKI, CHAYA S.; RAPOPORT, ROBERT N.; and RAPOPORT, RHONA. "Families and Work." In Marvin B. Sussman and Suzanne K. Steinmetz (eds.), *Handbook of Marriage and the Family*. New York: Plenum Press, 1987, pp. 251–283.
PLECK, JOSEPH H., and SAWYER, JACK, eds. *Men and Masculinity*. Englewood Cliffs, N.J.: Prentice-Hall, 1974.

PLIVEN, FRANCES FOX, and CLOWARD, RICHARD. *Why Americans Don't Vote.* New York: Pantheon, 1988.
POLIT, DENISE F., and FALBO, TONI. "Only Children and Personality Development: A Quantitative Review." *Journal of Marriage and the Family* 49, 1987.
POMEROY, WARDELL B. *Dr. Kinsey and the Institute for Sex Research.* New York: Harper & Row, 1972.
POPE, LISTON. *Millhands and Preachers.* New Haven: Yale University Press, 1942.
POPENOE, DAVID. "Beyond the Nuclear Family: A Statistical Portrait of the Changing Family in Sweden." *Journal of Marriage and the Family* 49, 1987.
POPULATION REFERENCE BUREAU. *1988 World Population Data Sheet.* Washington, D.C.: Population Reference Bureau, 1988.
POULANTZAS, NICOS. *Political Power and Social Classes.* London: NLB and Sheed and Ward, 1973.
POUSSAINT, ALVIN F. "A Negro Psychiatrist Explains the Negro Psyche." In Norman R. Yetman and C. Hoy Steele. *Majority and Minority: The Dynamics of Racial and Ethnic Relations.* Boston: Allyn and Bacon, 1971.
POWELL, DAVID E. "Soviet Society Today." In Uri Ra'anan and Charles M. Perry (eds.), *The USSR Today and Tomorrow: Problems and Challenges.* Lexington, Mass.: Lexington Books, 1987.
POWELL, DOUGLAS H., and DRISCOLL, PAUL F. "Middle-Class Professionals Face Unemployment." In Peter I. Rose (ed.), *Socialization and the Life Cycle.* New York: St. Martin's Press, 1979.
POWELL, G. BINGHAM. "Voter Turnout in Comparative Perspective." *American Political Science Review* 80, 1986.
POWERS, WILLIAM K. "Indians of the Plains." In Mircea Eliade (ed.), *The Encyclopedia of Religion.* New York: MacMillan, 1987.
PRADOS, JOHN. *Presidents' Secret Wars.* New York: William Morrow, 1986.
PRATT, BETH. "Many Profess to Feel Holy Presence." *Lubbock Avalanche-Journal*, August 16, 1988.
PREBISH, C.S. "Heavenly Father, Divine Goalie. Sport and Religion." *Antioch Review* 42, 1984.
PRESSER, HARRIET B. "Shift Work and Child Care among Young Dual-Earner American Parents." *Journal of Marriage and the Family* 50, 1988.
PRESTHUS, ROBERT VANCE. *The Organizational Society*, rev. ed. New York: St. Martin's Press, 1978.
PRESTON, SAMUEL H. *Biological and Social Aspects of Mortality and the Length of Life.* Leige: Ordina, 1982.
PRESTON, SAMUEL H. "Children and the Elderly: Divergent Paths for America's Dependents." *Demography* 21, 1984.
PRINCETON RELIGIOUS RESEARCH CENTER. *The Unchurched American.* Princeton, N.J.: Princeton Religious Research Center and the Gallup Organization, 1978.
PRITCHARD, LINDA K. "Religious Change in Nineteenth-Century America." In Charles Y. Glock and Robert N. Bellah (eds.), *The New Religious Consciousness.* Berkeley: University of California Press, 1976.
PROSEN, ROSE MARY. "Looking Back." In Michael Novak (ed.), *Growing Up Slavic in America.* Bayville, N.Y.: EMPAC. 1976.
QUINN, JAMES F. "Sex Roles and Hedonism Among Members of 'Outlaw' Motorcycle Clubs." *Deviant Behavior* 8, 1987.
RADIN, PAUL, ed. *Crashing Thunder: The Autobiography of a Winnebago Indian.* New York: D. Appleton, 1926. Published in 1920 as Part 1 of the autobiography.
RAINES, HOWELL. *My Soul Is Rested.* New York: Bantam Books, 1978.
RAINWATER, LEE. "The Lower Class: Health, Illness and Medical Institutions." In Irwin Deutscher and Elizabeth J. Thompson (eds.), *Among the People: Encounters with the Poor.* New Yor : Basic Books, 1968.
RASCHKE, HELEN J. "Divorce." In Marvin B. Sussman and Suzanne K. Steinmetz (eds.), *Handbook of Marriage and the Family.* New York: Plenum Press, 1987.
RASOR, DINA. *The Pentagon Underground.* New York: Random House—Times Books, 1985.
RAVITCH, DIANE. *The Schools We Deserve: Reflections on the Educational Crises of Our Time.* New York: Basic Books, 1985.
READ, KENNETH E. *The High Valley.* New York: Columbia University Press, 1980.
REED, EVELYN. "Is Biology Woman's Destiny?" *International Socialist Review*, 1971.
REEDER, LEO G. "The Patient-Client as a Consumer: Some Observations on the Changing Professional-Client Relationship." *Journal of Health and Social Behavior* 13, 1972.
REIMAN, JEFFREY H. *The Rich Get Richer and the Poor Get Prison.* New York: John Wiley, 1979.
REINHOLD, ROBERT. "In the Middle of L.A.'s Gang Warfare." *New York Times Magazine*, May 22, 1988.
REISS, IRA L. *The Social Context of Premarital Sexual Permissiveness.* New York: Holt, Rinehart & Winston, 1967.
REISS, IRA L. *Journey into Sexuality: An Explanatory Voyage.* Englewood Cliffs, N.J.: Prentice-Hall, 1986.
REISS, IRA L., and LEE, GARY R. *Family Systems in America*, 4th ed. New York: Holt, Rinehart & Winston, Inc., 1988.

REMINI, ROBERT V. *Andrew Jackson and the Course of American Democracy, 1833–1845*. New York: Harper & Row, 1984.

RENSBERGER, BOYCE. "African Women Save Energy Using Head for Heavy Loads." *Washington Post*, February 23, 1986.

RENSBERGER, BOYCE. "Sexual Competition and Violence." *Washington Post*, February 29, 1988.

RESKIN, BARBARA F., and HARTMAN, HEIDI, eds. *Women's Work, Men's Work: Sex Segregation on the Job*. Washington, D.C.: National Academy Press, 1986.

RICH, SPENCER. "Nursing Shortage Called Widespread." *Washington Post*, July 17, 1988.

RICHARDSON, LAUREL. *The New Other Woman: Contemporary Single Women in Affairs with Married Men*. New York: The Free Press, 1985.

RICHEY, RUSSELL E., and JONES, DONALD G. *American Civil Religion*. New York: Harper & Row, 1974.

RICHMOND-ABBOTT, M. *Masculine and Feminine: Sex Roles Over the Life Cycle*. Reading, Mass.: Addison-Wesley, 1983.

RIESMAN, DAVID. *The Lonely Crowd*. New Haven, Conn.: Yale University Press, 1961.

RILEY, MATILDA WHITE; FONER, ANNE; and WARING, JOAN. "Sociology of Aging." In Neil J. Smelser (ed.), *Handbook of Sociology*. Beverly Hills, Calif.: Sage, 1988.

RITZER, GEORGE. "Work-linked Equity in Sweden: Implications for America." In Irving Louis Horowitz (ed.), *Equity, Income and Policy: A Comparative Developmental Context*. New York: Praeger, 1977.

RITZER, GEORGE. "The McDonaldization of Society." *Journal of American Culture* 6, 1983.

RITZER, GEORGE. *Sociological Theory*, 2d ed. New York: Alfred A. Knopf, 1988.

RITZER, GEORGE, and WALCZAK, DAVID. *Working: Conflict and Change*, 3d ed. Englewood Cliffs, N.J.: Prentice-Hall, 1986.

RITZER, GEORGE, and WALCZAK, DAVID. "Rationalization and the Deprofessionalization of Physicians." *Social Forces* 66, 1988.

ROBERTS, ELIZABETH; KLINE, DAVID; and GAGNON, JOHN. *Family Life and Sexual Learning: A Study of the Role of Parents in the Sexual Learning of Children*. Cambridge, Mass.: Population Education, 1978.

ROETHLISBERGER, FRITZ, and DICKSON, WILLIAM J. *Management and the Worker*. New York: John Wiley & Sons, 1964. Originally published in 1939.

ROHLEN, THOMAS P. *Japan's High Schools*. Berkeley: University of California Press, 1983.

ROLLINS, B.C., and GALLIGAN, R. "The Developing Child and Marital Satisfaction of Parents." In R.M. Lerner and G.B. Spanier (eds.), *Child Influences on Marital and Family Interaction*. New York: Academic Press, 1978.

ROMAN, MEL, and HADDAD, WILLIAM. *The Disposable Parent: The Case for Joint Custody*. New York: Penguin Books, 1978.

ROOF, WADE CLARK, and HADAWAY, C. KIRK. "Denominational Switching in the Seventies: Going Beyond Stark and Glock." *Journal for the Scientific Study of Religion* 18, 1979.

ROOF, WADE CLARK, and MCKINNEY, WILLIAM. *American Mainline Religion: Its Changing Shape and Future*. New Brunswick, N.J.: Rutgers University Press, 1987.

ROSE, ARNOLD. *The Power Structure*. New York: Oxford University Press, 1967.

ROSE, PETER I., ed. *Socialization and the Life Cycle*. New York: St. Martin's Press, 1979.

ROSEBERRY, WILLIAM. *Coffee and Capitalism in the Venezuelan Andes*. Austin: University of Texas Press, 1983.

ROSECRANCE, JOHN. "Compulsive Gambling and the Medicalization of Deviance." *Social Problems* 32, 1985.

ROSEN, ELLEN ISRAEL. *Bitter Choices: Blue-Collar Women in and Out of Work*. Chicago: University of Chicago Press, 1987.

ROSEN, SHERWIN, and TAUBMAN, PAUL. "Changes in the Impact of Education and Income on Mortality in the U.S." In Linda DelBene and Foritz Schueren (eds.), *Statistical Uses of Administrative Records with Emphasis on Mortality and Disability Research*. Washington, D.C.: U.S. Department of Health, Education and Welfare, 1979.

ROSENBAUM, JAMES E. *Making Inequality: The Hidden Curriculum of High School Tracking*. New York: John Wiley, 1976.

ROSENBERG, MORRIS. *Conceiving the Self*. New York: Basic Books, 1979.

ROSENBERG, NATHAN. *Perspectives on Technology*. New York: Cambridge University Press, 1976.

ROSENTHAL, ROBERT, and JACOBSON, LENORE. *Pygmalion in the Classroom*. New York: Holt, Rinehart & Winston, 1968.

ROSNOW, RALPH L., and FINE, GARY ALAN. *Rumor and Gossip*. New York: Elsevier, 1976.

ROSS, CATHERINE E., and DUFF, RAYMOND S. "Returning to the Doctor: The Effect of Client Characteristics, Type of Practice, and Experience with Care." *Health and Social Behavior* 23, 1982.

ROSS, CATHERINE E.; MIROWSKY, JOHN; and HUBER, JOAN. "Dividing Work, Sharing Work, and In Between:

Marriage Patterns and Depression." *American Sociological Review* 48, 1983.

ROTH, JULIUS A. *Timetables: Structuring the Passage of Time in Hospital Treatment and Other Careers*. Indianapolis: Bobbs-Merrill, 1963.

ROTH, JULIUS A. "Treatment of the Sick." In J. Kosa, Aaron Antonovsky, and Irving Kenneth Zola (eds.), *Poverty and Health*. Cambridge, Mass.: Harvard University Press, 1969.

ROTHMAN, DAVID. *The Discovery of the Asylum: Social Order and Disorder in the New Republic*. Boston: Little, Brown, 1971.

ROWAN, BRIAN, and MIRACLE, ANDREW W., JR. "Systems of Ability Grouping and the Stratification of Achievement in Elementary Schools." *Sociology of Education* 56, 1983.

ROY, DONALD. "Efficiency and the 'Fix': Informal Intergroup Relations in a Piecework Machine Shop." *American Journal of Sociology* 60, 1954.

ROY, DONALD. "Banana Time: Job Satisfaction and Informal Interaction." *Human Organization* 18, 1959–1960.

RUBIN, LILLIAN BRESLOW. *Worlds of Pain: Life in the Working Class Family*. New York: Basic Books, 1976.

RUBIN, ZICK; PEPLAU, LETITIA A.; and HILL, CHARLES T. "Loving and Leaving: Sex Differences in Romantic Attachments." *Sex Roles* 7, 1981.

RUBINSON, RICHARD, and RALPH, JOHN. "Technical Change and the Expansion of Schooling in the United States, 1890–1970." *Sociology of Education* 57, 1984.

RUDIN, A.J. "America's New Religion." *The Christian Century* 89, 1972.

RUNCIE, JOHN F. "By Days I Make the Cars." *Harvard Business Review*, May–June 1980.

RUNDALL, THOMAS G., and WHEELER, JOHN R.C. "The Effect of Income on Use of Preventive Care: An Evaluation of Alternative Explanations." *Journal of Health and Social Behavior* 20, 1979.

RUSH, GARY B., and DENISOFF, R. SERGE. *Social and Political Movements*. New York: Appleton-Century-Crofts, 1971.

RUSHING, WILLIAM A. "The Supply of Physicians and Expenditures for Health Services with Implications for the Coming Physician Surplus." *Journal of Health and Social Behavior* 26, 1985.

RYAN, WILLIAM. *Blaming the Victim*. New York: Pantheon Books, 1971.

SABATO, LARRY J. *The Rise of Political Consultants: New Ways of Winning Elections*. New York: Basic Books, 1981.

SACHAR, HOWARD M. *A History of Israel, Volume II, From the Aftermath of the Yom Kippur War*. New York: Oxford University Press, 1987.

SADKER, MYRA, and SADKER, DAVID. "Sexism in the Schoolroom of the '80s." *Psychology Today*, March, 1985.

SAFILIOS-ROTHSCHILD, C. "Study of Family Power Structure: 1960–1969." *Journal of Marriage and the Family* 32, 1970.

SANDAY, PEGGY REEVES. *Female Power and Male Dominance*. New York: Cambridge University Press, 1981.

San Diego Tribune. February 7, 1986.

SASSER, W. EARL, JR., and LEONARD, FRANK. "Let First-Level Supervisors Do Their Job." *Harvard Business Review*, 58, 1980.

SAUNDERS, DANIEL G. "When Battered Women Use Violence: Husband-Abuse or Self-Defense?" *Violence and Victims* 1, 1986.

SAVETH, EDWARD N. *American Historians and European Immigrants*. New York: Columbia University Press, 1948.

SAXE, LEONARD, and FINE, MICHELLE. *Social Experiments: Methods for Design and Evaluation*. Beverly Hills, Calif.: Sage, 1981.

SCANZONI, JOHN. *Sexual Bargaining: Power Politics in the American Marriage*. Englewood Cliffs, N.J.: Prentice-Hall, 1972.

SCANZONI, JOHN. "Social Processes and Power in Families." In Wesley R. Burr, Reuben Hill, F. Ivan Nye, and Ira L. Reiss (eds.), *Contemporary Theories About the Family: Research-Based Theories*, Vol. I. New York: The Free Press, 1979.

SCANZONI, LETHA DAWSON, and SCANZONI, JOHN. *Men, Women, and Change: A Sociology of Marriage and the Family*. New York: McGraw-Hill, 1981.

SCHAEFER, WALTER E.; OLEXA, CAROL; and POLK, KENNETH. "Programmed for Social Class: Tracking in High School." *Trans-Action* 7, 1970.

SCHEFF, THOMAS J. *Being Mentally Ill*. Chicago: Aldine, 1966.

SCHLAFLY, PHYLLIS. *The Power of the Positive Woman*. New Rochelle, N.Y.: Arlington House, 1977.

SCHRAM, MARTIN. *The Great American Video Game: Presidential Politics in the Television Age*. New York: William Morrow, 1987.

SCHUMAN, HOWARD; STEEH, CHARLOTTE; and BOBO, LAWRENCE. *Racial Attitudes in America: Trends and Interpretations*. Cambridge, Mass.: Harvard University Press, 1985.

SCHUMM, WALTER R., and BUGAIGHIS, MARGARET A. "Marital Quality over the Marital Career: Alternative Explanations." *Journal of Marriage and the Family* 48, 1986.

SCHUR, EDWIN. *Crimes Without Victims: Deviant Behavior and Public Policy*. Englewood Cliffs, N.J.: Prentice-Hall, 1965.

SCHUR, EDWIN M. *The Americanization of Sex*. Philadelphia: Temple University Press, 1988.

SCHWALBE, MICHAEL L. *The Psychosocial Consequences of Natural and Alienated Labor*. Albany, N.Y.: State University of New York Press, 1986.

SCHWARTZ, HILLEL. *Never Satisfied: A Cultural History of Diets, Fantasies and Fat*. New York: The Free Press, 1986.

SCOTT, DANIEL T. *Technology and Union Survival: A Study of the Printing Industry*. New York: Praeger, 1987.

SEDLAK, MICHAEL W.; WHEELER, CHRISTOPHER W.; PULLIN, DIANA C.; and CUSIK, PHILIP A. *Selling Students Short: Classroom Bargains and Academic Reform in the American High School*. New York: Teachers College Press, 1986.

SENNETT, RICHARD, and COBB, JONATHAN. *The Hidden Injuries of Class*. New York: Vintage Books, 1972.

SEWELL, WILLIAM H. "Inequality of Opportunity for Higher Education." *American Sociological Review* 36, 1971.

SHAIKEN, HARLEY. *Work Transformed: Automation and Labor in The Computer Age*. Lexington, Mass.: Lexington Books, 1986.

SHANK, SUSAN E. "Women and the Labor Market: The Link Grows Stronger." *Monthly Labor Review* 111, 1988.

SHANNON, LYLE W. "Assessing the Relationship of Adult Criminal Careers to Juvenile Careers." In C. Abt (ed.), *Problems in American Social Policy*. Cambridge, Mass.: Abt Books, 1980.

SHAPIRO, CONSTANCE H. "Sexual Learning: The Short-Changed Adolescent Male." *Social Work* 25, 1980.

SHAPIRO, MARGARET. "Saturday Night Fervor." *Washington Post*, April 11, 1988.

SHAVIT, YOSSI, and FEATHERMAN, DAVID L. "Schooling, Tracking, and Teenage Intelligence." *Sociology of Education* 61, 1988.

SHEFFIELD, CAROLE J. "Sexual Terrorism: The Social Control of Women." In Beth B. Hess and Myra Marx Ferree (eds.), *Analyzing Gender: A Handbook of Social Science Research*. Beverly Hills, Calif.: Sage, 1987.

SHELL, ELLEN RUPPEL. "The Getting of Respect." *The Atlantic*, February, 1988.

SHEPHERD, GORDON, and SHEPHERD, GARY. *A Kingdom Transformed: Themes in the Development of Mormonism*. Salt Lake City: University of Utah Press, 1984.

SHERIF, MUZAFER. "A Study of Some Social Factors in Perception." *Archives of Psychology* 27, 1935.

SHERIF, MUZAFER. *Groups in Harmony and Tension*. New York: Harper & Brothers, 1953.

SHERMAN, LAWRENCE W., and BERK, RICHARD A. "The Specific Deterrent Effects of Arrest for Domestic Assault." *American Sociological Review* 49, 1984.

SHERMAN, LAWRENCE W., and COHN, ELLEN G. "The Impact of Research on Legal Policy: A Case Study of the Minneapolis Domestic Violence Experiment." *Law and Society* 23, 1989.

SHORTER, EDWARD. *A History of Women's Bodies*. New York: Basic Books, 1982.

SIEGEL, JACOB S., and TAEUBER, CYNTHIA M. "Demographic Perspectives on the Long-Lived Society." *Daedalus* 115, 1986.

SILBERMAN, CHARLES E. *Crisis in the Classroom: The Remaking of American Education*. New York: Random House, 1970.

SILVER, MARC L. *Under Construction: Work and Alienation in the Building Trades*. Albany, N.Y.: State University of New York Press, 1986.

SILVESTRI, GEORGE T., and LUKASIEWICZ, JOHN M. "A Look at Occupational Employment Trends to the Year 2000." *Monthly Labor Review* 110, 1987.

SILVESTRI, GEORGE T.; LUKASIEWICZ, JOHN M.; and EINSTEIN, MARCUS E. "Occupational Employment Projections Through 1995." *Monthly Labor Review* 106, 1983.

SIMMEL, GEORG. "The Dyad and the Triad." In Kurt Wolf (ed.), *The Sociology of Georg Simmel*. Glencoe, Ill.: The Free Press, 1950.

SIMMEL, GEORG. "The Metropolis and Mental Life." In Donald Levine (ed.). *Georg Simmel: Individuality and Social Forms*. Chicago: University of Chicago Press, 1971. Originally published 1903.

SIMMONS, J.L. "Public Stereotypes of Deviants." *Social Problems* 13, 1965.

SIMMONS, J.L., and MCCALL, GEORGE J. *Social Research: The Craft of Finding Out*. New York: Macmillan, 1985.

SIMON, JULIAN L. *The Ultimate Resource*. Princeton, N.J.: Princeton University Press, 1981.

SIMONS, LEWIS M. *Worth Dying For*. New York: William Morrow and Co., 1987.

SIMPSON, GEORGE EATON, and YINGER, J. MILTON. *Racial and Cultural Minorities: An Analysis of Prejudice and Discrimination,* 5th ed. New York: Plenum, 1985.

SINGER, MILTON. *When a Great Tradition Modernizes*. New York: Praeger, 1972.

SINGH, J.A.L., and ZINGG, ROBERT M. *Wolf Children and Feral Man*. New York: Harper & Row, 1942.

SITKOFF, HARVARD. *The Struggle for Black Equality: 1945–1980*. New York: Hill and Wang, 1981.

SLOMCZYNSKI, KAZIMIERZ M.; MILLER, JOANNE; and KOHN, MELVIN L. "Stratification, Work, and Values: A Polish-United States Comparison." *American Sociological Review* 46, 1981.

SMITH, ADAM. *The Wealth of Nations.* New York: The Modern Library, 1937.

SMITH, DOUGLAS A., and GARTIN, PATRICK R. "Specifying Specific Deterrence: The Influence of Arrest on Future Criminal Activity." *American Sociological Review* 54, 1989.

SMITH, HEDRICK. *The Russians.* New York: Quadrangle Books, 1976.

SMITH, JAMES D. "Trends in the Concentration of Personal Wealth in the United States, 1958 to 1976." *Review of Income and Wealth* 30, 1984.

SMITH, KEVIN B., and BYLUND, ROBERT A. "Cognitive Maps of Class, Racial, and Appalachian Inequalities Among Rural Appalachians." *Rural Sociology* 42, 1983.

SNIPP, C. MATTHEW. "American Indians and Natural Resource Development." *American Journal of Economics and Sociology* 45, 1986.

SNYDER, THOMAS D. *Digest of Educational Statistics 1987.* Washington, D.C.: U.S. Government Printing Office, 1987.

SOLDO, BETH J., and AGREE, EMILY. "America's Elderly." *Population Bulletin* 43, 1988.

SOLLIE, D., and MILLER, B. "The Transition to Parenthood as a Critical Time for Building Family Strengths." In N. Stinnet and P. Knaub (eds.), *Family Strengths: Positive Models of Family Life.* Lincoln: University of Nebraska Press, 1980.

SOLZHENITSYN, ALEXANDER I. *The Gulag Archipelago.* New York: Harper & Row, 1973.

SOMMER, ROBERT; BURSTEIN, EMILY; and HOLMAN, SANDY. "Tolerance of Deviance as Affected by Label, Act, and Actor." *Deviant Behavior* 9, 1988.

SORENSEN, GLORIAN, et al. "Sex Differences in the Relationship Between Work and Health: The Minnesota Heart Survey." *Journal of Health and Social Behavior* 26, 1985.

SOROKIN, PITIRIM A. *The Crisis of Our Age.* New York: E.P. Dutton, 1941.

SOROKIN, PITIRIM A. *Social and Cultural Dynamics.* Boston: Porter Sargent, 1957.

SOUTH, SCOTT. "Economic Conditions and the Divorce Rate: A Time Series Analysis of the Postwar United States." *Journal of Marriage and the Family* 47, 1985.

SOUTH, SCOTT. "Sex Ratios, Economic Power, and Women's Roles: A Theoretical Extension and Empirical Test." *Journal of Marriage and the Family* 50, 1988.

SOUTHERN POVERTY LAW CENTER. "'Move-In' Violence: White Resistance to Neighborhood Integration in the 1980s." Montgomery, Ala.: Southern Poverty Law Center, 1987.

SPANIER, GRAHAM B. "Measuring Dyadic Adjustment: New Scales for Assessing the Quality of Marriage and Similar Dyads." *Journal of Marriage and the Family* 38, 1976.

SPANIER, GRAHAM B., and FURSTENBERG, FRANK F., JR. "Remarriage and Reconstituted Families." In Marvin B. Sussman and Suzanne K. Steinmetz (eds.), *Handbook of Marriage and the Family.* New York: Plenum Press, 1987.

SPECTOR, MALCOLM. "Legitimizing Homosexuality." *Society*, July/August 1977.

SPINDLER, GEORGE D., and SPINDLER, LOUISE. "Anthropologists View American Culture." *Annual Review of Anthropology* 12. Palo Alto, Calif.: Annual Reviews, Inc., 1983.

SPITZE, GLENNA. "Work and Family." *Journal of Marriage and the Family* 50, 1988.

SPITZER, CINDY. "The Invisible Toll on Rescue Workers." *Washington Post-Health*, May 10, 1988.

"The Sport of Religion: The Ritual Athletes of Iran." CBS television program, February 9, 1972.

SPRECHER, SUSAN; MCKINNEY, KATHLEEN; and ORBUCH, TERRI L. "Has the Double Standard Disappeared? An Experimental Test." *Social Psychology Quarterly* 50, 1987.

STACK, STEVEN. "The Effect of the Decline in Institutionalized Religion on Suicide, 1954–1978." *Journal for the Scientific Study of Religion* 22, 1983.

STAFFORD, MARK, and GIBBS, JACK. "A Major Problem with the Theory of Status Integration and Suicide." *Social Forces* 63, 1985.

STAFFORD, MARK, and GIBBS, JACK. "Change in the Relation Between Marital Integration and Suicide Rates." *Social Forces* 66, 1988.

STARK, RODNEY, and BAINBRIDGE, WILLIAM SIMS. "Of Churches, Sects, and Cults: Preliminary Concepts for a Theory of Religious Movements." *Journal for the Scientific Study of Religion* 18, 1979.

STARR, PAUL. *The Social Transformation of American Medicine.* New York: Basic Books, 1982.

STEBBINS, ROBERT. "The Meaning of Academic Performance: How Teachers Define a Classroom Situation." In Peter Woods and Martyn Hammersley (eds.), *School Experience.* New York: St. Martin's Press, 1977.

STEIN, LEONARD I. "Male and Female: The Doctor–Nurse Game." In James P. Spradley and David W. McCurdy (eds.), *Conformity and Conflict: Readings in Cultural Anthropology*, 2d ed. Boston: Little, Brown, 1974.

STEINBERG, LAURENCE, and SILVERBERG, SUSAN B. "Influences on Marital Satisfaction During the Middle Stages of the Family Life Cycle." *Journal of Marriage and the Family* 49, 1987.

STEINMETZ, SUZANNE K. "Family Violence." In Marvin B. Sussman and Suzanne K. Steinmetz (eds.), *Handbook of Marriage and the Family*. New York: Plenum Press, 1987.

STELLMAN, JEANNE, and DAUM, SUSAN M. *Work Is Dangerous to Your Health*. New York: Vintage Books, 1973.

STERN, JOYCE D., and CHANDLER, MARJORIE O. eds. *The Condition of Education: 1987 Edition*. Washington, D.C.: U.S. Government Printing Office, 1987.

STERN, PHILIP M. *The Best Congress Money Can Buy*. New York: Pantheon, 1988.

STEVENS, ROSEMARY. *American Medicine and the Public Interest*. New Haven, Conn.: Yale University Press, 1971.

STOCKWELL, EDWARD G., and GROAT, H. THEODORE. *World Population: An Introduction to Demography*. New York: Franklin Watts, 1984.

STRAUS, MURRAY A. "Victims and Aggressors in Marital Violence." *American Behavioral Scientist* 23, 1980.

STRAUS, MURRAY A., and GELLES, RICHARD J. "Societal Change and Change in Family Violence from 1975 to 1985 As Revealed by Two National Surveys." *Journal of Marriage and the Family* 48, 1986.

STRAUS, MURRAY A.; GELLES, RICHARD J.; and STEINMETZ, SUZANNE K. *Behind Closed Doors: Violence in the American Family*. Garden City, N.Y.: Anchor/Doubleday, 1980.

STRICKLAND, W.P., ed. *Autobiography of Peter Cartwright, The Backwoods Preacher*. New York: Carlton and Porter, 1856.

STRONG, PHILIP. "Medical Errands: A Discussion of Routine Patient Work." In A. Davis and G. Horobin (eds.), *Medical Encounters: The Experience of Illness and Treatment*. New York: St. Martin's Press, 1977.

STROUSE, JEREMIAH, and FABES, RICHARD A. "Formal Versus Informal Sources of Sex Education: Competing Forces in the Sexual Socialization of Adolescents." *Adolescence* 20, 1985.

SUMNER, WILLIAM GRAHAM. *Folkways: A Study of the Sociological Importance of Usages, Manners, Customs, Mores, and Morals*. Boston: Ginn, 1906.

SUPLEE, CURT. "The Electronic Sweatshop." *Washington Post-Outlook*, January 3, 1988.

SUSSER, MERVYN W.; HOPPER, KIM; and RICHMAN, JUDITH. "Society, Culture, and Health." In D. Mechanic (ed.), *Handbook of Health, Health Care, and the Health Professions*. New York: The Free Press, 1983.

SUTHERLAND, EDWIN H. *Principles of Criminology*, 4th ed. Chicago: Lippincott, 1947.

SWAFFORD, MICHAEL. "Sex Differences in Soviet Earnings." *American Sociological Review* 43, 1978.

SYME, S. LEONARD, and BERKMAN, LISA F. "Social Class, Susceptibility, and Sickness." In Peter Conrad and Rochelle Kern (eds.), *The Sociology of Health and Illness*. New York: St. Martin's Press, 1981.

SZINOVACZ, MAXIMILIANE. "Family Power." In Marvin B. Sussman and Suzanne K. Steinmetz (eds.), *Handbook of Marriage and the Family*. New York: Plenum Press, 1987.

TALESE, GAY. *Thy Neighbor's Wife*. New York: Doubleday, 1980.

TANNER, NANCY. "Matrifocality in Indonesia and Africa and Among Black Americans." In M.Z. Rosaldo and L. Lamphere (eds.), *Women, Culture, and Society*. Stanford, Calif.: Stanford University Press, 1974.

TAVRIS, CAROL, and SADD, SUSAN. *The Redbook Report on Female Sexuality*. New York: Delacorte, 1977.

TAYLOR, KATHRYN M. "Telling Bad News: Physicians and the Disclosure of Undesirable Information." *Sociology of Health and Illness* 10, 1988.

TAYLOR, VERTA. "Good News About Disaster." *Psychology Today*, October, 1977.

TEACHMAN, JAY D. "Early Marriage, Premarital Fertility, and Marital Dissolution: Results for Blacks and Whites." *Journal of Family Issues* 4, 1983.

TEITELBAUM, MICHAEL S., and WINTER, JAY M. *The Fear of Population Decline*. New York: Academic Press, 1985.

TERKEL, STUDS. *Working*. New York: Pantheon Books, 1974.

THIO, ALEX. *Deviant Behavior*. Boston: Houghton Mifflin, 1978.

THOITS, PEGGY A. "Self-Labeling Processes in Mental Illness. The Role of Emotional Deviance." *American Journal of Sociology* 91, 1985.

THOREAU, HENRY D. *Walden: Or, Life in the Woods*. Boston: Ticknor and Fields, 1854.

THORNBERRY, TERENCE P., and FARNSWORTH, MARGARET. "Social Correlates of Criminal Involvement: Further Evidence on the Relationship Between Social Status and Criminal Behavior." *American Sociological Review* 47, 1982.

THORNTON, ARLAND. "Cohabitation and Marriage in the 1980s." *Demography* 25, 1988.

THORNTON, ARLAND, and FREEDMAN, DEBORAH. "The Changing American Family." *Population Bulletin*, 38 1983.

THORNTON, RUSSELL. *American Indian Holocaust and Survival*. Norman: University of Oklahoma Press, 1987.

TIGER, LIONEL. *Men in Groups*. New York: Random House, 1969.

TIMBERLAKE, MICHAEL, ed. *Urbanization in the World-Economy*. New York: Academic Press, 1985.

TIMBERLAKE, MICHAEL, and KENTOR, JEFFREY. "Economic Dependence, Overurbanization, and Economic Growth: A Study of Less Developed Countries." *The Sociological Quarterly* 24, 1983.

Time, "The Battle over Abortion." April 6, 1981.

Time. "Racism on the Rise." February 2, 1987.

Time. "Fed Up, Fearful and Frazzled." March 14, 1988a.

Time. "A Move to the Right." November 14, 1988b.

TITTLE, C.R.; VILLEMEZ, W.J.; and SMITH, D.A. "The Myth of Social Class and Criminality: An Empirical Assessment of the Empirical Evidence." *American Sociological Review*. 43. 1978.

TOFFLER, ALVIN. *Future Shock*. New York: Random House, 1970.

TOMASSON, RICHARD. *Iceland: The First New Society*. Minneapolis: University of Minnesota Press, 1980.

TOENNIES, FERDINAND. *Community and Society*. New York: Harper Torchbooks, 1957. Originally published 1887.

TOREN, NINA. "The Bus Driver: A Study in Role Analysis. *Human Relations* 26, 1973.

TREIMAN, DONALD. *Occupational Prestige in Comparative Perspective*. New York: Academic Press, 1977.

TRICE, HARRISON M. "The 'Outsider's Role in Field Study." In William J. Filstead (ed.), *Qualitative Methodology: Firsthand Involvement with the Social World*. Chicago: Markham, 1970.

TRICE, HARRISON M., and ROMAN, PAUL. "Delabeling, Relabeling and Alcoholics Anonymous." *Social Problems* 17, 1970.

TRILLIN, CALVIN. "Black or White." *The New Yorker*. 62. April 14, 1986.

TROELTSCH, ERNST. *The Social Teachings of the Christian Churches*. New York: Macmillan, 1931.

TSCHETTER, JOHN. "Producer Services Industries: Why Are They Growing So Rapidly." *Monthly Labor Review* 110, 1987.

TUMIN, MELVIN M. *Social Stratification*, 2d ed. Englewood Cliffs, N.J.: Prentice-Hall, 1985.

TURKLE, SHERRY. *The Second Self: Computers and the Human Spirit*. New York: Simon and Schuster, 1984.

TURNER, JONATHAN H., and MARYANSKI, ALEXANDRA. *Functionalism*. Menlo Park, Calif.: Benjamin/Cummings, 1979.

TURNER, JONATHAN H.; SINGLETON, ROYCE, JR.; and MUSICK, DAVID. *Oppression: A Socio-History of Black-White Relations in America*. Chicago: Nelson-Hall. 1984.

TURNER, RALPH H., and KILLIAN, LEWIS M. *Collective Behavior*, 2d ed. Englewood Cliffs, N.J.: Prentice-Hall, 1972.

UNITED NATIONS DEPARTMENT OF INTERNAL ECONOMIC AND SOCIAL AFFAIRS. "National Accounts Statistics: Compendium of Income Distribution Statistics." *Statistical Papers*. Series M. No. 79. New York: United Nations. 1985.

UNITED NATIONS. *World Population Trends and Policies, 1987 Monitoring Report*. Population Studies No. 103. New York: United Nations, 1987.

U.S. BUREAU OF JUSTICE STATISTICS. *Report to the Nation on Crime and Justice: The Data*. Washington, D.C.: U.S. Government Printing Office, 1983.

——. *Crime in the United States: 1987, Uniform Crime Reports for the United States*. Washington, D.C.: U.S. Government Printing Office, 1988a.

——. *Justice Expenditures and Employment Extracts: 1982 and 1983—Data from the Annual General Finance and Employment Surveys*. Washington, D.C.: U.S. Government Printing Office, 1988b.

——. *Prisoners in 1987*. Washington, D.C.: U.S. Government Printing Office, 1988c.

U.S. BUREAU OF THE CENSUS. *1980 Census of Population, vol. 1, Characteristics of the Population, Part 1. U.S. Summary*. Washington, D.C.: U.S. Government Printing Office, 1982.

——. *Statistical Abstract of the United States, 1985*. Washington, D.C.: U.S. Government Printing Office, 1984.

——. "Household Wealth and Asset Ownership: 1984." *Current Population Reports*. Series P-20, No. 7. Washington, D.C.: U.S. Government Printing Office, 1986.

——. "Rural and Urban Farm Population: 1987." *Current Population Reports*. Series P-27, No. 61. Washington, D.C.: U.S. Government Printing Office, 1987a.

——. *Statistical Abstract of the United States, 1988*. Washington, D.C.: U.S. Government Printing Office, 1987b.

——. "Educational Attainment in the United States: March 1987 and 1986." *Current Population Reports*. Series P-20, No. 428. Washington, D.C.: U.S. Government Printing Office, 1988a.

——. "Fertility of American Women: June 1987." *Current Population Reports*. Series P-20, No. 427. Washington, D.C.: U.S. Government Printing Office, 1988b.

——. "Money Income and Poverty Status in the United States: 1987." *Current Population Reports*. Series P-60, No. 161. Washington, D.C.: U.S. Government Printing Office. 1988c.

——. "Money Income of Households, Families, and Persons in the United States: 1986." *Current Population Reports*, Series P-60, No. 159. Washington, D.C.: U.S. Government Printing Office, 1988d.

——. "Poverty in the United States: 1986." *Current Population Reports*. Series P-60, No. 160. Washington, D.C.: U.S. Government Printing Office, 1988e.

——. "Projections of the Population of States, by Age, Sex, and Race: 1988 to 2010." *Current Population Reports*. Series P-25, No. 1017. Washington, D.C.: U.S. Government Printing Office, 1988f.

——. "School Enrollment—Social and Economic Characteristics of Students: October 1986." *Current Population Reports*. Series P-20, No. 429. Washington, D.C.: U.S. Government Printing Office, 1988g.

——. *Statistical Abstract of the United States, 1989*. Washington, D.C.: U.S. Government Printing Office, 1988h.

——. "The Hispanic Population of the United States." *Current Population Reports*. Series P-20, No. 418. Washington, D.C.: U.S. Government Printing Office, 1988i.

——. "Voting and Registration in the Election of November 1988." *Current Population Reports*. Series P-20, No. 435. Washington, D.C.: U.S. Government Printing Office, 1989.

U.S. Centers for Disease Control. "Premature Mortality by Income Level—Multnomah County, Oregon, 1976–1984." *Morbidity and Mortality Weekly Report* 37(10), 1988.

U.S. Commission on Civil Rights *The Economic Status of Americans of Asian Descent*. Washington, D.C.: U.S. Government Printing Office, 1988.

U.S. Department of Agriculture. *Budget Estimates for the United States Department of Agriculture*. Washington, D.C.: U.S. Government Printing Office, 1986.

U.S. News and World Report. "When Blocks Battle to Stay Lily-White." December 9, 1985.

Useem, Elizabeth L. *Low Tech Education in a High Tech World: Corporations and Classrooms in the New Information Society*. New York: The Free Press, 1986.

Useem, Michael, and Karabel, Jerome. "Pathways to Top Corporate Management." *American Sociological Review* 51, 1986.

Uys, Pieter-Dirk. "Chameleons Thrive Under Apartheid." *New York Times*, September 23, 1988.

Van der Tak, Jean; Haub, Carl; and Murphy, Elaine. "A New Look at the Population Problem." *The Futurist*, April, 1980.

Van Houten, Donald R. "The Political Economy and Technical Control of Work Humanization in Sweden During the 1970s and 1980s." *Work and Occupations* 14, 1987.

Vaught, Charles, and Smith, David L. "Incorporation and Mechanical Solidarity in an Underground Coal Mine." *Sociology of Work and Occupations* 7, 1980.

Veblen, Thorstein. *The Theory of the Leisure Class: An Economic Study of Institutions*. New York: Macmillan, 1899.

Verbrugge, Lois M. "Females and Illness: Recent Trends in Sex Differences in the United States." *Journal of Health and Social Behavior* 17, 1976.

Verbrugge, Lois M. "Gender and Health: An Update on Hypotheses and Evidence." *Journal of Health and Social Behavior* 26, 1985.

Voydanoff, Patricia. "Work Role Characteristics, Family Structure Demands, and Work/Family Conflict." *Journal of Marriage and the Family* 50, 1988.

Wade, Nicholas. *The Nobel Duel*. Garden City, N.Y.: Anchor Books, 1981.

Waite, Linda J.; Haggstrom, Gus W.; and Kanouse, David E. "The Consequences of Parenthood for the Marital Stability of Young Adults." *American Sociological Review* 50, 1985.

Waitzkin, Howard. "Information Giving in Medical Care." *Journal of Health and Social Behavior* 26, 1985.

Waldo, Gordon, and Griswold, David. "Issues in the Measurement of Recidivism." In Lee Sechrest, Susan O. White, and Elizabeth D. Brown (eds.), *The Rehabilitation of Criminal Offenders*. Washington, D.C.: National Academy of Sciences, 1979.

Waldron, Ingrid. "Sex Differences in Illness Incidence, Prognosis and Mortality: Issues and Evidence." *Social Science & Medicine* 17, 1983.

Wallace, Anthony F.C. *Religion: An Anthropological View*. New York: Random House, 1966.

Wallace, Anthony F.C. *The Death and Rebirth of the Seneca*. New York: Vintage/Random House, 1969.

Wallerstein, Immanuel. *The Modern World-System*. New York: Academic Press, 1974.

Wallerstein, Immanuel. *The Capitalist World Economy*. Cambridge, England: Cambridge University Press, 1979.

Wallerstein, Immanuel. *The Modern World-System II: Mercantilism and the Consolidation of the European World-Economy, 1600–1750*. New York: Academic Press, 1980.

Wallerstein, James S., and Wyles, Clement J. "Our Law-Abiding Law-Breakers." *Probation* 25, 1947.

WALLERSTEIN, JUDITH S., and KELLY, JOAN B. "The Effects of Parental Divorce: Experiences of the Preschool Child." *The Journal of the American Academy of Child Psychiatry* 14, 1975.

WALLERSTEIN, JUDITH S., and KELLY, JOAN B. "Effects of Parental Divorce: Experience of Children in Later Latency." *American Journal of Orthopsychiatry* 46, 1976.

WALTERS, VIVIENNE. "Company Doctors' Perceptions of and Responses to Conflicting Pressures from Labor and Management." *Social Problems* 30, 1982.

WARNER, W. LLOYD, and LUNT, PAUL S. *The Social Life of a Modern Community*. New Haven, Conn.: Yale University Press, 1941.

WASBURN, PHILO C. *Political Sociology: Approaches, Concepts, Hypotheses*. Englewood Cliffs, N.J.: Prentice-Hall, 1982.

Washington Post. "Pope Emphasizes Motherhood Role." January 11, 1979.

Washington Post. "More Money for Male Doctors." February 16, 1988a.

Washington Post. "Why Nurses Quit: The Frustration Behind the Shortage." July 12, 1988b.

Washington Post. "Tuesday's Turnout." November 13, 1988c.

WATSON, J. MARK. "Outlaw Motorcyclists: An Outgrowth of Lower Class Cultural Careers." *Deviant Behavior* 2, 1980.

WAX, ROSALIE. *Doing Field Work*. Chicago: University of Chicago Press, 1971.

WEBER, MAX. *From Max Weber: Essays in Sociology*. H.H. Gerth and C. Wright Mills (eds.). New York: Oxford University Press, 1946. Originally published 1918.

WEBER, MAX. *The Methodology of the Social Sciences*. New York: The Free Press, 1949. Originally published 1903–1917.

WEBER, MAX. *The Protestant Ethic and the Spirit of Capitalism* (Talcott Parsons, trans.). New York: Oxford University Press, 1958. Originally published 1904–1905.

WEBER, MAX. *Economy and Society: An Outline of Interpretative Sociology*, 3 vols. Guenther Roth and Claus Wittich (eds.). New York: Bedminster Press, 1968. Originally published 1921.

WEED, JAMES A. "National Estimates of Marriage Dissolution and Survivorship." *Vital and Health Statistics*, Series 3, No. 19. Washington, D.C.: U.S. Government Printing Office, 1980.

WEGMANN, ROBERT. "Classroom Discipline: An Exercise in the Maintenance of Social Reality." *Sociology of Education* 49, 1976.

WEISHAUS, SYLVIA, and FIELD, DOROTHY. "A Half Century of Marriage: Continuity or Change?" *Journal of Marriage and the Family* 50, 1988.

WEISMAN, STEVEN R. "Broken Marriage and Brawl Test a Cohesive Caste." *New York Times*, February 21, 1988.

WEISS, ROBERT S. *Marital Separation*. New York: Basic Books, 1975.

WEISS, ROBERT S. *Going It Alone: The Family Life and Social Situation of the Single Parent*. New York: Basic Books, 1979.

WEITZ, ROSE, and SULLIVAN, DEBORAH. "License Lay Midwifery and the Medical Model of Childbirth." *Sociology of Health and Illness* 7, 1985.

WEITZMAN, LENORE J. *Sex Role Socialization: A Focus on Women*. Palo Alto, Calif.: Mayfield, 1979.

WEITZMAN, LENORE J. *The Divorce Revolution: The Unexpected Social and Economic Consequences for Women and Children in America*. New York: The Free Press, 1985.

WELLMAN, BARRY. "The Community Question: The Intimate Networks of East Yorkers." *American Journal of Sociology* 84, 1979.

WELTER, BARBARA. "The Cult of True Womanhood: 1820–1860." *American Quarterly*, Summer 1966.

WENGER, DENNIS E.; DYKES, JAMES D.; SEBOK, THOMAS D.; and NEFF, JOAN L. "It's a Matter of Myths: An Empirical Examination of Individual Insight into Disaster Response." *Mass Emergencies* 1, 1975.

WERTZ, DOROTHY C.; SORENSON, JAMES R.; and HEEREN, TIMOTHY. "Can't Get No (Dis)Satisfaction." *Work and Occupations* 15, 1988.

WERTZ, RICHARD W., and WERTZ, DOROTHY C. "Notes on the Decline of Midwives and the Rise of Medical Obstetricians." In Peter Conrad and Rochelle Kern (eds.), *The Sociology of Health and Illness: Critical Perspectives 1986*. New York: St. Martin's Press, 1986.

WEST, CANDACE. "Actions Speak Louder Than Words: Communicating Control in a Cross-Sex Conversation." Paper presented at the Annual Meeting of the Southern Sociological Society, New Orleans, 1978.

WEST, CANDACE. "When the Doctor Is a 'Lady': Power, Status, and Gender in Physician–Patient Encounters." *Symbolic Interaction* 7, 1984.

WESTOFF, CHARLES F. "Coital Frequency and Contraception." *Family Planning Perspectives* 6, 1974.

WESTOFF, CHARLES F. "Fertility in the United States." *Science* 234, 1986.

WHITE, LYNN K.; BOOTH, ALAN; and EDWARDS, JOHN. "Children and Marital Happiness: Why the Negative Correlation?" *Journal of Family Issues* 7, 1986.

WHITE, MERRY. *The Japanese Educational Experience: A Commitment to Children*. New York: The Free Press, 1987.

WHYTE, MARTIN KING, and GU, S.Z. "Popular Response to China's Fertility Transition." *Population Development and Review* 13, 1987.

WICKER, TOM. "The Hispanic Factor." *New York Times*, September 9, 1988.

WILCOX, CLYDE. "PACs and Pluralism: Interest Group Formation and Partisanship." *Polity* 21, 1988.

WILDAVSKY, AARON, ed. *The Presidency*. Boston: Little, Brown, 1969.

WILEY, NORBERT. "The Micro-Macro Problem in Social Theory." *Sociological Theory* 6, 1988.

WILLIAM T. GRANT FOUNDATION. *The Forgotten Half: Pathways to Success For America's Youth and Young Families*. Washington, D.C.: The W.T. Grant Commission Office, 1988.

WILLIAMS, ROBIN M., JR. *American Society: A Sociological Interpretation*, 3d ed. New York: Alfred A. Knopf, 1970.

WILLIAMS, TANNIS M., and BOYES, MICHAEL C. "Television-Viewing Patterns and Use of Other Media." In Tannis M. Williams (ed.), *The Impact of Television: A Natural Experiment in Three Communities*. Orlando, Fla.: Academic Press, 1986.

WILLIAMS, TANNIS M., ed. *The Impact of Television: A Natural Experiment in Three Communities*. Orlando, Fla.: Academic Press, 1986.

WILLIAMS, TERRY, and MAJOR, TED. *The Secret Language of Snow*. New York: Sierra Club/Pantheon Books, 1984.

WILLIAMSON, JEFFREY G., and LINDERT, PETER H. *American Inequality*. New York: Academic Press, 1980.

WILSON, WILLIAM JULIUS. *The Declining Significance of Race*. Chicago: University of Chicago Press. 1978.

WILSON, WILLIAM JULIUS. *The Truly Disadvantaged: The Inner City, the Underclass, and Public Policy*. Chicago: University of Chicago Press, 1987.

WILSON, WILLIAM JULIUS. "The Cost of Racial and Class Exclusion in the Inner City." *Annals of the American Academy of Political and Social Sciences*, 501, 1989.

WOLFE, TOM. "The 'Me' Decade and the Third Great Awakening." *New York*, August 23, 1976.

WOLFF, EDWARD N. "Estimates of Household Wealth Inequality in the United States, 1962–1983." *The Review of Income and Wealth* 33, 1987.

WOLINSKY, FREDRIC D. *The Sociology of Health: Principles, Practitioners, and Issues*, 2d ed. Belmont, Calif.: Wadsworth, 1988.

WOLINSKY, FREDRIC D.; MOSELY, RAY R., II; and COE, RODNEY. "A Cohort Analysis of the Use of Health Services by Elderly Americans." *Journal of Health and Social Behavior* 27, 1986.

WOLINSKY, FREDERIC D., and WOLINSKY, SALLY R. "Expecting Sick-Role Legitimation and Getting It." *Journal of Health and Social Behavior* 22, 1981.

WOLPE, PAUL ROOT. "The Maintenance of Professional Authority: Acupuncture and the American Physician." *Social Problems* 32, 1985.

WORLD BANK. *World Development Report 1984*. New York: Oxford University Press, 1984.

WORLD BANK. *World Development Report 1988*. New York: Oxford University Press, 1988.

WRONG, DENNIS. "The Oversocialized Conception of Man in Modern Sociology." *American Sociological Review* 26, 1961.

WUTHNOW, ROBERT. "Sociology of Religion." In Neil J. Smelser (ed.), *Handbook of Sociology*. Beverly Hills, Calif.: Sage Publications, 1988a.

WUTHNOW, ROBERT. *The Restructuring of American Religion: Society and Faith Since World War II*. Princeton, N.J.: Princeton University Press, 1988b.

WYLIE, C. *Village in the Vaucluse*, 2d ed. Cambridge, Mass.: Harvard University Press, 1961.

YARROW, M.R.; CLAUSEN, J.A.; and ROBBINS, P.R. "The Social Meaning of Mental Illness." *Journal of Social Issues* 11, 1955.

YETMAN, NORMAN R. *Majority and Minority: The Dynamics of Race and Ethnicity in American Life*. Boston: Allyn and Bacon, 1985.

YINGER, J. MILTON. "Contraculture and Subculture." *American Sociological Review* 25, 1960.

YOUSSEF, NADIA HAGGAG. *Women and Work in Developing Societies*. Westport, Conn.: Greenwood Press, 1974.

ZELNIK, MELVIN, and KANTNER, JOHN. "Sexual Activity, Contraceptive Use and Pregnancy Among Metropolitan Area Teenagers: 1971–1979." *Family Planning Perspectives* 12, 1980.

ZELNIK, MELVIN, and SHAH, FARIDA K. "First Intercourse Among Young Americans." *Family Planning Perspectives* 15, 1983.

ZIMDARS-SWARTZ, SANDRA L. "The Virgin Mary: Mother as Intercessor and Savior of Society." In Sharon S.

Brehm (ed.), *Seeing Female: Social Roles and Personal Lives*. Westport, Conn.: Greenwood Press, 1988.

ZIMDARS-SWARTZ, SANDRA L. "Popular Devotion to the Virgin: The Marian Phenomena at Melleray, Republic of Ireland." *Archives de Sciences Sociales des Religions*, 1989a.

ZIMDARS-SWARTZ, SANDRA L. "Religious Experience and Public Cult: The Case of Mary Ann Hoof." *Journal of Religion and Health* 28, 1989b.

ZORZA, VICTOR. "When Brothers Share Wives, Age Counts." *Washington Post*, May 2, 1982.

ZUCKERMAN, EDWARD. *Almanac of Federal PACs*. Washington, D.C.: Amward Pubs. Inc., 1988.

ZUCKERMAN, LAURENCE. "The Made-for-TV Campaign." *Time*, November 14, 1988.

ZUKIN, SHARON. "Gentrification: Culture and Capital in the Urban Core." *Annual Review of Sociology* 13. Palo Alto, Calif.: Annual Reviews, Inc., 1987.

NAME INDEX

SUBJECT INDEX

Photo Credits (continued from copyright page).

Chapter Three Chapter Opener: Robert Harding Picture Library. p. 70TL: Harvey Lloyd/The Stock Market. p. 70TR: Tim Gibson/Envision. p. 70B: Wolfgang Kahler. p. 77: Roberto Koch/Picture Group. p. 82: Marc & Evelyne Bernheim/Woodfin Camp & Assoc. p. 84: G. Chauvel/Sygma. p. 85: Mark Richards/Picture Group. p. 89: Michael Grecco/Picture Group. p. 91: Jim Brown/Offshoot. p. 93: Randy Taylor/Sygma. p. 95: Mark Richards/Picture Group.

Chapter Four Chapter Opener: Llewellyn. p. 103: David Dempster/Offshoot. p. 106: Abe Rezny/The Image Works. p. 108: Bob Daemmrich/The Image Works. p. 110: Mary Ellen Mark. p. 111: MacDonald Photography/Envision. p. 115: Andrew Popper/Picture Group. p. 120: Topham/The Image Works. p. 122B: Jim Brown/Offshoot. p. 126: Diego Goldberg/Sygma. p. 129: Russ Schleipman/Offshoot. p. 130: Ben Asen/Envision.

Chapter Five Chapter Opener: Tim Gibson/Envision. p. 138L: Susanne Page. p. 138R: Ted Horowitz/The Stock Market. p. 139: Mark Antman/The Image Works. p. 143: Fred Bodin/Offshoot. p. 148: MacDonald Photography/Envision. p. 154: Rob Nelson/Picture Group. p. 156: D. Fineman/Sygma. p. 158: Jim Brown/Offshoot. P. 159: Rob Nelson/Picture Group. p. 160: David Burnett/Contact Press. p. 164: Brad Power/Picture Group.

Chapter Six Chapter Opener: Lawrence Migdale/Photo Researchers, Inc. p. 172: Susanna Pashko/Envision. p. 179: Charles Gatwood/The Image Works. p. 182: Mario Ruiz/Picture Group. p. 189: Michael Grecco/Picture Group. p. 190: Jane Rosett/Sygma. p. 195: Grace Harrington/The Image Works.

Chapter Seven Chapter Opener: Robert Harding Picture Library. p. 207: Tim Gibson/Envision. p. 208: Topham/The Image Works. p. 209: Brown Brothers. p. 212: Charles Gatewood/The Image Works. p. 213T: Charles Gatewood/The Image Works. p. 213B: Mark Antman/The Image Works. p. 217: Jim Brown/Offshoot. p. 218: Jim Brown/Offshoot. p. 220: Howard Dratch/The Image Works. p. 225: Bob Daemmrich/The Image Works. p. 234: Jim Caccavo/Picture Group. p. 237: John Griffin/The Image Works.

Connections—The Homeless p. 241: Ricki Rosen/Picture Group. p. 242: Bob Daemmrich/The Image Works.

Chapter Eight Chapter Opener: Bob Daemmrich/Stock Boston. p. 255TL: John Curtis/Offshoot. p. 255TR: Bettmann Newsphotos. p. 255BL: Russ Schleipman/Offshoot. p. 255BR: Ben Barnhart/Offshoot. p. 260: G. Rancinan/Sygma. p. 261: Fred Bodin/Offshoot. P. 264T: Picture Group. p. 264B: JP Laffont/Sygma. p. 265: JP Laffont/Sygma. p. 272: J. Langavin/Sygma. p. 277: Russ Schleipman/Offshoot.

Chapter Nine Chapter Opener: Gabe Palmer/The Stock Market. p. 285: Sygma. p. 290: Glenn Short/Sygma. p. 293: Russ Scheilpman/Offshoot. p. 296: Ira Wyman/Sygma. p. 298: Gabe Palmer/The Stock Market. p. 299: JP Laffont/Sygma. p. 301: Randy Taylor/Sygma. p. 302: University of Washington. p. 307: Rob Nelson/Picture Group. p. 313: Bisson/Sygma.

Chapter Ten Chapter Opener: Eastcott/Momatiuk/The Image Works. p. 326: Marc & Evelyne Bernheim. p. 327: Andy Hernandez/Picture Group. p. 328: Tom Gibson/Envision. p. 331L: Baldev/Sygma. p. 331R: Eastcott/Momatiuk/The Image Works. p. 334: David Pollack/The Stock Market. p. 336: Ben Barnhart/Offshoot. p. 342L: Ben Barnhart/Offshoot. p. 342R: Dore Gardner. p. 345: Sue Owrutsky/ Picture Group. p. 353: Frank Siteman. p. 356: JP Laffont/Sygma.

Connections—U.S.-Mexican Border p. 362: Eddie Adams/Sygma. p. 365: Eddie Adams/Sygma. p. 366: A. Tannenbaum/Sygma.

Chapter Eleven Chapter Opener: Eastcott/Momatiuk/Woodfin Camp & Assoc. p. 373: Billy Black/Envision. p. 374: Ben Barnhart/Offshoot. p. 375: Nancy S. Dituri/Envision. p. 380: Harriet Gans/The Image Works. p. 382: David Leifer/Offshoot. p. 385: Fred Bodin/Offshoot. p. 386: John Curtis/Offshoot. p. 395: Sygma. p. 403: Doug Menuez/Picture Group.

Chapter Twelve Chapter Opener: David Dempster/Offshoot. p. 410: North Wind Picture Archives. p. 413: Jon Feingersh. p. 415T: Jim Brown/Offshoot. p. 415B: Dan Ford Connelly/Picture Group. p. 417: Alain Nogues/Sygma. p. 420: Ken Straiton/The Stock Market. p. 423: MacDonald Photography/Envision. p. 426: Seth Resnick/Picture Group. p. 429: MacDonald Photography/Envision. p. 434: Seth Resnick/Picture Group. p. 438: MacDonald Photography/Envision.

Chapter Thirteen Chapter Opener: Robert Harding Picture Library. p. 448: Bettmann Archive. p. 452: Bruce Stromberg/The Stock Market. p. 454: Richard Howard/Offshoot. p. 458T: Bill Campbell/Picture Group. p. 458B: David Pollack/The Stock Market. p. 459: Ricki Rosen/Picture Group. p. 467: Mark Antman/The Image Works. p. 468: Gabe Palmer/The Stock Market. p. 472: A. Tannenbaum/Sygma. p. 473: Russ Schleipman/Offshoot.

Chapter Fourteen Chapter Opener: Ted Horowitz/The Stock Market. p. 480: Tim Gibson/Envision. p. 481T: Paul Steele/The Stock Market. p. 481B: Roy Morsch/The Stock Market. p. 482: Michael J. Okoniewski/The Image Works. p. 484: Dion Ogust/The Image Works. p. 489: Brent Peterson/The Stock Market. p. 492: MacDonald Photography/Envision. p. 500: Gabe Palmer/The Stock Market. p. 502: Jim Brown/Offshoot. p. 507: Charles West/The Stock Market.

Chapter Fifteen Chapter Opener: Luis Villota/The Stock Market. p. 518T: Baldev/Sygma. p. 518B: Topham/The Image Works. p. 519: Richard Steedman/The Stock Market. p. 522: D. Goldberg/Sygma. p. 530: David E. Dempster/Offshoot. p. 536: Ira Wyman/Sygma. p. 542: Minosa-Scorpio/Sygma. p. 543: Dore Gardner/Offshoot. p. 545: G. Giansauti/Sygma. p. 548: Frank Siteman.

Chapter Sixteen Chapter Opener: John Curtis/Offshoot Stock. p. 557: Bill Gentitle/Picture Group. p. 561: Michael Gordon Edrington/The Image Works. p. 566: JL Atlan/Sygma. p. 568: Arthur Grace/Sygma. p. 572: Koch/Contrasto/Picture Group. p. 578: JL Atlan/Sygma. p. 580: Ricki Rosen/Picture Group. p. 581: Jack McKigney/Picture Group. p. 582: Andy Hernandez/Picture Group. p. 584: Sygma.

Connections—Latchkey Children p. 588: Ted Cordingley/Offshoot. p. 591: Frank Siteman/Stock Boston.

Chapter Seventeen Chapter Opener: Russ Schleipman/Offshoot. p. 598: Envision. p. 602: Bob Daemmrich/Image Works. p. 603: Steve Connolly/Sygma. p. 607: Jim Brown/Offshoot. p. 610: Sygma. p. 614: JP Laffont/Sygma. 618: Alain Keler. p. 625: Rob Nelson/Picture Group. p. 628: Walter Weissman/Envision. p. 631: Jim Brown/Offshoot.

Chapter Eighteen Chapter Opener: Bryce Flynn/Picture Group. p. 642: J. Pavlovsky/Sygma. p. 647: Robyn Wishna/Picture Group. p. 647: N. Tully/Sygma. p. 651: Tony Suau/Black Star. p. 653: Sygma. p. 655: Matsumoto/Sygma. p. 657: Dore Gardner/Offshoot. p. 661: W. Eastep. p. 663: JP Laffont/Sygma. p. 665: Russ Schleipman/Offshoot. p. 666: H. Collart Odinetz/Sygma.

Connections—Reproductive Technology p. 670: Dan McCoy/Black Star. p. 673: A. Tannenbaum/Sygma.